A Dictionary
of Pseudonyms and Their Origins

A Dictionary of Pseudonyms and Their Origins, with Stories of Name Changes

by
Adrian Room

McFarland & Company, Inc., Publishers
Jefferson, North Carolina, and London

British Library Cataloguing-in-Publication data are available

Library of Congress Cataloguing-in-Publication Data

Room, Adrian.
  A dictionary of pseudonyms and their origins, with stories of name
changes / by Adrian Room.
    p. cm.
  Rev. ed. of: Naming names. 1981.
  Includes bibliographical references.
  ISBN 0-89950-450-7 (lib. bdg. : 50# alk. paper) ∞
  1. Anonyms and pseudonyms—Dictionaries. 2. Anonyms and
pseudonyms. I. Room, Adrian. Naming names. II. Title.
Z1041.R66 1989
929.4'03 – dc20   89-42750
                                                              CIP

Manufactured in the United States of America

McFarland and Company, Inc., Publishers
  Box 611, Jefferson, North Carolina 28640

Contents

Acknowledgments

I am indebted for this revision to those people who kindly helped with the research and typing of the first work, published in 1981, and although I do not repeat their names all over again here, I am just as grateful to them now as I was then.

No acknowledgments are really complete without the name of *one* individual or body, I would like to express my thanks to Leslie Dunkling, president of the Names Society, who ever since the first edition has kept me permanently tuned in to the "name wavelength," and who has supplied much useful material, whether privately or through his own books on the subject.

Introduction

This is a revised, expanded, and updated version of the book that first appeared in 1981 under the title of *Naming Names*, subtitled *Stories of Pseudonyms and Name Changes, with a Who's Who*.

It turned out that while many readers appreciated the introductory chapters, explaining how and why people adopt false names or change their names, and were glad to have the fairly comprehensive "Who's Who" so they could check who was or had been who, what they really liked and enjoyed were the so-called "Name Stories" themselves. These gave the background, mostly by means of extracts from biographies, autobiographies or similar material, to *why* a person had changed his or her name, and told how the change actually came about.

This aspect of name changing or pseudonymity is certainly entertaining, as well as eminently readable. I have therefore, in this new edition, greatly increased the "stories" and the background information, while at the same time adding what I hope are judicious or considered comments on various individual name changes. And instead of having two separate sections, one the "Name Stories," and the other the "Who's Who," as previously, I have now combined the information in a single listing. This makes the whole thing much handier and avoids the frequent cross-referral that was required in the original arrangement.

Moreover, apart from the many extra names and name stories, all the material from the first edition has been both updated and, where necessary, corrected for the new edition, which will make the book as a whole that much more valuable and accurate. The Bibliography, too, has been updated.

The introductory chapters have been similarly revised and updated, where necessary, and additional information has been added about the process of changing one's name upon marriage, which some reviewers rightly noted was absent from the first edition.

In short, the new edition aims to be more readable, more comprehensive and more orderly. But above all, it aims to present the fascinating world of pseudonyms and name changes as a worthy field of study in its own right, and to illustrate that field by as many apposite stories and origins as possible.

As for your name, I offer you the whole firmament to choose from.
— Opening words of "On Choosing a Name"
by Alpha of the Plough. The sentence was spoken by
the editor of the *Star* as an invitation to the English essayist
to write for that paper under a pseudonym (see page 75)

1. The Nature of a Name

With a name like yours, you might be any shape, almost. (Lewis Carroll, "Through the Looking-Glass")

"What's in a name?" agonized lovelorn Juliet, for she was a Capulet, and he, her roaming romantic Romeo, was a Montague, and the two families were deadly enemies.

Shakespeare himself well knew what was in a name. One need only mention his Aguecheek and Ariel, his Benvolio and Malvolio, his Pistol and Doll Tearsheet and of course his Romeo—was there ever a more evocative name?—to see and sense the charm of well chosen names.

We shall be examining in due course and in some detail "what's in a name," but first we should touch on a more basic question: what *is* a name?

We all of us have a name. Conventionally, at any rate in the Western world, we have, as an accepted and acceptable minimum, a forename, or Christian name, and a surname, or family name. We are John Smith, or Mary Brown, or Clark Gable, or Betty Grable, or even, like the famous social leader from Houston, Texas, Ima Hogg. The names are different, and serve different purposes—a forename is essentially private property, and a surname public—but in their respective and differing ways both names carry equal weight, both actually and legally, as a means of identification.

By custom and tradition, our first name is given us us soon after we are born, at a christening or baptismal or naming ceremony, while our last name is already there, and we simply become one more member of the family to share it. In most cases, we get our names from our parents, since our forename is chosen for us by our parents and we inherit our parents' surname.

Our first name is our special individual property—although there may be hundreds of other people who also bear it—and it lasts as long as our life lasts. Our surname may well have existed for centuries and generations before us, in one form or another, and will probably continue to be borne by our own children long after our own life has ended.

Assuming that our ancestors did not deliberately change the surname that we now bear, how far back can we trace this name? Theoretically, at least, must there not have been a time, going back as far as we can, when we come to the first of our forebears to be so named? How did *he* get his name? In other words, more generally, where did the very first names of all come from?

It is worth taking a look at this original process of name creation, since this is the process that we are chiefly concerned with in this book.

1

Many English and some Americans can trace their surnames back in written form to the Domesday Book of the late eleventh century. If your name is Gridley, for example, there is a chance, admittedly an extremely slim one, that Albert Greslet was one of your ancestors. His name was recorded by the Domesday Book in Cheshire in 1086. Or if you are a Tallboy, perhaps Ralph Tailgebosc of Hertford-shire, who likewise lived nearly a millennium ago, was one of the greatest of your great-grandfathers. Both Albert and Ralph have names that to our modern eyes are recognizably personal names, in the familiar forename-surname form. A number of names cited and recorded in the Domesday Book, however, are single names, or are for example names that belong to a person who is said to be the "filius" or son of someone else. The name that today is Jarrold or Gerald, for instance, occurs in the Domesday Book as Robertus filius Geraldi—"Robert Geraldson," as it were—while people today named Bishop will find, at any rate in Northamptonshire in 1066, that their Domesday ancestor was simply called Biscop.

The Domesday Book thus also records the early stages of our present binomial (forename-plus-surname) system. Originally, therefore, people had only one name. One person with one name; quite enough. But we want to go back even further. Where did these names come from in turn? Did they have a meaning? For example, was the original Tallboy (actually Tailgebosc, as we have seen) a tall boy, and was the early Bishop a bishop? What does Gridley (or Greslet) mean, and where did Gerald come from?

The answer is both simple and complex. Simple, in that all these original names did indeed have a meaning. Complex, in that many of these early names do not mean what they seem to mean. Ralph Tailgebosc was not a tall boy but was himself the descendant of someone who was a woodcutter, from the Old French *tailler* "to cut," and *bosc*, "wood." Over the centuries his surname became smoothed and assimilated to something that had an *English* meaning and pronunciation. The original Bishop, too, although his name has not changed anything like as radically as Ralph's, was almost certainly not a bishop but a man who looked like one or, more likely, had the manners or deportment of one—an episcopal posture, if you like. His name was thus more what we today would call a nickname. Albert Greslet's surname was really a nickname, too: it means "pockmarked," literally "marked by hail," also from Old French, while Gerald, these days more common as a Christian name, meant "spear-ruler."

Woodcutter, Bishop-like person, Pockmarked person, and One Who Ruled with His Spear. An impressive foursome! But we can go further back than that. We are limited by written or pictographic records, of course, but we have evidence that some time before 3050 B.C. there was a man named Sekhen, a predynastic king of Upper Egypt. And further back still, some two thousand years before him, in about 5000 B.C., there lived a Sumerian queen named Ninziddamkiag, which is believed to mean "the queen [who] loves the faithful husband"...

Romeo was not the only one to have had an evocative name...

Our names thus have their origin where language itself has its cradle—with this Egyptian king and that Sumerian queen. More specifically, they originated where the English language did: with the Greeks, the Romans, the Celts, the

Germanic peoples such as the Anglo-Saxons and the Vikings, and the Normans. All these races in fact had a naming system that was in many ways similar, since although it developed into the binomial system as we know it today, or, earlier, the famous trinomial system of the Romans (praenomen, nomen and cognomen), it originally involved the conferring of a single name that had a meaning.

This single meaningful name was in many cases what we might today think of as a nickname, as we have seen, or as a descriptive title. As such, it related directly or indirectly to the person named. If directly, it perhaps described his appearance, manner, gait or general image – either what he was or what he might become. The name might consist of a single element, as the Celtic word *ruadh*, "red," for someone who was of ruddy complexion (today the name is Roy), or a double element, as the Gerald mentioned, whose name derives from the Germanic *ger*, "spear," and *vald*, "rule." (This latter name was not so much an actual description but a desirable description: the child Gerald was so named in the hope that he would grow up to be a fearless ruler-by-the-spear. Might not his name help him to do this? Even today the power or suggestiveness of a name is strong. Kirk is probably more likely to be a modern "spear-ruler" than, say, Kevin.) If a name related indirectly to a person, it would usually derive from his or her family, home area, or occupation. If the first of these, it would often derive from the name of the father or grandfather. The Greeks, for example, named the eldest son after his paternal grandfather and later children after other relatives. Sometimes, however, a Greek boy bore the same name as his father. This was the case with Demosthenes, the orator, whose name, like the Germanic Gerald, was a two-element one and meant "people-strength." (Like Gerald, too, it is a desirable image name.)* Examples of names deriving respectively from a person's place of residence and his occupation are the Anglo-Saxon Grene (modern Green), for someone who lived near the village green, and Cupere (Cooper), for a man who made or repaired wooden casks.

The categories – descriptive, familial, residential and occupational – form the basis for most modern European and transatlantic surnames.

An interesting study, which regrettably would take up too much space to be made in this present book, would be to trace the fortunes and popularity of the original names as they evolved down the centuries, and to consider why many such names became fixed as surnames only (in the modern sense), while others remain in common use as Christian names or forenames. Of the few names we have already mentioned, for example, Bishop, Green and Cooper are more familiar today as surnames, while Gerald and Roy, although also occurring as surnames, are probably more frequent as forenames. Generally speaking, it can be said that *any* surname is capable of being put into use as a forename – Dudley and Sidney were English surnames that made this transition in the sixteenth century, just as later in America Chauncey and Washington were adopted as Christian names – but that many surnames, in particular familial, residential and occupational ones, just never made it.

Women's names were formed similarly but with a feminine ending. An unmarried Greek woman would derive her name from her father, a married woman from her husband, a widow from her son.

As to why surnames exist at all, the answer is much more straightforward. Surnames were found necessary to distinguish one particular person from others, perhaps many others, who had the same single name. And the simplest way to find another name—as we shall also see when we come to look specifically at pseudonyms—is to use your own father's name, as well as your own. This, after all, is what a surname is—a name that is "super" to, or added to, your own. (The word *surname* is not related to *sir*. As the sixteenth-century English historian and antiquary William Camden concisely but carefully put it, in his *Remains Concerning Britain,* "The French and we termed them Surnames, not because they are the names of the *Sire,* or the father, but because they are *super*-added to Christian names.") And to make it clear that you are using your father's name in your capacity as a son, many surnames came to incorporate an element that actually means "son." One we have already seen, since the Latin *filius* in the Domesday Book's Robertus filius Geraldi survives, in assimilated French form, as the Fitz- that begins many surnames, while a number of recognizable Christian names have become surnames by the simple process of having the actual word "son" tacked on to them. Thus both a Fitzwilliam and a Williamson had, originally, a father named William. Parallels to this I-am-the-son-of-my-father label exist in many other languages besides English. The Jewish equivalent, and a far more ancient one, is the *bar* or *ben*, meaning "son," in such names as the biblical Simon-bar-Jonas and the Talmudic Joshua ben Hananiah (*bar* is the Aramaic form, and *ben*, the Hebrew), while although not a surname in the modern sense, the Russian patronymic—the middle of three names that all Russians have, as Lev *Nikolayevich* Tolstoy or Maya *Mikhailovna* Plisetskaya—is still obligatory.

Subsequently, once a surname had been acquired, it became a family name proper and passed on, ordinarily, from father to son and daughter in the manner we have long become accustomed to. Perhaps it is a pity that in English we call this name, at times misleadingly, as we have seen, a "surname." The French, with their *nom de famille,* and the Germans, who know it as a *Familienname*, are much nearer to the real nature of the thing.

We have referred, too, to one of the four categories of surname as *nicknames*. This also is perhaps not quite the right word here, since properly, a nickname is an additional name or an extra name, and how can one refer to a single name as an extra name when it is the only one there is? (Even the work *nickname* has become distorted. By rights it should be not "a nickname" but "an ickname," since it derives from the now rare word *eke* meaning "also.") On the other hand to call such names *descriptive* names is to be almost too wide-ranging, since in a sense the other three categories are also descriptive. A reasonable alternative might be to call such direct names, which relate to the person him- or herself, *characterizing names*.

But we have so far mentioned only once the type of name that this book is really about, the *pseudonym*. And since we shall be using the word continually we must define it here, before going any further.

Literally, of course, a pseudonym is a "false name," as the two Greek elements that make up the word indicate. The term is a relatively new one. The *Oxford*

English Dictionary records its earliest appearance only as late as 1846, although the adjective "pseudonymous" dates back to 1706. The most recent (seventh, 1982) edition of the *Concise Oxford Dictionary* defines a pseudonym as a "fictitious name, especially one assumed by an author." Not a false name, a "fictitious" one. The same dictionary defines *fictitious* as "assumed," when applied to a name. And this, basically, is the sense in which we shall be using "pseudonym" in the present book: as a name that, whether it subsequently becomes a person's "proper" or permanent name or not, is one that has been consciously assumed or taken on instead of, or in addition to, the person's real name. In fact, it would be better to play down the "fictitious" side to such a name and emphasize the "assumed" aspect, since we shall be considering name changes of all kinds, even legal ones undertaken by such means as a deed poll. Is there in fact any point in saying that an assumed name is a false one? Name is a name is a name, as Gertrude Stein so nearly said. (Well, she was talking about Rose, and everyone knows what would smell as sweet.)

2. Why Another Name?

A good name is better than precious ointment. (Ecclesiastes 7:1)

Who are the people who choose to adopt a pseudonym or to change their name, and why do they do it?

Broadly speaking people assume a new or additional name because they have to, because they are expected to, or simply because they want to. The name that they assume is then made known to the public at large, to a particular group of people, or just to one other person. An actor, for example, wants his whole public to know his new name, while a spy or secret agent operates under a cover name that is known only to a select few. An individual, on the other hand, can communicate a message to a friend or loved one in a press announcement, for example, by using a disguised name that is known to his or her correspondent alone.

Let us see who exactly the main groups of people are.

One of the most common and striking situations in which people will change their original names for new ones is the act, to a greater or lesser degree traumatic, of emigration and subsequent naturalization. A person leaves his or her native country for some reason – often driven out by war, persecution or destitution – and, arriving in another, where very likely a new language is spoken, officially or tacitly starts a new life, assumes a new identity, and takes on a new name to go with it. One of the greatest migrations in history was the mass emigration to America by around 35 million people from all parts of Europe between 1820 and 1930. In their flight from poverty, famine and persecution, inhabitants of Great Britain and Ireland, Germany and Scandinavia, Italy and the Balkans, Russia and the Austro-Hungarian Empire, many of them Jews, poured into America in the hope of setting up a new life in a country that seemed to offer refuge and opportunities. And when they eventually reached the immigrant depot at Ellis Island – "Heartbreak Island" many of them called it, for fear of being denied entry – they were faced with a number of questions, of which the first was always, "What is your name?"

Immigrant names were a constant source of difficulty. Many of the newly arrived were barely literate and could not even spell their names, with the result that officials frequently simplified or anglicized them haphazardly. This meant that a number of immigrants left Ellis Island with a new name, perhaps not even realizing this, although many, especially the more literate, acquired a new name only in due course.

There are two well known stories about "on-the-spot" name changes of this kind.

The first concerns a German Jew named Isaac. Confused by all the questioning, he replied, when asked his name, "Ich vergessen" ("I forget" in Yiddish). The immigrant officer recorded his name as Fergusson.

The second incident is an occurrence in Elia Kazan's film *America, America* (1963). A Greek shoeshine boy, Stavros Topouzoglou, frightened that he may not be allowed into the country, answers to the name of a dead friend, Hohannes Gardashian. The officer tells him that if he wants to be an American, he must change his name for something shorter. "Hohannes – that's *all* you need here!" And he writes the name "Joe Arness," adding, "Well, boy, you're reborn, you're baptized again. And without benefit of clergy. Next. . . "

Whimsical though such tales are, they illustrate some important realities about the process of changing one's name. First a name change can be quite an arbitrary thing. Indeed, although many of the changes recorded in this book were undertaken consciously and deliberately, thousands of American immigrants came to have their names changed by random and gradual processes – a letter dropped here, a respelling adopted there – and changed most of all, perhaps, by what Howard F. Barker, one of America's greatest authorities on surnames, called "the abrasion of common speech." Second, the immigrant officer's comment, "You're reborn," states a basic philosophy that underlies virtually all name changes. For a human being, after all, a name is far more than a mere identification tag. It is not like a place name, for example, where *London* denotes "the capital of Great Britain" and *Fort Knox* signifies "military reservation and air base in Kentucky, where most of the U.S. gold reserves are stored." Our names not only identify us, they *are* us: they announce us, advertise us and embody us. Stavros the shoeshine boy, like many other immigrants, had his name changed for him, but many people choose a new name simply because they feel that the name itself can bestow a new image and a new persona. "In assuming a new name," the French literary critic Jean Starobinski wrote of Stendhal, who assumed over a hundred pseudonyms, "he not only grants himself a new face, but a new destiny, a new social rank, new nationalities." On a rather different plane, but approached by the same path, the pop singer Elton John commented, on adopting his new stage name, "I'm still the same guy, but a new name gave me a new outlook on life, and a new drive to do things."

Short of an actual physical reincarnation, a change of name is one of the most popular and efficacious ways, many believe, of becoming a new or a different person.

For the many Jews in this great immigration, the adoption of a new name was nothing new in itself. A hundred years previously, for example, Jews in many European countries had been ordered to assume fixed family names as the result of a radical change in the political and cultural climate. It was at this time, in fact, that many Germanic Jewish names arose, such as Weiss, Schwartz, Gross and Klein. These particular four names (White, Black, Large, Little) were in turn often random names, given or acquired with no relevance to the person who came to be so named. In many communities in Hungary, for instance, Jews were divided into four arbitrary groups and each of these names was assigned to every person in one of the groups.

Now, a century later, many immigrant Jews were obliged to change their name again, to an English-style surname. So widespread was the change, and so diffuse, that today it is virtually impossible to identify a given surname as Jewish: there are thousands of Smiths, Browns and Joneses who were originally, perhaps, Kovacs, Brand or (with utter dissimilarity) Edelstein. On the other hand, it is clear that today such name changes, foreign or Jewish to English, for example, are not taking place on anything like the scale that they did in the nineteenth century. In 1977 the director of the U.S. Immigration and Naturalization Service stated that each year about 142,000 people assume American nationality and of these only 7,000, or 15 percent, change their name, mainly by shortening it so that it is easier to pronounce in English. As the Russian U.S. émigré newspaper *Novoye Russkoye Slovo* commented: "In recent years the number of immigrants changing their name has fallen considerably. Many newcomers to the States prefer to maintain their ties with their homeland by keeping their real name and continuing to speak their native language" (September 1, 1977).

The practical advantages of changing a foreign name to an English-sounding one are obvious, and have already been mentioned. It is self-evident that if a person wishes to assimilate fully and successfully into a community, a name that blends with the others' will be of considerable assistance. Of course, equally, there is an obverse side to this: a person who does not change his or her name will be conspicuous as a foreigner, and this may be at least a hindrance, at most a positive and highly undesirable branding, especially in time of war. This was noticeably so in the First World War, when many Anglophones with Germanic names keenly regretted their "alien" name or were prompted to change it. The English poet, ultimately of Dutch origin, John Betjeman related in his verse autobiography *Summoned by Bells* how he was taunted at school about his name ("Betjeman's a German spy/ Shoot him down and let him die"), and in the British royal family King George V changed the family name from Wettin to Windsor by proclamation on July 17, 1917, while Queen Mary's family changed their name from Teck to "of Cambridge" and the Battenbergs became the Mountbattens. (See page 14, Chapter 3, for more on royal name changes.)

Would people ever change their English names to foreign ones, or to ones not native to them? The immigrants, of course, changed their native names to nonnative ones, but occasions when an English name has been changed to a foreign one, except for frivolous or satirical reasons, are not common, although cases have been recorded of Jews changing *back* to their original name from the English one that they adopted on immigration. There are perhaps two exceptions to this tendency not to change to a foreign name. The first is for groups such as ballet dancers, who may find it helpful to assume a foreign-sounding name, especially a Russian one. Thus the dancer Hilda Boot assumed the surname Butsova, while Patrick Healey-Kay became the well known ballet star Anton Dolin. In some instances it comes as a surprise to find that a ballerina did not originally have the Russian name by which she became famous. Tamara Karsavina was born Tamara Karsavina, but Lydia Sokolova began her dancing career as plain Hilda Munnings.

Then, apart from special instances such as that of disguise, when the national of one country aimed to pass himself off as the citizen of another, there have been occasions when some writers have assumed a foreign name with the aim of describing their impressions of their own country apparently through the eyes of an alien observer. Oliver Goldsmith did this for his *Chinese Letters*, which originally appeared as purportedly written by a Chinese philosopher named Lien Chi Altangi. This was in the mid-eighteenth century. On similar lines, but at the beginning of the last century, Robert Southey's *Letters of Espriella* claimed to be a collection of letters written from England by a young Spaniard, giving a picture of the times. There have been other examples of "foreigners' letters," most of which were inspired by the *Lettres Persanes* (Persian Letters) of the French writer Montesquieu. These letters comprised the supposed correspondence of two Persians, Rica and Usbek, making observations about life and *mœurs* in Paris at the end of the reign of Louis XIV.

All name changes, of course, are in the last resort voluntary affairs, although political or social pressure may be very great to make the change. Possibly the only category of person who is virtually compelled to make a name change is someone who has undergone a sex change. To undergo such a radical physical and emotional transformation and retain one's old opposite sex name would seem most undesirable. In recent times one such change (of sex and name) that became widely publicized, simply because the person concerned was, and is, a distinguished writer in his — now her — own right, was that of the distinguished English author and former editor Jan Morris, formerly James Morris. Jan Morris describes the whole experience and its consequences in her book *Conundrum* (1974). (See also her entry on page 227.)

A category where a name change is normally mandatory is that of persons entering a religious order, the motivation behind the change being the spiritual rebirth undergone by the entrant. We shall examine the various types of religious names adopted in Chapter 5; suffice it to say here that as a result of the second Vatican Council of 1962–1965 many Roman Catholic religious orders have dropped the giving of a name in religion altogether. In the Roman Catholic church, too, it is the usual practice, although not obligatory, for a person to take an additional name at Confirmation. The acquisition of a religious name of any kind is regarded as so significant that the bearer of the name, which is often that of a saint, will celebrate his "name-day" annually as a type of birthday — perhaps one should say "rebirth" day — on the feast day of the particular saint. In the Eastern Orthodox church the baptismal name is marked in this way, since the bearer will very likely have been named after the saint on whose feast day he or she was born.

The motivation that lies behind the assuming of a religious name — both a rebirth and a rejection of one's former worldly identification — seems to have influenced a category of name change that has been regularly observed since the eleventh century. This is the change of name undertaken by a pope upon his election. It is not actually obligatory for a pope to assume a new name, but an old custom. Although two popes, in fact, did not change their name — Adrian VI (pope in 1522–1523) and Marcellus II (in 1555) — in practice every pope has changed his name since Peter, bishop of Pavia, assumed the name John in 983. It is believed that he made this change out of reverence for St. Peter, the first pope, since in his *Epitaph* he says that he took on a new name "quia Petrus antea existerat" ("because Peter existed before"). Most popes have come to assume the name of a predecessor—the present pope, John Paul II, took the names of *two* predecessors—but there is one name that no pope will adopt. This name is Peter, and a tradition exists, or a superstition, if one dare mention such a thing with regard to the head of the Roman Catholic church, that if a pope named "Peter II" is elected he will be the last of all popes.

The very early popes changed their names simply because their original names were pagan: John II (pope in 533–535) was formerly Mercurius, and John XII (955–964) was Octavianus. On similar lines, and encouraged by the example of John XIV, the former Peter, the first transalpine pontiffs, Bruno of Carinthia and Gerbert of Aurillac, changed their barbarous names to genuine Roman ones, respectively Gregory V (966) and Sylvester II (999). In more recent times the motives for a papal name change have become a good deal more complex, and have included such factors as veneration for a particular predecessor of the same name, a "specialization" in the works of a predecessor, or simply a coincidence of election date or of place or region of origin. Papal names form a sufficiently distinctive and interesting category for us to treat them separately, as special names, in Chapter 7.

Turning from saints to sinners, we have a noted category of name adopters in criminals of all kinds. Here, perhaps, the desire for a new name is motivated not so much by the wish to start life afresh—no spiritual rebirth here!—but to dissociate oneself with one's former, "real" self. In this, at least, renegades and members of religious orders share a common reasoning. In the case of a criminal, of course, one important objective is to avoid detection or identification, and so an actual physical disguise is often accompanied by a change of name. The name itself may be unimportant: what *is* important is that the criminal should have a name of some kind, since truly and permanently anonymous human beings do not exist. Ideally, to have no name at all would be an excellent idea, since then the murderer would stand a good chance of escaping undetected, and no one would know whodunit. But if you start life with a name, as we all do, you cannot simply abandon it without replacing it somehow. Even the Man in the Iron Mask had a name, although what it was has still not been established with any degree of certainty.

A special type of name assumed by a criminal, or even a suspect, is, of course, an alias. The word is Latin in origin, meaning "otherwise," a sense that is indicated more obviously in the alternative term for an alias—"a.k.a," or "also known as," an abbreviation rather more common in the United States than in Britain.

Like misfortunes, aliases rarely come singly, especially when a criminal or suspect is on the run, and they are changed as often as the bearer's route and disguise. The ideal alias is one that is contained in a stolen or forged passport, which is essential if the criminal is escaping to another country. Cases of criminals with forged or illegal passports are legion. One that hit the headlines in 1977, largely because of its lurid details and bizarre nature—it actually combined sex and religion—was that of the "Mormon kidnap." A young Mormon missionary, one Kirk Anderson, claimed to have been "kidnapped and held handcuffed and manacled for three days on the orders of a wealthy lovesick woman" (*Sunday Times*,

September 18, 1977). The rich and randy lady in question was Joyce, or Joy, McKinney. Among aliases used by McKinney in forged passports on her subsequent flight from the police were Mrs. Bosler, Kathie Vaughn Bare, Cathy Van Deusen, Heidi Krasler, and Mrs. Palmquist. Traveling with her as her supposed husband was Keith Joseph May, a.k.a. Bob Bosler, alias Paul Van Deusen. Miss McKinney was something of an old hand at assuming a different name, it seemed. She had previously appeared as a model in a girlie magazine as Lexi Martin, and had advertised herself ("Gorgeous Former 'Miss USA' Contestant Desires Work!") in the *Los Angeles Free Press* as Joey.

The range of uses to which a name change can be put illegally or criminally is very wide. At one end there is the murderer and his alias. At the other is the child at school who answers "Here!" at rollcall to cover up for a friend who is playing hookey. This is a trivial but genuine case of impersonation. A number of cases are known of one person temporarily or even permanently succeeding in passing himself off as another. Among the more unusual, since they involve an impersonation of the opposite sex, are the histories of the seventeenth-century Spanish nun Catalina de Eranso, who served with the Spanish army in Chile and Peru as Alonso Díaz Ramírez de Guzmán, and of Barbara Ann Malpass, who spent four months in Jefferson County jail in 1959 claiming to be Charles Richard Williams. In the latter case the impersonation was made for the simple, practical reason that the prisoner reckoned she could more easily pass as a male runaway than a female.

It is certainly a fact that many pseudonyms are adopted for nefarious purposes, or at least for disguise. The code names and cover names taken by spies and undercover agents are well known, from the famous, although fictional, 007 (James Bond), to the infamous Cicero, who supplied top secret documents to the Germans in the Second World War — for a sizeable consideration — and who turned out to be, or so he claimed in a book published in London in 1953, one E. Bazna. Espionage is a world of forged papers, fake identities and secret passwords, a dark world of aliases, incognitos and assumed names. Experts in the art — or science — of espionage distinguish between a cover name and an operational name. A cover name is the name adopted by an agent when he embarks on his actual operation. In doing this, he assumes the identity of either a real person or a fictional one. If the former, he will also be impersonating that person. Thus the cover name of the Russian spy K.T. Molody was Gordon Lonsdale. An operational name, by contrast, is the name by which an agent is known to his chiefs, so that he can be identified without reference being made to his real name or his cover name. Thus the British-Russian agent whose real name was Allan Nunn May had the operational name Alek.

In considering the various categories of people who assume another name, we have briefly mentioned ballerinas and, in a very limited application, a few writers. These are members of a creative profession whose names — stage names and pen names — are probably the most familiar to the world since they are in a most popular sector of society. But before considering these special people, in Chapter 4, let us take a look at the more common majority who change their names for traditional or legal reasons.

3. Changing Names

Why, this is flat knavery, to take upon you another man's name. (Petruchio in "The Taming of the Shrew")

Both historically and actually, in past and present, name changes have long been a feature of the human scene.

History tends to concentrate on personalities, and the consequences of their actions. But behind some of the most familiar names there are some surprises, and we find that some of the best-known names are not really what they seem.

Oliver Cromwell, for example, was not really a Cromwell at all, but a Williams.

How did this come about? A certain Welsh gentleman, named Morgan Williams, married the sister, Katherine, of Thomas Cromwell, who had himself been created Earl of Essex by Henry VIII. Morgan Williams's son was Richard Williams, who received the patronage of Thomas Cromwell and who adopted his name in consequence, as sometimes happened. He was thus an ancestor of Oliver Cromwell (himself the great-great-grandson of Morgan Williams), and the Lord Protector of England was aware of his family line and former family name, even signing himself on occasions as "Oliver Williams, *alias* Cromwell."

Again, look up the Duke of Wellington, the "Iron Duke" who routed Napoleon at the Battle of Waterloo (1815), in any standard encyclopedia, and you will find that his name is given as Arthur Wellesley. Yet he was the grandson of a man named Richard Colley, or Cowley, who adopted the name of an Irish cousin, Garrett Wesley, on succeeding to his estates in 1728, and who later changed this name to Wellesley.

Even the great Mowbray family, whose name became that of the Earls of Northumberland and subsequently (by marriage) of the Earls of Nottingham, was really de Albini. The baronial house was founded at the Norman Conquest by Geoffrey de Montbrai, Bishop of Coutances. His nephew and heir, Robert de Mowbray, Earl of Northumberland (died 1125), rebelled against William Rufus and was consequently imprisoned at Windsor. He had married Mathilde de l'Aigle, but when he was imprisoned his wife was granted permission by the pope to dissolve the marriage and to marry instead Nigel de Albini (d'Aubigny), another nephew of the Bishop of Coutances. Nigel thus founded the second house of Mowbray, changing his name to this from de Albini together with his son, Roger, by order of Henry I, on the king's granting him the vast estates of his imprisoned uncle. This line of Mowbrays lasted until 1476, when John Mowbray, sixteenth Baron Mowbray and fourth Duke of Norfolk, died without leaving any male issue. On the death of his daughter Anne (in 1481), the dukedom of Norfolk passed to the Howard family.

12

In a similar fashion, the Dukes and Earls of Northumberland (distinct from the Mowbray already mentioned) are traditionally associated with the family name Percy, after the Norman baron, William de Percy, who accompanied William the Conqueror to England. Yet Sir Hugh Percy (1715–1786), first Duke of Northumberland of the third creation, was originally Sir Hugh Smithson. He gained the honors of the house of Percy through his grandmother-in-law, Lady Elizabeth Seymour, née Percy, heiress of the eleventh Earl of Northumberland, assuming her name and arms in 1750 on succeeding to the earldom through his wife, Lady Elizabeth's granddaughter, whom he had married ten years earlier. (The lady's grandfather, Charles Seymour, sixth Duke of Somerset, was not happy about the marriage, but it went ahead anyway.)

A glance through the many pages of the great *Dictionary of National Biography* reveals not only these name changes, but many others of a similar nature, brought about through various terms and conditions pertaining to family inheritances and marriages. To put it fairly crudely, Mr. A inherits the estate of his uncle, Mr. B, so changes his name from A to B. Or else Mr. C marries Miss D, herself an heiress, and on her succession to the inheritance changes his name (C) to hers (D), instead of the other way around, as usually happens. (Of which more below in due course.)

The examples quoted happen to be well-known families, but the same sort of name change can be found for other, less widely known families. Here are just a couple more examples:

Francis Egerton, first Earl of Ellesmere (1800–1857), was born the younger son of George Granvile Leveson-Gower (pronounced "Loosson-Gor"), 2nd Marquis of Stafford. On the death of his father in 1833, he changed his name from Leveson-Gower to Egerton, this being the name of his bachelor uncle, Francis Henry Egerton, eighth Earl of Bridgewater (died 1829), who left him property estimated at the then colossal evaluation of around £90,000 per annum. (The uncle died an eccentric in Paris, his house filled with dogs and cats dressed up as men and women.)

Then there was Sir Thomas Hugh Clifford Constable (1762–1823), topographer and botanist, born the son of Thomas Clifford and his wife Barbara, née Aston. In 1821 he succeeded to the estates of Francis Constable, of Burton Constable, and two years later was granted royal permission to adopt the name of Constable as his surname.

Sir Thomas Constable did not acquire his new name until a few months before his death, at the age of 61, unlike Francis Egerton, who was almost half this age when he made his name change. But the changes were equally valid and equally dependent on succession to an estate, and were typical of their time, which after all was not all *that* long ago, historically speaking.

The estate or property acquired need not necessarily be held by a member of the family, but can belong to a quite unrelated person. There is a nice example in literature of a name change resulting from an acquisition of property. In Thomas Hardy's *Tess of the D'Urbervilles*, where the author deploys so much genealogical skill, one John Stoke buys property in a part of England different from the one in which he had actually made his fortune. The acquisition prompts him to change his name, and he visits the British Museum, London, to study the county histories. He comes across the name "D'Urberville" and, in Hardy's words, "considered that D'Urberville looked and sounded as well as any of them: and D'Urberville accordingly was annexed to his own name for himself and his heirs eternally." His family thus became "Stoke-D'Urberville," but subsequently dropped the "Stoke." (The novel centers on Tess Durbeyfield, whose father John, a poor villager, has his head turned when he learns that he is descended from the ancient family of D'Urberville. Meanwhile Tess is seduced by Alec D'Urberville, son of the former John Stoke, whose claim to the name, as we have seen, is at best doubtful.)

Name changes of a somewhat different kind have taken place over the past century in the British royal family.

British kings and queens have never had individual surnames in the accepted sense, but instead have had "house" names, that is, names of dynasties. The further back one goes in time, the more general do the dynastic names seem, with William the Conqueror, for example, regarded as belonging to the "House of Normandy," and his great-grandson, Henry II, being the first of the "House of Plantagenet." (The latter name is essentially a nickname, given to Henry's father, Geoffrey, for his habit of wearing a sprig of broom, Latin *planta genista*, in his hat. Paradoxically, a case could be made for arguing that this name is much closer to a modern surname in its origin than many recent royal dynastic names. The only other royal house names resembling a genuine modern surname are those of "Tudor," this being the family name of a line of Welsh gentry, and "Stuart," originating as an occupational name, that of "steward," i.e. an officer of the Scottish royal household.)

George I was the first of the "House of Hanover," which concluded with Queen Victoria, who died in 1901. She was succeeded by Edward VII, of the "House of Saxe-Coburg." He took this dynastic name because Victoria's husband, Albert, had been Prince of Saxe-Coburg and Gotha. The German connection, which had been all too evident in the British royal family since the accession of George I (in 1714) as the son of the Elector of Hanover, would soon become an embarrassment. Edward VII died in 1910, and his successor, George V, was a cousin of the German Kaiser, Wilhelm II. Not so convenient when the First World War broke out in 1914, and a dilemma for the British royal family, who found themselves with a regal foot (so to speak) in the enemy's camp. At this time, too, several members of the royal family had German names and titles. What to do?

The solution adopted by the king was for the royal family to take a (British) *surname*, which would at the same time serve as a dynastic name. Similarly, British surnames were adopted in place of German family titles by other members of the royal family.

The first set of royal name changes was decreed in an order that appeared in the press on June 20, 1917 (somewhat late in the day, but better late than never). It ran as follows: "The King has deemed it desirable, in the conditions brought about by the present war, that those princes of his family who are his subjects and bear German names and titles should relinquish these titles, and henceforth adopt British surnames." This resulted in the creation of four new peerages: the Duke of Teck and his brother, Prince Alexander, became respectively Marquess of

Cambridge and Earl of Athlone, while the Princes Louis and Alexander of Battenberg became Marquesses of Milford Haven and Carisbrooke, respectively. Other members of the Teck family took the surname "Cambridge," while members of the Battenberg family assumed the surname "Mountbatten." (The latter, it will be noticed, is merely a part translation of the original German name.)

The next step was for King George, at a meeting of the Privy Council on July 17, to announce his intention, set forth in a royal proclamation of the same date, that "the Name of Windsor is to be borne by His Royal House and Family and Relinquishing the use of All German Titles and Dignities" to determine that his house and family "shall be styled and known as the House and Family of Windsor."

Why Windsor? The answer, of course, is in the Royal Castle of Windsor, in the town of this name in Berkshire by the banks of the Thames. Virtually every king and queen since William the Conqueror has had a hand in the building. Henry II (already mentioned) erected the first stone buildings, including the famous Round Tower, and the defenses are largely to this day those built under Henry III. Edward III was born there, and almost all succeeding monarchs down to George IV, including the two queens, expanded or altered the building. Windsor itself is also an ancient place-name, recorded even before the Norman Conquest of 1066, so on that ground is equally suitable. The name itself was proposed for the royal family by George V's private secretary, Arthur John Bigge, Baron Stamfordham. But he seems not to have been aware that as long ago as the fourteenth century, King Edward III had been styled as "Sir Edward de Windsor, King of England"!

The subsequent history of the royal family and its new surname is also not without interest. An intriguing situation developed when Queen Elizabeth II came to the throne in 1952. Before her accession, she had been married to the Duke of Edinburgh, so that her surname would have been the same as that of her husband, in other words, Mountbatten. It was possible to argue that on her succession, the royal house was in effect not the House of Windsor, but the House of Mountbatten. The new queen clarified the situation in a declaration of April 9, 1952, just two months after her succession, when she decreed that she and her descendants, other than females who marry, and their descendants, should bear the name of Windsor.

The Duke of Edinburgh, of course, was not a British subject in origin, and was naturalized six months before his marriage to the future queen in 1947, taking the surname of his uncle, Mountbatten. Before his naturalization, as a prince of the royal house of Greece and Denmark, his surname had been the impressively Germanic Schleswig-Holstein-Sonderburg-Glucksberg.

The tale of the Windsor surname was even now not quite complete, for in 1960, when the queen had been on the throne for eight years, she made a further declaration in Council with regard to it. This declaration brings us right up to date, and even into the future, so is worth quoting in full:

> Whereas on the 9th day of April, 1952, I did declare in Council My Will and Pleasure that I and My children shall be styled and known as of the House and Family of Windsor, and that my descendants, other than female descendants who marry and their descendants, shall bear the

name of Windsor. And whereas I have given further consideration to the position of those of My descendants who will enjoy neither the style, title or attribute of Royal Highness, nor the titular dignity of Prince, and for whom therefore a surname will be necessary. And whereas I have concluded that the Declaration made by Me on the 9th day of April, 1952, should be varied in its application to such persons: Now therefore I declare my Will and Pleasure that, while I and My children shall continue to be styled and known as the House and Family of Windsor, My descendants other than descendants enjoying the style, title or attribute of Royal Highness and titular dignity of Prince or Princess and female descendants who marry and their descendants shall bear the name of Mountbatten-Windsor.

This declaration could only apply to the grandchildren of the present Prince of Wales, Prince Charles, apart from the eldest grandson, and of the queen's subsequent other sons (Prince Andrew and Prince Edward). (Under a ruling of George V, the title and style of Prince and Princess were restricted to his grandchildren.) And so now, for the first time in British history, members of the royal family will have a hyphenated surname.

It goes without saying that the surname Windsor exists in its own right, as do surnames derived from many similarly ancient British place-names.

But just supposing that for some reason – not necessarily antiroyalist ones – you are named Windsor and do not like your name. How can you legally change it?

In the United States, a legal name change (except change of a woman's surname due to marriage) is a special proceeding of the local civic court. With this proceeding completed, you can then apply to the Social Security Administration for a new card (retaining your original number). The application must include Form SS5, available at local Social Security offices, and the original court document showing the name change (photocopies are not acceptable).

A woman who changes her name on marriage must also complete Form SS5 if she wishes official recognition of the change in the form of a Social Security card. Her application must include her original (not photocopied) marriage license.

In Britain, a name change is much easier. You simply change it, then advertise the fact, traditionally in the local or national press. This is what is known in legal terms as acquisition of a new name "by use and reputation." Cases of such lawful name changes can still be spotted, if irregularly, in the press, and are usually couched in fairly formal wording, on the lines of the following: "I, William Windsor, of 246 Main Street, Windsor, Berkshire, pastrycook, heretofore called and known by the name of William Wilberforce Windsor, hereby give notice that I have renounced and abandoned the name of William Wilberforce Windsor, and that I have assumed and intend henceforth on all occasions whatsoever and at all times to sign and use and to be called and known by the name of Frederick Makepeace Cook, in lieu and in substitution for my former name of William Wilberforce Windsor. Dated this 10th day of April, 1990." (Most such announcements, however, are much less wordy. Even so, they still have full legal force.)

Some changes of this type have remained memorable, if only because an obviously undesirable name was changed to a more acceptable one. The classic example, still quoted, is that of one Joshua Bug, who in the June 26, 1862, issue of *The Times* announced that he had assumed the new name of "Norfolk Howard." As a result, "Norfolk Howard" became a colloquial term for a bug for several years after.

The other, more formal and official British method of effecting a name change, is the so-called "deed poll." This is a fairly common and convenient way to evidence a name change, and consists of a declaration similar to the one above, but made before a witness, ideally a professional one such as Commissioner for Oaths. (The somewhat strange term originally designated a deed that was "polled," that is, the document was cut evenly along its sides, unlike an indenture, where the jagged edges of the two documents, one made by each party, were cut so as to fit into each other when the two deeds were placed together. In the case of a deed poll, the declaration is made by one person only, so there is no need for a second matching document.)

Naturally, there are many situations where a name change may be desirable, apart from those already mentioned. But the most common situation of all is that of marriage, the changer being the woman, who relinquishes her maiden name and takes the surname of her husband.

The tradition or custom is an old one, regarded as having symbolic significance, chiefly of a religious nature. The attitude was well summarized by the seventeenth-century English antiquary William Camden, who in his *Remains Concerning Britain* (1674), in which there is much of interest on personal and other names, wrote: "Here might I note that women with us at their marriage do change their surnames, and pass into their husbands' names, and justly, for that then *Non sunt duo, sed caro una* [They are not two, but one flesh]". Camden does go on to note, however, that not all countries observed this practice, and cites France and the Netherlands, where "The better sort of women will still retain their name with their husband's." (He comments: "But I fear husbands will not like this note, for that some of their dames may be ambitiously over pert and too-too forward to imitate it.")

The intention, thus, was for a unification of surname. But if two people have different names, as they of course almost always will, then naturally *one* will have to make a change. And in more recent times feminists of even the least militant kind have not been slow to point out that the change is traditionally made by the woman, not the man. The name change is thus seen as a subservient act, involving not merely a change of identity, but a loss of individuality. The abandoning of one's own family name, after all, is a highly personal and deeply felt affair. Hence the various devices used to avoid such an adoption and loss. One of the most widely favored is the practice commonly found in the United States, where a woman, on marrying, simply adds her husband's name to her own, which she retains. This results in a situation where, say, Jane Shore marries a John Strand, and becomes, however incongruously, Jane Shore Strand. In a traditional British family, the same lady would be Jane Strand, née Shore, with the latter name used only for documentation purposes, as when filling out an official application form of some kind.

Another solution, of course, is for the woman either not to undertake a legally binding marriage, so that no name change is involved, or to continue to use her maiden name. Many professional women retain their maiden name after marriage, if only in order to avoid complications from the point of view of the public, who will have become accustomed to the original name. On the other hand, a compromise can be effected by which a married woman uses her husband's surname in private life, but retains her original name for her business or public life.

Whatever the solution to the situation, any woman who does change her name on marriage has to deal with a whole host of incidental matters resulting from the change, not least involving the notification of a sizeable number of official organizations or bodies to which she belongs, such as banks, building or savings societies, doctors' registers, passport authorities and the like. A man will encounter a similarly tiresome procedure only when he changes his address, when of course it is the address only that changes, not his own personal name.

And this is to say nothing of the further difficulties that can ensue for a married woman if she obtains a divorce and then remarries! In the latter case, she may well feel that it is simply not worth all the bother of informing the relevant authorities of a further name change, even if she does actually adopt the surname of her second husband. In fact, there is evidence showing that many women do *not* advertise or publicly notify their new surname on remarriage, which can result in a number of administrative problems or at least misunderstandings. A writer in *The Times* (November 11, 1985) explains her attitude to the situation that she found herself in after her second marriage: "As time went on I felt a strange reluctance to change. I don't know why. When I remarried I had no strong feelings about losing the old name. True, I'd had it for 22 years, so you could say I was well used to it. . . . I just went along with the convention that women change their names when they marry; and after five years of trouble, odd looks and embarrassment later, I'm still juggling with two names. Seems I'm just reluctant to let the old one go." (Christine Brown, "The name I never dropped. . . .") The writer explained that although her new married name was on her two credit cards, the old name remained on her bank account, check book, banker's card and cash card. (The new name was on the credit cards because her husband paid the bills.) The article goes on to detail the difficulties the writer encountered, as when presenting a check (in her new name) for deposit in her building society account (in the old name), or buying plane tickets in her new name while traveling with her passport still in her old name. The latter experience resulted in a ground hostess's recommendation that she should carry her marriage certificate with her when she next flew, and so avoid delay.

This particular twice-married woman reached the following conclusion about her situation: "I wish I could claim I was making some kind of statement about holding on to my old name, but I'm not. I can hardly say it's a feminist thing since both names belong originally to men. I've known women who, for professional reasons, hold on to their name from a previous marriage and hyphenate it with the second. I refuse to do that since anything hyphenated with Brown sounds silly to me."

But what if the divorcee does not remarry? She may well wish to retain her married name, with all its associations. But she may equally well decide to revert to her maiden name. That road may certainly be paved with good intentions, but it can involve similar obstacles and result in unexpected personal unease, even trauma.

A second writer, also in *The Times* (January 9, 1987), gives her account of what happened (Doreen Stanfield, "Rebirth of a maiden by any other name").

The lady postponed making any decision on the matter for some four years after her divorce, and only tackled the situation because she needed to renew her passport. "Having taken the plunge, gone to a lawyer and made a statutory declaration I began to feel surprisingly enthusiastic about the whole thing. I could hardly wait to shed my old identity and assume my new one in all areas of my life." She accordingly notified all the usual bodies and authorities, sent change-of-name cards to her friends, and went about her life in her new persona. But when her mail continued to arrive in the old name, she realized there was more to the business than met the eye. "The whole process seemed to have assumed a symbolic significance for me; it was rather like some sort of rebirth. I was a chrysalis which is almost a butterfly, but not quite." The writer described how she began to feel positively schizophrenic, so that when, for instance, she had to sign a check in her old name, while waiting for her new book to arrive, it "seemed to symbolize a regression into at best the cocoon of non-identity." She discovered that she attached much greater significance to her name than she had previously realized, and that she resented being reminded by correspondents who used her old name that she was still "old Mrs. X," and that she was "not quite out of the cocoon yet."

Eventually, after several months, the writer's metamorphosis was complete, and she was fully established (or re-established) in her maiden name. Now, "I am able to take the odd regressive missive addressed to Mrs. X in my stride. She now seems a different person from me, someone I once knew."

The two accounts summarized here well illustrate the technical and emotional hazards that accompany a name change. And although they respectively concern a remarriage and a divorce, there is no reason why, for some women, the mere adoption of another surname on marriage in the first place may not be equally complex and traumatic.

No wonder that some women prefer not to change their name at all! Here is the view of the British Member of Parliament Emma Nicholson, the wife of business executive Sir Michael Caine: "I do not believe it is necessary for women to take their husbands' names. I rather like my name and I am sticking to it. My father was in Parliament, he has no son and I want to carry it on for him. I enjoy the feeling of carrying the banner forward. People will address us as Sir Michael Caine and Emma Nicholson" (*The Times*, January 6, 1988).

A name change of another sort involves adopting a new first name (Christian name). Some people come to have an intense dislike of their first name, and wish to change it for another.

There is no legal problem in this. One simply starts using the new chosen name. The only difficulty arises when a person seeks to abandon a genuine Christian name, conferred at baptism. But in order to avoid ecclesiastical or other negotiations, most legal advisers recommend simply retaining the original Christian name, but not actually using it. In such instances, a person does not actually change a first name, therefore, but merely adopts an additional name.

The extreme distaste that some people feel for a first name that has undesirable associations, real or imaginary, is typified by the following letter from a reader to the "agony aunt" of the *TV Times* (January 23–29, 1988), the latter lady being none other than the Italian-born TV personality Katie Boyle (whose own name story appears in this book on page 100). The reader writes as follows: "How I wish that each of us could legally choose our own Christian names when we reach the age of majority. My parents christened me Elsie Maud, after my father's favorite sisters. How I dislike my first name, and I never even admit to my second. Have you noticed that Elsie is always the least intelligent creature in a film or TV play, and in comic-book stories it is always the name chosen for dimwits? I always laugh but, deep down, I feel hurt and mad! I really think my name has given me an inferiority complex. Do you understand, Katie?" As ever, Katie did, and came up with sound practical advice and even a new name for the long-suffering lady. "Indeed I do. Baptized Caterina and brought up in Italy, I loathed my own name. Now I am known by lots of other versions, such as Catherine, Kate, Katie and, by many Italian friends, Caterinella. This has helped, so why don't you just switch the letters round and become known as Elise. Say straight out you have always hated the name Elsie, never felt like an Elsie, and laugh at the switch, so others laugh with you, not at you. It's the giggle which will get you over any embarrassment and keep people sympathetically on your side. I shall be the first to send you warmest wishes, dear Elise."

In short, if the Queen of England can make a declaration adopting a new name, so can any of her subjects, and so indeed can anyone anywhere else. But the decision whether to adopt a new name at all in the first place is one for the individual, and may be the hardest aspect of the whole area of name changes.

4. Names for a Living

Who hath not own'd, with rapture-smitten frame,
The power of grace, the magic of a name?
(Thomas Campbell, "Pleasures of Hope")

"Words, words, words" — and rather more — are the medium by which most full-time actors and writers earn their living, and in both of these creative categories the adoption of a pseudonym is a long-standing tradition.

Let us consider each group in turn, taking those of the stage first. And here it must be said that the term actor (and actress) should be taken in its widest sense, to embrace all men and women who perform or entertain or dance or sing or play on the stage or screen, or over radio or television — all who practice the performing arts, in fact.

Many stage names are very familiar to the public, who may indeed not realize that they *are* stage names. Actors, after all, become stars and achieve fame and win awards, and their names take on a particularly exalted or important significance.

Why do actors adopt a different name?

Many would perhaps reply, "Because it's the tradition." Some might add, "It's automatic." But if we look at the motives more closely, we can see more specific reasons.

First, in their line of work, actors assume other identities in any case. They change their true selves and become someone else, if only for one evening. This is particularly true of professional stage and film actors and actresses. In playing a part, whether it is major or a minor role, an actor will also assume not only the identity and character of another person, but also the name of that person. A name change is thus part of the job. Therefore a new name is assumed as if to emphasize that such "dual personality" is anyway part and parcel of the actor's real life. An actor is thus versatile and gifted, and in changing his own name adapts his own persona to the bread-winning business of becoming someone else, night after night. A stage name is, then, very important: not for nothing is an actor's name usually referred to as his or her "professional" name.

And apart from the psychological motive, there is also a historical one. For some years in the past, acting, especially in "higher" circles of society, was regarded as an inferior, degrading or even decadent way of life. Actors would thus change their names to avoid this undesirable stigma, and to dissociate their true name — and the good name of their family — from their vocation.

Again, actors are, even today, superstitious people, believing in good fortune and fame only when it happens, and a change of name may help to avoid a possible

21

failure on the stage. After all, if you are a flop, it is not the real you that has failed but your alter ego. A different name may perhaps actually help to bring good luck in your performance, as well as ward against failure. We recall the reasoning behind the name change made by Elton John in Chapter 2. For him at any rate, the transformation seemed to work!

There are also, of course, sound practical reasons for making an actor's name change desirable. We have already mentioned some of these and should now enumerate them more specifically.

(1) An actor's real name may be a very ordinary or common one. He or she therefore wishes to change it to something rather more glamorous and memorable. Thus Peggy Middleton became Yvonne de Carlo, Merle Johnson turned into Troy Donahue, and Norma Jean Baker was metamorphosed as Marilyn Monroe. Even a change of one name is enough, so that Thomas Connery became Sean Connery, and a simple tiny addition or alteration of one letter can make all the difference: Coral Brown lost her common touch when she became Coral Browne, and Frankie Howard made people look again when he restyled his name as Frankie Howerd.

(2) A real name may be awkward or ugly or even have undesirable connotations. Change it—to something euphonious and mellifluous! Thus did Virginia McSweeney become Virginia Valli, Nadine Judd turn into Nadia Nerina, and Jean Shufflebottom move upmarket to Jeannie Carson. Actresses, in particular, are anxious to avoid a name smacking of impropriety, which prompted Dora Broadbent to change to Dora Bryan, Diana Fluck to be reborn as Diana Dors, and Joanne La Cock to make her name as Joanne Dru.

(3) Very much from the practical point of view, a stage name may simply be too long for billing. A shorter rather than a longer name is always more memorable, too. So it was not surprising that Michael Dumbell Smith turned into Michael Crawford, Deborah Kerr-Trimmer became trimmer as Deborah Kerr, and Roger Ollerearnshaw, the TV announcer, became Roger Shaw. A shortened name can often be an improved one, too. The popular singer Gracie Fields had a name much more melodious and pleasantly evocative than her real name of Grace Stansfield.

(4) As applies to all names, a foreign name is often best changed by an actor to an English one. So Bernard Schwartz, Dino Crocetti and Daniel Kaminsky must have thought, to change their respectively German, Italian and Polish-sounding names to Tony Curtis, Dean Martin, and Danny Kaye. Many stage name changes are of this type.

(5) It may happen that an actor's name is similar, or even identical, to the name of another actor. In this case he is well advised to change it, simply to avoid confusion. In fact the British actors' trade union, Equity, makes it a condition that no actor may perform with the same name as another. So James Stewart, the British film actor, changed his name to Stewart Granger so as not to be confused with James Stewart, the American actor, and Melvin Kaminsky, the film comedy writer and producer changed to Mel Brooks so as not to be muddled with Max Kaminsky, the trumpet player.

When it comes to writers, the use of a pseudonym is much more flexible, and less stereotyped, than with an actor. A written, recorded name, after all, can be much more subtly manipulated than the stage name that an actor bears in the manner of a true name. Unlike an actor's name, it can be used for a single piece of writing or genre of writing. For example; it can be permanent or temporary, meaningful or arbitrary, resemble a real name or be quite unlike a conventional name. A writer, too, can have more than one pseudonym – even as many as a hundred – and can jettison at will one pseudonym to adopt another, for whatever reason, as easily as setting pen to paper. Indeed, by the very term "pseudonym" most people understand a writer's assumed name rather than an actor's (many dictionaries will define the word in terms of a writing name), and although a stage name will undoubtedly, because of the charisma of its bearer, often acquire a "star" quality, it is the name adopted by a writer that will almost always be the more telling.

We have already touched on one or two reasons that prompt a writer to adopt another name (for disguise, or to gain prestige). We should now have a closer look at the motives for adopting a pen name – some of which, in fact, are virtually the same as the motives that lead to a stage name.

Unlike an actor, a writer may well keep two professional lives on the go at once: his "bread-and-butter" one, which exercises his conventional abilities and qualifications, and which provides him with a regular paycheck and a good degree of security – his "job," in fact – and his dedicated work as a writer, which, at any rate to begin with, may not give him the same degree of security or reward him with the same regular income, but which does give him a considerable creative satisfaction. In such cases, when a man or woman is both these, professional person and vocational writer, he or she may find it convenient or desirable to adopt a pen name for the writing activities, if only to differentiate the two sides to a single person's life. When this happens, it is the pen name that will be the better known, of course, since this is the writer's more public face. We all know James Bridie, the playwright, much better than we know the Scottish doctor Osborne Henry Mavor; we are more likely to be familiar with the detective stories of Michael Innes than the English critical studies by J.I.M. Stewart. On the other hand, both sides of a person's creative activity may be equally well known, so that Cecil Day Lewis, the poet, has a status almost equalled by Nicholas Blake, the detective fiction writer. To distinguish, thus, the work of A.B. the breadwinner from Y.Z. the literary creator, is one of the prime functions of a pen name. Often, of course, a person's writing may be so successful that he is able to abandon his traditional career. In such a case his literary name usually "takes over" and becomes the whole individual. This happened, for example, to Richard Gordon, who gave up his professional work as a doctor in 1952 and devoted himself entirely to writing, and to John Le Carré, who as a result of the success of his third novel of espionage, *The Spy Who Came in from the Cold,* was able to leave the foreign service in 1964 and concentrate on full-time writing.

A writer may also assume a different name not in order to distinguish between the writing self and the professional self, but to differentiate between one aspect of his or her writing and another. A travel writer, for example, may turn his hand to mystery fiction, and will take on a second pseudonym (or a first, if he writes under his real name) to be reserved for this type of book. Or a literary critic may publish some verse under a different name. The New Zealand writer whose real name was Ruth France, for example, assumed the name Paul Henderson for her poetry. (She also adopted a male name. We shall be considering such "cross-sexing" shortly). Again, it may be convenient to use a different name for books or work written over a particular period, or even for a single publication. Christopher Caudwell, the British Marxist writer of studies of poetry and prose literature, reversed the usual process in this way, using his *real* name (Christopher St. John Sprigg) for seven detective novels written between 1933 and 1939. The Welsh-born novelist Cecil Blanche Woodham-Smith adopted the name Janet Gordon for just three novels – *April Sky* (1938), *Tennis Star* (1940), and *Just Off Bond Street* (1940) – and Leslie Seldon Truss, the British thriller writer, used the name George Selmark for a single novel, *Murder in Silence* (1939).

For a different type of distinction, a writer may choose to take on another name for contributions to a particular magazine, or when submitting work to a different publisher. The Scottish poet William Aytoun used the unconventional name Augustus Dun-shunner for his contributions to *Blackwood's Magazine*, and George Darley, the Irish writer, contributed to the *London Magazine* as John Lacy.

The reasons that motivate a writer to choose another name on practical grounds do not end there. Jean-Raymond De Kremer, the bilingual Belgian writer, called himself Jean Ray when writing in French, and John Flanders for his books in Flemish, and Andrey Sinyavsky, the Russian writer, used the name Abram Tertz for his allegedly subversive writings published in the West.

A different genre, a different period, a different approach, a different publisher, a different language, a different self – a writer can identify the difference by simply adopting a new name.

If the situation requires it, there is of course no reason why a writer should not assume more than one pen name. There may be a good practical value in this. From the sheer commercial side, for example, a single writer can submit articles to different journals under different names, and writers who are particularly prolific may indeed prefer to "parcel out" their writings in this way. Science fiction and fantasy writers frequently employ a whole range of names, as do crime novelists, and many publishers have stocks of ready-made pen names, so called "house names," that they allocate to their authors. And when descending to a more undemanding level of writing (and reading), such as light romantic fiction and "pulp" magazines (although some such work has turned out to be above average), the adoption of a battery of pen names has for some years been standard practice.

As to the number of pen names that a writer can adopt, there are few limits. John Creasey, the crime novelist, wrote his 560 books under 28 pseudonyms. Stendhal, the French novelist, had over a hundred pen names, with "Stendhal" itself the best known, and Voltaire, also a pseudonym – and one of the most famous in world literature – totalled at least 173, which would seem to be something of a record (see Appendix I, pages 326–28). For the majority of writers, however, a handful of pseudonyms suffices for most practical purposes.

It goes without saying that many of the reasons that encourage an actor to change his name (an unsuitable real name, for dissociation, for ease of distinction from a similar name, for memorability) also apply to writers, although not perhaps to quite the same extent. An actor's name is very much part of his or her image and stage personality, and it is billed and promoted in a much more blatant and "public" way than the name of a writer. An actor's name, therefore, really matters. With a writer, on the other hand, although the name is indeed of considerable significance, it is *what* is written that counts. It obviously helps to have a memorable and easily pronounceable and attractive name, but for a writer a name is much more a means of pure identification than it is for an actor. Anthony Trollope's novels achieved their classic status without their author's feeling it necessary to adopt another name, nor was Oscar Wilde ever tempted in this respect. But how far would mellifluously named Marilyn Monroe have got as Norma Jean Baker? It is interesting to speculate. (Not that there is anything wrong or repugnant or detractive in the name—it proved no hindrance to Josephine Baker, Carroll Baker or Hylda Baker—it is just that Marilyn Monroe sounds and looks more like the name of a glamorous actress, that it has more "favorable free associations," as the ad writers say.)

There are, however, particular motivations for a writer's name change that will hardly ever apply to an actor.

The chief of these is the so called "literary mask," the need or desirability for writers to conceal their true identity (which actors will hardly wish to do). The motivation here is not so much to find a name as to escape from one. In other words, the name is regarded as a "cover-up" name, much as we saw it was for a spy or criminal in Chapter 2.

Why should a writer wish to hide his or her identity?

One reason may be that he wishes to avoid censorship. When a writer has something important to say, whether as fact or fiction, and when it may be difficult to say it under his real name, either because of his own standing or because it is controversial or even unlawful or hostile to authority, the adoption of a pseudonym may be the only solution. In the past many anticlerical or generally antiestablishment writers have sought refuge in an assumed name. Voltaire, imprisoned in the Bastille for writing a scurrilous lampoon on the French regent (the notorious libertine Philippe II, Duke of Orleans), assumed his pseudonym on his release (1718) with the aim of pursuing his powerful philosophical and skeptical writings. A century before him a fellow Frenchman, Agrippa d'Aubigne, an ardent Protestant, attacked the evils of the establishment, in particular French monarchs such as Catherine de Médicis and her sons Charles IX and Henri III, in his classic poem *Les Tragiques* (1616). For this he assumed the initials L.B.D.D. Only some 300 years later were these letters deciphered as standing for "Le Bouc du Désert" ("The Scapegoat"). This was known to have been a nickname used for d'Aubigné— moreover at one time he lived in a small village in Brittany actually called Le Désert. D'Aubigné's poem was both antiroyalist and anticlerical. Specifically anticlerical was the work of yet another outstanding French writer, Blaise Pascal. For a bitter yet objective attack on the Jesuits he entitled his famous eighteen letters *Lettres de Louis de Montalte à un Provincial de Ses amis et aux RR. PP. Jésuites sur la Morale et la Politique de Ces Pères* (1656) ("Letters from Louis de Montalte to a Provincial Friend and to Their Reverend Fathers the Jesuits Concerning the Morality and the Policy of Those Fathers"). The work dealt the Jesuits a blow from which they never recovered. (It was subsequently placed on the Index and ordered to be burned by the Royal Council in 1660.)

In these three literary masks we incidentally see good examples of a permanent "take-over" pseudonym (Voltaire) and of names used for specific single works (L.B.D.D. and Louis de Montalte). It is merely a coincidence that all three may well have derived from place-names.

Thus critics and satirists of all ages have adopted a disguised name, from d'Aubigné in the seventeenth century to the wry American humorist Mr. Dooley (real name Finley Peter Dunne) in the twentieth. It is understandable, too, that not just critics and humanists but political activists and revolutionaries will wish to adopt a "cover" name, since the publishing of their ideology in printed form will be one of the most effective ways of disseminating their message. Escaping the watchful eye of the censor here is all-important. It was largely in order to publicize — and publish, even if only in the "underground" press — his views and theories on society and the economy that led Vladimir Ilich Ulyanov to adopt a whole number of pseudonyms, of which one, Lenin, was to make him internationally known as a professional revolutionary. (His views and activities had in fact caused the censor and the police to keep an eye on him even at the early age of 17. For him to have published anything under his real name would have been out of the question.) Lenin first used this particular name some time before the Revolution, in 1901. Many other Russians, both before and since the Revolution, have been obliged to adopt a pseudonym for fear of censorship or reprisals.

Another category of writers who undergo a name change are the plagiarists — those who "steal" the writing of someone else and put their own name to it. (The word "plagiarist" derives from the Latin for "kidnapper.") In this case, more rarely, there is not the normal change to another name but *from* another name to one's own. The filching or pirating of other people's works was common among Elizabethan playwrights, when hacks would openly steal the plays of others and present them as their own. Today, of course, the stringent laws of copyright make such thieving very difficult, if not impossible.

In some instances, however, the "plagiary" may be by mutual agreement between the "thief" and his victim. At the beginning of his career, for example, Bernard Shaw found it difficult to get his writing published. He was aided by his friend, the musical conductor George Lee. Shaw would write the musical reviews and Lee would have them printed over his own name. A similar situation in which a helping hand was given arose when Jack London aided his friend George Sterling. Sterling simply could not get his story "The First Poet" accepted. London included it in his collection of short stories entitled *Turtles of Tasman* (1916). Only some time later did Sterling reveal that he, not London, was the author of that particular story.

Very many writers, of course, are influenced by the writings of others and may unwittingly borrow from them. This is not deliberate, conscious, wholesale stealing, but simply unconscious (or possibly subconscious) borrowing or adaptation, and as such is not really plagiary. Milton, for example, was greatly influenced by Spenser who in turn owed a good deal to Chaucer, and Keats was influenced by all three. This does not mean that any of the four can be accused of plagiary – even if Chaucer, in turn, had borrowed from French and Italian writers!

Another type of writing involving the adoption of a different name is parody. One famous case of parody was the work entitled *Les Déliquescences d'Adoré Floupette*, a collection of *poèmes décadents* that appeared in Paris in 1885. These were taken seriously by the critics – at first, at any rate. Yet who was the delightfully named Adoré Floupette? It turned out that there was no such person, but the poems themselves were clever, if rather malicious, parodies of poems by the early French Symbolist poets – Verlaine, Mallarmé, Rimbaud, Moréas and others. The *Déliquescences* (meaning approximately "Meltings" or "Liquefactions") were actually the work of two young poets, Gabriel Vicaire and Henri Beauclair.

Many examples of parody, however, do not involve a name change at all. When Stella Gibbons wrote *Cold Comfort Farm* (1932) as a caricature of a novel by Mary Webb, she did not claim to *be* Mary Webb or anyone apart from her real self.

Cases of plagiary and parody may often be quite intriguing, even if one might think twice about reading the actual works involved. Even more interesting, and a further motive for adopting another name, are literary hoaxes. These occur when a writer claims to be someone other than who he really is – the converse of a plagiarist, in fact, and closer to a parodist. Literary hoaxes involve the donning of a real literary mask.

There are some classic examples of such hoaxes.

Washington Irving, the "Father of American Literature," began his career with a double hoax. Having already used the pseudonym Jonathan Oldstyle, Gent., for a series of satirical letters published in the *Morning Chronicle* (1802–1803), he got together with his brother William and the writer James K. Paulding to publish a series of satirical essays and poems entitled *Salmagundi; or, the Whim-Whams and Opinions of Launcelot Langstaff, Esq., and Others*. These were first published as pamphlets and subsequently (1808) in book form. But Irving was not content to stop here. The following year a number of American newspapers carried announcements signed by one Handiside, manager of the New York Columbia Hotel, to the effect that a hotel resident named Diedrich Knickerbocker had checked out of the hotel leaving a manuscript behind. The announcements described Knickerbocker's appearance and character and requested anyone who knew of his whereabouts to contact Mr. Handiside who at the same time declared that if Mr. Knickerbocker did not return to the hotel he, Handiside, would publish the manuscript to recover his losses, since the aforesaid Mr. Knickerbocker had not settled his account. All this was in fact the work of Irving, intended as a build-up for his famous burlesque whose full title was *A History of New York, from the Beginning of the World to the End of the Dutch Dynasty, by Diedrich Knickerbocker* (1809). Neither Knickerbocker nor Handiside existed, of course. Thanks to this unusual publicity the work enjoyed immense success, and a few months after publication Irving revealed himself as the true author and thus "blew" his hoax. After this he published under his real name.

Irving set something of a fashion for literary hoaxes with humorous names of this kind, especially among American writers. In the March 21, 1861, issue of the Findlay (Ohio) *Jeffersonian*, for example, there appeared a letter from one "Petroleum Vesuvius Nasby, late pastor uv the Church uv the New Dispensation, Chaplain to his excellency the President, and p.m. at Confederate x roads, kentucky." This illiterate and seemingly dissolute country preacher from the South appeared to be extolling slavery and supporting those who approved of it. Astute readers could see, however, that in fact his arguments were absurd and that his apparent support for the South was given ironically. The author of this letter – it was to be the first of a series – was in fact the editor of the *Jeffersonian*, whose real name was David Ross Locke.

Locke in turn was followed by C.F. Browne, who as Artemus Ward feigned an illiterate style not simply to entertain but in order to satirize insincerities and sentimentality. Like Shakespeare's Touchstone, he "uses his folly like a stalking horse, and under the presentation of that he shoots his wit."

Two more literary hoaxes deserve mention here. The French writer Prosper Mérimée published in 1825, at the start of his career, a selection of plays about Spanish life in the manner of Lope de Vega. Wary of possible criticism by supporters of the classical school, he ascribed the plays to a nonexistent Spanish actress, one Clara Gazul. He did more than this. A foreword to the plays, written by someone named Joseph Létrange (significantly, "Joseph the Strange") gave an account of Clara's life to date – how she had been brought up, how she had escaped from a nunnery to join a roving band of actors, and the like – and backed up this verbal background to the supposed authoress by an actual portrait of Clara, as a frontispiece to the plays. This portrait was executed by the painter Delescluze – and was in fact of the 22-year-old Mérimée wearing a mantilla and a necklace! Thus as Clara Gazul and Joseph Létrange, Mérimée not only donned a literary mask (a double one, in fact) but extended his hoax to a visual impersonation.

Pierre Louÿs (originally Louis), also a Frenchman, concocted another type of mystification. He claimed, in 1894, to have discovered and translated the songs of the unknown Greek poetess Bilitis, who had, it seemed, lived in the sixth century B.C. According to Louÿs, one Dr. Heim, an archaeologist, had discovered the tomb of the Greek woman lyricist, and as if to support the claim for her existence, subsequent editions of the *Chansons de Bilitis* even contained "her" portrait, as Mérimée's plays had done. But all of it was devised by Louÿs: there was no Bilitis, no Dr. Heim, and the portrait was simply a copy of a statue in the Louvre. The poems themselves were written by Louÿs in the style of Sappho.

Such pranks must have been highly satisfying to their perpetrators.

The ultimate in literary masks, however, is to take no name at all – to write anonymously. Many writers began their career in this way, believing that if what they wrote was worth reading, the public would buy it for its own sake, irrespective of whoever the author might be. Censor-dodgers, too, will obviously favor the anonymous approach. The trouble with such a system is – if your work has no name to it, how can the public obtain more if they want it? All that can be done is to resort to a cumbersome phrase such as "The Author of 'Confessions of a Convict'" or whatever it was called. Unless the author chooses to reveal his true identity immediately, he too will have to employ a similar awkward designation in order to be recognized as the writer of the original work.

A classic case of this kind is well illustrated by Sir Walter Scott. After a writing career that had already been under way for some twenty years—so he was not the typical anonymous beginner in this respect—Scott decided to change from verse romances, in which he was anyway largely overshadowed by Byron, to novels. There duly appeared, anonymously, in 1814, his now famous historical novel *Waverley*. Would it be a success? Scott was apprehensive: he was known as a poet, not a novelist. The book was indeed well received, but Scott was still cautious, with the result that all his following novels, up to 1827, were published as "by the Author of 'Waverley'." After this, confident that his reputation as a writer of historical fiction was assured, Scott wrote under his real name.

Among other works that were first published anonymously are Tennyson's *Poems by Two Brothers* (1827), Robert Browning's first poem "Pauline" (1833), James Fenimore Cooper's first novel *Precaution* (1820), Thomas Hardy's two novels *Desperate Remedies* (1871) and, surprisingly, *Far from the Madding Crowd* (1874), and Arthur Conan Doyle's first short stories in the *Cornhill Magazine* (1879).

Thus caution, apprehension and evasion are among the motives that prompt a writer to mask his true identity.

But why should a writer wish to disguise his or her sex?

To be more precise: why should a female writer—since in this respect the women easily outnumber the men—choose to adopt a masculine name?

However successful modern feminism may or may not be, there have certainly been times, many quite recent, when a woman writer has been obliged to assume a male name in order that her book should be widely read, or even that it should be published at all. In the Victorian era, for example, when a woman's role was basically regarded as that of wife and mother, for a feminine pen to turn out anything more powerful or unconventional than a little light romantic verse or a cozy daily diary would have been virtually unthinkable. And that a woman should produce a stark, passionate *roman d'amour* or a radical, serious work exposing the evils of racialism would have been as unlikely as for a woman to have become an M.P. or even a Prime Minister of Britain. Yet we now know, barely a hundred years later, such things are not only possible but fully acceptable.

It was simply that "serious" and innovative writing of any kind, especially where it went against commonly held moral, religious and social beliefs, was expected to come, if it came at all, from a male author, not a female. The woman's place was not only in the home, it was as a dilettante, and if a lady took to the pen at all it was more often for the execution of elegant artwork than for the creation of a great literary masterpiece.

The year before Charlotte Brontë wrote her masterpiece *Jane Eyre*—in 1847, when good queen Victoria had been on the throne only ten years—she and her two sisters Emily and Anne had felt it prudent or even essential to adopt, if not actually male names, at any rate ones that were not so obviously feminine as their own. (For

Charlotte's own account of the motive behind the sisters' name change, see her entry under Currer **Bell**, page 89.)

These "ambiguous" names were in fact short-lived. The following year (1848) Charlotte admitted to being the author of *Jane Eyre*, while Emily revealed herself as the writer of *Wuthering Heights* and Anne as that of *The Tenant of Wildfell Hall* – but for a while the three sisters had been so successful in masking their sex that many reviewers believed the authors to be three brothers.

It was not only the early Victorian authoresses who assumed a name of the opposite sex. Nearly forty years after Currer Bell, another woman writer would take a name that was more than masculine. This was Olive Schreiner, who in 1883 published *The Story of an African Farm* under the name of Ralph Iron. The book was a novel, but no light romance: it was an expressly feminist and anti–Christian work, which because of its fine descriptive style and originality achieved instant success. It was a controversial book, however, and when the sex of the author was revealed the controversy became a storm – which proves that the South African author was fully justified in her decision to adopt a cross-sex pseudonym.

Some two centuries before any of these andronymous authors, a number of French women writers had taken to adopting male pen names. Madeleine de Scudéry, known to her friends as "Sapho," wrote more than one novel under the name of her brother George. Her verbose pseudo-historical romances *Clélie* (1654–60) and *Artamène, ou le Grand Cyrus* (1649–53), each ten volumes in length, depicted distinguished persons of her day under disguised names. But Mlle de Scudéry made no secret of the fact that she was the author of these works: her pseudonym was more an incognito, which she had not assumed with any great degree of seriousness.

Among other well known French authoresses who wrote under a masculine pen name were Amandine Dudevant (as George Sand), Marie de Flavigny, comtesse d'Agoult (as Daniel Stern), and Delphine de Girardin (as Charles de Launay).

The practical advantages of adopting a male name, especially when it came to having your writing accepted for publication, were commented on by the French revolutionary writer Louise Michel: "I more than once had occasion to notice that when I submitted articles to a newspaper under the name Louise Michel I could wager a hundred to one that they would not be printed; but if I signed myself Louis Michel the chances of being published were much greater!" (*Mémoires*, Paris 1886).

A more straightforward way out of the difficulty that attended a woman writer was for her to sign herself simply "A Lady." Only a few authoresses so called appear in this present book, but there were very many who took the name. Indeed, in 1880 the bibliophile and pseudonymist Ralph Thomas – otherwise "Olphar Hamst" of the work listed in the Bibliography – published a fascinating volume entitled *Aggravating Ladies: being a list of works published under the pseudonym of "A Lady."* This contains over 50 identifiable "ladies" who put their pens to paper thus. Actually, the pseudonym is more satisfactory than it appears: it enables a woman writer to retain her anonymity while remaining loyal to her sex, and at the same time it has an air of respectability and appears aristocratic.

Except trivially or humorously, it has been a much rarer thing for a man to assume a female pseudonym. Whereas a female writer, to enter a male literary world, may frequently have found that the most effective passport is the adoption of a man's name, a male author is already in his man's world, and the same motives will not operate. In fact the only reason for a man to take on a female name as a writer is simply the reason that prompts him to adopt another name anyway – for any of the practical or aesthetic motives we have already mentioned.

Male writers who have thus adopted a female name are few and far between and mostly little known or of small consequence.

One exception, however, was that of the Scottish author Fiona Macleod, whose real name was William Sharp. This was primarily a "distinction" name, used consistently for his mystical and quasi–Celtic romances and plays from 1893 until his death in 1905 – he had earlier written some poetry and biography under his real name – but perhaps there was also a genuine femininity in the writing or the personality of the man himself that motivated this particular choice of name. His pen name was so successful that the true identity of the author of the books by Fiona Macleod was not known until after Sharp's death. (For more about his name, see his entry, page 210.)

In referring to women authors who chose to write as "A Lady" we were really dealing with a type of aristocratic name. Many writers of both sexes have chosen to devise a pseudonym that in one way or another suggests an aristocratic origin, even a royal one. This is of course a rather obvious way to enhance one's literary status, but it has been a steadily popular one over the centuries. The mechanics consist largely in assuming a name that includes an aristocratic particle or "honorific" such as the French *de* or German *von*. (For other ways of upgrading your name, see the next chapter.) The reasoning here is fairly straightforward, the argument being: aristocrats are more important than other people and receive greater attention; if I adopt an aristocratic name or title the public will pay more attention to my writing and will rate it highly (since the author is apparently an aristocrat) even before they have read it. But such "self-promotion," in the literal sense, became over-popular as a pseudonymous device, and consequently lost its initial impact. Ralph Thomas's "aggravating ladies" were not tiresome because it was difficult attempting to track them down – there were simply too many of them. And half the "mystique" of being an aristocrat, even if a spurious one, is of course the fact that you belong to the select few, not the repetitive many.

Rather more interesting is the adoption by a genuine aristocrat of an ordinary or "common" name. This can occur either when the writer's lofty status makes it difficult for him or her to have a work published under his or her name – this applies in particular to royalty – or when the nature of the work, and its subject matter, make it desirable for the high-ranking author to adopt a more lowly stance.

Since a "flight from fame" has been resorted to on more than one occasion by a king or queen, who even for private correspondence may well choose to become Mr. or Mrs. Thus Sarah Churchill, Duchess of Marlborough (1660–1744) corresponded with Queen Anne of England as Mrs. Freeman – a doubly symbolic name – while Queen Anne in turn wrote to the Duchess as Mrs. Morley.

One of the most prolific royal writers of the nineteenth century was Queen Elizabeth of Romania, who published several books of verse and prose as Carmen Sylva—a name perhaps more lyrical than lowly—while Elizabeth itself was the pen name chosen by Countess von Arnim, later Countess Russell, for her novels, beginning with *Elizabeth and Her German Garden* (1898). (Elizabeth was her mother's first name.)

The motives that thus urge an actor or writer to assume another name are many and varied, with several factors bearing on the actual choice of name.

And now that we have considered *why* the adoption of a pseudonym may be desirable or necessary, we must see *how* such a new name is devised.

5. How Do You Make a Name for Yourself?

A self-made man may prefer a self-made name.
(Judge Learned Hand, as Samuel Goldfish changed his name to Samuel Goldwyn)

Whatever the motivation for changing your name, temporarily or permanently, the big practical question is—how do I change my name? Where do I get my new name from?

Taking all pseudonyms and changed names on the broadest possible basis, it may be said that the new name is either ready-made to a greater or lesser degree, that is, it is based on an already existing name, or else it is an invented name, derived from random or meaningful letters, syllables or words. In this chapter we shall be considering the larger of these two categories—and the one that is the more interesting, since the names mainly look like real personal names—"ready-made" names. In Chapter 6 we shall then have a look at the invented ones.

The obvious place to start is with your own name. Your own real name, that is. Many people, especially those who are changing their name more for convenience than for special effect, will prefer to choose a name that in some way echoes or suggests their original name.

If your original name is foreign-sounding to English-speaking people, the easiest thing to do is to "anglicize" it. This can usually be arranged by modifying a section of the name to resemble an English name. In some instances, especially with Germanic names, such a modification can simultaneously be a translation, as English -*son* for German -*sohn*. In other cases it will suffice simply to switch to an English name that only vaguely resembles the original. Examples are Hardy Albrecht to Hardie Albright, Vladimir Dukelsky to Vernon Duke, Gertrude Konstam to Gertrude Kingston, and George Wenzlaff to George Winslow.

In many cases such an "anglicization" is also accompanied by a shortening, so that the surnames Reizenstein, Liebermann, Kirkegaard and Breitenberger become Rice, Mann, Kirk, and Byrnes. Two classic examples of this type are Spiro Anagnostopoulos, whose father had anglicized the family name to Agnew—Greek surnames are notable for their length—and Nathan Birnbaum, better known as the comedian George Burns. It is noticeable that transformations like this often pay little regard to the actual literal meaning of the original name, that is, there is frequently no attempt to translate the name into English, even when this would preserve the similarity. Elsy Steinberg changed her name to Elaine Stewart, not Elaine Stone, and Nathan Weinstein, the American novelist, became Nathaniel

West, not Nathaniel Vine or Nathaniel Stone. (But then he claims that Horace Greeley, the American journalist who founded the *New Yorker*, told him to "Go West, young man"—and he did!)

English-style modifications form a sizeable group, but bearers of foreign names who change to an English name quite unlike their own easily outnumber them. Thus Max Showalter became Casey Adams, Eugene Klass became Gene Barry, Louise Dantzler was reborn as Mary Brian, and Nathalie Belaieff turned into the nicely alliterative Nathalie Nattier. And even though such names are not based on the person's true name, at least they are an actual genuine or genuine-sounding English name, so in that respect are "ready-made." In practice, too, many people who favor this type of change already have an English-sounding forename which they retain (Leon Ames was Leon Waycoff, Geraldine Brooks was Geraldine Stroock, Kitty Carlisle was Catherine Holzman, and Cecil Parker was at least Cecil Schwabe).

But returning to "own-name-based" names, we find that many pseudonyms are not anglicized versions of a foreign name but merely simplified or abbreviated variants. This is the least concession that can be made to an English-speaking environment: at least they will be easier to read, remember and say, even if they do not actually look like an English name. But here again, it could be that a change of this type is intentionally made—the bearer of the name thus retains something of his or her native provenance, and so the resulting name is a convenient compromise, neither conspicuously foreign nor wholly English but somewhere between the two. In fact, such a name will still be sufficiently unusual to make it more memorable than an ordinary English name such as Jones or Adams. Examples of such names are Lionel Bart, who was Lionel Begleiter, Howard Da Silva, formerly Harold Silverblatt, Milton Berle, previously Mendel Berlinger, and Peter Tork, once Peter Torkelson. Even in non–English environments the same method can be used, with Jacques Tatischeff becoming Jacques Tati in France, and Franz von Strehlenau assuming the simplified but not specifically German name Nikolaus Lenau in Austria.

In fact a change of this kind may often result, as we have noted, from Howard F. Barker's "abrasion of common speech." A foreign-sounding name may become smoothed down and even abbreviated by the attempts of an English-speaking tongue to pronounce it. Several actual (legal) name changes have thus come about, so that such famous American names as those of General Custer, General Pershing, General Longstreet, and Herbert C. Hoover were, several generations back, respectively Köster, Pfoersching, Langestraet and Huber.

How else may one vary one's real name? The answer is: in any number of ways, often combining two or more devices. Among the more popular are the following:

(1) Omit your surname. Often a person's second or middle name may actually look like a surname anyway—it is often a family name, such as one's mother's maiden name—and the advantage of such a modification is that it is both simplicity itself and that it enables a person to retain his or her original name unchanged. In such a fashion, changing your name means no change at all, since your new name is your old, and your "pseudonym" is not even "pseudo"! Not surprisingly, this is a very common procedure. Thus, Edward Ashley Cooper became Edward Ashley,

William Bolitho Ryall became William Bolitho, Ernest Bramah Smith, author of the *Kai Lung* novels, dropped his prosaic Smith to assume (i.e., retain) his orientally exotic middle name as a surname, and Elizabeth Allen Gillease preferred to be known as just Elizabeth Allen. (To have a middle name that is at once a Christian name and a surname is indeed a stroke of good fortune.)

Of course, variants of this procedure are possible. While dropping your surname, you can simultaneously change your second name in some way, as can be done to a surname proper. George Augustus Andrews dropped his surname and altered his middle name to become George Arliss, for example. Or you can alter your *first* name while dropping your surname, often assuming instead a pet form of it or a nickname. Thus James Barry Jackson became Michael Barry, and William Berkeley Enos became Busby Berkeley. Then if you are blessed with two middle names, you can drop both your first name and your surname and use these two as first name and surname. This is what the humorist George Anthony Armstrong Willis did, to become Anthony Armstrong. Sherwood Bonner did likewise: originally she was Katherine Sherwood Bonner Macdowell. Again, you can omit your surname and reverse the order of your two first names, even omitting a forename in the process. This was what George Barrington Rutland Fleet did, to become Rutland Barrington. Similarly, by process of omission and reversal, Edward Thomas Andrulewicz became Thomas Andrew.

The dropping of one half of a double-barreled surname is also an expedient device, whatever else you may do with the rest of your name. Angela Baddeley was born Madeleine Angela Clinton-Baddeley, and Sir Felix Aylmer was originally Felix Edward Aylmer-Jones.

The permutations and combinations that apply in the category can also, of course, be employed in other methods.

(2) More straightforwardly, you can simply use a forename on its own. This is a method favored by cartoonists, who like a short name for signing purposes, by artists of all kinds—both painters and "artistes"—who like a single, stylish name, and is standard practice for several types of religious names, from saints to members of religious orders. (We shall be considering religious names as a separate category later in this chapter.) Such a name is usually a person's first name, or an abbreviated or pet form of this, but can be any forename. Examples are Fabian Forte Bonaparte, who became simply Fabian, Sabu Dastagir, known better as just Sabu ("the Elephant Boy"), and the pianist Solomon Cuttner, known professionally as Solomon. Beryl Botterill Antonia Yeoman decided that the best name for signing her cartoons was Anton, and the political cartoonist Vicky was born Victor Weisz. Cherilyn Sarkasian LaPier teamed with Sonny to become popular as simply Cher, and the film actress Ann-Margret has a double-barreled first name that she finds quite sufficient to enable her to drop her surname Olson. One of the most sensible things the Belgian wife of emperor Maximilian of Mexico did was to assume the single name Carlota. Originally, in her regal grandeur, she was Marie-Charlotte-Amélie-Augustine-Victoire-Clémentine-Léopoldine. (Royalty are renowned for their lavish endowment of Christian names.) A variation of this is to use your forename as a full-length pseudonym (forename plus surname) by splitting it into

two. Maybritt Wilkens did this to become May Britt, and Isaiah Edwin Leopold to be Ed Wynn. The use of a forename alone preceded by "Madame" or "Mademoiselle" or "Miss" is also popular with a number of lady artistes, from fortune-tellers to stage actresses. Mlle Augusta, the French ballerina, was born Caroline Augusta Josephine Thérèse Fuchs, and Mlle Clairon, the famous tragic actress of the Comédie Française, started life as Claire-Josèphe Hippolyte Léris de la Tude.

(3) As a kind of converse of this, you can simply use your surname alone. This is perhaps least of all a pseudonym, since the use of surname alone is established, in certain situations and for certain conventions, in a number of countries. For this reason, only a few examples are included in this book. However, Liberace is here, if only to prove that it was indeed the real surname of Wladziu Liberace, and the cartoonists Giles and Low are here for similar reasons: these are the real surnames, not concocted names, of Carl Giles and David Low. Even less of a pseudonym is a real surname preceded by "Mr." or "Mrs." Yet if we take it that a full, true name consists of a forename and a surname, this must be at least partly a pseudonym since there is an element of disguise. How many people, for example, know the Christian name of Mrs. Beeton, even less her maiden name? The famous cookbook writer was born Isabella Mary Mayson. Topol, incidentally, is the true surname of the actor Chaim Topol.

(4) A common disguise for one's real name, and one popular with writers of all kinds, is to use one's initials. Such a device is so frequently resorted to, both by established writers and private individuals alike — can you honestly say that you have never signed your name by your initials? — that, again, it hardly figures in our present collection of pseudonyms. But of course Q appears in our collection (see pages 256–57), and a few other initialisms will similarly be found. (Initials that stand for something other than the bearer's real name are another matter, and they are much more obviously genuine pseudonyms.)

(5) Much more enterprisingly and ingeniously, a favorite method of forming a pseudonym is to "juggle" with one's real name in some way. This can be done by reversing the order of names, for example, by making an anagram out of it or by reading it back to front (as a reversal), or simply by "recasting" the original name in a mixture of ways, adding or subtracting letters where convenient. The thriller writer John Dickson Carr, for instance, selected as two of his pseudonyms the names Carr Dickson and Carter Dickson. Edith Caroline Rivett, the writer of detective novels, took the initials of all three of her names plus the chief element of her middle name reversed to become E.C.R. Lorac (at one time she wrote also as Carol Carnac), and Patrick Reardon Connor dropped one name and altered one vowel in each of the other two to become Rearden Conner. For examples of full-blooded anagrammatic and reversal pseudonyms we need to quote the French poet and short-story writer Théophile Dondey who used an Irish-style transformation to become Philothée O'Neddy, and the English comedian Tommy Trinder who back-pedaled his surname to form the early stage name Red Nirt. A glance in the Bibliography at the end of this book will show that even one of the source authors, himself an expert on pseudonyms, appears under his pseudonymous name. This is Olphar Hamst, who was in reality the English nineteenth-century bibliophile

Ralph Thomas. The classic example of an anagrammatic name is, of course, that of Voltaire, formed from his real surname of Arouet (with *u* equating with *v*) plus the initials "L.J." (*j* becoming *i*), said to stand for "Le Jeune."

(6) An extension of a pseudonym consisting solely of initials, as already mentioned, is a name that is a marked contraction of the real name. These, like the "forename only" pseudonyms, are especially popular with cartoonists for a short, snappy name that can be quickly and compactly signed. Among such names are Batt (Oswald Barrett), Jak (Raymond Jackson), Jon (W.P. John Jones), and Gus (George W. Smith). This last name is formed from initials, and thus offers another possibility for a brief name. Erté, the French costume designer, devised his name from the two initials, as they sound in French, of his full name Romain de Tirtoff, and the French cartoonist François Lejeune did similarly to produce his pen name Jean Effel. The clown Coco had a name that came from the two -*ko*- syllables of his full name Nikolai Poliakoff, and the author of *The Book of Artemas: Concerning men, and the things that men did do at the time when there was a war* (1917), and subsequent "Artemas" books, took his name from the first syllables of his complete name Arthur Telford Mason. Here, once again, all kinds of variations are possible. Julia L.M. Woodruff, author of now unread nineteenth-century novels *(Holden with Cords* and *Shiloh),* took her initials, reversed them, turned the fourth into a surname, and wrote as W.M.L. Jay! The crosswordist Afrit had a name that was not only directly derived from his real name (Alistair Ferguson Ritchie) but one that additionally denotes a powerful devil in Islamic mythology, one that "inspires great dread," as every dedicated crossword compiler hopes he does in his solvers. (For a look at this fearsome class of pseudonymous devisers, see Chapter 7.)

Any name actually devised from an initial comes in this group, whether forming part of a conventional pseudonym, as Danny Kaye, who began life as Daniel Kaminsky, or used on its own, as above. Obviously, some letters of the alphabet are more suitable than others for forming a traditional English-type name — if that is what is wanted. Among them are B (Bee), D (Dee), G (Gee), J (Jay), and the popular K (Kay or Kaye).

How else can a pseudonym be evolved from your real name?

You can translate it!

Of course, you can only do this if your real name in any way resembles an ordinary translatable word or words. But to translate your name is a method of creating a pseudonym that has a well established and highly respectable antecedence. Such a method was established in the Renaissance period mainly by German scholars of the sixteenth and seventeenth centuries. These men were the "new aristocracy," and felt it appropriate to translate or in some way render their often very ordinary or even laughably earthy names into an elevated Latin or Greek form. As Paul Tabori remarked, "Schurtzfleisch (Apronflesh) or Lämmerschwanz (Sheeptail) were scarcely the right names under which to climb Mount Olympus" *(The Natural Science of Stupidity,* 1959). For examples of such classical pseudonyms and their vernacular originals, see in the main listing, among others, Agricola, Bucer, Copernicus, Fabricius, Melanchthon, Mercator, Praetorius, and Sagittarius.

Today, thinking little of it, we have come to accept the classical version of the name as the "real" one, so that we learn at school of Mercator's geographical projection and at university, possibly, of the Arminian doctrine rejecting predestination. We might even add a far more famous "classical" name to this list—that of Christopher Columbus, whose original Italian name was Cristoforo Colombo.

Some such names seemed particularly popular. Four Agricolas (or Agricolae) are cited here, but there were a number more. The translation was not always a faithful one. Kremer the mathematician took the opportunity of not only translating himself but promoting himself from a "tradesman" to a "wholesale merchant," *Mercator*. And where a name could not be easily translated—and even sometimes when it could—a favorite device was simply to "latinize" the name by adding "-us," as with Copernicus and Arminius. (The French theologian born Chauvin called himself Calvinus. Today, English-speakers know him as Calvin.)

In more recent times, as we have already seen (in Chapter 1), foreign immigrants to Anglophone countries have taken to translating their names—especially, like the scholars two or three centuries before them, those with German names. Schneider then becomes Taylor, Schönkind becomes Fairchild, and Weiss becomes White. Most such transformations are of Jewish names.

It is of course possible to translate or "render" from any one language to any other, as circumstances require, with the new name being a permanent acquisition or simply a temporary, even frivolous, pen name. The Laotian nationalist and author of resistance pamphlets thus adopted the name William Rabbit for one of his works, this being a translation (in part) of his real name Katay Don Sasorith, while the composer born in Italy as Giovanni Battista Lulli gallicized his name when he came to settle in France as Jean-Baptiste Lully. Some translations are almost unrecognizable, at least to an English speaker. The film star Judy Holliday started life as Judith Tuvim, her surname being Hebrew for "holiday." And how about Xanrof? This was the name adopted by Léon Fourneau, the French songwriter who wrote for the diseuse Yvette Guilbert at the turn of the century. He took his surname, translated it into Latin (*fornax*, "furnace"), then reversed it.

While considering translations and renderings, we should not overlook a type of converse procedure when a standard English name is turned into a foreign version. We quoted in Chapter 2 the need felt by a number of ballet dancers, for example, to russify their name. Hilda Boot and Patrick Healey-Kay we instanced, but there were also Ethel Liggins, who turned into Ethel Leginska, and Lilian Marks, famous as Alicia Markova. Richard Adama, the American ballet dancer who became director of the Bremen State Opera Ballet in Germany, was born Richard Adams, and—in the world of opera this time rather than ballet—the American singer Lillian Norton preferred to modify her name to the more distinguished Lillian Nordica. A variation on the theme was performed by the Scottish music hall dancer Elizabeth McLauchlan. Teaming with her husband Raoul (né Hugh Duff McLauchlan) she gallicized and prettified her first name to become just Babette.

Babette is a diminutive of Elizabeth, of course, and different enough almost to be regarded as a pet name or nickname. In this it offers another possibility for evolving a pseudonym: adopt your own pet name or nickname.

There can be few people who have not had an affectionate or teasing name given them at some stage in their lives, even if only in their school days, and this could make an ideal "ready-made" pseudonym.

Many well known names, from classical times to the present, originated as nicknames. The Roman emperor Caligula had a name that arose from his upbringing among soldiers: as a boy running around camp he wore small size *caligae*, the Latin word used for the stout iron-nailed shoes worn by soldiers. His name thus literally means "Little Boots." (And how much nicer that is than Gaius Julius Caesar, his real name.) In complete contrast, the film actor Zero Mostel, really Samuel Mostel, got "zero" for his subjects at school. In spite of the uncomplimentary nickname, he chose to adopt it as his screen name. School nicknames are notorious, in fact, and have been turned to advantage by a number of personalities for use as an adopted name. Ginger Rogers was called Ginger at school, Jack Oakie (Lewis Offield) was called "Oakie" at school as he came from Oklahoma, and Dana, the singer, has a school nickname that is Irish for "mischievous" or "naughty." (It is also a Christian name — and coincidentally a surname — in its own right, which makes it an even better name.) Other nicknames also originate in childhood, whether at school or not, and these too can be adopted. Bing Crosby's first name was a childhood nickname, and Cyd Charisse derived her first name from her baby brother's attempt to say "sister." Bebe Daniels made her first film when she was only seven — a "baby" — and the disc jockey Kid Jensen (really David Allen Jensen) was Radio Luxembourg's youngest DJ when he was still a mere kid of 18.

In a somewhat unexpected quarter, and of much more venerable vintage, it is interesting to see that many of the names of famous classical painters originated as nicknames. Botticelli — a name that itself is sometimes used as a humorous word or name today for a person's posterior — was really Alessandro Filipepi, all those five hundred years ago. His name means "little barrel," and was the nickname used by his elder brother Giovanni. Similarly Canaletto means "little Canale" (Canale was his father's real name), Masaccio means "huge great Tom" (it has the Italian augmentative ending), and Tintoretto means "little dyer" — his father was a dyer. One of Masaccio's pupils was Masolino, whose name means "little Tom" — not only in reference to his master but as a diminutive of his own name Tommaso. It is difficult to see why the sixteenth-century Italian painter Giovanni Antonio Bazzi should have chosen to adopt his hardly flattering nickname of Il Sodoma, "the sodomite," but, whether flaunting it or vaunting it, Sodoma he became.

Many nicknames actually look like real names, even Red Buttons — Aaron Schwatt was a red-haired bellboy in his teens — but some are obviously an everyday word used as a name, such as Twiggy (Lesley Hornby), and these "word-into-name" pseudonyms we shall be considering in Chapter 6, not here.

Very many possibilities are thus open for a pseudonym to be derived from your own name — whether your real name, or part of it, or your pet name or nickname. But supposing you want to find your ready-made name some other way?

The obvious answer is, of course, that you can get your name from someone else. The only question is — who? Who is to be the person whose name you are to adopt? What is special about him or her, or his or her name? Where do you start?

Many pseudonyms, like charity, begin at home. That is, within the family. And one of the commonest methods of all is to adopt your mother's maiden name.

This is an eminently satisfactory method, since it is not only a genuine surname that you are acquiring but one that is in every sense of the word a real family name. From the practical point of view, too, it enables you to extend the life of a name that might otherwise have disappeared from the family. Indeed, many people already bear their mother's maiden name as one of their own middle names, in which case to adopt such a name as a pseudonym is all too easy. You simply drop your surname.

Examples of "mother's maiden name" adoptions are easy to find. Here are a dozen people who all made this particular adoption: Constance Cummings, Ann Dvorak, Dulcie Gray, Helen Hayes, Viola Keats, Jeremy Kemp, Elsa Lanchester, Mario Lanza, Yvonne Mitchell, Anna Neagle, Romy Schneider, Simone Signoret (thus making a satisfying alliterative match)... The list can be extended considerably.

And if not your mother's name, you can always take a name from some other member of the family, whether a near and dear one or a more remote relative.

Julie Andrews adopted her stepfather's name, as did Truman Capote. Diana Dors took that of her maternal grandmother. Vivien Leigh took her husband's middle name, rather unusually, and George Scrope, the nineteenth-century English geologist and MP, rather more unconventionally, took his wife's maiden name. (He did this on marrying, thus reversing the usual role—a fine tribute to his 24-year-old bride, who was the daughter of William Scrope, the last of the old earls of Wiltshire.) For further instances of this kind, where a man adopted his wife's name on marriage (and on inheriting), see Chapter 3, p. 12.

Some people choose to take a really historic family name. Josephine Tey, the novelist, adopted that of her great-great-grandmother, and Owen Meredith, the British statesman and poet, went way back in time to take his first name from Owen Gwynnedd ap Griffith, king of North Wales, and Meredith ap Tudor, the great-grandfather of Henry VII. Edward Robert Bulwer Lytton, as Meredith is better known (his pseudonym was for his writing), was a lineal descendant of both of these royal forebears.

It is almost axiomatic that an adoptee should acquire the name of his step-parents, usually his stepfather. But he may well have had a real name of his own to begin with, which he will relinquish. This happened to Leslie Lynch King, better known as Gerald R. Ford, and to the famous author Jack London, whose actual father's name was Chaney.

The usual variations can be arranged. Paul Hamlyn, the publisher, adopted and also adapted his mother's maiden name of Hamburger, and Maria Karnilova, the American ballet dancer, changed her mother's maiden name from Karnilovich to supersede her real surname of Dovgolenko. Jacques Offenbach, the composer, took his father's nickname, "Der Offenbacher" (he was born in Offenbach-am-Main) and Kay Hammond assumed her mother's stage name. (Kay's maiden name was Standing, and her married name Clements.) Working down-family instead of up, Mike Todd, whose original first name was Avrom, took the first name of his son, Michael, and Mme Champseix, the nineteenth-century French writer, comosed her pen name, André Léo, from the Christian names of both her sons.

If not from a relation, then you can always borrow someone else's name. The scope here is almost infinite, since the person whose name you choose may be known to you or not. He or she may be a public or private hero, an admired figure, a friend, a colleague—even an enemy! The act of adopting the particular person's name may be intended as a mark of homage or respect, or virtually a near-random affair. You may simply be attracted by the name itself: when pop singer Gerry Dorsey turned himself into Engelbert Humperdinck it was not because of his admiration for the German classical composer's works. The adopted name may in turn already be a pseudonym. This was the case with the American comic film actress Eve Arden, born Eunice Quedens. She based her name on that of Elizabeth Arden (Florence Graham), the Canadian cosmetician, who herself had taken her first name from that of Elizabeth, author of *Elizabeth and Her German Garden* (1898)—who was actually Mary Annette von Arnim.

Something of the wealth of possibilities can be seen by running through the names in the main listing (p. 68), but among the borrowings will be found the names of a leading lady (Busby Berkeley), a schoolteacher friend (Richard Burton), an admired pop singer (Elvis Costello), a bishop (Lorenzo da Ponte), some benefactors (Carlo Farinelli), a prison guard (O. Henry), a noted golfer (Ted Ray), and a general of the American Revolution (John Wayne). For Lorenzo da Ponte to adopt the name of the bishop who christened him was not so much a personal tribute but a standing convention, since this was customary by many converts to Catholicism—much as in London, in the thirteenth and fourteenth centuries, it was quite normal for an apprentice to assume the name of his master, and even earlier, for Roman slaves to take the names, as mentioned in Chapter 1, of *their* masters.

In Chapter 7 we shall be having a special look at the name assumed by crossword compilers, but suffice it to say here that many of them gleefully (and gloatingly) adopted the names of Spanish Grand Inquisitors, a custom initiated by one of the doyen crosswordists, Torquemada.

Another special category of creative person is the Welsh bardic poet, for whom it is traditional to adopt the name of an ancient versifier: Robert Ellis, a nineteenth-century minister and poet, thus took as his bardic name that of the most important Welsh poet of the twelfth century, Cynddelw, which itself is also sometimes chosen as a suitable forename for a Welsh baby boy.

A much larger and more important category of name adoption is that followed by members of religious orders, and many congregations of nuns, sisters, and brothers, as well as several religious orders and congregations of men, still retain the practice of assuming the name of a saint or venerated member of the church on their admission to the community (which in the Christian church is usually at the ceremony of clothing). Until recently, too, this meant that members of many orders, such as the Catholic Friars Minor, Carmelites and Capuchins, abandoned their surname altogether on taking their new religious name—although Capuchins added to their religious name the name of their place of origin, as for example

Father Pius of Chester. The adoption of a saint's name is not dependent on the sex of the novice—nuns have often received the name of a male saint.

Today, since the Second Vatican Council (as mentioned in Chapter 2), many orders have dropped the giving of a name in religion. However, the custom is by no means moribund, and the realities of the process of choosing a name are decribed by Suzanne Campbell-Jones in her account of the clothing of novice Franciscan sisters: "The girl put up her own choice of names, and usually two or three devolved on a favorite saint or even a favorite sister, teacher or friend. One nun took the name Ita, not because it meant in chains, but because she knew a very nice nun by that name. Sisters still used their baptismal names for legal documents or transactions outside the convent life" *(In Habit...*, 1979).

Not surprisingly, the names of members of the Holy Family are regarded with special favor among Christian postulants. Nuns choose Mary (the mother of Christ) and Elizabeth (Mary's cousin, and mother of John the Baptist); male novices choose Joseph (Mary's husband) and John (Elizabeth's son, the Baptist). Other popular choices are names of the apostles and disciples and outstanding New Testament figures, among them Andrew, Barnabas, Bartholomew, James, John (the Baptist or the Apostle), Luke, Mark, Martha, Mary (Magdalene, if not the Virgin), Matthew, Paul, Peter, Philip, Simon (also the name of Christ's brother), Stephen, and Timothy. For nuns, too, a desirable name to acquire is Teresa, who was the founder of the reformed (discalced, i.e., "unshod") Carmelite order. The Albanian-born Mother Teresa of Calcutta, who was originally Agnes Bojaxhiu, took the name of this sixteenth-century Spanish Mother Teresa.

Many of the later saints have come to be known by their own Christian names, so that the mystical theologian and poet St. John of the Cross was actually baptized as John (more precisely, Juan), and St. Bernadette was christened Marie-Bernarde, with her name simply a standard French feminine diminutive (so spelled, minus the second "r") of Bernard.

Names of popes, some of which are those of saints (John, Paul) and some not (Pius, Innocent)—although these may be the names of earlier popes who were themselves saints—are especially interesting, and will be dealt with separately in Chapter 7.

Religious names are thus almost always, indeed exclusively, adopted as a mark of veneration and affection.

But if in your search for a pseudonym all else fails in your hunt for a human being with a ready-made name that you can adopt, there is another recourse. This is to adopt a fictional name—meaning not so much a fictitious name (in a sense, all pseudonyms are fictitious) but a name from fiction.

There are probably characters in fiction whom we admire as much as we would if they were real flesh and blood—possibly more, since many fictional characters are idealized—and an effective way of expressing our private liking for one of them is to adopt his or her name as our own.

Here, too, the range is very wide, although naturally not as unlimited as when choosing a real person's name. And as for who, exactly, is to be the chosen character—the selection is very much a matter of personal taste and inclination. An actor or actress may choose the name of a character in a play, whether they have actually taken the part or not; a novelist or short story writer may prefer the name of some greater or lesser hero or heroine in a similar work—or even in his or her *own* work. The actress Elizabeth Ashley, when still Elizabeth Cole, took her new surname from the first name of Ashley Wilkes, as acted by Leslie Howard (originally Leslie Stainer) in *Gone with the Wind,* and Tom Jones, who began life as Thomas Woodward, reputedly derived his name from the hero of the film (of the book) *Tom Jones.* On the other hand the two famous fictional detectives Ellery Queen and Paul Temple gave their names respectively to two two-man teams of crime novelists: the Americans Frederic Dannay and Manfred B. Lee, and the British writers Francis Durbridge and James McConnell (who used Paul Temple as their joint pen name for mystery novels *not* about the eponymous detective!).

To adopt the name of a character that you have yourself created is not merely a way of going on a literary ego trip, but more a reward for the sweat, toil and tears—and doubtless satisfaction—that you have experienced in creating that character. You have put something of your own world into him, now let him be identified with you, his creator.

The usual variety abounds, with names deriving from a girl in a song (Nelly Bly), the heroine of one of the writer's own novels (Margaret Howth), the hero of an opera (Mario Lanza), a biblical hunter (Nimrod), a Shakespearean comic character (Peter Quince), and a character in Proust (Françoise Sagan). Dame Rebecca West took her name from an Ibsen play, and Dinah Shore from the song "Dinah." And what could be finer than Edward Bradwardine Waverley, the name chosen by John Croker from *two* characters in Sir Walter Scott's novel *Waverley* to reply to one Malachi Malagrowther—who was Scott himself in the guise of one of his own characters in *The Fortunes of Nigel.*

Fiction, of course, covers several genres and generations, from classical times to the present, and we have already mentioned the Renaissance fashion for classical names. Classical names—those of ancient mythological characters or even real Latin and Greek authors—have always found steady favor as a rather chic pseudonym, often, one suspects, almost as much for the impressive appearance of the name as for any actual association with the original bearer of the name.

Janus, for example, is a good example of a symbolic classical name, being that of the "two-faced" Roman god of beginnings and endings (hence January). His name has been adopted by a number of writers, including the two German theologians Johann von Döllinger and Dr. Johannes Friedrich, and the French journalist and novelist Robert le Bonnières. We have seen how the name of Cassandra was used by William Connor; it was also adopted, perhaps less symbolically, by the Russian-born French graphic artist and stage designer (in the form Cassandre) Adolphe Mouron. The name of Alcibiades, the Athenian general and politician, was assumed by two noblemen—Albert, Margrave of Brandenberg, and George Villiers, Duke of Buckingham. It was also used by Alfred, Lord Tennyson, for an article in *Punch* published in March, 1846. The eighteenth- and nineteenth-century reformer and politician John Thelwell took the name Sylvanus Theophrastus. "Sylvanus" was a name used for one of the wood gods that followed Pan;

Theophrastus was a Greek philosopher and scientist, a disciple of Aristotle. (It was also one of the real names of Paracelsus: literally it means "god-guided.") The American nineteenth-century novelist Emma Embury adopted the name Ianthe for her contributions to periodicals. In Greek mythology Ianthe was a Cretan girl who fell in love with another girl called Iphis—who subsequently (or consequently?) changed into a boy and married Ianthe.

With such classical borrowings, it is often difficult to tell whether the name derives from the original character or from a later character of the same name, for example, in a play by Shakespeare or Racine. The English poet laureate Alfred Austin, for instance, in using the name Lamia for editing *The Poet's Diary,* may have taken this name directly from classical sources—Lamia lured strangers so that she could devour them—or from Keats's *Lamia* (1820). Again, there were often more than one classical personage of the same name, and without more precise indication it is impossible to tell whether Lady Mary Montagu, the eighteenth-century English writer of letters and poems, had in mind the Queen of Halicarnassus or the sister of Mausolus when she took the name Artemisia. And if she actually based the name on that of Artemis—who was also, as goddess of the moon, called Diana, Cynthia, Delia, Hecate, Luna, Phoebe and Selene—we are even more in the dark, since this name has also been alluded to scores of times by Shakespeare and several poets.

Today, the vogue for classical pseudonyms is less in evidence, although columnists and journalists frequently favor a name of this type. (On of the most popular is Atticus, who still writes regularly in the *Sunday Times.* Atticus was an elegant Roman scholar and master of Greek, and a publisher and patron of the arts. His real name was Titus Pomponius. The pseudonym itself literally means "coming from Attica," i.e., from Athens, and was an epithet given by Romans to distinguished scholars and writers.)

If classical names do not appeal, the pseudonym searcher can always derive a name in a random fashion, by taking any name in existence and adopting it. That is to say, you can take any standard "ready-made" name and use it, without reference to a particular person of this name. Such names can be styled as arbitrary, since although real enough as names they have no specific origin.

On one of its lower levels of application "Mr. and Mrs. Smith" is an arbitrary name when used by an (unmarried) couple to check in at a hotel. They have not taken the name from a particular Mr. and Mrs. Smith, but have simply chosen the commonest surname in the English language as a transparent disguise.

Even so, there are degrees of arbitrariness, since the actual name adopted may be specifically that of a particular person, even though the adopter knows absolutely nothing about the person. In other words, the name is taken on simply as a name, nothing more. When David Cornwell became John Le Carré he took the name from a shopfront in London which he had seen while sitting on the top deck of a bus. Adam Faith, on the other hand, found his name in a "Naming the Baby" book. No doubt somewhere in the English-speaking world there is a real Adam Faith, perhaps several Adam Faiths, but Terence Nelhams had none of them specifically in mind when he chose his name.

Lists of arbitrary names are, or were, frequently held by agents and managers when engaging a new performer, much as many firms today hold lists of arbitrary trade names, evolved by computer, for possible use for a new product. Cary Grant came by his name from such a list. And of course an excellent source of ready-made names suitable for adoption in this way is a telephone directory! Walden Cassotto is said to have found his name Bobby Darin in a phone book, as did Martha Raye, the American radio and TV comedienne who was born Margaret Reed.

An arbitrary name can, naturally, be an invented one, such as Cantinflas or Pele, in which case it does not belong in this chapter but the next.

Some pseudonyms result from a mistake such as a misprint. They do belong here since they are certainly "ready-made," even if inadvertently.

As names of this type can be instanced those of F. Anstey, the novelist, and Irving Berlin, the great songwriter. They were the results of printer's errors of their real names, respectively, T. Anstey Guthrie and Israel Baline. A "mistake" name may also be a misprint of an already chosen pseudonym, not a true name. The American essayist Donald Grant Mitchell had adopted the name J.K. Marvel for his contributions to the *Morning Courier and New York Enquirer* in 1846. A typo gave him his permanent pen name of Ik Marvel. Such misprints more readily occur when the native of one country is billed in another, in a foreign tongue. This happened to the English music hall entertainer Percy Henry Thompson, who took his stage name, Percy Honri, from the way the French printer had announced his appearance at the Folies Bergère. (There must have been many such instances. I am reminded of a friend who, on holiday in Spain, saw a movie poster announcing a film starring "Dirt Bogarde.")

When considering the evolution of personal names in Chapter 1, we saw that one source of surnames was place-names. In their more evolved form, place-names can also serve as a suitable pseudonym, especially when they indicate a place with which the name adopter has a special connection, for example as a birthplace. (Strictly speaking, the classical name Atticus, mentioned above, is a pseudonym of place-name origin, although in translated and adjectival form.)

In this category we must interpret "place-name" in its widest form, to include not just standard geographical names but names of houses, estates, streets, and fields, for example – that is, anywhere that is a place with a name. Since many place-names frequently resemble a personal name – indeed, many of them actually are a personal name (as Alberta, Washington, and, after all, America) – it is often relatively easy to convert them or adapt them as a pseudonym.

To illustrate the scope place-names in the wide sense of the word offer, we need only consider Conway Twitty (Conway, Arkansas, and Twitty, Texas), George Orwell (river Orwell), Clemence Dane (church of St. Clement Danes, London), Arthur Lucan (Lucan Dairy, Dublin), Cyril Hare, the British crime novelist (Cyril Mansions, Battersea, London), Gordon Craig (the Scottish island Ailsa Craig), and Cardinal Mindszenty (native Hungarian village of Szehimindszenty). Sometimes the pseudonym refers to the place name less obviously, more allusively, as with Nellie Melba (Melbourne, Australia), the British novelist George Woden (Wednesbury, West Midlands, itself named after Woden, the Scandinavian god of war and wisdom), and Stainless Stephen, the English music hall comedian (born in Sheffield, of stainless steel fame).

Some centuries back it was in fact almost standard practice for certain sectors of society to assume the name of their native town or village. This was noticeably the case with Italian painters of the Renaissance school: Caravaggio, Perugino, and Veronese, for example, whose real names were respectively Merisi, Vanucci and Cogliari, took the names of their birthplaces Caravaggio, Perugia and Verona. But in many cases of this kind, the native place-name would have often been a conventional addition to the real name to start with, so that Caravaggio was properly Michelangelo Merisi da [from] Caravaggio. Another Renaissance painter, although a German one, not an Italian, was Lucas Cranach, born Lucas Müller. He also adopted the name of his birthtown, then spelled Cranach (now Kronach). (This was Lucas Cranach the Elder; his son, Lucas Cranach the Younger, kept the name.) A later painter, the Frenchman Claude Gellée, became known as Claude Lorrain, from his birthplace in the historic province of Lorraine. (It is incorrect to spell his adopted name Claude Lorraine: his surname has no "e" as it is the French adjective meaning "from Lorraine," "Lotharingian," not the name of the province itself.)

An enjoyable game is hunting for places that are named after pseudonymous persons: there are rather more than one might imagine, from all the places in Soviet Russia named for Lenin (many of them previously for Stalin), to London Peak, Oregon, named for Jack London.

Place-names, when used as personal names, can be regarded just as properly "ready-made" as any name of a human being. The name, after all, is already there, in existence. It does not have to be invented. Moreover, as we have seen, it frequently *looks* like a personal name. To convert an ordinary word or phrase into a pseudonym, however, is to invent a name, since by definition a word (in this sense) is not already a name.

These, then, are the chief sources of ready-made pseudonyms—people and places. Who actually provides the name or produces it is another matter: people can adopt a name themselves or they can be suggested or noted for them. We have mentioned more than one instance of an actor or performer's being given a name by an agent or manager. Then again, in Chapter 2, it was noted that many foreign immigrants to the United States were presented with a new name on an *ad hoc* basis by the immigration officer almost as soon as they had set foot on land.

We now pass to the much more obviously "pseudo" class of invented names.

6. Invented Names

Francis Matthews is a lousy name for the theatre. Perhaps I should have called myself Clint Thrust. (Francis Matthews, interviewed in *TV Times*, May 25, 1978.)

Most of the names that we have so far been considering have actually looked like real names, usually comprising a "forename" and a "surname" element. Such names resemble the conventional names that we know in our daily lives.

Names that do *not* resemble conventional names we can perhaps call "invented names," and they are the subject of this chapter.

In general, invented names can be divided into three distinct types: those that are standard words, singly or grouped; those that are an artificial combination of letters or syllables (a rarish category, as will be seen); and those that are represented by signs or symbols other than conventional letters. Of course, some names are a blend of one or more of these types, just as some names are a mixture of a "true" name and an invented name or element.

In the first category come many names that are essentially descriptive titles. These are very common. Oliver Goldsmith, for instance, used the name "The Citizen of the World," the novelist Chiang Yee wrote as "The Silent Traveller," Hector McNeile published his Bulldog Drummond stories as "Sapper," and one of Daniel Defoe's many pseudonyms was "An English Gentleman." Many women writers identified themselves simply as "A Lady," as already mentioned.

Descriptive names of this type, especially the brief or single-word ones, are sometimes adopted by journalists and columnists, when they may belong to an individual regular contributor or to a series of writers. Examples of such names are "Spectator," "Onlooker," "Linesman" (a nice punning name for a sports journalist), or "Diplomat." Even a multiple name such as "Our City Staff," in the financial pages of a British newspaper, is really a pseudonym of this type. After all, the writers do not reveal their proper individual names. But most newspapers and magazines, even so, will now have reports and features written under the real name of the contributor, and there has been a marked trend in the second half of the twentieth century away from pseudonymous (and anonymous) articles.

In the eighteenth and nineteenth centuries, the author of a first novel that sold well frequently resorted to a standard pseudonym for any subsequent book, which was published as being by "The Author of. . ." In his *Handbook of Fictitious Names*, Olphar Hamst identifies more than 160 such writers, from "The Author of *Abbeychurch*" (Charlotte M. Yonge, who often favored this type of pseudonym) to "The Author of *Zohrab*" (James Morier, "a great Oriental traveller, and writer of tales"). The respective works that appeared under these pseudonyms were *Scenes and Characters; or, Eighteen Months at Beechcroft* (1847) and *Ayesha, the Maid of Kars* (1834), both now mostly or even wholly unread.

But by no means were all adopters of this style of pseudonym as obscure, and most readers will readily recognize the true identity of "The Author" of *Handley Cross* (Surtees), *Peter Simple* (Marryat), *Tom Brown's Schooldays* (Hughes), and *Uncle Tom's Cabin* (Harriet Beecher Stowe).

As the name or pseudonym of an author frequently follows the title of the actual work, and is (or was) preceded by the word "By . . . ," this gives scope for the pseudonym to refer to the title itself as a factual statement. An example of such a name (quoted by Hamst) is *"The Art of Making Catalogues of Libraries; or, A Method to Obtain in Short Times a Most Perfect, Complete, and Satisfactory Printed Catalogue of the British Museum Library* By a Reader Therein." The author of this lengthily titled work was actually an Italian, the bibliographer Andrea Crestadoro, who wrote in English.

Descriptive pseudonyms are frequently allusive, even punningly so, such as "Sealion" for the English naval writer Geoffrey Bennet, and "Beachcomber" for the *Daily Express* columnist D.B. Wyndham Lewis, as well as his successor, J.B. Morton. Names of this type that consist of two words frequently come close to resembling genuine "forename-surname" names, and only the incongruity of the words themselves indicates that they are not so. An example is the name of the British professional wrestler "Giant Haystacks," real name Martin Ruane.

In cases where names like this have been deliberately selected to incorporate a standard word that happens to resemble or be identical to a personal name, the actual artificiality of the name may remain undetected. A classic example is the name "Mark Twain," adopted by Samuel L. Clemens. "Mark Twain" was actually the call of pilots on the Mississippi River (see the full story on pp. 304–05), but "Mark" suggests that the name is a genuine one. In such cases the adopter of the name has donned a double disguise, choosing a name that is not his own anyway, and one that is not even a personal name at all! There are other forenames besides Mark that lend themselves to such treatment, among them April, Bill, Bob, Cherry, Daisy, Dawn, Frank, Guy, Holly, King, Lance, May, Pat, Peg, Pip, Ray, Rob, Rose, Tony, and Will. (Fruit and flower names and pet names generally are the best candidates.) And this is to say nothing of the punning distortions familiar from our childhood as the names of bogus authors (Eileen Dover, Cora Napple, and so on). Of the creating of such silly names there is (fortunately) no end, and the Australians have added to the name-fund with Emma Chizit, Gloria Soame, and classically, Afferbeck Lauder. These are all so-called "Strine" creations (see the last name's entry on p. 198). Among real people with names of this type, we have Stepin Fetchit, Lemmie B. Good, Will B. Good, Orpheus Seeker, Marti Caine, and Luke Sharp, invented names all.

Nor are other languages immune from exploitation in this way. The following resemble genuine names (and we make allowances for their foreignness), but they are devised from standard words in the relevant language: Caran d'Ache (Russian), Felix Carmen (Latin), Mata Hari (Malay), Dita Parlo (Italian).

Names that consist of a genuine forename with a standard word as surname also come into the "invented" category, at least partially, and obviously the scope is much wider here than when selecting a forename of this type, where the choice is restricted to existing names. Among the many examples, thus, are Jimmy Driftwood, Dion Fortune, Gary Glitter, Peter Porcupine, and Vera Vague. Again the language may not be English, as for Maxim Gorky (Russian) or Danny La Rue (French). And where the surname *does* coincide with a standard word, we have the converse of a "Mark Twain"-style name. An example is that of Veronica Lake (whose invented surname was chosen to describe her lake-blue eyes). In some cases, both forename and surname may seem genuine, but actually be standard words recruited into name service. A good example is that of Patience Strong, whose name (albeit selected from a book title) embodies the human qualities that the writer wished to personify.

As another variation on the "standard word" theme, a forename may be preceded by an adjective or a noun. Popular choices here are for common words such as "Big," "Little," "Aunt," "Uncle," the latter two formerly favored by children's writers and broadcasters. Examples of such names are Big Maybelle, Little Richard, Aunt Effie, and Uncle Mac. Other adjectives can equally be commandeered, to give names such as Woody Allen (the reference is to woodwind instruments), Muddy Waters (the apparent surname is an invention), and Shakin' Stevens. Nouns are equally adopted, as for Giant Haystacks (already mentioned), Guitar Slim, and Washboard Sam. Place-names may function as forenames, too, as for the various people named (originally doubtless nicknamed) "Tex," and country singer Conway Twitty derived his name entirely from place-names. But of course such names are *already* names, so differ from the standard words that we are considering here.

Standard words are in particular used for a special category of pseudonym that is as much private as the ones already mentioned are public. These are the "love names" as characteristically resorted to by placers of personal ads in the press on Valentine's Day. Most lovers anyway use a standard word or words (or a pet distortion of it) for their loved one, and this is therefore the latter's name. Perhaps we should refer to such names as "intimate names," as distinct from the pet names that are fairly conventional abbreviations or alterations of a standard forename. Thus a girl named Susan will almost certainly become "Sue" or "Susie" or something similar to her close friends and family, and even at first to her boyfriend or lover. But for an intimate relationship she can progress to almost any kind of descriptive name, depending both on her personal characteristics or nature and the intimate naming habits or inclinations of her lover. (There are patterns of naming, though, as we shall see.)

A few examples of such "love names" will be enough to show the sort of descriptive techniques traditionally used by one lover to address another. The following appeared in *The Times* for Valentine's Day (February 14) 1988 (the names are extracted from the actual messages or *déclarations d'amour* and are those of the recipient): Baby Doll, Cuddly Sniggle, Chipmunk, Badger, Barrel Body, Big Nose, Bright Eyes, Bunny, Chocolate Buttons, Curly, Darling Porker, Dearest Dimples,

Diddlie Wumps, Frog Eyes, Honey Bunny, Kissyface, Lady Luck, Lollipop, Monster, Pooch, Princess, Purring Lady, Scrummybum, Snugglebum, Sweet Boy, The Lizard, Village Girl, Woolly Bear. (True, many of the ads open with the addressee's real name, but purely in order to draw her—it is mostly her, not his—attention to the message.)

Such names may be nonce names or permanent designations, but they are pseudonyms either way right enough, and are formed from standard words or "babytalk" adaptations of such words. The British lexicographer Robert Burchfield analyzed the appellations in an article that subsequently appeared in *The Times* (March 6, 1988), and noted some interesting naming practices, which include the use of childish words and word elements ("bum," "bun," "-kin"), as well as the use of animal names of this type ("bunny," "puss," "pig," "bear"), the high frequency of words describing physical characteristics ("Big Ears," "Big Nose"), and a large proportion of amorous-sounding invented words, some covertly (or even overtly) sexual ("Higgle Huggle," "Boofuls," "Sexorexic Fish," "Angeldrawers"). Many such inventions have meanings that can be fairly readily guessed at, or at least intuited, but others (such as "Lion Poxie Nin") remain truly private. The reduplication of sound or letter that is generally popular with pseudonym-adopters is very marked here, and is found in such names as "Grottie Smottie," "Fottlebot," "Finjin Minjin," and some of those already cited above.

Such concoctions are also found for standard "public" pseudonyms, such as Boz (for Charles Dickens, although admittedly derived from a childish pronunciation), Mistinguett (by "Miss Hellyet" out of "Vertinguette") and Woon (from the surname Wotherspoon). A few pseudonyms have no meaningful origin, but have been simply devised to match an existing name or merely to serve as a name and nothing more. Examples are the name of Grock, the circus clown, which was invented to match that of Brick (yet differ from that of Brock), and, at least partially, Squibob, although this does at least suggest "squib." Genuinely meaningless names are thus rare, and even the name "X" traditionally indicates that the named person wishes to remain anonymous.

Initials or letters are, however, a very common method of devising a pseudonym. Such letters may derive from existing names or from standard words, and it will be impossible to tell without an explanation. One famous actress was known by initials that could be interpreted both ways: "BB" denoted both Brigitte Bardot and *bébé* ("baby"). Coincidentally, Lewis Carroll adopted "B.B." as an early pen name, although it is still not certain what the letters or initials stood for.

A few pseudonymists have carried the use of letters to a deliberate excess, as for the eighteenth- and nineteenth-century French novelist Xavier de Maistre, who for his *Voyage Autour de Ma Chambre* ("Journey Around My Room") of 1794 adopted the name "M. le ch. X. o. a. s. s. d. s. M. S." This lengthy abbreviation stood for "Monsieur le chevalier Xavier, officier ancien sur survice de sa Majesté Sardinienne" ("Sir Knight Xavier, former officer in the service of His Majesty of Sardinia"). A different device was resorted to by the seventeenth-century German writer Hans Jakob Christoffel von Grimmelshausen, better known as "Simplicissimus," who for *Das wunderbarliche Vogel-Nest* ("The Wondrous Bird's Nest")

(1672) signed himself on the title page as "A.c.eee.ff.g.hh.ii.ll.mm.nn.oo.rr.sss. t.uu," these letters being simply those of his own name arranged in alphabetical order.

But back in the world of standard invented names, we must not overlook the traditional *non*-standard method of forming a pseudonym, which is to utilize signs and symbols that are not ordinary letters. The standard symbol for anonymity or at least pseudonymity is the asterisk (*) or the dash (–), with such devices either assuming the role of individual letters or standing for an entire name. Frequently, asterisks are used in a number that corresponds to the number of letters in the real name. Thus Olphar Hamst, in his work already mentioned above, succeeded in identifying one **** ******, who wrote the *Letter to *, &c., on the Rev. W.L. Bowles's strictures on the Life and writings of Pope* (1821), purportedly by "The Right Hon. Lord Byron," to be actually John Murray (1778–1843), son of John Murray, the founder of the well-known London publishing house that bears his name. The deciphering of asterisms (as they may be called) is a hard task, however, and the number of asterisks may not in fact be significant at all, but purely random. It seems to have been so in the case of **********, the author of *Letters of Advice from a Lady of Distinction to her Niece, the Duchess of *, &c., shortly after her Marriage* (1819). Hamst could not handle this one, and it is quite likely that the author was not after all a true "Lady of Distinction," nor the addressee a "Duchess." Nor did Hamst tell his readers who Θ was, as the author of *The Book of God* (1866).

Names like these, created from signs and symbols, will not occur elsewhere in this book. This is not to belittle them, however, for * is just as valid a pseudonym as George Orwell or Mark Twain, although far less original. (It also creates a practical difficulty when it comes to reading it out: how does one pronounce an asterism?)

7. Names with a Difference

Quo nomine vis vocari? ("By what name do you wish to be called?" — traditionally asked of a pope-elect by the Dean of the Sacred College of Cardinals)

This chapter is dedicated to names that are special: carefully chosen names, significant names, ambiguous names, popular names, outrageous names, baffling names, vocational names and traditional names. We shall be considering names so evocative and meaningful that they almost eclipse their bearer, and names so trivial that they are mostly long forgotten. We shall also take a necessarily speculative view of certain "open-ended" names — ones whose story is still incomplete or unexplained. And finally, in the light of our examination of the many aspects of pseudonyms and name-changes, we shall pose once again, but this time perhaps more subjectively and philosophically, the question, "What *is* a name?"

Let us at once proceed to the specific. What did the bearers of these names have in common? Linus, Anacletus, Evaristus, Telesphorus, Hyginus, Anicetus, Soter, Eleutherius, Zephyrinus, Urban, Pontian, Auterus, Fabian, Cornelius. . . .

Roman emperors? Greek gods? Classical authors? Esoteric underground "cover" names?

Here are some more, whose owners still have the same common identity: Paul, John, Pius, Benedict, Leo, Gregory, Clement, Innocent. . . .

You probably guessed correctly: all the names are those of popes, with the "classical" names above being the (real) names of very early popes, and the more familiar names that follow being those that were assumed by some popes.

We considered papal names as a special category of pseudonym in Chapter 2, where we saw that the motives for choosing a particular name can be clearly stated on the one hand or obscure on the other. Here we should take a closer look at some of the more popular names that popes have used, and try to see why they have enjoyed such favor. Why, for example, have several popes been named John, yet none chose Matthew, Mark or Luke? (True, there was one pope named Mark, but this was his real name. He pontificated for nine months in 336, many years before the first assumed name.)

It is in fact the name John that is easily "top of the popes." No less than 23 popes have assumed the name in its "neat" form — the last of these being Angelo Roncalli, who became John XXIII in 1958 — with the name used in combined form by two recent popes, John Paul I (Albino Luciani, elected 1978 and in office for only 33 days), and John Paul II, his successor (Karol Wojtyla, elected that same year, and the first non–Italian pope since 1522).

John has long been a popular Christian name at all levels, in many countries, largely thanks to the two important New Testament characters, John the Baptist and St. John the Evangelist, "the two men who were closest to Christ the Lord"—as Angelo Roncalli designated them when explaining his own reasons for choosing the name. Roncalli's account of his motives for assuming the name John, in fact, gives us as clear a picture as any regarding the popularity of the name, as well as an insight into one individual pope's choice. Apart from the biblical pedigree, the name was dear to him, he said, since it was his father's name, it was the dedication of the village church in Lombardy where he was baptized as well as that of many cathedrals throughout the world, including the Lateran basilica of San Giovanni in Rome, and of course it was the name of 22 of his predecessors. For the future John XXIII, therefore, the name was selected on a careful combination of historical, religious, and personal grounds. Significantly, the name was in turn adopted, with specific reference to John XXIII's reforming spirit, by his two successors John Paul I and John Paul II, with the latter combining homage to both John XXIII and John Paul I, whose policies he intended to pursue.

John was thus not only the first papal name to be assumed (in 983, see Chapter 2), but flourishes as a still popular papal choice a thousand years after. What name could have a better pedigree than that!

The next most common papal name is Gregory, which has been adopted 16 times—the most recently by Bartolommeo Alberto Cappellari, pope for 15 years from 1831. Just as John owes its popularity to two saints, so there seems to be little doubt that Gregory owes much of its charisma to the first pope of the name, St. Gregory the Great, of *non Angli sed angeli* fame (with reference to the English slave boys he saw in Roman marketplaces). It is almost certain that St. Gregory himself was so named after the two fathers of the Eastern church Gregory of Nazianzus and Gregory of Nyssa ("The Wonderworker"). It is a characteristically "papal" name, which may explain why its general use in Western Europe and the New World has not been particulary favored. In English-speaking countries, indeed, it is today more likely to be associated with a surname rather than a Christian name.

Following Gregory in frequency comes another typically papal name, Benedict. In English-speaking countries this is even more unpopular, except among Roman Catholics, than Gregory, although it still flourishes in Latin countries. (Its meaning, "blessed," derives directly from Latin, whereas Gregory, "watchman," comes from Greek, and John, "the Lord is gracious," originated in Hebrew.) Who was the original Benedict who prompted 15 popes to assume the name, from Niccolò Boccasini in the fourteenth century to Giacomo della Chiesa ("James Church"!) in the twentieth? As with John and Gregory and most common papal names, there were other saints of this name, the best known probably being the founder of the Benedictine order. It seems likely, however, that apart from personal references (an identification with this saint or previous pope Benedict), many popes chose the name because of its highly favorable meaning. If a pope is not "blessed," who is?

Following Benedict in frequency comes an equally meaningful name, Clement. Fourteen popes took the name, from the eleventh-century Suidger to Giovanni Ganganelli in the eighteenth century. Can we ascribe their name to a Saint Clement? If we can, it must be to the first pope of this name, who died at the end of the first century and who has by some been identified with one of the fellow laborers of St. Paul mentioned in Paul's epistle to the Philippians (4, 3). This St. Clement was famous for the letter he sent from the church of Rome to the church of Corinth, which represented the first known example of a bishop of Rome intervening in the affairs of another church. Mild (the literal meaning of Clement) the first pope of the name may have been, but clearly not meek, and subsequent popes Clement may have had him in mind when choosing the name for their pontifical position. Again, possibly the literal interpretation of the name may have been regarded as an auspicious one.

Clement has not been a particularly popular name for English speakers, and even less popular—in fact, almost nonexistent—has been the next most common papal name, Innocent. This patently obvious name was first borne by St. Innocent in the fifth century (it was his real name), and the most recently by Michelangiolo Conti, elected as Innocent XIII in 1721. St. Innocent was hardly a distinguished man, however, either as saint or pope, and the adoption of the name by later popes would appear to be either a personal tribute to an earlier allonymous pontiff or, again, the acquisition of a favorably descriptive name. Another possibility would be a link that one of the popes of the name had with the feast day of St. Innocent (June 22) or of the Holy Innocents (December 28), or perhaps with a church dedicated to the saint or the Holy Innocents.

Seen through twentieth-century eyes, the name Innocent seems a curiously bland and watery one for a pope—emphatically meek *and* mild. Just the opposite is Leo, "lion," a name adopted by exactly the same number of popes as those who chose Innocent—13. The choice of this particular name by a pope is much more likely to be an act of homage to a previous Leo than an intention to suggest a lion-like character! Indeed, we know that Leo IX, himself a saint, chose the name as a tribute to Leo the Great (Leo I), since he aimed to put the papacy, in the eleventh century, on the same sound foundations as those laid by his namesake over half a century before. Again, Leo XIII, adopting the name on his election in 1878, was paying tribute to Leo XII, whom he had always admired for his interest in education, understanding attitude towards temporal governments, and desire to make active links with lapsed Catholics. The reasonable popularity of the Christian name Leo among present-day Catholics derives largely in turn from Leo XIII himself, since this pope, the last of the name, was the first world authority to codify the duties and rights of workers and their employers (1890). We thus find, coincidentally, that the papal bearers of this name that hints at strength and power have indeed been strong-natured and of powerful spiritual stature.

The only other name that has attracted over ten popes is Pius, which once more has a transparent meaning and an apt one (if rather obviously so). Twelve popes assumed this name, over half of them comparatively recently (seven since 1775). As with Innocent, we must assume either a personal compliment or simply a desirable, and traditional, epithet behind the adoption of the name. The first pope so called (it was his actual name) was the second-century ex-slave saint who combatted Gnosticism. Not until over a thousand years later, in 1458, did another pope come to adopt the name, with the most recent bearer being Pius XII (died 1958).

Pius IX (also known euphoniously as "Pio Nono") had the longest of all pontificates (1846–1878), and we know that he took his name in deference to the memory of Pius VII, who had been his friend and who also, like himself, had been bishop of Imola. Earlier and later Piuses appear to have adopted the name on more or less conventional grounds. As a Christian name, Pius is effectively a nonstarter.

Of other names favored by popes, many are unremarkable Christian names, as Stephen (selected nine or ten times, depending on the reckoning), Alexander (eight), Paul and Adrian (six each), Nicholas (five), and Victor (three). Among the typically "papal" names have been Boniface (nine popes so called), Urban (eight), and Sixtus (five). The latter three have meanings that are all of Latin origin, respectively "doing good," "townsman" and, oddly, "sixth." (It is thought that the first pope Sixtus was so named as he was the sixth pope in line after St. Peter. It was Sixtus IV who gave his name to the fine Sistine Chapel, the pope's private chapel next to St. Peter's in Rome, famous for Michelangelo's ceiling fresco.) Most of these were adopted for reasons we have seen, with an implied or specific personal, historical or abstract reference.

In the twentieth century there has been a trend away from "adjectival" names of the Benedict, Innocent and Pius type, with a reversion to genuine Christian names. The four popes since the last Pius have thus been (apparently unoriginally but with particular personal reference) John, Paul, John Paul and John Paul. Interestingly, and almost prophetically, the first John Paul was instantly allotted the ordinal number "the First" by the media in many countries, thus prompting one letter writer to appear in *The Times* asking, "How long are we to wait for Pope John Paul II?" (J.C. Davis, September 1, 1978). On the last day of the month in which this letter was printed, the same newspaper would publish John Paul I's obituary.

Among the names, true and assumed, of the 265 popes elected to date (1989), some curiosities may be noted:

►Of the six popes named Adrian, the fourth was the only English one (Nicholas Breakspear) and the sixth the only Dutch (Adrian Boeyens). The latter was the last non–Italian pope before the election of the Polish cardinal Karol Wojtyla as John Paul II in 1978.

►Paul VI was baptized as John the Baptist (Giovanni Battista).

►All the popes named Stephen with an ordinal number higher than II could also be one number higher, i.e., Stephen III could be Stephen IV, Stephen IV is sometimes known as Stephen V, and so on. This is because there are two popes Stephen II, the first of whom was not consecrated (he died a few days after his election) and so was not listed in the official book of popes (*Liber Pontificalis*). This means that his successor was a "real" Stephen II or actually a Stephen III.

►The first pope named Boniface — otherwise St. Boniface, the "Apostle of Germany" — was originally named Wynfrid, a Germanic name meaning "friendpeace." He was renamed Boniface by Paul Gregory II.

►Martin V, born Oddone Colonna, was elected pope in 1417. He was only the third pope so named, however, not the fifth, since the two popes, "Martin II" and

"Martin III" never existed. A thirteenth-century scribe misread the names of the two popes Marinus (as Martinus)—hence the error.

►Sixtus IV is not the only pope whose name has passed, specifically or generally, into the English language (see above). Gregory XIII gave his name to the Gregorian calendar, introduced by him in 1582 (and still in force), while Gregorian chant, or plainsong, is named after the first pope so named, St. Gregory the Great. The once popular card game called Pope Joan was *not* derived from a pope named John or even from the mythical female pope of this name (who was supposed to have been elected pope as John VIII in about 855 and who was allegedly born in England), but apparently comes from the French term for the game, *nain jaune* ("yellow dwarf").

Passing from popes to lesser mortals, we must now turn our attention to another special category of names, one that in fact often nicely combines a distortion of a religious name and a play on words. This category comprises the ingenious names chosen by crossword compilers.

Where papal names are historically and spiritually significant, crossword compilers' names, as is to be expected, are linguistically so. Some of them, indeed, are as satisfying to "crack" as a neat clue is to solve.

As far as the English language crossword is concerned, the way was led by compilers whose classic names (in more senses than one) have gone down in cruciverbal history, in particular names derived from Spanish Inquisitors, as Torquemada (Edward Mathers), pioneer of the cryptic clue, his successor Ximenes (D.S. Macnutt), and *his* successor Azed (Jonathan Crowther). (See the main listing, p. 68, for accounts of all three names.) Some names of crosswordists pay homage, directly or indirectly, to this tortuous—and torturous—trio, such as Apex (Eric Chalkley), who aimed to "ape X," or imitate Ximenes, and Machiavelli (Mrs. Joyce Cransfield, a rare woman compiler). Most names, however, are neat and apt versions of the compilers' true names, or have a similarly punning and/or erudite origin.

Some of the finest British crossword compilers have become known to solvers through the medium of the radio and TV journal *The Listener,* which publishes their work regularly. For private circulation, two "Who's Whos" of *Listener* crossword setters were compiled in 1965 and 1978, giving many of the origins of setters' pseudonyms. Let us see, therefore, how some British crosswordists devised their names. (None of these names appears in the central listing of the present work.)

Most crosswordists favor a variation on their real name, whether using the whole name, the surname alone (or the first name alone), or simply the initials. Thus "Ad" is Alfred Adams, "Dogop" is Donald George Puttnam, "Eli" is Ivor Neame Ellis, "ffancy" (with its fancy aristocratic doubled "f") is Robert Caffyn, and "Klick" is Robert William Killick. "Mog" is J.E. Morgan, "Ram" is Reginald A. Mostyn, "Smada" is Arthur Adams, "Twudge" is Tom W. Johnson, and a pronunciation of his initials, and "Leon" is Noel Anthony Longmore. ("Noel" reversed *and* letters from his surname.)

Sometimes the wordplay, as might be expected, is more erudite. "Philipontes" is Philip Bridges, with his surname rendered into Latin to join his already Greek first name. "Ploutos" is Michael Rich, whose surname is similarly translated, although this time into Greek. (The bearer of this name had been given a classical education, and was actually taught the subject at school by the great Ximenes already mentioned above.) "Rhombus" is not only Robert Holmes, of which name it is a partial anagram, but is also a reference to the profession of the bearer, who is a mathematician.

Some of the allusions can never be guessed, and an explanation is necessary for them to be appreciated. Thus, "Algol" is F. Fereday, who was formerly a mathematician, and "Buff", or Colin Clarke, derives from the name of a Durham pub, the Buffalo's Head, where the bearer of the name spent much time as a student. "Loki" and "Thor" not only took their respective names from Norse mythology, but are husband and wife, the former being Eve McLaughlin and the latter Terence McLaughlin. At the same time, of course, Loki's name actually suggests her surname, and Thor's name hints at his *first* name. Cunning people, these crosswordists!

"Sam" is in the same vein, for this was the name given Albert John Hughes when he was at school. Similarly, it is impossible to deduce by the name alone that "Topher," otherwise John R. Cheadle, took his name from his son, Christopher. Andrew Bremner took the name "Sabre," apparently adding an initial convenient "S" to letters from his real name. "Merlin" is not only a "wizard with words," but took a name that hints at his home address, Marlin Ridge, Pucklechurch. "Smokey" is David A. Crossland, and his name derives from that of a favorite but recently deceased dog. And "Egma," who in everyday life is David Michael, adopted a Shakespearian word for his name, that of Costard's attempt at "enigma" in *Love's Labour's Lost*. The title of this play itself epitomizes the fate of many a would-be crossword solver.

Crossword setters' pseudonyms are thus frequently found in the "lit. & fig." style that they frequently favor when devising their cryptic clues.

Pseudonyms among crossword solvers seem to be rarely used, presumably since they seek publicity, not obscurity. However an instance is known of two setters-turned-solvers who assumed false names to enter Ximenes competitions. These were the cocompilers Dorothy Taylor and Alec Robins (Zander), who assumed the respective names of Mrs. B. Lewis (a next-door neighbor of Miss Taylor, with no interest in crosswords) and L.F. Leason (Mr. Robins is Jewish: "L.F." indicates the Hebrew letter aleph – or "A" – for his first name, and his mother's name was Leah, with Robins himself thus being "Leah's son" or Leason). In recent years the couple have been banned from Azed crosswords in *The Observer* for such deviousness!

Crossword setters may well have the occasional mental tussle before they can come up with a satisfactory word to fill an awkward "light," or a good clue for a word once they have entered it in their grid.

Tusslers of another sort, physical not mental, are wrestlers, and many of those who do battle in the ring will select a suitable pseudonym for themselves.

Some ring names are fairly conventional, and could apply to almost any person who has adopted a pseudonymous name. You cannot tell that Bobby Becker, Don

Eagle, Paul Jones and Dusty Rhodes, for example, are wrestlers simply by their ring names. But many wrestlers specialize in some kind of act, costume, or gimmick, or fall into a particular physical or ethnic group, and as such choose a name that reflects their special quality. Let us look at some of these categories.

►"The toffs": Some wrestlers like to pose as members of the nobility, and so have names like Lord Duncum, Lord Charles Montague, Sir Norman Charles, Lord Patrick Lansdowne, and Lord Bertie Topham. One "blue blood" wrestler in Los Angeles, James Blears, changed his name legally to Lord Blears.

►"The hillbillies": Where the "lords" enter the ring wearing cloaks and monocles, the "hillbillies" appear in blue denim and rope belts. They have names like Hillbilly Spunky, Logger Larsen, Klondike Bill, Farmer Jack, Elviry Snodgrass, and Country Boy Humphrey.

►"The Indians": If you have cowboys in the ring, then you must also have Red Indians. Many wrestlers in this category are called "Chief," as Chief White Owl, Chief Kit Fox, Chief Little Wolf, Chief Big Heart, Chief Thunderbird, Chief Sunni War Cloud, and Chief Indio Cherokee. Women wrestlers of this kind are usually "Princess," as Princess Tona Tomah, Princess Rose White Cloud, and Princess War Star. Many of these really are Indians, although not chiefs or princesses. Others have names such as Billy Two Rivers, Johnny War Eagle, Danny Little Bear, and Tiny Roebuck.

►"The terrible Turks": A good guise for a wrestler, with bald head and fearsome moustache. Among them have been Ali Bey the Turkish Terror, Youssouf the Terrible Turk, and Humid Kala Pasha (so called because of his "excessive humidity" when wrestling). There has also, of course, been an Ali Baba.

►"The fatties": Their names speak for themselves: Haystack Calhoun, Giant Haystacks, Man Mountain Dean, and The Blimp. A woman wrestler in this generous group is Heather Feather. She weighs in and wades in at just under 390 pounds and trains on sausage pizzas.

►"The angels": Handsome wrestlers? Far from it! These are the big men with uneven eyes, hideous hooters, misshapen mouths, and fiddle-case feet. Their names are often variations on their category: The Golden Angel, The Swedish Angel, The Super Swedish Angel (billed as "the world's ugliest wrestler"), The Czech Angel, and the Polish Angel. There was even a bald woman wrestler named The Lady Angel.

After such a show of power—an amateur tackles a *Listener* crossword or a professional wrestler at his peril—we should perhaps come down to more homely and familiar names.

Peter Anthony, for example, and Judith M. Berrisford. These are such ordinary names that one might not even suspect they are pseudonyms. Yet they are, and moreover, to justify their mention in this chapter—are somewhat out of the ordinary run of pen names. They are in fact the names of not two individuals, but two couples—respectively Peter Shaffer and his brother Anthony, and Clifford Lewis and his wife Mary. Where two people work together like this, whether as family relatives or not, it is only natural that if they assume a pseudonym, they should take a single name.

For a couple to adopt a single pen name is fairly common, and in forming their pseudonym the usual devices are resorted to—with perhaps a wider scope for "own name" creation, since there are twice as many real names to work on. The Shaffer brothers, for example, simply used their first names as a forename and surname, while the Lewises based their joint name on the maiden name of Mary Lewis's mother (Berrisford). (What is rather unusual is that the husband-and-wife team decided in favor of a feminine pen name; normally such double pen names are masculine.)

As with all pseudonyms, variations in formation and application are possible here. A Citizen of New York for example, was not a single citizen, nor even two, but turns out to be three distinguished writers—Alexander Hamilton, "King of the Feds," and James Madison, fourth U.S. President, and John Jay, jurist and statesman. The pseudonym Patrick Quentin conceals the identity of no less than four writers (Richard Webb, Hugh Wheeler, Martha Kelly, and Mary Aswell), and the clearly concocted name Smectymnuus was the joint name of five English Presbyterian ministers.

Very occasionally an inversion of this type of name occurs, when a pseudonym consisting of two names turns out to be a single individual. This is the case with "William and Robert Whistlecraft," who were not a father-and-son or fraternal team but just one man—John Hookham Frere, the early nineteenth-century English diplomat and author. He used the name for his humorous poem *The Monks and the Giants* (1817–1818), a mock-romantic Arthurian work—to be precise, the first four cantos of it—which came to provide a model for the much better known poem *Don Juan* by Byron, begun a year later (1819).

In all pseudonym creations there is often present a latent whimsicality. If you are "making a name for yourself," why not devise something witty and clever, and enjoy yourself in the process? An amusing or punning name will often be remembered much more vividly and effectively than a prosaic and commonplace one. One suspects, for example, that if Patsy Sloots, the film actress, had retained her real name instead of changing it to the mildly attractive but rather ordinary Susan Shaw, she would have made a greater impact on her public. (Why, her real name almost *looks* like a stage name! Could she really be Posy Slatts?)

It is not surprising, therefore, that some pseudonym bearers have turned to the creation of a comical name, or several comical names, with considerable relish. The novelist William Makepeace Thackeray must have enjoyed inventing George Savage Fitzboodle, Jeames de la Pluche, Major Gahagan, Ikey Solomons, Michael Angelo Titmarsh, Charles James Yellowplush and their kind, much as Charles Dickens and P.G. Wodehouse, in their respective fictional works, had a genius for devising names for their characters that are often witty, occasionally outrageous, and usually entirely fitting. (The study of names of fictional characters is an important and enlightening subject, as yet mostly left untreated except by a few dedicated literary or linguistic experts. We hinted at the aptness of many Shakespearean names at the beginning of Chapter 1, for example: there is a virgin field that would richly pay the pioneer cultivator.)

And lest it be thought that the prerogative of humorous pseudonym creation belongs exclusively to writers, especially the classic American humorists (Josh Billings and Diedrich Knickerbocker among them), let us here cite some of the most enjoyable pseudonyms ever concocted. These are the names used by W.C. Fields, whose offbeat imagination gave us, among others: Mahatma Kane Jeeves, Otis Criblecolis, Egert Souse, Cuthbert J. Twillie, Professor Eustace McGarde, Elmer Prettywillie, Samuel Bisbee, Elmer Finch, Gabby Gilfoil, Professor Quail, Augustus Winterbottom, T. Frothingwell Bellows, Larson E. Whipsnade, and Woolchester Cowperthwaite. Ridiculous names, of course—yet somehow many of them not quite beyond the bounds of possibility as actual names.

Multiple pseudonyms like this are found in several spheres of creative activity. Among names used for his recordings by George Harrison, of the Beatles, for example, were L'Angelo Misterioso, George O'Hara, Hari Georgeson, P. Roducer, Jai Raj Harisein, George H., George O'Hara Smith, Son of Harry, George Harrysong, and The George O'Hara Smith Singers. This last name referred to the fact that the recording was of his own voice overdubbed many times.

Even John Lennon resorted to the occasional musical pseudonym, such as Noel Nohnn and John O'Cean, while Paul McCartney recorded under the names of Apollo C. Vermouth (almost a Fields creation) and Paul Ramon. Some of these are nonce usages, of course, but nonetheless genuine for that.

In the more familiar world of literature, there have been several multiple pseudonyms (maybe we could call them "multinyms"). Erle Stanley Gardner, the U.S. writer of detective fiction, used the names of Kyle Corning, A.A. Fair, Charles M. Green, Charlton Kendrake, Charles J. Kenny, Robert Parr, and Les Tillray, while John Creasey, the English crime novelist, used almost 30 different pseudonyms, including Gordon Ashe, Michael Halliday, Brian Hope, Kyle Hunt, Abel Mann, J.J. Marric, Richard Martin, Rodney Mattheson, Anthony Morton, Tex Riley, and Jeremy York. These are not as enterprising as Fields' names, but they are wide-ranging enough.

But 30 pen names is chicken feed beside the "centenarians," those writers who adopted 100 or more pseudonyms. Nor are they all English-speakers.

In his great four-volume *Dictionary of Pseudonyms,* we find Masanov, thus, listing the 106 names used by V.M. Doroshevich (1864–1922), the Russian journalist and satirical writer (including Ivanov Son of Influenza, and Wandering Minstrel, Professor of Striped and Spotted Dark Green Magic—who says the Russians are a humorless race?), and the 107 pseudonyms assumed by the writer, actor and journalist A.M. Gerson (1851–1888), from the obvious "A.G." to the unexplained "S.S." The palm, however, must go to the Russian humorist Konstantin Arsenyevich Mikhaylov (1868–   ), who boasted no less than 325 pen names, from "Ab." to "Z." Most of them are in fact abbreviations and variants of a particular pseudonym such as G., G-ver, Gl., Glv., Gllivr, and the like, which all seem to indicate "Gulliver", while others are rather pedestrian descriptive names such as Passenger, Pedagogue and Reformer. For a humorist, indeed, the majority are not even specially amusing. Still, the record stands, and must therefore be duly noted.

Far more interesting than these are the full 173 pseudonyms adopted by Voltaire. Since, as far as I am aware, these have never appeared before in their entirety in an English-language publication, whether in original French or in translation, I am allocating Appendix I to them (pages 326–28) in the hopes that they will satisfy the reader's curiosity and also be a useful passage of reference for all who need them. Appendix II, which may serve as a comparison, lists the 198 names used by Daniel Foe, otherwise Daniel Defoe, author of *Robinson Crusoe*.

With the two enjoyable names of Doroshevich, quoted above, we are reminded of the playful nature that many pseudonyms assume. Indeed, the humor and wit – and sheer outrageousness – of many pen names is one of their most popular attributes. Everyone likes a funny name, simply because everyone enjoys a joke or relishes a pun. At the same time, the actual *use* of a humorous pseudonym may be a dead serious one. A frivolous name may mask a biting satire or cruel travesty. Thus Thomas Nash, the sixteenth-century English satirical pamphleteer and dramatist, chose the apparently lighthearted name Adam Fouleweather for his *Wonderful, strange, and miraculous Astrologicall Prognostication* (1591) that was an acrid reply to the savage denunciation of him by the astrologer Richard Harvey, and two hundred years later William Cobbett, the British author and politician, chose the amusing name Peter Porcupine for his perfectly serious pro–British pamphlets published in America in the 1790s.

It is the lengthy, descriptive names, however, that make the most entertaining reading, whatever their purpose, and for their own sakes we can introduce a few more.

Lord John Russell, the nineteenth-century English statesman, entitled himself "A Gentleman who has left his Lodgings" for his *Essays and Sketches of Life and Character* (1820). This originally had a preface signed "Joseph Skillet," allegedly the lodging-house keeper who published the essays to pay the rent that the "Gentleman" had neglected to pay. In the same style, but a few years earlier, Charles Snart, an attorney of Newark, Nottinghamshire, had published a book on fishing called *Practical Observations on Angling in the River Trent* (1812). For this purpose the author described himself as "A Gentleman Resident in the Neighbourhood, who has made the Amusement his Study for upwards of Twenty Years." In both cases, as with similar diverting titles, the name of the book would precede the pen name of the author, so that Lord Russell's essays and sketches were "By a Gentleman who . . ." and Charles Snart's discourse on angling was written "By a Gentleman . . . ." Such names as "One who . . ." are also of this type, as *A Peep at the Wiltshires Assizes, a Serio-Ludicrous Poem* (1820) by "One who is but an Attorney" (George Butt, a Salisbury, Wiltshire, solicitor), and *English History for Children, from four to ten years of Age* (1832–1833), by "One who loves the Souls of the Lambs of Christ's Flock" (the Rev. Richard Marks, a Buckinghamshire vicar). (Hamst, quoting this last multipartite name, says, "We dare not allow ourselves to comment upon a person who uses such a pseudonym as this.")

Infinitely more entertaining than these long-winded names, though, are those that combine description with fantasy, as the two Doroshevich names. Russian nineteenth-century writers, in fact, seem to have made such names something of a specialty. Dmitriev quotes two fine specimens.

The first was devised by V.A. Zhukovsky, a minor poet, for a frivolous "Greek ballad rendered in the Russian style" entitled *Yelena Ivanovna Protasova, or Friendship, Impatience, and Cabbage* (1811). For this, Zhukovsky assumed the name "Maremyan Danilovich Zhukovyatnikov, President of the Commission on the Construction of the Muratov House, Author of the Crowded Stables, Fire-breathing Ex-president of the Old Kitchen Garden, Knight of the Three Livers, and Commander of the Gallimaufry." Zhukovsky wrote this curiosity while staying with his friends, the Protasov family, at their estate at Muratovo, just outside Moscow.

A friend of Zhukovsky, one Alexander Pleshcheyev, wrote some "critical comments" on this same ballad under what must be one of the lengthiest and weirdest pseudonyms ever devised by any writer: "Aleksandr Pleshchepupovich Chernobrysov, Active Mameluke and Bogdohan, Choirmaster of the Cowpox, Privileged Galvanist of the Canine Comedy, Publisher of a Topographical Description of Wigs, and Delicate Arranger of Divers Musical Tummy-Rumblings, Including the Fully Scored Howlings Herewith Appended." The preposterous personal name that heads the pseudonym, although based on Pleshcheyev's real name, has a meaning that works out something like "Alexander Splashnavelovich Shooblackcatoff." (The Mameluke and Bogdohan in the name are mellifluous titles of, respectively, classes of Egyptian rulers and Chinese emperors.)

A glance through the alphabetical listing that forms the main section of this book will show that some pseudonymous surnames seem specially favored, and have been adopted by several individuals. Among the most popular are (with variant spellings) Carol, Douglas, Field, Ford, Hay, John, Jones, Page and Williamson, and not far behind come names such as Adams, Alexander, Allan, Anthony, Barry, Bell, Blair, Brook, Brown and others. A consideration of such popular names will reveal that many of them are alternate first names and surnames (Allan, Carol, Douglas, John, and the like). It also appears that names denoting a color are often adopted (Brown, Gray, White), as are both "countryside" names (Brook, Field, Ford, Hay, Lane) and "good image" names (Home, Hope, King, Ray). Gray (or Grey) occurs several times, as does that popular name Lee, which is in the versatile "first-name-or-surname" category.

Overall the most popular and frequently recurring names, too, are the briefest, and for a standard, run-of-the-mill surname, a monosyllabic name is often preferred. In some cases this may be because the brevity and simplicity of the name is refreshingly welcome after a difficult foreign name or an unduly long one. In other cases the ease of spelling and pronunciation, and the ready recognition of the name, are attractive factors.

Both Lynn and Carol are unusual in being girls' names popular as male assumed surnames. (They exist as real surnames, but not as widely as other names listed here.) It is tempting to ascribe the popularity of Carol to that most popular of pseudonymous writers, Lewis Carroll, but there is no evidence for this. Nor is there any evidence against it, since of the ten Carrolls (or variant spellings) listed, nine were born later than the author of *Alice in Wonderland* and could indeed have been inspired to adopt this name, consciously or subconsciously. Of the other names, a few may simply have occurred here as the result of random selection – that is, it may be sheer chance that eight Drakes are listed, and nine Shaws.

The great popularity of Page or Paige would not seem to be randomly indicated, though. Why should this name be desirable? Again, apart from being a short and simple name, it may be that one or more of the bearers suggested the name to the others—perhaps Patti Page or Janis Paige.

However, there are two names that are even more popular than these, at least as represented in our selection in this book. These are Gray or Grey, which occurs 20 times as a pseudonymous surname, and Lee, which comes 18 times.

These two names doubtless have more to them than simply being monosyllabic color and nature names. Lee, for instance, is also a fairly popular given name, especially in the United States. Gray is not a forename, but seems to be popular simply because it is a pleasant name, a reasonably euphonious one, and a name with "gentle" associations (although as a common adjective, it has a number of undesirable meanings, such as "dull," "pale," "old"). Add to Gray names such as Grayson and Greyson (four of one and one of the other), and we have the most frequently occurring pseudonymous surname in the book.

Both names have a high frequency in other collections of pseudonyms also. Of his total 3400 names, for example, Clarke has 11 Greys and 13 Lees, and Atkinson, in his "over 6000" English and American literary pseudonyms, has 11 Greys and 18 Lees. (For the record, Clarke also lists 11 Allens, 11 Carols or Carrolls, 11 Fords or Fordes, and 10 Joneses. Atkinson has 17 Allans or Allens, 20 Blakes, 14 Craigs, 22 Graemes or Grahams, 14 Hamiltons, 13 Hills, 14 Jameses, 22 Johnses or Joneses, 20 Kings, 23 Martins, 12 Millers, 13 Peterses, 16 Robertses or Robertsons, 24 Scotts, 22 Smiths, 31 Stewarts or Stuarts [11 Stewarts, 20 Stuarts], 18 Thomases, 15 Wests, 15 Williamses [and one Williamson], and 18 Wilsons. Neither author has any name more common than these. Clarke's number one name is thus Lee, as ours almost is, while Atkinson's is Stuart or Stewart. The majority of their top-scoring names are, as ours also are, "dual-purpose" forenames-surnames.) It may even be that the popularity of such pseudonymous surnames may encourage the use of such names as real given names.

Looked at less statistically, can it be said that the pseudonyms adopted by men differ in any way from those chosen by women?

On the whole, there is very little difference, especially among the more conventional names. Take all those Lees, for example. In virtually every case the first name, whether male or female, is quite unremarkable: Andrew, Bruce, Canada, Dickey, Steve, William for the men, and Anna, Brenda, Dixie, Dorothy, Gypsy Rose, Holm, Lila, Michele, Patty, Peggy, Vanessa, Vernon (a sex disguise name) for the women. A more random dip in the alphabetical listing will show that most men adopt rather routine, traditional masculine names (John Abbot, Richard Amberley, John Oldcastle, Drew Pearson), and that women do likewise with their feminine names (June Allyson, Doris Day, Sheilah Graham, Lana Turner).

It is certainly noticeable, however, that men who care about their specifically masculine image—film actors playing tough roles, for example—do tend to choose "rugged," rather aggressive-sounding names, as Rock Hudson, Tab Hunter, and Paul Temple. (Note the verbal associations: rocks, hunters, temples.) Some women, too, who wish to project an exclusively feminine image – as "cuties" and "sweeties" of song or the cinema, or as sex symbols of one sort or another – likewise choose (or are given) a name that is intended to have associations of romance or glamour (Renée Adorée, Eve Arden, Veronica Lake, Penny Singleton).

It should also not go unnoticed that the actual letters incorporated in a name are often important, with men frequently choosing "forceful" letters, such as "k" and "x," and women opting for soft, seductive letters, as "l" and "s." Gutturals can be gutsy, and sibilants sexy!

A large number of pseudonyms also turn out to have a common syllabic pattern. That most frequently favored is bisyllabic forename plus bisyllabic surname, as Casey Adams, Stella Martin, Henry Oscar, with the first syllable of each name accented. But this is also a fairly common phenomenon among ordinary names, and even a brief look at the *real* names of pseudonymous writers will show that there are several of this type, as David Bingley, Douglas Christie, Mary Douglas, Walter Gibson, Eric Hiscock. Perhaps an unusually high proportion of pseudonyms, however, are alliterative, with the forenames and surnames both beginning with the same letter. One has only to think of the names of some well-known movie stars to see this: Anouk Aimée, Brigitte Bardot (if hers is indeed a pseudonym), Claudette Colbert, Diana Dors, Greta Garbo, Marilyn Monroe and Simone Signoret are good examples.

But among all these facts and figures, all these personal particulars and calculated analyses, are there not any pseudonyms, it will be asked, whose real identity we cannot crack? Are there not still some disguised figures whose masks have not yet been removed? The answer is yes, of course. And here we are thinking not so much of the criminal or secret agent whose false name or cover name has not yet been revealed, but of the individual whose pseudonym has successfully concealed his true identity in spite of serious and scholarly attempts to unveil it.

In some cases, of course, a person's true identity may not be disclosed until after his death – this happened, for example, with the writer Fiona Macleod and the broadcaster A.J. Alan – but there are one or two names whose real bearers are still unknown or at most conjectured.

Probably the most famous of all "uncracked" pseudonyms is that of Junius, the eighteenth-century author whose letters, 70 in number, in the London *Public Advertiser* between January 21, 1769, and January 21, 1772, revealed many intimate scandals of the day and were generally "agin the government" and antiroyalist (one of the letters was an impudent one addressed to King George III in person). Even today, over two hundred years later, and after much ingenious detective work and extremely thorough searching of contemporary documents, the identity of the infamous writer remains in doubt. Almost always using the name Junius, but occasionally switching to Lucius, Brutus and possibly Nemesis, the author clearly had the objective of ruining the ministry of the Duke of Grafton, Britain's incapable and ineffective prime minister for the three years 1767 to 1770 and lord privy seal from 1771 to 1775.

Who was he? After a consideration of his style – he had an original and fine command of language – his classical name (but to which Junius, actual or fictional, was the allusion, if there indeed was an allusion?), and all the other many historical and political facets of the time, some 50 names were proposed as the real author. The most likely of these is popularly held to be Sir Philip Francis (1740–1818), an Irish-born politician, who was known to have written a number of letters to the papers under pseudonyms. But this is only a conjecture. Other names suggested as the true author have been Edward Gibbon, Edmund Burke, John Wilkes, Lord Chesterfield, Thomas Paine, Lord Chatham (whom Junius loyally and actively supported), Lord Shelburne, Horace Walpole, Isaac Barré, George Grenville, Lord Temple, Henry Grattan, Alexander Wedderburn, Lord George Sackville, and Horne Tooke.

"The mystery of Junius increases his importance," wrote the author himself, and this proved to be so, if only in the form of several imitators, with pseudonyms such as Junius Ridivivus, Junius Secundus, Philo-Junius, and Junius itself. "I am the sole depository of my own secret, and it shall perish with me," also wrote the sharp-tongued satirist, whom even twentieth-century technology has failed to unmask.

The *Letters of Junius* in fact made a significant contribution to journalistic history in that they established the fashion for the anonymity of leading articles in the press today.

Somewhat earlier than this, another literary name had attracted wide attention. This was one George Psalmanazar. As with Junius, his real name is unknown to this day, but unlike Junius he was an outrageous, if cunning, impostor. George Psalmanazar claimed to be a native from Formosa, which at the time of his arrival in London in 1703 was virtually an unknown island. The following year Psalmanazar published an account of Formosa with a grammar of the language spoken there. This "language" was, however, a fabrication from start to finish – he had simply concocted it. At the time literary London was taken in, but his imposture was soon exposed by Roman Catholic missionaries who had been to Formosa and who proved that the language set forth in Psalmanazar's grammar was nothing like the actual native tongue. Realizing that he had been revealed for the fraud he was, the bogus scholar publicly confessed his hoax and applied himself to more orthodox works, in particular the study of Hebrew. He died in 1763 having become a man of some repute and even the friend of Dr. Johnson.

Psalmanazar may possibly have actually been a Frenchman, or perhaps a Swiss. His year of birth is uncertain, although the year 1679 has been conjectured. He seems to have taken his name from Shalmaneser, an Assyrian prince mentioned in the Bible (2 Kings 17: 3), although it is not known what particular significance this name had for him, if any. (The name Shalmaneser itself means nothing more than "Shalman be propitious." However, the Assyrian king "took" Samaria and "carried away" Israel just as the impostor "took" London and "carried away" much of the cultural world of the capital.)

A man with a false name disseminating false scholarship in a country that was not even his own and claiming to be from a country where he had never set foot takes some beating for sheer impudence!

Most of the pseudonyms assumed by false claimants to the throne and bogus pretenders have in due time come to be exposed: you cannot go about calling yourself Prince Louis or Lady Maria for long without some kind of reaction and disclosure. There is one royal pretender, however, who still remains unidentified. She was an almost exact contemporary of Junius, and although less well known than he, has a story that intrigues considerably.

This was the so-called Princess Elizaveta Tarakanova, a Russian girl born probably in 1745 who claimed to be the daughter of the Empress Elizabeth and Count Razumovsky and who in 1772, when in Paris, declared herself to be the pretender to the Russian throne under the name of Princess Vladimirskaya. Her precise origin and true name have still not been revealed. All that is certainly known is her fate — a typically "Russian" one, both romantic and tragic. In February 1775 she was arrested in Italy by Count Orlov, who 13 years before had been instrumental in putting Catherine the Great on the throne by forcing Peter III to abdicate. Orlov brought her back to Russia where the self-styled princess was imprisoned in the notorious Petropavlovsk Fortress, in St. Petersburg, where she died of tuberculosis on December 4, 1775. (A popular Russian painting by Flavitsky shows Tarakanova trapped in her cell by a rising flood: the waters of the River Neva rush through the prison bars while the wretched princess vainly seeks refuge by standing on her bed. This is melodramatic fiction, however, since the great St. Petersburg flood occurred not that year but two years later, in 1777. No doubt Flavitsky, painting his picture nearly a century later, in 1864, felt that enough mystery already shrouded the subject of his portrait to enable him to depict a more poignant fate than death by TB.)

One or two other pseudonyms of the hapless princess are known, as Miss Frank, and Mrs. (or Madame) Tremouille, but her true identity remains a secret. (Her main name of Tarakanova exists as a genuine Russian surname, meaning — somewhat unromantically, although in the end appropriately, perhaps — "cockroach.")

In the event it was Paul I who succeeded his mother Catherine to the throne in 1796.

In more recent times there has been considerable speculation about the true identity of the horror and fantasy fiction writer M.Y. Halidom. (The name itself clearly originates in the oath "by my halidom," with *halidom* meaning a holy place or thing.) The name no doubt hid the identity of more than one writer, and superseded the previously used name Dryasdust, which was that given for the author of the trilogy *Tales of the Wonder Club* (1899, 1900). This trilogy was reissued under the "Halidom" name in three separate parts a year or two later: Volume I in 1903, II in 1904, and III in 1905. The "Dryasdust" name had first appeared in 1890 for *The Wizard's Mantle*, a story about a cloak of invisibility during the Spanish Inquisition. This was reprinted, under the name Halidom, in 1903. The last story to appear by this still unidentified writer or group of writers was "The Poison Ring" (1912).

Even today there are writers active whose true identity is a closely guarded secret. Kremlinologists, for example, long paid special attention to the articles that appeared in the Soviet newspaper *Pravda* written by one "I. Alexandrov." No one knows for sure who he really was, but the name was believed to be that of a party official whose words carried high-level Kremlin approval. In similar fashion the English publishing trade journal *The Bookseller* carries a regular column by Quentin Oates. His role is a special and influential one, for he reviews not books but the actual reviews written by literary critics. Literary editors therefore pay special heed to his words. Acerbic Quentin Oates is widely known to be, but his identity is publishing's best-kept secret.

The professional activity of Messrs. Alexandrov and Oates is of course more narrowly directed than those of Junius, and arguably less damaging. So far, however, their masks remain firmly fixed in place, even if one day they will eventually drop and the three writers will stand revealed as their true selves.

We must mention one more name that hides an as yet unestablished true identity. This was the poet and satirist Pietro Aretino, who lived and wrote some years before any of our other "mystery men," more than two hundred years even before Junius.

Aretino, we know, was the son of a shoemaker in Arezzo, north central Italy. Pietro was born in Arezzo, we also know, on April 20, 1492. Later, he pretended to be the bastard son of a nobleman, deriving his "adopted" name from that of his native town—Aretino means "belonging to Arezzo." Over the 60 years of his life (he died in Venice on October 21, 1556) the cobbler's son gained fame (or notoriety) as a writer of vicious satires and lewd sonnets and as a leader of dissolute society in the grand style. It was his writings, especially his five comedies, that really established his reputation as a literary figure of considerable standing, above all his lively and amusing *La Cortigiana* ("Life at Court") (1534), which is an enjoyable account of lowerclass life in contemporary Rome.

We thus have a good deal of information about Aretino the man and his work. We even know what he looked like, for Titian painted his portrait (currently in the Frick Collection, New York). But we still do not know the one thing that interests us here in this book—his real name!

Yet if we are honest, we will probably admit that the mystery behind the pseudonym of the seven masked figures mentioned here—there are of course many more—actually adds to their status. The concealed or undiscolosed identity of Junius makes him more powerful, just as it makes Psalmanazar more outrageous, Princess Tarakanova more tragic, M.Y. Halidom (and Dryasdust) more ghoulish, I. Alexandrov more authoritative, Quentin Oates more influential, and Aretino more colorful. The image that they hold, with the names by which they are known, is quite complete as it is, and we do not wish our picture of them to be disturbed. It is simply *because* we know that their name is not their true name that their standing in our eyes is enhanced.

The world will be a duller place when the true identity of the Man in the Iron Mask is revealed.

Pseudonyms and Name Changes
and Their Origins

This lengthy alphabetical listing presents some 4000 pseudonymous names to the reader, and not only gives the original names of the bearers but in many instances gives an account of the name change, often in the bearer's own words. Where a first-hand account of a name change is not quoted, there will frequently be a "gloss" or comment on the name. In some cases this is speculative. In others the reader's attention is drawn to some aspect of the name change which is of interest, and which may possibly otherwise be overlooked.

The listing does not, of course, aim to be comprehensive. There are other books of pseudonyms that come closer to that unattainable goal, among them the compilations by Jennifer Mossman and Harold Sharp (see Bibliography, pp. 341, 342). But those works do not give the stories behind the names that his present book aims to give. So that where they score in quantity, they lack in background, and where we lose by selectivity, we gain by detail and authentic documentation. Overall, too, we gain by giving the reader a better "read," while at the same time the facts of the individual name changes are set out for easy reference.

I have done my best to come up with a "name history" wherever possible, and spent many hours tracking down the required biographies and autobiographies in public libraries for this purpose. Of course, such biographies are the most accessible when the person is well known, and this explains the lack of background stories for some of the lesser-known names. But although the general emphasis is on the well-known, or at least the familiar, the pseudonymous net has been cast quite wide, and has captured many specimens of interest and originality that have now been displayed on the pages that follow. For our purposes, therefore, Ron Moody is just as important as Marilyn Monroe, and has been granted exactly the same factual data, even if he lacks the desired background story.

What are the factual data that the reader can expect to find?

All entries aim to be consistent and to give: (a) the person's *pseudonym* or *changed name*, followed by (b) his or her *original name*, (c) *years of birth and death*, as appropriate, followed by (d) *nationality*, and (e) *occupation* or *status*.

Despite general consistency, there are departures from the norm in some instances. A person's year of birth (or death) may be unknown, for example, in which case there will be a question mark (?). The year may be uncertain, in which case it will be preceded by a question mark (to denote an approximation) or the letter "*c.*" (for Latin *circa*, "about"), this denoting a closer approximation than a question mark. A person may well have been born in one country, but lived and worked mainly in another (often as not the United States), and such "dualities" are mostly noted. The person's profession or occupation may be much fuller and more complex than it appears, and only a general indication is usually given of the relevant main activity, chiefly for purposes of identification, but also because the actual occupation may have a bearing on the professional name chosen for it.

The original or "real" name of the person is sometimes given in full. In many cases, however, simply the forename and surname are enough for the purpose. But a married woman's maiden name may well be important, and have influenced the choice of adopted name, so that in many instances it will be quoted.

There are a few multiple names, chiefly of the "one for all" type, where a single name has been adopted by more than one person as a joint name. In such cases, the names of the original persons are linked by a plus sign (+). For an example, see Wade Miller (Robert Wade plus Bill Miller), or the fivefold Smectymnuus.

In a few instances, the person concerned will have acquired a familiar nickname, and I have added this where appropriate, if only for interest or for the sake of completeness. Gilbert M. Anderson (who was originally Max Aaronson) became known as "Bronco Billy," for example, and Ann Sheridan (who began life as Clara Lou Sheridan) was dubbed "the Oomph Girl."

Where a story or quotation accompanies a name, its source will frequently be given, usually (for a book) with the name of the author, the title of the quoted work, and its year of publication. Sometimes the background material or anecdote may have been taken from a work listed in the Bibliography. In such cases the author's name alone is given, together with the page(s) of the work where the quotation occurs. Several quotes come from the pages of newspapers and magazines, and in such instances the title of the periodical is given together with the date of the issue copied. The same procedure is followed for information gained directly from radio or television, with the name of the program and the date of its broadcast.

But enough of introductory explanations! The reader is invited to plunge in and enjoy the wealth of names and notes that follows. Many of the names will be familiar enough, but the stories behind them may well be eye-openers. . . .

A.A.: Anthony Armstrong *(q.v.)*.

Anthony **Abbot:** Charles Fulton Oursler (1893–1952), U.S. journalist, playwright, novelist.

John **Abbot:** Vernon John (1896–1943), U.S. music hall singer.

Russ **Abbot:** Russell Allan Roberts (1947–   ), Eng. TV comedian.

Bud **Abbott:** William A. Abbott (1895–1974), U.S. film comedian, teaming with Lou Costello *(q.v.)*.

Johann Philip **Abelin:** Johann Ludwig Gottfried (*c.*1600–1634), Ger. historian.

Ab-o'-th'-Yate: Benjamin Brierley (1825–1896), Eng. dialect writer. Benjamin Brierley was an English weaver who came to write stories and verse in the Lancashire dialect. His early stories were narrated by a character called "Owd Ab" (Old Abe), and this gave his basic pen name, with "Yate" being a Lancashire form of "gate," meaning not "gate" but "street" as in many street names in northern

English towns (such as Briggate [="Bridge Street"], Leeds). Ben Brierley was thus "Abe from the street," or a typical old world townee character.

Acanthus: H. Frank Hoar (1909–1976), Eng. cartoonist. The acanthus is a prickly plant; perhaps the cartoonist regarded himself as a "prickly" commentator?

Johnny **Ace:** John Marshall Alexander, Jr. (1929–1954), U.S. black rock musician.

Richard **Adama:** Richard Adams (1928–   ), U.S. ballet dancer. A typical ballet foreign-style adaptation of a standard English (American) name.

Casey **Adams:** Max Showalter (1917–   ), U.S. film actor.

Don **Adams:** Donald James Yarmy (1926–   ), U.S. TV comedian. "Adams" could be regarded as extracted from "Donald James."

Edie **Adams:** Elizabeth Edith Enke (1927–   ), U.S. film actress, singer.

Fay **Adams:** Faye Scruggs (–   ), U.S. blues singer.

Maud **Adams:** Maud Wikstrom (1945–   ), Swe.-born film actress.

Maude **Adams:** Maude Kiskadden (1872–1953), U.S. stage actress. Adopted mother's maiden name.

Moses **Adams:** George William Bagby (1828–1883), U.S. humorist, lecturer.

Nick **Adams:** Nicholas Adamschock (1932–1968), U.S. film actor.

Stephen **Adams:** Michael Maybrick (1844–   ), Eng. composer, singer.

Max **Adeler:** Charles Heber Clark (1847–1915), Ger.-born U.S. humorous writer.

Renée **Adorée:** Jeanne de la Fonte (1898–1933), Fr.-born U.S. film actress. "Renée" suggests "reborn;" "Adorée" suggests both "adored" and "gilded."

Adrian IV: Nicholas Breakspear (c. 1100–1159), Eng. pope.

Adrian V: Ottobono Fieschi (?–1276), It. pope.

Adrian VI: Adrian Florensz Boeyens (1459–1523), Du. pope. The last pope to retain his own baptismal name as a papal name.

Gilbert **Adrian:** Adrian Adolph Greenberg (1903–1959), U.S. film costume designer. "Gilbert" doubtless from "Greenberg."

Iris **Adrian:** Iris Adrian Hostetter (1913–   ), U.S. film actress.

Max **Adrian:** Max Bor (1903–1973), Ir.-born Eng. stage actor.

Æ (or AE, A.E.): George William Russell (1867–1935), Ir. poet, artist. The name derives from the initial letter of "Æon," a pseudonym used by Russell for an article, and itself meaning "eternity," from the Greek. The printer had queried the spelling of the name in this way, so that Russell opted for the digraph alone.

Affable Hawk: [Sir] Desmond MacCarthy (1878–1952), Br. dramatic, literary critic. The American Indian-style name was chosen by MacCarthy for his articles in the *New Statesman* to match that of his predecessor, Solomon Eagle *(q.v.)*.

Afrique: Alexander Witkins (1907–   ), S.A. music hall singer. French for "Africa."

Afrit: Alistair Ferguson Ritchie (1887–1954), Br. crossword compiler. The name partly derives from the initial elements of his own name (*A*listair *F*erguson *Rit*chie), partly represents Afrit, a powerful devil in Muslim mythology. A crossword compiler likes to inspire dread in his hapless solvers!

Luigi **Agnesi:** Louis Ferdinand Léopold Agniez (1833–1975), Belg. bass opera singer.

Spiro **Agnew:** Spiro Theodore Anagnostopoulos (1918–), U.S. politician, of Gk. parentage. Typical (and necessary) shortening of one of the notoriously lengthy Greek surnames.

Shmuel Yosef **Agnon:** Samuel Josef Czaczkes (1888–1970), Hebrew novelist, short story writer. Jewish name taken from his story *Agunot* (1908) ("Forsaken Wives"), his literary debut.

Maria de **Agreda:** María Fernandez Coronel (1602–1665), Sp. abbess, mystic. Abbess (also known as María de Jesus) was head of Franciscan monastery in Spanish town of Agreda, where she was also born and where she died.

Georgius **Agricola:** Georg Bauer (1494–1555), Ger. scholar and humanist. Latin *agricola* meant "ploughman," "farmer," to which German *Bauer* ("farmer," "smallholder") corresponds. Compare the next three names below.

Johan **Agricola:** Johannes Sneider (later Schnitter) (1494–1566), Ger. Lutheran reformer. Schneider first latinized his name as *Sartor* (German *Schneider,* "tailor"), but then adopted name of Agricola (see entry above).

Martin **Agricola:** Martin Sore (or Sohr) (1486–1556), Ger. composer, teacher, writer of music. Sore was self-taught, and was thus called to music "from the plough;" hence adoption of name Agricola (Latin, "ploughman").

Rodolphus **Agricola:** Roelof Huysman (1443–1485), Du. humanist. Dutch surname means "man of the house," here interpreted through Latin *agricola* (see above).

Ernst **Ahlgren:** Victoria Benedictsson (1850–1888), Swe. writer.

Juhani **Aho:** Johannes Brofeldt (1861–1921), Finnish author. Both names appear to derive from letters of "Johannes."

Gustave **Aimard:** Olivier Gloux (1818–1883), Fr.-born U.S. romantic novelist.

Anouk **Aimée:** Françoise Sorya (1932–), Fr. film actress. Actress named herself after character in one of her early films.

Patricia **Ainsworth:** Patricia Nina Bigg (1932–), Austral. writer.

Ruth **Ainsworth:** Ruth Gilbert (1908–), Br. writer of children's fiction.

Catherine **Aird:** Kinn Hamilton McIntosh (1930–), Eng. mystery writer.

Catherine **Airlie:** Jean Sutherland MacLeod (1908–), Sc. writer.

Anna **Akhamatova:** Anna Andreyevna Gorenko (1889–1966), Russ. poet. When Anna Gorenko was 17, and an aspiring poet, her father objected to her writings, calling her a "decadent poetess," and saying she would shame the family name. Anna retorted, "I don't need that name," and instead chose a Tatar name, that of her great-grandmother. The southern Tatars had always seemed mysterious and fascinating to the girl who came to be one of Russia's greatest modern poets [Amanda Haight, *Anna Akhmatova: A Poetic Pilgrimage,* 1976].

Alain: Emile-Auguste Chartier (1868–1951), Fr. philosopher, essayist. Alain took his pseudonym from the fifteenth-century poet Alain Chartier, whom (romantically) Margaret of Scotland is said to have kissed on the lips as he slept, so as to honor the beautiful words and thoughts that issued from them (she explained).

Alain-Fournier: Henri-Alban Fournier (1886–1914), Fr. novelist. New name selected to be distinguished from writer Edouard Fournier (1819–1880).

A.J. **Alan:** Leslie Harrison Lambert (1883–1940), Br. broadcaster, story-teller.

Jane **Alan:** Lillian Mary Chisholm (1906–), Eng. short story writer.

Antony **Alban:** Antony Allert Thomson (1939–   ), Br. author.

Mme **Albani:** Marie Louise Emma Cecile Lajeunesse (1847–1930), Can. opera singer.

Joe **Albany:** Joseph Albani (1924–1988), U.S. bop pianist.

Eddie **Albert:** Eddie Albert Heimberger (1908–   ), U.S. stage, film, TV actor. Said to have adopted name because he grew tired of announcers referring to him as "Eddie Hamburger."

Martha **Albrand:** Heidi Huberta Freybe Loewengard (1914–   ), Ger.-U.S. spy novelist. Name is that of great-grandfather.

Hardie **Albright:** Hardy Albrecht (1903–1975), U.S. film actor.

Alceste:[1] Alfred Assolant (1827–1886), Fr. writer; [2] Hippolyte de Castile (–   ), Fr. writer; [3] Louis Belmontet (1799–1879), Fr. writer; [4] Edouard Laboulaye (1811–1883), Fr. writer. Doubtless one or more of these derive from opera *Alceste* (Lully, Gluck) or from character of this name in Molière's *Le Misanthrope*, where he is the misanthropic hero. But operatic Alceste is based on Euripides' play *Alcestis*, where the name is that of the heroine!

Alcibiades: [1] Albert, Margrave of Brandenburg (1522–1557), Ger. prince; [2] Alfred, Lord Tennyson (1809–1892), Eng. poet; [3] George Villiers, Duke of Buckingham (1627–1688), Eng. courtier. Original Alcibiades was Athenian general of fifth century BC, appearing in later literature.

Alan **Alda:** Alphonso D'Abruzzo (1936–   ), U.S. stage actor. "Alda" derived from first two letters of real names, as it did for his father, Robert Alda *(q.v.)*.

Frances **Alda:** Frances Davies (1883–1952), N.Z. opera singer.

Robert **Alda:** Alfonso Giuseppe Giovanni Roberto D'Abruzzo (1914–1986), It.-born U.S. film actor, father of Alan Alda (see above).

Mark Aleksandrovich **Aldanov:** Mark Aleksandrovich Landau (1889–1957), Russ. writer. Near-anagram of non–Russian name "Landau."

G.R. **Aldo:** Aldo Graziani (1902–1953), It. cinematographer.

Adair **Aldon:** Cornelia Lynde Meigs (1884–1973), U.S. educator, author, playwright.

Louis **Aldrich:** Louis Lyon (1843–1901), U.S. actor.

Shalom **Aleichem:** Solomon Rabinowitz (1859–1916), Russ.-born Jewish novelist, working in U.S. Name is familiar Yiddish greeting derived from Hebrew, meaning "peace be with you."

O **Aleijadinho:** António Francisco Lisbôa da Costa (?1730–1814), Brazilian sculptor, architect. Architect was born deformed, and name is Portuguese for "the little cripple."

Aleksandr Nikolayevich **Aleksandrov:** Aleksandr Nikolayevich Fedotov (1903–1971), Russ. circus artiste.

Grigory Vasiliyevich **Aleksandrov:** Grigory Vasiliyevich Mormonenko (1903–1983), Russ. film director.

Vladimir Borisovich **Aleksandrov:** Vladimir Borisovich Keller (1898–1954), Russ. literary critic.

Jean le Rond d'**Alembert:** Jean-le-Rond Destouches (1717–1783), Fr. mathematician. Mathematician was illegitimate son of hostess Mme de Tencin and one of her lovers, the chevalier Destouches. As a baby, he was abandoned on the steps of the Paris church of Saint-Jean-le-Rond, and this gave his first name. However, he was enrolled in school as Jean-Baptiste Daremberg, and presumably latter name was altered for reasons of euphony to give "d'Alembert."

Alexander III: Rolando Bandinelli (*c.* 1105–1181), It. pope.

Alexander IV: Rinaldo [Count] of Segni (1199–1261), It. pope.

Alexander V: Pietro di Candia (*c.* 1339–1410), It. antipope.

Alexander VI: Rodrigo Borgia (1431–1503), Sp.-born It. pope.

Alexander VII: Fabio Chigi (1599–1667), It. pope.

Alexander VIII: Pietro Vito Ottoboni (1610–1691), It. pope.

Mrs. **Alexander:** Annie Hector, née French (1825–1902), Ir.-born Br. popular novelist. Name was her husband's first name.

Ben **Alexander:** Nicholas Benton Alexander (1911–1969), U.S. film actor.

Dair **Alexander:** Christine Campbell Thomson (1897–   ), Eng. writer.

[Sir] George **Alexander:** George Alexander Gibb Samson (1858–1918), Br. stage actor, theatre manager.

Jane **Alexander:** Jane Quigley (1939–   ), U.S. film, TV actress.

Joan **Alexander:** Joan Pepper (1920–   ), Br. author.

John **Alexander:** Jeremy Taylor (1613–1667), Eng. bishop, author.

Alexis: Sergei Vladimirovich Simansky (1877–1970), Russ. churchman, Patriarch of Moscow and All Russia.

Willibald **Alexis:** Georg Wilhelm Heinrich Haring (1798–1871), Ger. historical novelist.

Claudie **Algeranova:** Claudie Leonard (1924–   ), Br. ballet dancer.

Muhammad **Ali:** Cassius Marcellus Clay (1942–   ), U.S. black boxer. The famous boxer adopted his new name in 1964 on joining the Black Muslim movement after becoming the new world heavyweight champion as a result of his contest against Sonny Liston. The name was given him by Elijah Muhammad *(q.v.)*, leader of the Black Muslims in the U.S. Ali made the following announcement to reporters in Miami Beach two days after gaining the title: "From now on my name is Muhammad Ali. Don't call me by my slave name. Cassius Clay was a slave name. It was given to my family by my white masters. I'm a Black Muslim now. That's my religion, the religion of Elijah Muhammad. And my name is Muhammad Ali. I want you to call me that from now on." The name itself means "praiseworthy noble one" [1. Muhammad Ali with Richard Durham, *The Greatest: My Own Story*, 1977; 2. Larry Bortstein, *Ali*, 1976].

Rashied **Ali:** Robert Patterson (1935–   ), U.S. pop musician.

Alien: Louise Alien Baker (1858–   ), U.S. novelist.

Alkan: Charles-Henri Valentin Morhange (1813–1888), Fr. pianist, composer.

George **Allan:** Mite (or Marie) Kremnitz, née Marie von Bardeleben (1852–1916), Ger. writer.

Johnnie **Allan:** John Guillot (1938–   ), U.S. pop musician.

Paula **Allardyce:** Ursula Torday (–   ), Br. thriller writer.

Chesney **Allen:** William Ernest Chesney Allen (1896–1982), Br. music hall comedian, teaming with Bud Flanagan *(q.v.)*.

Dave **Allen:** David Tynan O'Mahoney (1936–   ), Ir. TV entertainer. When the entertainer began his career, and was eager for engagements, he changed his name to Allen, which began with "A" and would thus come near the top of any agent's list.

Major E.J. **Allen:** Allan Pinkerton (1819–1884), Sc.-born U.S. detective.

Elizabeth **Allen:** Elizabeth Allen Gillease (1934–   ), U.S. stage, film actress.

F.M. **Allen:** Edmund Downey (1856–1937), Ir. humorous writer. Adopted wife's maiden name.

Fred **Allen:** John F. Sullivan (1894–1956), U.S. radio comedian, film actor. John F. Sullivan was at first a juggler, taking the name Fred St. James. He then dropped the "St." to become simply Fred James. Later (1921) he grew tired of telling people that he wasn't a member of the Jesse James Gang, and so changed his name to Fred Allen "as a tribute to Ethan Allen who had stopped using the name after the revolution." (Ethan Allen was the famous soldier and frontiersman who captured Ft. Ticonderoga, New York, in the U.S. War of Independence.)

Ronald **Allen:** Alan Ayckbourn (1939–   ), Br. playwright. Name partly from his own first name, partly from his wife's maiden name, Roland.

Rosalie **Allen:** Julie Marlene Bedra (1924–   ), U.S. country singer.

Terry **Allen:** Edward Albert Govier (1924–1987), Br. boxer. Govier gave two accounts of his change of name. "Mate of mine called Terry Allen got killed, so I took his name for boxing. Sort of keeps it goin', like," was his original version. Later, however, he recalled how, when on the run from the Navy, he stole the identity card of a newspaper boy he knew in Islington, called Terry Allen. His birthday, which many of the record books have accepted as Govier's own, was August 11, 1925 [*The Times*, April 9, 1987].

Woody **Allen:** Allen Stewart Konigsberg (1935–   ), U.S. stage, film actor, playwright. "Woody" arose as a nickname, for the actor's fondness for the clarinet, a woodwind instrument. He added his first name to this to serve as a "surname."

Alfred **Allendale:** Theodore Edward Hook (1788–1841), Eng. novelist.

Mary **Allerton:** Mary Christine Govan (1897–   ), U.S. author.

Ellen **Alleyne:** Christina Georgina Rossetti (1830–1894), Eng. poet.

Claud **Allister:** Claud Palmer (1891–1970), Eng. film actor.

David **Allyn:** Albert DiLello (1923–   ), U.S. popular singer.

June **Allyson:** Ella Geisman (1917–   ), U.S. dancer, singer, film actress.

Alma: Charlotte Mary Yonge (1823–1901), Eng. novelist, writer. In her own *History of Christian Names* (1863), Charlotte M. Yonge interprets the name Alma as meaning either "fair" or "all good," and perhaps she intended this sense for herself. But she also rightly relates the name to the Battle of Alma (1854), the first of the Crimean War, and possibly she adopted the pen name at about this time for her early writing. It may be no more than a coincidence that her own Christian names contain the letters (in sequence) of "Alma."

E.M. **Almedingen:** Martha Edith von Almedingen (1898–1971), Russ.-born Eng. novelist, poet, biographer. The initials are those of her two first names, reversed.

A.L.O.E.: Charlotte Maria Tucker (1821–1893), Br. writer, children's author. The initials were intended to stand for "A Lady of England," and the suggestion of "aloe" (the plant, and the associated bitter drug) appears to be merely coincidental.

Alicia **Alonso:** Alicia Ernestina de la Caridad dei Cobre Martinez Hoyo (1921–   ), Cuban ballet dancer.

V. **Alov:** Nikolay Vasilyevich Gogol (1809–1852), Russ. novelist, playwright. Gogol used the name, doubtless formed from letters in his full name, for his early poem of German idyllic life, *Hanz Küchelgarten* (1828), published at his own expense. When it was derided by the critics, he bought up all the copies and destroyed them. At least he had preserved his true identity!

Alpha of the Plough: Alfred George Gardiner (1865–1946), Br. essayist. The pseudonym was intended to be astronomical (see the epigraph on p. viii), referring to the brightest star (Alpha Ursae Majoris) in the Plough (Big Dipper), the famous formation in the constellation of Ursa Major (Great Bear). But there are certain other links, which may or may not have been intentional. "Alpha" suggests "Alfred," and the name George, meaning literally "tiller of the soil," "farmer," appears to be echoed in the "Plough." Even Gardiner has a similar rustic association with the latter. But this may simply be to read too much into the name.

[Mother] **Alphonsa:** Rose Hawthorne (1851–1926), U.S. author, nun, medical worker.

Peter **Altenberg:** Richard Engländer (1859–1919), Austr. writer. One can appreciate the desire to change a nationally misleading name in this instance.

Althea: Althea Braithwaite (1940–   ), Br. children's writer, illustrator.

Robert **Alton:** Robert Alton Hart (1903–1957), U.S. film director.

Alun: John Blackwell (1797–1840), Welsh poet, prose writer. The name is a bardic one. John Blackwell was born in Flintshire, and the Welsh forename Alun is associated with the name of the Alyn River, which flows through Flintshire.

Don **Alvarado:** José Paige (1900–1967), U.S. film actor, playing "latin lover" roles.

Albert **Alvarez:** Raymond Gourron (1861–1933), Fr. opera singer.

Lucine **Amara:** Lucine Armaganian (1927–   ), U.S. opera singer, of Armenian descent.

Giuseppe **Amato:** Giuseppe Vasaturo (1899–1964), It. film producer.

Richard **Amberley:** Paul Bourquin (1916–   ), Br. writer.

Don **Ameche:** Dominic Felix Amici (1908–   ), U.S. film actor. The respelled surname is designed to prompt an accurate pronunciation of the Italian original "Amici." But does it succeed? Does it even mislead?

Adrienne **Ames:** Adrienne Ruth McClure (1909–1947), U.S. film actress.

Jennifer **Ames:** Maysie Sopoushek, née Greig-Smith (1901–1971), Austral.-born romantic novelist.

Leon **Ames:** Leon Waycoff (1903–   ), U.S. stage, film, TV actor.

Ramsay **Ames:** Ramsay Philips (1919–   ), U.S. film actor.

Arthur **Amyand:** [Major] Andrew Charles Parker Haggard (1854–?1923), Br. novelist, historian.

Dulce **Anaya:** Dulce Esperanza Wöhner de Vega (1933–   ), Cuban ballet dancer.

An Craoibhín Aoibhinn: Douglas Hyde (1860–1949), Ir. writer and statesman. Douglas Hyde was the founder of the Gaelic League and a campaigner for the native Gaelic (Irish) language. His Gaelic name means "the fair maiden," and comes from the title of a traditional Irish song, "An craoibhín aoibhinn álainn óg," – "The fair excellent young maid." The pseudonym is pronounced approximately "Un creen een."

Merry **Anders:** Merry Anderson (1932–   ), U.S. film actress.

Daphne **Anderson:** Daphne Carter, née Scrutton (1922–1977), Eng. stage, film actress.

G.M. **Anderson:** Max Aronson (1882–1971), U.S. film actor ("Bronco Billy")

[Dame] Judith **Anderson:** Frances Margaret Anderson (1898–   ), Austral. film actress. Presumably "Judith" has a (?Jewish) charisma that "Frances Margaret" does not have.

R. **Andom:** Alfred Walter Barratt (1869–   ), Eng. humorist. A rather transparent pun for a humorous writer.

Fern **Andra:** [Baroness] Fern Andra von Weichs (–   ), U.S. film actress.

Andrea del Sarto: Andrea d'Agnolo (1486–1531), It. painter. The painter's family had been craftsmen and tradesmen, and his father was a tailor. Hence "del Sarto," from Italian *sarto*, "tailor."

Stephen **Andrew:** Frank G. Layton (1872–1941), Eng. novelist.

Thomas **Andrew:** Edward Thomas Andrulewicz (1932–1984), U.S. ballet dancer, choreographer.

Julie **Andrews:** Julie Elizabeth Wells (1935–   ), Eng. film actress. The actress assumed the name of her stepfather, Ted Andrews, a Canadian singer. In 1969 she married the U.S. writer-producer-director Blake Edwards *(q.v.)* and used a combination of her name and his, Julie Andrews Edwards, for her book *Mandy* (1972).

Tige **Andrews:** Tiger Androwaous (?1923–   ), Lebanese-born U.S. film actor.

Pierre **Andrezel:** Karen Blixen, née Dinesen (1885–1962), Dan. novelist. Karen Blixen, also writing as Isak Dinesen *(q.v.)*, used the French name for her book *Gengoedelsens Beje* (translated as "The Angelic Avengers") (1944), criticizing the German occupation of Denmark. Andrezel is the name of a village east of Paris.

Pier **Angeli:** Anna Maria Pierangeli (1932–1971), It. film actress. The actress's surname conveniently divides to form a forename and new surname, although suggesting a man (as if "Peter Angel"), not a woman.

Fra **Angelico:** [Fra] Giovanni da Fiesole (1387–1455), It. painter. The great Renaissance painter's real (lay) name was Guido di Pietro, and his religious name, as a Dominican monk, is thus the one given here, with "Fra" meaning "brother." But the name by which he is now best known originated as a nickname, "Beato Angelico," (literally "blessed angelic one"), because of the angelic beauty of his character. This name became established only after his death.

Angelina: Harriet Martineau (1802–1876), Eng. author.

[Sir] Norman **Angell:** Ralph Norman Angell Lane (1872–1967), Eng. writer.

Battista **Angeloni:** John Shebbeare (1709–1788), Eng. political writer. John Shebbeare used the Italian-style name for his political satire, purporting to be a translation, attacking the Duke of Newcastle. Its full title was *Letters on the English Nation, by Battista Angeloni, a Jesuit resident in London* (1756).

Muriel **Angelus:** Muriel Angelus Findlay (1909–), Sc. film actress.

Angelus à Sancto Francisco: Richard Mason (1601–1678), Eng. Franciscan priest. The name can be understood as "angel of St. Francis."

Margit **Angerer:** Margit von Rupp (1905–1978), Hung.-born Austr. opera singer.

[Mother] **Ann:** Ann Lee (1736–1784), U.S. mystic, founder of Shaker movement.

Annabella: Suzanne Georgette Charpentier (1909–), Fr. film actress. The actress adopted her name from Edgar Allan Poe's poem *Annabel Lee.*

Annette: Annette Funicello (1947–), U.S. film actress.

Ann-Margret: Ann-Margret Olsson (1941–), Swe.-born U.S. film actress.

Anodos: Mary Elizabeth Coleridge (1861–1907), Eng. poet. Mary Elizabeth Coleridge was the granddaughter of the elder brother of the poet and critic Samuel Taylor Coleridge. She adopted her name from the Greek word for "healthy."

Another Lady: Marie Dobbs, née Catton (c. 1920–), Austral. author. The name was used by Marie Dobbs for her completion (published 1975) of Jane Austen's unfinished novel *Sanditon* (written 1817), so that the combined authorship was credited to "Jane Austen and Another Lady," in the style of Jane Austen's day. Marie Dobbs also wrote as "Anne Telscombe."

[Père] **Anselme:** Pierre de Guibours (1625–1694), Fr. genealogist, friar.

Ansky: Solomon Rappoport (1863–1920), Jewish ethnologist, playwright.

F. **Anstey:** Thomas Anstey Guthrie (1856–1934), Eng. author, children's writer. The writer intended his pseudonym to be "T. Anstey," from his first two names. A printer misprinted this as "F. Anstey," which he allowed to remain.

Adam **Ant:** Stuart Leslie Goddard (1954–), Br. rock singer. Stuart Goddard was at the Hornsey College of Art, London, when he asked a friend to design a tattoo for his upper left arm. This was a heart pierced with a dagger, the word ADAM on top, PURE and SEX on either side, the whole thing set just above his vaccination mark. From then on, he called himself "Adam." "When I had the tattoo done," he said, "I really went in for it. Adam is a very strong name; it's the *first* name – you know – the Garden of Eden. I associate it with strength." The strength was further incorporated by adding "ant" to make "adamant," and "Ant" thus became his surname. ("Mr. Ant for you," said the girl on the telephone.) He soon adopted the surname for the group of four he sang with, so that he was "Adam and the Ants" [*Observer Magazine*, January 10, 1982].

[Archbishop] **Anthony:** Andrew Borisovich Bloom (1914–), Swiss-born Russ. churchman.

C.L. **Anthony:** Dorothy ("Dodie") Gladys Smith (1896–), Eng. playwright, novelist.

Evelyn **Anthony:** Evelyn Ward Thomas (1928–), Br. romantic and suspense novelist.

John **Anthony:** Ronald Brymer Beckett (1891–), Eng. writer.

Joseph **Anthony:** Joseph Anthony Deuster (1912–), U.S. stage actor, director.

Julie **Anthony:** Julie Nutt, née Lush (1952–), Austral. cabaret singer, dancer.

Lysette **Anthony:** Lysette Chodzka (1963–   ), Eng.-born Pol. TV actress. Interviewed for the *Telegraph Sunday Magazine* (April 17, 1983), Lysette Anthony explained the evolution of her name. "My father appeared with Ivor Novello *(q.v.)* in *King's Rhapsody* and decided that Chodzki was no good as a stage name: so he became Michael Anthony. When I first went to school at a convent I was asked my name and got terribly confused. I said my father's name was Michael Anthony, my mother was Bernadette Milnes and my name was Lysette Chodzka – the female version of the [Polish] family name. That was complicated enough, but then when I was ten I played a precocious kitten in *Pinocchio* in the West End and decided to call myself Lysette Elrington, after my grandmother. But at 16 I started fashion modeling and adopted my father's stage name and became Lysette Anthony – anyway, if your name starts with letter A you are always first in the casting directories"!

Piers **Anthony:** Piers Anthony Dillingham Jacob (1934–   ), Eng.-born U.S. SF writer.

Ray **Anthony:** Raymond Antonini (1922–   ), U.S. pop musician.

Dr. Pessimist **Anticant:** Thomas Carlyle (1795–1881), Sc. philosopher, writer.

Antoine: Antek Cierplikowski (1884–   ), Pol.-born Fr. hairdresser.

Anton: Beryl Botterill Antonia Yeoman (?1914–1970), Austral.-born Br. cartoonist. Cartoonists need short names: this one comes from the cartoonist's third name.

[Brother] **Antoninus:** William Everson (1912–   ), U.S. poet, Dominican lay brother.

António: António Ruíz Soler (1922–   ), Sp. dancer.

Peter **Antony:** Peter Levin Shaffer (1926–   ), Eng. playwright + Anthony Joshua Shaffer (1926–   ), Eng. playwright, twin brothers.

Christopher **Anvil:** Harry C. Crosby (–   ), U.S. SF writer.

Ape: Carlo Pellegrini (1839–1889), It. cartoonist, working in England. The cartoonist chose his pen name to reflect the essentially mischievous nature of his work, as a cartoon or caricature "apes" its subject. Ape's first effort, drawn over the name "Singe" (French for "monkey"), appeared in the fashionable magazine *Vanity Fair* in 1869. Another contributor to this magazine was Spy *(q.v.)*.

Apex: Eric Chalkley (1917–   ), Eng. crossword compiler. In typical "cryptic crossword" fashion, the name has a double sense, indicating not only a "top compiler," but one who aimed to "ape X," that is, to imitate Ximenes *(q.v.)*.

Guillaume **Apollinaire:** Guillaume Apollinaire de Kostrowitsky (1880–1918), Fr. poet.

Johnny **Appleseed:** John Chapman (1774–1847), U.S. orchardist. The name, strictly speaking a nickname, was given to the man who planted fruit trees for the frontier settlers in Pennsylvania, Ohio, Indiana and Illinois. He adopted it, however, so can legitimately be included here.

Aquanetta: Burnu Davenport (1920–   ), U.S. film actress.

Thoinot **Arbeau:** Jehan Tabourot (1519–1596), Fr. author of books on dancing. The name is a precise anagram, taking "j" as "i." Thoinot is a genuine forename, as a diminutive version of "Antoine."

Madame d'**Arblay:** Frances ("Fanny") Burney (1752–1840), Eng. novelist, diarist. The writer's adopted name was that of her husband, General d'Arblay, a French refugee in England.

John **Archer:** Ralph Bowman (1915–), U.S. film actor. A synonymous name change!

Archimedes: [Sir] James Eward Edmonds (1861–1956), Eng. military historian.

Elizabeth **Arden:** Florence Nightingale Lewis, née Graham (1878–1966), Can. cosmetician. A cosmetician needs a carefully selected and suitable name. Florence Nightingale Graham was felt to be not sufficiently glamorous. Miss Graham rather liked the name Elizabeth Hubbard, which was that of the original owner of the New York salon where she set up her business. (The name was still on the window, although the lady herself had moved two doors further down Fifth Avenue.) However Elizabeth Graham did not sound quite right, so she instead chose that of Elizabeth Arden. The usual explanation behind the name is that "Elizabeth" came from the author of *Elizabeth and her German Garden* (see **Elizabeth**), and that "Arden" came from Tennyson's poem *Enoch Arden*. But would Miss Graham have really been so closely familiar with these Victorian works? It is said that she actually made the final choice of name after posting letters to Elizabeth Arden "in care of Graham" to see what impact the name made on the envelope. She liked it! Miss Arden's keen rival in the cosmetic field was Helena Rubinstein (Elizabeth Arden was thus the "Miss" of the cosmetics world, Helena Rubinstein the "Madame," and Coco Chanel the "Mademoiselle") [Margaret Allen, *Selling Dreams*, 1981].

Eve **Arden:** Eunice West, née Quedens (1912–), U.S. comic film, TV actress. Eunice Quedens took her stage name from the label on a coldcream jar, which read: "Evening in Paris, by Elizabeth Arden." The first word of this gave "Eve," and the last word "Arden." For the origin of the latter name, see the entry above!

Pietro **Aretino:**? (1492–1556), It. satirist, dramatist (the "scourge of princes"). The writer's real name is unknown (see p. 67). "Aretino" means "of Arezzo," his native town.

La **Argentina:** Antonia Mercé y Luque (1888–1936), Argentine-born Sp. ballet dancer.

La **Argentinita:** Encarnación Lopez Julves (1895–1945), Argentine-born Sp. ballet dancer. La Argentinita was younger than La Argentina, so rightly took a diminutive form of the name, "the little Argentinian."

Pearl **Argyle:** Pearl Wellman (1910–1947), Br. ballet dancer, stage actress.

Carina **Ari:** Carina Janssen (1897–1970), Swe. ballet dancer. An unusual extraction of a surname from an existing forename.

Arion: [1] George Laval Chesterton (1856–), Eng. sporting correspondent; [2] William Falconer (1732–1769), Eng. "sailor-poet." According to legend, the ancient Greek poet Arion was cast into the sea by mariners but subsequently brought back to land by a dolphin. His name is thus suitable for both sporting and maritime associations.

Ariosto: [Rev.] Edward Irving (1792–1834), Sc. clergyman, founder of Holy Catholic Apostolic Church. The name of Lodovico Ariosto, the sixteenth-century romantic epic Italian poet, was widely adopted by "great" men, or used as a nickname for important writers of the eighteenth and nineteenth centuries. Goethe, for example, was "The Ariosto of Germany," and Walter Scott "The Ariosto of the North." Possibly Irving had the latter specifically in mind.

Harold **Arlen:** Hyman Arlock (1905–1986), U.S. composer of musicals.

Michael **Arlen:** Dikran Kuyumjian (1895–1956), Bulgarian-born Br. novelist, of Armenian descent.

Richard **Arlen:** Cornelius R. Van Mattimore (1898–1976), U.S. film actor. It may be significant that all three Arlens above were born within the same decade.

Arletty: Arlette-Léonie Bathiat (1898–   ), Fr. stage, film actress.

George **Arliss:** George Augustus Andrews (1868–1946), Eng. stage, film actor, related to Leslie Arliss (see next entry).

Leslie **Arliss:** Leslie Andres (1901–1988), Br. film director.

Armand: Friedrich Armand Strubberg (1806–1889), Ger.-born author, working in U.S.

Jacobus **Arminius:** Jakob Harmensen (1560–1609), Du. Protestant churchman. Conventional latinization of surname.

Anthony **Armstrong:** George Anthony Armstrong Willis (1897–1976), Can.-born Br. humorist, novelist.

Henry **Armstrong:** Henry Jackson (1912–1988), U.S. boxer. What more apposite name for a "lord of the ring?"

Robert **Armstrong:** Donald Robert Smith (1890–1973), U.S. film actor.

Dudley (or Ernest) **Armytage:** William Edward Armytage Axton (1846–   ), Eng. journalist, writer.

Desi **Arnaz:** Desiderio Alberto Arnaz y de Acha (1915–1986), Cuban-born U.S. film, TV actor.

Peter **Arne:** Peter Arne Albrecht (1920–1983), Br.-U.S. film actor.

James **Arness:** James Aurness (1923–   ), U.S. film, TV actor.

Peter **Arno:** Curtis Arnous Peters, Jr. (1906–1968), U.S. cartoonist, illustrator.

Sig **Arno:** Siegfried Aron (1895–1975), Ger. film comedian, working in U.S.

Edward **Arnold:** Guenther Edward Arnold Schneider (1890–1956), U.S. film actor.

Françoise **Arnoul:** Françoise Annette Marie Mathilde Gautsch (1931–   ), Algerian-born Fr. film actress.

Sonia **Arova:** Sonia Errio (1927–   ), Bulgarian-born Br. ballet dancer.

Bill **Arp:** Charles Henry Smith (1826–1903), U.S. humorist. The name is almost certainly intended to suggest a comic rendering of "Wyatt Earp," the name of the famous lawman of the Wild West. Bill Arp began his career as a writer by contributing letters to a newspaper of his native Georgia addressed to "Mr. Abe Linkhorn," this being a similar eccentric spelling of a famous real name.

Artemas: Arthur Telford Mason (*fl.* 1917), Br. author. The name was formed from the first letters of the writer's real name (*Ar*thur *T*el*ford* *Mas*on), but at the same time suggests a classical name such as Artemon, Artemidorus, or even Artemisia (as for the next entry below).

Artemisia: [Lady] Mary Wortley Montagu (1689–1762), Eng. writer of letters, poems. Artemisia was the name of queens of Asia Minor, one being the sister (and wife) of King Mausolus, to whom she erected the famous tomb known as the Mausoleum.

Arthénice: Catherine de Vivonne, Marquise (Madame) de Rambouillet (1588–1665), Fr. social leader. The classical-looking name is an exact anagram of "Catherine."

Beatrice **Arthur:** Bernice Frankel (1923–   ), U.S. film actress.

George K. **Arthur:** George K. Arthur Brest (1899–   ), Sc. film actor.

Jean **Arthur:** Gladys Georgianna Greene (1905–   ), U.S. film actress.

Julia **Arthur:** Ida Lewis (1869–1919), Can. stage actress.

Peter **Arthur:** Arthur Porges (1915–   ), U.S. writer of detective stories, SF, horror fiction.

Robert **Arthur:** [1] Robert Arthur Feder (1909–   ), U.S. film producer; [2] Robert Arthaud (1925–   ), U.S. film actor, previously radio announcer.

Nikolay **Arzhak:** Yuly Daniel (1925–1988), Russ. dissident writer.

Oscar **Asche:** John Stanger Heiss (1871–1936), Br. stage actor, of Scandinavian descent.

Clifford **Ashdown:** Richard Austin Freeman (1862–1943), Eng. mystery writer + John James Pitcairn (1860–1936), Eng. mystery writer.

Gordon **Ashe:** John Creasey (1908–1973), Br. crime novelist.

Renée **Asherson:** Renée Ascherson (1920–   ), Eng. stage, film actress.

Edward **Ashley:** Edward Ashley Cooper (1904–   ), Br. film actor.

Elizabeth **Ashley:** Elizabeth Cole (1939–   ), U.S. film actress. The actress took her new surname from the forename of Ashley Wilkes, acted by Leslie Howard *(q.v.)* in the motion picture of Margaret Mitchell's novel, *Gone with the Wind.*

Lena **Ashwell:** Lena Margaret Pocock (1872–1957), Br. stage actress, producer.

Grégoire **Aslan:** Kridor Aslanian (1908–1982), Fr.-Turkish film actor. A French version of the Turkish name, with "Aslan" (meaning "lion") retained from the original name.

Asper: Samuel Johnson (1709–1784), Eng. lexicographer, critic. Latin for "rough," "severe," as a critic can be.

Assiac: Heinrich Fraenkel (1897–   ), Ger.-born Eng. writer on Nazi Ger. history.

Fred **Astaire:** Frederick Austerlitz (1899–1987), U.S. dancer, stage, film actor. The name change was not made by the dancer himself, but by his parents, Frederic and Ann Gelius Austerlitz, when the future movie star was only two years old. The suggestion of "star" in the name is appropriate!

Anne **Aston:** Anne Lloyd (1948–   ), Sc. TV hostess. "Lloyd" is a typical Welsh name, not a Scottish one.

James **Aston:** Terence Hanbury White (1906–1964), Br. novelist.

Mary **Astor:** Lucille Vasconcellos Langhanke (1906–1987), U.S. film, TV actress, of Ger. parentage.

Mustafa Kemal **Atatürk:** Mustafa Kemal [Pasha] (1881–1938), Turkish soldier, statesman. The famous Turkish leader adopted his surname, meaning "father of the Turks," in 1934 when as president of the Turkish Republic he introduced compulsory registration of surnames.

William **Atheling:** Ezra Pound (1885–1972), U.S. poet.

William **Atherton:** William Knight (1947–   ), U.S. TV actor.

Charles **Atlas:** Angelo Siciliano (1893–1972), U.S. bodybuilder. In Greek mythology, Atlas was the Titan god who supported the heavens on his shoulders.

Philip **Atlee:** James Atlee Philips (1915–   ), U.S. spy novelist.

Joseph **Atterley:** George Tucker (1775–1861), U.S. essayist, satirist.

Atticus: [1] Joseph Addison (1672–1719), Eng. poet, dramatist; [2] Junius *(q.v.)*; [3] Richard Hebes (1773–1833), Eng. bibliomaniac. The name of Atticus, a Roman literary patron of the second century BC, has been adopted by many writers and diarists. See p. 44.

Attila the Hun: Raymond Quevedo (1892–1962), Trinidad calypso singer.

Cécile **Aubry:** Anne-José Benard (1929–   ), Fr. film actress.

Michel **Auclair:** Vladimir Vujovic (1922–   ), Fr. film actor.

Maxine **Audley:** Maxine Hecht (1923–   ), Eng. stage actress.

Stéphane **Audran:** Colette Suzanne Jeannine Dacheville (1939–   ), Fr. film actress.

Mischa **Auer:** Mischa Ounskowsky (1905–1967), Russ.-born U.S. film actor. Name taken from his uncle, Leopold Auer, a violinist.

Jan **August:** Jan Augustoff (?1912–1976), U.S. popular pianist.

John **August:** Bernard Augustine de Voto (1897–   ), U.S. novelist.

Mlle **Augusta:** Caroline Augusta Joséphine Thérèse Fuchs, Comtesse de Saint-James (1806–1901), Fr. ballet dancer. Mlle Augusta was probably right to select her second name as the most "international" for professional use.

Georgie **Auld:** John Altwerger (1919–   ), Can. jazz musician.

Marie **Ault:** Mary Cragg (1870–1951), Br. stage, film actress. If Ault is not a family name, presumably the semantic correspondence between Ault and Cragg was intentional, via French *haut*, "height," or Welsh *allt*, "cliff"?

Jean-Pierre **Aumont:** Jean Pierre Salomons (1909–   ), Fr. film actor, working in U.S.

Charles **Austin:** Charles Reynolds (1879–1942), Eng. music hall comedian.

Gene **Austin:** Eugene Lucas (1911–1972), U.S. popular singer.

Lovie **Austin:** Cora Calhoun (1887–1972), U.S. black jazz pianist.

Florence **Austral:** Mary Wilson (1894–1968), Austral. opera singer.

Frankie **Avalon:** Francis Thomas Avallone (1939–   ), U.S. pop singer, film actor.

Richard **Avery:** Edmund Cooper (1926–   ), Eng. SF writer, reviewer.

Tex **Avery:** Fred Bean Avery (1907–1980), U.S. film animator. Like other people so named or nicknamed, Tex Avery was born in Texas.

Catherine **Aydy:** Emma Christina Tennant (1937–   ), Br. novelist, journalist.

Dan **Aykroyd:** Daniel Agraluscasacra (1951–   ), Can. film actor.

[Sir] Felix **Aylmer:** Felix Edward Aylmer-Jones (1889–1979), Br. stage, film actor.

Allan **Aynesworth:** Edward Abbot-Anderson (1865–1959), Eng. stage actor.

Agnes **Ayres:** Agnes Hinkle (1896–1940), U.S. film actress.

Lew **Ayres:** Lewis Ayer (1908–   ), U.S. film actor.

John **Ayscough:** Francis Browning Drew Bickerstaffe-Drew (1858–1938), Eng. writer of religious novels.

Azed: Jonathan Crowther (1942–   ), Eng. crossword compiler. The compiler's crossword clues cover "A to Z," while at the same time being tortuous, or even torturous, like the Spanish grand inquisitor whose name is reversed here, Don Diego de Deza. This association is all the more meaningful when it is known that Jonathan Crowther succeeded Ximenes *(q.v.)* as chief compiler for the *Observer* newspaper. Earlier, he had compiled for other publications as "Gong," an early childhood pronunciation of "Jonathan."

Charles **Aznavour:** Shahnour Aznavurjan (1924–   ), Fr. film actor, singer, of Armenian parentage.

Azorin: José Martínez Ruíz (1873–1967), Sp. author, literary critic. The writer took his pen name from that of the eponymous hero of his autobiographical novel *António Azorín* (1903), with the name itself deriving from the Spanish for "hawklike." (Compare the name of the Azores, "islands of hawks," although there the language of origin is Portuguese.)

Babette: Elizabeth McLauchlan (1925–   ), Sc. music hall dancer. Babette is one of the many affectionate forms of "Elizabeth," albeit a French one.

Jean **Babilée:** Jean Gutman (1923–   ), Fr. ballet dancer, choreographer, actor.

Alice **Babs:** Alice Nilson (1924–   ), Swe. popular singer, film actress.

Lauren **Bacall:** Betty Joan Perske (1924–   ), U.S. stage, film actress. The actress's mother left Romania for America when she (the mother) was only a year or two old, together with her own parents. On arriving at the immigration office on Ellis Island, the family gave their name, Weinstein-Bacal, meaning "wineglass" in German and Russian (the latter properly *bokal*, itself from French *bocal*). The immigration officer must have written just the first half of the name, so that the husband and wife were Max and Sophie Weinstein (Lauren Bacall's grandparents), with their daughters Renee and Nathalie (her mother) and their son Albert. Nathalie married William Perske, but soon divorced him, and then took instead the second half of the original "double" name for herself and her daughter. Then when the future Lauren was eight years old, her mother became Nathalie Bacal, and the little girl was Betty Bacal. By the time she was 8, Betty had added another "l" to her name, as "there was too much irregularity of pronunciation": some people rhymed the name with "cackle," others pronounced it "Bacahl." She felt the second "l" would ensure that the second syllable of the name would be pronounced correctly, as in "call." When she began her film career, director Howard Hawks wanted to find a good name to go with her surname, and asked if there was a suitable one somewhere in her family. Betty's grandmother's name, Sophie, did not seem to be quite right, and Hawks said he would think of something. Later, over lunch one day with Betty, he said he had found a name for her. It was "Lauren," and he was going to tell everyone that it was an old family name of Betty's, even that it had been her great-grandmother's. "What invention!" commented Lauren, who is actually said to dislike the name [Lauren Bacall, *By Myself,* 1979].

Backsight-Forethought: [Sir] Ernest Dunlop Swinton (1868–1951), Br. army officer, writer. Major-General Swinton used the pseudonym for his treatise on minor tactics entitled *The Defence of Duffer's Drift* (1904), which came to be recommended reading for young officers. His better-known pen name was Ole Luke-Oie *(q.v.)*.

Angela **Baddeley:** Madeleine Angela Byam Shaw, née Clinton-Baddeley (1904–1976), Eng. stage, film actress, sister of Hermione Baddeley *(q.v.)*

Hermione **Baddeley:** Hermione Willis, née Clinton-Baddeley (1906–1986), Eng. stage, film actress.

George **Bagby:** Aaron Marc Stein (1906–   ), U.S. mystery writer.

Bahā' Allāh: [Mirza] Hoseyn Ali Nuri (1817–1892), Muslim religious leader, founder of the Baha'i faith. Bahā' Allāh claimed to be the manifestation of the unknowable God; his religious name means "Glory of God," from the Arabic.

Guy **Bailey:** [Professor] Cedric Keith Simpson (1907–   ), Eng. pathologist, forensic expert. "Guy" is a reference to Guy's Hospital, London, where Professor Simpson was Head of the Department of Forensic Medicine; "Bailey" refers to the Old Bailey, the Central Criminal Court of England, also in London.

Mildred **Bailey:** Mildred Rinker (1907–1951), U.S. popular singer, film actress.

Art **Baker:** Arthur Shank (1898–1966), U.S. film actor.

Leon **Bakst:** Lev Samoylovich Rosenberg (1866–1924), Russ. theatrical designer, scenic artist. The artist's adopted name was that of his grandfather.

George **Balanchine:** Georgy Melitonovich Balanchivadze (1904–1983), Russ.-born U.S. ballet dancer.

Edward **Baldwin:** William Godwin (1756–1836), Eng. philosopher, novelist, writer.

Neil **Balfort:** Robert Lionel Fanthorpe (1935–   ), Eng. writer of horror stories.

Clara **Balfour:** Felicia Dorothea Hemans, née Browne (1793–1835), Eng. poet.

Ina **Balin:** Ina Rosenberg (1937–   ), U.S. film actress.

Bobby **Ball:** Robert Harper (1944–   ), Eng. TV comedian, teaming with Tommy Cannon *(q.v.)*.

Harry **Ball:** William Henry Powles (? –1888), Eng. music hall singer, father of Vesta Tilley *(q.v.)*.

Lucille **Ball:** Lucille Hunt (1911–1989), U.S. stage, TV actress, comedienne. The stage name apparently developed from Lucille Hunt's original assumed name as a fashion model, which was "Diane Belmont." Maybe "Ball" was an endeavor to resist the commonly used "Bell."

Kaye **Ballard:** Catherine Gloria Balotta (1926–   ), U.S. film comedienne.

Balthus: Balthasar Klossowski de Rola (1908–   ), Fr. painter, of Pol. parentage.

Micah **Balwidder:** John Galt (1779–1839), Sc. novelist.

Honoré de **Balzac:** Honoré Balzac (1799–1850), Fr. novelist. The honorific "de" was self-styled. The surname of Balzac's grandfather was Balssa, which was changed to Balzac by his father because of its peasant connotations.

D.R. **Banat:** Raymond Douglas Bradbury (1920–   ), U.S. SF writer.

Anne **Bancroft:** Anna Maria Luisa Italiano (1931–   ), U.S. stage, film actress. Anne Bancroft was born in New York as the daughter of Italian immigrants, and even her original name came as the result of a misunderstanding. Her father, on arriving at Ellis Island, thought he was being asked his nationality and said

"Italiano, Italiano." This was recorded as his name (which was what he was really being asked). Anna Maria first acted as Anne Marno, but subsequently selected the name Anne Bancroft when she made her first film, *Don't Bother to Knock* (1952).

Albert **Band:** Alfredo Antonini (1924–), It.-born film director, working in U.S.

Monty **Banks:** Mario Bianchi (1897–1950), It. film actor, director. Mario Bianchi not only anglicized his name but did it in such a way as to suggest "mountebank," the term for a charlatan.

Vilma **Banky:** Vilma Lonchit (or Konsics) (1898–), Austr.-Hung. film actress.

Margaret **Bannerman:** Margaret Le Grand (1896–), Can. stage actress.

Baptiste: Nicolas Anselme (1761–1835), Fr. sentimental comedy actor.

Theda **Bara:** Theodosia Goodman (1890–1955), U.S. stage, film actress. For publicity purposes, as the first "vamp," Theodosia Goodman claimed to be the daughter of an eastern potentate, so that her name was an anagram of "Arab death." But at least Theda is something like Theodosia.

Imamu Amiri **Baraka:** Everett LeRoi Jones (1934–), U.S. black playwright, poet, novelist.

W.N.P. **Barbellion:** Bruce Frederick Cummings (1889–1919), Eng. essayist, diarist, naturalist. The writer adopted this name, taken from the front of a confectioner's shop in Bond Street, London, when he published entries from his diary in book form under the title *The Journal of a Disappointed Man* (1919). He claimed that the initials stood for "Wilhelm Nero Pilate," all men of bravado.

Barbette: Van der Clyde Broodway (1899–1972), U.S. music hall female impersonator.

David **Barclay:** David Poole Fronabarger (1912–1969), U.S. stage actor.

Gabriel **Barclay:** Manly Wade Wellman (1903–), U.S. SF, fantasy, mystery writer.

Roy **Barcroft:** Howard H. Ravenscroft (1901–1969), U.S. film actor.

Countess **Barcynska:** Marguerite Florence Helene Evans, née Jervis (1894–1964), Br. writer.

The **Bard:** Edward Jerringham (1727–1812), Eng. poet, dramatist of Della Cruscan school.

Samuel A. **Bard:** Ephraim George Squier (1821–1888), U.S. archeologist, traveler, author.

Wilkie **Bard:** William Augustus Smith (1870–1944), Eng. music hall comedian. The actor had a high, domed forehead, like that of Shakespeare: hence his nickname and subsequent stage name.

Brigitte **Bardot:** Camille Javal (1934–), Fr. film actress. This real name (if that is what it is) is consistently quoted in all his editions by Halliwell (see Bibliography), although biographies of the actress do not mention it. A genuine pseudonym used by Brigitte Bardot, however, was "BB" *(q.v.)*.

Lynn **Bari:** Marjorie Bitzer (or Fisher) (1913–), U.S. film actress.

Victor **Barna:** Győző Braun (1911–1972), Hung.-born Eng. table tennis player. The significance of "Victor" for a sportsman should not be overlooked!

Barney **Barnato:** Barnett Isaacs (1852–1897), Eng. financier, diamond magnate, formerly a vaudeville artiste.

Louis **Barnaval:** Charles De Kay (1848–1935), U.S. editor, writer.

Binnie **Barnes:** Gertrude Maude Barnes (1908–1983), Eng. film actress.

L. David **Barnett:** Barnett D. Laschever (1924–   ), U.S. journalist, writer.

Baron: Baron de V. Nahum (1906–1956), Eng. photographer.

Jacques **Baroncelli:** Jacques Baroncelli-Javon (1881–1951), Fr. film director.

Ida **Barr:** Maud Barlow (1882–1967), Eng. music hall comedienne.

Richard **Barr:** Richard Baer (1917–   ), U.S. stage director, producer.

Ray **Barra:** Raymond Martin Barallobre (1930–   ), U.S. ballet dancer.

Judith **Barrett:** Lucille Kelly (1914–   ), U.S. film actress.

Rona **Barrett:** Rona Burstein (1937–   ), U.S. gossip columnist.

Amanda **Barrie:** Shirley Ann Broadbent (1939–   ), Eng. stage, film, TV actress.

J.J. **Barrie:** Barry Authors (1936–   ), Can. pop singer.

Mona **Barrie:** Mona Smith (1909–   ), Austral. film actress.

Wendy **Barrie:** Marguerite Wendy Jenkins (1912–1978), Br. film actress. Marguerite Jenkins was the goddaughter of the writer J.M. Barrie, author of *Peter Pan,* and she took her surname from him. She was already named Wendy, after the heroine of the play, Wendy Darling.

E. **Barrington:** Eliza Louisa Moresby Beck (? –1931), Br. romantic, historical novelist.

Rutland **Barrington:** George Barrington Rutland Fleet (1853–1922), Eng. actor, singer.

Blue **Barron:** Harry Friedland (1911–   ), U.S. trombonist, bandleader.

David **Barry:** Merig Wyn Jones (1944–   ), Eng. TV actor.

Don **Barry:** Donald Barry d'Acosta (1912–1980), U.S. film actor.

Gene **Barry:** Eugene Klass (1921–   ), U.S. film, TV actor.

Joan **Barry:** Joan Tiarks, née Bell (1901–1989), Eng. stage, film actress, society hostess.

John **Barry:** John Barry Prendergast (1933–   ), Eng. rock musician.

Len **Barry:** Leonard Borisoff (1942–   ), U.S. pop singer.

Michael **Barry:** James Barry Jackson (1910–   ), Eng. musician, writer.

Ethel **Barrymore:** Ethel Mae Blythe (1879–1959), U.S. stage, film actress. Both Ethel Blythe and her brothers John and Lionel Blythe (see next two entries below) adopted the stage name of their father, Maurice Barrymore *(q.v.).*

John **Barrymore:** John Blythe (1882–1942), U.S. stage, film actor.

Lionel **Barrymore:** Lionel Blythe (1878–1954), U.S. stage, film actor.

Maurice **Barrymore:** Herbert Blythe (1847–1905), Eng. actor, father of Ethel, John, and Lionel Barrymore (see above). Maurice Barrymore adopted his stage name from an old playbill hanging in the Haymarket Theatre, London. It was in turn adopted by his three children, Ethel, John and Lionel, who made their name on the American stage, where Maurice Barrymore himself went in 1875.

Michael **Barrymore:** Michael Parker (1952–   ), Eng. TV entertainer.

Louis **Barsac:** Ernest James Oldmeadow (1867–1949), Br. journalist, writer.

Lionel **Bart:** Lionel Begleiter (1930–   ), Br. lyricist, composer. Lionel Begleiter adopted his professional name from Bart's, the popular name of St. Bartholomew's

Hospital, London. Oddly enough, his real name means (in German) "musical accompanist."

Freddie **Bartholomew**: Frederick Llewellyn (1924–), Eng. child film actor, working in U.S. The young actor was brought up by his aunt, Millicent Bartholomew, and adopted her name.

Bartimeus: Lewis Anselmo da Costa Ricci (1886–1967), Br. author of naval stories. The best-known Bartimeus is the biblical one, the blind beggar healed by Jesus. Possibly the author intended this reference in some sense?

Sy **Bartlett**: Sacha Baraniev (1909–1978), Russ.-born U.S. screenwriter, film producer.

Eva **Bartok**: Eva Szöke (1926–), Hung. film actress.

Fra **Bartolommeo**: Bartolommeo di Pagolo del Fattorino (or Baccio della Porta) (1472–1517), It. painter.

Count **Basie**: William Basie (1904–1984), U.S. black jazz musician. During a broadcast from the Reno Club, Kansas City, the announcer of an experimental radio program introduced Basie as the "Count," and he adopted the nickname. Compare the name of Duke Ellington *(q.v.)*.

Ivan **Baskoff**: Henri Meilhac (1832–1897), Fr. dramatist, author.

Lina **Basquette**: Lina Belcher (1907–), U.S. film actress.

Hogan Kid **Bassey**: Okon Bassey Asuquo (1932–), Nigerian boxer.

Florence **Bates**: Florence Rabe (1888–1954), U.S. film actress. The actress took her stage name from the character of Miss Bates that she played in a stage adaptation (1835) of Jane Austen's novel *Emma*.

Batt: Oswald Barrett (–), Br. cartoonist.

Battling Siki: Louis Phal (1897–1925), Senegalese boxer, working in U.S.

Beryl **Baxter**: Beryl Gross, née Ivory (1926–), Br. stage, film actress.

Jane **Baxter**: Feodora Forde (1909–), Br. stage, film actress.

Keith **Baxter**: Keith Baxter-Wright (1933–), Welsh stage actor.

Nora **Bayes**: Dora Goldberg (1880–1928), U.S. vaudeville, musical comedy actress.

William **Baylebridge**: Charles William Blocksidge (1883–1942), Austral. poet, short story writer.

Beverly **Bayne**: Pearl von Name (1894–1982), U.S. film actress.

Hervé **Bazin**: Jean-Pierre Hervé-Bazin (1911–), Fr. poet, novelist, short story writer.

B.B. [1] Lewis Carroll *(q.v.)*; [2] Denys James Watkins-Pitchford (1905–), Eng. writer of books about the countryside; [3] Brigitte Bardot *(q.v.)*. [2] and [3] here usually used the name in the form "BB." Denys Watkins-Pitchford chose the initialism for *The Sportsman's Bedside Book* (1937), and derived it from the designation of the particular size of lead shot he used for shooting wild geese, BB being 0.18 inches in diameter. Brigitte Bardot's own initials are of course B.B., and "BB" was first used in print for her appearance as a cover girl on the French magazine *Elle* in 1948. The initials have added point when it is remembered that in French they are said exactly the same as *bébé*, "baby." Brigitte Bardot was still a teenager at the time.

Beachcomber: [1] Dominic Bevan Wyndham Lewis (1894–1979), Br. humorous columnist; [2] John Cameron Andrieu Bingham Michael Morton (1893–1979), Br. humorous columnist. The name was passed down by [1] to [2] in 1924, when Morton succeeded Lewis as columnist on the *Daily Express.* The reference is to the essential "gleaning" activity of a beachcomber. The columnists looked for interesting news items, just as a beachcomber searches the shore for valuables.

John **Beal:** James Bliedung (1909–   ), U.S. stage, film actor.

Orson **Bean:** Dallas Frederick Burroughs (1928–   ), U.S. stage actor, comedian. Dallas F. Burroughs began his stage career as a magician, and chose this randomly bizarre name for his work.

Allyce **Beasley:** Allyce Schiavelli, formerly Sansocie, née Tannenberg (*c.*1950–   ), U.S. film, TV actress.

Beatrice: Anne Manning (1807–1879), Eng. novelist, miscellaneous writer.

Warren **Beatty:** Warren Beaty (1937–   ), U.S. film actor. Warren Beaty made a minor adjustment to his real name by doubling a letter for his screen name. His sister, Shirley Maclaine *(q.v.),* made a similar small alteration.

Philip **Beauchamp:** George Grote (1794–1871), Eng. historian.

Beauchâteau: François Chastelet (*fl.*1625–1665), Fr. actor.

Balthasar de **Beaujoyeux:** Baldassare di Belgiojoso (? –1587), It. violinist, composer. A name that is part rendered, part translated, from Italian to French.

Pierre-Augustin Caron de **Beaumarchais:** Pierre-Augustin Caron (1732–1799), Fr. dramatist. Beaumarchais took his writing name from that of a small property owned by his first wife. There are several villages of the name (meaning "beautiful marsh") still to be found in the north of France today.

Beauménard: Rose-Perrine le Roy de la Corbinaye (1730–1799), Fr. actress, wife of Bellecour *(q.v.).*

André **Beaumont:** Jean Conneau (1880–1937), Fr. aviator.

Charles **Beaumont:** Charles Nutt (1929–1967), U.S. SF writer.

Susan **Beaumont:** Susan Black (1936–   ), Br. film actress.

Beauval: Jean Pitel (*c.*1635–1709), Fr. actor.

Roger de **Beauvoir:** Edouard Roger de Bully (1809–1866), Fr. novelist.

Christopher **Beck:** Thomas Charles Budges (1868–1944), Eng. writer of stories for boys.

Lily Adams **Beck:** Eliza Louisa Moresby Beck (? –1931), Eng. author.

Cuthbert **Bede:** [Rev.] Edward Bradley (1827–1889), Br. humorist. The author of *The Adventures of Mr. Verdant Green* (1853) was educated at the University of Durham, and took his name from the two patron saints of this city, St. Cuthbert and the Venerable Bede.

Donald **Bedford:** Henry James O'Brien Bedford-Jones (1887–1949), Can.-born U.S. writer of historical adventures.

Demyan **Bedny:** Yefim Alekseyevich Pridvorov (1883–1945), Russ. Socialist poet. The pen name of Yefim Pridvorov derives from Russian *bedny,* "poor," reflecting the conditions of the peasants and working classes before the 1917 Revolution. (Compare the name of Maxim Gorky, *q.v.).* It was originally a nickname. He had brought a poem entitled "Demyan Bedny, the Harmful Peasant" to his editors, and when he next visited the office they exclaimed "It's Demyan Bedny!" Demyan was actually the first name of his uncle, who was a peasant. The poet would also have certainly wished to avoid the aristocratic associations of his real surname, Pridvorov, which suggests *pridvorny*, "of the court."

Widow **Bedott:** Frances Miriam Whitcher (1814–1852), U.S. humorous writer.

Jon (or George) **Bee:** John Badcock (? –c.1830), Br. sporting writer.

Janet **Beecher:** Janet Beecher Meysenburg (1884–1955), U.S. film actress.

Francis **Beeding:** John Leslie Palmer (1885–1944), Br. thriller writer + Hilary Aidan St. George Saunders (1898–1951), Br. thriller writer. A single name for a two-man writing partnership. Palmer had always liked the name Francis; Saunders had once owned a house in the Sussex village of Beeding.

Captain **Beefheart:** Don Van Vliet (1941–   ), U.S. pop singer.

Beggerstaff Brothers: [Sir] William Newzam Prior Nicholson (1872–1949), Eng. poster artist + James Pryde (1866–1941), Eng. poster artist.

Maurice **Béjart:** Maurice-Jean de Berger (1927–   ), Fr. ballet dancer, opera director.

Barbara **Bel Geddes:** Barbara Geddes Lewis (1922–   ), U.S. stage, film actress.

Belita: Gladys Jepson-Turner (1924–   ), Br. ice skater, dancer, film actress.

Ivan Petrovich **Belkin:** Aleksandr Sergeyevich Pushkin (1799–1837), Russ. poet, dramatist. Pushkin used the name for the supposed narrator of his own *Tales of the Late Ivan Petrovich Belkin* (1831). He did not use the name for any other work.

Acton **Bell:** Ann Brontë (1820–1849), Eng. novelist, poet, sister of Currer Bell *(q.v.)*.

Currer **Bell:** Charlotte Brontë (1816–1855), Eng. novelist, sister of Acton Bell (above) and Ellis Bell (below). When the three sisters, Ann, Charlotte and Emily Brontë, first published some poems in 1846, they named themselves as "Currer, Ellis, and Acton Bell," leading many people to think that the authors were three brothers, and therefore writing to them as men. In due course, Charlotte Brontë would give the following account of the assumption of these names: "Averse to publicity, we veiled our own names under those of Currer, Ellis, and Acton Bell; the ambiguous choice being dictated by a sort of conscientious scruple of assuming Christian names positively masculine, while we did not declare ourselves women, because—without at the time suspecting that our mode of writing and thinking was not what is called 'feminine,'—we had a vague impression that authoresses are liable to be looked on with prejudice." (quoted in Mrs. Gaskell, *The Life of Charlotte Brontë* (1857). Charlotte Brontë first published *Jane Eyre* (1847) as "Currer Bell," and that same year Emily Brontë's *Wuthering Heights* also appeared, with the author given as "Ellis Bell." Their guise was soon penetrated and when Charlotte Brontë received a letter from her contemporary, Harriet Martineau, it began "Dear Madam," although "Currer Bell, Esq." appeared on the envelope.

Ellis **Bell:** Emily Brontë (1818–1848), Eng. novelist (see above).

Josephine **Bell:** Doris Bell Ball, née Collier (1897–1987), Eng. detective novelist, doctor.

Marie **Bell:** Marie-Jeanne Belon-Downey (1900–1985), Fr. stage, film actress.

Neil **Bell:** Stephen H. Critten (1887–1964), Eng. novelist, short story writer.

Paul **Bell:** Henry Fothergill Chorley (1808–1872), Eng. journalist, novelist, music critic.

Rex **Bell:** George F. Beldam (1905–1962), U.S. film actor.

William **Bell:** William Yarborough (1939–), U.S. soul singer.

George **Bellairs:** Harold Blundell (1902–), Eng. mystery novelist.

Madge **Bellamy:** Margaret Philpott (1903–), U.S. film actress.

Bellecour: Jean-Claude-Gilles Colson (1725–1778), Fr. playwright, comic actor, husband of Beauménard *(q.v.)*.

Belleroche: Raymond Poisson (*c.*1630–1690), Fr. actor.

Bellerose: Pierre Le Messier (*c.*1592–1670), Fr. actor.

Belleville: Henri Legrand (*c.* 1587–1637), Fr. actor. This was the name Legrand assumed for his tragic roles. For his comic parts he used the name Turlupin *(q.v.)*.

Louie **Bellson:** Louis Paul Balassoni (1924–), U.S. pop musician.

Bessie **Bellwood:** Elizabeth Ann Katherine Mahony (1847–1896), Ir. music hall artiste.

N. **Beltov:** Georgy Valentinovich Plekhanov (1857–1918), Russ. Socialist. Plekhanov adopted the name from *Whose Fault?* (1841–1846), a novel by Herzen *(q.v.)*.

Andrey **Bely:** Boris Nikolayevich Bugayev (1880–1934), Russ. symbolist poet, writer, critic. When Bugayev wanted to publish some poetry as a student, in 1901, his father objected. The pseudonym Andry Bely was proposed for him by his editor, M.S. Solovyov, who devised it simply for its euphony, even though Russian *bely* means "white." Bugayev had initially preferred the name "Boris Burevoy," suggesting Russian *burevoy*, "stormy." But Solovyov said that people would only pun on the name, seeing it as *Bori voy*, "Borya's howl." So Andrey Bely it was.

Benauly: Benjamin Vaughan Abbott (1830–1890), U.S. author + Austin Abbott (1831–1896), U.S. author, + [Rev.] Lyman Abbott (1835–1922), U.S. author, his brother. The composite name consists of the first syllables of each of the three brothers' forenames, in strict order of seniority!

Bendigo: William Thompson (1811–1889), Br. boxer, prizefighter. The name is a corruption of "Abednego," one of the three "certain Jews" (Shadrach, Meshach and Abednego) who were ordered, according to the Bible story, to be cast into King Nebuchadnezar's burning fiery furnace for not serving his gods or worshipping his golden image. The boxer's own ring name was given in turn to the Australian mining town of Bendigo, which was developed in the gold rush of 1851 by an admirer of his who had adopted his name to boost his own reputation as a boxer.

Benedict XI: Niccolò di Boccasini (1240–1304), It. pope.

Benedict XII: Jacques Fournier (? –1342), Fr. pope.

Benedict XIII: Pierfrancesco Orsini (1649–1730), It. pope.

Benedict XIV: Prospero Lambertini (1675–1758), It. pope.

Benedict XV: Giacomo Della Chiesa (1854–1922), It. pope. This last Benedict's real name happens to translate as "James Church."

Dirk **Benedict:** Dirk Niewoehner (1944–), U.S. TV actor.

Richard **Benedict:** Riccardo Benedetto (1916–1984), U.S. film actor.

David **Ben-Gurion:** David Gruen (1886–1973), Pol.-born Israeli prime minister. David Gruen adopted the ancient Hebrew name of Ben-Gurion when working as a farmer in northern Palestine, where he came in 1906. The name means "son of strength." It assimilates well to his former surname, which means "green."

Bruce **Bennett:** Herman Brix (1909–), U.S. film actor.

Compton **Bennett:** Robert Compton-Bennett (1900–1974), Eng. film director.

Harve **Bennett:** Harvey Fischman (1930–), U.S. TV series producer.

Lennie **Bennett:** Michael Berry (1938–), Eng. stage, TV entertainer.

Tony **Bennett:** Anthony Dominick Benedetto (1926–), U.S. popular singer.

Jack **Benny:** Benjamin Kubelsky (1894–1974), U.S. stage, radio, TV comedian. When Benjamin Kubelsky began his career (1918) he called himself "Ben Benny." But this was too close to the name of Ben Bernie, bandleader and comedian. He therefore changed again to "Jack Benny." When he first saw the name in lights he said, "I got the strangest feelings. . . as if this wasn't me and I was an impostor and someday the audience would find me out" [Irving A. Fein, *Jack Benny: An Intimate Biography*, 1976].

Carl **Benson:** Charles Astor Bristed (1820–1874), U.S. author.

Robby **Benson:** Robert Segal (1956–), U.S. juvenile film actor.

Brook **Benton:** Benjamin Franklin Peay (1931–), U.S. black rock singer.

Gertrude **Berg:** Gertrude Edelstein (1899–1966), U.S. TV, radio, film actress.

Teresa **Berganza:** Teresa Vargas (1935–), Sp. opera singer. Spanish *varga* means "hill," and doubtless the singer chose a name that interpreted this in a more recognizable form (through German *Berg* and related words).

Polly **Bergen:** Nellie Burgin (1929–), U.S. stage, radio, TV singer, film actress.

E. **Berger:** Elizabeth Sara Sheppard (1830–1862), U.S. novelist. The link must surely have been between French *berger* and English *shepherd*.

Helmut **Berger:** Helmut Steinberger (1944–), Austr. film actor.

Ludwig **Berger:** Ludwig Bamberger (1892–1969), Ger. film director.

Elisabeth **Bergner:** Elisabeth Ettel (1897–1986). Pol.-born Br. film actress, working in U.S.

Ballard **Berkeley:** Ballard Blascheck (1904–1988), Eng. stage, film, TV actor.

Busby **Berkeley:** William Berkeley Enos (1895–1976), U.S. director of film musicals. Busby Berkeley adopted his new first name from the actress Amy Busby.

Milton **Berle:** Mendel Berlinger (1908–), U.S. TV, stage, film comedian.

Irving **Berlin:** Israel Baline (1888–), Russ.-born U.S. composer, popular song writer. Israel Baline, the son of a penniless itinerant synagogue cantor, published his first sheet music in 1907, and the printer misprinted his surname as "Berlin." The composer kept it that way, and "anglicized" Israel to Irving.

Paul **Bern:** Paul Levy (1889–1932), U.S. film director.

[Saint] **Bernadette:** Marie-Bernarde Soubirous (1844–1879), Fr. peasant girl, visionary. The saint's name derives from one half of her own Christian name. The other half would have given "St. Mary," which would have been unacceptable.

Carl **Bernhard:** Andrea Nicolai de Saint-Aubin (1798–1865), Dan. novelist, chronicler.

Sarah **Bernhardt:** Henriette-Rosine Bernard (1844–1923), Fr. tragic actress. The actress was born as the illegitimate daughter of Judith Van Hard, a Dutch courtesan who had settled in Paris, and Edouard Bernard, a law student. Her Germanic-looking surname was devised to reflect the names of both.

Ben **Bernie:** Benjamin Angelvitz (1891–1943), U.S. bandleader.

L'Abbé **Bernier:** Paul Thiry, Baron d'Holbach (1723–1789), Fr. materialist, atheist writer. The atheist philosopher and encyclopaedist used the name sardonically for his *Théologie portative, ou Dictionnaire abrégé de la religion chrétienne* (1786). Holbach also wrote as Nicolas Boulanger and Jean Mirabeau *(q.v.)*.

Bert **Berns:** Bert Russell (1929–1967), U.S. pop writer, producer.

Claude **Berri:** Claude Langmann (1934–   ), Fr. film director.

Judith M. **Berrisford:** Mary Lewis (1921–   ), Eng. writer of books on animals for children + Clifford Lewis (1912–   ), Eng. writer of books on animals for children, her husband. The two writers based their joint name on the maiden name, Berrisford, of Mary Lewis's mother.

Chuck **Berry:** Charles Edward Anderson Berry (1926–   ), U.S. blues songwriter, singer. "Chuck" is a common American familiar form of "Charles."

Dave **Berry:** David Grundy (1941–   ), Eng. pop singer. Dave Berry adopted his new surname from that of Chuck Berry *(q.v.)*

Jules **Berry:** Jules Paufichet (1883–1951), Fr. film actor.

Francesca **Bertini:** Elena Seracini Vitiello (1892–   ), It. film actress.

Vic **Berton:** Vic Cohen (1896–1953), Fr. film actor.

Charles **Bertram:** James Bassett (1853–1907), Eng. magician.

Mary **Berwick:** Adelaide Anne Proctor (1825–1864), Eng. poet. Adelaide Anne Proctor, the daughter of Barry Cornwall *(q.v.)*, contributed to Charles Dickens's periodical *Household Words* under the pseudonym of Mary Berwick. Her assumed surname seems to have been chosen as one geographically opposed to that of her father. Cornwall is in the extreme southwest of England, while Berwick is in the extreme northeast.

Don **Betteridge:** Bernard Newman (1897–1968), Br. novelist, travel writer.

Bettina: Bettina Ehrlich (1903–   ), Austr. children's book illustrator, working in U.K.

Billy **Bevan:** William Bevan Harris (1887–1957), Eng.-born U.S. film actor.

Isla **Bevan:** Isla Buckley (1910–   ), Br. film actress.

Clem **Bevans:** Clement Blevins (1879–1963), U.S. film actor.

Bhaskar: Bhaskar Roy Chowdhury (1910–   ), Indian ballet dancer, teacher, working in U.S.

Ernesto **Bianco:** Oscar Ernesto Pelicori (1923–1977), Argentine stage actor.

Jacob **Bibliophile:** Paul Lacroix (1806–1884), Fr. historical writer.

John **Bickerdyke:** [1] Jonathan Swift (1667–1745), Ir.-born Br. satirist, cleric; [2] [Sir] Richard Steele (1672–1729), Ir. essayist, dramatist; [3] Benjamin West (1730–1813), U.S. mathematician. Swift used the name for a pamphlet of 1708 attacking the almanac-maker John Partridge Steele used it for launching *The Tatler* the following year; West adopted it for a series of almanacs published in 1768 in Boston. Swift was thus the first to use the name, and he is said to have taken it from a smith's sign, adding the common Christian name Isaac. There was a real Isaac Bickerstaffe (with a final "e"), as an Irish playwright. But he lived after both Steele and Swift (from about 1735 to about 1812), so the name could have not derived from him.

Big Bopper: Jaye P. Richardson (1930–1959), U.S. rock singer/songwriter.

Big Daddy: Shirley Crabtree (1935–), Eng. heavyweight wrestler. The popular wrestler began his career as "Shirley Crabtree, The Blond Adonis," and as the rather corny "Mr. Universe." By the time he was in his early 30s, he was wrestling as "The Battling Guardsman." It was then that he met and married his wife Eunice, and she suggested a new name to improve his "bad guy" image, as she knew he had a gentle side to him. Thus, in 1975, "The Battling Guardsman" became the softer, cuddlier "Big Daddy" [*TV Times Magazine*, October 16–22, 1982].

Hosea **Biglow:** James Russell Lowell (1819–1891), U.S. humorist, satirist, poet. Lowell used the name for the purported author, a young New England farmer, of *The Biglow Papers*, two series of satirical verses in Yankee dialect published in the mid–1840s.

Big Maybelle: Mabel Smith (1926–1972), U.S. blues singer.

Big Youth: Manley Buchanan (*c.* 1949–), Jamaican pop singer, DJ.

Bilitis: Pierre Louÿs (1870–1925), Belg.-born Fr. novelist. The famous "hoax" name is that of the supposed Greek poetess Bilitis (see full story, p. 28).

Vladimir Naumovich **Bill-Belotserkovsky:** Vladimir Naumovich Belotserkovsky (1884–1970), Russ. dramatist. English-speakers have long had problems with Russian names, and when Belotserkovsky was in the U.S., Americans gave up on his full name and called him by its first syllable, as "Bill." The writer liked this, and (to make matters worse, had he but known) added it to his existing name.

Josh **Billings:** Henry Wheeler Shaw (1818–1885), U.S. humorist. Henry W. Shaw used the name for his first book, *Josh Billings, His Sayings*, publication of which was arranged in 1865 by C.F. Browne (see Artemus **Ward**). The name is not as crackpot as most of Shaw's writings, which incorporate an amazing display of ridiculous spellings, deformed grammar, incongruous statements, and the like.

Billy the Kid: William H. Bonney (1859–1881), U.S. desperado.

Bim: Ivan Semyonovich Radunsky (1872–1955), Russ. circus clown, teaming with Bom (*q.v.*). Bim was always accompanied by Bom, and Bom always went with Bim. The team of *Bim-Bom*, in fact, was a single interdependent entity. It comprised a pair of Russian clowns, who first performed under the name in 1891. (The name is a meaningless one, but perhaps suggests something like "bang-bang" or "boom-boom"). There was always a single *Bim* in the person of Ivan Radunsky, a Pole by origin, but there were no less than four *Boms:* a Russianized Italian named Cortesi, a fellow Pole called Stanevsky, a Czech by the name of Viltzak, and finally a Russian named Kamsky. The duo began as an eccentric but versatile couple, both amusing and acrobatic, lively and highly literate (they spoke "good" Russian, as distinct from the broken Russian affected by a number of clowns). After the tragic death by drowning of Cortesi in 1897, the second Bom presented a different image, dressing not as a conventional clown but as a gay "man about town," wearing evening dress, complete with top hat and a chrysanthemum in his buttonhole. The pair now played down the acrobatics in favor of verbal satire. In 1901–1904 the two toured Europe. After the Revolution, Stanevsky emigrated to his native Poland, and Bim followed suit. He returned in 1925, however, and in his partnership with Viltzak now concentrated more on the musical aspect of his turns. (The third Bom was an accomplished if unorthodox musician. One of his specialties was playing on two concertinas at once, Bim finally teamed up with Kamsky in the war years (1941–6). The first half of the 1920s produced a number of Bim-Bom imitators, such as Bib-Bob (Rashkovsky and Vorontsov), Viys-Vays (Sidelnikov and Solomenko), Din-Don, Rim-Rom, Fis-Dis and the like [Shneyer, p. 67].

Satane **Binet:** Francisque Sarcey (1828–1899), Fr. dramatic critic, novelist.

W. **Bird:** Jack Butler Yeats (1871–1957), Ir. painter, cartoonist.

Tala **Birell:** Natalie Bierle (1908–1959), Pol.-Austr. film actress, working in U.S.

George A. **Birmingham:** [Rev.] James Owen Hannay (1865–1950), Ir.-born Br. author of light novels. James Hannay chose the pen name "Birmingham" not because he had some connection with that city, but simply because it was (and still is) a fairly common name in Co. Mayo, where he was rector in the town of Westport. The more usual spelling of the name, however, is Bermingham.

Joey **Bishop:** Joseph Abraham Gottlieb (1918–   ), U.S. TV, film comedian. Joey Bishop adopted the name of his roadie, Glenn Bishop.

Julie **Bishop:** Jacqueline Wells Brown (1914–   ), U.S. film actress.

Stacey **Bishop:** George Antheil (1900–1957), U.S. novelist, opera composer. Stacey can be either a man's or a woman's name, and the novelist does not seem to have been seeking any special ambiguity in choosing it.

George **Bizet:** George Tulloch Bisset-Smith (1863–   ), Sc. sociologist, writer.

Brynjolf **Bjarme:** Henrik Ibsen (1828–1906), Norw. poet, dramatist.

Dinna **Bjørn:** Dinna Bjørn Larsen (1947–   ), Dan. ballet dancer.

Cilla **Black:** Priscilla Maria Veronica White (1943–   ), Eng. popular singer, film, TV actress. "Cilla" as a pet form of "Priscilla"; "Black" by contrast, of course, with "White." The name is said to have been used of her early in her career by a feature writer in the magazine *Merseybeat*, who had forgotten her real name. Of the two, Black is probably a more common surname than White, after all.

Gavin **Black:** Oswald Wynd (1913–   ), Sc. thriller writer.

Ivory **Black:** Thomas Allibone Janvier (1849–1913), U.S. novelist.

Karen **Black:** Karen Ziegler (1942–   ), U.S. film actress.

Lionel **Black:** Dudley Barker (1910–1980), Eng. novelist, nonfiction writer.

Harry **Blackstone:** Henri Bouton (1885–1965), U.S. magician.

Scrapper **Blackwell:** Frankie Black (1903–1962), U.S. black jazz guitarist.

Vivian **Blaine:** Vivienne Stapleton (1921–   ), U.S. film actress.

David **Blair:** David Butterfield (1932–1976), Eng. ballet dancer.

Janet **Blair:** Martha Lafferty (1921–   ), U.S. film actress.

Joyce **Blair:** Joyce Sheridan Taylor, née Ogus (1932–   ), Eng. stage actress.

Lionel **Blair:** Lionel Ogus (1934–   ), Eng. stage actor, dancer, choreographer, TV performer.

Anne **Blaisdell:** Elizabeth Linington (1921–   ), U.S. writer of historical, mystery novels.

Amanda **Blake:** Beverly Louise Neill (1929–1989), U.S. stage, film actress.

Marie **Blake:** Blossom MacDonald (1896–1976), U.S. film actress.

Nicholas **Blake:** Cecil Day-Lewis (1904–1972), Ir.-born Br. poet. The poet's name derives from that of his son, Nicholas, and one of his mother's family names. (She was Kathleen Blake Squires.)

Robert **Blake:** Michael Gubitosi (1933–   ), U.S. film actor.

Neltje **Blanchan:** Neltje Doubleday, née de Graff (1865–1918), U.S. writer on nature subjects.

Alexander **Bland:** Nigel Gosling (1909–1982), Eng. ballet critic + Maude Gosling, née Lloyd (1908–   ), S.A.-born Eng. ballet dancer, critic, his wife.

Fabian **Bland:** Hubert Bland (1856–1914), Br. author + Edith Bland, née Nesbit (1858–1924), Br. author, his wife. The joint pseudonym was used for *The Prophet's Mantle* (1888), with "Fabian" a reference to the Fabian Society, of which Hubert Bland was a prominent member. Edith Nesbit was well-known as a children's writer under the name of simply "E. Nesbit," with the bare initial deliberately concealing her sex. This led to the common assumption on the part of librarians that she was a man, which delighted her. She enjoyed her masculine role, and many of her stories had a male narrator.

Ralph **Blane:** Ralph Uriah Hunsecker (1914–   ), U.S. film composer, lyricist.

Sally **Blane:** Elizabeth Jane Young (1910–   ), U.S. film actress, sister of Loretta Young *(q.v.)*.

Docteur **Blasius:** Paschal Grousset (1845–1919), Fr. journalist.

Charles Stuart **Blayds:** Charles Stuart Calverley (1831–1884), Br. poet, parodist. Charles Stuart Calverley's father was the Rev. Henry Blayds, and a descendant of the old Yorkshire family of Calverley. The poet assumed the ancient name in 1852, when he became 21 and of full age.

Christopher **Blayre:** Edward Heron-Allen (1861–1943), Eng. writer of fantasy fiction.

Henri **Blaze:** Ange Henri Blaze de Bury (1813–1888), Fr. author.

Oliver **Bleeck:** Ross Thomas (1926–   ), U.S. mystery writer.

Emile **Blémont:** Léon-Emile Petitdidier (1839–1927), Fr. critic, dramatist, writer.

Carla **Bley:** Carla Borg (1938–   ), U.S. jazz, rock composer.

Belinda **Blinders:** Desmond F.T. Coke (1879–1931), Br. novelist.

Helen **Bliss:** Helena Louise Lipp (1917–   ), U.S. stage actress, singer.

Reginald **Bliss:** Herbert George Wells (1866–1946), Eng. novelist, sociological writer. H.G. Wells used the name for his novel *Boon* (1915), in which Reginald Bliss was the friend and literary executor of the main character, the popular playwright and novelist, George Boon.

Levi **Blodgett:** Theodore Parker (1810–1860), U.S. religious writer.

Charles **Blondin:** Jean-François Gravelet (1824–1897), Fr. tightrope walker. French *blondin* means "fair-haired person," as Gravelet was. It exists as a surname (of this origin) in its own right.

Buster **Bloodvessel:** Douglas Trendle (1958–   ), Br. rock singer.

Claire **Bloom:** Claire Blume (1931–   ), Eng. stage, film actress.

Kurtis **Blow:** Kurt Walker (–   ), U.S. black rock singer, rapper.

Ben **Blue:** S. David Cohen (1941–1982), U.S. pop music writer. Cohen was renamed by his friend Bob Dylan *(q.v.)*.

Miss **Bluebell:** Margaret Leibovici, née Murphy (originally Kelly) (1912–   ), Ir. dancer, teacher, founder of "Bluebell Girls" dancing troupe. The dancer was born in Dublin to a Mrs. Kelly. Only a fortnight after the birth, however, her mother gave away her baby to a spinster, Mary Murphy, who would raise the child. Later, a doctor visiting the little girl, who was thin and delicate, was mesmerized by her clear blue eyes and nicknamed her "Bluebell." Margaret Murphy adopted the name for herself and passed it on to her dancers [*Sunday Times Magazine*, August 23, 1981].

Blue Boy: Austin Lyons (1955–   ), Trinidad calypso singer.

Jake **Blues:** John Belushi (1949–1982), U.S. soul singer (Blues Brothers).

Nelly **Bly:** Elizabeth Cochrane Seaman (1867–1922), U.S. journalist. Elizabeth Seaman's name was suggested by the managing editor of *The Pittsburgh Dispatch*, for which she began writing at the age of 18. The name comes from a character in a song by Stephen Foster, writer of such world-famous hits as "The Old Folks at Home," "O Susanna," and "Jeanie with the Light Brown Hair."

Larry **Blyden:** Ivan Lawrence Blieden (1925–   ), U.S. stage actor, director.

Betty **Blythe:** Elizabeth Blythe Slaughter (1893–1972), U.S. film actress.

Jimmy **Blythe:** Sammy Price (1908–   ), U.S. black jazz pianist.

Tim **Bobbin:** John Collier (1708–1786), Eng. author, painter.

Bobèche: Antoine Mandelard (1791–c.1840), Fr. comic actor, teaming with Galimafré *(q.v.)*. French *bobèche* is a slang word for "head," so can be understood as something like "nut," "noddle."

Willie **Bobo:** William Correa (1934–   ), U.S. jazz musician.

Bocage: Pierre-Martinien (or François) Tousez (1797–1863), Fr. actor.

Dirk **Bogarde:** Derek Gentron Gaspart Ulric van den Bogaerde (1921–   ), Br. stage, film actor, of Du. descent.

Boisgilbert: Ignatius Donnelly (1831–1901), U.S. author, politician.

Marc **Bolan:** Marc Feld (1947–1977), Br. pop musician. Marc Feld cut his first disc in 1965 as "Mark Bowland," a name given him by Decca, the recording company. That same year he made this more distinctive as Marc Bolan.

Rolf **Boldrewood:** Thomas Alexander Browne (1826–1915), Eng.-born Austral. author of popular novels.

Richard **Boleslavsky:** Boleslaw Ryszart Srzednicki (1889–1937), Pol.-born U.S. stage director.

William **Bolitho:** William Bolitho Ryall (1831-1930), S.A.-born Br. journalist, author.

Florinda **Bolkan:** José Suarez Bulcão (1941–   ), It. film actress, of Brazilian parentage.

Isabel **Bolton:** Mary Britton Miller (1883–   ), U.S. poet, novelist.

Bom [1] F. Cortesi (? –1897), It.-born Russ. circus clown, teaming with Bim *(q.v.)*; [2] Mechislav Antonovich Stanevsky (1879–1927), Russ. clown, of Pol. parentage teaming with Bim; [3] Nikolay Iosifovich Viltzak (1880–1960), Russ. clown of Cz. parentage, teaming with Bim; [4] N.A. Kamsky (1894–1966), Russ. clown, teaming with Bim.

Bombardinio: William Maginn (1793–1842), Ir. author.

Fortunio **Bonanova:** Luis Moll (1895–1969), Sp. film actor, singer.

Father **Bonaventura:** Charles Edward Stuart (1720–1788), Sc. prince ("The Young Pretender").

Beulah **Bondi:** Beulah Bondy (1892–1981), U.S. film actress.

Gary U.S. **Bonds:** Gary Anderson (1939–), U.S. rock composer. The rock musician's new name originated with his first manager, who sent copies of his hit "New Orleans" to radio stations in sleeves marked "Buy U.S. Bonds."

Captain Ralph **Bonehill:** Edward Stratemeyer (1863–1930), U.S. writer of fiction for boys.

Bon Gaultier: William Edmonstone Aytoun (1813–1865), Sc. poet + [Sir] Theodore Martin (1814–1909), Sc. poet. The name was first used for the joint work, *Bon Gaultier Ballads* (1845), in which the poets parodied the verse of the day. The name comes from Rabelais, who in the Prologue to *Gargantua* used the words in a sense meaning "good fellow," "good companion," Gaultier being a generalized personal name.

Ali **Bongo:** William Wallace (–), Eng. TV magician. The fairly traditional magician's name was first used by Wallace in a performance in a village pantomime. He was assistant to magician David Nixon (1919–1978) in TV shows.

Jacques **Bonhomme:** Guillaume Cale (or Caillet) (? –1358), Fr. peasant leader. The generic name (something like "Jack Goodfellow") was one given to the peasantry in the fourteenth century. Its sense was derogatory, however, not approbatory, and it implied serfdom.

[St.] **Boniface:** Wynfrith (or Winfrid) (?680–755), Eng. missionary, martyr. Wynfrith, the "Apostle of Germany," was renamed by Pope Gregory II in 719 for the third-century saint Boniface who had been martyred at Tarsus.

Boniface VIII: Benedetto Caetani (?1355–1404), It. pope.

Issy **Bonn:** Benjamin Levin (1903–1977), Eng. radio comedian, singer. A typical Jewish nickname for the comedian, who was popular on radio in the 1930s. He also occasionally appeared in the cinema as "Benny Leven." "Issy" implies Israel, and "Bonn" represents Benjamin.

Richard **Bonnelli:** Richard Bunn (–), U. S. opera singer.

Sherwood **Bonner:** Katherine Sherwood Bonner Macdowell (1849–1883), U.S. short story writer.

Jessie **Bonstelle:** Laura Justine Bonesteele (1872–1932), U.S. stage actress, theatre manager.

Roger **Bontemps:** Roger de Collerye (?1470–1540), Fr. poet.

William **Boot:** Tom Stoppard *(q.v.)*. Tom Stoppard used the name for early pieces as a drama critic when writing for the magazine *Scene* (1962). He took it from the hero of Evelyn Waugh's *Scoop,* who was a nature columnist. Stoppard used the name Boot for several characters in his plays, often complemented by another character called Moon. In 1964 he wrote a TV play called *This Way Out with Samuel Boot*, which actually featured a *pair* of Boots, representing contrary attitudes towards material possessions.

Adrian **Booth:** Virginia Davis, née Pound (1918–   ), U.S. film actress. Adrian is sometimes found as a woman's name in the U.S., as also (rarely) in the U.K.

Edwina **Booth:** Josephine Constance Woodruff (1909–   ), U.S. film actress. Edwina Booth took her stage name from the actor Edwin Booth, the outstanding tragedian of the nineteenth century, and the first American actor to make his reputation in Europe.

James **Booth:** James Geeves-Booth (1930–   ), Eng. stage, film actor.

Shirley **Booth:** Thelma Booth Ford (1907–   ), U.S. stage actress.

Cornell **Borchers:** Cornelia Bruch (1925–   ), Ger. film actress.

Olive **Borden:** Sybil Tinkle (1909–1947), U.S. film actress.

Petrus **Borel:** Joseph-Pierre Borel (or Borel d'Hauterive) (1809–1858), Fr. poet, novelist.

Ernest **Borgnine:** Ermes Borgnino (1918–   ), U.S. film actor.

Ludwig **Börne:** Löb Baruch (1786–1837), Ger. political writer, satirist. Löb Baruch took his new name on converting from Judaism to Christianity in 1818.

Francesco **Borromini:** Francesco Castelli (1599–1667), It. architect.

Bos: Thomas Peckett Prest (*c.*1810–1879), Eng. author of stories for boys. Prest, and others like him, originally intended to ascribe their virtual piracies of writings by Dickens to "Boaz," after Dickens's own pen name Boz *(q.v.)*. This was ruled out, however, as being rather too close, and also rather too biblical. The genre of Prest's particular fiction came to be known as the "penny dreadful."

Hieronymus **Bosch:** Jerom van Aeken (?1450–?1516), Du. painter. Bosch took his new name from his birthplace, the Dutch town of 's Hertogenbosch.

Abbé **Bossut:** [Sir] Richard Phillips (1767–1840), Eng. writer. Phillips was a great pseudonymist. He used "Abbé Bossut" (after the genuine French mathematician of the name, his near contemporary) for a series of French, Italian and Latin word books and phrase books; "Rev. J. Goldsmith" for geographical and scientific works; "Rev. David Blair," "Rev. C.C. Clarke," "Rev. John Robinson," "Rev. S. Barrow," "Mrs. (or Miss) Pelham," for other writings.

Boston Bard: Robert S. Coffin (1797–1827), U.S. poet.

A **Bostonian:** Edgar Allan Poe (1809–1849), U.S. poet, short story writer. Poe was born in Boston, Mass.

Sandro **Botticelli:** Alessandro di Mariano dei Filipepi (1445–1510), It. painter. The painter adopted the nickname given to his elder brother Giovanni, a rotund pawnbroker. "Botticello" means "little barrel" (Italian *botte*, "barrel," with diminutive ending as for "violoncello").

Anthony **Boucher:** William Anthony Parker White (1911–1968), U.S. editor, SF, detective story writer.

Barbara **Bouchet:** Barbara Gutscher (1943–   ), U.S. film actress, of Ger. parentage.

Dion **Boucicault:** Dionysius Lardner Boursiquot (?1820–1890), Ir.-born U.S. actor, dramatist. The actor, who was of Huguenot extraction, began his career under the name of "Lee Moreton" in 1838, subsequently adopting the new spelling of his original name in 1841, after the success (in London) of his own play *London Assurance.*

Nicolas **Boulanger:** Paul Thiry, Baron d'Holbach (1723–1789), Fr. materialist, atheist writer. Holbach took this name, one of several, from the French philosopher Nicolas-Antoine Boulanger, his contemporary.

Houari **Boumédienne:** Mohammed Ben Brahim Boukharrouba (1927–1978), Algerian head of state. The military leader adopted his new name as a *nom de guerre* when he joined a guerrilla unit in 1955. "Boumédienne" is the French spelling of Arabic *Bum-ed-Din,* "Owl of religion."

Benjamin **Bounce:** Henry Carey (?1687–1743), Eng. poet, composer. Carey used the exuberant name for his equally lively dramatic burlesque *Chrononhoton-thologos,* "the Most Tragical Tragedy that ever was Tragediz'd by any Company of Tragedians" (1734). In this, Chrononhotonthologos was the king of Queerummania, and two other characters were Aldiborontiphoscophornia and Rigdum-Funnidos, names which Walter Scott later gave to his printer and publisher, the brothers James and John Ballantyne, for the pomposity of the former and the cheerfulness of the latter.

George **Bourne:** George Sturt (1863–1927), Eng. writer of books on rural subjects. Sturt took his pen name from his birthplace, Lower Bourne, Farnham, Surrey.

Bourvil: André Raimbourg (1917–1970), Fr. film comedian. The actor's screen name comes from the village of Bourville, northwest of Paris, where he was raised. At the same time it half suggests the latter half of his real surname.

B. **Bouverie:** William Ewart Gladstone (1809–1898), Br. prime minister, author.

Marjorie **Bowen:** Gabrielle Margaret Vere Long, née Campbell (1886–1952), Eng. novelist, biographer.

David **Bowie:** David Robert Hayward-Jones (1947–   ), Eng. rock musician. The singer changed his name to Bowie in 1966 so as not to be confused with Davy Jones of The Monkees, with his new name allegedly for the bowie knife. (Why precisely this is uncertain, although the letters of "Bowie" can be found in his full real name.) In the early 1970s he adopted a stage persona under the name of "Ziggy Stardust."

Edgar **Box:** Gore Vidal (1925–   ), U.S. novelist.

Boxcar Willie: Lecil Travis Martin (1932–   ), U.S. country musician. Lecil Martin took his name after being impressed by the way in which, during the American Depression, unemployed men would climb onto the roofs of boxcars so as to travel aross the States by freight train. His own father was a railroad man, and the family house lay only a few feet from the track. On assuming the name, Boxcar Willie adopted the stage guise of an unshaven, unkempt, cigar chompin' hobo in a battered hat.

Boy: Tadeusz Żeleński (1874–1941), Pol. writer.

John **Boyd:** Boyd Bradfield Upchurch (1919–   ), U.S. SF writer.

Nancy **Boyd:** Edna St. Vincent Millay (1892–1950), U.S. poet.

Stephen **Boyd:** William Millar (1928–1977), Ir. film actor, working in U.S.

Katie **Boyle:** Caterina Irene Helen Imperiali di Francavilla (1926–   ), It.-born Eng. TV panelist, writer, columnist. "Katie" for Caterina; "Boyle" for her first husband, Richard Bentinck Boyle (Viscount Boyle) subsequently the Earl of Shannon. They divorced in 1955. (See also p. 20.)

René **Boylesvé:** René-Marie-Auguste Tardiveau (1867–1926), Fr. novelist.

Boz: Charles Dickens (1812–1870), Eng. novelist. Dickens used this name both in reports of debates in the House of Commons in *The Morning Chronicle* (1835) and, more famously, in his collection of articles entitled *Sketches by Boz* (1836–1837). He explained the name as being "the nickname of a pet child, a younger brother, who I had dubbed Moses (after Moses Primrose in Goldsmith's *The Vicar of Wakefield*) [. . .] which being pronounced Boses, got shortened to Boz." The name was pronounced "Boze."

Dame Hilda **Bracket:** Patrick Fyffe (*c.*1950–   ), Br. female impersonator, teaming with Dr. Evadne Hinge *(q.v.)* (as "Hinge and Bracket").

Edward P. **Bradley:** Michael Moorcock (1939–   ), Eng. SF writer.

Will **Bradley:** Wilbur Schwichtenberg (1912–   ), U.S. trombonist.

Scott **Brady:** Gerald Tierney (1924–1985), U.S. film actor.

June **Brae:** June Bear (1917–   ), Eng. ballet dancer.

Eric **Braeden:** Hans Gudegast (–   ), Ger. film actor.

John **Braham:** John Abraham (?1774–1856), Eng. opera singer.

Otto **Brahm:** Otto Abrahamsohn (1856–1912), Ger. stage director, literary critic.

Caryl **Brahms:** Doris Caroline Abrahams (1901–1983), Eng. writer, humorist.

Ernest **Bramah:** Ernest Bramah Smith (1868–1942), Br. author.

Christianna **Brand:** Mary Christianna Lewis (1907–1988), U.K. thriller writer.

Max **Brand:** Frederick Schiller Faust (1892–1944), U.S. novelist.

John **Brandane:** John MacIntyre (1869–1947), Sc. dramatist.

Henry **Brandon:** Henry Kleinbach (1910–   ), U.S. film actor.

Willy **Brandt:** Herbert Ernst Karl Frahm (1913–   ), West Ger. politician. Herbert Frahm fled to Norway as a political refugee in 1933, adopting Willy Brandt as his party (Social Democrat) name.

Brassaï: Gyula Halesz (1899–1984), Hung.-born Fr. photographer. Brassaï adopted his name from that of his birth town, Brassó, Hungary (now Braşov, Romania).

Pierre **Brasseur:** Pierre-Albert Espinasse (1905–1972), Fr. stage, film actor, playwright. Brasseur was the maiden name of the actor's mother.

Wellman **Braud:** Wellman Breaux (1891–1966), U.S. black jazz bassist.

Brécourt: Guillaume Marcoureau (1638–1683), Fr. actor, dramatist.

Hans **Breitmann:** Charles Godfrey Leland (1824–1903), U.S. humorous writer, editor. Leland had received a university education in Germany, and he used the name for his amusing dialect poems, collected in *Hans Breitmann's Ballads* (1914).

Marie **Brema:** Minny Fehrmann (1856–1925). Eng. opera singer.

Brenda: Mrs. G. Castle Smith (*fl.*1875), Br. children's writer.

Edith **Brendall:** Eddy Charly Bertin (1944–   ), Ger.-born Belg. writer of horror stories.

Evelyn **Brent:** Mary Elizabeth Riggs (1899–1975), U.S. film actress.

George **Brent:** George Brent Nolan (1904–1979), Ir.-born U.S. film actor.

Romney **Brent:** Romulo Larralde (1902–1976), Mexican-born U.S. stage, film actor, dramatist.

Edmund **Breon:** Edmund MacLaverty (1882–1951), Ir. stage, film actor, working in U.S., U.K.

Ford **Brereton:** Samuel Rutherford Crockett (1860–1914), Sc. novelist, journalist.

Jeremy **Brett:** Peter Jeremy William Huggins (1935–   ), Eng. stage, film actor.

David **Brian:** Brian Davis (1914–   ), U.S. film actor.

James **Brian:** Arthur George Street (1892–1966), Eng. author of books on country life.

Mary **Brian:** Louise Dantzler (1908–   ), U.S. film actress.

Fanny **Brice:** Fannie Borach (1891–1951), U.S. singer, comedienne. Fannie Borach grew so weary of having her name mispronounced as "Bore-ache" and "Bore-act" that she changed it to something simpler. Lauren Bacall *(q.v.)* had similar problems.

Bricktop: Ada Beatrice Queen Victoria Louise Virginia Smith (1894–1984), U.S. cabaret singer, entertainer. From rolling royalty (with a common touch in "Smith") to basic brevity. Bricktop, the daughter of black parents, but with a part-Irish mother, took her name from the chic Bricktop café in Paris where she was the proprietress and where she entertained many famous expatriate U.S. writers, such as Hemingway and Scott Fitzgerald.

Ann **Bridge:** [Lady] Mary Dolling O'Malley, née Sanders (1891–1974), Eng. novelist. Ann Bridge took her pen name from her birthplace, the hamlet of Bridge End, Surrey. (Reverse the two halves of this name, and you get something that can be turned into "Ann Bridge.")

Bonar **Bridge:** [Rev.] W.W. Tulloch (1846–1920), Sc. biographer, editor. Tulloch took his name from the Scottish village of Bonar Bridge, Sutherland.

James **Bridie:** Osborne Henry Mavor (1888–1951), Sc. playwright. As a doctor, Osborne Henry Mavor needed a pseudonym for his distinctive dramatic writing. His first play was *The Sunlight Sonata* (1928), which he wrote as "Mary Henderson." He subsequently adopted his grandmother's surname for later plays, with the first under the Bridie name being *The Anatomist* (1930). He continued in general medical practice until 1938.

Bright Eyes: Susette La Flesche (1854–1903), U.S.-Indian writer, lecturer. Susette was the daughter of an Omaha chief who was himself the son of a French trader and an Omaha woman. "Bright Eyes" was her Indian name, which she came to use when involved in her people's struggle for justice.

Carl **Brisson:** Carl Pedersen (1895–1958), Dan. film actor, working in U.K.

Elton **Britt:** James Britt Baker (1917–1972), U.S. country singer, yodeller.

May **Britt:** Maybritt Wilkens (1933–   ), Swe. film actress.

Morgan **Brittany:** Suzanne Cupito (1953–   ), U.S. child film, TV actress.

Barbara **Britton:** Barbara Brantingham Czukor (1919–1980), U.S. film actress.

Colonel **Britton:** Douglas E. Ritchie (1905–   ), Br. radio news director.

Lynn **Brock:** Alister McAllister (1877–1943), Ir. author.

Lea **Brodie:** Lea Dregham (1951–   ), Eng. TV actress. Lea Dregham came to adopt her husband's former pseudonym for her professional work.

Steve **Brodie:** John Stevens (1919–   ), U.S. film actor.

James **Brolin:** James Bruderlin (1940–   ), U.S. film, TV actor.

John **Bromfield:** Farron Bromfield (1922–   ), U.S. film actor.

Charles **Bronson:** Charles Buchinsky (1921–   ), U.S. film actor. Bronson's grandfather was Charles Dennis Bunchinsky, the son of Russian immigrants from Lithuania. The family dropped the middle "n," and Charles Buchinsky changed to "Bronson" for his third film, *Drum Beat* (1954). "With the hounds of McCarthyville skulking round Hollywood Slavic names didn't seem so fashionable," he reasoned [David Downing, *Charles Bronson*, 1982].

Lesley **Brook:** Lesley Learoyd (1916–   ), Br. film actress.

Hillary **Brooke:** Beatrice Peterson (1914–   ), U.S. film actress.

Elkie **Brooks:** Elaine Bookbinder (1945–   ), Eng. popular singer. As a youngster, Elaine Bookbinder took singing lessons from the cantor of her local synagogue in Lancashire, and she chose the name Elkie as a Yiddish equivalent for "Elaine," while simultaneously shortening her long surname to "Brooks" [*The Times*, March 21, 1987].

Geraldine **Brooks:** Geraldine Stroock (1925–1977), U.S. film actress. "Brooks" is a more manageable name than "Stroock," to which it nevertheless retains a kind of resemblance.

Leslie **Brooks:** Leslie Gettman (1922–   ), U.S. film actress. Presumably Leslie Gettman was unaware of Lesley Learoyd, who became Lesley Brook *(q.v.)*.

Mel **Brooks:** Melvin Kaminsky (1926–   ), U.S. film comedy writer, producer. Melvin Kaminsky changed his name so as not to be confused with trumpet player Max Kaminsky. His new name arose as a contraction of his mother's maiden name, Brookman.

Phyllis **Brooks:** Phyllis Weiler (1914–   ), U.S. film actress.

Joyce **Brothers:** Joyce Bauer (1928–   ), U.S. TV psychiatrist.

Arthur **Brown:** Arthur Wilton (1944–   ), Eng. rock musician, comedian.

Carter **Brown:** Alan Geoffrey Yates (1923–1985), Br.-born Austral. thriller writer.

Georgia **Brown:** Lillian Klot (1933–   ), Eng. stage, film, TV actress.

Teddy **Brown:** Abraham Himmebrand (1900–1946), U.S. music hall instrumentalist. "Brown" could be regarded as an assimilation of "Abraham," while also hinting at the latter half of "Himmebrand."

Vanessa **Brown:** Smylla Brind (1928–   ), U.S. film actress. "Brown" here must represent "Brind." The actress's real name is memorable, but so unusual as to be meaningless in popular terms: everyone can identify "Vanessa Brown."

Coral **Browne:** Coral Brown (1913–   ), Austral. stage actress.

Henriette **Browne:** Sophie de Saux, née de Boutellier (1829–1901), Fr. painter, etcher.

Matthew **Browne:** William Brightly Rands (1823–1882), Br. writer of poems, fairy tales for children.

H. **Brownrigg:** Douglas William Jarrold (1803–1857), Eng. author, playwright, humorist.

Thomas **Brown the Younger:** Thomas Moore (1779–1852), Ir. poet, satirist.

Arthur Loring **Bruce:** Francis Welch Crowninshield (1872–   ), U.S. editor.

David **Bruce:** Marden McBroom (1914–1976), U.S. film actor.

Lenny **Bruce:** Leonard Alfred Schneider (1925–1966), U.S. comedian.

Leo **Bruce:** Rupert Croft-Cooke (1903–1979), Br. detective novelist.

Virginia **Bruce:** Helen Virginia Briggs (1910–1982), U.S. film actress.

Erik **Bruhn:** Belton Evers (1928–1986), Dan. ballet dancer, director, working in U.S.

Henri **Brulard:** Stendhal *(q.v.)*.

Bruscasmbille: Jean Deslauriers *(fl.* 1610–1634), Fr. actor. The name appears to represent French *brusque en bille,* "brusque in the head," with *bille* a slang word for "head," something like English "nut," "noddle."

Dora **Bryan:** Dora May Lawton, née Broadbent (1923–   ), Eng. stage, film, TV comedienne. Dora Broadbent's surname was "not a name for the stage," as Noel Coward put it. She therefore looked for an alternative, which would at the same time suggest the original. At first she selected "Bryant," from the match manufacturers, Bryant & May, but when the program arrived from the printers, the final "t" was missing and she settled for the "Bryan" instead.

Jane **Bryan:** Jane O'Brien (1918–   ), U.S. film actress.

Rudy **Bryans:** Bernard Godet (*c.*1945–   ), Fr. ballet dancer.

James **Bryce:** Alexander Anderson (1862–1949), Sc. novelist.

Bryher: Annie Winifred Ellerman (1894–1983), Eng. novelist. The novelist took her name from the island of Bryher, in the Isles of Scilly.

Yul **Brynner:** Taidje Kahn (1915–1985), U.S. film actor. The famous actor's mother was part Russian, and his father part Swiss. At first he spelled his name Youl Bryner. Some years later, a New York theatrical agent told him that "Youl" sounded too much like "you-all," and "Bryner" as though he was soaked in brine and pickled. To clarify the pronunciation, if not the origin of the name, Youl Bryner therefore respelled his name as Yul Brynner, pronounced "Yool Brinner" [Jhan Robbins, *Yul Brynner: The Inscrutable King,* 1988].

Bubbles: John William Sublett (1902–1986), U.S. black tapdancer. A near anagram of the dancer's real surname.

Martin **Bucer:** Martin Kuhhorn (1491–1551), Ger. Protestant reformer. In the fashion of his time, the theologian translated his German name (literally "cow horn") into Greek, with "Bucer" the latinized form of Greek *boukeros* (from *bous,* "ox," and *keras,* "horn"). The name is pronounced "Bootser."

Buffalo Bill: William Frederick Cody (1846–1917), U.S. scout, showman. William Frederick Cody was so named by Ned Buntline *(q.v.),* when Cody provided buffalo meat for rail construction crews.

Bunny: Carl Emil Schultze (1866–1939), U.S. cartoonist.

Ned **Buntline:** Edward Zane Carroll Judson (1823–1886), U.S. adventurer, trapper, author. Ned Buntline, as a writer of so-called "dime novels," simply took a ridiculous word for his pen name, with "Ned" representing his real first name,

Edward. A buntline is a line fastened to the foot of a square sail when it has to be hauled up for furling. Ned Buntline named Buffalo Bill *(q.v.)*, and depicted him in his writings.

Eleanor **Burford:** Eleanor Alice Burford Hibbert (1906–), Eng. novelist.

David **Burg:** Alexander Dolberg (1933–), Russ.-born Eng. writer, translator.

Annekatrin **Bürger:** Annekatrin Rammelt (1937–), Ger. film actress.

Anthony **Burgess:** John Burgess Wilson (1917–), Eng. novelist, critic. The well-known novelist explained how he came by his pen name in his autobiography: "I was christened John Burgess Wilson and was confirmed in the name of Anthony. When I published my first novel I was forced to do so in near-disguise. I was an official of the Colonial Office at the time, and it was regarded as improper to publish fiction under one's own name. So I pulled the cracker of my total name and unfolded the paper hat of Anthony Burgess. [. . .] Burgess was the maiden name of the mother I never knew [. . .] a dancer and singer [. . .] named the Beautiful Belle Burgess on music hall posters. She married a Manchester Wilson but was right to insist that her slightly more distinguished surname get on to my baptismal certificate. There have always been too many plain Wilsons around" [Anthony Burgess, *Little Wilson and Big God,* 1986].

Betty **Burke:** Charles Edward Stuart (1720–1788), Sc. prince ("The Young Pretender"). One of the prince's many disguise names, in this instance when rescued by Flora Macdonald after the Battle of Culloden (1746) and taken secretly by her to the island of Skye disguised as her maid. The prince was 26 at the time, and Flora two years younger.

Billie **Burke:** Mary William Ethelbert Appleton Burke (1885–1970), U.S. stage, film actress. In this case "Billie" represents "William" (normally a man's name, of course), but Billie was a popular name among chorus girls for some time.

Fielding **Burke:** Olive Dargan, née Tilford (1869–1968), U.S. poet, novelist.

Jonathan **Burn:** Henry Jonas Jonathan Burn-Forti (1939–), Eng. stage, TV actor.

George **Burns:** Nathan Birnbaum (1896–), U.S. stage, TV comedian.

Katherine **Burns:** Katharine Hepburn (1909–), U.S. stage, film actress. Katharine Hepburn used this name for her first stage performance in New York, when she appeared in *Night Hostess* (1928). Her film debut followed only four years later.

Ellen **Burstyn:** Edna Rae Gillooly (1932–), U.S. film actress. The actress's stage name is that of her third husband, Neil Burstyn.

Richard **Burton:** Richard Walter Jenkins (1925–1984), Welsh stage, film actor. When a schoolboy in Port Talbot, south Wales, Richard Jenkins showed signs of promise as an actor. As such, he became the protégé of the English teacher and school play producer Philip H. Burton, who made the 18-year-old his legal ward and gave him his name. The document that spelled out the change was dated December 17, 1943. Philip Burton would have adopted his pupil if it had been legally possible, but the difference between their ages was 20 days short of 21 years, the minimum required by law at that time. This ruled out official adoption.

Instead, an agreement was drawn up between Philip Burton and the real father making the "infant" a ward until he reached the age of 21. Part of the document declared that Richard Jenkins shall "absolutely renounce and abandon the use of the surname of the parent and shall bear and use the surname of the adopter and shall be held out to the world and in all respects treated as if he were in fact the child of the adopter" [Paul Ferris, *Richard Burton,* 1981].

[Sir] Alexander **Bustamente:** William Alexander Clark (1884–1977), Jamaican prime minister. William Clarke, the son of an Irish father and Jamaican mother, had worked for some time in Cuba as a police inspector. He assumed the name of the Cuban lawyer and politican Antonio Sánchez Bustamente y Sirvén, his near contemporary. The Cuban lawyer was the jurist who drew up the Bustamente Code dealing with international private law.

Prince **Buster:** Buster Campbell (1938–   ), Jamaican ska, rock musician.

The **Busy-Body:** Benjamin Franklin (1706–1790), U.S. statesman, scientist, philosopher. Franklin used the name for articles written in 1728.

Hilda **Butsova:** Hilda Boot (*c.*1897–1976), Eng. ballet dancer.

William **Butterworth:** Henry Schroeder (1774–1853), Eng. topographer, engraver.

Myra **Buttle:** Victor William Williams Saunders Purcell (1896–1965), Br. author of books on China.

Red **Buttons:** Aaron Schwatt (1918–   ), U.S. stage, screen, TV comedian. At the age of 16, Aaron Schwatt was a singing bellhop at Dinty Moore's City Island Tavern in the Bronx. For this job he had to wear a uniform with 48 prominent buttons. He had red hair, so was nicknamed after these two distinctive features – and came to adopt the name himself in place of his immigrant name.

Max **Bygraves:** Walter William Bygraves (1922–   ), Eng. TV entertainer. On his first night in the Royal Air Force, aged 17 (and having lied about his age to enlist), Walter William Bygraves impersonated his idol, Max Miller *(q.v.),* and thereafter assumed his first name.

Robert **Byr:** Karl Robert Emmerich von Bayer (1815–1902), Austr. novelist, writer on military subjects.

James **Byrne:** Edward William Garnett (1868–1937), Br. writer, literary adviser.

Edd **Byrnes:** Edward Breitenberger (1933–   ), U.S. juvenile TV actor.

Marion **Byron:** Miriam Bilenkin (1911–   ), U.S. film actress.

Walter **Byron:** Walter Butler (1899–1972), U.S. film actor.

Roy **C:** Roy Charles Hammond (1943–   ), U.S. pop singer. Roy Charles Hammond adopted this short, distinctive name in order not to be confused with either pop musician Roy Hamilton or singer Ray Charles *(q.v.).*

James **Caan:** James Cahn (1938–   ), U.S. film actor.

Bruce **Cabot:** Etienne Jacques de Bujac (1904–1972), U.S. film actor, of Fr. descent.

Susan **Cabot:** Harriet Shapiro (1927–1986), U.S. film actress.

Cadenus: Jonathan Swift (1667–1745), It. satirist, cleric. The name is an anagram of Latin *decanus,* "dean." Swift had become Dean of St. Patrick's Cathedral, Dublin, in 1699, hence his common nickname of "Dean" Swift. He used the name Cadenus for his poem *Cadenus and Vanessa* (1713) addressed to Esther Vanhomrigh, thereby incidentally creating the woman's name Vanessa. (Swift formed the name from the first three letters of "Vanhomrigh" plus "Essa," a pet form of Esther.)

Caffarelli: Gaetano Majorano (1710–1783), It. male soprano singer.

Nicolas **Cage:** Nicolas Coppola (1964–   ), U.S. film actor, nephew of Francis Coppola.

Sammy **Cahn:** Samuel Cohen (1913–   ), U.S. film lyricist.

Marti **Caine:** Lynda Denise Ives, formerly Stringer, née Crapper (1945–   ), Eng. TV singer, entertainer, comedienne. Needing a stage name, Lynda Crapper opened a gardening book at random in 1968 and lighted on the entry "Tomato cane." That gave her name—or so the story goes!

Michael **Caine:** Maurice Joseph Micklewhite (1933–   ), Eng. film, TV actor, working in U.S. The actor took his first name from his nickname, Mike (no doubt itself based on his surname), and his second name from the film *The Caine Mutiny*. He had to pick a screen name in a hurry in 1954, and happened to see a Leicester Square, London, cinema advertising the film. The name appealed to him for its brevity and strength [*Telegraph Sunday Magazine*, May 9, 1982].

Calamity Jane: Martha Burk (or Canary) (?1852–1903), U.S. popular heroine of the West. Calamity Jane was a colorful character who wore men's clothing, carried a gun, indulged in drinking sprees—and prophesied "doom and gloom." Hence her nickname which became the name by which she is generally known to-day, having featured (in a much more attractive guise) in dime novels of the 1870s and 1880s. "Jane" has long been a nickname for a woman, especially a distinctive or disreputable one. Martha Burk was a prostitute in various frontier towns.

Taylor **Caldwell:** Janet Miriam Taylor Reback, née Caldwell (1900–1985), Eng.-born U.S. novelist. It is not clear to what extent Taylor Caldwell wished to disguise her sex, if at all, or to what extent she wished to be associated with the contemporary (and better-known) novelist, Erskine Caldwell. Taylor is hardly a common woman's name.

Louis **Calhern:** Carl Henry Vogt (1895–1956), U.S. stage, film actor. The actor was obliged to adopt a stage name under pressure from his uncle, who regarded the profession as shameful. The new name came from a combination of his first two names for "Calhern" and from the city of St. Louis for his first name.

Rory **Calhoun:** Francis Timothy McGown, later Durgin (1922–   ), U.S. film actor.

Caligula: Gaius Julius Caesar (12–41), Roman emperor. The name means "Little Boots," and was the pet name given to Gaius Caesar by his father's soldiers when he ran around the camp as a young boy. It is strange that such an agreeable name should come to be adopted by such a cruel despot.

Calixtus II: Guido di Borgogna (? –1124), It. pope.

Calixtus III: Alfonso Borgia (1378–1458), Sp. pope.

Michael **Callan:** Martin Caliniff (1935–   ), U.S. dancer, film actor.

Maria **Callas:** Cecilia Sophia Anna Maria Meneghini, née Kalogeropoulos (1923–1977), U.S. opera singer, of Gk. parentage. A classic example of a necessary shortening of a typical lengthy Greek surname. The abbreviating was done not by the opera singer but by her father, shortly after his arrival with his family in the U.S. in 1923, the year of Maria's birth.

Joseph **Calleia:** Joseph Alexander Herstall Vincent Calleja (1897–1976), Maltese-born U.S. film actor.

Emma **Calvé:** Rosa Noémie Emma Calvet de Roquer (1858–1942), Fr. opera singer.

Phyllis **Calvert:** Phyllis Bickle (1915–   ), Eng. stage, film, TV actress. Phyllis Bickle was requested to change her name by film producer Herbert Wilcox. The actress selected Calvert as she felt it "had a sort of ring to it." Apparently, she did not feel a need to alter Phyllis.

Corinne **Calvet:** Corinne Dibos (1925–   ), Fr. film actress.

Henry **Calvin:** Wimberly Calvin Goodman, Jr. (1918–1975), U.S. film comedian.

Marie **Camargo:** Marie Anne de Cupis (1710–1770), Belg. ballet dancer, of Spanish descent. The dancer adopted her mother's Spanish maiden name as her professional name.

Elizabeth **Cambridge:** Barbara K. Hodges, née Webber (1893–1949), Br. novelist, short story writer.

John **Cameron:** Archibald Gordon Macdonell (1895–1941), Sc. author.

Rod **Cameron:** Nathan R. Cox (1910–1983), Can. film actor, appearing in U.S. films.

Camillus: [1] Alexander Hamilton (1755–1804), U.S. statesman, pamphleteer, author; [2] Fisher Ames (1758–1808), U.S. statesman, orator, political writer. Both men adopted the name of Camillus, the Roman soldier and statesman who saved Rome from the Gauls and who was instrumental in securing the passage of the so-called Licinian laws, introducing measures in favor of the rights of the plebeians.

Herbert Edward **Campbell:** Herbert Edward Story (1844–1904), Br. music hall artiste.

Judy **Campbell:** Judy Birkin, née Gamble (1916–   ), Eng. stage, screen, TV actress, mother of film actress Jane Birkin (1946–   ). The actress adopted the surname assumed by her father, Joseph Arthur Campbell, né Gamble.

Mrs. Patrick **Campbell:** Beatrice Stella Campbell, née Tanner (1865–1940), Eng. stage actress. The actress was always known by her husband's name. Not really a pseudonym, of course, but a distinctive stage name of sorts. Beatrice Tanner eloped when she was 19 to marry Patrick Campbell, a London businessman.

Cañadas: Henry Higgins (1944–1978), Colombian-born Eng. bullfighter, working in Spain. Henry Higgins was the only Englishman to have qualified as a matador in the Spanish bull ring. In the bullfighting tradition, he adopted a Spanish ring name. It means "glens," "narrow valleys" (related to English "canyon"). Such valleys are a feature of the countryside around Bogotá, Colombia, where Higgins was born. The Spanish themselves usually referred to him as simply "El Inglés" ("the Englishman").

Canaletto: Giovanni Antonio Canal (1697–1768), It. painter. "Canaletto" means "little Canal." It is uncertain how the painter came to acquire this version of his surname, as he was not noticeably small. Possibly it was to distinguish him from his father, Bernardo Canal, who was a theatrical scene painter. Giovanni often assisted his father in his work, so that the Italian diminutive-*etto* ending (as in "stiletto") more or less equated to "Jr."

Ann **Candler:** Ann More (1740–1814), Eng. poet (the "Suffolk Cottager"). Not really a pseudonym but the poet's married name, here recorded purely for interest.

Edward **Candy:** Barbara Alison Neville (1925–   ), Br. novelist.

Denis **Cannan:** Denis Pullein-Thompson (1919–   ), Br. actor, playwright. The actor adopted his mother's maiden name as his stage and pen name.

Charles **Cannell:** Evelyn Charles Vivian (1882–1947), Eng. writer of adventure, detective stories.

Effie **Canning:** Effie Carlton, née Crockett (1857–1940), U.S. stage actress.

Dyan **Cannon:** Samille Diane Friesen (1937–   ), U.S. film actress. The film producer who gave Samille Friesen her new name was Jerry Ward, who arranged her first screen test. Folklore (which may nevertheless contain something of the true origin) claims that one day he looked at her and exclaimed, "I see something explosive. Terrific! Bang! Cannon!" [*TV Times,* June 1–7, 1985].

Freddy **Cannon:** Frederick Anthony Picariello (1940–   ), U.S. rock musician.

Tommy **Cannon:** Thomas Darbyshire (1938–   ), Eng. TV comedian, teaming with Bobby Ball *(q.v.).* The two men, formerly Lancashire welders, began their entertaining acts as the Harper Brothers (after Ball's real name), working in social clubs and cabaret. They changed their joint name to "Cannon and Ball" for an appearance on the TV talent show *Opportunity Knocks,* in 1973. Cannon is the bigger and older of the two, with Ball his "feed" (providing his "ammunition," as it were).

Cantinflas: Mario Moreno Reyes (1913–   ), Mexican circus clown, bullfighter, stage and film comedian. The name looks meaningful (Spanish *cantina,* "buffet" suggests itself), but it is apparently without meaning, and was given as a nickname to the performer by one of his fans.

Eddie **Cantor:** Edward Israel (or Isidore) Itskowitz (1892–1964), U.S. singer, entertainer, film actor. Latin *cantor* means "singer," whether understood as the Jewish leader of a synagogue service (as suitable for the actor, who was Jewish) or for the leader of some other type of worship. "Cantor" is a Jewish surname in its own right.

Robert **Capa:** Endre Ermö Friedmann (1913–1954), Hung.-born U.S. photographer. The new name was created in the mid–1930s. At that time, Friedmann was publishing his work simply as "André." He felt that this made him sound like a hairdresser, however, so he and his girl friend Gerda Pohorylles, who helped him to promote this work, devised a different name. This was "Robert Capa," supposedly the name of an already successful American photographer who was so rich that he refused to sell his photos at normal prices. The name itself was arbitrary in origin, although André (Endre) claimed that "Robert" came from the movies, and in particular from Robert Taylor, who in 1936 was starring as Greta Garbo's lover in *Camille.* But both words of the name were easy to pronounce, in many languages, and "Capa" looked like any nationality. Gerda could thus tell French editors that Capa was American, but also tell American editors that the photographer was

French. And when the newly christened Capa went to Spain, his surname sounded conveniently Spanish. This ambiguity must have appealed to André, and the name was perfect for a stateless person. In a letter to his mother shortly after, Capa wrote: "I am working under a new name. They call me Robert Capa. One could almost say that I've been born again, but this time it didn't cause anyone any pain." Gerda also changed her name at about this time. Instead of Gerda Pohorylles, she became Gerda Taro, the new name borrowed from a young Japanese painter working in Paris. Not only was her new name easy to pronounce (as Capa's was), but it suggested "tarot," with its connotations of gypsies and fortune-telling. What's more the new name as a whole sounded rather like "Greta Garbo," who in 1936 was at the peak of her fame. [Richard Whelan, *Robert Capa: A Biography*, 1985].

Truman **Capote:** Truman Streckfus Persons (1924–1984), U.S. writer. Truman Capote's surname was adopted from his stepfather.

Al **Capp:** Alfred Gerald Caplin (1909–1979), U.S. cartoonist.

Capucine: Germaine Lefebvre (1933–   ), Fr. stage, screen actress.

Caran d'Ache: Emmanuel Poiré (1858–1909), Fr. caricaturist. The artist was born in Moscow, and took his name as a French arrangement of the Russian word *karandash*, meaning "pencil." Compare the name of **Karandash.**

Caravaggio: Michelangelo Merisi (da Caravaggio) (1573–1610), It. painter. The painter's name is that of his birthplace, Caravaggio, near Bergamo in northern Italy.

Francis **Carco:** François Marie Alexandre Carcopino-Tussoli (1886–1958), Fr. poet, writer.

Cardini: Richard Valentine Pitchford (1895–1973), Welsh magician. The name suggests a blend of "cards" and "Houdini." See the latter name for its own origin.

Christine **Carere:** Christine de Borde (1930–   ), Fr. film actress.

Carette: Julien Carette (1897–1966), Fr. film actor.

Edwin **Carewe:** Jay Fox (1883–1940), U.S. film director.

Karl **Carl:** Karl Andreas von Bernbrunn (1789–1854). Austr. actor, dramatist, impresario.

Richard **Carle:** Charles Carleton (1871–1941). Br. film actor.

Kitty **Carlisle:** Catherine Holzman (1915–   ), U.S. opera singer, film actress.

Carlo-Rim: Jean-Marius Richard (1905–   ), Fr. film writer, director. The name appears to be loosely based on the writer's real name, with "Carlo" representing "Richard" and the letters of "Rim" from "Marius."

Carlota: Marie-Charlotte-Amélie-Augustine-Victoire-Clémentine-Léopoldine (1840–1927), Belg.-born empress of Mexico. The wife of Emperor Maximilian adopted a Spanish version of the second element of her seven-part French name as a mercifully single name for standard use. Royal personages usually acquire strings of names like this in an attempt to preserve the names of earlier members of the family.

Richard **Carlson:** Albert Lea (1914–1977), U.S. film actor, director.

Felix **Carmen:** Frank Dempster Sherman (1860–1916), U.S. poet. The poet's adopted name translates as the Latin for "happy song."

Carmen Sylva: Elizabeth, Queen of Romania, née Pauline Elisabeth Ottilie Luise, Princess of Wied (1843–1916), Romanian verse, prose writer. The royal pen name was probably meant to be evocative more than directly meaningful. As it stands, it suggests Latin *carmen*, "song," and *silva*, "wood." But both Carmen and Sylva are German women's names in their own right. (Elizabeth's works were mostly in German.)

Carmontelle: Louis Carrogis (1717–1806), Fr. painter, dramatist.

Carol **Carnac:** Edith Caroline Rivett (1894–1958), Br. detective novelist. The writer seems to have evolved her *nom de plume* by using letters from "Caroline," some more than once. She also wrote as E.C.R. Lorac *(q.v.)*.

Judy **Carne:** Joyce Botterill (1939–   ), Eng. TV actress, working in U.S. The actress took her screen name "from a character she played years ago in a school play." [*TV Times Magazine,* June 5–11, 1982].

Martine **Carol:** Marie-Louise Mourer (1922–1967), Fr. film actress.

Norman **Carol:** Sydney Edward Brandon (1890–   ), Eng. music hall comedian.

Sue **Carol:** Evelyn Lederer (1907–1982), U.S. film actress.

Catherine **Carr:** Rosalind Herschel Seymour, née Wade (1909–   ), Eng. novelist.

Glyn **Carr:** Showell Styles (1908–   ), Br. detective novelist.

Jane **Carr:** Rita Brunstrom (1909–1957). Br. film actress.

Philippa **Carr:** Eleanor Alice Burford Hibbert (1906–   ), Eng. author of historical romances.

Vikki **Carr:** Florencia Bisenta de Casillas Martinez Cardona (1938–   ), U.S. pop singer.

Edward **Carrick:** Edward Anthony Craig (1905–   ), Br. art director, film actor. "Carrick" means the same as "Craig," that is, "rock," the former name being a Celtic variant of the English (which corresponds to "crag").

Andrea **Carroll:** Andrea Lee DeCapite (1946–   ), U.S. pop singer.

Diahann **Carroll:** Carol Diann Johnson (1935–   ), U.S. black TV singer, actress.

Elisabeth **Carroll:** Elisabeth Pfister (1937–   ), U.S. ballet dancer.

Joan **Carroll:** Joan Felt (1932–   ), U.S. child film actress. The actress changed her name when she was only eight, choosing a name that seemed "musical."

John **Carroll:** Julian la Faye (1905–1979), U.S. film actor, singer.

Lewis **Carroll:** Charles Lutwidge Dodgson (1832–1898), Eng. children's writer. One of the most famous and best-loved names in nineteenth-century English literature, whom most people know as the author of *Alice in Wonderland* and *Through the Looking-Glass,* was really Charles Lutwidge Dodgson, a mathematical lecturer at Oxford University. His pseudonym is a transposition and translation (or rendering) of his first two names, of course – Lutwidge to Lewis and Charles to Carroll. (Compare German Ludwig and Latin Carolus). He was requested to produce a pen name by Edmund Yates, editor of the humorous paper *The Train,* to which Dodgson was contributing (1856, six years before he told, and began to write, the story of *Alice*). He first offered Yates the name Dares, after his birthplace Daresbury, but Yates thought this "too much like a newspaper signature." So Dodgson tried again, and on February 11, 1856, wrote in his diary: "Wrote to Mr. Yates sending him a choice of names: 1. *Edgar Cuthwellis* (made by transposition out of "Charles Lutwidge"). 2. *Edgar U.S. Westhill* (ditto). 3. *Louis Carroll* (derived from Lutwidge . . . Ludovic . . . Louis, and Charles). 4. *Lewis Carroll* (ditto)."

Yates made his choice, saving all Alice lovers from Edgar Cuthwellis, and on March 1 Dodgson duly recorded in his diary "Lewis Carroll was chosen." This was not in fact his first pseudonym, since his early contributions to *The Train* were signed as "B.B." (it was this that prompted his editor to ask for a proper *nom de plume*). The precise origin of B.B. is not clear, although Dodgson had shown a fondness for writing over mysterious initials as self-appointed editor of the Dodgson family journal, *The Rectory Magazine*. In this, as a 15-year-old schoolboy, he contributed pieces as V.X., F.L.W., J.V., F.X., Q.G.–and B.B. In her biography of Carroll, Anne Clark suggests that B.B.–which would appear to be one of the few initialized pseudonyms Dodgson retained for use in adult life–might perhaps stand for "Bobby Burns," since a number of the pieces contributed by the youthful author to *The Rectory Magazine* were mournful ballads in the style of Robert Burns.

On the other hand in *Poverty Bay: A Nondescript Novel* (1905), by Harry Furniss, the illustrator chosen by Dodgson for *Sylvie and Bruno*, the following is found: "He was known at Eton as "B.B.," short for Beau Brummell, the exquisite, whom he was supposed, by the boys at school, to emulate." Furniss was here perhaps consciously or unconsciously using Dodgson's own nickname, which had been confided to him some years before and which he now remembered. This seems quite a likely explanation for the strange double-letter name. Additionally, Francis King, reviewing Anne Clark's book in the *Sunday Telegraph* (September 9, 1979), points out that many of the names in Carroll's *The Hunting of the Snark* began with B, including all the crew members (Bellman, Barrister, Broker, Billiardmarker, Beaver, etc.) and the Snark itself, which ultimately turns out to be a Boojum! [1. Anne Clark, *Lewis Carroll: A Biography*, 1979; 2. John Pudney, *Lewis Carroll and His World*, 1976].

Madeleine **Carroll:** Marie-Madeleine Bernadette O'Carroll (1906–1987), Br. film actress.

Nancy **Carroll:** Ann La Hiff (1905–1965), U.S. film actress.

Sydney W. **Carroll:** George Frederick Carl Whiteman (1877–1958), Austral.-born Br. stage actor, critic, theatre manager.

Arthur **Carron:** Arthur Cox (1900–1967), Eng. opera singer.

Jasper **Carrott:** Robert Davies (1945–), Eng. comedian. Robert Davies explains how he came by his name: "Jasper is a nickname I picked up when I was nine, I don't know why. There is no reason for it. I added Carrott when I was 17. I was on a golf course with a friend, when he met somebody, and said: 'Oh, this is Jasper.' Carrott was the first name that came into my head. No one since school days has ever called me, or even known me, by my original name, Bob Davies" [*TV Times*, February 15, 1979]. "Jasper" is actually a nickname for any person, meaning little more than "person." As such, it now has its own entry in the *Oxford English Dictionary (Supplement*, Volume II, 1976).

Arthur **Carson:** Peter Brooke (1907–), Eng.-born U.S. thriller writer.

Jeannie **Carson:** Jean Shufflebottom (1928–   ), Br. film actress.

John **Carson:** John Derek Carson-Parker (1927–   ), Br. stage, TV actor.

John Paddy **Carstairs:** John Keys (1910–1970), Eng. film director, screenwriter.

Peter **Carsten:** Pieter Ransenthaler (1929–   ), Ger. film actor, working in U.S.

Bruce **Carter:** Richard Alexander Hough (1922–   ), Eng. children's writer, publisher.

Helena **Carter:** Helen Rickerts (1923–   ), U.S. film actress.

Jack **Carter:** John Chakrin (1922–   ), U.S. TV comic.

Janis **Carter:** Janis Dremann (1917–   ), U.S. film actress.

Mrs. Leslie **Carter:** Caroline Louise Dudley (1862–1937), U.S. stage actress. An actress who, like Mrs. Patrick Campbell *(q.v.)*, appeared professionally under her husband's name. She took to the stage in 1889, after her nine-year-old marriage broke up. Despite initial objection to her status as divorcee, she soon won popular acclaim for her fine performances.

Nick **Carter:** [1] John R. Coryell (1848–1924), U.S. popular fiction writer; [2] Thomas Chalmers Harbaugh (1849–1924), U.S. popular fiction writer; [3] Frederick Van Rensselaer Day (?1861–1922), U.S. popular fiction writer. The name was adopted by the author (or authors) of a series of detective novels that appeared in the U.S from about 1870. The character Nick Carter, who gave the name, is said to have been invented by [1] and passed on by him to [2] and [3].

Anna **Carteret:** Anna Wilkinson (1942–   ), Br. stage actress. Carteret was the maiden name of the actress's mother.

Richard Claude **Carton:** Richard Claude Critchett (1856–1928), Br. actor, dramatist.

Louise **Carver:** Louise Spilger Murray (1868–1956), U.S. film actress.

Lynn **Carver:** Virginia Reid Sampson (1909–1955), U.S. film actress.

Ivan **Caryll:** Félix Tilken (1861–1921), Belg. operetta composer, working in U.K. and U.S.

Maria **Casares:** Maria Casares Quiroga (1922–   ), Fr.-Sp. film actress.

Justin **Case:** Hugh Barnett Cave (1910–   ), Eng.-born U.S. horror fiction writer. A corny name, but a mention here just to show that at least one writer had to use it!

Bill **Casey:** William Weldon (1909–   ), U.S. black blues singer, guitarist.

Sir Edwin **Caskoden:** Charles Major (1856–1913), U.S. novelist.

Cassandra: [Sir] William Neil Connor (1909–1967), Eng. columnist. Sir William Connor was columnist for the *Daily Mirror* from 1935, and was noted for his gloomily prophetic articles. His pen name reflects this, as in Greek mythology Cassandra was the daughter of Priam, king of Troy, who received the gift of prophecy from Apollo. However, when she refused the god's advances, he decreed that no one would believe her predictions, although they were invariably true. Her name has thus come to denote any "prophet of doom." The columnist did not choose the name himself; it was given him by Harry Bartholomew, one of the newspaper's directors. Connor commented: "I was a bit surprised to discover that I had changed my sex; was the daughter of the King of Troy; that I could foretell in the stars when the news was going to be bad; [. . .] that nobody believed me when I spoke the unpleasant truth" [Robert Connor, *Cassandra: Reflections in a Mirror*, 1969].

Jean-Pierre **Cassel:** Jean-Pierre Crochon (1932–   ), Fr. film actor.

Butch **Cassidy:** Robert Le Roy Parker (1866–1909), U.S. bank robber. "Butch" was given as a nickname, since the bank robber worked as a butcher for a time when on the run from the law. "Cassidy" was an alias.

Billie **Cassin:** Joan Crawford *(q.v.)*.

Don **Castle:** Marion Goodman, Jr. (1919–1966), U.S. film actor.

Frances **Castle:** Evelyn Barbara Leader, née Blackburn (1898–   ), Eng. novelist, playwright.

Irene **Castle:** Irene Foote (1893–1969), U.S. cabaret dancer, teaming with Vernon Castle *(q.v.)*.

Vernon Blythe **Castle:** Vernon Blythe (1885–1918), Br. cabaret dancer, aviator.

William **Castle:** William Schloss (1914–1977), U.S. horror film director. "Castle" translates "Schloss" (as a German word).

Harry **Castlemon:** Charles Austin Fosdick (1842–1915), U.S. writer of adventure stories for boys.

Gilbert **Cates:** Gilbert Katz (1934–   ), U.S. film director.

Christopher **Caudwell:** Christopher St. John Sprigg (1907–1937), Br. Marxist writer.

Christopher **Caustic:** Thomas Green Fessenden (1771–1837), U.S. author, inventor, lawyer.

C.P. **Cavafy:** Konstantinos Petrou Kavaphes (1863–1933), Gk. poet.

Alberto **Cavalcanti:** Alberto de Almeida-Cavalcanti (1897–1926), Brazilian film actor.

Pier Francesco **Cavalli:** Pier Francesco Caletti di Bruno (1602–1676), It. opera composer. The composer assumed the name of his Venetian patron, Federico Cavalli.

Cavendish: Henry Jones (1831–1899), Br. authority on whist. The writer took his name from his club, the Cavendish, in Cavendish Square, London.

Kay **Cavendish:** Kathleen Murray (–   ), Br. classical pianist, crooner, broadcaster.

Pisistratus **Caxton:** [Lord] Edward George Earle Lytton Bulwer Lytton (1803–1873), Eng. novelist, playwright, statesman. One of several pseudonyms used at different times by the writer. This one was no doubt semi-seriously derived from Pisistratus, the fifth-century B.C. "Tyrant of Athens," and William Caxton, the first English printer.

Henry **Cecil:** Henry Cecil Leon (1902–1976), Br. author, playwright.

Ceiriog: John Hughes (1832–1887), Welsh poet, folk musicologist. Ceiriog was the poet's bardic name, taken from that of the village where he was born, Llanarmon Dyffryn Ceiriog, and itself named after the river Ceiriog on which it stands.

Celestine II: Guido di Città di Castello (? –1144), It. pope.

Celestine III: Giacinto Orsini (*c.*1106–1198), It. pope.

Celestine IV: Goffredo Castiglioni (? –1241), It. pope.

Celestine V: Pietro da Morrone (*c.*1209–1296), It. pope.

Céline: Odette Sansom (1912–   ), Fr.-born Br. wartime agent.

Louis-Ferdinand **Céline:** Louis Ferdinand Destouches (1894–1961), Fr. novelist.

Blaise **Cendrars:** Frédéric Sauser-Hall (1887–1961), Fr. novelist, poet, of Swiss parentage.

Luigia **Cerale:** Luigia Cerallo (1859–1937), It. ballet dancer.

C.W. **Ceram:** Kurt W. Marek (1915–1972), Ger.-born U.S. writer, archeologist. The writer's pen name reversed his real name.

Frederick **Cerny:** Frederick Guthrie (1833–1886), Eng. physicist. The scientist used his pen name for two poems published early in his life. "Cerny" looks as if it bears some relation to "Guthrie," although it may have had some other origin.

Cham: [Comte] Amédée de Noé (1819–1879), Fr. caricaturist. As one might expect from an artist of this genre, the name is a quiet pun. "Cham" is the French for "Ham," the second son of Noah, for whom the French equivalent is "Noé."

Champfleury: Jules-François-Félix Husson (1821–1889), Fr. novelist, journalist. Jules Husson was Jules Fleury before he became Champfleury, and the latter name seems to have developed from the former. It was no doubt suggested by the sixteenth-century work *Champfleury,* by the grammarian Geoffrey Tory. This encouraged the writing of learned works in French, as against the traditional Latin.

Marge **Champion:** Marjorie Belcher (1921–), U.S. film actress, dancer.

James **Chance:** James Siegfried (1953–), U.S. rock musician.

Gene **Chandler:** Eugene Dixon (1937–), U.S. pop singer, record producer.

Jeff **Chandler:** Ira Grossel (1919–1961), U.S. stage, film actor.

Fay **Chandos:** Irene Maude Swatridge, née Mossop (*c.*1905–), Eng. novelist.

Stockard **Channing:** Susan Williams Antonia Stockard (1944–), U.S. film comedienne.

Mlle **Chantilly:** Marie-Justine-Benoiste Duronceray (1727–1772), Fr. actress.

Saul **Chaplin:** Saul Kaplan (1921–), U.S. film music composer, musical director.

Jacques **Chardonne:** Jacques Boutelleau (1884–1968), Fr. novelist.

Cyd **Charisse:** Tula Ellice Finklea (1921–), U.S. film actress. Many filmographies give the actress's "real" name as shown here. And indeed that was how she started life. But Charisse is equally "real," as it is the name of her first husband, the ballet teacher Nico Charisse. She retained the name although soon divorcing Charisse and marrying actor and singer Tony Martin. If anything, "Cyd" is the name that is not genuine. When a young child she was called "Sid" by her baby brother, in his attempt to say "sister." She adopted the name, but respelled it "Cyd." Much more of a pseudonym was that of "Felia Sidorova," which Tula used when she first danced (in 1939). This was derived from "Finklea" and the same "Sid" in mock-Russian form.

Bobby **Charles:** Robert Charles Guidry (1938–), U.S. black rock songwriter.

Maria **Charles:** Maria Zena Schneider (1929–), Br. film, TV actress.

Pamela **Charles:** Pamela Foster (1932–), Eng. stage actress, singer. The actress adopted her father's first name as her stage name.

Ray **Charles:** Ray Charles Robinson (1930–), U.S. black popular singer. Ray Charles Robinson dropped his surname in order not to be confused with the champion boxer, Sugar Ray Robinson *(q.v.).*

Charlotte Elizabeth: Charlotte Elizabeth Tonna (1790–1846), Eng. writer of evangelical books for children.

John **Charlton:** Martin Charlton Woodhouse (1932–   ), Eng. author. Woodhouse selected a family name for his "rather violent detective story," *The Remington Set* (1975). This was full of cops and robbers and four-letter words, so a different name was desirable in order not to shock his regular readers.

Charo: Maria del Rosario Pilar Martinez Molina Baeza (1948–   ), Can. folk singer.

Leslie **Charteris:** Leslie Charles Bowyer Yin (1907–   ), Singapore-born U.S. crime novelist, of joint Eng.-Chin. parentage. The pseudonym appears to be based on the writer's second name, although "Charteris" occurs in fictional works, such as Sir Patrick Charteris in Scott's *The Fair Maid of Perth* and Leonard Charteris in Shaw's *The Philanderer*.

Alida **Chase:** Alida Anderson (1951–   ), Austral. ballet dancer.

Beatrice **Chase:** Olive Katharine Parr (1874–1911), Eng. novelist.

Charlie **Chase:** Charles Parrott (1893–1940), U.S. film comedian.

James Hadley **Chase:** René Brabazon Raymond (1906–1985), Eng. thriller writer. The name appears to be a fairly random one (possibly more American than British) for a writer who also used other pseudonyms, such as "James L. Docherty," "Ambrose Grant," and "Raymond Marshall."

Geoffrey **Chater:** Geoffrey Robinson (1921–   ), Eng. stage actor.

Daniel **Chaucer:** Ford Madox Ford *(q.v.)*.

Mary **Chavelita:** Mary Chavelita Dunne (1860–1945), Austral. novelist.

Paddy **Chayevsky:** Sidney Stychevsky (1923–1981), U.S. film, TV writer.

Chubby **Checker:** Ernest Evans (1941–   ), U.S. black pop musician. The name originated as a nickname, comparing the musician to Fats Domino *(q.v.)*, whom he resembled when young. ("Checker" because he checked with him, or resembled him.) The nickname is said to have been bestowed by the wife of U.S. pop promoter Dick Clark.

Cheiro: [Count] Louis Hamon (1866–1936), Br. writer on palmistry. From the Greek element that gives the word "cheiromancy," otherwise palmistry, Greek *cheir* meaning "hand."

Antosha **Chekhonte:** Anton Pavlovich Chekhov (1860–1904), Russ. short story writer, dramatist. The name was humorously given to the young Anton by Father Pokrovsky, his scripture teacher at school in Taganrog, and Chekhov adopted it for several early, lighter writings in various magazines. In 1886 he wrote to the noted journalist Suvorin: "The pseudonym 'A. Chekhonte' may seem somewhat weird and recherché, but it arose back in the hazy days of my youth. I have grown accustomed to it, and so no longer regard it as strange." Father Pokrovsky did not select only Chekhov for this treatment, however; he liked giving amusing names to his students generally.

Pierre **Chenal:** Pierre Cohen (1903–   ), Fr. film director.

Cher: Cherilyn Sarkasian LaPier (1946–   ), U.S. pop singer, film actress, formerly teaming with husband Sonny *(q.v.)*.

Rose **Chéri:** Rose-Marie Cizos (1824–1861), Fr. actress.

Gwen **Cherrell:** Gwen Chambers (1926–), Eng. stage actress.

Weatherby **Chesney:** Charles John Cutliffe Wright Hyne (1865–1944), Eng. fiction writer.

Peter **Cheyney:** Reginald Evelyn Peter Southhouse-Cheyney (1896–1951), Ir. crime novelist.

Walter **Chiari:** Walter Annichiarico (1924–), It. film comedian.

Chief Thundercloud: [1] Victor Daniels (1899–1955), U.S. Indian film actor; [2] Scott Williams (1901–1967), U.S. radio, film actor, of Indian descent.

Charles B. **Childs:** Charles Vernon Frost (1903–), Eng. mystery writer.

Alice **Cholmondeley:** Elizabeth *(q.v.)*.

Linda **Christian:** Blanca Rosa Welter (1923–), Mexican film actress.

Christian-Jaque: Christian Albert François Maudet (1904–), Fr. film director, writer.

Lou **Christie:** Geno Lugee Salo (1943–), U.S. (male) pop singer.

John **Christopher:** Christopher Sam Youd (1922–), Eng. SF short story writer, novelist.

June **Christy:** Shirley Luster (1925–), U.S. jazz singer.

Korney Ivanovich **Chukovsky:** Nikolay Vasilyevich Korneychuk (1882–1969), Russ. critic, poet. The writer used his surname to form a new first and last name, employing his pseudonym before the 1917 Revolution.

Chung Ling Soo: William Ellsworth Campbell (1861–1918), U.S. conjuror. He modelled himself on a real Chinese conjuror, Ching Ling Foo, who had toured successfully in the U.S. Ching accused Campbell of being an impostor, and he admitted it. However, this impersonation made him all the more popular with his audiences. On first performing, Campbell had used the name "William E. Robinson."

Marcus Tullius **Cicero:** William Melmoth the Elder (1666–1743), Eng. religious writer, lawyer. The three-part name was the full one of the famous Roman orator.

The **Cid:** Rodrigo Diaz de Bivar (?1040–1099), Sp. national hero. The name, also familiar as "El Cid," was the popular one given to the military leader, and it represents Spanish Arabic *as-sıd,* "the lord."

Cimabue: Bencivieni di Pepo (or Benvenuto di Giuseppe) (before 1251–1302), It. painter, mosaicist. The name reveals something of the artist's proud and impetuous nature. It arose as a nickname, and means effectively "Bullheaded," from Italian *cima,* "top," "head," and *bue,* "ox."

Paul **Cinquevalli:** Paul Kestner (1859–1918), Pol.-born U.S. juggler. The performer adopted the name of his tutor in the art, Cinquevalli.

A **Citizen of New York:** Alexander Hamilton (1737–1804), U.S. statesman + James Madison (1751–1836), U.S. president + John Jay (1745–1829), U.S. jurist, statesman. The three men adopted the unified name for their essays in the *Federalist* in favor of the new U.S. Constitution (1787–1788). They subsequently adopted the joint name Publius *(q.v.)*.

René **Clair:** René-Lucien Chomette (1898–1981), Fr. film director. The famous director first adopted the name as an actor in 1920. No doubt he wanted to avoid the undesirable associations of the name Chomette, which to a French ear suggests being out of work *(chômeur,* "unemployed person").

Ina **Claire:** Ina Fagan (1892–1985), U.S. stage, film actress.

Mlle **Clairon:** Claire-Josèphe-Hippolyte Léris de la Tude (1723–1803), Fr. tragic actress. "Clairon" not only suggests the actress's first name, but is meaningful in French as the word for "bugle."

Ada **Clare:** Jane McElheney (1836–1874), U.S. writer of passionate poetry and fiction.

Claribel: Charlotte Alington-Barnard (1830–1869), Ir. writer of popular ballads. The name occurs occasionally for characters in classical literature, suggests both "clear" and "beautiful" (as the voice or words of a balladeer should be), and also represents the writer's full real name.

Clarín: Leopoldo Alas (1852–1901), Sp. novelist, critic. The writer's pen name means "bugle," and refers to his prominent critical "voice." As a critic, Alas was one of the most influential of his time, and his articles were noted for their biting and belligerent style.

Clarinda: Agnes Maclehose, née Craig (1759–1841), Sc. correspondent of Sylvander *(q.v.)*. Both names are typical of classical literature. Clarinda occurs in Spenser's *Faerie Queene*, for example.

Dane **Clark:** Bernard Zanville (1913–   ), U.S. film actor.

The Rev. T. **Clark:** John Galt (1779–1839), Sc. novelist. The novelist used the name for *The Wandering Jew* (1820). For the really astute reader, he encoded his actual surname in the initial letters of the words beginning the book's last four sentences. These were "Greatness," "All," "Literally," "To."

John **Clarke:** Richard Cromwell (1626–1712), Eng. soldier, politician. Richard Cromwell, eldest son of Oliver Cromwell, used this name for living in seclusion in Paris from 1659 to 1680.

Mae **Clarke:** Violet Klotz (1907–   ), U.S. film actress.

Madame **Claude:** Fernande Grudet (1924–   ), Fr. procureuse.

Claude Lorrain: Claude Gellée (1600–1682), Fr. landscape painter. "Lorrain" is not the painter's surname, as sometimes supposed, but represents Lorraine, the region of France where he was born and where, for a short period in 1625, he worked. The name distinguished him from other artists named Claude.

Mrs. Mary **Clavers:** Caroline Matilda Kirkland, née Stansbury (1801–1864), U.S. short story writer, novelist.

Bertha M. **Clay:** Charlotte Monica Braeme (1836–1884), Eng. author of romantic novels. It may be unintentional, but all except one of the letters in the writer's pseudonym can be found in her real full name. (And all letters if one counts "i" as "y.")

Richard **Clayderman:** Philippe Pages (1954–   ), Fr. popular pianist. The pianist's name was altered by composers and record producers Olivier Toussaint and Paul de Senneville to one that could not be mispronounced abroad. But why clumsy "Clayderman"?

Lucie **Clayton:** Evelyn Florence Kark, née Gordine (1928–   ), Eng. fashion designer.

Jedediah **Cleishbotham:** [Sir] Walter Scott (1771–1832), Sc. poet, novelist. One of the humorous pen names devised by the great Scottish writer. (Others were

Chrystal Croftangry and Captain Cuthbert Clutterbuck.) This particular name was used for the four series of his *Tales of My Landlord* (1816), with the author supposedly a schoolmaster and parish clerk. The name ties in well with these two occupations: "Jedediah" is a typical Puritan name, and "Cleishbotham" means "whipbottom" (Scottish dialect *cleish*, "to whip").

Clement II: Suidger (? –1047), It. pope.

Clement III: Paolo Scolari (? –1191), It. pope.

Clement IV: Guy le Gros Folques (? –1268), Fr. pope.

Clement V: Bertrand de Got (*c*.1260–1314), Fr. pope.

Clement VI: Pierre Roger (1291–1352), Fr. pope.

Clement VII: Giulio de' Medici (1478–1534), It. pope.

Clement VIII: Ippolito Aldobrandini (1536–1605), It. pope.

Clement IX: Giulio Rospigliosi (1600–1669), It. pope.

Clement X: Emilio Bonaventura Altieri (1590–1676), It. pope.

Clement XI: Giovan Francesco Albani (1649–1721), It. pope.

Clement XII: Lorenzo Corsini (1652–1740), It. pope.

Clement XIII: Carlo della Torre Rezzonico (1693–1769), It. pope.

Clement XIV: Giovanni Vincenzo Antonio Ganganelli (1705–1774), It. pope.

Hal **Clement:** Harry Clement Stubbs (1922–   ), U.S. SF writer.

E. **Clerihew:** Edmund Clerihew Bentley (1875–1956), Eng. writer, inventor of the *clerihew*. The writer's unusual second name, which he used as a pen name and which has now passed into the language in its own right, was the maiden name of his mother.

Jimmie **Cliff:** James Chambers (1948–   ), Jamaican pop singer ("reggae's first superstar").

Laddie **Cliff:** Clifford Perry: (1891–1937), Br. film comedian, composer.

Charles **Clifford:** William Henry Ireland (1777–1835), Eng. Shakespearean forger.

Martin **Clifford:** Frank Richards *(q.v.)*.

Patsy **Cline:** Virginia Patterson Hensley (1932–1963), U.S. country singer.

Clio: [1] Joseph Addison (1672–1719), Eng. poet, dramatist, essayist; [2] Thomas Rickman (1761–1834), Eng. bookseller, reformer. These two names have different origins. For [1], the letters of the name were taken to represent "*C*helsea, London, *I*slington, the *O*ffice," as being the places where Addison lived and worked. (He was a civil servant, so that "Office" means "government office.") But the letters could equally represent his initials in a signature. And of course they also stand for the name of Clio, the Muse of History, which was the sense chosen for [2]. It arose as a nickname when he was a student, for his precocity as a poet and his taste for historical subjects.

Colin **Clive:** Colin Clive-Greig (1898–1937), Br. film actor, working in U.S.

Kitty **Clive:** Catherine Raftor (1711–1785), Eng. actress. Not exactly a pseudonym, but the actress's married name. Her short-lived marriage was to George Clive, a barrister, and she kept his name as a stage name.

Clodion: Claude Michel (1738–1814), Fr. sculptor. The artist fashioned his first name into a classical mold.

Anacharsis **Cloots:** Jean-Baptiste du Val-de-Grace, Baron de Cloots (1755–1794), Fr. revolutionary, of Prussian descent. The self-styled "Orator of the human race" chose a name that punningly mocked his aristocratic ancestry, for Greek *anacharsis* means "graceless."

Upton **Close:** Josef Washington Hall (1894–1960), U.S. journalist, novelist. When the journalist held a government post in Shantung (1916–1919), he learned of the Japanese invasion and put "up close" on his messages to indicate his position near the front. This notation later produced his pen name.

Frank **Clune:** Francis Patrick (1909–1971), Austral. author.

June **Clyde:** June Tetrazini (1909–   ), U.S. film actress, singer, dancer.

Lee J. **Cobb:** Leo Jacoby (1911–1976), U.S. stage, film actor. The stage and screen name derive from the actor's real name, dropping the final "y."

William **Cobb:** Jules Hippolyte Lermina (1839–1915), Fr. novelist.

Charles **Coburn:** Colin Whitton McCallum (1852–1945), Sc.-born Br. music hall comedian. The artiste took his name from the Coburn Road, east London. He should not be confused with Charles D. Coburn, the U.S. actor and manager, who was his virtual contemporary.

Pindar **Cockloft:** William Irving (1766–1821), U.S. poet.

Coco: Nikolai Poliakov (1900–1974), Russ.-born Eng. circus clown. The much-loved clown's ring name represents the "-ko-" syllable that is found in each of his real names. "Coco" has now become a popular name for any clown, both in English-speaking countries and elsewhere. There was another Coco (more precisely "Koko") as a well-known Russian clown who was a virtual contemporary of Poliakov. His real name was Alfons Frantsevich Luts (1885–1945).

Commander **Cody:** George Frayne (*c.*1940–   ), U.S. rock musician.

Lew **Cody:** Louis Joseph Cote (1884–1934), Fr.-born U.S. film actor.

Captain **Coe:** Tom Cosgrove (1902–1978), Eng. sports writer, editor.

Joshua **Coffin:** Henry Wadsworth Longfellow (1807–1882), U.S. poet.

Emile **Cohl:** Emile Courte (1857–1938), Fr. film cartoonist.

Claudette **Colbert:** Lily Claudette Chauchoin (1905–   ), Fr. stage, film actress, working in U.S.

Nat "King" **Cole:** Nathaniel Adams Coles (1919–1965), U.S. singer, jazz pianist. The musician's own name, with his nickname of "King," plus the name of his group, the King Cole Trio, resulted in a performing name that was additionally associated with the "Old King Cole" of the children's nursery rhyme. Nathaniel Coles dropped the "s" of his name in 1937, when he formed his trio.

Cy **Coleman:** Seymour Kaufman (1929–   ), U.S. popular musician.

Manning **Coles:** Adelaide Frances Oke Manning (1891–1959), Eng. spy, detective novelist + Cyril Henry Coles (1901–1965), Eng. spy, detective novelist, her husband. A fairly uncommon combination of two surnames to make a united first name and surname.

Colette: Sidonie-Gabrielle Claudine Colette (1873–1954), Fr. novelist. A single name that suggests a first name rather than the surname that it actually is. The writer's early books were written under the pen name of her husband, Willy *(q.v.)*.

She used her own name, in combination with his (as Colette-Willy), for *Dialogues de Bêtes* (1904). She divorced Willy two years later, but continued to write as Colette-Willy until 1916, after which she wrote as Colette alone.

Bonar **Colleano:** Bonar William Sullivan II (1924–1958), U.S. film actor. The adopted surname seems to have evolved somehow from "Sullivan."

Constance **Collier:** Laura Constance Hardie (1878–1955), Eng. stage, film actress.

Lois **Collier:** Madelyn Jones (1919–   ), U.S. film actress.

Patience **Collier:** René Collier, née Ritcher (1910–1987), Eng. stage actress.

William **Collier:** William Senior (1866–1944), U.S. stage, film actor.

Michael **Collins:** Dennis Lynds (1924–   ), U.S. mystery writer, journalist.

Sam **Collins:** Samuel Thomas Collins Vagg (1827–1865), Eng. music hall singer, manager.

Tom **Collins:** Joseph Furphy (1843–1912), Austral. novelist. It is not impossible that the novelist took his pen name from the cocktail. At least, it is historically possible.

Tommy **Collins:** Leonard Raymond Sipes (1930–   ), U.S. country singer.

Carlo **Collodi:** Carlo Lorenzini (1826–1890), It. writer. The author of *Le Avventure di Pinocchio* (1883) took his pen name from his mother's birthplace. He himself was born in Florence.

Bud **Collyer:** Clayton Johnson Heermanse, Jr. (1908–1969), U.S. TV personality, brother of June Collyer *(q.v.)*.

June **Collyer:** Dorothy Heermanse (1907–1968), U.S. film actress.

Colon: Joseph Dennie (1768–1812), U.S. essayist, satirist, collaborating with Spondee *(q.v.)*.

Jessi **Colter:** Miriam Johnson (c.1940–   ), U.S. country singer. The singer claimed to have an ancestor Jessi Colter who was a member of the Jesse James Gang. She therefore adopted his name as her stage name.

Coluche: Michel Gérard Josèphe Colucci (1944–1986), Fr. radio, stage, film comedian, of It. parentage.

Christopher **Columbus:** Joseph C. Morris (1903–   ), U.S. black jazz drummer, bandleader.

Silas Tomkyn **Comberback:** Samuel Taylor Coleridge (1772–1834), Eng. poet, critic. The name was used by the poet, retaining his initials, when he enlisted in the army (15th Dragoons) in 1793.

Betty **Comden:** Elizabeth Kyle, née Cohen (1918–   ), U.S. film, stage writer, actress.

Jan Ámos **Comenius:** Jan Ámos Komenský (1592–1670), Czech educationist, Moravian bishop.

Cuthbert **Comment:** Abraham Tucker (1705–1774), Eng. moralist. For the occasion of this pleasant name, see Edward **Search.**

Perry **Como:** Pierino Roland Como, formerly Nick Perido (1912–   ), It.-U.S. crooner, film actor.

Fay **Compton:** Virginia Lillian Emmeline Compton Mackenzie (1894–1978), Br. stage actress, sister of author Compton Mackenzie (1883–1972).

Frances Snow Compton: Henry Brooks Adams (1838–1918), U.S. historian, novelist.

Joyce Compton: Eleanor Hunt (1907–   ), U.S. film actress.

Comus: Robert Michael Ballantyne (1825–1894), Sc. novelist for boys. Comus was the name of the pagan god invented by Milton for his pastoral entertainment ("masque") of the name (1634).

Confucius: K'ung Fu-tze (*c.*551–479 BC), Chin. philosopher, teacher of ethics. "Confucius" is the westernized (latinized) form of the philosopher's name, which itself means "Master K'ung," K'ung being his family name.

Chester **Conklin:** Jules Cowles (1888–1971), U.S. film actor.

F. Norreys **Connell:** Conal Holmes O'Connell O'Riordan (1874–1948), Ir. dramatist, novelist.

John **Connell:** John Henry Robertson (1909–1965), Br. novelist, biographer.

Rearden **Conner:** Patrick Reardon Connor (1907–   ), Ir. novelist, short story writer.

Ralph **Connor:** Charles William Gordon (1860–1937), Can. writer of religious novels. The novelist intended to use the name "Cannor," from the letter heading "Brit. Can. Nor. West Mission," but his editor copied this as "Connor" and added "Ralph" to give a full name.

Michael **Connors:** Kreker Jay Michael Ohanian (1925–   ), U.S. film, TV actor, of Armenian parentage.

Owen **Conquest:** Frank Richards *(q.v.).*

Con **Conrad:** Conrad K. Dober (1893–1938), U.S. songwriter.

Jess **Conrad:** Gerald James (1936–   ), Br. pop singer.

Joseph **Conrad:** Jósef Teodor Konrad Nałęcz Korzeniowski (1857–1924), Pol.-born Br. novelist, writing in English. Conrad became a British naturalized subject in 1886 and anglicized his first and third names.

Robert **Conrad:** Conrad Robert Falk (1935–   ), U.S. TV, film actor.

Will **Conroy:** Harry Champion (1866–1942), Eng. music hall comedian.

Michael **Constantine:** Constantine Joanides (1927–   ), Gk.-born U.S. TV, film actor.

Albert **Conti:** Albert de Conti Cedassamre (1887–   ), Austr. film actor.

Gloria **Contreras:** Carmen Gloria Contreras Roeniger (1934–   ), Mexican ballet dancer, teacher.

Gary **Conway:** Gareth Carmody (1938–   ), U.S. film, TV actor.

Hugh **Conway:** Frederick John Fargus (1847–1895), Eng. novelist.

Russ **Conway:** Trevor Stanford (1927–   ), Eng. popular musician.

Shirl **Conway:** Shirley Crossman (1914–   ), U.S. TV actress.

Tom **Conway:** Thomas Charles Sanders (1904–1967), Eng. film actor.

William Augustus **Conway:** William Augustus Rugg (1789–1828), Ir. actor.

Coo-ee: William Sylvester Walker (1846–   ), Austral. novelist. "Coo-ee" was (and is) the traditional Australian bush call.

Susan **Coolidge:** Sarah Chauncy Woolsey (1845–1905), U.S. writer of books for girls. The author of *What Katy Did* (1872) and subsequent stories based her pen name on that of her sister, who called herself "Margaret Coolidge."

Alice **Cooper:** Vincent Furnier (1948–   ), U.S. pop singer. The feminine name was chosen by the "shock-horror" performer in 1969 to illustrate his theory that "people are both male and female biologically." A session with a Ouija board allegedly indicated that Alice Cooper had been a seventeenth-century witch, who was now reincarnated as Furnier.

Frank **Cooper:** William Gilmore Simms (1806–1870), U.S. novelist.

Gary **Cooper:** Frank J. Cooper (1901–1961), U.S. film actor. How come that "Coop" changed "Frank" for "Gary"? The metamorphosis was the work of his Hollywood agent, Nan Collins. She came from Gary, Indiana. She explained "'My home town was named after Elbert H. Gary. I think Gary has a nice poetic sound to it. I'd like to see you take Elbert Gary's last name for your first. 'You mean,' he interrupted, 'Gary Cooper?' 'Yes – Gary Cooper. Say it again. Gary Cooper. Very nice. I like it. Don't you?' Gary Cooper. He ran the name around in his mind a few times. He spoke it again, 'Gary Cooper.' Then he smiled. 'I like it.' 'You see,' Miss Collins said. 'I knew you would. And you'll have to agree, Gary Cooper doesn't sound as tall and lanky as Frank Cooper'" [George Carpozi, Jr., *The Gary Cooper Story,* 1971]. By assuming the name, the actor gave the name a popular boost to make it one of the most common first names of the mid-twentieth century.

Jackie **Cooper:** John Cooperman, Jr. (1921–   ), U.S. film actor.

Jefferson **Cooper:** Gardner Francis Fox (1911–   ), U.S. writer of historical romances.

William **Cooper:** Harry Summerfield Hoff (1910–   ), Ir. novelist. He was obliged to choose another name for his writings when employed as a civil servant.

Joan **Copeland:** Joan Maxine Miller (1922–   ), U.S. stage actress, singer.

Coram: Thomas Whitaker (1883–1937), Eng. ventriloquist. Latin *coram* means "openly," "in public." A ventriloquist is a paradoxical performer; he conceals his voice, but does so for public entertainment.

Le **Corbusier:** Charles Edouard Jeanneret (1887–1965), Fr. architect, of Swiss descent. The precise reason for the architect's adoption of this particular name is not clear. It may well have been a family name. But a story tells how Jeanneret nicknamed a cousin "Le Corbeau" because of his resemblance to a crow (French *corbeau),*and that the name originated from that. Corbusier exists in its own right as a French (Walloon) name, meaning "shoemaker."

Ellen **Corby:** Ellen Hansen (1913–   ), U.S. film actress.

Alex **Cord:** Alexander Viespi (1931–   ), It.-born U.S. film actor.

Mara **Corday:** Marilyn Watts (1932–   ), U.S. film actress. It is possible that Marilyn Watts was influenced in her choice of acting name by that of the Swiss actress Paule Corday, who also used the names Rita Corday and Paula Corday. There was also Charlotte Corday, the French revolutionary. But she is hardly likely to have been the inspiration for the name. "Mara" represents "Marilyn," of course.

El **Cordobés:** Manuel Benítez Pérez (*c.*1936–   ), Sp. bullfighter. The bullfighter's ring name means "the Cordoba man." However, he was not born in Cordoba, but in Palma del Rio. The name came, it is said, from a monument in Cordoba to the great matador Manolete *(q.v.),* from whom Benítez derived his inspiration to excel in the bullring.

Raymond **Cordy:** Raymond Cordiaux (1898–1956), Fr. film comedian.

Marie **Corelli:** Mary Mackay (1855–1924), Br. novelist. The novelist Mary (or Minnie) Mackay was of illegitimate birth, and knowing this created the myth that her father, actually Charles Mackay, a songwriter, was Italian. In a letter to *Blackwood's Magazine* she thus claimed to be "a Venetian, and a direct descendant (through a long line of ancestry) of the great Michael Angelo Corelli, the famous composer." Mary chose the name initially for a possible musical career, with a second choice of name being "Rose Trevor." Earlier she had written as "Vivian Earle Clifford." Arcangelo Corelli (rather than Michael Angelo) was a real enough person, and an Italian violin virtuoso and composer of the seventeenth and early eighteenth century [Brian Masters, *Now Barabbas Was a Rotter: The Extraordinary Life of Marie Corelli*, 1978].

Jill **Corey:** Norman Jean Speranza (1935–   ), U.S. pop singer.

Lewis **Corey:** Louis C. Fraina (1894–1953), U.S. Marxist critic.

Don **Cornell:** Dominico Francisco Connello (1921–   ), U.S. popular singer.

Corno di Bassetto: George Bernard Shaw (1856–1950), Ir. dramatist, critic, novelist. Shaw used the waggish name when writing as a music critic for *The Star* (1888–1890). The corno di bassetto is (in its Italian notation, familiar in music scores) the basset horn, which two words suggest "Bernard Shaw."

Barry **Cornwall:** Bryan Waller Procter (1787–1874), Eng. poet, songwriter. The name chosen by the poet for his work is a near anagram of his real name, give or take a few letters.

Correggio: Antonio Allegri (da Correggio) (1494–1534), It. painter. As was the tradition of his day, the painter adopted the name of his birthplace (which was also the town where he died). Correggio is in northern Italy, near Reggio.

Adrienne **Corri:** Adrienne Riccoboni (1930–   ), Sc. film actress, of It. descent. The actress was renamed by Gordon Harbord, who also renamed Laurence Harvey and who nearly gave Diana Dors another name. The letters of "Corri" come from the actress's real name. Presumably Harbord selected a name like this, rather than the more obvious "Ricci," for unambiguity of pronunciation.

Ray "Crash" **Corrigan:** Ray Benard (1903–1976), U.S. film actor.

Ricardo **Cortez:** Jacob Krantz (1899–1977), U.S. film actor, brother of Stanley Cortez *(q.v.)*.

Stanley **Cortez:** Stanley Krantz (1908–   ), U.S. cinematographer.

Baron **Corvo:** Frederick William Serafino Austin Lewis Mary Rolfe (1860–1913), Br. writer. The idiosyncratic author claimed to have received the title of Baron Corvo from the Duchess Sforza-Cesarini when living in Italy in the 1880s – a claim that has been neither confirmed nor disproved. The enigmatic writer himself gave three versions of the origin of his pseudonym: that it was a style offered and accepted for use as a *tekhnikym* or trade name when he denied sacred orders and sought a secular livelihood, that it came from a village near Rome and was assumed when he was made a baron by the Bishop of Emmaus, who was on a visit to Rome, and that it was bestowed by the aforementioned duchess. Rolfe had other pseudonyms, as "Frederick Austin," "King Clement," and "Fr. Rolfe." He wrote autobiographically as "Nicholas Crabbe" in *Nicholas Crabbe* and *The*

Desire and Pursuit of the Whole, and as "George Arthur Rose" in (and as) *Hadrian the Seventh. Corvo* is Italian for "raven," moreover, and he had already adopted the raven as a heraldic device. (Perhaps Crabbe has a similar symbolic significance.) George Arthur Rose is said to derive from St. George "of the Roses" and Duke Arthur (of Brittany) murdered by King John in 1203. In C.S. Lewis's *That Hideous Strength* there is a jackdaw called Baron Corvo [1. A.J.A. Symons, *The Quest for Corvo,* 1940; 2. Donald Weeks, *Corvo,* 1971].

Michael **Costa:** Michele Andrea Agniello (1808–1884), It. opera composer, of Sp. descent, working in U.K.

Elvis **Costello:** Declan McManus (1954–   ), Br. rock singer, songwriter. When his parents divorced and separated, Declan McManus took his mother's maiden name, Costello, and moved with her from London to Liverpool. He then returned to London and sang as a solo singer in folk clubs as "D.P. Costello." In 1977 Jake Riviera signed him for Stiff Records and gave him the name Elvis, for Elvis Presley, if only so that he could promote him with the Presley slogan, "Elvis is King." The singer's original name is Irish in origin.

Lou **Costello:** Louis Cristillo (1906–1959), U.S. film comedian, teaming with Bud Abbott *(q.v.).*

A.V. **Coton:** Edward Haddakin (1906–1969), Eng. ballet, critic, writer.

François **Coty:** Francesco Giuseppe Spoturno (1874–1934), Corsican-born Fr. perfume manufacturer.

Johnny **Cougar:** John Cougar Mellencamp (1951–   ), U.S. rock singer.

Nicole **Courcel:** Nicole Andrieux (1930–   ), Fr. film actress.

George Victor Marcel **Courteline:** Georges Victor Marcel Moinaux (1858–1929), Fr. humorist, dramatist.

Peregrine **Courtenay:** Winthrop Mackworth Praed (1802–1839), Eng. poet. The names have an aristocratic ring for a Cambridge man, as Praed was.

Jerome **Courtland:** Jerome Jourolmon (1926–   ), U.S. film actor.

John **Coventry:** John Williamson Palmer (1825–1906), U.S. journalist.

Joe **Cowell:** Joseph Leathley Hawkins-Witchett (1792–1863), Eng. stage comic, working in U.S.

Jane **Cowl:** Grace Bailey (1883–1950), U.S. playwright, stage, film actress.

Richard **Cowper:** Colin Middleton Murry (1926–   ), Eng. SF writer.

Charles Egbert **Craddock:** Mary Noailles Murfree (1850–1922), U.S. novelist, short story writer. Mary Murfree, who wrote novels and short stories in dialect, took her (masculine) name from that of the hero of an early story in *Appleton's Journal.* It was not until 1885, the year after the publication of her first collection of stories, *In the Tennessee Mountains,* that the editor of the *Atlantic Monthly,* to which she contributed, discovered the author of the tales of mountaineers and their hard life to be in reality a frail, crippled spinster.

A.A. **Craig:** Poul William Anderson (1926–   ), U.S. SF writer.

Alisa **Craig:** Charlotte Macleod (1922–   ), U.S. thriller writer.

Gordon **Craig:** Henry Edward Godwin Terry (1872–1966), Br. stage actor, designer, producer. The actor was the illegitimate son of the actress Ellen Terry and Edwin Godwin, an architect. He was known as Edward Godwin until his mother married (1877) the actor Charles Wardell, when he became Edward Wardell. Ten years later his mother renamed him Henry, for the great Scottish actor, Henry Irving, and Gordon for her friend, Lady Gordon. Craig came from the Scottish island Ailsa Craig, a name which appealed to her. "What a magnificent name for an actress!" she said.

James **Craig:** John Meador (1912–1985), U.S. film actor.

Michael **Craig:** Michael Gregson (1928–   ), Eng. film actor.

Lucas **Cranach** (the Elder): Lucas Müller (1472–1553), Ger. painter. The painter adopted the name of his birthtown, Cranach (now Kronach, West Germany). He first indicated his adoption of the name by signing his painting *Rest on the Flight into Egypt* (1504) as "LC." His son, Lucas Cranach the Younger (1515–1586), kept the name.

Phyllis **Crane:** Phyllis Francis (1912–   ), U.S. film actress.

Vincent **Crane:** Vincent Rodney Cheesman (1943–   ), Eng. rock musician.

Hawes **Craven:** Henry Hawes Craven Green (1837–1910), Eng. theatre scene-painter.

Joan **Crawford:** Lucille Le Sueur (1904–1977), U.S. film actress. The actress first appeared in a film (1925) under her real name ("Well, honey, you certainly picked a fancy one," a Hollywood producer is alleged to have commented, when she told him her name). She was soon to become Billie Cassin, however, Cassin being her stepfather's name. Later the same year (1925) she acquired her lasting stage name of Joan Crawford. This was as the result of a sponsored contest in *Movie Weekly*, with $1,000 offered in prizes. The top prize of $500 would go to the person who could find a name "simple to pronounce," "euphonious," and one to match her personality—"energetic, ambitious and typically American." The contest closed on May 2, 1925. The winning name was Joan Arden (nicely suggesting "ardent"), and Billie duly assumed the name. Only a week later, however, this was discovered to be the name of an extra, so the second-prize name was chosen instead. Joan was not too keen on the surname, complaining that it sounded like "crawfish." Film actor William Haines commented: "You're lucky it isn't cranberry—you could be dished up every Thanksgiving with the turkey." But the name brought fame (Lucille Le Sueur had been thought "contrived" and "too theatrical") [Joan Crawford with Jane Kesner Ardmore, *A Portrait of Joan: The Autobiography of Crawford*, 1963].

Kathryn **Crawford:** Kathryn Crawford Moran (1908–   ), U.S. film actress.

Michael **Crawford:** Michael Dumbell Smith (1942–   ), Eng. stage, film, TV actor. The actor initially adopted his step-father's name, calling himself Michael Ingram. He then opted for a more distinctive stage name, and selected "Crawford" from a passing biscuit truck in 1965. He subsequently adopted this name legally.

Captain **Crawley:** George Frederick Pardon (1924–1884), Eng. writer on sports, pastimes. The writer adopted the literary name of Sir Pitt Crawley, the coarse, brutal, wife-bullying old man in Thackeray's *Vanity Fair*. It is not clear to what extent he actually wished to identify himself with the character's disagreeable nature.

Geoffrey **Crayon:** Washington Irving (1783–1859), U.S. humorous writer. Irving used the name for *The Sketch Book* (1819–1820), a collection of familiar essays and tales. The pen name is appropriate for the title of the work.

Joseph **Crehan:** Charles Wilson (1884–1966), U.S. film actor.

Kid **Creole:** August Darnell *(q.v.)*.

Dormer **Creston:** Dorothy Julia Colston-Baynes (*c.*1900–   ), Br. biographer. The writer seems to have deliberately selected a sexually ambiguous pen name. "Dormer" occurs as a surname in a number of fictional works, such as the schoolmaster in Hugh Walpole's *Mr. Perrin and Mr. Traill* (1911). Of course, "Dormer Creston" also suggests "Dorothy Colston," the author's real name.

Paul **Creston:** Joseph Guttoveggio (1906–   ), U.S. composer.

Paul **Creyton:** John Townsend Trowbridge (1827–1916), U.S. novelist, poet, author of books for boys.

Otis **Criblecolis:** W.C. Fields *(q.v.)*.

Jimmy **Cricket:** James Mulgrew (1945–   ), Ir.-born Br. TV entertainer. The comedian undoubtedly based his name on the interjection of surprise, "jiminy cricket!"

Edmund **Crispin:** Robert Bruce Montgomery (1921–1978), Eng. crime, SF writer, musical composer. The writer composed music under his own name, leaving this pseudonym for his crime and SF fiction. The pen name appears to be composed of two saints' names, St. Edmund and St. Crispin, who may possibly have had some significance for the writer.

Peter **Criss:** Peter Crisscoula (1947–   ), U.S. rock musician.

Linda **Cristal:** Victoria Maya (1936–   ), Mexican film actress, working in U.S.

Estil **Critchie:** Arthur J. Burks (1898–1974), U.S. fantasy fiction writer.

Richmal **Crompton:** Richmal Crompton Lamburn (1890–1969), Eng. (female) author of books for boys.

Richard **Cromwell:** [1] Richard Williams (–   ), Welsh great-grandfather of Oliver Cromwell; [2]Roy Radabaugh (1910–1960), U.S. film actor. With regard to [1], the *Dictionary of National Biography* records that the father of Oliver Cromwell (1599–1658) was the "grandson of a certain Richard Williams, who rose to fortune by the protection of Thomas Cromwell, earl of Essex, and adopted the name of his patron." Richard Williams's own father was Morgan Williams, a Welsh farmer from Glamorganshire, who married Thomas Cromwell's elder sister, Katherine. Thomas Cromwell's dates are usually given as (?1485–1540). (See also p. 12.)

Hume **Cronyn:** Hume Blake (1911–   ), Can. film actor.

Bing **Crosby:** Harry Lillis Crosby (1904–1977), U.S. crooner, film actor. Harry Crosby enjoyed the comic strip "Bingville Bugle" as a kid, with its hero a character named Bing. Either because of his fondness for this character, or (some say) his resemblance to it, he was nicknamed "Bing" and later adopted the name.

David **Crosby:** David Van Cortland (1941–   ), U.S. rock singer.

Amanda **Cross:** Carolyn Heilbrun (1926–   ), U.S. detective fiction writer.

Christopher **Cross:** Christopher Geppert (*c.*1951–   ), U.S. pop singer. Obviously a mild pun on "criss-cross" is intended here.

Henri Edmond **Cross:** Henri Delacroix (1856–1910), Fr. neoimpressionist painter. Presumably the painter translated his name to promote his national name internationally.

Christopher **Crowfield:** Harriet Elizabeth Beecher Stowe (1811–1896), U.S.

novelist. The famous author of *Uncle Tom's Cabin* used the masculine name for some of her lesser writings.

Alfred **Crowquill:** Alfred Henry Forrester (1805–1872), Eng. illustrator, cartoonist + Charles Robert Forrester (1803–1850), Eng. illustrator, cartoonist, his brother. A crow quill is a special type of artist's pen, capable of drawing very fine lines. It was originally made from crows' quills.

James **Cruze:** Jens Cruz Bosen (1884–1942), U.S. film director, of Dan. parentage.

Guy **Cullingford:** Constance Lindsay Taylor (1907–   ), Br. detective novelist.

Constance **Cummings:** Constance Cummings Levy, née Halverstadt (1910–   ), U.S. stage, film actress. The actress's second name is her mother's maiden name.

Robert **Cummings:** Charles Clarence Robert Cummings (1910–   ), U.S. film actor. The actor's regular screen name is not as original as the one under which he passed himself off when he went to England to acquire the accent. For this purpose he was "Blade Stanhope Conway," and as such he succeeded in obtaining a part in Galsworthy's play *The Roof.*

Grace **Cunard:** Harriet Jeffries (1893–1967), U.S. film actress.

E.V. **Cunningham:** Howard Fast (1914–   ), U.S. mystery writer.

Le **Curé d'Ars:** Jean-Baptiste-Marie Vianney (1786–1859), Fr. Roman Catholic saint. The priest and saint gains his most familiar name from the village of Ars-en-Dombes, where he was in charge of the parish from 1817 to the end of his life.

Finlay **Currie:** Finlay Jefferson (1878–1968), Sc. stage, film actor.

Avon **Curry:** Jean Bowden (1920–   ), Sc. writer of romantic novels, thrillers.

Alan **Curtis:** Harold Neberroth (1909–1953), U.S. film actor.

Ken **Curtis:** Curtis Gates (1925–   ), U.S. TV actor.

Peter **Curtis:** Norah Lofts, née Robinson (1904–   ), Br. novelist.

Tony **Curtis:** Bernard Schwartz (1925–   ), U.S. film actor, of Hung. parentage. The actor's name change was proposed by Hollywood producer Bob Goldstein, who said: "Schwartz ain't a name to get you into the big time. Not even George Bernard Schwartz." Bernard had reckoned on being something like "Ricardo Cortez," but unfortunately there was already an actor of that name. After a process of elimination, therefore, Universal Pictures came up with "Anthony Curtis." The first name was soon shortened to "Tony" [Michael Munn, *The Kid from the Bronx: A Biography of Tony Curtis,* 1984].

Michael **Curtiz:** Mihály Kertész (1888–1962), Hung. film actor, working in U.S.

Cynddelw: Robert Ellis (1810–1875), Welsh poet. The Baptist minister adopted a traditional bardic name for his poetry. Cynddelw was the name of a famous twelfth-century Welsh court poet. The name itself means "chief form."

Morton **Da Costa:** Morton Tecosky (1914–   ), U.S. stage, musical, film director.

Dagmar: Virginia Ruth Enger (*c.*1930–   ), U.S. TV comedienne. Dagmar is a royal Danish name.

Dagonet: George Robert Sims (1847–1922), Br. writer. Dagonet was the name of King Arthur's fool in Malory's *Le Morte d'Arthur.*

Lil **Dagover:** Marta-Maria Daghofer, née Lillets (1897–1980), Javanese-born Ger. film actress, of Du. parentage.

Julian **D'Albie:** D'Albiac Luard (1892–1978), Ir.-born Eng. stage, radio, TV actor.

Charles **Dale:** Charles Marks (1881–1971), U.S. vaudeville, film actor.

Jim **Dale:** James Smith (1935–   ), Br. film actor, comedian.

Margaret **Dale:** Margaret Bolan (1922–   ), Br. ballet dancer, choreographer, TV director.

Cass **Daley:** Catherine Dailey (1915–1975), U.S. film comedienne.

Vernon **Dalhart:** Marion Try Slaughter (1883–1948), U.S. country singer.

Dalida: Yolande Christina Gigliotti (1933–1987), Egyptian-born Fr. film actress, singer. The actress was of Italian parentage, and her stage name may have been an affectionate form of her first name, Yolande, or else a form of Delilah, Samson's mistress in the Bible.

Marcel **Dalio:** Israel Moshe Blauschild (1900–1983), Fr. film comedian, working in U.S. The actor took his screen name from the character Prince Danilo, in Lehár's opera *The Merry Widow.*

John **Dall:** John Tenner Thompson (1918–1971), U.S. film actor.

Toti **Dal Monte:** Antonietta Meneghelli (1893–1975), It. opera singer. "Toti" is undoubtedly an affectional form of the singer's first name.

Charles **Dalmorès:** Henry Alphonse Brin (1871–1939), Fr. opera singer, working in U.S.

Lacy J. **Dalton:** Jill Byrem (1948–   ), U.S. country, rock singer.

Hamlin **Daly:** Edward Hoffman Price (1898–   ), U.S. adventure fiction writer.

Rann **Daly:** Edward Vance Palmer (1885–1959), Austral. writer.

Lili **Damita:** Lilliane Carré (1901–   ), Fr. film actress.

Stuart **Damon:** Stuart Michael Zonis (1937–   ), U.S. stage, TV actor, director.

Vic **Damone:** Vito Farinola (1929–   ), U.S. film actor, singer.

Claude **Dampier:** Claude Cowan (1885–1955), Br. stage, film comedian.

Dana: Rosemary Scallon, née Brown (1952–   ), Ir.-born Br. pop singer. The popular singer from Northern Ireland took her name from her nickname at school: Irish *dana* means "naughty," "mischievous." It also happens to be a first name (and even a surname) in its own right. The singer pronounces her name to rhyme with "Ghana," not "gainer."

Violet **Dana:** Viola Flugrath (1897–1987), U.A. film actress.

Frank **Danby:** Julia Frankau (1864–1916), Br. popular novelist.

Clemence **Dane:** Winifred Ashton (1888–1965), Eng. novelist, playwright. The writer took her name from the London church of St. Clement Danes, itself possibly so named as built on an ancient Danish burial site. Winifred Ashton first went on stage in 1913 under the name of "Diana Coris."

Hal **Dane:** Haldane M'Fall (1860–1928), Eng. soldier, author, art critic.

Karl **Dane:** Karl Daen (1886–1934), Dan. film actor.

John **Dangerfield:** Oswald Crawford (1834–1909), Eng. novelist, travel writer.

Mlle **Dangeville:** Marie-Anne Botot (1714–1796), Fr. actress.

Dangle: Alexander M. Thompson (1861–   ), Eng. journalist, editor. Dangle is a character in Sheridan's play *The Critic.*

Suzanne **Danielle:** Suzanne Morris (1957–), Eng. TV actress.

Bebe **Daniels:** Virginia Daniels (1901–1971), U.S. film actress, radio entertainer, teaming with husband Ben Lyon. The actress was originally Virginia Dougherty, and made her first screen appearance when she was still a virtual "baby." Ben Lyon changed her first name to "Bebe" (from "baby") and her surname to the smoother and more attractive "Daniels." The two worked together on radio and television in England. Some sources give the actress's original first names as Norma Jean.

Lisa **Daniely:** Elizabeth Bodington (1930–), Eng. film, TV actress. The actress used this stage name for what she defined as "sexy, undistinguished movies." She reverted to her real name in the 1970s with "a new middleaged persona," as she put it.

Gabriele **D'Annunzio:** Gabriele Rapagnetta (1863–1938), It. poet, novelist, dramatist. The writer was almost certainly capitalizing on his first name to refer to the Archangel Gabriel, who in the Bible story told Mary of the forthcoming birth of Jesus, this happening known as the Annunciation. Italian *annunzio* means "announcement."

Dante: Harry Jansen (1882–1955), Dan.-born U.S. conjuror. A name that combines a reference to the performer's nationality with a comic suggestion of the great Italian poet.

Michael **Dante:** Ralph Vitti (1931–), U.S. film director.

Helmut **Dantine:** Helmut Guttman (1917–1982), Austr. film actor, working in U.S.

Caleb **D'Anvers:** Nicholas Amhurst (1697–1742), Eng. poet, political writer. The writer used the name for the influential political journal, the *Craftsman*, which he edited from 1726.

Lorenzo **da Ponte:** Emmanuele Conegliano (1749–1838), It. opera librettist. The librettist of many of Mozart's most famous operas was born a Jew. On being converted to the Roman Catholic religion he took the name of the bishop who baptized him, Monsignor Lorenzo da Ponte, as was the custom then.

Kim **Darby:** Deborah Zenby (1947–), U.S. film actress.

Mireille **Darc:** Mireille Aigroz (1938–), Fr. film actress.

Denise **Darcel:** Denise Billecard (1925–), Fr. film actress, working in U.S. The actress extracted her new surname from her original one.

Alex **D'Arcy:** Alexander Sarruf (1908–), Egyptian film actor.

Roy **D'Arcy:** Roy F. Guisti (1894–), U.S. film actor.

Phyllis **Dare:** Phyllis Dones (1890–1975), Eng. musical comedy actress, sister of Zena Dare *(q.v.)*.

Simon **Dare:** Marjorie Huxtable (1897–), Br. author of romantic novels.

Zena **Dare:** Florence Hariette Zena Dones (1887–1975), Br. film actress.

Bobby **Darin:** Walden Robert Cassotto (1934–1973), U.S. pop singer, film actor. The singer found his new surname in a phone book.

Rubén **Darío:** Félix Rubén García Sarmiento (1867–1916), Nicaraguan poet, essayist. The poet's adopted second name is the Spanish for "Darius." Possibly he chose the name for the famous king of Persia, Darius the Great.

August **Darnell:** Thomas August Darnell Browder (1951–   ), U.S. rock singer, of Dominican/Fr.-Can. parentage. The singer is also familiar as King Creole, a name referring to his mixed parentage.

Linda **Darnell:** Monetta Eloyse Darnell (1921–1965), U.S. film actress.

Peter **Darrell:** Peter Skinner (1929–1987), Br. dancer, choreographer.

James **Darren:** James William Ercolani (1936–   ), U.S. film actor, pop singer.

Frankie **Darro:** Frank Johnson (1917–1976), U.S. film actor.

John **Darrow:** Harry Simpson (1907–   ), U.S. film actor.

Bella **Darvi:** Bayla Wegier (1927–1971), Pol.-Fr. film actress, working in U.S.

Jane **Darwell:** Patti Woodward (1880–1967), U.S. film actress. Patti Woodward claimed to have taken her acting name from "a character in fiction." But who was Jane Darwell?

Comtesse **Dash:** Marquise Gabrielle Saint-Mars (1804–1872), Fr. writer.

Howard **Da Silva:** Harold Silverblatt (1909–1978), U.S. film actor, director. A neat conversion of a German (Jewish) name into a Portuguese-style one, in the process turning a silver leaf (*Silberblatt*) into a bramble bush (*silva*)!

Jean **Dauberval** (or d'Auberval): Jean Bercher (1742–1806), Fr. ballet dancer, choreographer.

Claude **Dauphin:** Claude Legrand (1903–1978), Fr. stage, film actor.

Victor **d'Auverney:** Victor-Marie Hugo (1802–1885), Fr. novelist.

Dauvilliers: Nicolas Dorné (c.1646–1690), Fr. actor.

Lewis **Davenport:** George Ryan (1883–1916), Eng. conjuror.

Jocelyn **Davey:** Chaim Raphael (1908–   ), Eng. crime novelist.

Nina **Davey:** Margaret Symonds (1902-1977), Eng. stage actress.

Hugh **David:** David Williams Hughes (1925–1987), Welsh TV director.

Thayer **David:** David Thayer Hersey (1926–1978), U.S. film actor.

Lawrence H. **Davidson:** David Herbert Lawrence (1885–1930), Eng. novelist, short story writer. Although resembling his real name, this early pen name used by D.H. Lawrence derived from Davidson Road School, Croydon, where the future novelist taught for a brief period. Appropriately, he assumed the name for a school textbook, *Movements in European History* (1921).

Marion **Davies:** Marion Cecilia Douras (1897–1961), U.S. film actress.

Siobhan **Davies:** Sue Davies (1950–   ), Eng. ballet dancer, teacher, choreographer.

Gordon **Daviot:** Elizabeth Mackintosh (1897–1952), Br. novelist, playwright.

Billie **Davis:** Carol Hedges (1945–   ), Eng. (white) soul singer.

Danny **Davis:** George Nowlan (1925–   ), U.S. trumpeter, popular singer.

David **Davis:** William Eric Davis (1908–   ), Eng. broadcaster, children's radio storyteller.

Nancy **Davis:** Anne Frances Robbins (1923–   ), U.S film actress. "Nancy" was the actress's nickname from infancy (probably from "Anne Frances"). "Davis" was the name of her stepfather, a Chicago surgeon. And the lady herself is now of course Nancy Reagan, the former U.S. President's wife. The two married in 1952 when they were both Hollywood actors. Her school records, incidentally, give her date of birth as 1921.

Skeeter **Davis:** Mary Frances Penick (1931–   ), U.S. country singer. Mary Penick took her singing name from that of her schoolfriend, Betty Jack Davis, with whom she formed the Davis Sisters group in 1953 (and, who, sadly, was killed that year). "Skeeter" is the fairly common nickname (from "mosquito") for a person who "bites" or is energetic.

William **Davis:** Adolf Günther Kies (1933–   ), Ger.-born Eng. writer, editor. Possibly "Davis" was formed from "Adolf Kies," with the "f" serving for the "v."

Peter **Dawlish:** James Lennox Kerr (1899–1963), Br. writer of boating stories for boys. Dawlish is a coastal resort near the mouth of the Exe River in Devon.

Bobby **Day:** Robert Byrd (1934–   ), U.S. pop singer.

Dennis **Day:** Eugene Denis McNulty (1917–1988), U.S. film actor, singer, radio and TV entertainer.

Doris **Day:** Doris von Kappelhoff (1924–   ), U.S. film actress, singer. The new name was suggested for the actress by Barney Rapp, a Cincinnati band leader. At first, however, he wanted to rename her as "Doris Kapps," based on her real name. (He himself had similarly shortened his name, from Rappaport to Rapp.) But the final name to emerge was "Doris Day," based on the singer's well-known song, "Day After Day." This particular name, too, also symbolized a new career, a "new day." However, the actress never really came to enthuse about her name: "I never did like it. Still don't. I think it's a phony name," she would write [Doris Day and A.E. Hotchner, *The Sentimental Journey: Doris Day's Own Story*, 1976].

Frances **Day:** Frances Schenk (1908–1984), U.S. film actress.

Josette **Day:** Josette Dagory (1914–1978), Fr. film actress.

Laraine **Day:** Laraine Johnson (1917–   ), U.S. film actress. The actress adopted the name of her drama teacher, Elias Day.

Henri **de Alleber:** Henri de Lapomeraye (1839–1891), Fr. critic, lecturer.

Eddie **Dean:** Edgar Dean Glossop (?1908–   ), U.S. film actor.

Isabel **Dean:** Isabel Hodgkinson (1918–   ), Eng. stage, film actress.

James **Dean:** James Byron (1931–1955), U.S. film actor.

Jimmy **Dean:** Seth Ward (1928–   ), U.S. country singer. The age difference is probably small enough for the singer to have adopted the name of James Dean *(q.v.)*, otherwise Jimmy Dean, and in fact the movie actor was already making his name in the early 1950s, when Seth Ward was similarly starting his career as a singer.

Charles **Deane:** Edward Saunders (1866–1910), Eng. music hall singer, songwriter.

Colonel W. **de Basil:** Vassili Grigorievitch Voskresensky (1881–1951), Russ. impresario. "Vassili" is the Russian equivalent of "Basil."

Jean-Gaspard **Deburau:** Jan Kaspar Dvořák (1796–1846), Fr. pantomime actor, of Cz. parentage. A French rendering (but not translation) of the original Czech name.

Yvonne **de Carlo:** Peggy Yvonne Middleton (1922–   ), Can. film actress.

Eleanora **de Cisneros:** Eleanor Broadfoot (1878–1934), U.S. opera singer.

Arturo **de Cordova:** Arturo Garcia (1908–1973), Mexican film actor.

Dave **Dee:** David Harmon (1943–   ), Eng. pop singer, TV actor. "Dee" represents "David," the singer's first name, and originally arose as a school nickname. He first used the name on stage for his group Dave Dee and the Bostons. Later, this same group was reorganized under the cumbersome name of Dave Dee, Dozy, Beaky, Mick and Tich, those being the individual school nicknames of the classmates who formed it. (Dozy was Trevor Davies; Beaky was John Dymond; Mick was Michael Wilson; Tich was Ian Amey.) Dave Dee left the group in 1969.

Joey **Dee:** Joseph Dinicola (1940–   ), U.S. rock musician.

Kiki **Dee:** Pauline Matthews (1947–   ), Eng. pop singer, stage actress. The singer's name suggests "chickadee," but may have a family pet name as origin. She rejected the suggestion of "Kinky Dee" as her first stage name.

Nicholas **Dee:** Joan Aiken (1924–   ), Eng. thriller, children's book writer.

Ruby **Dee:** Ruby Ann Wallace: (1924–   ), U.S. black film actress.

Sandra **Dee:** Alexandra Zuck (1942–   ), U.S. film actress.

André **Deed:** André Chapuis (1884–1938), Fr. film comedian. The actor gained a remarkable collection of nicknames in different European languages, once his particular brand of destructive lunacy became popular. In France itself he was known as Boireau (from *boire*, "to drink"), in Italy Beoncelli ("little drunkard," from *beone*, "tippler"), in Spain Sanchez, and so on. When he worked for the Itala Company of Turin, Italy, he gained further names, such as Cretinetti (Italy), Gribouille (France, "simpleton"), Toribio (Spain, ditto) Glupishkin (Russia, *glupy*, "silly"), Foolshead (England).

Eduardo **de Filippo:** Eduardo Passarelli (1900–1984), It. film actor, director, playwright.

Daniel **Defoe:** Daniel Foe (?1660–1731), Eng. journalist, novelist. It is just possible that the famous author of *Robinson Crusoe* (1719) was originally Daniel Defoe. But records show that he was probably Daniel Foe, and that he came to be known as "Mr. D. Foe" to distinguish himself from his father, James Foe. The initial then became the aristocratic particle "de."

Louis **de Funès:** Carlos Louis de Funès de Galarza (1908–1982), Fr. film actor, comedian, of Portuguese parentage.

Richard **Dehan:** Clotilde Inez Mary Graves (1863–1932), Ir. playwright, humorous novelist.

John **Dehner:** John Forkum (1915–   ), U.S. film actor.

Elmyr **de Hory:** Palmer Hoffer (1906–1976), Hung. copier of master painters. The painter's assumed name is more or less a copy of his original name, allowing for artistic license.

Maurice **Dekobra:** Ernest Maurice Tessier (1885–1973), Fr. novelist.

De Kolta: Joseph Buartier (1847–1903), Fr. magician, working in U.S., U.K.

E.M. **Delafield:** Edmee Elizabeth Monica Dashwood, née de la Pasture (1890–1943), Eng. novelist. The writer's assumed surname is essentially an English translation of her French original.

Theodore **de la Guard:** Nathaniel Ward (*c.*1578–1652), Eng. poet, novelist. The writer chose this pseudonym for *The Simple Cobler of Aggawam* (1647), in the process translating his first name from its Hebrew original into Greek (they both mean "gift of God") and his surname from French to English. The same name, therefore, only different!

Isidore **de Lara:** Isidore Cohen (1858–1935), Eng. opera composer.

Abbé **de la Tour:** Isabelle de Charrière, née Isabella van Tuyll van Servoskerken (1840–1905), Du.-born Fr. novelist, autobiographer. The novelist seems to have devised a pen name that worked on more levels than one. As it stands, it translates as "abbot of the tower." But "Abbé" could equally well represent "Isabelle" (or "Isabella"), and "Tour" may have evolved from "Tuyll." In other words, "Abbé de la Tour" is a sort of meaningful "Isabella van Tuyll." Servoskerken is a Dutch place-name, "Servos' church," also suggesting a holy man and a tower. The lady also used the pen name Zélide *(q.v.).*

Le Vicomte Charles **de Launey:** Delphine de Girardin, née Gay (1804–1855), Fr. writer. The writer used the masculine name for a weekly gossip column in the 1830s, published in book form in 1842 as *Lettres parisiennes.* The name Launay (de Launay) has associations of the Bastille for French people: Bernard de Launay was the governor of the Bastille, and the diarist Mlle de Launay (as Mme de Staal called herself) was long imprisoned in the Bastille.

Bernard **Delfont:** Boris (later Barnet) Winogradsky (1909–   ), Russ.-born Eng. theatre, TV manager, presenter, brother of Lew Grade *(q.v.).*

Jean **de L'Isle:** Alphonse Daudet (1840–1897), Fr. novelist, short story writer.

Belinda **Dell:** Jean Bowden (1920–   ), Sc. writer of romantic novels, thrillers.

Claudia **Dell:** Claudia Dell Smith (1910–   ), U.S. film actress.

Dorothy **Dell:** Dorothy Goff (1915–1934), U.S. film actress.

Gabe **Dell:** Gabriel del Vecchio (1920–1988), U.S. film actor, one of "Dead End Kids."

Della Crusca: Robert Merry (1755–1798), Eng. poet. Merry was the leader of the so-called Della Cruscans, a band of poets who produced affected, sentimental verse in the latter half of the eighteenth century. They took their name (and so therefore did he) from the Della Crusca, the literary academy established in Florence in 1582 with the aim of purifying the Italian language. The name literally means "of the chaff," referring to the "sifting" process to which the academy submitted the language.

Florian **Deller:** Florian Drosendorf (1729–1773), Austr. violinist, composer.

Florentina **del Mar:** Carmen Conde (1907–   ), Sp. poet, novelist, short story writer. The pseudonym suggests "flower of the sea."

Danielle **Delorme:** Gabrielle Girard (1926–   ), Fr. film actress.

Josèphe **Delorme:** Charles-Augustin Sainte-Beuve (1804–1869), Fr. literary critic. The writer used this name for his *Vie, Poésie et Pensées de Josèphe Delorme* (1829), a collection of romantic autobiographical poems. "Josèphe Delorme" was supposedly a friend of Sainte-Beuve who had died young when a medical student.

Victoria **de Los Angeles:** Victoria Lopez Cima (1923–   ), Sp. opera singer. The name should suggest "Victoria of the angels" rather than "Victoria of Los Angeles"!

Dolores **del Rio:** Lolita Dolores Martinez Asunsolo Lopez Negrette (1905–1983), Mexican film actress. The actress's real name appears in many versions, of which the one here is that given by Lloyd and Fuller (see Bibliography, p. 343). But "del Rio" was actually the name of her first husband, Jaime del Rio, and "Lolita" is simply a pet form of "Dolores" anyway. Most sources settle for an original name of just "Dolores Asunsolo."

Michael **Delving:** Jay Williams (1914–1978), U.S. mystery writer.

Alice **Delysia:** Alice Kolb-Bernard, née Douce (1889–1979), Fr. stage, film actress, working in U.K.

Katherine **De Mille:** Katherine Lester (1911–), U.S. film actress.

Tirso **de Molina:** Gabriel Téllez (c.1571–1848), Sp. dramatist. When censorship threatened his writing, the dramatist changed his name to "Tirso de Molina," "Tirso from the mill."

Louis **de Montalte:** Blaise Pascal (1623–1662), Fr. philosopher, physicist. Pascal's pen name contains a latinized reference to the "high mountain" of Puy-de-Dôme, near Clermont-Ferrand, where he conducted several of his scientific experiments into atmospheric pressure.

Peter **de Morny:** Esme Wynn-Tyson (1898–), Eng. novelist, dramatist, critic.

Terry **Dene:** Terence Williams (1938–), Eng. rock singer.

Catherine **Deneuve:** Catherine Dorléac (1943–), Fr. film actress, sister of actress Françoise Dorléac (1942–1967).

Richard **Denning:** Ludwig (then Louis) Albert Denninger (1914–), U.S. film actor.

Les **Dennis:** Leslie Heseltine (1954–), Eng. TV comedian.

Reginald **Denny:** Reginald Leigh Daymore (1891–1967), Br. stage, film actor.

John **Denver:** John Henry Deutschendorf, Jr. (1943–), U.S. country singer, songwriter.

Karl **Denver:** Angus Mackenzie (1934–), Sc. pop musician.

Lynsey **De Paul:** Lynsey Rubin (1951–), Br. popular singer.

Madame Marguerite **de Ponti:** Stéphane Mallarmé (1842–1898), Fr. poet. The symbolist poet used this name when acting as editor of the fashion magazine *La Dernière Mode* (1897).

Dan De **Quille:** William Wright (1829–1898), U.S. humorist, historian of the Far West. There is no doubt a pun here on "quill" and "write."

Thomas **de Quincey:** Thomas Quincey (1785–1859), Eng. essayist. There is some uncertainty whether the writer added the aristocratic "de" himself, to claim Norman descent, or whether his father was already named De Quincey. According to the *Dictionary of National Biography*, the author liked to alphabetize his name under "Q," which seems to suggest the reverse of this.

John **Derek:** Derek Harris (1926–), U.S. film actor.

Tristan **Derème:** Philippe Huc (1889–1942), Fr. poet.

Rick **Derringer:** Rick Zehringer (1947–), U.S. rock musician.

Father **Desiderius:** Peter Lenz (1832–1928), Ger. artist, architect.

Florence **Desmond:** Florence Dawson (1905–), Eng. revue artiste, impersonator. The actress was renamed as a child dancer by a matron overseeing the group she was in at the time.

Johnny **Desmond:** Giovanni di Simone (1920–1987), U.S. actor, singer.

Paul **Desmond:** Paul Breitenfeld (1924–1977), U.S. saxophonist.

William **Desmond:** William Mannion (1878–1949), Ir. film actor, working in U.S.

Jerry **Desmonde:** James Robert Sadler (1908–1967), Eng. music hall comedian.

Philippe Nicolas **Destouches:** Philippe Nicolas Néricault (1680–1754), Fr. playwright.

Andre **de Toth:** Endre Antai Mihály Sásvrái Farkasfawi Tóthfalusi Toth (1913–), Hung. film actor. If this is indeed the actor's real name (it is so quoted, albeit in garbled form, by Lloyd and Fuller), then how can we begrudge him his aristocratic "de"? He's surely earned it.

Jacques **Deval:** Jacques Boularan (1890–1972), Fr. playwright, working in U.S.

[Dame] Ninette **de Valois:** Edris Connell, née Stannus (1898–), Ir.-born Br. ballet dancer, director, teacher. "And where did the name de Valois come from?" "My mother thought of it, because our family had French connections." (Part of interview on occasion of interviewee's 90th birthday, *Sunday Times Magazine*, May 29, 1988.) Valois is a historic region and duchy in northern France.

David **Devant:** David Wighton (1868–1941), Eng. magician.

Mlle **de Villedieu:** Marie Catherine H. Desjardins (1631–1683), Fr. author.

Justin **de Villeneuve:** Nigel Davies (1939–), Br. manager of Twiggy *(q.v.)*.

Andy **Devine:** Jeremiah Schwartz (1905–1977), U.S. film comedian.

Dominic **Devine:** David McDonald Devine (1920–1980), Eng. thriller writer.

Magenta **de Vine:** Kim Porter (1960–), Br. TV reporter.

Patrick **Dewaere:** Jean-Marie Bourdeau (1947–1982), Fr. film actor.

Billy **de Wolfe:** William Andrew Jones (1907–1974), U.S. stage, film comedian, of Welsh parentage. Bill Jones (as he was usually known) was told by a theatre manager that his real name would not do for a star. He therefore took the manager's own name. Simple.

Al **Dexter:** Albert Poindexter (1902–), U.S. country singer, composer.

Anthony **Dexter:** Walter Fleischmann (1919–), U.S. film actor.

William **Dexter:** William T. Pritchard (1909–), Eng. writer on magic. The writer's pen name may well have been based on "dexterous," given his specialty.

Robert **Dhéry:** Robert Foullcy, originally Héry (1921–), Fr. film comedian.

Fra **Diavolo:** Michele Pezza (1771–1806), It. brigand chief. The semilegendary brigand adopted his nickname, which means "Brother Devil," and was given him by victimized peasants on account of his ferocity. It was rumored, moreover, that Pezza had originally been a monk named Fra Angelo. Fra Diavolo was the subject of Auber's opera of this name.

Thomas John **Dibdin:** Thomas John Pitt (1771–1833), Eng. actor, playwright. The actor was illegitimate, so adopted his mother's maiden name.

Angie **Dickinson:** Angeline Brown (1931–), U.S film actress.

Carr **Dickson:** John Dickson Carr (1905–1977), U.S. detective novelist.

Carter **Dickson:** John Dickson Carr (1905–1977), U.S. detective novelist.

Gloria **Dickson:** Thais Dickerson (1916–1945), U.S. film actress.

Bo **Diddley:** Ellas McDaniel (1928–), U.S. black jazz musician. Ellas

McDaniel acquired his name when he was training to be a boxer at the local gym. A "bo diddley" is a one-stringed African guitar. The musician (and guitar player's) name was originally Bates. His mother, however, was too poor to raise him and he was adopted by his mother's first cousin, a Sunday school teacher in Chicago, and he adopted her name, McDaniel.

Didi: Waldir Pereira (1928–   ), Brazilian footballer.

Marlene **Dietrich:** Marie Magdalene Dietrich von Losch (1901–   ), Ger.-born U.S. film actress, singer. The actress's first name is a telescoping of "Marie Magdalene." Dietrich was the name of her father, an officer in the Royal Prussian Police. A year or two after her birth, Marie's family moved from Berlin to Weimar, where her mother remarried, her new husband being Edouard von Losch. In the popular mind, the name of Marlene Dietrich is mixed up with that of Lilli Marlene, the girl in the German song (borrowed by the British) that was popular in the Second World War, as Dietrich herself was. Doubtless the German/English association helped. But the song originated in a poem written in the First World War, even though it was actually composed in 1938. So the two ladies are quite distinct. ("Lilli Marlene" was sung by the Swedish singer, Lale Andersson.)

Phyllis **Diller:** Phyllis Driver (1917–   ), U.S. film actress, comedienne.

Izak **Dinesen:** Karen Christentze Blixen, née Dinesen (1885–1962), Dan.-born Eng. novelist. A male name used by the author for her English writings, including several volumes of short stories. She also used the name Pierre Andrezel *(q.v.)*.

Ding: Jay Norwood Darling (1876–1962), U.S. cartoonist. From his surname.

Ding Ling: Jiang Weizhi (Chiang Wei-chih) (1904–1986), Chin. (female) novelist, Communist.

Ronnie James **Dio:** Ronald Padavona (1949–   ), U.S. rock singer.

Dion: Dion DiMucci (1939–   ), U.S. rock musician.

Discobolus: Donald Williams Aldous (1914–   ), Eng. writer on sound recording, engineering. The writer's name is Latin for "discus thrower," or in modern terms "disc thrower" (that is, one who "throws" discs on to a record player, or who records on such discs in the first place).

Dick **Distich:** Alexander Pope (1688–1744), Eng. poet. Pope used this pseudonym for writing in the *Guardian,* a distich being a verse couplet.

Dito und Idem: Elizabeth, Queen of Romania (1843–1916), Romanian verse, prose writer + Mite (or Marie) Kremnitz (1852–1916), Ger. writer. This was the joint pseudonym used by the already pseudonymous Carmen Sylva *(q.v.)* and George Allan *(q.v.)* when the two ladies wrote as coauthors. The words (respectively in Italian, German, and Latin) translate as "the same and the same." A mildly learned joke.

Divine: Harris Glenn Milstead (1946–1988), U.S. film actor, drag artist. Nicknamed, with some justification, "The Filthiest Man Alive," the gross actor (300 pounds in weight) obviously selected a screen name that was fundamentally the reverse of his sluttish persona.

Dorothy **Dix:** Elizabeth Meriwether Gilmer (1861–1951), U.S. writer of advice to the lovelorn. The same name was used by the English journalist Jean Nicol (died 1986) when employed by the *Daily Mirror* at the start of her career in the 1930s.

Richard **Dix:** Ernest Carlton Brimmer (1894–1949), U.S. film actor.

Marmaduke **Dixey:** Geoffrey Howard (1889–1973), Eng. novelist, poet.

Diz: Edward Jeffrey Irving Ardizzone (1900–1979), Br. cartoonist, illustrator.

Don Leucadio **Doblado:** Joseph Blanco White *(q.v.)*.

Issay **Dobrowen:** Ishok Israelevich Barabeychik (1891–1953), Russ. conductor, pianist, working in Germany, Sweden.

Lew **Dockstader:** George Alfred Clapp (1856–1924), U.S. vaudeville artist, "Blackface" performer. The performer acquired his stage name through his partnership in a minstrel troupe with Charles Dockstader, billed as the Dockstader Brothers. When Charles died in 1883, Clapp kept the name, even after the troupe had disbanded.

Q.K. Philander **Doesticks,** P.B.: Mortimer Neal Thomson (1831–1875), U.S. humorist. The name is simply a frivolous one, although the writer claimed that "P.B." stood for "Perfect Brick."

Sir Iliad **Doggrel:** [Sir] Thomas Burnet (1694–1753), Eng. writer + George Ducket (? –), Eng. member of parliament.

Dolbokov: Hannes Vayn Bok (1914–1964), U.S. SF writer, artist + Boris Dolgov (–), U.S. artist.

R. **Doleman:** Robert Parsons (1546–1610), Eng. Jesuit missionary, plotter. Robert Parsons, who founded the English province of the Society of Jesus, used this name for *A Conference about the Next Succession to the Crown of England,* published in 1594. Parsons used several pseudonyms, many of them simply initials.

Anton **Dolin:** Sydney Francis Patrick Chippendall Healey-Kay (1904–1983), Eng. ballet dancer, choreographer. The dancer assumed his stage name in 1921, when he joined Diaghilev's Ballets Russes. "Anton" is said to have been a tribute to Anton Chekhov. "Dolin" was apparently suggested by a fellow ballet student. It is not only a genuine Russian name, as appropriate for a ballet dancer, but equally suggests the common Irish surname Dolan. Healey-Kay's mother, Helen Maude Kay, née Healey, was Irish.

Jenny **Dolly:** Janszieka Deutsch (1893–1941), U.S. film actress, singer, teaming with twin sister Rosie Dolly *(q.v.)*.

Rosie **Dolly:** Roszika Deutsch (1893–1970), U.S. film actress, singer. The twin sisters, Jenny and Rosie Dolly, were of what might best be described as "Central European" origin. They succeeded in converting their foreign names into attractive English ones.

Léon **Dominique:** Léon Aronson (1893–1984), Russ.-born Fr. restaurateur, drama critic. Léon Aronson adopted the name of the Russian restaurant he founded (in 1927) in Paris, the Dominique, as a pseudonym for his second profession as drama critic.

Fats **Domino:** Antoine Domino (1928–), U.S. black jazz musician. The musician's surname is his real one. "Fats" was the (accurately descriptive) nickname given him by band leader Bill Diamond when he first started playing, as a ten-year-old, at the Hideaway Club, New Orleans. In 1949 his first record was called "The Fat Man." He was the inspiration for the name of Chubby Checker *(q.v.)*.

Troy **Donahue:** Merle Johnson (1936–), U.S. film actor.

Pauline **Donalda:** Pauline Lightstone (1882–1970), Can. opera singer.

Donatello: Donato di Niccolo di Betto Bardi (?1386–1466), It. sculptor. The artist's adopted name arose as a straightforward nickname, "little Donato."

Lonnie **Donegan:** Anthony James Donegan (1931–   ), Eng. pop musician. The singer took his new first name from his co-musician, Lonnie Johnson.

Donovan: Donovan Philip Leitch (1946–   ), Sc. rock musician.

Dick **Donovan:** Joyce Emmerson Preston Muddock (1843–1934), Eng. journalist, detective fiction writer.

Mr. **Dooley:** Finley Peter Dunne (1867–1936), U.S. humorist. Mr. Dooley, in a series of the writer's works, was a typical Irish saloon keeper with a typical Irish name.

Mary **Doran:** Florence Arnot (1907–   ), U.S. film actress.

Dolores **Dorn:** Dolores Dorn-Heft (1935–   ), U.S. stage, film actress.

Philip **Dorn:** Hein van der Niet (1901–1975), Du. film actor, working in U.S. He appeared in early movies as Fritz van Dongen.

Sandra **Dorne:** Joanna Smith (1925–   ), Br. film actress.

Marie **Doro:** Marie Stewart (1882–1956), U.S. film actress.

Diana **Dors:** Diana Mary Fluck (1931–1984), Eng. stage, film, TV actress. The actress was nearly called "Diana Scarlett," a name that her agent Gordon Harbord (who also named Laurence Harvey and Adrienne Corri, *(q.v.)*) had chosen for her. But Diana was not keen on this, and her final stage name came about as described in her autobiography: "To be born with the name of Fluck, particularly if one is a girl, can be nothing less than disastrous. Originally my reason for changing it was no more than a young girl's ambition to become a film star [. . .] but when I was cast in my first film the director tried gently to explain that the second part of my name would have to be altered [. . .] I was only fourteen and did not quite understand his well meant reasoning then, but as I wished to call myself something much more exotic anyway, I agreed willingly, and the search for a new surname was on! My agent had suggested Scarlett [. . .] and I toyed with that for a while. My own fantasy of Diana Carroll also seemed a possibility but my father was incensed that the family name was not to be used [. . .] Finally my mother in a moment of brilliance decided that I *would* stick to a family name after all, and because my grandmother's maiden name had been Dors, she felt it sounded good to have two names with the same initial. So Dors it was and we were all happy! [Diana Dors, *Behind Closed Dors*, 1979].

Fifi **D'Orsay:** Angelina Yvonne Cecil Lussier D'Sablon (1907–1983), Can.-born U.S. stage, film actress. The actress claimed that her new surname was adopted from a bottle of French perfume, and that "Fifi" was what other girls called her when she was in the Greenwich Village Follies chorus in the 1920s. Fifi is certainly a typical chorus girl's name, like Gigi and Mimi. "D'Orsay" would be a "prestige" name for a commercial product, suggesting the Quai d'Orsay, the French foreign office (named after its location in Paris).

Marie **Dorval:** Marie Delaunay (1798–1849), Fr. actress.

Gabrielle **Dorziat:** Gabrielle Moppert (1880–1979), Fr. film actress.

Dosso **Dossi:** Giovanni di Lutero (?1479–1542), It. painter.

Dottsy: Dorothy Brodt (1954–   ), U.S. country singer.

Catherine **Doucet:** Catherine Green (1875–1958), U.S. stage, film actress.

Craig **Douglas:** Terence Perkins (1941–   ), Eng. popular singer.

Donald **Douglas:** Douglas Kinleyside (1905–1945), U.S. film actor.

Donna **Douglas:** Doris Smith (1933–   ), U.S. TV actress.

Felicity **Douglas:** Felicity Dowson, née Tonlin (1910–   ), Eng. stage, film, TV, radio author.

George **Douglas:** George Douglas Brown (1869–1902), Sc. author.

Kirk **Douglas:** Issur Danielovitch Demsky (1916–   ), U.S. film actor, of Russ.-Jewish parentage. The actor chose his new first name because he felt it was "snazzy," and his surname out of his admiration for Douglas Fairbanks, Jr. *(q.v.)*. His adoption of "Kirk" (in 1941) gave the name a popular boost, especially with its "rugged" and respectable associations ("church").

Melvyn **Douglas:** Melvyn Edouard Hesselberg (1901–1981), U.S. stage, film actor, producer, director.

Mike **Douglas:** Michael Delaney Dowd, Jr. (1925–   ), U.S. TV host.

Olive **Douglas:** Anna Buchan (? –1948), Sc. novelist, sister of writer John Buchan.

Robert **Douglas:** Robert Douglas Finlayson (1909–   ), Br. stage, film actor, working in U.S.

Wallace **Douglas:** Wallace Finlayson (1911–   ), Can. stage director.

Frederick **Douglass:** Frederick Augustus Washington Daily (?1817–1895), U.S. black lecturer, writer.

Kent **Douglass:** Robert Douglas Montgomery (1908–1966), U.S. film actor. The actor also used the name Robert Douglass *(q.v.)*. He adopted both names as there was already a Robert Montgomery *(q.v.)*, as well as a Robert Douglas *(q.v.)*. Note the additional "s" to aid the distinction, essential in the second case.

Robert **Douglass:** Robert Douglas Montgomery (1908–1966), U.S. film actor. The actor also used the name Kent Douglass *(q.v., above)*.

Stephen **Douglass:** Stephen Fitch (1921–   ), U.S. stage actor, singer. The actor adopted his mother's maiden name.

Billie **Dove:** Lilian Bohny (1904–   ), U.S. film actress.

Peggy **Dow:** Margaret Varnadow (1928–   ), U.S. film actress.

Eddie **Dowling:** Joseph Nelson Goucher (1894–1976), U.S. stage actor, producer, playwright. The actor adopted his mother's maiden name.

Major Jack **Downing:** Seba Smith (1792–1868), U.S. humorist. Major Jack Downing was the supposed name of a Down East Yankee who began to publish letters in the *Portland Courier* (founded by Smith in 1829) in 1830. He had a comic turn of speech and an essentially homespun sagacity that soon won him popularity among his readers. Note the echo of "Down East" in his name.

Lynn **Doyle:** Leslie Alexander Montgomery (1873–1961), Ir. humorous novelist, playwright.

Alfred **Drake:** Alfredo Capurro (1914–   ), It.-born U.S. stage singer, dancer.

Charles **Drake:** Charles Ruppert (1914–   ), U.S. film actor.

Charlie **Drake:** Charles Springall (1925–   ), Eng. TV, film, stage comedian.

Dona **Drake**: Rita Novella (1920–   ), Mexican singer, dancer, film actress. What was wrong with her pleasantly memorable original name?

Fabia **Drake**: Fabia Drake McGlinchy (1904–   ), Br. film actress.

Frances **Drake**: Frances Dean (1908–   ), U.S. film actress.

Samuel **Drake**: Samuel Drake Bryant (1768–1854), Br.-born U. S. actor-manager.

Tom **Drake**: Alfred Alderdice (1918–1982), U.S. film actor.

M.B. **Drapier**: Jonathan Swift (1667–1745), Ir. satirist, cleric. A "nonce" pseudonym adopted by the famous author of *Gulliver's Travels*. He used the name for *The Drapier's Letters* (1724), written in the guise of a Dublin draper. A patent had been granted to the Duchess of Kendal for supplying copper coins for use in Ireland, and this she sold to one William Wood for £10,000. The profit on the patent would have been, it is said, around £25,000, and Swift published four letters prophesying ruin to the Irish if "Wood's halfpence" were admitted into circulation. The letters were effective, and the government was forced to abandon the plan and to compensate Wood.

Sir Alexander **Drawcansir**: Henry Fielding (1707–1754), Eng. novelist, playwright. Fielding used the pseudonym as editor of *The Covent-Garden Journal* (1752). The original Drawcansir was the burlesque tyrant portrayed, as a caricature of Dryden's Almanzor, in Buckingham's farcical comedy *The Rehearsal* (1672). The name itself is obviously a parody of "Almanzor," while possibly intentionally suggesting someone who enjoys *draw*ing a *can* of liquor. The original Drawcansir has only three lines in the play, of which two are: "He that dares drink, and for that drink dares die, And, knowing this, dares yet drink on, am I." This parodied Almanzor's: "He who dares love, and for that love must die, And, knowing this, dares yet love on, am I."

Alfred **Drayton**: Alfred Varick (1881–1949), Br. film actor.

Mikey **Dread**: Michael Campbell (–   ), Jamaican reggae producer.

Carl **Dreadstone**: John Ramsey Campbell (1940–   ), Eng. writer of horror fiction.

Sonia **Dresdel**: Lois Obee (1908–1976), Eng. stage, film actress.

Louise **Dresser**: Louise Kerlin (1881–1965), U.S. film actress.

Marie **Dressler**: Leila Marie Koerber (1869–1934), Can.-born U.S. stage, film comedienne.

Ellen **Drew**: Terry Ray (1915–   ), U.S. film actress. There seem to be theatrical overtones in the actress's stage name. Her substitution of "Ellen" for "Terry" suggests the name of Ellen Terry (1847–1928), the famous English stage actress, while "Drew" is also a well-known acting name, as for Mrs. John Drew (1820–1897), the American actress and theatre manager.

Jimmy **Driftwood**: James Morris (1917–   ), U.S. country singer.

Adam **Drinan**: Joseph Todd Gordon Macleod (1903–1984), Br. author, play producer, radio newsreader. The well-known British newsreader, Joseph Macleod, chose the name "Adam Drinan" for three books of verse about the Hebrides, selecting the pseudonym because some of his ancestors had come from Drinan in the Isle of Skye.

Droch: Robert Seymour Bridges (1844–1930), Eng. poet. The poet's early pen name is a Celtic rendering of his surname. Scottish Gaelic *drochaid,* for example, is "bridge."

Joanne **Dru:** Joanne Letitia La Coque (or Laycock) (1923–   ), U.S. film actress. When a stage actress (briefly), Joanne La Coque performed as "Joanne Marshall." She later selected the name of "Dru" after a Welsh ancestor. It was director Howard Hawkes who encouraged her to change her name.

The **Druid:** Henry Hall Dixon (1822–1870), Eng. sporting writer.

Ivor **Drummond:** Roger Longrigg (1929–   ), Br. writer of spy adventures. The name suggests "Bulldog Drummond," the chief character in the thrillers by Sapper *(q.v.).*

Dryasdust: M.Y. Halidom *(q.v.).*

The Rev. Dr. **Dryasdust:** [Sir] Walter Scott (1771–1832), Sc. novelist. The famous author used the mock self-deprecatory name in the introduction to several of his novels.

Leo **Dryden:** George Dryden Wheeler (1862–1939), Eng. singer of patriotic songs in the music hall.

Doggerel **Drydog:** Charles Clark (1806–1880), Br. sporting writer.

Edward **Dryhurst:** Edward Roberts (1904–   ), Br. film producer, actor.

Sieur **du Baudrier:** Jonathan Swift (1667–1745), Ir. satirist, cleric. Swift used the name for his *New Journey to Paris* (1711).

Jack **Duchesne:** Michel Jacques Saint-Denis (1897–1971), Fr.-born Eng. stage actor, producer.

Thomas **du Clévier:** Bonaventure Des Périers (*c.*1500–1543), Fr. storyteller, humanist writer. The writer used the name for his *Cymbalum Mundi* (1537), four satirical dialogues in the style of Lucian. "Du Clévier" is an anagram of French *incrédule* ("unbeliever"), with "Thomas" referring to the biblical Doubting Thomas. The work was supposedly translated by du Clévier, and sent by him to his friend Tryocan. But the latter was also a pseudonym used by Des Périers, and is an anagram of *croyant* ("believer"). The work is an attack on the Christian faith and its liturgy and discipline. It was officially suppressed, and only one copy survived.

Mlle **Duclos:** Marie-Anne de Châteauneuf (1668–1748), Fr. actress.

Pete **Duel:** Peter Deuel (1940–1971), U.S. film actor.

Dufresne: Abraham-Alexis Quinault (1693–1767), Fr. actor.

Dugazon: Jean-Baptiste-Henri Gourgaud (1746–1809), Fr. actor.

Doris **Duke:** Doris Curry (*c.*1940–   ), U.S. soul singer.

Vernon **Duke:** Vladimir Dukelsky (1903–1969), Russ.-born U.S. popular music composer.

Germaine **Dulac:** Charlotte Elisabeth Germaine Saisset-Schneider (1882–1942), Fr. film director, actress.

Alexandre **Dumas:** Alexandre Davy de la Pailleterie (1802–1870), Fr. novelist, playwright. Yes, this *is* the famous author of *The Count of Monte Cristo,* otherwise "Dumas *père.*" His parents were Creoles, and "Dumas" was the name of his West Indian grandmother. To be fair, however, it was his father that adopted the name, rather than the writer himself.

Mlle **Dumesnil:** Marie-Françoise Marchand (1712–1803), Fr. tragic actress.

Margaret **Dumont:** Margaret Baker (1889–1977), Ger.-U.S. ballet dancer, teacher.

Steffi **Duna:** Stephanie Berindey (1913–   ), Hung. dancer, film actress.

Irma **Duncan:** Irma Dorette Henriette Ehrich-Grimme (1897–1977), Ger.-U.S. ballet dancer, teacher.

Michael **Dunn:** Gary Neil Miller (1934–1973), U.S. dwarf film actor.

Augustus **Dun-shunner:** [Professor] William Edmonstone Aytoun (1813–1865), Sc. poet. The writer used this name for his contributions to *Blackwood's Magazine.* A "dun" is a debt collector, so that a "dun-shunner" is someone who avoids debt collectors or creditors.

Amy **Dunsmuir:** Margaret Oliphant Oliphant, née Wilson (1828–1897), Sc. novelist. (Margaret Wilson married her cousin, Francis Oliphant.)

Thomas Edward **Dunville:** Thomas Edward Wallen (1868–1924), Eng. eccentric music hall comedian.

Carolus **Duran:** Charles-Auguste-Emile Durand (1837–1917), Fr. genre portrait painter.

Henry Fowle **Durrant:** Henry Welles Smith (1822–1881), U.S. lawyer, lay preacher. The lawyer changed his name so as not to be confused with the many other Henry Smiths.

Deanna **Durbin:** Edna Mae Durbin (1921–   ), Can. film actress, singer. The actress juggled the letters of her fairly common first two names and came up with the more esoteric "Deanna," counting "m" as "n" and losing the "y" in the process.

Slim **Dusty:** David Gordon Kirkpatrick (1927–   ), Austral. singer.

Frank **Duveneck:** Frank Decker (1848–1919), U.S. painter, etcher, sculptor. The artist adopted his stepfather's name.

Henri **Duvernois:** Henry Schwabacher (1875–1937), Fr. novelist, playwright.

Ann **Dvorak:** Anna McKim (1911–1979), U.S. film actress. The actress adopted her mother's maiden name.

Bob **Dylan:** Robert Allen Zimmerman (1941–   ), U.S. rock musician, poet, composer. The commonly held theory is that Bob Dylan adopted the name of the Welsh poet, Dylan Thomas. But the musician himself has specifically denied this: "I knew about Dylan Thomas, of course, but I didn't deliberately pick his name" [Anthony Scaduto, *Bob Dylan: An Intimate Biography,* 1979]. Which leaves us uncertain as to *why* he chose "Dylan." Among other recording names used by Dylan are "Blind Boy Grunt," "Bob Landy," and "Robert Milkwood Thomas" [Stuart Hoggard and Jim Shields, *Bob Dylan: An Illustrated Discography,* 1978].

Solomon **Eagle:** [Sir] John Collings Squire (1884–1958), Br. poet, essayist, short story writer.

Sheena **Easton:** Sheena Orr (1959–   ), Sc. popular singer.

Barbara **Eden:** Barbara Huffman (1934–   ), U.S. film actress.

Sir John **Edgar:** [Sir] Richard Steele (1672–1729), Eng. essayist, dramatist.

Paul **Edmonds:** Henry Kittner (1915–1958), U.S. fantasy fiction writer.

G.C. **Edmondson:** José Mario Garry Ordonez Edmondson y Cotton (1922–   ), Guatemalan-born U.S. SF writer.

Willie **Edouin:** William Frederick Bryer (1846–1908), Eng. pantomime actor.

George Alden **Edson:** Paul Frederick Ernst (1902–   ), U.S. writer of horror stories.

Albert **Edwards:** Arthur Bullard (1879–1929), U.S. journalist, writer.

Blake **Edwards:** William Blake McEdwards (1922–   ), U.S. film producer, director.

Gus **Edwards:** Gustave Edward Simon (1881–1945), U.S. songwriter.

Vince **Edwards:** Vincento Edouardo Zoine (1926–   ), U.S. film actor.

Jean **Effel:** François Lejeune (1918–1982), Fr. cartoonist. The artist's new surname represented his initials, "F.L.," pronounced in French as in English. He preceded this with the most common French forename, Jean. The name as a whole was shorter than the original, too, and so more suitable for signatures on his cartoons.

Aunt **Effie:** Jane Euphemia Browne (1811–1898), Br. children's writer.

Philippe **Egalité:** Louis Philippe Joseph, duc d'Orléans (1747–1793), Fr. statesman. The duke assumed his (literally) egalitarian name in order to court the favor of the people when he became Deputy for Paris (1792) in the *Convention Nationale.* In the *Convention* he voted for the death of Louis XVI, his cousin — and was himself executed the following year. So much for egalitarianism.

Lesley **Egan:** Elizabeth Linington (1921–   ), U.S. mystery writer. The writer's pen name is a sort of part-anagram of her real name. Perhaps this was intentional, for a mystery writer?

H.M. **Egbert:** Victor Rousseau Emanuel (1879–1960), Eng.-born U.S. pulp magazine writer.

George **Egerton:** Mary Chavelita Dunne (1860–1945), Austral. novelist. Mary Dunne was married twice, and her pen name derives from that of her first husband, George Egerton Clairemont. Her second marriage, in 1901, was to a theatrical agent, Reginald Golding Bright. She herself was of Irish-Welsh parentage and was brought up in Ireland.

John **Eglinton:** William Kirkpatrick Magee (1868–1962), Ir. essayist, poet, biographer.

Britt **Ekland:** Britt-Marie Eklund (1942–   ), Swe. film actress.

Florence **Eldridge:** Florence McKechnie (1901–   ), U.S. stage actress.

Gus **Elen:** Ernest Augustus Elen (1862–1940), Eng. music hall artist, singer of Cockney songs.

Avril **Elgar:** Avril Williams (1932–   ), Eng. stage actress. The actress assumed her father's third name as her stage name.

El Hakim: Barry Walls (1937–   ), Eng. circus fakir. The name is a stock one for fake fakirs, and is Arabic for "the wise one."

Elia: Charles Lamb (1775–1834), Eng. writer, poet. The well-known writer first used his pen name in his *Essays of Elia,* which appeared in *The London Magazine* in 1820–1823. The subject of the first essay was an Italian clerk named Elia who worked at South Sea House, headquarters of the East India Company, where Lamb had worked and where his brother was still employed at the time of the appearance of the *Essays.* The name is said to have been originally pronounced "Ellia."

George **Eliot:** Mary Ann (later, Marian) Evans (1819–1880), Eng. novelist. The famous author of *The Mill on the Floss* (1860), took her male name from that of her lover, the philosopher and writer George Henry Lewes (who himself wrote as Slingsby Lawrence *(q.v.)*). Her surname she chose because it was a "full-mouthed, easily-pronounceable name." She first used her pen name in 1858 for her novel entitled *Scenes of Clerical Life.* Two years after the death of Lewes in 1878 Marian Evans married John Walter Cross, an American banker. She died that same year, but Cross lived on until 1924. Such is the generally accepted story behind her name. In his diverting book *Pribbles and Prabbles* (1906), however, Major-General Patrick Maxwell points out an unusual coincidence: that some time in the 1840s a young officer of the Bengal cavalry called George Donnithorne Eliot was accidentally drowned in a lake in the Himalayas. Not only does this officer's name contain the pen name assumed by Marian Evans, but in her *Adam Bede* (1859) there is a character named Arthur Donnithorne. That the Bengal officer was, however, an early flame of Marian Evans seems highly unlikely, although the young authoress could have read about him.

Elizabeth: Mary Annette, Countess von Arnim (later Russell), née Beauchamp (1866–1941), Austral. author. The author assumed her mother's first name for her novels, and it occurs in the title of her best known work, *Elizabeth and Her German Garden,* published anonymously in 1898.

Duke **Ellington:** Edward Kennedy Ellington (1899–1974), U.S. black jazz musician. "Duke" has long been used in the U.S. as a nickname for a smart or accomplished person, especially one who dresses and behaves stylishly. This certainly suited the greatest and most prolific jazz musician of the twentieth century.

Cass **Elliott:** Ellen Naomi Cohen (1942–1974), U.S. pop singer.

Jack **Elliott:** Elliott Charles Adnopoz (1931–), U.S. folk singer.

Maxine **Elliott:** Jessie Dermot (1868–1940), U.S. stage actress. Jessie Dermot adopted her stage name at the suggestion of Dion Boucicault *(q.v.).*

William "Wild Bill" **Elliott:** Gordon Nance (1903–1965), U.S. film actor.

Mary **Ellis:** Mary Elsas (1900–), U.S. film actress, singer.

Patricia **Ellis:** Patricia Gene O'Brien (1916–1970), U.S. film actress.

James **Ellison:** James Ellison Smith (1910–), U.S. film actor.

Ziggy **Elman:** Harry Finkelman (1914–1969), U.S. jazz trumpeter.

Isobel **Elsom:** Isobel Reed (1893–1991), Br. stage, film actress, working in U.S.

Julian **Eltinge:** William Julian Dalton (1882–1941), U.S. female impersonator.

Geoffrey Rudolph **Elton:** Geoffrey Rudolph Ehrenberg (1921–), Ger.-born Eng. historian. The well-known historian changed his name to Elton in 1944 under an Army Council Instruction. This was of course in the Second World War.

Paul **Eluard:** Eugène Grindel (1895–1952), Fr. poet.

Maurice **Elvey:** William Seward Folkard (1887–1967), Br. film director.

Violetta **Elvin:** Violetta Prokhorova (1925–), Russ. ballet dancer.

Ron **Ely:** Ronald Pierce (1938–), U.S. athlete, TV actor.

Gilbert **Emery:** Gilbert Emery Bensley Pottle (1875–1945), Eng.-born U.S. film actor, playwright.

Pierre **Emmanuel:** Noël Jean Mathieu (1916–1984), Fr. poet and Resistance fighter.

Emmwood: John Musgrove-Wood (1915–), Eng. cartoonist.

Frederick **Engelheart:** Lafayette Ronald Hubbard (1911–), U.S. fantasy fiction writer, founder (1951) of Scientology.

Ephemera: Edward Fitzgibbon (1803–1857), Eng. journalist, writer of books on angling. There is a nice pun here: "ephemera" on the one hand denotes something short-lived, such as a journalist writes about; on the other hand it is a term for the mayfly, whose artificial form is used as a bait by anglers.

Desiderius **Erasmus:** Gerhard Gerhards (or Geert Geerts) (?1466–1536), Du. humanist, theologian. The great Renaissance scholar was born as the second child of Margaret, a physician's daughter, and Roger Gerhard (or Geert), a priest. He was thus illegitimate, or a "love child," and the name that he adopted reflects this, as both "Desiderius" and "Erasmus" means "desired one," that is, "loved one," from Latin *desiderare*, "to want," "to desire" and Greek *erasmios*, "beloved." Compare the next name below.

Thomas **Erastus:** Thomas Lieber (or Liebler) (1524–1583), Ger.-Swiss theologian, physician. "Erastus" translates the theologian's real name, which itself means "lover." Compare the name of Desiderius Erasmus (above).

Leif **Erickson:** William Anderson (1911–1986), U.S. film actor.

John **Ericson:** Joseph Meibes (1927–), Ger.-born U.S. film actor.

Erratic Enrique: Henry Clay Lukens (1838–?1900), U.S. humorous writer, poet, journalist.

Erté: Romain de Tirtoff (1892–), Russ.-born Fr. costume designer. The designer's brief pseudonym, suitable for signing, derives from his initials "R.T." as pronounced in French (approximately "air-tay").

Patrick **Ervin:** Robert E. Howard (1906–1936), U.S. SF writer.

Uncle **Esek:** Henry Wheeler Shaw (1818–1885), U.S. humorist. The humorist's best known pen name was Josh Billings *(q.v.)*.

Carl **Esmond:** Willy Eichberger (1905–), Austr. film actor, working in U.K., U.S.

Henry Vernon **Esmond:** Henry Vernon Jack (1869–1922), Eng. state actor-manager, dramatist. The actor appears to have been influenced in his choice of professional name by that of the central character in Thackeray's *Henry Esmond.*

Dr. **Esperanto:** [Dr.] Lazar Ludwik Zamenhof (1859–1917), Pol. physician, inventor of Esperanto. The inventor's name translates (in Esperanto) as "Dr. Hoping One" (compare French *espérer*, "to hope" and related words in other languages). He used the name for his book introducing the language, *Langue Internationale: Préface et Manuel Complet* (1887). His hopes have to some extent been justified, as Esperanto is easily the most widely used artificial language.

David **Essex:** David Albert Cook (1947–), Eng. pop singer.

Martin **Esslin:** Martin Julius Pereszlenyi (1918–), Eng. radio producer, drama critic, of Austr.-Hung. parentage.

Partenio **Etiro:** Pietro Aretino *(q.v.).* An obvious anagram of the Italian satirist's pseudonym.

Robert **Eton:** Lawrence Walter Meynell (1899–1989), Eng. author.

Eugenius III: Bernardo Paganelli (or Pignatelli) (? –1153), It. pope.

Eugenius IV: Gabriele Condolmieri (*c.*1383–1447), It. pope.

Eusébio: Eusébio Ferreira da Silva (1942–   ), Mozambiquan-born Port. footballer (the "Black Panther").

Dale **Evans:** Frances Octavia Smith (1912–   ), U.S. film actress.

Gil **Evans:** Ernest Gilmore Green (1912–1988), Can.-born jazz composer.

Joan **Evans:** Joan Eunson (1934–   ), U.S. film actress.

Linda **Evans:** Linda Evanstad (1942–   ), U.S. TV actress, of Norw. descent.

Judith **Evelyn:** Judith Evelyn Allen (1913–1967), U.S. stage, film actress.

Chad **Everett:** Raymon Lee Cramton (1937–   ), U.S. TV, film actor.

Kenny **Everett:** Maurice James Christopher Cole (1944–   ), Eng. radio, TV DJ, entertainer, presenter. Maurice Cole was working for a pirate radio station when the program controller, Ben Tony, told all on board the ship that they must change their names for legal purposes. The DJ explains how he made his own choice: "I think I'd just seen a movie with an actor called Edward Everett Horton. [. . .] I quite liked the name Everett so that came first, followed straightaway by Kenny" [Kenny Everett, *The Custard Stops at Hatfield*, 1982]. Edward Everett Horton (1887–1970) was an American star comic film actor, constantly popular from the 1920s to 1940s.

Evoe: Edmund George Valpy Knox (1881–1971), Eng. essayist, humorist. The writer's pseudonym is a blend of the initials of two of his names and the Latin cry *evoe* (from Greek *euoi*), used as an exclamation of joy in Bacchic rites. Evoe was editor of *Punch* from 1932 to 1949.

Tom **Ewell:** S. Yewell Tompkins (1909–   ), U.S. film comedian, stage actor. The actor adopted a form of his mother's maiden name, which he already had as his middle name.

Ex-Private X: Alfred McLelland Burrage (1889–1956), Eng. novelist, fantasy story writer.

Clive **Exton:** Clive Brooks (1930–   ), Eng. playwright.

An **Eye-Witness:** Charles Lamb (1775–1834), Eng. essayist, critic, poet. The writer, whose best-known pseudonym was Elia *(q.v.),* used this particular pen name for his verses entitled *Satan in Search of a Wife* (1831).

Fabian: Fabiano Forte (1943–   ), U.S. pop singer, film actor.

Nanette **Fabray:** Nanette Fabares (1920–   ), U.S. film comedienne, singer.

Philippe **Fabre d'Eglantine:** Philippe François Nazaire Fabre (1750–1794), Fr. playwright, revolutionary politician. The French writer, who was revolutionary in language as well as in politics—he invented new names for the months and days of the week—assumed this name after winning the *Prix de l'églantine* ("Wild Rose Prize") at the *Jeux Floraux* of Toulouse in his youth, although some say he won by means of a false claim.

Georg **Fabricius:** Georg Goldschmied (1516–1571), Ger. scholar. The scholar's assumed name is a latinization of his real name, which means "goldsmith." Compare the next two names below.

Barent **Fabritius:** Barent Pieterz (1624–1673), Du. painter, brother of Carel Fabritius (below).

Carel **Fabritius:** Carel Pieterz (1622–1654), Du. painter. Both brothers adopted the name Fabritius as a reference to their previous trade as carpenters (Latin *faber*, "carpenter"). Compare the name of Georg Fabricius (above).

Fabulous Moolah: Lillian Ellison (*c.*1930–   ), U.S. wrestler. The champion woman wrestler began her career in the ring at a tender age as "Slave Girl Moolah," the "prop" of a wrestler named Elephant Boy. Her ring name was effectively a nickname, from her announcement that she intended to wrestle for "all the moolah [money] I can get my hands on." She seems to have succeeded, and in the 1970s she claimed to be earning more than $100,000 a year.

A.A. **Fair:** Erle Stanley Gardner (1889–1970), U.S. crime novelist.

Douglas **Fairbanks,** Sr.: Douglas Elton Thomson Ullman (1883–1939), U.S. film actor. The film actor was the son of Hezekiah Charles Ullman and Ella Adelaide Marsh. When his parents divorced soon after he was born, his mother assumed the name of her first husband, John Fairbanks. Douglas Fairbanks adopted this name himself in 1900 and of course passed it down to his son, the film actor Douglas Fairbanks, Jr. (1909–   ).

Sydney **Fairbrother:** Sydney Tapping, later, Parselle, (1873–1941), Eng. film actress. The actress adopted her great-grandmother's name as her screen name.

Morgan **Fairchild:** Patsy McClenny (1950–   ), U.S. TV actress.

Frank **Fairleigh:** Francis Edward Smedley (1818–1864), Eng. novelist. The writer adopted the name of the fictional hero of his own novel, *Frank Fairleigh* (1850).

Michael **Fairless:** Margaret Fairless Barber (1869–1901), Eng. "inspirational" writer. The writer partly preserved her own name in her pseudonym, with the initial "M" of "Michael" representing that of "Margaret," and "Fairless" being her second name, which was the first name of her brother, Fairless Barber. But "Michael" was specific, in that it was the name of a young boy friend who often spent his summer holidays with her family. He was Michael McDonnell (1882–1956), later to become Sir Michael and Chief Justice of Palestine in the 1930s.

Adam **Faith:** Terence Nelhams (1940–   ), Eng. pop singer. The singer chose the name for the radio series *Six Five Special,* taking "Adam" from the boys' section of a book of names for children, and "Faith" from the girls' section. He commented: "I liked the sound of Adam. Adam, the first man. Short. Sweet. Easily memorized." On the name as a whole: "I liked the note of courage in it. Adam Faith. Yes, they seemed to match up" [Adam Faith, *Poor Me*, 1961].

Falco: Johann Holzel (1957–   ), Austrian pop singer.

Hans **Fallada:** Wilhelm Friedrich Rudolf Ditzen (1893–1947), Ger. novelist. The novelist adopted his new surname from the talking horse in the fairy tale "The Ugly Duckling," as recounted in *Grimms' Fairy Tales* (1812–1822).

Georgie **Fame:** Clive Powell (1943–   ), Eng. pop musician. The name was given to the singer by rock-'n'-roll producer Larry Parnes, who allegedly said, "The next kid to walk through my door, I'm gonna call Georgie Fame." The next kid to do so was Clive Powell, and Parnes hired him as a member of the Blue Flames, the backing group assigned to Billy Fury *(q.v.)* on a 1960 tour.

Violet **Fane:** Baroness Mary Montgomerie Currie, previously Singleton, née

Lamb (1843–1905), Eng. novel, verse writer. The author selected the name, that of a character in Disraeli's novel *Vivian Grey* (1827), for her first publication, a volume of verse entitled *From Dawn to Noon* (1872). The pseudonym was necessary to conceal her literary activity from her family.

Eben **Fardd:** Ebenezer Thomas (1802–1863), Welsh poet. "Eben" represents "Ebenezer," and "Fardd" simply means "poet" (Welsh *bardd*, "poet," "bard," here in its mutated form).

Donna **Fargo:** Yvonne Vaughn (1949–   ), U.S. country singer. Presumably "Fargo" for the famous pioneer expressman, Wells Fargo, with "Donna" meaning "lady." Although the singer's new surname also suggests her original surname.

Princess **Farida:** Safina Zulfikar (1920–1988), queen of Egypt. Safina Zulfikar changed her first name (Iranian for "pure rose") to Farida ("precious") in 1938, when she married King Farouk. The change complied with a tradition that all members of the Egyptian royal family must have names beginning with the same initial. King Farouk divorced his wife ten years later, however, when she failed to produce an heir to the throne, and Farida went to live in France with her three daughters.

Carlo **Farinelli:** Carlo Broschi (1705–1782), It. castrato singer. The singer adopted the surname of his benefactors, the brothers Farina. According to some accounts, he may have been their nephew. The brothers were of French origin, and appear to have been originally named Farinel.

Ralph Milne **Farley:** Robert Sherman Hoar (1887–1963), U.S. SF writer.

Chris **Farlowe:** John Henry Deighton (1940–   ), Eng. pop singer.

Marianne **Farningham:** Mary Anne Hearn (1834–1909), Eng. religious writer, hymnwriter. The writer adjusted her first two names to form a single Christian name, then changed her surname to that of the village in Kent where she was born.

Martha **Farquharson:** Martha Farquharson Finley (1828–1909), U.S children's writer.

Walli **Farrad:** Wallace D. Fard (*c*.1877–?1934), U.S. Black Muslim leader. This is one of the many names assumed by the Black Muslim leader, who became prominent in the 1930s in America. He is now revered by Black Muslims as Master Wallace Fard Muhammad, and to him are assigned all the attributes of God (Allah), so that he is referred to as "Creator of Heaven and Earth, Most Wise, All Knowing, Most Merciful, All Powerful, Finder and Life-Giver, Master of the Day of Judgment." Understandably one of the criticisms leveled at the Black Muslims by orthodox Muslims is that they worship Wallace Fard rather than Allah of the "true" Islam. Among the other names used by Fard were: Professor Ford, Farrad Mohammed, F. Mohammed Ali, Wallace Fard Muhammad, and God (Allah). His divinity was reinforced by his mysterious disappearance around 1935.

M.J. **Farrell:** Mary Nesta Keane, née Skrine (1905–   ), Ir. author. Mary (or Molly) Skrine began to write during a long spell in bed with suspected tuberculosis. The result was a romantic tale entitled *The Knight of Cheerful Countenance*, which was accepted by Mills & Boon. For this she selected the pen name Farrell, taking it from a bar she passed one day, riding home on her bicycle. She said, "I had to keep it a secret as long as I possibly could. Young men in that circle would have been afraid of you if they thought you read, let alone wrote" [*Sunday Times Magazine*, August 24, 1986].

Suzanne **Farrell:** Roberta Sue Ficker (1945–), U.S. novelist.

Catherine **Fawcett:** Catherine Ann Cookson, née McMullan (1906–), Eng. novelist.

Alice **Faye:** Alice Jeanne Leppert (1912–), U.S. film actress.

Joey **Faye:** Joseph Anthony Palladino (1910–), U.S. stage comedian.

Frank **Faylen:** Frank Ruf (1907–1985), U.S. film actor.

Irving **Fazola:** Irving Henry Prestopnik (1912–1949), U.S. jazz clarinettist. The musician's new name was created from the three musical notes *fa* (F), *so* (G), and *la* (A). No doubt one motive for a name change was that his Slavic surname Prestopnik means "criminal."

Dr. **Feelgood:** William Lee Perryman (1911–1985), U.S. blues singer. See also **Piano Red.**

Charles K. **Feldman:** Charles Gould (1904–1968), U.S. film producer.

Félix: Félix Fernandez Garcia (*c.*1896–1941), Sp. ballet dancer.

María **Félix:** María de los Angeles Felix Güerenã (1915–), Mexican film actress.

N. **Felix:** Nicholas Wanostrocht (1807–1876), Eng. schoolmaster, writer on cricket. The teacher and writer (and cricketer) used his pen name for his writings on the "great game," including the primer *Felix on the Bat,* a book sometimes found in the natural history section of public libraries. He also invented a device called the "catapulta," a kind of mechanical bowler. He was equally "N. Felix" when playing cricket, and is believed to have adopted this name "in deference [. . .] to the feelings of parents" (*Dictionary of National Biography*).

Elisaveta **Fen:** Lydia Jackson, née Jiburtovich (1900–1983), Russ.-born Eng. writer and translator.

Freddy **Fender:** Baldemar G. Huerta (1937–), U.S. country singer.

Shane **Fenton:** Alvin Stardust (*q.v.*).

Fanny **Fern:** Sara Payson Parton, née Willis (1811–1872), U.S. children's author.

Fernandel: Fernand-Joseph-Désiré Contandin (1903–1971), Fr. film comedian. The mother-in-law of the future comedian used to refer to him as "Fernand d'elle," that is, *her* Fernand, meaning her daughter's son, not her own. This is said to be the origin of the name.

Elizabeth X. **Ferrars:** Morna Doris Brown, née MacTaggart (1907–), Eng. novelist, mystery writer. The writer adopted her mother's maiden name.

José **Ferrer:** José Vincente Ferrer Otero y Cintrón (1909–), Puerto Rican-born U.S. stage, film actor.

Stepin **Fetchit:** Lincoln Theodore Monroe Andrew Perry (1902–1985), U.S. black film actor. The film actor, who made his name as a slow-moving, hardly nimble-witted black servant, originally adopted the stage name of "Skeeter" (which he wasn't). This became "Stepin Fetchit," however, when he was near destitute on one occasion, and bet his clothes against $30 on a horse of this name at an

Oklahoma race. He won, saved his clothes, and would soon write a comical song about his equine savior, whose own name obviously implies "Step and fetch it," or "Move fast and win the prize."

Edwige **Feuillère**: Caroline Edwige Cunati-Koenig (1907–), Fr. stage, film actress. Although a stage name, it should be pointed out that the actress used her married name, her husband being Pierre Feuillère. She began her stage career as "Cora Lynn" (from "Caroline").

Jacques **Feyder**: Jacques Frédérix (1888–1948), Belg.-born Fr. film director.

Michael **ffolkes**: Brian Davis (1925–1988), Eng. cartoonist. The cartoonist explained how his name came about: "I've always had a kind of attraction for multiple identity. I got ffolkes from *Burke's Peerage*. As an unusual name it has been very valuable. It was about the time of Sprods and Trogs and Smilbys [see **Trog** and **Smilby**]. I wanted a distinctive name. I don't think *Punch* knows, actually [. . .] Originally I wanted to write and called myself Brian Chorister, horrible name. Then I tried using the name Dedalus, based on the James Joyce character [. . .] I had just read Joyce. It shows a tendency to want to get away from the ordinariness of being Davis. Davis, plain Davis, is one of the commonest names in the country" [Michael Bateman, *Funny Way to Earn a Living*, 1966].

John **Field**: John Greenfield (1921–), Eng. ballet dancer, director.

Martyn **Field**: Frederick William Horner (1854–), Eng. politician, administrator, author. The writer took his name from the London church of St. Martin-in-the-Fields, where he was Chairman of the Works Committee.

Michael **Field**: Katharine Harris Bradley (1848–1914), Eng. poet + Edith Emma Cooper (1862–1913), Eng. poet.

Virginia **Field**: Margaret Cynthia Field (1917–), Eng. film actress.

Gabriel **Fielding**: Alan Gabriel Barnsley (1916–), Br. novelist. The novelist assumed his mother's maiden name, which in full was Fielding-Smith.

Benny **Fields**: Benjamin Geisenfeld (1894–1959), U.S. film actor, singer.

Gracie **Fields**: Grace Stansfield (1898–1979), Eng. popular singer, comedienne. The singer began her career in her native Rochdale, Lancashire, when she was only 13. After a performance one day, the girl brought up the matter of her name. "'Mumma,' said Grace, as they walked home together after the second house, 'T' manager says Grace Stansfield's a bit long as names go.' Mumma who was glowing inside with secret pride, tried it out for sound. Yes, it might be a bit costly to put a name like that up in lights. She wondered whether they should cut the name in half. 'How about, Fields?' she suggested. 'but let's get sommat posh to put in front, like Stana, or Anna!' 'What's wrong with Grace, Mumma?' Mumma rolled it over her tongue. 'Grace Fields! Bit too stiff-like. Now what about . . . Gracie. That's it, Gracie Fields!' The thirteen-year-old, newly-christened Gracie Fields gave a whoop of joy" [Muriel Burgess with Tommy Keene, *Gracie Fields*, 1980].

Lew **Fields**: Lewis Maurice Shanfields (1867–1941), U.S. stage comedian, teaming with Joseph Weber.

Tommy **Fields**: Thomas Stansfield (1908–), Eng. music hall comedian.

Totie **Fields**: Sophie Feldman (?1930–1978), U.S. nightclub, TV comedienne. "Totie" was undoubtedly a childish pronunciation of "Sophie."

W.C. Fields: William Claude Dukinfield (1879–1946), U.S. film comedian. This was the comedian's standard stage name. All the many others ranged from the bizarre to the grotesque, and were in the best tradition of American humorous pseudonyms. (For a selection, see Chapter 7). As an appetizer, note the (admittedly rather tame) first name that he assumed when he started his career as a boy juggler (1891). This was simply "Whitey, the Wonder Boy." He first used W.C. Fields in 1893. Claude was a name that he had always hated; the villains in his films were often called Claude. Many of the names that he subsequently adopted were based on the names used by Charles Dickens, whose books he admired [Carlotta Monti with Cy Rice, *W.C. Fields and Me,* 1974].

Figaro: Henry Clapp (1814–1875), U.S. journalist, editor. The name has been popular with many journalists and columnists. Another was Mariano Jose de Larra (1809–1837), the Spanish satirist and dramatist, who used the pseudonym for the contribution of humorous articles to various periodicals. *Le Figaro* is itself a leading French daily newspaper, founded in 1825. The name comes from the hero of Beaumarchais's *Le Barbier de Séville* (1775) and *Le Mariage de Figaro* (1784), where Figaro is a barber-turned-doorkeeper. And barbers (and doorkeepers), of course, hear all the gossip. The ultimate source of the name may be in Spanish *hígado,* "liver," in the sense of someone who has "pluck" and spirit.

Filandre: Jean-Baptiste Monchaingre (or Jean Mathée) (1616–1691), Fr. actor-manager.

Fin-Bec: William Blanchard Jerrold (1826–1884), Eng. playwright, novelist. French *fin-bec* (literally "fine beak") means "gourmet." Jerrold lives as much in Paris as in London, and was himself a gourmet, publishing the *Epicure's Year-Book* in 1867 and (as Fin-Bec) gastronomic works such as *Knife and Fork* (1871), *The Dinner Bell* (1878), and the like.

Peter **Finch:** Peter Ingle-Finch (1916–1977), Eng. stage, film actor.

Larry **Fine:** Laurence Feinberg (1911–1975), U.S. film comedian.

Fiore della Neve: Martinus Gesinus Lambert van Loghem (1849–1934), Du. poet, fiction writer. The writer's adopted Italian name means "flower of the snow."

John **Fiske:** Edmund Fisk Green (1842–1901), U.S. philosopher, historian.

Minnie Maddern **Fiske:** Marie Augusta Davey (1865–1932), U.S. stage actress. The actress made her stage debut with her parents when she was only three, appearing under her mother's maiden name, with "Minnie" referring to her smallness. The name of Fiske was that of her husband, Harrison Grey Fiske, whom she married in 1890.

Mary **Fitt:** Kathleen Freeman (1897–1959), Br. writer of books on Greek subjects, detective novelist.

Edward **Fitzball:** Edward Ball (1792–1873), Eng. dramatist.

George Savage **Fitz–Boodle:** William Makepeace Thackeray (1811–1863), Eng. novelist. One of the many eccentric noms de plume adopted by the famous writer. He used this one for his contributions to *Fraser's Magazine* (1842).

Barry **Fitzgerald:** William Joseph Shields (1888–1961), Ir. film actor. When William Shields began his acting career, he was working full time as a civil servant. Another name for this activity was therefore needed, and he chose a typical Irish name. By day he was thus William Shields, and by night, when he acted, he was Barry Fitzgerald – a dual personality.

Walter **Fitzgerald:** Walter Fitzgerald Bond (1896–1977), Eng. stage, film actor.

Paul **Fix:** Paul Fix Morrison (1901–1983), U.S. film actor.

Francis **Flagg:** Henry George Weiss (1898–1946), U.S. SF writer.

Bud **Flanagan:** Chaim Reuben Weintrop (1896–1968), Eng. stage, film comedian, of Pol.-Jewish parentage. The actor first trod the boards of the music hall as "Fargo the Boy Conjuror." This was in London. At the age of 13 he emigrated with his family to the United States and, after a brief interlude as a boxer with the unlikely ring name of Luke McGluke, tried his fortune on the vaudeville stage as Bobby Wayne. Back in Britain again at the start of the First World War he joined the army as Driver Robert Winthrop. But why Flanagan? The name was inherited from his army years. Apparently a mean sergeant-major seemed to have it in for the future actor and singer, and when Driver Winthrop was wounded in 1918 and took his leave of the service, his last words to his sergeant-major were, "I'll remember your name as long as I live." Flanagan, thus, was the name he assumed when resuming his career on the stage. (Later the sergeant-major became a barman in London, and Bud and he were reconciled.) After Flanagan and Allen's famous song *Underneath the Arches* was published in 1932 the profits began to roll in handsomely. With his share, Bud bought a house in the village of Angmering, Sussex, and named it *Arches*. His actual first break in show business was given him by Florrie Forde (*q.v.*) [Bill McGowran, "You See Him Everywhere," in *Late Extra: A Miscellany by "Evening News" Writers, Artists, and Photographers*, Associated Newspapers, *c.*1952].

Fléchelles: Hugues Guéru (? –1633), Fr. actor.

George **Fleming:** Constance Fletcher (1858–1938), U.S. novelist, playwright.

Oliver **Fleming:** Philip MacDonald (1900–1981), Eng. writer of detective novels.

Rhonda **Fleming:** Marilyn Louis (1922–   ), U.S. film actress.

Herbert **Flemming:** Arif Nicolaiih El-Michelle (1905–   ), Tunisian jazz trombonist.

George U. **Fletcher:** Fletcher Pratt (1897–1956), U.S. naval, American historian, fantasy writer.

Robert **Fletcher:** Robert Fletcher Wycoff (1923–   ), U.S. theatre designer.

Fleury: Abraham-Joseph Bénard (1750–1822), Fr. comic actor.

William Jermyn **Florence:** Bernard Conlin (1831–1891), U.S. comedian.

Floridor: Josias de Soulas, Sieur de Primefosse (?1608–1671), Fr. actor.

Florizel: George IV (1762–1830), king of Great Britain. King George IV adopted this name when still Prince of Wales for his correspondence with the actress Mrs. Mary Robinson. Florizel is the character in Shakespeare's *The Winter's Tale* who falls in love with Perdita. When Mrs. Robinson first attracted the royal attention, she was playing the part of Perdita, and indeed became generally known by this name after her fine enactment of the role in 1779. She left the stage the following year to become the Prince's mistress, thus in a curious sense living up to her stage name (which means "Lost One") See further details at Perdita.

Flotsam: Bentley Collingwood Hilliam (1890–1968), Eng. composer, pianist, entertainer, teaming with Jetsam *(q.v.)*. The comic singers always signed off their act with the phrase, "Yours very sincerely, Flotsam and Jetsam." Flotsam was a countertenor, as fitting for his name (flotsam *floats* on the surface of the water), while Jetsam was a bass (jetsam—at least according to some—*sinks* deeply when it is thrown overboard).

Barbara **Flynn:** Barbara McMurray (1948–   ), Eng. stage, TV actress.

Josiah **Flynt:** Josiah Flint Willard (1869–1907), U.S. writer on experiences as a tramp.

Nich **Foch:** Nina Fock (1924–   ), Du. stage actress, working in U.S.

Jonathan Lituleson **Fogarty:** James T. Farrell (1904–1979), U.S. novelist, critic.

Joan **Fontaine:** Joan de Beauvoir de Havilland (1917–   ), Eng.-born U.S. stage, film actress. The actress adopted the name Joan Fontaine in 1937, following her mother's divorce and subsequent remarriage to George M. Fontaine. Joan's elder sister, by one year, is the actress Olivia de Havilland.

Wayne **Fontana:** Glyn Geoffrey Ellis (1945–   ), Eng. rock musician. An American name for a purely English musician. But his first record was a version of "Road Runner," by Bo Diddley *(q.v.)*, and this was released on the Philips' *Fontana* label in 1963.

[Dame] Margot **Fonteyn:** Margot Fonteyn de Arias, née Margaret Hookham (1919–   ), Eng. ballet dancer. The ballet dancer originally changed her name from Margaret Hookham to "Margot Fontes," based on her Brazilian mother's maiden name. Later, on the advice of Ninette de Valois *(q.v.)*, she changed this to Margot Fonteyn.

Brenda **Forbes:** Brenda Taylor (1909–   ), Eng. stage actress. The actress adopted her mother's maiden name as her stage name.

Bryan **Forbes:** John Theobald Clarke (1926–   ), Eng. film actor, screenwriter. As the actor records in his autobiography, "Bryan Forbes is a stage fiction, chosen at random by the late Lionel Gamlin, the man who gave me my first professional job" [Bryan Forbes, *Notes for a Life*, 1974]. (Lionel Gamlin was a radio producer for the BBC.)

Meriel **Forbes:** Meriel Forbes-Robertson (1913–   ), Eng. stage, film actress.

Ralph **Forbes:** Ralph Taylor (1902–1951), Br. film actor, working in U.S.

Stanton **Forbes:** Deloris Stanton Forbes (1923–   ), U.S. mystery writer.

Elbur **Ford:** Eleanor Hibbert (1906–   ), Eng. novelist.

Emile **Ford:** Emile Sweetman (1937–   ), Bahamanian rock singer.

Ford Madox **Ford:** Ford Hermann Hueffer (1873–1939), Br. novelist, editor. The writer initially adopted the Christian names Joseph Leopold Madox—he was the grandson of the Victorian painter Ford Madox Brown—then, embarrassed in the First World War by his German surname, changed his name by deed poll (1919) to Ford Madox Ford. On the title pages of his books his name alternated between Ford Madox Ford and Ford Madox Hueffer: he used the former for his sequence of war novels with the central character Christopher Tietgens as well as for travel books and reminiscences. For *The Questions at the Well; With Sundry Other Verses for Notes of Music* (1893) he had earlier used the name "Fenil Haig."

Francis **Ford:** Francis Feeney (or O'Fearna) (1883–1953), U.S. film actor.

Frankie **Ford:** Frank Guzzo (1940–   ), U.S. rock singer.

Gerald Randolph **Ford,** Jr.: Leslie Lynch King, Jr. (1913–   ), U.S. president. When the future thirty-eighth President of the United States was still a baby, his parents divorced and his mother moved to Grand Rapids where she married Gerald R. Ford, Sr., who adopted the boy and gave him his name.

Glenn **Ford:** Gwyllyn Newton (1916–   ), Can. film actor, working in U.S.

John **Ford:** Sean Aloysius Feeney (or O'Fearna) (1895–1973), U.S. film director, of Ir. parentage.

Leslie **Ford:** Zenith Brown, née Jones (1898–   ), U.S. detective novelist.

Paul **Ford:** Paul Ford Weaver (1901–1976), U.S. stage actor. The actor adopted his mother's maiden name, which was already his middle name.

Wallace **Ford:** Samuel Jones Grundy (1897–1966), Eng.-born U.S. film actor.

Florrie **Forde:** Florence Flanagan (1876–1940), Austral.-born Eng. music hall singer.

Walter **Forde:** Thomas Seymour (1896–1984), Br. film director.

Keith **Fordyce:** Keith Marriott (1928–   ), Eng. radio, TV interviewer, DJ.

Mark **Forest:** Lou Degni (1933–   ), U.S. film actor.

Fanny **Forester:** Emily Chubbuck Judson (1817–1854), U.S. novelist. Did Emily Judson base her pen name on that of Fanny Fern *(q.v.)*? Or vice versa?

Frank **Forester:** Henry William Herbert (1807–1858), Eng. author, editor, working in U.S.

Forez: François Mauriac (1885–1970), Fr. novelist, playwright, poet. When working for the French Resistance, Mauriac wrote *Cahier Noir* (1943), choosing for this the name of the mountainous region in the Massif Central that Resistance workers found so suitable for cover.

George **Formby:** George Hoy Booth (1904–1961), Eng. film comedian, singer, ukelele player. The well-known comedian, whose middle name, Hoy, was his mother's maiden name, took the same stage name as his father, James Lawler Booth. How did Booth Senior come to acquire his name? As a young millworker, James would supplement his small wages by singing in the street, where he was "discovered" by a Mr. Brown, together with another boy who had teamed up with him, and sent to different Northern towns to earn a shilling or two for his "manager." Mr. Brown would pay James threepence a week and the other boy sixpence. To cut his expenses, Mr. Brown transported the boys in the traveling props basket, with the lid down, to avoid paying their train fares. "On one occasion, when they were travelling from Manchester to Bury, Jimmy happened not to be in the basket and sat watching coal wagons go by. A sign on one of the wagons showed that it came from Formby, Lancashire. The name appealed to him. He preferred it, in a theatrical sense, to his own name of Booth and decided there and then to make it his own. But Jimmy or James did not go with it. Beginning with the first letter of the alphabet he went through in his mind all the names he could think of and stopped when he got to 'G' and George. That was it—George Formby. It sounded right. It suited him. His change of name coincided with his desire to end the singing partnership " [Alan Randall and Ray Seaton, *George Formby,* 1974].

Sally **Forrest:** Katharine Scully Feeney (1928–   ), U.S. film actress.

Steve **Forrest:** William Forrest Andrews (1924–   ), U.S. film actor.

John **Forsell:** Carl Johan Jacob (1868–1941), Swe. opera singer.

Willi **Forst:** Wilhelm Anton Frohs (1903–1980), Austr. film actor.

Robert **Forster:** Robert Foster (1941–   ), U.S. film actor.

Bruce **Forsyth:** Bruce Joseph Forsyth Johnson (1928–   ), Eng. stage, TV actor, compère.

Jean **Forsyth:** Jean Newton McIlwraith (1871–1938), Can. short story, magazine article writer.

John **Forsythe:** John Lincoln Freund (1918–   ), U.S. stage, film actor.

Fortis: Leslie Forse (1907–1978), Eng. journalist, editor.

Dion **Fortune:** Violet Mary Firth (1890–1946), U.S. writer of occult novels.

Lukas **Foss:** Lukas Fuchs (1922–   ), Ger.-born U.S. composer, conductor.

Dianne **Foster:** Dianne Laruska (1928–   ), Can. film actress.

Norman **Foster:** Norman Hoeffner (1900–1976), U.S. film actor.

Richard **Foster:** Kendall Foster Crossen (1910–   ), U.S. author, journalist.

Susanna **Foster:** Susan De Lis Flanders Larson (1924–   ), U.S. film actress. She began her career as an opera singer and took her professional name from that of Stephen Foster and his song "Oh, Susanna." Compare the name of Nelly Bly.

Fougasse: Cyril Kenneth Bird (1887–1965), Eng. artist, cartoonist, editor. The former editor of *Punch* (succeeding Evoe, *q.v.*) adopted his unusual name in order to avoid confusion with another *Punch* artist calling himself Bird (although actually Yeats). He later explained that "fougasse" was an old technical term used by sappers for a rough-and-ready landmine that might or might not go off. A cartoonist always hopes that his drawings and captions *will* "go off," or make an impact.

Adam **Fouleweather:** Thomas Nashe (1567–1601), Eng. satirical pamphleteer, dramatist. The satirist used this name for his *Astrologicall Prognostication* (1591), in which he replied to the savage attack on him by Richard Hervey, the astrologer. His best-known pseudonym was Pasquil (*q.v.*).

Oliver **Foulis:** David Lloyd (1635–1692), Eng. miscellaneous writer.

Sidney **Fox:** Sidney Liefer (1910–1942), U.S. film actress.

William **Fox:** Wilhelm Fried (1879–1952), Hung.-born U.S. film executive ("Twentieth-Century Fox").

John **Foxx:** Dennis Leigh (*c.*1950–   ), Eng. rock musician.

Redd **Foxx:** John Elroy Sanford (1922–   ), U.S. film, TV comedian. The comedian was already known by his nickname of "Chicago Red" (for the Chicago baseball team), and to this he added an extra "d," taking his second name from the great baseball player Jimmie Foxx, who at one time played for Chicago.

Eddie **Foy,** Sr.: Edwin Fitzgerald (1856–1928), U.S. stage actor, vaudeville player.

Eddie **Foy,** Jr.: Edward Fitzgerald (1905–1983), U.S. stage actor, dancer, son of Eddie Foy, Sr. (*q.v.*). A good example of a necessary shortening of a lengthy name so that it fits easily on billboards.

F.P.A.: Franklin Pierce Adams (1881–1960), U.S. journalist, humorist. The writer usually signed his columns with his initials.

Harry **Fragson:** Leon Vince Philip Pott (1869–1913), Eng.-Belg. music hall comedian, singer.

Celia **Franca:** Celia Franks (1921–   ), Eng. ballet dancer, director, choreographer.

Anatole **France:** Jacques Anatole François Thibault (1844–1924), Fr. novelist, poet, dramatist. The writer assumed his pseudonym not so much to emphasize his nationality as to commemorate the fact that his father, who owned a bookshop, was called "Monsieur France" by his customers. (His first name was François.)

[Mother] **Frances Mary Theresa:** Frances Ball (1794–1861), Eng. religious founder of Loretto nuns, Ireland.

Anthony **Franciosa:** Anthony George Papaleo (1928–   ), It.-born U.S. film actor.

Arlene **Francis:** Arlene Kazanjian (1908–   ), U.S. TV personality.

Arthur **Francis:** Ira Gershwin (1896–1983), U.S. songwriter. Ira Gershwin used this name when, after an abortive literary start, he began writing the lyrics for his brother George's songs in the 1920s (see George Gershwin).

Connie **Francis:** Concetta Rosa Maria Franconero (1938–   ), U.S. pop singer, film actress, of It. descent.

Kay **Francis:** Katherine Edwina Gibbs (1903–1968), U.S. stage, film actress. The actress's stage name came from that of her first husband, James Dwight Francis.

M. E. **Francis:** Mary Blundell, née Sweetman (c.1855–1930), Ir. novelist. The writer adopted the first name of her husband, Francis Blundell.

[Saint] **Francis of Assisi:** Giovanni di Pietro di Bernadone (1182–1226), It. monk, preacher. The famous saint's father was away on business in France at the time of his son's birth and on his return changed the baby's name to Francesco (Francis) as a memorial to his visit.

Franco: L'Okanga La Ndju Pene Luambo Makiadi (1938–   ), Zaïre popular musician.

Harry **Franco:** Charles Frederick Briggs (1804–1877), U.S. journalist, author.

Pat **Frank:** Harry Hart (1907–   ), U.S. SF writer.

Melvin **Franklin:** David English (1942–   ), U.S. black Motown singer.

Jane **Frazee:** Mary Jane Frahse (1918–1985), U.S. singer, film actress. An original modification of a European name for an English-speaking audience.

Liz **Frazer:** Elizabeth Winch (1933–   ), Eng. film actress.

Frédérick: Antoine-Louis Prosper Lemaître (1800–1876), Fr. actor. The actor adopted his grandfather's name as his stage name.

Pauline **Frederick:** Beatrice Pauline Libbey (1883–1938), U.S. stage, film actress.

Vera **Fredowa:** Winifred Edwards (1896–1989), Eng. ballet dancer, teacher.

Arthur **Freed:** Arthur Grossman (1894–1973), U.S. film producer.

Mrs. **Freeman:** Sarah Churchill, Duchess of Marlborough (1660–1744), Eng. aristocrat. This was the symbolic name adopted by the Duchess for her correspondence with Queen Anne, otherwise Mrs. Morley (*q.v.*).

Cynthia **Freeman:** Bea Feinberg (?1915–1988), U.S. romantic novelist.

Peter **French:** John Nicholas ffrench (1935–), Welsh stage, TV actor.

Pierre **Fresnay:** Pierre-Jules-Louis Laudenbach (1897–1975), Fr. stage, film actor.

Aunt **Friendly:** Sarah S.T. Baker (1824–1906), Br. children's writer.

Trixie **Friganza:** Delia O'Callahan (1870–1955), U.S. actress, singer.

Freddie **Frinton:** Frederick Hargate (1911–1968), Eng. comedian. Perhaps from Frinton-on-Sea, a popular seaside resort (in Essex) since the 1880s?

Joachim **Frizius:** Robert Flud (1574–1637), Eng. physician, Rosicrucian.

David **Frome:** Zenith Brown, née Jones (1898–), U.S. novelist.

Christopher **Fry:** Christopher Harris (1907–), Eng. playwright. The writer adopted his grandmother's maiden name as his pen name.

Elmer **Fudpucker:** Hollis Champion (1935–), Can. country & western singer, comedian.

Fu Manchu: David Bamberg (1904–1974), U.S. magician, son of Okito *(q.v.)*.

Sofia **Fuoco:** Maria Brambilla (1830–1916), It. ballet dancer.

Robin **Furneaux:** Frederick William Robin Smith, 3rd Earl of Birkenhead (1936–1985), Br. author, historian.

Yvonne **Furneaux:** Yvonne Scatcherd (1928–), Fr. film actress, working in U.K.

Billy **Fury:** Ronald Wycherley (1941–1983), Eng. pop singer. The singer was so named by impresario Larry Parnes (who also named Georgie Fame and Marty Wilde, *(q.v.)*). The name is almost certainly an 'image' one, as were those of Fame and Wilde.

Johnny **G:** John Gotting (1949–), Eng. folk, pub rock singer.

Franceska **Gaal:** Fanny Zilveritch (1904–1972), Hung. film actress.

Jean **Gabin:** Jean Alexis Gabin Moncorgé (1904–1976), Fr. film actor. The actor adopted the same professional name as that of his father, a café entertainer.

Naum **Gabo:** Naum Neemia Pevsner (1890–1977), Russ. constructivist sculptor.

Zsa Zsa **Gabor:** Sari Gabor (1923–), Hung. film actress, working in U.S.

Sarah **Gainham:** Sarah Rachel Ames (1922–), Br. novelist.

Serge **Gainsbourg:** Lucien Ginzburg (1928–), Fr. popular singer, of Jewish-Russ. parentage. The singer changed his first name, as he regarded it as that of a typical hairdresser ("Lucien coiffeur pour hommes"). In any case, he had never liked it. His Jewish-Russian surname (representing the common Jewish name Ginsburg, ultimately from the Bavarian town of Gunzburg) he converted to a French-style equivalent [Lucien Roux, *Serge Gainsbourg*, 1986].

Vincenzo **Galeotti:** Vincenzo Tomaselli (1733–1816), It. ballet dancer, teacher.

Galimafré: Auguste Gérin (1790–1870), Fr. comic actor, tealing with Bobèche *(q.v.)*. The actor's stage name means "hotch-potch" (modern French *galimafrée*).

Anna **Galina:** Evelyne Cournand (1936–), U.S. ballet dancer. It is tempting to think that the ballerina formed her name from those of two great Russian artistes, the dancer *Anna* Pavlova and the singer *Galina* Vishnevskaya.

Geoffrey **Gambado:** Henry William Bembury (1750–1811), Eng. artist, caricaturist.

Sir Gregory **Gander:** George Ellis (1753–1815), Eng. author. The writer used the name for his *Poetical Tales by Sir Gregory Gander* (1778), which were immediately identified as coming from his pen.

Joe **Gans:** Joseph Gaines (1874–1910), U.S. lightweight boxer.

Greta **Garbo:** Greta Lovisa Gustafsson (1905–   ), Swe.-born U.S. film actress. That the world-famous movie star was originally Greta Lovisa Gustafsson there is little doubt. Exactly how she acquired her well-known screen surname is rather more uncertain. The name is generally thought to have been given to her by the Swedish film director Mauritz Stiller (although it is possible that someone other than Stiller was responsible for the name). But how did he devise it? One version says that he "toyed with Gabor after Gabor Bethlen, an ancient Hungarian king, then settled on the variation, Garbo" [Norman Zierold, *Garbo*, 1970].

One of the most detailed accounts of the origin of the name is given by Garbo's biographer, Robert Payne: "The name, which became so memorable, was the invention of Mauritz Stiller, who had long cherished it and was determined to bestow it on an actress worthy of it. In his imagination the name suggested fairyland, romance, beauty, everything he had associated in his childhood with the utmost happiness and the wildest dreams. Many explanations were later offered to explain the name. Someone wrote that he derived it from the first letters of a sentence he wrote describing Greta Gustafsson: *Gör alla roller berömvärt opersonligt* ("Plays all roles in a commendably impersonal fashion"). Others remembered that *garbo* in Spanish and Italian is a rarely used word describing a peculiar kind of grace and charm. Still others imagined it was derived from the name of Erica Darbo, a famous Norwegian singer of the time. A more plausible explanation can be found in the *garbon*, a mysterious sprite that sometimes comes out at night to dance to the moonbeams. This elfin creature was a descendant of the dreaded *gabilun* of Swedish and German folklore, who was killed by Kudrun. The *gabilun* breathed fire from its nostrils and could assume any shape at will, and some memory of his ancient power remained in the *garbon*, just as Robin Goodfellow retains some features of the Great God Pan. No one knows the true origin of the word. When asked about it, Stiller simply looked up in the air, smiled, and said, 'I really don't know. But it's right, isn't it?'" [Robert Payne, *The Great Garbo*, 1976].

Yet another theory, put forward by Frederick Sands and Sven Broman in their biography [*The Divine Garbo*, 1979], is that Greta had visited some relatives from time to time who live on a farm called "Garboda," and that this might perhaps be the explanation. The change was at any rate made officially on December 4, 1923. Finally, as if all this mystery was not enough, Garbo at times used other pseudonyms. Among these other names were Harriet Brown (her favorite), Gussie Berger, Mary Holmquist, Jean Clark, Karin Lund, Miss Swanson, Emily Clark, Jane Emerson, Alice Smith, and the unexpected male name Karl Lund.

Joyce **Gard:** Joyce Reeves (1911–   ), Br. children's writer.

Vincent **Gardenia:** Vincent Scognamiglio (1922–   ), U.S. film comedian.

Ava **Gardner:** Lucy Johnson (1922–   ), U.S. film actress. "Lucy Johnson" is stated to be the actress's "real" name by many sources. But it appears that she was indeed born Ava Lavinia Gardner, the daughter of Jonas and Mary Elizabeth Gardner, of Grabtown, North Carolina [John Daniell, *Ava Gardner*, 1982].

Ed **Gardner:** Edward Poggenberg (1901–1963), U.S. TV actor.

John **Garfield:** Jacob Julius Garfinkle (1912–1952), U.S. film actor.

Beverly **Garland:** Beverly Fessenden (1926–   ), U.S. film, TV actress.

Judy **Garland:** Frances Ethel Gumm (1922–1969), U.S. film actress. The actress changed her name in 1934 or 1935, when she was still only 12, for a singing act that she performed with her sisters (as the Gumm Sisters, who were on one occasion wrongly billed as the Glum Sisters). Young? Well, yes. But then Frances Gumm was one of the greatest child film stars, playing Dorothy in *The Wizard of Oz* when she was still in her teens. Her new name was given her by her agent, George Jessel, who based it on the name of *New York Post* theatre critic Robert Garland and the song *Judy*, by Hoagy Carmichael. This was popular at the time and her favorite – especially the line that went, "If she seems a saint, and you find she ain't, that's Judy!"

Robert **Garloch:** Robert Sutherland (1909–   ), Br. poet.

James **Garner:** James Baumgartner (1928–   ), U.S. film actor.

Edward **Garrett:** Isabella Fyvie Mayo (1843–1914), Br. novelist.

John **Garrick:** Reginald Doudy (1902–   ), Br. stage, film actor. The actor must surely have picked his name to commemorate the great eighteenth-century English actor David Garrick.

Garrincha: Manoel Francisco dos Santos (1933–   ), Chilean footballer.

Andrew **Garve:** Paul Winterton (1908–   ), Eng. journalist, mystery writer.

Romain **Gary:** Roman Kacewgary (1914–1980), Russ.-born (Georgian) Fr. author.

Jonathan **Gash:** John Grant (1935–   ), Br. mystery writer.

Pearly **Gates:** Viola Billups (1946–   ), U.S. black popular singer. The singer was so named by her manager, Bruce Welch, who told her she had "better learn how to spell it." But how else could you spell such a heavenly name?

Gath: George Alfred Townsend (1841–1914), U.S. journalist, war correspondent, fiction writer. The name represents the writer's initials with also, one suspects, an oblique pun on the biblical exhortation, "Tell it not in Gath."

Gaultier-Garguille: Hugues Guéru (*c.*1573–1633), Fr. actor.

Paul **Gavarni:** Sulpice Guillaume Chevalier (1804–1866), Fr. illustrator, caricaturist. The artist acquired his "canvas name" by a curious mistake. He once sent his paintings to a Paris exhibition from the Pyrenean village of Gavarnie. When displayed, the pictures were erroneously labeled as being by "Gavarnie," this name having appeared on the container. The exhibition was a success, and with a minor adjustment of spelling, the artist assumed the name attributed to him.

John **Gavin:** Jack Golenor (1928–   ), U.S. film actor.

Jack **Gawsworth:** Terence Ian Fytton Armstrong (1912–1970), Eng. poet, critic, editor, horror story writer.

William **Gaxton:** Arturo Gaxiola (1893–1963), U.S. entertainer. The name looks suspiciously like a variation on that of William Caxton, the famous English printer, with the first half of the original surname retained for distinction.

Maisie **Gay:** Maisie Munro-Noble (1883–1945), Eng. film actress.

Noel **Gay:** Reginald Armitage (1898–1954), Eng. popular songwriter and music publisher. The musician adopted the name when he was director of music and organist at St. Anne's Church, London. The aim was not to embarrass the church authorities, who might not have been too pleased to discover their music director writing musicals!

Crystal **Gayle:** Brenda Gail Webb (1951–   ), U.S. pop singer.

Janet **Gaynor:** Laura Gainor (1906–1984), U.S. film actress.

Mitzi **Gaynor:** Francesca Mitzi Marlene de Charney von Gerber (1930–   ), U.S. film actress.

Eunice **Gayson:** Eunice Sargaison (1931–   ), Br. film, stage actress.

Clara **Gazul:** Prosper Mérimée (1803–1870), Fr. novelist, historian. For the web of intrigue woven here, see the account on page 28.

Myles na **gCopaleen:** Brian O'Nolan (1912–1966), Ir. novelist. The name was used by the writer for many years for his contributions to the *Irish Times.* It was devised for him by Dion Boucicault *(q.v.)* and means "Myles of the hobby horse." He also wrote as Flann O'Brien *(q.v.)* and George Knowall.

George **Gé:** George Grönfeldt (1893–1962), Finnish ballet dancer, choreographer.

Nicolai **Gedda:** Nicolai Ustinov (1925–   ), Swe. opera singer, of Russ. descent.

Will **Geer:**William Ghere (1902–1978), U.S. stage actor.

Firmin **Gémier:** Firmin Tonnerre (1869–1933), Fr. stage actor, manager, director.

[Dame] Adeline **Genée:** Anina Jensen (1878–1970), Dan.-born Br. ballet dancer.

Genêt: Janet Flanner (1892–1978), U.S. foreign correspondent, novelist, art critic. The name represents her first name, and was possibly inspired by that of the French dramatist and novelist Jean Genet (1910–1986).

Genghis Khan: Temujin (or Temuchin) (1162–1227), Mongol conqueror. The great fighter adopted the title Genghis (or Chingis), meaning "perfect warrior," in 1206, adding "Khan" to mean "lord," "prince."

A **Gentleman of the University of Oxford:** Percy Bysshe Shelley (1792–1822), Eng. poet. Shelley used this name or title for his early "Gothic horror" verses, *St. Irvyne, or the Rosicrucian* (1811), published privately when he was a student at Oxford University.

A **Gentleman who has left his Lodgings:** [Lord] John Russell (1792–1878), Eng. poet. The earl adopted this nom de plume for his *Essays and Sketches of Life and Character* (1820).

A **Gentleman with a Duster:** Harold Begbie (1871–1929), Eng. novelist, biographer, religious writer.

Bobbie **Gentry:** Roberta Lee Streeter (1944–   ), U.S. pop musician, of Port. descent.

Mlle **George:** Marguerite-Joséphine Weymer (1787–1867), Fr. actress.

Boy **George:** George Alan O'Dowd (1961–   ), Eng. pop singer. The singer adopted the name in 1982, when he first began appearing, dressed as a girl (or at least androgynously), with his group Culture Club. He had himself billed as "Boy George" on the sleeve of his first single in order to answer the inevitable initial question, "Is it a boy or a girl?" The name would ensure that the apparent "she" was actually a "he" [*Pop Focus*, 1983].

Daniel **George:** Daniel George Bunting (1890–1967), Br. essayist, critic, anthologist.

Gladys **George:** Gladys Anna Clare (1904–1954), U.S. film actress.

Jim **Gerald:** Jacques Guenod (1889–1958), Fr. stage, film actor.

Geraldo: Gerald Bright (1904–1974), Br. dance-band leader. The dance-band leader added the "o" to his name after a visit to Brazil.

Stephen **Geray:** Stefan Gyergyay (1904–1976), Hung. film actor, working in U.K., U.S.

William **Gerhardie:** William Alexander Gerhardi (1895–1977), Russ.-born Eng. writer. The writer added an "e" to his name in the 1960s, saying that Dante, Shakespeare, Racine, Goethe and Blake had "e's" so why not he? [*The Times*, July 16, 1977].

Karl **Germain:** Charles Mattmueller (1878–1959), U.S. magician, of Ger. parentage.

[Sir] Edward **German:** Edward German Jones (1862–1936), Br. light opera composer.

Gene **Gerrard:** Eugene Maurice O'Sullivan (1892–1971), Br. music hall comedian, film actor.

George **Gershwin:** Jacob Gershvin (1898–1937), U.S. composer, of Jewish-Russ. parentage.

John **Gerstad:** John Gjerstad (1924–), U.S. stage actor, producer, director, playwright.

Gertrude: Jane Cross Simpson (1811–1886), Eng. poet, hymnwriter.

Tamara **Geva:** Tamara Gevergeyeva (1908–), Russ. ballet dancer, working in U.S.

Domenico **Ghirlandaio:** Domenico di Tommaso Bigordi (1449–1494), It. painter. The painter's professional name was based on his father's skill in making garlands (Italian *ghirlanda*).

Lewis Grassic **Gibbon:** James Leslie Mitchell (1901–1935), Sc. novelist, short story writer.

Henry **Gibbs:** Henry St. John Clair Rumbold-Gibbs (1910–1975), Br. spy novelist.

Terry **Gibbs:** Julius Gubenko (1924–), U.S. drummer, vibes player.

Chloë **Gibson:** Chloë Cawdle (1899–), Eng. stage director.

Theo **Gift:** Theodora Boulger, née Havers (1847–1923), Eng. writer of children's stories, fantasy fiction. The writer's pen name is a half-translation of her first name Theodora, as this means "God's gift."

Anthony **Gilbert:** Lucy Beatrice Malleson (1899–1973), Eng. writer of detective novels, short stories.

Jean **Gilbert:** Max Winterfield (1879–1942), Ger. operetta composer.

John **Gilbert:** [1] John Gibbs (1810–1889), U.S. actor; [2] John Pringle (1895–1936), U.S. film actor. John Pringle adopted his stepfather's name, Gilbert, as his screen name.

Lou **Gilbert:** Lou Gitlitz (1909–   ), U.S. stage actor.

Paul **Gilbert:** Paul MacMahon (1917–   ), U.S. film comedian, dancer.

Gilderoy: Patrick Macgregor (? –1638), Sc. robber, cattlestealer. The criminal's assumed name was perhaps ironically taken by him on the understanding that it meant "servant of the king." He was hanged in the year mentioned, thus giving the expression "to be hung higher than Gilderoy's kite," meaning "to be punished more severely than the worst criminal." The gallows where Gilderoy met his fate were 30 feet high.

Giles: Carl Ronald Giles (1916–   ), Br. cartoonist.

Jack **Gilford:** Jacob Gellman (1907–   ), U.S. film comedian.

André **Gill:** Louis-André Gosset (1840–1885), Fr. caricaturist.

Geneviève **Gilles:** Geneviève Gillaizeau (1946–   ), Fr. film actress.

Ann **Gillis:** Alma O'Connor (1927–   ), U.S. child film actress.

Virginia **Gilmore:** Sherman Virginia Poole (1919–1986), U.S. film actress, of Br. parentage.

Barbara **Gilson:** Charles Gibson (1878–1943), Eng. soldier, writer of children's stories.

Giorgione: Giorgio Barbarelli (da Castelfranco) (1477–1510), It. painter. The painter's name means "big Giorgio," implying that he was a large or tall man. The Italian "augmentative" suffix -*one* is found in some English words, such as "trombone" ("big trumpet," or *tromba).*

Albert **Giraud:** Marie Emile Albert Kayenbergh (1860–1929), Belg. poet.

Dorothy **Gish:** Dorothy de Guiche (1898–1968), U.S. film actress, sister of Lillian Gish *(q.v.).*

Lillian **Gish:** Lillian de Guiche (1896–   ), U.S. film actress.

Gertie **Gitana:** Gertrude Mary Ross, née Astbury (1889–1957), Br. music hall singer. The popular singer, famous for her rendering of the song *Nellie Dean,* derived her second name from the Spanish for "gypsy," referring to the gypsy costume she wore when she performed for the first time.

Siôn **Glanygors:** John Jones (1766–1821), Welsh satirical poet, social reformer. The poet took his name from his birthplace, the farm of Glan-y-Gors (=("Marshbank") near Ruthin (now in Clwyd).

Gary **Glitter:** Paul Francis Gadd (1944–   ), Eng. pop singer. According to some accounts, the singer's performing name originated as a nickname (no doubt with "Gary" deriving from his surname). Paul Gadd first began his recording career as "Paul Raven," probably referring to his thick, black hair. In the late 1960s, he toured clubs in Frankfurt and Hamburg, Germany, under the name of "Paul Monday." After considering other names such as "Terry Tinsel" and "Horace Hydrogen" he and his writer/producer Mike Leander settled on "Gary Glitter" in 1971.

Gluck: Hannah Gluckstein (1895–1978), U.S.-born Br. artist.

Alma **Gluck:** Reba Fiersohn (1884–1938), U.S. opera singer, of Rom. parentage.

Tito **Gobbi:** Tito Weiss (1915–   ), It. opera singer.

Paulette **Goddard:** Pauline Marion Goddard Levee (1911–   ), U.S. film actress.

John **Godey:** Morton Freedgood (1912–   ), U.S. writer of mystery short stories.

Charles **Godfrey:** Paul Lacey (1851–1900), Eng. music hall artist.

Michael **Gold:** Irwin Granich (1893–1967), U.S. Communist writer, critic.

Peter **Goldsmith:** John Boynton Priestley (1894–1984), Eng. novelist, essayist, dramatist + George Billam (–   ), Eng. writer.

Horace **Goldwin:** Hyman Goldstein (1873–1939), Polish-born U.S. illusionist.

Samuel **Goldwyn:** Schmuel Gelbfisz (1879–1974), U.S. film producer, of Pol.-Jewish parentage. When the future producer came to England in the 1890s, he anglicized his name as Samuel Goldfish. In 1916, he and his two brothers Edgar and Arch Selwyn formed the Goldwyn Pictures Corporation, its name formed from the two elements of *Gold*fish and Sel*wyn*. He himself then adopted this name. (The other way round he would have been "Samuel Selfish"!) In 1918 he officially adopted the name Samuel Goldwyn [A. Scott Berg, *Goldwyn: A Biography*, 1989].

Babs **Gonzales:** Lee Brown (1919–1980), U.S. popular singer.

Lemmie B. **Good:** Limmie Snell (*c*.1945–   ), U.S. pop singer. This joky name should be compared to the next name below.

Will B. **Good:** Rosco ("Fatty") Arbuckle (1887–1933), U.S. comic film actor, comedy director. This is the pseudonym that Arbuckle adopted when he attempted to become a movie director on resuming his work in the cinema after a ban of 11 years resulting from a scandal in 1921 (in which a starlet was killed at a party). Arbuckle was eventually cleared by the jury, but his reputation was ruined, and his subsequent career never recovered its former success.

Gale **Gordon:** Gaylord Aldrich (1906–   ), U.S. TV actor.

Janet **Gordon:** Cecil Blanche Woodham-Smith, née Fitzgerald (1896–   ), Welsh novelist.

Neil **Gordon:** Archibald Gordon Macdonell (1895–1941), Sc. writer.

Rex **Gordon:** Stanley Bennet Hough (1917–   ), Br. SF writer.

Richard **Gordon:** Gordon Ostlere (1921–   ), Br. novelist.

Ruth **Gordon:** Ruth Gordon Jones (1896–1985), U.S. stage, film actress, screenwriter.

Gorgeous George: George Raymond Wagner (1915–1963), U.S. wrestler.

Maxim **Gorky:** Aleksey Maksimovich Peshkov (1868–1936), Russ. writer. Early in his career, the young writer identified closely with the ordinary Russians, and for some time lived "among the people," sharing their poverty and daily struggle for existence. For many such people life was hard, hence his name, from Russian *gor'ky*, "bitter." He first used the name for his story *Makar Chudra* (1892). The name had in fact been used by earlier writers, such as the poet I.A. Belousov (1863–1930).

Tobio **Gorria:** Arrigo Boito (1842–1918), It. composer, librettist. A name that is both an anagram and a reversal of the two original names. "Tobio" suggests Italian *Tobia*, "Toby," and the composer could have devised a name to incorporate this genuine first name. Why not "Tobia Gorrio," for example?

Sirak **Goryan:** William Saroyan (1908–1981), U.S. novelist, short story writer, of Armenian parentage.

Jeremias **Gotthelf:** Albert Bitzius (1797–1854), Swiss novelist, short story writer. The writer was a pastor professionally, with strong Christian principles. He thus changed his name in order to express his convictions, with "Jeremias" for the great Old Testament prophet (whose own name means "God raise up") and "Gotthelf" as the German for "God's help."

Bernard **Gould:** [Sir] Bernard Partridge (1861–1945), Br. actor, cartoonist.

Elliott **Gould:** Elliott Goldstein (1938–), U.S. stage, film actor. The actor was given this simpler version of his name by his mother.

Robert **Goulet:** Stanley Applebaum (1933–), Can. singer, film, TV actor.

Caius **Gracchus:** François-Emile (or Noël) Babeuf (1760–1797), Fr. revolutionary politician. The political agitator was given the nickname "Gracchus" for the resemblance of his agrarian reforms to those of the second-century Roman statesman Gaius (or Caius) Gracchus. He later adopted the name, calling himself "Caius-Gracchus, Tribun du peuple."

[Baron] Lew **Grade:** Louis Winogradsky (1906–), Russ.-born Br. TV executive, brother of Bernard Delfont *(q.v.)*. The great show business personality changed his name in the 1920s, when he entered dancing competitions in London at the height of the Charleston craze. He won several prizes, and became an increasingly popular attraction. Soon realizing that his original name was "too much of a mouthful," shortened it to "Louis Grad." Subsequently, he became a professional dancer, and went on to perform at the Moulin Rouge, Paris. "A few days before my opening night, a big article appeared about me in the *Paris Midi* newspaper. It was great publicity, but the writer had spelt my name incorrectly. Instead of Louis Grad it came out as Lew Grade. I liked the look and sound of it – and Lew Grade it has been ever since" [Lew Grade, *Still Dancing*, 1987].

Bruce **Graeme:** Graham Montague Jeffries (1900–), Eng. novelist.

Rodney **Graeme:** Roderic Graeme Jeffries (1926–), Eng. mystery writer.

Bill **Graham:** Wolfgang Grajonca (1931–), Ger.-born U.S. rock promoter.

Sheilah **Graham:** Lily Sheil (1904–1988), Eng. writer, biographer. The English writer and companion (1937–1940) to Scott Fitzgerald married Major John Graham Gillam in the 1930s and went to Hollywood, where she became a gossip columnist. She once said, "The name Lily Sheil, to this day, horrifies me to a degree impossible to explain." Her new name was presumably based on her original surname and her husband's second name.

Gloria **Grahame:** Gloria Grahame Hallward (1924–1981), U.S. stage, film actress.

Sarah **Grand:** Frances Elizabeth McFall, née Clarke (1862–1943), Ir. novelist.

Grandmaster Flash: Joseph Saddler (1957–), U.S. rock singer, rapper.

J.J. **Grandville:** Jean-Ignace-Isidore Gérard (1803–1847), Fr. illustrator, caricaturist.

Stewart **Granger:** James Lablache Stewart (1913–), Eng. film actor. The actor changed his name in order to avoid confusion with the U.S. film actor James Stewart *(q.v.)*. As a British actor, he was anyway governed by the rules of Equity, the actors' union, which states that no two actors can have the same name.

Cary **Grant:** Alexander Archibald Leach (1904–1986), Eng. film actor, working in U.S. The story goes that when the actor was looking for a suitable stage name, his friend Fay Wray, the Canadian actress, suggested he should use the name of the character he had played in the musical comedy *Nikki*. This was "Cary Lockwood." Alexander Leach liked "Cary" but not "Lockwood," so "someone rummaged in a desk and brought out a notebook filled with page after page of names. [. . .] They came up with 'Grant' [. . .] I said it was fine" [Albert Govoni, *Cary Grant: An Unauthorized Biography,* 1973].

Gogi **Grant:** Audrey Brown (1924–   ), U.S. pop singer.

Joan **Grant:** Joan Kelsey, née Marshall (1907–   ), Eng. novelist. The writer adopted the name of her first husband, Arthur Leslie Grant.

Kathryn **Grant:** Olive Grandstaff (1933–   ), U.S. film actress.

Kirby **Grant:** Kirby Grant Hoorn (1911–1985), U.S. film actor, of Du.-Sc. parentage.

Lee **Grant:** Lyova Haskell Rosenthal (1926–   ), U.S. stage, film actress.

Peter **Graves:** Peter Aurness (1925–   ), U.S. film actor, brother of James Arness *(q.v.).*

Fernand **Gravet:** Fernand Martens (1904–1970), Fr. film actor.

Barry **Gray:** Robert Barry Coffin (1797–1857), U.S. author.

Colleen **Gray:** Doris Jensen (1922–   ), U.S. film actress.

Dobie **Gray:** Leonard Victor Ainsworth (1942–   ), U.S. soul singer.

Donald **Gray:** Eldred Tidbury (1914–1979), Eng. film, TV actor.

Dulcie **Gray:** Dulcie Winifred Catherine Denson, née Bailey (1919–   ), Eng. stage, film actress, thriller writer. The actress adopted her mother's maiden name.

E. Conder **Gray:** Alexander Hay Japp (1837–1905), Sc. author, publisher. The writer used several pseudonyms, of which the best known was probably H.A. Page *(q.v.).* "E. Conder Gray" appears to be a sort of representation of "Alexander Hay."

Elizabeth Janet **Gray:** Elizabeth Gray Vining (1902–   ), U.S. novelist.

Ellington **Gray:** Naomi Ellington Jacob (1889–1964), Eng. novelist.

Gilda **Gray:** Marianna Michalska (1901–1959), Pol. dancer, film actress, working in U.S.

Linda **Gray:** Linda Baxter (1910–   ), Eng. stage actress, singer. The actress used her mother's maiden name as her stage name.

Michael **Gray:** Michael Grealis (1947–   ), Eng. TV reporter.

Nadia **Gray:** Nadia Kujnir-Herescu (1923–   ), Russ.-Romanian film actress.

Sally **Gray:** Constance Vera Stevens (1917–   ), Br. film actress.

Simon **Gray:** [Sir] Alexander Boswell (1775–1822), Eng. antiquary, poet.

David **Grayson:** Ray Stannard Baker (1870–1940), U.S. essayist.

Diane **Grayson:** Diane Guinibert (1948–   ), Flemish-born Eng. stage, film, TV dancer, actress.

Kathryn **Grayson:** Zelma Kathryn Elizabeth Hedrick (1922–   ), U.S. film actress, singer.

Larry **Grayson:** William White (1923–   ), Eng. TV entertainer, compère. The entertainer, an illegitimate child, first started acting in the music hall at the age of 14 under the name of "Billy Breen." In 1956 he was spotted by agent Evelyn Taylor at London's Nuffield Centre. She signed him up, and began looking for a new name for him. "We sat there for ages going through different names. First we settled on Larry. And at the time there was a very popular Hollywood singing star Kathryn Grayson. 'That's it,' said Eve, 'Larry Grayson—write it down.' He did, liked it and has written it many thousands of times on autograph books since" [*TV Times*, August 20–26, 1983]. Of course, "Grayson" does in itself suggest a kind of relationship with "White." For the film actress mentioned, see the entry above!

The **Great Carmo:** Harry Cameron (1881–1944), Austral.-born Eng. magician. "Carmo" was an exotic reworking of "Cameron," of course.

The **Great Lafayette:** Sigmund Neuberger (1872–1911), Ger. magician, working in U.S. One wonders which particular Lafayette, if any, he had in mind. The "greatest" was doubtless the French statesman and officer of the eighteenth century, who defended Virginia (1781).

The **Great Macdermott:** Gilbert Hastings Farrell (1845–1901), Br. music hall artist.

The **Great Nicola:** William Mozart Nicol (1880–1946), U.S. illusionist.

The **Great Soprendo:** Geoffrey Durham (*c.*1950–   ), Br. magician. Like all magicians, The Great Soprendo produces surprises, as his name indicates (Spanish *sorprendo*, "I surprise").

El **Greco:** Domenikos Theotokopoulos (?1548–?1614), Gr.-born Sp. painter. The painter's name is Spanish for "the Greek." However, the painter himself never forgot his Greek origins, and usually signed his paintings with his full Greek name. He seems to have gained his name "El Greco" when first working in Italy, perhaps with "El" as Italian *Il* (unless *El* is a Venetian dialect form of the article). He first appeared in Spain in 1577.

Henry **Green:** Henry Vincent Yorke (1905–1973), Br. novelist.

Mitzi **Green:** Elizabeth Keno (1920–1969), U.S. child film actress.

Peter **Green:** Peter Greenbaum (1946–   ), Br. pop musician.

Max **Greene:** Mutz Greenbaum (1896–1968), Ger. cinematographer, working in U.K.

Shecky **Greene:** Sheldon Greenfield (1925–   ), U.S. TV comedian.

Grace **Greenwood:** Sara Jane (Clarke) Lippincott (1823–1904), U.S. poet, newspaper writer.

[Sir] Ben **Greet:** Philip Barling Greet (1857–1936), Br. stage actor, theatre manager. The actor first appeared on the stage in 1879 as "Philip Ben," the nickname "Benjamin" having been given to him as the youngest of eight children. He later adopted the name Ben in place of his original first names.

Gregory V: Brunone di Carinzia (972–1048), It. pope.

Gregory VI: Giovanni Graziano (Johannes Gratianus) (? –?1048), Ger.-born It. pope.

[Saint] **Gregory VII:** Hildebrand (*c.*1020–1085), It. pope.

Gregory VIII: Alberto di Morra (?1142–1187), It. pope.

Gregory IX: Ugo (or Ugolino) Dei Conti di Segni (? –1241), It. pope.

Gregory X: Teobaldo Visconti (1210–1276), It. pope.

Gregory XI: Pierre-Roger de Beaufort (1331–1378), Fr. pope.

Gregory XII: Angelo Correr (?1327–1417), It. pope.

Gregory XIII: Ugo Buoncompagni (1502–1585), It. pope.

Gregory XIV: Niccolo Sfondrati (1535–1591), It. pope.

Gregory XV: Alessandro Ludovisi (1554–1623), It. pope.

Gregory XVI: Bartolomeo Alberto Cappellari (1765–1846), It. pope.

Paul **Gregory:** Jason Lenhart (?1905–   ), U.S. impresario, film producer.

Maysie **Greig:** Maysie Sopoushek, née Greig-Smith (1901–   ), Austral. novelist.

Stephen **Grendon:** August William Derleth (1909–1971), U.S. writer of horror fiction.

Henry **Greville:** Alice Durand, née Fleury (1842–1902), Fr. novelist.

Leo **Grex:** Leonard Reginald Gribble (1908–   ), Eng. detective fiction writer.

Anne **Grey:** Aileen Ewing (1907–   ), Br. film actress.

Beryl **Grey:** Beryl Svenson, née Groom (1927–   ), Br. ballet dancer, artistic director. When Beryl Groom was beginning her dancing career at the age of 14, Ninette de Valois *(q.v.)* suggested this new name for her. "I called her Beryl Grey because there was an easy flow to it. If she had remained Groom people would have called her Broom or something. It's not a ballet name." Dame Ninette also suggested "Iris Grey," but Beryl resisted this. It took her about twenty years to get used to her new name [David Gillard, *Beryl Grey: a Biography,* 1977].

Joel **Grey:** Noel Katz (1932–   ), U.S. stage actor. The actor's father formed a group called Mickey Katz and His Kittens. When the father changed this name to Mickey Kats and His Kosher Jammers, Joel Katz went on the stage alone as "Joel Kaye," later changing this to "Joel Grey" [*The Times,* May 15, 1976].

Lita **Grey:** Lillita MacMurray (1909–   ), U.S. juvenile film actress.

Mary **Grey:** Ada Bevan ap Rees Bryant (1878–1974), Welsh stage actress.

Nan **Grey:** Eschal Miller (1918–   ), U.S. film actress.

Grey Owl: Archibald Stansfeld Belaney (1888–1938), Eng. author of books on the Canadian Indians. The writer was best known for his *Pilgrims of the Wild* (1935). He himself was the son of an English father who had married, in the U.S., a woman said by him to be of Indian descent. His pen name was that of an Indian chief, and was an English translation of the native form, Wa-sha-quon-asin.

R.E.H. **Greyson:** Henry Rogers (1806–1877), Eng. reviewer, Christian apologist. The writer's pen name is an anagram of his real name. He used it for two volumes of imaginary letters, *Selections from the Correspondence of R.E.H. Greyson, Esq.* (1857).

Gabbler **Gridiron:** Joseph Haselwood (1793–1833), Eng. antiquary.

Francis **Grierson:** Benjamin Henry Jesse Francis Shepard (1848–1927), Eng.-born U.S. writer, singer, pianist.

Ethel **Griffies:** Ethel Woods (1878–1975), Eng. stage, film actress, working in U.S.

Arthur **Griffinhoofe:** George Colman [the Younger] (1762–1836), Eng. dramatist.

Fred **Griffiths:** Frederick George Delaney (1856–1940), Eng. music hall hartist.

Romayne **Grigorova:** Romayne Austin (1926–   ), Eng. ballet dancer, teacher. The dancer's name is not a contrived Slavic-style one, but her own married name, that of Grigor Grigorov, a Bulgarian journalist whom she married in 1960. "At our wedding reception several colleagues suggested I use Grigorova all the time, as it would look good on the programmes: Romayne Grigorova, Ballet Mistress to the Covent Garden Opera" [personal letter from Romayne Grigorova, November 15, 1982].

Dod **Grile:** Ambrose Gwinett Bierce (1842–?1914), U.S. short story writer. The writer used this name for three collections of vitriolic sketches and witticisms published in the 1870s. The name *looks* like an anagram—but of what?

Carleton **Grindle:** Gerald W. Page (1939–   ), U.S. SF, horror fiction writer, editor.

Harry **Gringo:** Henry Augustus Wise (1819–1869), U.S. author of melodramatic novels.

David **Grinnell:** Donald A. Wollheim (1914–   ), U.S. SF, fantasy writer, publisher.

Juan **Gris:** José Victoriano Gonzalez (1887–1927), Sp.-born Fr. Cubist painter.

Grock: Charles Adrien Wettach (1880–1959), Swiss circus clown. The clown had originally been a partner of another clown named Brick, whose own former partner had been Brock. "Grock" went well with "Brick" but was distinctive from "Brock." For a similar twinning of clown names see **Bim.**

Gros-Guillaume: Robert Guérin (*fl.* 1598–1634), Fr. actor.

Anton **Grot:** Antocz Franziszek Groszewski (1884–1974), Pol. film art director, working in U.S.

Anastasius **Grün:** Anton Alexander von Auersperg (1806–1876), Austr. poet, statesman.

Matthias **Grünewald:** Matthias Gothardt (or Mathis Gothart Nithart) (*c.*1455–1528), Ger. painter. The painter's name arose from a seventeenth-century misprinting of "Gothardt" as "Grünewald," and this is now the standard form of his name.

Nathaniel **Gubbins:** Edward Spencer Mott (1844–1910), Eng. sporting writer. The writer also used the friendly "Gub-Gub."

Guercino: Giovanni Francesco Barbieri (1591–1666), It. painter, illustrator. The painter's name is Italian for "squint-eyed," which alas he was. This particular defect does not seem to have affected the quality of his paintings, however.

George **Guess:** Sequoyah (?1770–1843), U.S.-Indian language teacher, writer. The half-breed Cherokee, who devised a system of writing for his tribe, was probably the son of a British trader named Nathaniel Gist (or Guess). His Indian name (spelled Sequoia) was given to the giant redwoods of California and to Sequoia National Park in that state.

Che **Guevara:** Ernesto Guevara de la Serna (1928–1967), Argentine socialist revolutionary. Many Argentines have a verbal mannerism in that they punctuate their speech with the interjection *¡che!* Guevara did this, and the word became his nickname, which he subsequently adopted as a first name.

Bonnie **Guitar:** Bonnie Buckingham (*c.*1935–   ), U.S. country musician. Bonnie Buckingham changed her name to Bonnie Guitar in the mid–1950s, when she was hired as a studio guitarist by Favor Robinson, owner of Abbott Records in Los Angeles.

Guitar Slim: Eddie Jones (1926–1959), U.S. blues singer.

Norman **Gunston:** Garry McDonald (1948–   ), Austral. TV comedian.

Sigrid **Gurie:** Sigrid Gurie Hauklid (1911–1969), Norw.-born U.S. film actress.

Angelina **Gushington:** Charles Wallwyn Radcliffe-Cooke (1841–1911), Br. writer.

Impulsia **Gushington:** Helena Selina Sheridan (1806–1867), Eng. song, ballad writer. Helena Sheridan, who was successively Mrs. Blackwood, Lady Dufferin, and the Countess of Blackwood, used this name (which vies with the one above) for *Lispings from Low Latitudes; or Extracts from the Journal of the Hon. Impulsia Gushington* (1863), written when, as a widow, she accompanied her son on his travels up the Nile.

Johannes **Gutenberg:** Johann Gensfleisch (*c.*1398–1468), Ger. printing inventor. Understandably, the printing pioneer was not too happy about his surname, which literally translates as "gooseflesh." He therefore adopted the far pleasanter maiden name of his mother, which had the advantage of beginning with the same letter.

Edmund **Gwenn:** Edmund Kellaway (1877–1959), Eng. film actor.

Gwyndaf: Evan Gwyndaf Evans (1913–1986), Welsh poet. Gwyndaf, the poet's bardic name, was the name of a Celtic saint as well as his own middle name.

Anne **Gwynne:** Marguerite Gwynne Trice (1918–   ), U.S. film actress.

Greta **Gynt:** Margrethe Woxholt (1916–   ), Norw.-born Eng. film actress. The actress appears to have adopted the name of the hero of Ibsen's play *Peer Gynt.*

Gyp: Sibylle Gabrielle Marie Antoinette, née de Riquetti de Mirabeau, Comtesse de Martel de Janville (1850–1932), Fr. novelist. The novelist took her name from Jip, the little dog in Charles Dickens's *David Copperfield.* She pronounced the name "Zheep."

Buddy **Hackett:** Leonard Hacker (1924–   ), U.S. film comedian.

Albert **Haddock:** Alan Patrick Herbert (1890–1971), Eng. journalist, writer.

Christopher **Haddon:** John Leslie Palmer (1885–1944), Eng. novelist, theatre critic.

Peter **Haddon:** Peter Tildsley (1898–1962), Br. film actor.

Reed **Hadley:** Reed Herring (1911–1974), U.S. film actor.

Jean **Hagen:** Jean Verhagen (1924–1977), U.S. film actress.

William **Haggard:** Richard Henry Michael Clayton (1907–   ), Eng. author of spy, mystery novels. The writer assumed his mother's maiden name as his pen name.

Larry **Hagman:** Larry Hageman (1939–   ), U.S. film, TV actor.

Kevin **Haigen:** Kevin Higgenbotham (1954–   ), U.S. ballet dancer.

Haile Selassie: Ras Tafari Makonnen (1891–1975), Ethiopian emperor. The name adopted by the emperor, on assuming full authority in 1930, is effectively a title, meaning "Might of the Trinity." In his original name, "Ras" is an honorific, meaning "Prince." It was the emperor's original name that gave the title of the Rastafarians, the Jamaican sect who believe that Blacks are the chosen people, and that Haile Selassie was God Incarnate, and that he would secure their repatriation to their African homeland.

Alan **Hale:** Rufus Alan McKahan (1892–1950), U.S. film actor.

Binnie **Hale:** Bernice Hale Monro (1899–1984), Eng. stage comedienne, sister of Sonnie Hale *(q.v.).*

Creighton **Hale:** Patrick Fitzgerald (1882–1965), U.S. film actor.

Jonathan **Hale:** Jonathan Hatley (1892–1966), U.S. film actor.

Sonnie **Hale:** John Robert Hale Monro (1902–1959), Eng. stage, film comedian.

Fromental **Halévy:** Jacques Fromental Elie Lévy (1799–1862), Fr. musical composer.

Hugh **Haliburton:** James Logie Robertson (1846–1922), Sc. poet, prose writer.

M.Y. **Halidom:** ? (? – ?), Br. (?) horror story writer(s). The identity of the writer(s) is still uncertain, although the assumed name clearly derives from the oath "by my halidom," "halidom" being an old word for "holiness." See also p. 66.

Adam **Hall:** Elleston Trevor (1920–   ), Eng. spy thriller writer.

Holworthy **Hall:** Harold Everett Porter (1887–1936), U.S. novelist, short story writer.

Huntz **Hall:** Henry Hall (1920–   ), U.S. film actor.

James **Hall:** James Brown (1900–1940), U.S. film actor.

Jon **Hall:** Charles Hall Locher (1913–1979), U.S. film actor.

Ruth **Hall:** Ruth Hale Ibanez (1912–   ), U.S. film actress.

[Sir] Charles **Hallé:** Karl Halle (1819–1895), Ger.-born Eng. pianist, orchestra conductor.

Joseph **Haller:** Henry Nelson Coleridge (1798–1843), Eng. lawyer, writer.

Brett **Halliday:** Davis Dresser (1904–1977), U.S. author of "private eye" stories. The writer's new surname came from the name of the detective in his first novel. His publisher, however, had not liked the name Halliday and had changed it to Burke. The publisher's own name was Brett—and this was the one adopted by Dresser as his new forename. Among other names used by Dresser for pulp magazine short stories were Matthew Blood, Peter Shelley, Anthony Scott, Don Davis, Anderson Wayne, Hal Debrett (jointly with Kathleen Rollins), Asa Baker (for his first mystery), Sylvia Carson, and Kathryn Culver.

James **Halliday:** David Symington (1904–   ), Eng. writer on India, Africa.

Michael **Halliday:** John Creasey (1908–1973), Eng. crime novelist.

Johnny **Hallyday:** Jean-Philippe Smet (1943–   ), Fr. pop singer. The singer was virtually abandoned by his parents, and was brought up by an aunt, whose daughter and American son-in-law, Lee Halliday, were both dancers. Young Jean-Philippe accompanied his cousins on all their tours round Europe, and in due course adopted the name Halliday, but with a small distinctive change in spelling [*Sunday Times Magazine,* August 11, 1985].

Clive **Hamilton:** Clive Staples Lewis (1898–1963), Br. writer on literary, religious subjects, novelist, children's writer. C.S. Lewis adopted his mother's maiden name for his long narrative poem *Dymer* (1926).

Cosmo **Hamilton:** Cosmo Gibbs (1879–1942), Eng. playwright, novelist. The writer adopted his mother's maiden name as his pen name.

David **Hamilton:** David Pilditch (1939–   ), Eng. radio, TV announcer, compère. The broadcaster adopted his mother's maiden name (which is also his own middle name) when he began his career in radio. At the time he was carrying out his statutory National Service in the Royal Air Force at the base at Compton Bassett, Wiltshire, where John Dightam, the corporal who ran the forces broadcasting station, Compton Forces Network, suggested he should change his name. "Pilditch is too unusual. You'll need something people will remember easily if you ever make it to BFN [British Forces Network]" [David Hamilton, *The Music Game: An Autobiography*, 1986].

[Lady] Emma **Hamilton:** Amy Lyon (1765–1815), Eng. society leader, Nelson's mistress. At the age of 16, Amy Lyon was calling herself Emily Hart when she began to live with the nephew of the man who would become her husband, Sir William Hamilton. She married in 1791, at the age of 26, when Hamilton was 61. The nephew was Charles Francis Greville.

Gail **Hamilton:** Mary Abigail Dodge (1833–1896), U.S. popular writer, essayist. The writer, an agitator for women's suffrage, adapted her second name to provide her first name, taking her new surname from Hamilton, her home town in Massachusetts.

Paul **Hamlyn:** Paul Bertrand Hamburger (1926–   ), Br. publisher. The well-known publisher came to Britain as a German-Jewish refugee from Berlin in 1933, when he was only seven. He changed his name because as a child he did not like being nicknamed "Sausage" and "Wimpy." His brother is the poet and translator Michael Hamburger [*The Times*, July 30, 1985].

Hans **Hammergafferstein:** Henry Wadsworth Longfellow (1807–1882), U.S. poet.

Alexander **Hammid:** Alexander Hackenschmied (*c.*1910–   ), Cz. maker of film documentaries, working in U.S.

Kay **Hammond:** Dorothy Katherine Leon, later Clements, née Standing (1909–1980), Eng. stage, film actress. The actress adopted her mother's pseudonym as her stage name.

Pierre **Hamp:** Henri Louis Bourillon (1876–1962), Fr. novelist.

Walter **Hampden:** Walter Hampden Dougherty (1879–1955), U.S. stage, film actor.

Olphar **Hamst:** Ralph Thomas (*fl.*1832–1868), Br. bibliophile, pseudonymist. The anagrammatic pseudonym is one of the leading pseudonymists of the nineteenth century, professionally a barrister, but for our purposes much more importantly the author of the *Handbook of Fictitious Names* (1868) (see Bibliography).

Knut **Hamsun:** Knut Petersen (1859–1952), Norw. novelist.

John **Hanson:** John Watts (1922–   ), Can.-born Eng. stage actor, singer.

Han Suyin: Elizabeth Comber, née Chow (1917–   ), Br. novelist.

Robert **Harbin:** Ned Williams (1910–1978), S.A.-born Eng. conjuror.

Ephraim **Hardcastle:** William Henry Pyne (1769–1843), Eng. painter, author. The artist used his pseudonym for his literary activities, which he began by way of a series of anecdotes on art and artists in the 1820s.

Theo **Hardeen:** Theodore Weiss (1876–1944), U.S. illusionist, brother of Houdini *(q.v.).* The illusionist's assumed name resembles Houdini's own.

Ty **Hardin:** Orson Hungerford (1930–   ), U.S. TV, film actor. The actor's name suggests a pun on "tie hard in," suitable for his own "muscular" image. But this may not actually be the origin.

Wes **Hardin:** Clay Allison (1914–   ), Eng. writer of westerns.

Ann **Harding:** Dorothy Walton Gatley (1902–1981), U.S. stage, film actress.

Cyril **Hare:** Alfred Alexander Gordon Clark (1900–1958), Eng. crime novelist. The writer, professionally a lawyer and judge, took his pen name from *Cyril* Mansions, Battersea, London, where he settled after his marriage (1933), and *Hare* Court, Temple, where he worked.

[Sir] John **Hare:** John Fairs (1844–1921), Br. stage actor, theatre manager.

Martin **Hare:** Zoë Zajdler, née Girling (*c*.1907–   ), Ir. writer.

Marion **Harland:** Mary Virginia Terhune, née Hawes (1830–1922), U.S. popular writer.

Steve **Harley:** Steven Nice (1951–   ), Eng. pop musician.

Jean **Harlow:** Harlean Carpentier (1911–1937), U.S. film actress. The actress adopted both her mother's first name and her maiden surname as her own screen name. Her real first name was pronounced "Harley-Ann."

Rolf **Harolde:** Rolf Harolde Wigger (1899–1974), U.S. film actor.

Slim **Harpo:** James Moore (1924–1970), U.S. popular harmonica player, singer. The player made his initial public appearances as "Harmonica Slim" before settling to a slicker version of this as "Slim Harpo."

George G. **Harrington:** William Mumford Baker (1825–1883), U.S. clergyman, novelist.

Barbara **Harris:** Sandra Markowitz (1937–   ), U.S. film actress.

Jed **Harris:** Jacob Horowitz (1906–1979), U.S. theatrical impresario.

Rex **Harrison:** Reginald Carey Harrison (1908–   ), Eng. stage, film actor.

Uncle **Harry:** John Habberton (1842–1921), U.S. journalist, writer.

Dolores **Hart:** Dolores Hicks (1939–   ), U.S. film actress.

Simon **Harvester:** Henry St. John Clair Rumbold-Gibbs (1910–1975), Br. spy novelist.

Laurence **Harvey:** Larushka Mischa Skikne (1928–1973), Lithuanian-born U.S. film actor. Larry Skikne's name was changed by his agent, Gordon Harbord, who also created the names of Adrienne Corri *(q.v.)* and Diana Scarlet (see Diana Dors). "Larry" (itself from "Larushka") should be changed to "Laurence," he decided, while "Skikne" was "much too continental." "He always asked players their mothers' names or the names of their relatives. Larry Skikne's mother's name had been Zotnik. That would never do. The most English name he could think of was Harvey, as in the solid Knightsbridge store, Harvey Nichols. Not so English as Harrods perhaps, but they could hardly call him Laurence Harrods. Harbord was quite pleased with the name Laurence Harvey. 'But we have to be careful,' he told Skikne. Together they searched the pages of the theatrical directory, but they found no other actor named Harvey" [Des Hickey and Gus Smith, *The Prince, Being the Public and Private Life of Larushka Mischa Skikne, a Jewish Lithuanian Vagabond Player, otherwise known as Laurence Harvey,* 1975].

Lilian **Harvey:** Lilian Pape (1906–1968), Br. film actress, of Ger. parentage.

Signe **Hasso:** Signe Larsson (1910–   ), Swe. film actress.

Hugh **Hastings:** Hugh Williamson (1917–   ), Austral. stage actor, dramatist.

Henry **Hathaway:** Marcus Henry Leopold de Fiennes (1898–1985), U.S. film director.

June **Haver:** June McMurray, née Stovenour (1925–   ), U.S. film actress.

Phyllis **Haver:** Phyllis O'Haver (1899–1960), U.S. film actress.

June **Havoc:** Ellen Evangeline Hovick (1916–   ), U.S. stage, film actress, director.

Dale **Hawkins:** Delmar Allen Hawkins (1938–   ), U.S. rock musician.

Allan **Hawkwood:** Henry James O'Brien Bedford-Jones (1887–1949), Can.-born U.S. historical fiction, fantasy writer.

Alice **Hawthorne:** Septimus Winner (1827–1902), U.S. popular songwriter. The songwriter adopted the name of a famous ancestor on his mother's side, Nathaniel Hawthorne.

Rainey **Hawthorne:** Charlotte Eliza Lawson Riddell, née Cowan (1832–1906), Ir.-born Eng. writer. The pen name seems to be an arbitrary one, as probably was the writer's better-known pseudonym of F.G. Trafford *(q.v.)*.

Charles **Hawtrey:** George Hartree (1914–1988), Br. film comedian.

Ian **Hay:** John Hay Beith (1876–1952), Sc. novelist.

Linda **Hayden:** Linda Higginson (1951–   ), Br. film actress.

Melissa **Hayden:** Mildred Herman (1923–   ), Can.-U.S. ballet dancer, teacher.

Sterling **Hayden:** Christian Walter Hamilton (1916–1986), U.S. film actor.

Helen **Haye:** Helen Hay (1874–1957), Br. stage, film actress.

Helen **Hayes:** Helen Hayes MacArthur, née Brown (1900–   ), U.S. stage, film actress. The actress adopted her mother's maiden name, otherwise her own middle name, as her stage surname.

Henry **Hayes:** Ellen Warner Kirk, née Olney (1842–1928), U.S. popular fiction writer.

Giant **Haystacks:** Martin Austin Ruane (1947–   ), Br. wrestler, actor. The wrestler's name is descriptive of his vastness, but at the same time suggesting an inner softness.

Joan **Haythorne:** Joan Mary Shankland, née Haythornthwaite (1915–1987), Eng. stage, film actress.

Louis **Hayward:** Seafield Grant (1909–1985), S.A. film actor, working in U.S.

Susan **Hayward:** Edythe Marrener (1918–1975), U.S. film actress. How come this particular metamorphosis? Here's how Warner Brothers talent executive, Max Arnow, and talent agent Benny Medford, brought it about, after the actress's screen test in the role of Scarlett O'Hara: "The first item on the agenda was to change her name. Edythe was far too sedate for the screen image they had in mind. Edythe herself suggested the name of her grandmother, Katie Harrington, but Arnow felt it smacked of burlesque; so the brainstorming began. Another up-and-coming actress from Brooklyn, Margarita Cansino, had been doing rather well under the name Rita Hayworth. Hayworth, Haywood. . . . Arnow tossed it about in his mind. He had been working a lot lately with superagent Leland Hayward, and liked the sound of the name. Medford agreed. From his private garden of favorite names, Medford plucked Susan, and Susan Hayward was born. [. . .] Edythe viewed her name change with equanimity. It was, after all, a necessary step toward stardom" [Christopher P. Anderson, *A Star, Is a Star, Is a Star! The Lives and Loves of Susan Hayward*, 1981].

Richard **Haywarde:** Frederick Swartwout Cozzens (1818–1869), U.S. writer.

Rita **Hayworth:** Margarita Carmen Cansino (1918–1987), U.S. stage, film actress. Here's how the actress's agent, Ed Judson, brought about her change of name when introducing her to Harry Cohn of Columbia Pictures: "The signing of Rita Cansino couldn't have been a less significant event. Cohn took no interest at all in the unknown who had already flopped at Fox—except for her name. 'Latin types are out. She sounds too Mexican,' Cohn argued, even though she had been cast as a Spanish dancer in her first Columbia programmer. 'How about her mother's maiden name?' Judson asked. 'Her uncle Vinton has done okay at RKO.' Vinton Haworth [. . .] was by this time a successful character actor and radio star. [. . .] 'Haworth. If it's pronounced Hayworth,' said Cohn, 'why the hell isn't it spelled that way?' They added the 'y' and Rita Hayworth was born" [Edward Z. Epstein and Joseph Morella, *Rita: The Life of Rita Hayworth*, 1983].

Désiré **Hazard:** Octave Feuillet (1821–1890), Fr. novelist, dramatist.

Hy **Hazell:** Hyacinth Hazel O'Higgins (1920–1970), Br. revue, musical comedy actress.

H.D.: Hilda Doolittle (1886–1961), U.S. poet, novelist.

Matthew **Head:** John E. Canady (1907–   ), U.S. art critic, mystery novel writer.

David **Hedison:** Ara Heditsian (1926–   ), U.S. film, TV actor.

Jack **Hedley:** Jack Hawkins (1930–   ), Br. film, TV actor.

Van **Heflin:** Emmet Evan Heflin, Jr. (1910–1971), U.S. stage, film actor.

Gerard **Heinz:** Gerard Hinze (1903–1972), Ger. stage actor, working in U.K.

Ernest **Helfenstein:** Elizabeth Oakes Smith (1806–1893), U.S. popular novelist, magazine writer.

Heliogabalus (or Elagabalus): Varius Avitus Bassanius (204–222), Roman emperor. The crazed emperor was given a name which was that of the Syro-Phoenician sungod whose priest he became while still a child, with the first part of the name representing Greek *helios*, "sun," and the rest of the name said to relate to that of the Gabellus, a tributary of the Po River.

Richard **Hell:** Richard Myers (1949–   ), U.S. punk rock musician.

Robert **Heller:** William Henry Palmer (*c*.1830–1878), Eng. magician, working in U.S. The magician may have adopted a name that was a variant on that of Robert-Houdin, whom he greatly admired when young. See also **Houdini.**

Brigitte **Helm:** Gisela Eva Schiltenhelm (1907–   ), Ger. film actress.

Mary **Henderson:** James Bridie *(q.v.)*.

Paul **Henderson:** Ruth France (1913–1968), N.Z. novelist, poet.

Ray **Henderson:** Raymond Brost (1896–1970), U.S. film composer.

Jimi **Hendrix:** James Marshall Hendrix (1942–1970), U.S. black rock musician. On being discharged from the U.S. paratroopers in 1963 for medical reasons, Hendrix first played under the name Jimmy James. He then adopted his better-known name, with this becoming prominent on the formation of his group, the Jimi Hendrix Experience, in London in 1966.

Buck **Henry:** Buck Henry Zuckerman (1930–   ), U.S. film actor, screenwriter, director.

O. **Henry:** William Sydney Porter (1862–1910), U.S. short story writer. It should first be noted that the well-known writer's pen name is just so, and not, as sometimes seen, "O'Henry." Porter first used the name for his story *Whistling Dick's Christmas Stocking* (1899) written in prison at Columbus, Ohio, where he was serving a sentence for embezzlement (as a result of obtaining money for his sick wife). The pseudonym is sometimes said to have been taken from one of the prison guards, Orrin Henry, but the commonly accepted version of the origin says that it is presumed to be an abbreviation of the name of a French pharmacist, Etienne-Ossian Henry, found in the *U.S. Dispensatory*. This last was a reference work used by Porter when he was working as a prison pharmacist.

Paul **Henry:** Paul Henry Smith (1947–   ), Br. TV actor.

Gladys **Henson:** Gladys Gunn (1897–1983), Ir. stage, film actress.

Audrey **Hepburn:** Edda van Heemstra Hepburn-Ruston (1929–   ), Belg.-born U.S. film actress, of Br.-Du. parentage.

Holmes **Herbert:** Edward Sanger (1882–1956), Br. stage, film actor.

Herblock: Herbert Lawrence Block (1909–   ), U.S. cartoonist.

Hergé: George Rémi (1907–1983), Belg. cartoonist. The famous creator of Tintin, the boy detective, used a name that was simply the reversal of his initials in their French pronunciation ("R.G."="Ergé").

Eileen **Herlie:** Eileen Herlihy (1919–   ), Sc. stage, film actress.

Herman: Peter Blair Denis Bernard Noone (1947–   ), Eng. pop singer. The lead singer of the group Herman's Hermits, formed 1963, owed his name to a nickname. Members of the local Manchester group, the Heartbeats, with whom he sang previously, claimed that Noone resembled Sherman of the *Rocky and Bullwinkle* TV cartoon series. This name was then slightly shortened to "Herman" and used to blend in nicely with that of his own band. Peter Noone performed under his own name from 1970.

James A. **Herne:** James Ahearn (1839–1901), U.S. actor, playwright.

Robert **Heron:** John Pinkerton (1758–1826), Sc. writer.

James **Herriot:** James Alfred Wright (1916–   ), Eng. veterinary novelist. The Yorkshire veterinary surgeon, who did not begin to publish his famous books until 1970, when he was over 50, took his pen name quite ingenuously: "I had to have one because I didn't want to be accused of advertising by the Royal College of Veterinary Surgeons. And I was watching the telly one night when this footballer came on. He was the goalkeeper for Bristol City, I think. He was called James Herriot and I thought: 'That's a nice name.' So I used it" [*Telegraph Sunday Magazine*, June 7, 1981]. By a coincidence, the medieval word "heriot" was used for a death duty paid to a lord by his tenant in the form of the dead man's best beast.

Barbara **Hershey:** Barbara Herztine (or Herzstein) (1947–   ), U.S. film actress. Barbara Hershey gained fame (or notoriety) as the Hollywood actress who at the age of 20 changed her name to Barbara Seagull, after a dead seagull whose spirit she felt had entered her. She subsequently threw off her image as a typecast flower child actress, and settled to her name of Hershey.

Carl **Hertz:** Leib (or Louis) Morganstern (1859–1924), U.S. illusionist, working in U.K.

Hervé: Florimond Rongé (1825–1892), Fr. composer, organist, orchestra leader.

Irene **Hervey:** Irene Herwick (1910–   ), U.S. film actress.

Aleksandr Ivanovich **Herzen** (or Gertsen): Aleksandr Ivanovich Yakovlev (1812–1870), Russ. revolutionary writer. Aleksandr was an illegitimate child, the son of a Russian father and a German mother (Luise Haag). He was thus a "love child," and his new name, invented by his father, reflects this, deriving from the German for "heart," *Herz,* or even from the verb *herzen,* "to press to one's heart," "to hug."

Werner **Herzog:** Werner Herzog Stipetic (1942–   ), Ger. film director.

Catherine **Hessling:** Andrée Heuschling (1899–1979), Fr. film actress.

Charlton **Heston:** John Charles Carter (1924–   ), U.S. stage, film actor. The actor's stage name was adopted from that of his stepfather.

Martin **Hewitt:** Arthur Merrison (1863–1945), Eng. novelist, journalist. The writer adopted the name of the hero of his own detective stories.

Harrington **Hext:** Eden Phillpotts (1862–1960), Eng. novelist, poet, essayist, playwright. The novelist used the pen name for his mystery stories: "Hext" suggests "hexed," or "bewitched" (having a spell put on by a *hex* or witch or wizard).

Anne **Heywood:** Violet Pretty (1930–   ), Eng. film actress.

H.H.: Helen Maria Hunt Jackson, née Fiske (1830–1885), U.S. poet, novelist, children's writer. The initials are of course for the writer's first and third names. She also wrote as Saxe Holm *(q.v.).*

Ruth **Hiatt:** Ruth Redfern (1908–   ), U.S. film actress.

Harry **Hieover:** Charles Bindley (1795–1859), Eng. sporting writer. Both names suggest English field sports, involving harrying and hunting.

Nehemiah **Higginbottom:** Samuel Taylor Coleridge (1772–1834), Eng. poet, critic. The poet used this name for his contributions to the *Monthly Review,* in which he parodied his own style.

Jack **Higgins:** Henry Patterson (1929–   ), Eng. fiction writer.

Patricia **Highsmith:** Patricia Plangman (1921–   ), U.S. novelist. The novelist assumed the name of her adoptive parents as her pen name.

Headon **Hill:** Francis Edward Grainger (1857–1924), Eng. romantic novelist, detective fiction writer. Headon Hill is a hill on the Isle of Wright.

Jenny **Hill:** Elizabeth Pasta (1851–1896), Br. music hall artiste ("the Vital Spark").

Joe **Hill:** Joel Emanuel Hagglund (1879–1915), Swe.-born U.S. poet, composer.

Robin **Hill:** Robert Young (1811–1908), Eng. poet. There is a Staffordshire village called Robin Hill.

Steven **Hill:** Solomon Berg (1924–   ), U.S. stage, film actor. The actor translated his surname into English.

Terence **Hill:** Mario Girotti (1939–   ), It. film actor.

Wendy **Hiller:** Wendy Gow, née Watkin (1912–   ), Eng. stage, film actress. The actress adopted her mother's maiden name as her stage name.

Harriet **Hilliard:** Peggy Lou Snyder (1914–   ), U.S. film, TV actress.

Thomas **Hinde:** [Sir] Thomas Willes Chitty (1926–   ), Br. novelist. The novelist adopted his mother's maiden name as his pseudonym.

Jerome **Hines:** Jerome Heinz (1921–   ), U.S. opera singer.

Dr. Evadne **Hinge:** George Logan (*c.* 1950–   ), Sc. female impersonator, teaming with Dame Hilda Bracket *(q.v.)* (as "Hinge and Bracket").

Hi-Regan: [Captain] John Joseph Dunne (1837–1910), Eng. traveler, journalist, writer on sporting subjects, father of George Egerton *(q.v.)*.

Shere **Hite:** Shirley Diana Gregory (*c.*1935–   ), U.S. sexologist. The writer's professional name, the subject of some punning by journalists, is her married name, with "Shere," pronounced "Sherry," derived as a pet form of her first name.

H.L.L.: Jane Laurie Borthwick (1813–1897), Sc. hymnwriter. Together with her sister, Sarah Borthwick Findlater, Jane Borthwick made a series of translations (1854–1862) from the German, entitled the work *Hymns from the Land of Luther*, and used the initials of this to give her own pen name.

Rose **Hobart:** Rose Keefer (1906–   ), U.S. film actress.

John Oliver **Hobbs:** Pearl Mary Teresa Craigie, née Richards (1867–1906), U.S.-born Eng. novelist. The novelist, usually referred to as simply Mrs. Craigie, chose the name "Hobbes" simply because it was "homely," suggesting "hob by the hearth" and similar words. Pearl Richards's parents brought her to England when she was less than a year old.

Ho Chi Minh: Nguyen That Thanh (1890–1969), North Vietnamese president. The politician first became an active socialist in France in 1917 under the name of Nguyen Ai Quoc, "Nguyen the patriot." In 1942, however, he assumed the name by which he came to be best known, Ho Chi Minh, "He who enlightens." These were by no means his only names, and previously he had used several party pseudonyms.

Stephen **Hockaby:** Gladys Maude Winifred Mitchell (1901–1983), Eng. crime novelist.

Johnny **Hodges:** Cornelius Hodge (1905–1970), U.S. saxophonist.

John **Hodgkinson:** John Meadowcroft (1767–1805), Br. actor, working in U.S.

Dennis **Hoey:** Samuel David Hyams (1893–1960), Eng. film actor, working mainly in U.S.

Fay **Holden:** Fay Hammerton (1894–1973), Br. stage, film actress, working in U.S.

Jan **Holden:** Jan Wilkinson (1931–   ), Eng. stage actress.

Stanley **Holden:** Stanley Waller (1928–   ), Eng. ballet dancer.

William **Holden:** William Franklin Beedle, Jr. (1918–1981), U.S. film actor. A Paramount executive said that the actor's real name "sounds like an insect," so renamed him in 1958 after a newspaper friend.

Billie **Holiday:** Eleanora Fagan (1915–1959), U.S. black popular singer.

Judy **Holliday:** Judith Tuvim (1922–1965), U.S. stage, film actress. The actress translated her Jewish name from the Hebrew to English. Compare Yom Tov (literally "good day") as the term for a Jewish holy day or holiday.

Earl **Holliman:** Anthony Numenka (1928–   ), U.S. film actor.

Buddy **Holly:** Charles Hardin Holley (1936–1959), U.S. rock musician. There is a small difference between the rock pioneer's professional name and his original name. This arose when his surname was misspelled on his first recording contract in 1956, and he did not bother to have his name corrected [John J. Goldrosen, *Buddy Holly: His Life and Music*, 1979].

Hanya **Holm:** Johanna Kuntze, née Eckert (*c.*1900–   ), Ger. stage choreographer, director of musicals, working in U.S.

Ian **Holm:** Ian Holm Cuthbert (1931–   ), Eng. stage, film, TV actor.

Saxe **Holm:** Helen Maria Hunt Jackson, née Fiske (1830–1885), U.S. poet, novelist, children's writer. There are echoes of "Helen Jackson" in the name, but this may not be the actual origin. The author used the pen name for her earliest writings, after the death of her first husband, Captain Edward Hunt. She married William Jackson in 1875.

Gordon **Holmes:** Louis Tracy (1863–1928), Eng. journalist, fiction writer.

H.H. **Holmes:** William Anthony Parker White (1911–1968), U.S. thriller writer. Rather gruesomely, the writer adopted the name of the murderer H.H. Holmes for his pen name.

Patrick **Holt:** Patrick Parsons (1912–   ), Br. film actor.

Victoria **Holt:** Eleanor Alice Burford Hibbert (1906–   ), Eng. "Gothic" novelist.

Cecil **Home:** Julia Augusta Webster, née Davies (1837–1894), Br. poet, dramatist.

Evelyn **Home:** Peggy Makins, née Carn (1916–   ), Br. agony columnist. Evelyn Home was the long-serving agony columnist in the magazine *Woman* from 1937 to 1974. The name was one that Peggy Carn inherited on the magazine, deriving from Eve, symbolizing womanhood, and (obviously) Home, suggesting domestic happiness. The name itself was first chosen by a German Jewish woman psychologist who was writing for *Woman* when Peggy Carn took over. The columnist later wrote: "The 'Evelyn' contained Eve, the archetypal mother, the temptress, the sexy side of woman; the 'home' was what every woman is supposed to want. At the time I thought the name too phony to be taken seriously ever; I was totally mistaken" [Peggy Makins, *The Evelyn Home Story*, 1975]. The pseudonym was abandoned in 1974, when Peggy Makins was succeeded in turn by Anna Raeburn *(q.v.)*.

Homer: Henry D. Haynes (1917–1971), U.S. humorous country singer, teaming with Jethro *(q.v.)*.

Geoffrey **Homes:** Daniel Mainwaring (1901–   ), U.S. mystery novelist, screenwriter.

Harry **Honeycomb:** James Henry Leigh Hunt (1784–1859), Eng. essayist, poet. The famous poet used this semi-serious name, based on his second name and surname, for contributions to various journals, such as the *New Monthly Magazine*.

Honorius II: Lamberto Scannabechi (? –1130), It. pope.

Honorius III: Cencio Savelli (? –1227), It. pope, grand-uncle of Honorius IV *(q.v.)*.

Honorius IV: Giacomo (or Jacomus) Savelli (?1210–1287), It. pope.

Percy **Honri:** Percy Henri Thompson (1874–1953), Eng. music hall artiste. The performer adopted the misprinted version of his name "Henri" that appeared in a billing.

Anthony **Hope:** [Sir] Anthony Hope Hawkins (1863–1933), Eng. historical novelist, playwright. The author of *The Prisoner of Zenda* (1894) wrote the famous romantic adventure novel while practicing as a barrister in London. He therefore adopted a pseudonym, using his first two names only. The book was such a success that it enabled him to give up the law as a career and to become a fulltime novelist.

Ascott R. **Hope:** Ascott Robert Hope-Moncrieff (1846–1927), Br. editor, author of books for boys.

Bob **Hope:** Leslie Townes Hope (1904–   ), Eng.-born U.S. film comedian. The well-known actor originally adopted the name "Lester T. Hope," reasoning: "I thought that was a little more manish. . . I found a lot of girls would call me Leslie and I'd call them Leslie, and there was a sort of conflict of interests there so I changed it to 'Lester.'" He then thought that this name "still looked a little ginger around the edges," so changed "Lester" to "Bob." "I thought that was more chummy and audiences would get to like me" [Charles Thompson, *Bob Hope: The Road from Eltham*, 1981].

Laura Lee **Hope:** Edward L. Stratemeyer (1863–1930), U.S. author of stories for girls. The author used various pseudonyms for his fiction for boys and girls, choosing this feminine one for his stories about the Bobbsey Twins for girls. The name itself was doubtless random, but any name in "Hope" suggests wholesome good value, even excitement.

Laurence **Hope:** Adela Florence Nicolson, née Cory (1865–1904), Br. writer of "oriental" lyrics. Possibly "Laurence" was at least subconsciously suggested by the author's second name.

Antony **Hopkins:** Antony Reynolds (1921–   ), Eng. composer, conductor, broadcaster on music. Antony Hopkins (who must not be confused with Anthony Hopkins, the film actor) was adopted by Major and Mrs. Hopkins at the age of four, and thereafter assumed their name.

Hedda **Hopper:** Elda Furry (1890–1966), U.S. film actress, gossip columnist. The actress's second name is that of her husband, De Wolf Hopper, whom she married in 1913. He had been married four times already, and his wives had been named Ella, Ida, Edna, and Nella. In view of the similarity of Elda's own name to these, a numerologist was consulted. He recommended the name Hedda, which may be different numerologically but hardly otherwise.

Adam **Hornbrook:** Thomas Cooper (1805–1892), Eng. politician, author.

Isaac **Hortibonus:** Isaac Casaubon (1559–1614), Swiss theologian, classical scholar. The scholarly pseudonym seems to have been devised as an alteration of his real surname, with "Casaubon" (which actually means "in good state") interpreted as "good house." "Hortibonus" or "Hortusbonus," as he sometimes spelled it, thus meant "good garden."

Harry **Houdini:** Erik Weisz (1874–1926), Hung.-born U.S. escapologist. The escapologist was keen to escape from the ties of his real name. "Houdini" he adopted for his admiration of the French illusionist Robert-Houdin *(q.v.)*. But how come "Harry" from "Erik?" The name probably evolved gradually — according to one account, via Ehrich, Ehrie, and Erie — as befits the gradual emergence of an escapologist from his confines.

John **Houseman:** Jacques Haussman (1902–1988), Rom. stage, film director, working in U.S.

Renée **Houston:** Katherina Houston Gribbin (1902–1980), Sc. vaudeville artist, film actress.

The **Howadji:** George William Curtis (1824–1892), U.S. travel writer, newspaper correspondent. The author used this name for his travel writings, such as *Nile Notes of a Howadji* (1851) and *The Howadji in Syria* (1852). The name itself was probably an arbitrary mock-oriental concoction, vaguely suggesting "howdah."

Don **Howard:** Donald Howard Koplow (1935–   ), U.S. popular singer.

Elizabeth Jane **Howard:** Elizabeth Jane Liddon (1923–   ), Eng. writer, editor, reviewer. The writer adopted her mother's maiden name as her pen name.

H.L. **Howard:** Charles Jeremiah Wells (?1799–1879), Eng. poet.

John **Howard:** John Cox (1913–   ), U.S. juvenile film actor.

Keble **Howard:** John Keble Bell (1875–1928), Eng. playwright, journalist.

Leslie **Howard:** Leslie Stainer (1893–1943), Eng. stage, film actor, of Hung. parentage. The actor may have anglicized his original Hungarian name of László Horvarth.

Susan **Howard:** Jeri Lynn Monney (*c.*1948–   ), U.S. film, TV actress.

Thomas **Howard:** Jesse Woodson James (1847–1892), U.S. desperado. This pseudonym was used by the (in)famous Jesse James in his final days while living at St. Joseph, Miss. It seems to have been simply an "innocuous" name.

Frankie **Howerd:** Francis Alick Howard (1922–   ), Eng. stage, film, TV comedian. The actor chose the smallest of changes when adopting his stage name: "It seems to me that there were too many Howards: among them Trevor, Sidney and Arthur. So how to stay Howard, yet alter it? I hit on the idea of a change of spelling: Howerd — which, I argued, would have the added advantage of making people look twice because they assumed it to be a misprint" [Frankie Howerd, *On the Way I Lost It*, 1976].

Howlin' Wolf: Chester Arthur Burnett (1910–1976), U.S. black blues singer, songwriter.

Margaret **Howth:** Rebecca Blaine Harding Davis (1831–1910), U.S. novelist. The writer adopted the name of the heroine of her own novel, *Margaret Howth* (1862).

John **Hoyt:** John Hoysradt (1905–   ), U.S. film actor.

Rock **Hudson:** Roy Harold Fitzgerald, originally Roy Scherer (1925–1985), U.S. film actor. Rock Hudson had a more or less standard story to account for his screen name, which he said had been given him by his first agent, Henry Willson. Here is one version of it: "Henry thought he knew what was best for me. I remember he said, 'we have to change your name.' 'Why?' I asked. 'I don't want one of those silly names.' 'You have to,' he said, 'so it looks good on the marquee. Roy Fitzgerald is too long.' 'What about Geraldine Fitzgerald? Is that too long?' But Henry insisted. He hit me with Hudson. Then he had some really macho, cockamamie first names.

Like Dirk. Lance. Finally he said, 'What about Rock?' That clicked. 'Yeah, that sounds pretty good,' I said. It was not too far from Roy, and no one else had it. So that was it." But it is now known that it was actually Ken Hodge, Rock Hudson's friend and lover, who gave him his name, with "Rock" for strength, and "Hudson" taken from the Long Beach phone book. Even so, Willson *did* rename several famous actors, many of whom he gave names similar to "Rock Hudson." Among them were Tab Hunter, Troy Donahue, Rory Calhoun, and Rip Torn *(q.v.)* [Rock Hudson and Sara Davidson, *Rock Hudson: His Story*, 1986]. Although born Roy Scherer, the actor subsequently adopted the name of his stepfather, Wallace Fitzgerald.

Baby **Huey:** James Ramey (1944–1970), U.S. rhythm and blues singer.

Hazel **Hughes:** Hazel Heppenstall (1913–1974), S.A. stage actress. The actress adopted her mother's maiden name as her stage name.

Kathleen **Hughes:** Betty von Gerlean (1929–), U.S. film actress. Possibly the actress's surname suggested her new stage first name.

Josephine **Hull:** Josephine Sherwood (1884–1957), U.S. stage, film actress.

Richard **Hull:** Richard Henry Sampson (1896–1973), Eng. detective novelist.

Engelbert **Humperdinck:** Arnold George Dorsey (1936–), Eng. pop singer. The singer borrowed the name of the German classical composer (best known for his opera *Hansel and Gretel*) for his professional name. It was suggested to Dorsey by his manager, Gordon Mills, in 1965, who was looking through some old records of works by the composer at the time. Dorsey officially assumed the name the following year.

Evan **Hunter:** Salvatore A. Lombino (1926–), U.S. writer, popularly known as Ed McBain *(q.v.)*.

Jeffrey **Hunter:** Henry Hunter McKinnies, Jr. (1925–1969), U.S. film actor.

Kim **Hunter:** Janet Cole (1922–), U.S. stage, film actress. The actress's name was changed by David O. Selznick, who told her that Janet Cole could be anyone, but that Kim Hunter had individuality, and with a name like that she would go far.

Tab **Hunter:** Arthur Andrew Gelien (1931–), U.S. film actor. The actor's name was given him by his agent, Henry Willson (see Rock Hudson, above).

Veronica **Hurst:** Patricia Wilmshurst (1931–), Br. film actress.

Mary Beth **Hurt:** Mary Supinger (1948–), U.S. film actress.

Walter **Huston:** Walter Houghston (1884–1950), Can.-born U.S. stage, film actor.

Betty **Hutton:** Elizabeth Jane Thornburg (1921–), U.S. film actress. The actress's name was changed in 1937 by Vincent Lopez, a Detroit bandleader, after a numerologist had been consulted. Betty's sister Marion also changed her surname to Hutton (see next entry).

Marion **Hutton:** Marion Thornburg (1920–1987), U. S. singer, film actress, sister of Betty Hutton *(q.v.)*.

Robert **Hutton:** Robert Bruce Winne (1920–), U.S. film actor.

Père **Hyacinthe:** Charles-Jean-Marie Loyson (1827–1912), Fr. priest, writer.

Robin **Hyde:** Iris Guiver Wilkinson (1906–1939), S.A. novelist, poet, working in New Zealand.

Diana **Hyland:** Diana Gentner (1936–1977), U.S. stage, TV actress.

Jane **Hylton:** Gwendoline Clark (1927–1979), Br. film actress.

Ronald **Hynd:** Ronald Hens (1931–   ), Eng. ballet dancer, choreographer, director. Hynd is married to the former dancer Annette Page *(q.v.)*.

Janis **Ian:** Janis Eddy Fink (1951–   ), U.S. pop singer, song writer.

Ianthe: Emma Catherine Embury (1806–1863), U.S. novelist. The writer used this name for her contributions to various periodicals, no doubt borrowing it from one of the many literary Ianthes, such as the maiden in Shelley's *Queen Mab* or the young lady to whom Byron dedicated *Childe Harold's Pilgrimage.*

Abdullah **Ibrahim:** Adolph Johannes Brand (1934–   ), South African popular pianist, composer.

Billy **Idol:** William Broad (1955–   ), Eng. punk rock singer.

Idris: Arthur Henry Mee (1875–1943), Eng. journalist, editor, writer. The founder of the *Children's Encyclopaedia* (called *Book of Knowledge* in the U.S.) adopted this name for his journalistic writings, probably taking it from the Celtic giant of this name, who is said to have given the name of Cader Idris, the Welsh mountain.

Francis **Iles:** Anthony Berkeley Cox (1893–1971), Br. writer of detective stories.

Margaret **Illington:** Maude Ellen Light (1879–1934), U.S. stage actress. The actress's stage name was coined for her by the theatre manager, Daniel Frohman, who engaged her. He seems to have "upped" Maude to Margaret, and based "Illington" on her second name, or formed it as a sort of anagram of her two last names.

Immerito: Edmund Spenser (?1552–1599), Eng. poet. This was the pseudonym under which Spenser published his first major work, *The Shepheardes Calender* (1579), with the name meaning "undeservedly" in Latin.

Fay **Inchfawn:** Elizabeth Rebecca Ward (1881–   ), Br. popular writer. An unusual pen name which may possibly be based on a name such as Inchbald.

Frieda **Inescort:** Frieda Wightman (1900–1976), Sc.-born film actress, working in U.S.

Colonel Frederic **Ingham:** Edward Everett Hale (1822–1909), U.S. author, editor, Unitarian clergyman. The prolific author used the name for *The Ingham Papers* (1870) and other writings.

Mona **Inglesby:** Mona Kimberley (1918–   ), Br. ballet dancer.

Ingoldsby: [Rev.] James Hildyard (1809–1897), Eng. classical scholar. The writer adopted the name of the village in Lincolnshire where he had his living as a clergyman (from 1846). Compare the next name below.

Thomas **Ingoldsby:** [Rev.] Richard Harris Barham (1788–1845), Br. writer, antiquary. The well-known author of *The Ingoldsby Legends* (1837), whose full title was *The Ingoldsby Legends: or Mirth and Marvels, by Thomas Ingoldsby Esquire,* took his name from the Lincolnshire village of Ingoldsby, although he never held a living there, as did James Hildyard (see entry above).

Rex **Ingram:** Reginald Ingram Montgomery Hitchcock (1893–1950), It.-born film director, working in U.S.

Michael **Innes:** John Innes Mackintosh Stewart (1906–   ), Sc. writer of detective novels. J.I.M. Stewart, professionally a university lecturer in English literature, and a distinguished literary critic, used this name for his detective fiction. The name itself consists of the first names of two of his three sons. (Michael Stewart, born 1933, is the economist and author of *Keynes and After* and other works.)

Innocent II: Gregorio Papareschi dei Guidoni (? –1143), It. pope.

Innocent III: Giovanni Lotario dei Conti di Segni (1161–1216), It. pope.

Innocent IV: Sinibaldo (de') Fieschi (? –1254), It. pope.

Innocent V: Pierre de Tarentaise (*c.*1224–1276), Fr. pope.

Innocent VI: Etienne Aubert (? –1362), Fr. pope.

Innocent VII: Cosimo Gentile de' Migliorati (?1336–1406), It. pope.

Innocent VIII: Giovanni Battista Cibo (1432–1492), It. pope.

Innocent IX: Giovanni Antonio Facchinetti (1519–1591), It. pope.

Innocent X: Giovanni Battista Pamfili (1574–1655), It. pope.

Innocent XI: Benedetto Odescalchi (1611–1689), It. pope.

Innocent XII: Antonio Pignatelli (1615–1700), It. pope.

Innocent XIII: Michelangelo Conti (1655–1721), It. pope.

Michael **Ireland:** Darrell Figgis (1882–1925), Ir. poet, writer.

Irenaeus: Samuel Irenaeus Prime (1812–1885), U.S. clergyman, author.

Irene: Irene Lentz (1901–1962), U.S. film costume designer.

William **Irish:** Cornell George Hopley-Woolrich (1903–1968), U.S. mystery writer.

Ralph **Iron:** Olive Emilie Albertina Schreiner (1855–1920), Br. novelist. The masculine name was assumed by the (female) writer for *The Story of an African Farm* (1883) (see p. 30). The name seems to be loosely based on her first name and surname, but may have had some symbolic sense.

George **Irving:** George Irving Sheasky (1922–), U.S. stage actor, singer.

[Sir] Henry **Irving:** John Henry Brodribb (1838–1905), Br. stage actor, theatre manager. The actor changed his name in order to avoid embarrassing his parents, who were ashamed of his profession. The name itself was a tribute to two real Irvings: Edward Irving (1792–1834), a popular Scottish religious writer, and Washington Irving (1783–1859), his favorite boyhood author.

Jules **Irving:** Jules Israel (1925–), U.S. stage director.

May **Irwin:** Georgia Campbell (1862–1928), U.S. stage actress, music hall artist.

Iskander: Aleksandr Ivanovich Herzen *(q.v.).* The Russian revolutionary writer used the Turkish form of his first name as a pseudonym for *Notes of a Young Man* (1940) and other writings. For a similar name, compare Skanderbeg.

Burl **Ives:** Burl Icle Ivanhoe (1909–), U.S. stage, film actor, folk singer.

Ub **Iwerks:** Ubbe Ert Iwwerks, (1901–1971), U.S. film animator.

Kareem Abdul **Jabbar:** Lew Alcindor (1947–), U.S. basketball player. Alcindor converted to Islam when a student, under the influence of Malcolm X *(q.v.),* and subsequently changed his name to a Moslem one.

Wanda **Jackson:** Wanda Goodman (1937–), U.S. pop singer.

Frank **Jacson:** Ramon Mercader (1914–1978), Sp. assassinator of Leon Trotsky *(q.v.).*

Dean **Jagger:** Dean Jeffries (1903–1982), U.S. film actor.

Jak: Raymond Jackson (1927–), Eng. cartoonist.

Elmore **James:** Elmore Brooks (1918–1963), U.S. blues guitarist.

Etta **James:** Etta James Hawkins (*c.*1938–   ), U.S. soul singer.

James **James:** Arthur Henry Adams (1872–1936), N.Z. novelist, poet, playwright.

Jimmy **James:** James Casey (1892–1965), Eng. music hall comedian. The comedian changed his name when working in Wales, on being told that his name Casey would not be popular there.

Joni **James:** Joan Carmello Babbo (1930–   ), U.S. popular singer.

Polly **James:** Pauline Devaney (1941–   ), Eng. stage, TV actress.

Rick **James:** James Johnston (1955–   ), U.S. "punk funk" musician.

Sonny **James:** James Loden (1929–   ), U.S. country singer.

Tommy **James:** Thomas Jackson (1947–   ), U.S. pop singer.

Laurence M. **Janifer:** Larry Mark Harris (1933–   ), U.S. SF writer.

Elsie **Janis:** Elsie Bierbauer (1889–1956), U.S. stage actress.

Emil **Jannings:** Theodor Friedrich Emil Janenz (1884–1950), Swiss film actor, of U.S.-Ger. parentage.

Janosch: Horst Eckert (1931–   ), Ger. illustrator of children's books.

Sebastian **Japrisot:** Jean-Baptiste Rossi (1931–   ), Fr. novelist. The novelist's new surname consists of letters extracted from his whole name. Presumably his new first name must have some special significance.

David **Janssen:** David Meyer (1930–1980), U.S. film, TV actor.

Jacques **Jasmin:** Jacques Boé (1798–1864), Fr. poet, "troubadour."

W.M.L. **Jay:** Julia Louisa Matilda Woodruff, née Curtiss (1833–1909), Eng. author. The author's pen name consists of a reversal of her initials, with the "J" of "Julia" formed as a word.

Jennifer **Jayne:** Jennifer Jayne Jones (1932–   ), Br. film, TV actress.

Michael **Jayston:** Michael James (1936–   ), Eng. stage actor.

Gloria **Jean:** Gloria Jean Schoonover (1928–   ), U.S. film actress.

Ursula **Jeans:** Ursula Livesey, née McMinn (1906–1973), Eng. stage actress.

Mahatma Cane **Jeeves:** W.C. Fields *(q.v.).*

Anne **Jeffreys:** Anne Carmichael (1923–   ), U.S. stage actress, singer.

Allen **Jenkins:** Alfred McGonegal (1900–1974), U.S. film actor.

Caryl **Jenner:** Pamela Penelope Ripman (1917–   ), Eng. stage director, theatre manager.

Jenneval: Hippolyte Louis Alexandre Dechet (1801–1830), Fr. comedian, poet.

Kid **Jensen:** David Allen Jensen (1950–   ), Can.-born Eng. radio, TV DJ, compère. The radio and TV personality began working as a DJ when he was only 16. In 1968 he started working for Radio Luxembourg, where he was nicknamed "Kid" for his youth and youthful appearance. He adopted the name instead of his first name until about 1980, when he felt sufficiently mature to revert to "David." Even so, he still features as David "Kid" Jensen in later reference and publicity sources.

Suzie **Jerome:** Suzanne Willis (1960–1986), Br. film, TV actress.

Mary **Jerrold:** Mary Allen (1877–1955), Br. film actress.

Jethro: Kenneth C. Burns (1923–   ), U.S. humorous country singer, teaming with Homer *(q.v.).*

Jetsam: Malcolm McEachern (1884–1945), Austral. singer, stage, radio entertainer, teaming with Flotsam *(q.v.)*.

Jimmy Jewel: James Marsh (1911–   ), Eng. music hall, radio, TV comedian. Jimmy Jewel explains the genesis of his name: "We were really a family called Marsh, but father always worked as Jimmy Jewel. He wouldn't let me call myself Jimmy Jewel, Jr., so for years I worked as Maurice Marsh because I was always doing Chevalier impressions; then we kept changing our names on the bills so the audience wouldn't know it was all one family" [*The Times*, August 3, 1983].

Jillana: Jillana Zimmermann (1936–   ), U.S. ballet dancer.

Ann Jillian: Ann Jura Nauseda (1951–   ), U.S. TV actress.

Jodelet: Julian Bedeau (?1590–1660), Fr. comic actor, brother of L'Espy *(q.v.)*.

Robert Joffrey: Abdullah Jaffa Anver Bey Khan (1930–1988), U.S. ballet dancer, choreographer, of Afghan parentage.

John II: Mercurius (? –535), It. pope.

John III: Catelinus (? –574), It. pope.

John XII: Octavian (?937–964), It. pope.

John XIV: Pietro Canepanova (? –984), It. pope.

John XVII: Giovanni Siccone (? –1003), It. pope.

John XVIII: Giovanni Fasano (? –1009), It. pope.

John XXI: Pietro di Giuliano (*c*.1210 or 1220–1277), It. pope.

John XXII: Jacques d'Euse (1249–1334), Fr. pope.

John XXIII: Angelo Giuseppe Roncalli (1881–1963). See pp. 52–53 for a consideration of this pope's name, and those of other popes called John or John Paul.

Dr. John: Malcolm John ("Mac") Rebennack (1941–   ), U.S. rock musician.

Elton John: Reginald Kenneth Dwight (1947–   ), Eng. pop musician. Reg Dwight changed his name by deed poll, adopting his new first name from Elton Dean, saxophonist for the soul group Bluesology, and his surname from Long John Baldry, the rock singer. The pop singer's *full* stage name is in fact Elton Hercules John, the middle name added later since, as he explained, "It gave me something to look up to and to remind me always to be strong" (before changing his name, Reginald Kenneth Dwight had expressed his view that it "sounded like a cement mixer!") [Gerald Newman with Joe Bivona, *Elton John*, 1976].

Evan John: Evan John Simpson (1901–1953), Br. playwright, novelist.

Jasper John: Rosalie Muspratt Jones (1913–   ), Br. film, stage actress.

Rosamund John: Nora Rosamund Jones (1913–   ), Br. film actress.

[Saint] John of the Cross: Juan de Yepes y Alvarez (1542–1591), Sp. mystic, poet. The saint's title refers directly to his poetry, and in particular to his poem *Noche oscura del alma* ("Dark night of the soul"), in which he describes how the human soul sheds its attachment to everything and finally passes through a personal experience of the Crucifixion to attain the glory of Christ.

John Paul I: Albino Luciani (1913–1978), It. pope.

John Paul II: Karol Wojtyla (1920–   ), Pol. pope. For an account of the relationship between the various popes named John and John Paul, see pp. 52–53.

Foster Johns: Gilbert Vivian Seldes (1893–1970), U.S. journalist, drama critic, writer.

Crockett **Johnson:** David Johnson Leisk (1906–1975), U.S. cartoonist.

John **Johnson:** Guy Fawkes (1570–1606), Eng. conspirator. John Johnson was the name assumed by Guy Fawkes when he hired a house next to the Houses of Parliament with the aim of constructing a gunpowder mine in its cellars (the "Gunpowder Plot") so as to blow up the House of Lords while King James was present there for the official opening of parliament. "John Johnson" was to be the servant of one of the conspirators, Thomas Percy. The name seems arbitrary.

Kay **Johnson:** Catherine Townsend (1904–1975), U.S. film actress.

Rita **Johnson:** Rita McSean (1912–1965), U.S. film actress. The actress "translated" her Gaelic name into English to provide her stage name; "McSean" means "son of John."

Benjamin F. **Johnson of Boone:** James Whitcomb Riley (1854–1916), U.S. poet, journalist.

Al **Jolson:** Asa Yoelson (1885–1950), U.S. singer, stage film actor, of Jewish-Lithuanian descent. The famous singer first changed his forename Asa to Al when his elder brother changed his own name, Hirsh, to Harry. Later, in 1899, Fred E. Moore, an electrician in New York's Dewey Theatre, suggested he join him in a singing act as Harry Joelson. Eventually, four years later, the printer shortened "Joelson" to "Jolson" as the actor's original name seemed "long, foreign sounding" [Michael Freedland, *Al Jolson*, 1971].

Annie **Jones:** Annika Jasko (*c*.1967–), Austral. TV actress, of Hung. parentage.

Buck **Jones:** Charles Frederick Gebhardt (1889–1942), U.S. film actor.

Jennifer **Jones:** Phyllis Selznick, née Isley (1919–), U.S. film actress. An American reporter once asked Phyllis Isley how she came by her screen name. Her reply was: "My mother must have been reading an English novel, but I suppose they'll change it once I get to Hollywood." They didn't, though.

John Paul **Jones:** John Paul (1747–1792), Sc.-born U.S. naval hero. This is the man who is said to have given his name to the dance known as the Paul Jones.

L.Q. **Jones:** Justus Ellis McQueen (1927–), U.S. film actor.

Paul **Jones:** Paul Pond (1942–), Eng. stage actor, pop musician.

Richard **Jones:** Theodore Edward Hook (1788–1841), Eng. humorist, novelist.

Sheridan **Jones:** Ada Elizabeth Chesterton, née Jones (1870–1962), Br. journalist, writer. "Sheridan" was a family name on the paternal side, used by Ada Elizabeth Jones for many of her journalistic writings. Among her family and close friends she was known as "Keith."

T. Percy **Jones:** William Edmonstoune Aytoun (1813–1865), Sc. humorous writer.

Tom **Jones:** Thomas Jones Woodward (1940–), Welsh popular singer. The singer was renamed by his manager, Gordon Mills, reputedly after the hero of the book of the same name by Fielding, or, more precisely, from its filmed version (1963), in which the central figure, who undergoes many sexual escapades, is played by Albert Finney.

Mrs. Dorothy **Jordan:** Dorothea Bland (1762–1816), Ir. comedy actress. The actress was the illegitimate daughter of another actress by a gentleman named Francis

Bland, and she first went on the stage as "Miss Francis." In 1780 she was engaged by Richard Daly, the Irish theatre manager, for the Smock Alley Theatre, Dublin, but was seduced by him and two years later fled to England with her mother and sister. There, as she was clearly pregnant (although not married), she changed her name on the advice of friends to "Mrs. Jordan," and continued acting until, and even after, the birth of Daly's child. She chose this particular name as it suited the "matronly" role for the condition in which she then found herself: "jordan" is a term for a chamber pot, a receptacle (or an equivalent) to which pregnant women must frequently resort.

Joselito: José Gómez (1895–1920), Sp. bullfighter.

[Père] **Joseph:** François Leclerc du Tremblay (1577–1638), Fr. friar, diplomat. The French friar, equally well known by his nickname of *L'Eminence Grise* (he was advisor to Cardinal Richelieu, *L'Eminence Rouge*), seems to have adopted a biblical name for his religious role.

Josiah Allen's Wife: Marietta Holley (1836–1926), U.S. humorist. In the humorist's writings, much of the homely philosophizing by Samantha, the wife of a fictional character named Josiah Allen, served as propaganda for temperance and female suffrage.

Louis **Jourdan:** Louis Gendre (1919–   ), Fr. film actor. The actor's screen name seems to be a modification of his real surname.

Leatrice **Joy:** Leatrice Joy Zeidler (1894–1985), U.S. film actress.

Brenda **Joyce:** Betty Leabo (1918–   ), U.S. film actress.

Thomas **Joyce:** Arthur Joyce Lunel Carey (1888–1957), Ir. novelist.

J.S. of Dale: Frederic Jesup Stimson (1855–1943), U.S. author, lawyer. The initials presumably represent the author's middle name.

Aunt **Judy:** Margaret Scott Gatty (1809–1873), Eng. children's writer. The writer (Margaret Gatty, who married a Mr. Scott) took her name from that of the popular Victorian children's magazine, *Aunt Judy's Magazine*, of which she was editor. She was the mother of the well-known children's writer Juliana Horatia Ewing, and the magazine took its own name from the family pet name, Judy, for Juliana.

Julius II: Giuliano della Rovere (1443–1513), It. pope. The papal name (in Italian, Giulio) is not far removed from its bearer's real Christian name.

Julius III: Giammaria Ciocchi del Monte (1487–1555), It. pope.

June: June Tripp (1901–1985), Eng. revue actress, singer, working in U.S.

Jennie **June:** Jane Croly, née Cunningham (1829–1901), Eng.-born U.S. writer. The writer's pen name was doubtless a pleasant dual variation on her first name.

Junius: Sir Philip Francis (1740–1818), Ir. politician and writer. The writer is generally believed – although not conclusively – to be the most likely pseudonymous author of the so-called "Letters of Junius," that appeared in the *Public Advertiser*. (See pp. 64–65 for a further consideration of the author's identity, together with details of the letters themselves.) If the name is not a reference to a particular Roman personage of note, such as either of the conspirators Lucius Junius Brutus or Marcus Junius Brutus, who were both in the plot to kill Caesar, the intention may have been to indicate a youthful or *junior* person. Compare the next two entries below.

E. **Junius:** Adrien Emmanuel Rouquette (1813–1887), U.S. poet, novelist. The writer used the name for his *Critical Dialogue Between Aboo and Caboo* (1880), denouncing the depiction of Creoles in George Washington Cable's novel, *The Grandissimes* (1880). Rouquette, who was the son of a Creole mother, based his pen name on that of Junius *(q.v.)*, with "E." presumably for "Emmanuel."

Junius Americanus: Arthur Lee (1740–1792), U.S. diplomat. The diplomat, who used the name for some letters he published, adopted the pseudonym made famous by Junius *(q.v.)*.

Katy **Jurado:** María Cristina Estella Marcella Jurado García (1927–   ), Mexican film actress, working in the U.S.

John **Justin:** John Ledsma (1917–   ), Br. film actor.

Tonio **K.:** Steve Krikorian (1950–   ), U.S. rock singer, songwriter.

Kalanag: Helmut Schreiber (1893–1963), Ger. illusionist. The artist adopted the name from Kipling's *Jungle Book*, where it is that of an elephant, and is said to mean "Black Snake."

Lev Borisovich **Kamenev:** Lev Borisovich Rozenfeld (1883–1936), Russ. revolutionary, opponent of Stalin *(q.v.)*. The revolutionary's name is based on Russian *kamen'*, "stone," and presumably is in the same "symbolic" class as that of Stalin ("steel") himself. Ironically (or even as expected), in this case steel proved stronger than stone, for Kamenev was a victim of the Great Purge of the mid–1930s.

Eden **Kane:** Richard Graham Sarstedt (1942–   ), Eng. pop singer. The singer is said to have derived his name from the Orson Welles film *Citizen Kane*. He used it from the early 1960s, although he also featured briefly in 1973 with his brothers Robin and Peter Sarstedt under his own name, as the Sarstedt Brothers.

Helen **Kane:** Helen Schroeder (1904–1966), U.S. singer, film actress.

Karandash: Mikhail Nikolayevich Rumyantsev (1901–1983), Russ. circus clown. The name of the famous clown is the Russian word for "pencil." He adopted it in 1934 when appearing in Leningrad, taking it from the French cartoonist Caran d'Ache *(q.v.)*. Rumyantsev had earlier worked as a commercial artist. Hence the attraction of this particular name.

Anna **Karina:** Hanne Karin Blarke Bayer (1940–   ), Dan. film actress, working in France, U.S. One can see the direct origin of the actress's name in her two first names. At the same time the screen name strongly suggests that of Tolstoy's heroine, Anna Karenina, whether in the original novel or (more likely) in one of the filmed versions of it.

Barbara **Karinska:** Varvara Zhmoudsky (1886–1983), Russ.-U.S. ballet costume designer, maker.

Miriam **Karlin:** Miriam Samuels (1925–   ), Br. film revue comedienne.

Boris **Karloff:** William Henry Pratt (1887–1969), Eng. film actor, working mainly in U.S. The actor, noted for his portrayal of the monster in *Frankenstein* (1931) derived his Russian-sounding name from one of his maternal ancestors. "I dredged up 'Karloff' from Russian ancestors on my mother's side, and I picked 'Boris' out of the chilly, Canadian air."

Phil **Karlson:** Philip N. Karlstein (1908–1986), U.S. film director.

Maria **Karnilova:** Maria Dovgolenko (1920–   ), U.S. ballet dancer, of Russ.

parentage. The dancer adopted (and adapted) her stage name from her mother's maiden name, which was Karnilovich.

Fred **Karno:** Frederick John Westcott (1866–1941), Eng. music hall comedian. The actor adopted his name in 1887 when he and two gymnast colleagues filled in at a London music hall for a troupe called "The Three Carnos." His agent, Richard Warner, suggested they change the "C" to a more distinctive "K" [J.P. Gallagher, *Fred Karno, Master of Mirth and Tears*, 1971].

Kurt S. **Kasznar:** Kurt Serwischer (1913–), Austr. stage actor.

Isser **Katch:** Isser Kać (1896–1958), Pol. film actor, working in U.S.

Anna **Kavan:** Helen Woods Edmonds (1901–1968), Fr.-born SF writer, working in U.S., U.K.

Charles **Kay:** Charles Piff (1930–), Eng. stage actor.

John **Kay:** Joachim F. Krauledat (1944–), Ger.-born U.S. rock musician.

Karen **Kay:** Adrienne Judith Pringle (*c.*1948–), Eng. TV entertainer, singer.

Danny **Kaye:** David Daniel Kaminsky (1913–1987), U.S. stage, film, TV actor.

Nora **Kaye:** Nora Koreff (1920–1987), U.S. ballet dancer.

Elia **Kazan:** Elia Kazanjoglou (1909–), Turk.-born U.S. film director. The well-known director was taken by his family to the U.S. when he was only four, and they then shortened their name to Kazan. Later, when he was established in Hollywood, an unsuccessful attempt was made to change his name yet again to "Cezanne." Perhaps an artistic reference was intended?

Ernie **K-Doe:** Ernest Kador, Jr. (1936–), U.S. black rhythm and blues singer.

Buster **Keaton:** Joseph Francis Keaton (1895–1966), U.S. film comedian. It remains uncertain how the great silent film comedian came by his nickname. The popular account is that it was given him by Harry Houdini *(q.v.)* after seeing the boy Keaton tumble down a flight of stairs. On the other hand, there may be a link with the comic strip character Buster Brown. Either way the actor is quite unrelated to the actress Diane Keaton *(q.v.)*.

Diane **Keaton:** Diane Hall (1946–), U.S. stage, film actress. The actress adopted her mother's maiden name of Keaton as there was already a Diane Hall as a member of the actors' union, Equity, which has a ruling that no two members should have the same name.

Viola **Keats:** Viola Smart (1911–), Sc. stage actress. The actress adopted her mother's maiden name as her stage name.

Howard **Keel:** Harold Clifford Leek (1917–), U.S. stage, film actor, singer.

Malcolm **Keen:** Malcolm Knee (1887–1970), Br. film, stage actor, theatre manager.

Carolyn **Keene:** [1] Edward L. Stratemeyer (1863–1930), U.S. children's writer; [2] Harriet Stratemeyer Adams (1894–1982), U.S. children's writer, his daughter. The writer's daughter continued, and expanded on, the many series started by her father, especially that centering on Nancy Drew, the girl detective. Mrs. Adams was also the major author of the Hardy Boys series, begun by the Stratemeyer Syndicate, set up in 1914 to produce books that Stratemeyer himself outlined and edited. He also wrote as Laura Lee Hope and Arthur M. Winfield *(q.v.)*. But why did he not use "Carolyn Keene" for the name of the girl detective, and keep "Nancy

Drew" for himself ? They would have been much more appropriate that way round.

Laura **Keene:** Mary Moss (or Foss) (*c.*1830–1873), U.S. actress, theatre manager.

Tom **Keene:** George Duryea (1896–1963), U.S. film actor.

Keith: James Barry Keefer (–), U.S. pop singer. This name must surely have originated as a nickname.

David **Keith:** Francis Steegmuller (1906–), U.S. novelist, literary critic. The author of serious literary and biographical studies used this name for his crime fiction. He also wrote as Byron Steel *(q.v.).*

Ian **Keith:** Keith Ross (1899–1960), U.S. film actor.

Penelope **Keith:** Penelope Timson, née Hatfield (1940–), Eng. TV actress. The actress adopted her mother's maiden name.

Harry **Kellar:** Harry Keller (1849–1922), U.S. magician.

Will P. **Kellino:** William P. Gislingham (1873–1958), Br. circus clown, film actor, director. The performer's new surname was created out of his original name.

Kem: Kimon Evan Marengo (1906–), Egyptian-born Br. political cartoonist. A neat combination of an acronym (from the artist's initials) and a variant of his first name. It is brief, too, as an ideal artist's name should be for signing purposes.

Jeremy **Kemp:** Jeremy Walker (1934–), Eng. film, TV actor. The actor adopted his mother's maiden name as his stage name.

Kempferhausen: Robert Pearse Gillies (1788–1858), Eng. litterateur and autobiographer. The writer adopted the name under which he featured in the series of dialogues known as the *Noctes Ambrosianae* published in *Blackwood's Edinburgh Magazine* between 1822 and 1835. Compare the name of Christopher North.

Joan **Kemp-Welch:** Joan Green (1906–), Eng. stage actress, theatre director. The actress borrowed her mother's maiden name to use as her stage name, rather unusually preserving its lengthy (for theatrical purposes) "double-barrelling."

Geoffrey **Kendal:** Geoffrey Bragg (*c.*1910–), Br. stage actor, theatre manager, father of TV actress Felicity Kendal (1947–) and film actress Jennifer Kendal (1934–1984). As a young man, Geoffrey Bragg was dismissed from his job as an engineering apprentice, and decided instead to try his luck on the stage with his surname changed to that of his home town in the English Lake District, Kendal. "Bragg," at that time, didn't sound too good, although today it is associated with the English novelist, journalist and broadcaster Melvyn Bragg (1939–), to whom Geoffrey Kendal may be distantly related. The Kendal family spent some time in India in the 1940s and 1950s (interrupted by Felicity's birth) touring the country and staging Shakespeare's plays. In 1965 the film *Shakespeare Wallah* presented a version of the Kendal family's Indian adventures, and itself featured father and both daughters, with Jennifer marrying the film's leading man, the Indian actor Shashi Kapoor [1. *The Sunday Times,* August 22, 1982; 2. Geoffrey Kendal with Clare Colvin, *The Shakespeare Wallah: The Autobiography of Geoffrey Kendal,* 1986].

William Hunter **Kendal:** William Hunter Grimston (1843–1917), Br. stage actor, theatre manager. The actor assumed the name Kendal for his theatrical debut as Louis XIV in *A Life's Revenge* (1861), possibly basing it on the name Kemble, that of a noted acting family. The intermingling of the names Kemble, Kendal and Kendall in the acting world generally is remarkable. See the next entries below as well as Geoffrey Kendal (above).

Kay **Kendall:** Justine McCarthy Kendall (1926–1959), Eng. film actress. Presumably "Kay" is an extraction from "Kendall."

Suzy **Kendall:** Frieda Harrison (1944–   ), Eng. film actress.

Merna **Kennedy:** Maude Kahler (1908–1944), U.S. film actress.

Milward **Kennedy:** Milward Rodon X. Burge (1894–1968), Eng. journalist, mystery writer.

Dee Dee **Kennibrew:** Delores Henry (1945–   ), U.S. pop singer. This looks like a couple of nicknames at work, with "Kennibrew" an embellished variant on "Henry."

Charles J. **Kenny:** Erle Stanley Gardner (1889–1970), U.S. crime novelist.

Barry **Kent:** Barry Sautereau (1932–   ), Eng. stage actor.

Jean **Kent:** Joan Mildred Summerfield (1921–   ), Eng. film actress.

Richard **Kent:** Frank Owen (1893–1968), Eng. writer of "oriental" mystery fiction.

Jomo **Kenyatta:** Kamau (?1894–1978), African statesman, nationalist leader. The president of Kenya was born as Kamau, the son of Ngengi. He was baptized in 1914 as Johnstone Kamau, with "Jomo" a pet form of his Christian name. His second name derived from a Kikuyu word for a fancy belt, which he affected.

Alfred **Kerr:** Alfred Kempner (1867–1948), Ger. theatre critic.

Deborah **Kerr:** Deborah Jane Viertel, née Kerr-Trimmer (1921–   ), Sc. film actress.

Frederick **Kerr:** Frederick Grinham Keen (1858–1901), Br. stage, film actor.

M.E. **Kerr:** Marijane Meaker (1932–   ), U.S. writer of teenage fiction. One might have expected the author to capitalize on her first name, instead of extracting initials from her surname. But no doubt she preferred to be more impersonal, or of unidentifiable sex, since she was writing for both sexes.

Orpheus C. **Kerr:** Robert Henry Newell (1836–1901), U.S. humorous journalist. The humorist's pen name is an obvious pun on "office seeker," and was suggested by the many political aspirants at the time of Lincoln's inauguration. It came to be used as the name of a stock character for political lampooning subsequently.

Norman **Kerry:** Arnold Kaiser (1889–1956), U.S. film actor.

Stanley **Ketchel:** Stanislaus Kiecal (1886–1910), U.S. middleweight boxer (the "Michigan Assassin").

Chaka **Khan:** Yvette Marie Stevens (1953–   ), U.S. black rock singer. The singer adopted her name in the late 1960s, when she was working on the Black Panthers' breakfast program, with "Chaka" an African name meaning "fire."

Kid Creole: August Darnell (*q.v.*).

Johnny **Kidd:** Frederick Heath (1939–1966), Eng. rock singer.

Michael **Kidd:** Milton Greenwald (1919–   ), U.S. dancer, choreographer, theatre director. The dancer adopted the name of the hero of Aaron Copland's ballet *Billy the Kid* (1938), which was the first work in which he publicly performed.

Bobbie **Kimber:** Robert Kimberley (1918–), Eng. ventriloquist, female impersonator.

Alan **King:** Irwin Kniberg (1924–), U.S. cabaret performer, film actor.

Albert **King:** Albert Nelson (1923–), U.S. blues singer, guitarist.

Andrea **King:** Georgetta Barry (1915–), Fr.-U.S. film actress.

B.B. **King:** Riley B. King (1925–), U.S. black blues guitarist. When a deejay in Memphis, Riley B. King used the radio name "Beale Street Blues Boy." This was later shortened to "B.B. King."

Ben E. **King:** Benjamin Earl Nelson (1938–), U.S. pop singer.

Carole **King:** Carole Klein (1942–), U.S. pop singer.

Dennis **King:** Dennis Pratt (1897–1971), Eng. opera singer, film actor. The actor adopted his mother's maiden name as his stage name, thus converting from the (potentially) ridiculous to the (equally potentially) sublime. (A good title for any biography of the singer would be "How a Pratt became a King.")

Earl **King:** Solomon Johnson (1934–), U.S. black rhythm and blues singer. Somehow the two aristocratic names do not seem excessive, doubtless because they are standard first names and surnames in their own right.

Edith **King:** Edith Keck (1896–), U.S. stage actress. A name change possibly even more necessary than that made by Dennis King (above).

Freddie **King:** Billy Miles (1934–), U.S. black rock musician.

Kennedy **King:** George Douglas Brown (1869–1902), Sc. novelist, of Ir. parentage. The novelist, best known under his pseudonym George Douglas (q.v.), used this particular pen name for a book for boys, *Love and a Sword* (1899).

Nosmo **King:** Vernon Watson (?1887–1949), Eng. stage comedian. The comedian entered the stage through double doors on which the warning NO SMOKING appeared in large letters. Five letters were on the left-hand door, and four on the right, and this made the actor's agreeable stage name.

Ben **Kingsley:** Krishna Bhanji (1944–), Anglo-Indian film actor. The actor, famous for his role in (and as) *Ghandi* (1982), reversed his Hindu names and then anglicized them. In a sense "Kingsley," suggesting "king," is a good match for "Krishna," as this is the name of the most famous of the Hindu deities.

Sidney **Kingsley:** Sidney Kieschner (1906–), U.S. stage, film actor, playwright.

Hugh **Kingsmill:** Hugh Kingsmill Lunn (1889–1949), Br. novelist, short story writer, biographer.

Gertrude **Kingston:** Gertrude Silver, née Konstam (1866–1937), Eng. stage actress, theatre manager. The actress's stage name was an anglicization of her maiden name.

Mme **Kinkel:** Elizabeth Sara Sheppard (1830–1862), U.S. novelist.

Klaus **Kinski:** Nikolaus Günter Nakszynski (1926–), Pol.-born Ger. stage, film actor.

Nastassia **Kinski:** Nastassya Nakszynski (1959–), Ger. film actress, working in U.S., daughter of Klaus Kinski (q.v.).

Phyllis **Kirk:** Phyllis Kirkegaard (1926–), U.S. film actress.

Edmund **Kirke:** James Roberts Gilmore (1822–1903), U.S. businessman, author.

Sergey Mironovich **Kirov:** Sergey Mironovich Kostrikov (1886–1934), Russ.

statesman, Communist leader. The well-known Soviet politician had a party name chosen for him in the office of the Vladikavkaz newspaper *Terek* by the selection of the rare first name Kir from a calendar. This was in 1912. Earlier, he had signed himself "S. Mironov," from his patronymic, Mironovich, but this was regarded as not being sufficiently "secret."

Louise **Kirtland:** Louise Jelly (1905–   ), U.S. stage actress.

Lord **Kitchener:** Aldwyn Roberts (*c.*1921–   ), Trinidad calypso singer.

Alf **Kjellin:** Christian Keleen (1920–   ), Swe. film actor, working in U.S.

Klabund: Alfred Henschke (1890–1928), Ger. Expressionist poet, playwright, novelist. The unusual pseudonym derives from a blend of German *Klabautermann,* "hobgoblin," and *Vagabund,* "vagabond." Henschke felt such a name would be apt for the eternally seeking, wandering poet which he envisaged himself to be.

Tristan **Klingsor:** Léon Leclerc (1875–   ), Fr. poet, art critic. The poet adopted the names of two legendary medieval characters: Tristan (or Tristram) fell in love with Iseult (Ysolde) after they both mistakenly drank a love potion; Klingsor was an evil magician in German legend.

Diedrich **Knickerbocker:** Washington Irving (1783–1859), U.S. humorist. The great humorist used this name for the supposed Dutch author of his *History of New York* (1809). But where did he get the name itself? Very likely from a Dutch family of the name who came to live in Albany County around 1674. The family name, which may originally have been "Knickerbacker," probably meant "baker of knickers," the latter being clay marbles. Irving's pseudonym became popular from the illustrations to his burlesque history drawn by George Cruickshank, showing Dutchmen in wide, loose knee breeches. Hence the adoption of "knickerbockers" (and later "knickers") as a word for breeches, or trousers, whether outerwear or (as in British use) underwear.

David **Knight:** David Mintz (1927–   ), U.S. film, stage actor. The actor's stage name is his mother's maiden name.

Ted **Knight:** Tadewurz Wladzui Konopka (*c.*1925–   ), U.S. TV actor. The actor's name seems to be a fairly casual anglicization of his Slavic name.

Edward **Knoblock:** Edward Knoblauch (1874–1945), U.S. dramatist, working in U.K.

Teddy **Knox:** Albert Edward Cromwell-Knox (1896–1974), Eng. stage comedian, teaming with Jimmy Nervo *(q.v.).*

Ruth **Kobart:** Ruth Maxine Kohn (1924–   ), U.S. stage actress, singer.

Konimo: Daniel Amponsah (1934–   ), U.S. popular musician.

Al **Koran:** Edward Doe (1916–1972), Br. conjuror. The conjuror seems to have chosen a name that simply means "The Koran," otherwise the holy book of Islam, taking the Arabic definite article as the English name "Al" (short for "Alfred"). Presumably he was aware of the meaning, and did not intend any disrespectful reference.

[Sir] Alexander **Korda:** Sandro Kellner (1893–1956), Hung.-born Br. film producer. At the age of 15, young Sandro Kellner migrated from the Hungarian countryside to Budapest, the capital, where he was befriended by a Catholic priest who got him a job on a local paper. As the boy was legally too young to have a job, he had to find a pseudonym for himself, and as a compliment to his patron, took the phrase "Sursum Corda" ("Lift up your hearts" from the Roman mass). This had the additional advantage of being close to his original name [Michael Korda, *Charmed Lives*, 1980]. Alexander Korda was the brother of Vincent Korda and Zoltán Korda (*qq.v.*).

Vincent **Korda:** Vincent Kellner (1897–1979), Hung.-born film art director.

Zoltán **Korda:** Zoltán Kellner (1895–1961), Hung.-born film director.

Alexis **Korner:** Alexis Koerner (1928–1984), Fr.-born jazz and pop musician, working in U.S., U.K.

Fritz **Kortner:** Fritz Nathan Kohn (1892–1970), Austr. film actor.

Sonia **Korty:** Sophia Ippar (1892–1955), Russ. ballet dancer, choreographer, teacher.

Charles **Korvin:** Geza Kaiser (1907–   ), Czech-born U.S. film actor.

Henry **Koster:** Hermann Kosterlitz (1905–1988), Ger. film director, working in U.S.

Billy J. **Kramer:** William Howard Ashton (1943–   ), Eng. pop singer. The singer's adopted name looks like a cross between the tennis champions Billie-Jean King (coincidentally born the same year as Ashton) and Jack Kramer. But the actual origin may simply be American-style arbitrary.

Kukryniksy: Mikhail Vasilyevich Kupriyanov (1903–   ) + Porfiry Nikitich Krylov (1902–   ), + Nikolai Aleksandrovich Sokolov (1903–   ), Russ. artists, satirical cartoonists. The three artists adopted a joint name comprising elements from each of their three respective names, adding the Russian plural ending (-*y*).

Thomas **Kyd:** Alfred Bennett Harbage (1901–   ), U.S. educator, Shakespeare scholar, detective story writer. Thomas Kyd was the name of a sixteenth-century English dramatist.

Barbara **Laage:** Claire Colombat (1925–   ), Fr. film actress.

Louise **Labé:** Louise Charly (?1524–1566), Fr. poet. The poet was nicknamed "La Belle Cordière" as her husband was a ropemaker (French *cordier*). Her pseudonym arose as an abbreviation of this.

Patti **LaBelle:** Patricia Louise Holt (1944–   ), U.S. black rock singer. The singer's professional name arose simultaneously with that of her group, now known (since 1971) as Labelle but formed in 1961 as Patti LaBelle and the Blue Belles.

Simon **Lack:** Simon Macalpine (1917–1980), Sc. stage actor. The actor's stage surname was extracted from the middle of his real surname (reversed).

Ed **Lacy:** Len Zinberg (1911–1968). U.S. mystery story writer.

John **Lacy:** George Darley (1795–1846), It. poet, novelist, critic.

Steve **Lacy:** Steven Lackritz (1934–   ), U.S. popular musician.

Cheryl **Ladd:** Cheryl Stoppelmoor (1951–   ), U.S. TV actress.

Diane **Ladd:** Diane Ladnier (1932–   ), U.S. film actress.

Léon **Ladulfi:** Noël du Fail (1520–1591), Fr. writer. Cryptic crossword buffs will soon spot the anagram here.

A **Lady of Quality:** Enid Algerine Bagnold (1889–1981), Eng. novelist, playwright. An earlyish pseudonym used by the writer who actually became "A Lady of Quality" in 1920 when she married Sir Roderick Jones.

La Fleur: Robert Guérin (*fl.*1598–1634), Fr. actor. The actor used this stage name for his serious roles in tragedy, keeping his other name of Gros-Guillaume *(q.v.)* for farce. His son-in-law, François Juvenon (*c.*1623–1674), adopted the same name when he played the parts of kings in succession to Montfleury *(q.v.)*. Juvenon's son, also an actor, was La Tuillerie *(q.v.)*.

La Grange: Charles Varlet (1639–1692), Fr. actor.

Bert **Lahr:** Irving Lahrheim (1895–1967), U.S. stage, film comedian.

Cleo **Laine:** Clementine Dinah Dankworth, née Campbell (1927–   ), Eng. jazz singer, actress. The singer presumably adopted her professional name from that of her first husband, George Langridge.

Denny **Laine:** Brian Arthur Haynes (1944–   ), Eng. pop musician.

Frankie **Laine:** Frank Lo Vecchio (1913–   ), U.S. pop singer, actor, of Sicilian parentage.

Hugh **Laing:** Hugh Skinner (1911–1988), Barbados-born U.S. ballet dancer.

Arthur **Lake:** Arthur Silverlake (1905–1986), U.S. film actor.

Veronica **Lake:** Constance Ockleman (1919–1973), U.S. film actress. The actress, who made her debut as Constance Keane in *Sorority House* (1939), was given her famous name by the Paramount producer Arthur Hornblow, Jr., in 1940, when she was 20, for the film *I Wanted Wings* (1941). The actress tells how the name was arrived at in her autobiography: "'Believe me' [said Hornblow], 'the right name, a name that the public can latch on to and remember can make all the difference. It isn't just a matter, though, of creating a name that can be remembered. If that were all it took, we'd just name you Maude Mudpie or Tilly Tits or something and they'd remember the name. [. . .] Picking a name involves coming up with something that associates in the fan's mind the person attached to that name. The name has to . . . well, it has to be the person, or at least what the fan thinks that person is. [. . .] Connie, here's how I came to choose your new name. I believe that when people look into those navy blue eyes of yours, they'll see a calm coolness – the calm coolness of a lake.' The first thing that crossed my mind was that I was going to be named Lake something or other. That doesn't sound very outlandish these days with Tab and Rock, but in those days names stuck closer to the norm. [. . .] 'And your features, Connie, are classic features. And when I think of classic features, I think of Veronica.' Lake Veronica! Oh! Veronica Lake. Of course. And then it hit me. My mother was sometimes called Veronica. Of all the goddamn names in the world to choose. [. . .] I broke down and bawled like a baby into the couch cushions" [Veronica Lake with Donald Bain, *Veronica*, 1969].

Barbara **La Marr:** Rheatha Watson (1896–1926), U.S. film actress.

Hedy **Lamarr:** Hedwig Eva Maria Kiesler (1913–   ), Austr. film actress, working in U.S. The actress was given her screen name by MGM's Louis B. Mayer, after "the most beautiful star he had ever seen" – Barbara La Marr *(q.v.)*. It is not all that frequently that one stage name engenders another like this.

Louis **Lambert:** Patrick Sarsfield Gilmore (1829–1892), Ir.-born U.S. bandmaster.

La Meri: Russell Meriwether Hughes (1898–   ), U.S. ballet dancer, ethnologist, writer. The dancer's name derives from the first part of her middle name.

La Messine: Juliette Adam, née Lamber (1836–1936), Fr. novelist, editor. The writer's pen name means "the woman of Metz." She also wrote as Comte Paul Vasili *(q.v.)*.

Lamia: Alfred Austin (1835–1913), Eng. poet. The poet used this name for some of his autobiographical writing, as when he edited *The Poet's Diary* (1904). He presumably took it with reference to the witch of the name, who was said to suck the blood of children, and who is the subject of Keats's poem *Lamia* (1820).

Dorothy **Lamour:** Dorothy Mary Leta Lambour (1914–   ), U.S. film actress. Different sources give different original names for the actress. Among them are Mary Dorothy Stanton (Wlaschin), Mary Leta Dorothy Kaumeyer (Lloyd and Fuller), Mary Dorothy Slaton (Quinlan), and simply Dorothy Kaumeyer (Halliwell and others). Evidence seems to suggest, however, that she was actually Dorothy Mary Leta Lambour, the latter name being that of her mother's second husband, Clarence Lambour, and that she then altered this to "Lamour" (which happens to suggest "love") [Dorothy Lamour, *My Side of the Road,* 1981].

Lana: Alan Kemp (1938–   ), Eng. female impersonator. By adjusting his (male) first name, the performer achieved a (female) stage name.

G.B. **Lancaster:** Edith Joan Balfour Lyttleton (?1865–1948), N.Z. writer.

Elsa **Lanchester:** Elizabeth Sullivan (1902–1986), Br. stage, film actress, working in U.S. The actress adopted her mother's maiden name as her stage name.

Harald **Lander:** Alfred Bernhardt Stevnsborg (1905–1971), Dan.-Fr. ballet dancer, teacher.

Lew **Landers:** Lewis Friedlander (1901–1962), U.S. film director.

Elissa **Landi:** Elisabeth-Marie-Christine Kühnelt (1904–1948), Austr.-It. film actress.

Carole **Landis:** Frances Lillian Mary Ridste (1919–1948), U.S. film actress.

Jessie Royce **Landis:** Jessie Royce Medbury (1904–1972), U.S. stage, film actress.

Jane **Landon:** Frances Jane Leach (1947–   ), Austral. ballet dancer.

Michael **Landon:** Eugene Maurice Orowitz (1937–   ), U.S. film, TV actor.

Avice **Landone:** Avice Spitta (1910–1976), Eng. stage actress.

Allan "Rocky" **Lane:** Harold Albertshart (1901–1973), U.S. film actor.

Burton **Lane:** Burton Levy (1912–   ), Br. composers of musicals.

Christy **Lane:** Eleanor Johnstone (*c.*1940–   ), U.S. country singer.

Jane **Lane:** Elaine Dakers, née Kidner (? –1978), Eng. writer of historical novels, children's books, biographies. The writer adopted her grandmother's maiden name as her pen name.

Lola **Lane:** Dorothy Mullican (1909–1981), U.S. film actress, sister of Priscilla Lane *(q.v.)*.

Lupino **Lane:** Henry George Lupino (1892–1959), Br. stage, film comedian. The actor added the surname of his great-aunt Sara Lane (1823–1899) to his own surname, using the latter as a first name for his new stage name. Sara Lane was an actress of note in her own right.

Priscilla **Lane:** Priscilla Mullican (1917–   ), U.S. film actress, sister of Lola Lane *(q.v.)*.

Eddie **Lang:** Salvatore Massaroa (1903–1933), U.S. jazz guitarist.

June **Lang:** June Vlasek (1915–   ), U.S. film actress.

Launcelot **Langstaff:** Washington Irving (1783–1859), U.S. story writer, essayist, historian + William Irving (1766–1821), U.S. politician, satirist, his brother + James Kirk Paulding (1778–1860), U.S. writer. The joint pseudonym was used by the three men for the satirical essays and poems published as *Salmagundi; or the Whim-Whams and Opinions of Launcelot Langstaff, Esq. and Others* (1808). The pen name doubtless had an implied punning reference to the satirist who uses his pen as a 'lance' or a 'staff' to point his barbs.

E.B. **Lanin:** Dr. Emile Joseph Dillon (1854–1933), Ir.-born Br. newspaper correspondent. The writer's name is a reference to his native Dublin, which is known as "Eblana," its historic name, in literary imprints.

Jörg **Lanner:** Jörg Langenstrass (1939–   ), Ger. ballet dancer.

Joi **Lansing:** Joyce Wasmannsdorf (1928–1972), U.S. film actress.

Robert **Lansing:** Robert H. Broom (1929–   ), U.S. TV actor.

Mario **Lanza:** Alfredo Arnold Cocozza (1921–1959), It.-born U.S. opera singer. The singer took his first name from the hero of his favorite opera, Puccini's *Tosca*, in which Floria Tosca falls in love with Mario Cavaradossi, and his second name from his mother's maiden name, Lanza.

Eddie **Large:** Edward Hugh McGinnis (1942–   ), Sc.-born Br. TV comedian, teaming with Syd Little *(q.v.)* (as "Little and Large").

Rod **La Rocque:** Roderick la Rocque de la Rour (1896–1969), U.S. film actor.

Laroque: Pierre Régnault Petit-Jean (*c.*1595–1676), Fr. actor.

Rita **La Roy:** Ina Stuart (1907–   ), Fr. film actress, of Eng. descent.

Larry: Terence Parkes (1927–   ), Eng. cartoonist. The artist's name arose as a nickname given him by school pupils when he was a teacher in Peterborough. The nickname in turn came from the film then showing locally, *The Jolson Story* (1946), in which the actor Larry Parkes played Al Jolson *(q.v.)*.

Danny **La Rue:** Daniel Patrick Carroll (1927–   ), Ir.-born Br. revue artist, female impersonator. The actor was given his name by the comedian and producer Ted Gatty for his revue *Men Only*, allegedly because Carroll was said to have looked "as long as a street" when wearing drag [Peter Underwood, *Life's a Drag! Danny La Rue and the Drag Scene*, 1974].

Jack **La Rue:** Gaspare Biondolillo (1903–1984), U.S. film actor.

Denise **Lasalle:** Denise Craig (*c.*1947–   ), U.S. pop singer, songwriter.

Lady Caroline **Lascelles:** Mary Elizabeth Maxwell, née Braddon (1837–1915), Eng. novelist.

Orland di **Lasso** (or Orlandus Lassus): Roland Delattre (?1532–1594), Belg. musical composer. Many reference sources give the composer's real name as above, although some dispute this particular origin. (The *Oxford Companion to Music*, in its entry for him, says specifically "not Roland de Lattre as often stated.") Perhaps it arose in the belief that his more familiar name was a latinized version of a French original, with the "true" name thus reconstructed from this.

Yusef **Lateef:** William Evans (1921–   ), U.S. popular musician.

Frank **Latimore:** Frank Kline (1925–   ), U.S. film actor.

La Tuillerie: Jean-François Juvenon (1650–1688), Fr. actor, dramatist, grandson of Gros-Guillaume *(q.v.).*

Afferbeck **Lauder:** Alistair Morrison (1911–   ), Austral. writer. The writer introduced "Strine" to the world (in 1964) as the characteristic Australian pronunciation of English. "Strine" is "Australian" in Strine, and "Afferbeck Lauder" is "alphabetical order"!

Laura: Mary Robinson, née Darby (1758–1810), Eng. actress, novelist, poet. The writer adopted the name used to refer to her in William Gifford's satire, *The Maeviad* (1795), directed against current poets and their schools.

Stan **Laurel:** Arthur Stanley Jefferson (1890–1965), Eng. film comedian, working in U.S., teaming with Oliver Hardy. The familiar "thin one" of the comic pair originally appeared on the stage as Stan Jefferson. One day, however, he noticed that his name had 13 letters, so substituted the shorter and more obviously propitious "Laurel" for his surname.

Paula **Laurence:** Paula de Lugo (1916–   ), U.S. stage actress.

Piper **Laurie:** Rosetta Jacobs (1932–   ), U.S. film actress, of Russ.-Pol. parentage.

Comte de **Lautréaumont:** Isidore-Lucien Ducasse (1846–1870), Fr. poet. The poet adopted the name of the hero of the novel *Latréaumont* by Eugène Sue *(q.v.).*

Hector **Lavoe:** Hector Perez (1946–   ), U.S. popular singer, bandleader.

Anthony **Lawless:** Philip MacDonald (1900–1981), Br. writer of detective novels.

Jody **Lawrance:** Josephine Lawrence Goddard (1930–   ), U.S. film actress.

Lars **Lawrence:** Philip Stevenson (1896–1965), U.S. author.

Marc **Lawrence:** Max Goldsmith (1910–   ), U.S. film actor.

Slingsby **Lawrence:** George Henry Lewes (1817–1878), U.S. philosopher, literary critic. Slingsby seems to have been a vogue pseudonym among English writers in the nineteenth century. Slingsby Lawrence was the name used by George Henry Lewes, lover of George Eliot *(q.v.),* for adaptations of French plays. Others of the name were Jonathan Freke Slingsby (John Francis Waller), who adopted the pseudonym for his contributions to the *Dublin University Magazine,* and Philip Slingsby (Nathaniel Parker Willis), the American poet, who used the name when in England for a collection of sketches, *Inklings of Adventure* (1836). No doubt there was some mutual borrowing of the name, but who started it? There is a village Slingsby in North Yorkshire, with ruins of the seventeenth-century Slingsby Castle, but none of the writers seems to have had any connections here.

Steve **Lawrence:** Sidney Leibowitz (1935–   ), U.S. pop singer. The singer borrowed the first names of his two nephews for his professional name, with "Lawrence" at the same time not all that far removed from his original surname.

Henry Hertzberg **Lawson:** Henry Hertzberg Larsen (1867–1922), Austral. poet, short story writer.

W.B. **Lawson:** George Charles Jenks (1850–1929), Br. printer, journalist, fiction writer, working in U.S.

Wilfred **Lawson:** Wilfred Worsnop (1900–1966), Br. stage, film actor.

Frank **Lawton:** Frank Lowaton Mokeley, Jr. (1904–1969), Br. film, stage actor.

Halldór Kiljan **Laxness:** Halldór Kiljan Gudjonsson (1902–   ), Icelandic poet, novelist, playwright. The writer's name looks very much like an Icelandic place-name, itself meaning "salmon cape."

Dilys **Lay:** Dilys Laye (1934–   ), Eng. stage actress.

Joe **Layton:** Joseph Lichtman (1931–   ), U.S. choreographer, stage director.

Leadbelly: Huddie Ledbetter (1889–1949), U.S. folk singer.

Evelyn **Lear:** Evelyn Schulman (1928–   ), U.S. opera singer.

[Major] **Le Caron:** Thomas Miller Beach (1841–1894), Br. secret agent, working in U.S.

John **Le Carré:** David John Moore Cornwell (1931–   ), Eng. spy story writer. When starting his career as a writer, Cornwell was employed as a civil servant by the Foreign Office, and was advised to adopt another name, as it would have been frowned on for a serving diplomat to publish novels under his own name. The story goes that Cornwell saw the name on a London shoe shop one day, when riding on a bus, and decided to adopt it. He first used it in 1962 for *A Perfect Spy.*

Jean-Paul **Le Chanois:** Jean-Paul Dreyfus (1909–1985), Fr. film director. During the Second World War the actor was with the French Resistance, and adopted the undercover name Le Chanois. After 1945, he retained this as his professional name.

Andrew **Lee:** Louis (Stanton) Auchinloss (1917–   ), U.S. novelist.

Anna **Lee:** Joanna Boniface Winnifrith (1913–   ), Br. film actress, working in U.S.

Brenda **Lee:** Brenda Mae Tarpley (1944–   ), U.S. country singer. Spot the "Lee": it's at the end of the singer's original surname.

Bruce **Lee:** Lee Yuen Kam (1940–1973), U.S. film actor, of Chin. parentage. The actor's original name was the one given him by his mother, when he was born in San Francisco to a touring Hong Kong vaudeville family. A hospital nurse, however, gave him the more American name of Bruce Lee.

Canada **Lee:** Leonard Lionel Cornelius Canegata (1907–1952), U.S. black stage, film actor. The actor is said to have adopted his name when an announcer had difficulty pronouncing "Lee Canageta." "Lee" comes from "Leonard."

Dickey **Lee:** Dick Lipscomb (1941–   ), U.S. pop singer. "Lee" comes from the singer's original surname.

Dixie **Lee:** Wilma Wyatt (1911–1952), U.S. film actress.

Dorothy **Lee:** Marjorie Millsop (1911–   ), U.S. film actress.

Gypsy Rose **Lee:** Rose Louise Hovick (1913–1970), U.S. stage, film actress, sister of June Havoc *(q.v.).* The actress took the name "Gypsy" for her burlesque striptease acts, with "Rose Lee" based on her two first names. In her act, too, her stage mother was "Madame Rose."

Holme (or Holm) **Lee:** Harriet Parr (1828–1900), Eng. novelist. The author, who wrote around 30 "refined" but sentimental novels, adopted a *nom de plume* that was intended to be understood as "homely."

Lila **Lee:** Augusta Apple (1902–1973), U.S. film actress.

Laura **Lee:** Laura Lee Rundless (1945–   ), U.S. soul singer.

Michele **Lee:** Michele Dusiak (1942–   ), U.S. film actress, singer.

Patty **Lee:** Alice Cary (1920–1971), U.S. poet, novelist.

Peggy **Lee:** Norma Deloris Engstrom (1920–   ), U.S. nightclub singer, film actress. When the singer was working on the radio station WDAY, manager Ken Kennedy nicknamed her "Peggy Lee," doubtless after the existing singer of this name.

Steve **Lee:** Michael Patrick Parry (1947–   ), Eng. writer, anthologist.

Vanessa **Lee:** Winifred Ruby Moule (1920–   ), Eng. stage actress, singer.

Vernon **Lee:** Violet Paget (1856–1935), Fr.-born Eng. essayist, art critic, novelist, working in Italy. The writer adopted her pseudonym in 1875, taking "Lee" from the surname of her stepmother, Matilda Lee-Hamilton, whom her father married in 1855, when he was tutor to the widow's son Eugene Lee-Hamilton, the poet and novelist. "Vernon" was a masculine adaptation of her first name, Violet.

William **Lee:** William S. Burroughs (1914–   ), U.S. novelist. The author used this pen name for *Junkie* (1953), his frank account of his life as a drug addict. He continued the account under his real name in *The Naked Lunch* (1959).

Richard **Leech:** Richard Leeper McClelland (1922–   ), Ir. stage, film, TV actor.

Andrea **Leeds:** Antoinette Lees (1914–1974), U.S. film actress.

Herbert I. **Leeds:** Herbert I. Levy (?1900–1954), U.S. film director.

Thomas **Leer:** Thomas Wishart (*c.*1955–   ), Sc. new wave singer.

Ethel **Leginska:** Ethel Liggins (1890–   ), Eng. pianist, conductor, composer.

Janet **Leigh:** Jeanette Helen Morrison (1927–   ), U.S. film, TV actress.

Vivien **Leigh:** Vivian Mary Hartley (1913–1967), Eng. stage, film actress. The actress married Herbert Leigh Holman in 1932 and the same year adopted his middle name, at the same time "refining" her first name from "Vivian" to "Vivien."

Eino **Leino:** Armas Eino Leopold Lönnbohm (1878–1926), Finn. poet.

Erich **Leinsdorf:** Erich Landauer (1912–   ), U.S. conductor, of Austr. parentage.

Murray **Leinster:** William Fitzgerald Jenkins (1896–1975), U.S. SF writer.

Henri-Louis **Lekain:** Henri-Louis Caïn (1729–1778), Fr. actor.

L.E.L.: Letitia Elizabeth Landon (1802–1838), Eng. poet, novelist.

Sara **Leland:** Sally Harrington (1941–   ), U.S. ballet dancer.

[Sir] Peter **Lely:** Pieter van der Faes (1618–1680), Du. portrait painter, working in England. Although some doubt remains regarding the origin of the painter's name, one account tells how his father, a military captain, was known by the nickname of "Lely" for the prominent lily on the house where he was born. The son is then said to have adopted the name as his new surname.

Francis **Lemarque:** Nathan Korb (1917–   ), Fr. popular singer, poet, of Jewish-Pol. (or Latvian) parentage. The singer's new name evolved from that of "Les Frères Marc," a duo formed with his elder brother Maurice ("Marc") in 1936.

Lemmy: Ian Kilminster (1945–   ), Eng. punk rock musician.

Lenare: Leonard Green (1883–   ), Eng. society photographer. Lenare opened his studio in 1923. Since in those days a French-sounding name was the fashion for dressmakers and photographers, he took the first syllable of "Leonard" and added what he believed to be a French-style ending. When asked about the origin of the name, he would point to his bald head and say, "Look, Len no 'air" [*Sunday Times Magazine*, November 13, 1977]. It is really a variant of "Leonard."

Nikolaus **Lenau:** Franz Niembsch Edler von Strehlenau (1802–1850), Austr. poet.

Leonid **Lench:** Leonid Sergeyevich Popov (1905–   ), Russ. writer, dramatist. The writer regarded his surname as too ordinary, so a member of the editorial staff of the magazine where he worked—the Krasnodar *Krasnoye Znamya*—devised the name "Lench" from "Lenchik," one of the diminutive forms of his first name.

Vladimir Ilyich **Lenin:** Vladimir Ilyich Ulyanov (1870–1924), Russ. Communist party founder, head of state. The origin of the Communist leader's name, famous though it is, is still uncertain. Lenin first used it in 1901—some time before the Revolution—for an article in the revolutionary journal *Iskra*, then published in Munich. The traditional explanation is that the name derives from the river Lena, Siberia, where there had been disturbances. Ulyanov had been exiled to Siberia, although not to the Lena but to the village of Shushenskoye, on the river Yenisey. So why this particular river? According to one authority, the choice was a more or less random one: he would have chosen a name based on the river Volga, but this was already "booked" (as Volgin) by the Marxist Plekhanov. He therefore took the next big river to the east [Louis Fisher, *The Life of Lenin*, 1966].

The uncertainty of the origin of the pseudonym is emphasized by the person who should have known its derivation—Lenin's wife. In 1924, the year of his death, she wrote a letter to the magazine *Komyacheyka:* "Dear Comrades, I don't know why Vladimir Ilyich took the name 'Lenin'; I never asked him about it. His mother was named Mariya Aleksandrovna, his late sister Olga. The events on the river Lena happened after he took his pseudonym. He was never in exile on the Lena. Probably the name was chosen by chance " [Dmitriev, p.44]. Another tentative explanation is that the name came from a girl classmate, Lena. The true origin may perhaps be revealed one day . . .

Dan **Leno:** George Wilde Galvin (1860–1904), Eng. music hall artist. The well-known music hall performer began his career by playing slapstick sketches with "the Leno family," this being the stage name of his stepfather, whose real surname was Wilde. His first name was changed from George to "Dan" " . . . owing to a misapprehension on the part of either the printer or deviser of a playbill. The boy's stepfather appreciated the accidental change and saw the value of it, and as Dan Leno the stage name was crystallised" [*Dictionary of National Biography*].

Rula **Lenska:** [Countess] Roza-Maria Lubienska (1947–   ), Pol.-born Br. TV actress.

Lotte **Lenya:** Karoline Blamauer (1900–1981), Austr. stage actress, opera singer.

[Saint] **Leo IX:** Bruno of Egisheim (1002–1054), Alsatian pope.

Leo X: Giovanni de' Medici (1475–1521), It. pope.

Leo XI: Alessandro Ottaviano de' Medici (1535–1605), It. pope.

Leo XII: Annibale Sermattei della Genga (1760–1829), It. pope.

Leo XIII: Vincenzo Gioacchino Pecci (1810–1903), It. pope.

André **Léo:** Léonie Champseix, née Béra (1829–1900), Fr. writer, campaigner for women's rights. The writer adopted the first names of her two sons as her pseudonym.

Benny **Leonard:** Benjamin Leiner (1896–1947), U.S. lightweight boxer.

Hugh **Leonard:** John Keyes Byrne (1926–   ), Ir. dramatist.

Sheldon **Leonard:** Sheldon Bershad (1907–   ), U.S. film actor, TV producer.

Baby **Le Roy:** Le Roy Overacker (1931–   ), U.S. film actor.

Carole **Lesley:** Maureen Carole Lesley Rippingdale (1935–1974), Br. film actress. The actress originally worked under the name of Lesley Carol, before settling to the two names by which she was best known.

Frank **Leslie:** Henry Carter (1821–1880), Eng. engraver, publisher, working in U.S. The artist used the name early in his career when he was being brought up by his father and uncle to learn the glove-making business, and he did not wish to incur their wrath by his taste for drawing, sketching, and engraving. He emigrated to New York in 1848 and changed his name legally from Henry Carter to Frank Leslie.

Joan **Leslie:** Joan Agnes Theresa Sadie Brodel (1925–   ), U.S. film actress. The actress changed her name to escape the suggestion of "broad" in her surname, as did Amanda Barrie and Dora Bryan *(qq.v.)*, respectively Shirley Broadbent and Dora Broadbent.

Natasha **Leslie:** Nathalie Krassovska (properly Krasovskaya) (1919–   ), Russ.-U.S. ballet dancer. The dancer reverted to her Russian name in 1952.

L'Espy: François Bedeau (? –1663), Fr. actor, brother of Jodelet *(q.v.)*.

Bruce **Lester:** Bruce Lister (1912–), S.A. film actor, working in U.S., U.K.

Daniel **Lesueur:** Jeanne Lapauze, née Loiseau (1860–1921), Fr. writer.

Letine: George Gorin (1853–1880), Eng. music hall artiste, acrobatic cyclist.

Daniel **Levans:** Daniel Levins (1953–   ), U.S. ballet dancer.

Les **Levante:** Leslie George Cole (1892–1978), Austral. illusionist ("The Great Levante").

Samuel **Levene:** Samuel Levine (1905–1980), U.S. stage actor.

Gary **Lewis:** Gary Levitch (1946–   ), U.S. pop musician, son of Jerry Lewis *(q.v.)*.

Jerry **Lewis:** Joseph Levitch (1926–   ), U.S. film comedian, teaming with Dean Martin *(q.v.)*. Jerry Lewis used the same surname as the one adopted by his parents, who were also in show business. He once quipped, "How could anyone called Levitch get laughs?"

Mel **Lewis:** Melvin Sokoloff (1929–   ), U.S. popular musician.

Smiley **Lewis:** Overton Amos Lemons (1920–1966), U.S. pop musician.

Ted **Lewis:** Theodore Friedman (1889–1971), U.S. bandleader, entertainer, film actor.

Val **Lewton:** Vladimir Ivan Leventon (1904–1951), Russ.-born U.S. horror movie director.

Ben **Lexcen:** Robert Miller (1936–1988), Austral. yachtsman, marine architect.

George **Leybourne:** Joe Saunders (1842–1884), Eng. music hall artiste ("Champagne Charlie").

Liberace: Wladziu Valentino Liberace (1919–1987), U.S. popular pianist, film actor, entertainer, of It. parentage. "Call me Lee," the "Casanova of the Keyboard" would say. And somehow his real surname, which he used as his professional name, perfectly suited him, with its suggestion of "liberal," "liberty," "libertine," and even "libidinous." He originally adopted the name of "Walter Busterkeys" when playing (as a minor attraction) in Las Vegas in the 1930s. But he soon reverted to his real name, which became well-known with his television appearances.

David **Lichine:** David Liechtenstein (1910–1972), Russ.-U.S. ballet dancer, choreographer. A neat conversion of a lengthy Germanic-sounding (albeit Russian) name to a more genuine-seeming one.

Serge **Lido:** Serge Lidoff (1906–1984), Russ.-Fr. ballet photographer.

Winnie **Lightner:** Winifred Hanson (1901–1971), U.S. film comedienne.

Beatrice **Lillie:** [Lady] Constance Sylvia Peel, née Munston (1894–1989), Can.-born Eng. stage actress.

Limahl: Christopher Hamill (*c.*1960–), Eng. pop singer. A clear anagrammatic adaptation for the singer of the group Kajagoogoo, which split up in 1986.

Frank **Lin:** Gertrude Franklin Atherton, née Horn (1857–1948), U.S. novelist.

Abbey **Lincoln:** Anna Marie Woolridge (1930–), U.S. black film actress.

Elmo **Lincoln:** Otto Elmo Linkenhelt (1889–1952), U.S. film actor.

Anya **Linden:** Anya Sainsbury, née Eltenton (1933–), Eng. ballet dancer.

Hal **Linden:** Harold Lipshitz (1931–), U.S. stage actor, singer.

Max **Linder:** Gabriel-Maximilien Leuvielle (1883–1925), Fr. film comedian.

Margaret **Lindsay:** Margaret Kies (1910–1981), U.S. film actress.

Bambi **Linn:** Bambi Linnemeier (1926–), U.S. stage actress, dancer.

Carolus **Linnaeus:** Carl von Linné (1707–1778), Swe. botanist.

Virna **Lisi:** Virna Lisa Pieralisi (1936–), It. film actress.

Emanuel **List:** Emanuel Fleissig (1890–1967), Austr.-born U.S. opera singer.

Frances **Little:** Fannie Macaulay, née Caldwell (1863–1941), U.S. novelist.

Syd **Little:** Cyril John Mead (1942–), Eng. TV comedian, teaming with Eddie Large *(q.v.)* (as "Little and Large"). The comedians have descriptive names: Eddie Large is plump and taller than Syd Little, who is thin and bespectacled.

Thomas **Little:** Thomas Moore (1779–1852), Ir. poet, satirist. The Irish writer used this name on occasions to denote his small stature, and was referred to under the name by Byron in the latter's *English Bards and Scotch Reviewers* (1809). Moore also used names such as "Thomas Brown the Younger," "One of the Fancy," and "Trismegistus Rustifucius, D.D."

Little Anthony: Anthony Gourdine (1941–), U.S. pop singer.

Little Eva: Eva Narcissus Boyd (1945–), U.S. pop singer.

Little Milton: Milton James Campbell (1934–), U.S. blues musician.

Little Richard: Richard Wayne Penniman (1935–), U.S. rock musician.

Little Tich: Harry Relph (1868–1928), Br. music hall comedian. The personality is one of the few "Littles" not to take his real first name. The dwarfish comedian was given the nickname "Little Tich" as a child because he resembled the portly so-called "Tichborne claimant." The reference is to a nineteenth-century legal case, in which one Arthur Orton claimed in 1866 to be Roger Charles Tichborne, the heir to an English baronetcy, who had been lost at sea. Orton was eventually discredited and imprisoned in 1874. In assuming the name "Little Tich," Harry Relph bequeathed the word "tichy" or "titchy" to the English language, meaning "very small," "tiny."

Mark **Littleton:** John Pendleton Kennedy (1795–1870), U.S. politician, educationist, author. The writer used this pseudonym for *Swallow Barn* (1832), a series of Virginia sketches.

Little Walter: Marion Walter Jacobs (1930–1968), U.S. blues harmonica player.

Little Willie John: William John Woods (1937–1968), U.S. soul singer.

Maksim Maksimovich **Litvinov:** Meir Walach (1876–1951), Russ. revolutionary, diplomat. The Soviet politician used the name Litvinov as one of several party cover names. Others were "Papasha" ("Daddy"), "Maximovich," and "Felix," all fairly arbitrary.

Mary **Livingstone:** Sadye Marks (*c.*1903–), U.S. radio, TV comedienne.

Emma **Livry:** Emma-Marie Emarot (1842–1863), Fr. ballet dancer.

Michael **Lland:** Holland Stoudenmire (1924–1989), U.S. dancer, ballet master.

Richard **Llewellyn:** Richard Dafydd Vivian Llewellyn Lloyd (1907–1983), Welsh novelist, dramatist.

Charles **Lloyd:** [Sir] Charles Lloyd Birkin (1907–), Eng. horror story writer.

Lucy Vaughan **Lloyd:** John Keats (1795–1821), Eng. poet. An unexpected name used by the poet for an unfinished poem, *The Cap and Bells* (1820). The adoption of a pseudonym by Keats when he was already well established suggests that he intended the poem to be somehow directed against the Lake Poets. Robert Gittings points out that Lucy suggests Wordsworth (real person or not, Lucy was the subject of a number of Wordsworth's poems), while Charles Lloyd was a poet and neighbor of Wordsworth. Keats's poem written under the pseudonym was first published only in 1848, 26 years after his death [Robert Gittings, *John Keats*, 1968].

Marie **Lloyd:** Matilda Alice Victoria Wood (1870–1922), Eng. music hall artist. The famous music hall performer first used the name Bella Delmere when she began her career on the stage at the age of 14. The name probably evolved from that of the "Fairy Bell Minstrels," a troup of little girl singers and actresses that she formed when herself only a young child. Later, she adopted the name Marie Lloyd, taking this from the financial journal *Lloyds Weekly News*.

Lobo: Kent Lavoie (1943–), U.S. pop guitar player, singer, of Fr.-Indian descent. The singer took the name, Spanish for "wolf," when he first recorded "Me and You and a Dog Named Boo," reasoning that he could hide behind his anonymity if he failed to make the charts. He needn't have worried — the record was a huge hit on both sides of the Atlantic in 1971. Thereafter he kept the name.

Gary **Lockwood:** John Gary Yusolfsky (1937–), U.S. film, TV actor.

Margaret **Lockwood:** Margaret Mary Day (1911–), Eng. film, TV actress.

John **Loder:** John Muir Lowe (1898–1988), Br. film actor.

Cecilia (or Cissie) **Loftus:** Marie Cecilia M'Carthy (1876–1943), Sc. stage, film actress, working in U.S.

Ella **Logan:** Ella Allan (1913–1969), Sc.-born U.S. singer, actress.

Jimmy **Logan:** James Short (1922–   ), Sc. stage, TV actor, comedian.

Herbert **Lom:** Herbert Charles Angelo Kuchačevič ze Schluderpacheru (1917–   ), Cz.-born Br. film actor.

Carole **Lombard:** Jane Alice (or Janice) Peters (1908–1942), U.S. film comedienne.

George **London:** George Burnstein (1920–1985), Can. opera singer, producer, of Russ.-U.S. parentage.

Jack **London:** John Griffith Chaney (1876–1916), U.S. author. The famous author was the illegitimate son of William Henry Chaney, an itinerant astrologer, and Flora Wellman. Nine months after his birth his mother married John London, a ruined farmer. Jack London's surname is thus that of his stepfather.

Julie **London:** Julie Peck (1926–   ), U.S. film actress, singer.

Pietro **Longhi:** Pietro Falca (1702–1785), It. painter. The artist apparently adopted the name of the well-known family of Italian architects, Longhi (or Lunghi).

Frederick **Lonsdale:** Lionel Frederick Leonard (1881–1954), Eng. dramatist. The playwright adopted the name Lonsdale officially in 1908, and seems to have based it on his original surname.

E.C.R. **Lorac:** Edith Caroline Rivett (1894–1958), Eng. writer of detective novels. One does not have to be much of a detective to deduce that the writer's pen name is a combination of her initials and a reversal of the first two-thirds of her second name.

Jack **Lord:** John Joseph Ryan (1922–   ), U.S. film, TV actor.

Jeremy **Lord:** Ben Ray Redman (1896–1961), U.S. journalist, writer.

Sophia **Loren:** Sofia Scicolone (1934–   ), It. film actress, working in U.S. The charismatic actress was an illegitimate child, the daughter of Riccardo Scicolone and Romilda Villani. Her original name was thus Sofia Villani Scicolone. It would not be long, however, before people would be telling her that her real surname "sounded like a chunk of Italian sausage," and before long she changed it to her famous present name. The choice of name is popularly supposed to have been made by Carlo Ponti, whom she married (in 1957). A biography of Loren suggests otherwise, however. Originally, it seems, a magazine editor had suggested the name "Sofia Lazzaro," from the New Testament story of Lazarus (with presumably a symbolic reference to a "rebirth"). Then the Italian producer, Goffredo Lombardo, who had been working with the Swedish actress Martha Toren, said that "Lazzaro" sounded more like a corpse than its resurrection and proposed a further change. Taking "Toren" as a basis, he worked through the alphabet, stopping at "Loren." "Yes," was his verdict, "Loren—it suits you. . . ." Subsequently Sofia changed to Sophia, with the changed letters "adding a touch of class" [Donald Zec, *Sophia: An Intimate Biography*, 1975].

Constance **Lorne:** Constance MacLaurin (1914–   ), Sc. stage actress.

Marion **Lorne:** Marion Lorne MacDougal (1886–1968), U.S. stage, film comedienne.

Tommy **Lorne:** Hugh Gallagher Corcoran (1890–1935), Sc. music hall comedian.

Claude **Lorrain:** *see* **Claude Lorrain**

Peter **Lorre:** Laszlo Löwenstein (1904–1964), Hung. film actor, working in U.S.

Joan **Lorring:** Magdalen Ellis (1926–   ), Eng.-Russ. film actress, working in U.S.

Amy **Lothrop:** Anna Bartlett Warner (1827–1915), U.S. novelist, sister of Elizabeth Wetherell *(q.v.)*.

Pierre **Loti:** Louis-Marie-Julien Viaud (1850–1923), Fr. naval officer, traveler, writer. The naval officer's tours of duty took him to Tahiti, where the native women nicknamed him "Loti," meaning "rose." He adopted the name professionally.

Joe **Louis:** Joseph Louis Barrow (1914–1981), U.S. black heavyweight boxer.

Morris **Louis:** Morris Bernstein (1912–1962), U.S. abstract Expressionist painter.

Aunt **Louisa:** Laura B.J. Valentine (1814–1899), Br. children's writer.

Anita **Louise:** Anita Louise Fremault (1915–1970), U.S. stage, film actress.

Tina **Louise:** Tina Louise Blacker (1934–   ), U.S. film actress.

Pierre **Louÿs:** Pierre Louis (1870–1925), Belg.-born Fr. novelist, poet. For the poet's enactment of his best-known pseudonym, see **Bilitis** (and also p. 28).

Bessie **Love:** Juanita Horton (1898–1986), U.S. film actress, working in U.K. The actress was renamed in 1916 by Frank Woods, head of scenario for D.W. Griffith, right before the cast of her first film, *The Flying Torpedo:* "Bessie, because any child can pronounce it; and Love, because we want everyone to love her!" [*Sunday Times Magazine,* September 18, 1977].

Darlene **Love:** Darlene Wright (1938–   ), U. S. pop singer. The singer also records under her real name, but her adopted name presumably means what it looks and sounds as if it means.

Mrs. **Lovechild:** [Lady] Eleanor (or Ellenor) Fenn, née Frere (1743–1813), Eng. writer of books of instruction for children. The writer, who had no children of her own, found some solace in her pen name. She also wrote as "Solomon Lovechild" and "Mrs. Teachwell."

Linda **Lovelace:** Linda Boreman (1952–   ), U.S. porno movie actress. The actress's screen name was given her by Gerry Damiano, director of her best known film, *Deep Throat.* He "came up with the name Linda Lovelace for the character in his movie. There had been a BB [Brigitte Bardot] and an MM [Marilyn Monroe] and now he wanted an LL." The actress commented: "In time I came to dislike the name, Linda Lovelace, because of what it stood for" [Linda Lovelace with Mike McGrady, *Ordeal,* 1981]. Lovelace, of course, was the name of the handsome rake who loves Clarissa Harlowe in Samuel Richardson's famous novel *Clarissa* (1748), as well as being a (genuine) name suggesting someone who "loves lace." (The former actress's present married name is, exceptionally, not given in this entry, in order to protect her identity. She no longer uses the name Lovelace. The jacket of the book cited here reveals simply that she "lives on Long Island with her husband, Larry, and their two children.")

Lena **Lovich:** Marlene Premilovich (*c.*1955–   ), U.S. rock singer, of Eng.-Yugoslav parentage. It is a fortunate coincidence that the singer's stage name, extracted from her real name, happens to alliterate and to suggest "love."

Low: [Sir] David Alexander Cecil Low (1891–1963), N.Z.-born Eng. cartoonist, caricaturist. It would have been interesting to know what brief signatory name the artist would have adopted if he had not already had an ideally short surname.

Robert **Lowery:** Robert Lowery Hanks (1916–1971), U.S. film actor.

Woytec **Lowski:** Wojciech Wiesidlowski (1939–), Pol. ballet dancer.

Myrna **Loy:** Myrna Williams (1905–), U.S. film actress. The actress took her new name in 1932 when she felt that "the plain old Welsh name of Williams just didn't seem flossy enough."

Antonella **Lualdi:** Antonietta de Pascale (1931–), It. film actress.

Arthur **Lucan:** Arthur Towle (1887–1954), Eng. music hall female impersonator, film actor. The comedian was on tour in 1913 at the Lucan Dairy, Dublin, and this provided a handy stage name for the creator of the character "Old Mother Riley."

Victoria **Lucas:** Sylvia Plath (1932–1963), U.S. poet. The poet adopted this name for her semi-autobiographical novel *The Bell Jar* (1963), reissued later (1966) under her own name. The author was devastated when her pseudonym was revealed in the original year of publication.

Lucas van Leyden: Lucas Hugenz (or Lucas Jacobsz) (1494–1533), Du. painter, engraver. The artist adopted the name of his birthplace (and also the place of his death), the Dutch town of Leiden.

Lucius II: Gherardo Caccianemici (? –1145), It. pope.

Lucius III: Ubaldo Allucingoli (?1097–1185), It. pope.

Aunt **Lucy:** Lucy Bather (1836–1864), Eng. children's writer.

Johnny **Ludlow:** Ellen Wood, née Price (1814–1887), Eng. novelist. Mrs. Henry Wood (as she is more usually known) used this name for her series of tales which appeared in the *Argosy* magazine from 1868. She did not admit to their authorship until 1879.

Bela **Lugosi:** Béla Ferenc Denzso Blaskó (1882–1956), Hung. film actor, working in U.S. The actor took his name from his birthplace, Lugos, Hungary (now Lugoj, Romania).

Luigi: Eugene Louis Facciuto (1925–), U.S. ballet dancer, teacher. An italianization of the dancer's second name.

Marcel **Luipart:** Marcel Fenchel (1912–), Ger.-Austr. ballet dancer, choreographer, teacher.

Luisillo: Luis Perez Davilla (1928–), Mexican ballet dancer, choreographer.

Paul **Lukas:** Pál Lukász (1895–1971), Hung.-born U.S. film actor.

Jean-Baptiste **Lully:** Giovanni Battista Lulli (1632–1687), It.-born Fr. composer. The composer gallicized his name after being brought to France as a teenager.

Lulu: Marie McDonald McLaughlin Lawrie (1948–), Sc. popular singer, stage, TV actress. When the singer was only 14 she was appearing at various clubs in Glasgow. At one such club, the Lindella, she was recommended by her manager, Marian Massey, as being a "lulu of a kid," meaning that she was outstanding for her age. She adopted the name, and two years later, with her group Lulu and the Luvvers, hit the charts with her recording of "Shout."

Lulu Belle: Myrtle Eleanor Cooper (1913–), U.S. country singer, teaming with Scotty *(q.v.)*.

Sidney **Luska:** Henry Harland (1861–1905), U.S. novelist, working (from 1890) in U.K. Henry Harland liked to pose as a writer of Russian origin, and as having a European education. He used this Slavic-style name for his novels about immigrant Jews, including *As It Was Written: A Jewish Musician's Story* (1885).

Annabella **Lwin:** Myant Myant Aye (1966–   ), Burmese-born Br. rock singer.

David **Lyall:** [1] Annie Shepherd Swann (1860–1943), Sc. novelist; [2] Helen Buckingham Reeves, née Mathers (1853–1920), Eng. novelist. Is it possible that one or both writers based their pen names on that of Edna Lyall *(q.v.)*? They were contemporaries, all three.

Edna **Lyall:** Ada Ellen Bayly (1857–1903), Eng. writer of popular novels. It is not too difficult to extract the letters of "Edna Lyall" from the writer's original name.

Le **Lycanthrope:** Petrus Borel (1809–1859), Fr. poet, novelist. The writer apparently adopted this name, from the Greek word for "wolf-man," with reference to the classic saying, "Man is a wolf to man." His name is associated with melodramatic horror novels, such as *Madame Putiphar* (1839).

Viola **Lyel:** Violet Watson (1900–1972), Eng. stage, film actress.

John **Lymington:** John Newton Chance (1911–   ), Br. SF writer.

Moura **Lympany:** Mary Defries, née Johnstone (1916–   ), Eng. concert pianist. The pianist's change of name was made at the suggestion of conductor Basil Cameron. She therefore adapted her Cornish mother's maiden name, Limpenny, to Lympany, while simultaneously modulating her own Mary to the softer Moura [*Telegraph Sunday Magazine*, June 10, 1979].

Barre **Lyndon:** Alfred Edgar (1896–1972), Br. playwright, screenwriter, working in U.S. The writer's pen name looks very much like that of the hero of Thackeray's novel, *The Luck of Barry Lyndon* (1844).

Carol **Lynley:** Carolyn Lee (1942–   ), U.S. juvenile film actress.

Barbara **Lynn:** Barbara Lynn Ozen (1942–   ), U.S. blues singer.

Diana **Lynn:** Dolores Loehr (1924–1972), U.S. film, stage, TV comedienne.

Ethel **Lynn:** Ethelinda Beers, née Eliot (1827–1879), U.S. poet.

Dr. H.S. **Lynn:** Hugh Simmons (1836–1899), Eng. conjuror.

Jeffrey **Lynn:** Ragnar Lind (1909–   ), U.S. film actor.

Loretta **Lynn:** Loretta Webb (1935–   ), U.S. country singer, sister of Crystal Gayle *(q.v.)*.

Vera **Lynn:** Vera Margaret Welch (1917–   ), Eng. popular singer. The former "Forces' Sweetheart" explains how she arrived at her new name: "I ought to adopt a more comfortable name than Vera Welch. My main concern was to find something that was short, easily remembered, and that would stand out on a bill— something that would allow for plenty of space round each letter. We held a kind of family conference about it, and we found the answer within the family too. My grandmother's maiden name had been Lynn; it seemed to be everything a stage name ought to be, but at the same time it was a real one. From then on, I was to be Vera Lynn" [Vera Lynn, *Vocal Refrain: An Autobiography*, 1975].

Gillian **Lynne:** Gillian Land, née Pyrke (1926–   ), Eng. ballet dancer, director, choreographer.

Lynx: Rebecca West *(q.v.)*.

Leonard **Lyons:** Leonard Sucher (1906–1976), U.S. columnist.

Maarten **Maartens:** Jozua Marius Willem van der Poorten-Schwartz (1858–1915), Du.-born Eng. novelist.

Uncle **Mac:** Derek McCulloch (1897–1967), Eng. children's author, broadcaster.

McArone: George Arnold (1834–1865), U.S. poet, humorist. In enjoying the (macaronic?) pun, do not overlook the strong echo of the humorist's real surname.

Ed **McBain:** Salvatore A. Lombino (1926–), U.S. writer, novelist.

C.W. **McCall:** William Fries (1928–), U.S. country singer.

Greg **McClure:** Dale Easton (1918–), U.S. film actor. An instance where the actor's real name looks more like a screen name, and vice versa.

Kent **McCord:** Kent McWhirter (1942–), U.S. TV actor.

F.J. **McCormick:** Peter Judge (1891–1947), Ir. stage, film actor.

Kid **McCoy:** Norman Selby (1873–1940), U.S. boxer. According to some, the boxer was the original "real McCoy," although the term has been recorded as early as 1883, which makes Selby just a wee bit too youthful.

Sylvester **McCoy:** Percy James Patrick Kent-Smith (1943–), Sc. TV actor.

Ruth **McDevitt:** Ruth Shoecraft (1895–1976), U.S. film actress.

Hugh **MacDiarmid:** Christopher Murray Grieve (1892–1978), Sc. poet, critic, translator. The origin of the writer's pen name remains a mystery. He first used it in 1922, when supporting the revival of the Scots dialect as a literary medium. His only comment on his name appears to be that quoted in his obituary in *The Times* (September 11, 1978): "It was an immediate realization of this ultimate reach of the implications of my experiment in writing in Scots which made me adopt, when I began writing Scots poetry, the Gaelic pseudonym of Hugh MacDiarmid (Hugh has a traditional association and essential rightness in conjunction with Mac-Diarmid)."

Marie **McDonald:** Marie Frye (1923–1965), U.S. film actress ("The Body").

Murray **Macdonald:** Walter MacDonald Honeyman (1899–), Sc. stage director, manager.

Ross **Macdonald:** Kenneth Millar (1915–1983), U.S. novelist, mystery writer.

Geraldine **McEwan:** Geraldine Crutwell, née McKeown (1932–), Eng. stage, TV actress.

Stephen **Macfarlane:** John Keir Cross (1911–1967), Sc. fantasy fiction, children's writer.

Mike **McGear:** Michael McCartney (1944–), Eng. pop musician, stepbrother of Paul McCartney (of the Beatles). The singer seems to have adopted a name that matched those of the fellow members of his trio, subsequently known as the Scaffold: John Gorman and Roger McGough. At the same time it no doubt refers to "gear" in some slang sense. (As an adjective, "gear" meant "very fashionable" in the mid–1960s, when McCartney was becoming established.)

Fibber **McGee:** James Jordan (1897–), U.S. film actor, radio comedian, teaming with his wife Molly McGee (*q.v.*).

Molly **McGee:** Marion Jordan (1898–1967), U.S. film actress, radio comedienne.

Arthur Machen: Arthur Llewellyn Jones (1863–1947), Welsh horror fiction, ghost story writer.

Machito: Frank Grillo (1912–1984), U.S.-born Afro-Cuban jazz musician. The name suggests a diminutive of Spanish *macho*, "manly," although no actual word *machito* exists as such.

Bunny Mack: Cecil Bunting MacCormack (*c.*1940–   ), African singer.

Connie Mack: Cornelius Alexander McGillicuddy (1862–1956), U.S. baseball manager.

Helen Mack: Helen McDougall (1913–1986), U.S. film actress.

Marion Mack: Joey Mario McCreery (1902–1989), U.S. film actress.

Warner Mack: Warner McPherson (1938–   ), U.S. country singer.

Kenneth McKenna: Leo Mielziner (1899–1962), U.S. film actor, director.

Charles Macklin: Charles M'Laughlin (1700–1797), Ir. actor, playwright.

Bridget Maclagen: Mary Borden (1886–1968), U.S.-born Eng. novelist.

Shirley Maclaine: Shirley Maclean Beaty (1934–   ), U.S. film actress, sister of Warren Beatty *(q.v.).* The actress dropped her surname and adopted the spelling of her mother's maiden name for her screen name.

Fiona Macleod: William Sharp (1855–1905), Sc. author. The writer used the feminine name for his mystic Celtic tales and romances of peasant life in the manner of the so-called "Celtic twilight" movement. The name Fiona, now a popular (and "uppish") girls' name, was first used by Sharp, and is based on Gaelic *fionn*, "white," "fair." Sharp maintained the fiction of "Fiona Macleod" until after his death, and even had a bogus entry for the lady in *Who's Who*, the prestigious British record of important persons, in which he described her recreations as "boating, hill-climbing, and listening."

Frank McLowery: Clay Allison (1914–   ), Eng. writer of westerns.

Edward McLysaght: Edward Lysaght (1888–1986), Eng.-born Ir. historian, genealogist. The distinguished First Herald of Ireland was born in England, a fact that he was never too keen to reveal. On completing his education at Oxford, he moved to Ireland and became gradually involved with the "Irish Ireland" political movement, eventually adding "Mc" to his name in 1920 so as to indicate its Gaelic origin more obviously.

Brinsley Macnamara: John Weldon (1891–1963), Ir. stage actor, dramatist.

Gus McNaughton: Augustus Howard (1884–1969), Br. film actor.

Pierre Mac Orlan: Pierre Dumarchey (1882–1970), Fr. novelist.

Butterfly McQueen: Thelma McQueen (1911–   ), U.S. black stage, film actress. Early in her career (1938), the actress played the part of Butterfly in *Brown Sugar*, and the character's name stuck as a nickname, which she then adopted. It is just right to suggest comic flightiness.

Seán MacStiofáin: John Edward Drayton Stephenson (1928–   ), Br.-born leading IRA member. The Irish name is a rendering of the English "John Stephenson."

Ralph McTell: Ralph May (1944–   ), Br. folk songwriter.

Minnie Maddern: *see* Minnie Maddern **Fiske.**

Rose Maddox: Roseea Arbana Brogdon (1926–   ), U.S. country singer.

Jean **Madeira:** Jean Browning (1918–1972), U.S. opera singer.

Madeleine: Noor Imayat Khan (1914–1944), Br. agent, working in France.

Guy **Madison:** Robert Moseley (1922–   ), U.S. film actor.

Noël **Madison:** Nathaniel Moscovitch (1898–1975), U.S. film actor.

Madonna: Madonna Louise Ciccone (1959–   ), U.S. pop singer. The singer's real first name accorded well with her chart-topping album of 1985, *Like a Virgin*, and cutely contrasted with her lacy, somewhat tacky image.

Johnny **Maestro:** John Mastrangelo (1939–   ), U.S. rock singer.

Magic Sam: Sam Marghett (1937–1969), U.S. black magician. How clever to adopt a name that descriptively alludes to the performer's real surname.

Hyacinthe **Maglanowich:** Prosper Mérimée (1803–1890), Fr. novelist, historian. Just one of the pseudonyms adopted by the writer who also deluded his readers as Clara Gazul *(q.v.)* and Joseph Létrange.

Philip **Magnus:** [Sir] Philip Magnus-Allcroft (1906–   ), Eng. biographer.

Magnus **Magnusson:** Magnus Sigursteinsson (1929–   ), Icelandic-born Br. broadcaster, writer. The well-known quizmaster was born in Scotland to Icelandic parents. His father, the Icelandic Consul-General for Scotland, was Sigursteinn Magnusson, and according to the traditional Icelandic practice, Magnus automatically acquired a surname directly based on his father's first name, as Sigursteinsson ("son of Sigursteinn"). However, he instead adopted his father's own surname, for ease of memorability and pronunciation (and no doubt for its agreeable alliteration). Just as sons add *-son* to their father's first name, so daughters add *-dottir* (Magnus's mother was Ingibjorg Sigurdardottir), and Icelandic women do not change their name on marriage, as conventionally elsewhere in Europe. The difficulties consequently created in Icelandic telephone directories is (fortunately) outside the scope of this present book.

Taj **Mahal:** Henry Saint Clair Fredericks (1942–   ), U.S. black blues-rock musician. An "Indian" name of obvious derivation. For the record, the name of the famous Indian mausoleum is actually a corruption of the title of the emperor's wife who was buried there. This was Mumtaz Mahal, "choice one of the palace."

Maharaj Ji: Pratap Singh Rawat (1957–   ), Indian guru. The guru's assumed name is really a title meaning "perfect master." (Compare the Indian princely title "maharajah," literally "great king.")

Jock **Mahoney:** Jacques O'Mahoney (1919–   ), U.S. film actor.

Marjorie **Main:** Mary Tomlinson Krebs (1890–1975), U.S. film actress. The actress, famous in her role as "Ma Kettle," took her screen name from the title of Sinclair Lewis's novel *Main Street*.

Charles Eric **Maine:** David McIlwain (1921–   ), Br. SF writer.

John Wilson **Maitland:** [Sir] William Watson (1858–1935), Eng. poet.

Thomas **Maitland:** Robert Williams Buchanan (1841–1901), Eng. poet, novelist. The poet used the name for his article "The Fleshly School of Poetry," attacking Pre-Raphaelites, and especially Rossetti, in the October 1871 edition of the *Contemporary Review*.

Maître Adam: Adam Billaut (1602–1662), Fr. carpenter, poet.

Earl **Majors:** Alan Garreth (1953–1978), Eng. motorcycle stunt rider.

Lee **Majors:** Harvey Lee Yeary II (1942–   ), U.S. film actor.

[Archbishop] **Makarios III:** Mikhail Khristodolou Mouskos (1913–1977), Cypriot head of state. The religious name adopted by the archbishop is the Greek word for "blessed."

Mala: Ray Wise (1906–1952), Eskimo film actor, working in U.S.

Malachi **Malagrowther:** [Sir] Walter Scott (1771–1832), Sc. poet, novelist. Scott's nom de plume was adopted from the character of Sir Mungo Malagrowther in his own novel *The Fortunes of Nigel* (1822).

Curzio **Malaparte:** Kurt Erich Suckert (1898–1957), It. writer, journalist. The writer adopted a surname that was intended to suggest the converse of that of (Napoleon) Bonaparte (or Buonaparte). The emperor's own name derives from a Corsican "auspicious" first name, meaning "goodly portion."

Karl **Malden:** Karl Mladen Sekulovich (1913–   ), U.S. film, TV actor.

Lucas **Malet:** Mary St. Leger Harrison, née Kingsley (1852–1931), Eng. novelist, daughter of novelist Charles Kingsley. The author formed her pseudonym from the surnames of two families related to the Kingsleys, adopting it because she did not want her novels to be judged on the well-known Kingsley name but on their own merit. She first used it for *Colonel Enderby's Wife* (1885).

Max **Malini:** Max K. Breit (1873–1963), Pol.-born U.S. magician.

David **Mallet:** David Malloch (?1705–1765), Sc. poet, miscellaneous writer. The poet adopted an anglicized version of his Scottish name in 1724, writing in a letter to a friend at the time that "there is not one Englishman that can pronounce [Malloch]." Dr. Johnson strongly disapproved of this change, and referred to it in his definition of the word "alias" in his *Dictionary*: "*alias* means otherwise, as Mallet *alias* Malloch, that is, otherwise Malloch."

Gina **Malo:** Janet Flynn (1909–1963), Ir.-Ger.-U.S. film actress, working in U.K.

Dorothy **Malone:** Dorothy Eloise Maloney (1925–   ), U.S. film, TV actress.

Louis **Malone:** Louis MacNeice (1907–1963), Ir. poet. The early pen name used by the poet was taken from his birthplace, Malone Road, Belfast.

Felix **Man:** Hans Baumann (1893–1985), Ger. pioneer photo-journalist, working in U.K.

Manchecourt: Henri Léon Emile Lavedan (1859–1940), Fr. playwright, novelist.

Georges **Mandel:** Jeroboam Rothschild (1885–1943), Fr. politician.

Miles **Mander:** Lionel Mander (1888–1946), Eng. stage, film actor.

Frederick **Manfred:** Frederick Feikema (1912–   ), U.S. novelist, of Frisian descent. The writer called himself Feike Feikema from 1944 to 1951.

Barry **Manilow:** Barry Alan Pinkus (1946–   ), U.S. popular singer.

Handsome Dick **Manitoba:** Richard Blum (1954–   ), U.S. rock singer.

Abby **Mann:** Abraham Goodman (1927–   ), U.S. screenwriter.

Anthony **Mann:** Emil Anton Bundesmann (1906–1967), U.S. film director.

Daniel **Mann:** Daniel Chugermann (1912–   ), U.S. film director.

Hank **Mann:** David Liebermann (1887–1971), U.S. film actor.

Herbie **Mann:** Herbert Jay Solomon (1930–   ), U.S. popular musician.

Manfred **Mann:** Michael Lubowitz (1940–   ), S.A.-born Eng. pop musician.

Theodore **Mann:** Theodore Goldman (1924–   ), U.S. stage producer, director.

Mary **Mannering:** Florence Friend (1876–1953), Eng. stage actress, working in U.S.

Charles **Manners:** Southcote Mansergh (1857–1935), Ir. opera singer, working in U.K.

David **Manners:** Rauff de Ryther Duan Acklom (1901–   ), Can. stage, film actor, novelist.

Mrs. Horace **Manners:** Algernon Charles Swinburne (1837–1909), Eng. poet. The poet used this name for his novel, *A Year's Letters*, originally serialized in 1877 but republished in 1905 as *Love's Cross Currents*.

Irene **Manning:** Inez Harvuot (1917–   ), U.S. film actress.

Manolete: Manuel Laureano Rodríguez Sánchez (1917–1947), Sp. bullfighter. The fighter's name is based on his first name, as that of his predecessor Joselito *(q.v.)* was based on his.

Jayne **Mansfield:** Vera Jane Palmer (1932–1967), U.S. film actress. The actress's familiar screen name is actually her married name, for she married Paul Mansfield in 1950 when she was 16. But at least she embellished her original plain "Jane" to a more distinctive "Jayne."

Katherine **Mansfield:** Kathleen Mansfield Murry, née Beauchamp (1888–1923), N.Z.-born Br. novelist, short story writer.

Paul **Mantee:** Paul Marianetti (1936–   ), U.S. film actor.

E. **Manuel:** Ernest L'Epine (1826–1893), Fr. writer. A confusing pen name, since it suggests the Fr. poet and dramatist Eugène Manuel (1823–1901), who wrote under his real name.

Maori: James Inglis (1845–1908), N.Z. author, journalist, politician.

Le **Mapah:** Ganneau (1805–1851), Fr. sculptor, religious leader. The name of the quasireligion founded by the Frenchman was *Évadisme*, which exalted the standing of woman and preached equality of the sexes. Its name is based on the first two letters of "Eve" and "Adam," while "Le Mapah" represents the first two letters of Latin *mater* and *pater*, "mother" and "father." The movement was founded in about 1835, but today remains as just one of a number of tried and tested but now long abandoned cults.

Adele **Mara:** Adelaida Delgado (1923–   ), Sp.-U.S. dancer, film actress.

Sally **Mara:** Raymond Queneau (1903–1976), Fr. writer.

Jean **Marais:** Jean Alfred Villain-Marais (1913–   ), Fr. film actor.

Marc: Charles Mark Edward Boxer (1931–1988), Br. cartoonist.

Félicien **Marceau:** Louis Carette (1913–   ), Belg. novelist, dramatist.

Marcel **Marceau:** Marcel Mangel (1923–   ), Fr. mime artist.

Frederic **March:** Ernest Frederick McIntyre Bickel (1897–1975), U.S. stage, film actor. The actor changed his name at the suggestion of film director John Cromwell, who felt that "Bickel" sounded too much like "pickle." So the star of *A Star Is Born* adapted his mother's maiden name of Marcher as his screen name. Some years later he commented, "I wish I'd left it as it was—after all, Theodore Bickel [the film actor] did all right."

Maxwell **March:** Margery Allingham (1904–1966), Br. crime novelist.

Rocky **Marciano:** Rocco Francis Marchegiano (1923–1969), U.S. heavyweight boxer.

Marevna: Maria Vorobiev (1892–1984), Russ. painter, working in France, U.K. The painter was given her professional name, based on her real name, by Maxim Gorky *(q.v.)*.

Margo: María Marguerita Guadelupe Boldao y Castilla (1918–1985), Mexican-born stage, film actress, dancer, working in U.S.

Marie-Jeanne: Marie-Jeanne Pelus (1920–   ), U.S. ballet dancer.

Mariemma: Emma Martinez (1920–   ), Sp. ballet dancer.

Marilyn: Peter Robinson (1963–   ), Eng. pop singer. The singer affected a blond, androgynous look, vaguely reminiscent of Marilyn Monroe *(q.v.)*.

J.-J. **Marine:** René Oppitz (1904–1976), Belg. poet, critic, detective story writer.

Frances **Marion:** Frances Marion Owens (1887–1973), U.S. screenwriter.

Mona **Maris:** Maria Capdevielle (1903–   ), Fr.-Argentine film actress, working in U.S.

Sari **Maritza:** Sari Deterling-Nathan (1911–   ), Anglo-Austr. film actress.

J. **Marjoram:** Ralph Hales Mottram (1883–1971), Eng. novelist, poet.

Chris **Marker:** Christian François Bouche-Villeneuve (1921–   ), Fr. film director.

Mrs. **Markham:** Elizabeth Penrose, née Cartwright (1780–1837), Eng. novelist, children's writer. The writer took her pen name from the village of Markham, Nottinghamshire, where she spent much of her childhood.

David **Markham:** Peter Basil Harrison (1913–1983), Eng. stage actor.

Robert **Markham:** Kingsley Amis (1922–   ), Eng. novelist, poet, playwright, short story writer. The writer used this name for *Colonel Sun: A James Bond Adventure* (1968). "It's easy to spell and easy to remember," he says.

[Dame] Alicia **Markova:** Lillian Alice Marks (1910–   ), Br. ballet dancer.

Louis **Marlow:** Louis Umfreville Wilkinson (1881–1966), Br. novelist, biographer.

Anthony **Marlowe:** Anthony Perredita (1913–   ), Eng. stage actor. The actor adopted his mother's maiden name as his stage name.

Hugh **Marlowe:** Hugh Hipple (1914–1982), U.S. film actor.

Julia **Marlowe:** Sarah Frances Frost (1866–1950), Eng.-born U.S. stage actress.

Vic **Marlowe:** Victor Hugh Etheridge (? –1987), Br. variety actor, dancer. All these Marlowe names, even where a genuine family name, share something of the charisma of the great sixteenth-century English dramatist Christopher Marlowe.

Florence **Marly:** Hana Smekalova (1918–1978), Fr.-Cz. film actress.

Martin **Marprelate:** John Penry (1559–1593), Welsh Puritan writer + John Udall (?1560–1592), Eng. Puritan preacher + Henry Barrow (? –1593), Eng. church reformer + Job Throckmorton (1545–1601), Eng. Puritan. The name, with its pun of "mar prelate" (i.e. "attack the episcopacy"), was used for a number of anonymous (or pseudonymous) tracts directed against the bishops and defending the Presbyterian system of discipline. The tracts were issued from a secret press in the two years from 1588, and the suspected authors were the Puritan pamphleteers mentioned. Penry and Barrow were executed, Udall died in prison, but Throckmorton, denying his complicity, escaped punishment.

J.J. Marric: John Creasey (1908–1973), Eng. crime novelist. Creasey used around two dozen pen names. This one, less orthodox than most, may have been intended to suggest his own first name and a version of "crime."

Moore **Marriott:** George Thomas Moore-Marriott (1885–1949), Br. film comedian.

Mlle **Mars:** Anne-Françoise-Hippolyte Boutet (1779–1847), Fr. actress.

Carol **Marsh:** Norma Simpson (1926–   ), Br. film actress.

Garry **Marsh:** Leslie Marsh Geraghty (1902–1981), Eng. stage, film actor. The actor seems to have used his surname as the basis of his new first name, retaining his middle name for his new surname.

Joan **Marsh:** Nancy Ann Rosher (1913–   ), U.S. film actress.

Marion **Marsh:** Violet Krauth (1913–   ), U.S. film actress.

Brenda **Marshall:** Ardis Ankerson Gaines (1915–   ), U.S. film actress.

Tully **Marshall:** Tully Marshall Phillips (1864–1943), U.S. film actor.

Paul **Martens:** Stephen H. Critten (1887–1964), Eng. novelist, short story writer.

Fred **Marteny:** Feodor Neumann (1931–   ), Cz.-Austr. ballet dancer, choreographer.

Martin IV: Simon de Brie (?1210–1285), Fr. pope.

Martin V: Oddone Colonna (1368–1431), It. pope.

Dean **Martin:** Dino Crocetti (1917–   ), U.S. film actor, teaming with Jerry Lewis *(q.v.)*. The well-known actor put himself over as a "cousin" of the Metropolitan Opera star Nino Martini, although quite unrelated to him. The adoption of this particular name and ruse was suggested by band leader Ernie McKay, at Walkers Café, Columbus, Ohio [Michael Freedland, *Dino: The Dean Martin Story*, 1984].

Ernest H. **Martin:** Ernest H. Markowitz (1919–   ), U.S. stage manager, producer.

Ross **Martin:** Martin Rosenblatt (1920–1981), Pol.-U.S. film actor.

Stella **Martin:** Georgette Heyer (1902–1974), Br. author of historical romances, detective novels.

Tony **Martin:** Alvin Maris (1912–   ), U.S. cabaret singer, film actor.

Jean Paul Egide **Martini:** Johann Paul Ägidius Schwarzendorf (1741–1816), Ger.-born Fr. composer.

Al **Martino:** Alfred Cini (1927–   ), U.S. pop singer.

L. **Martov:** Yuly Osipovich Tsederbaum (1873–1923), Russ. Menshevik leader. The name may have been intended to be meaningful (Russian *mart* means "March"), but otherwise the letters may have simply been extracted from the politician's real name.

Ik **Marvel:** Donald Grant Mitchell (1822–1908), U.S. essayist. The writer adopted the name "J.K. Marvel" in 1846 for his contributions to the *Morning Courier and New York Enquirer*. This was misprinted as "Ik Marvel," and he stuck with it. "Ik" would have been a short form of "Isaac."

Chico **Marx:** Leonard Marx (1891–1961), U.S. film comedian (see below).

Groucho **Marx:** Julius Henry Marx (1895–1977), U.S. film comedian (see below).

Gummo **Marx:** Milton Marx (1893–1977), U.S. film comedian (see below).

Harpo **Marx:** Adolph Arthur Marx (1893–1964), U.S. film comedian (see below).

Zeppo **Marx:** Herbert Marx (1901–1979), U.S. film comedian. In order of appearance, the Marx Brothers' cast was as follows: Chico (born Leonard), Harpo (Arthur), Groucho (Julius), Gummo (Milton), and Zeppo (Herbert). Chico, it seemed, had a reputation for always being "after the chicks"; Harpo, of course, played the harp; Groucho "had a naturally caustic view of life" (and according to another theory was characterized by the grouch-bag or briefcase in which he carried his stage equipment); Gummo always had holes in his shoes and wore rubbers, or gumshoes, over them; Zeppo—although nobody is quite sure—was born around the time the first Zeppelin was built. The names grew out of their characters. In a television interview (reported in *The Listener* of August 16, 1979) Groucho said of his name: "I always had a grim visage, because I handled the money, and the others didn't have too much confidence in me, and it became Groucho, and it was a nice name."

Aunt **Mary:** Mary Hughes, née Robson (*fl.*1820), Br. children's writer.

Masaccio: Tommaso di Giovanni di Simone Guidi (1401–1428), It. painter. The artist's name means "huge Tom," and must have alluded to his size or stature. (*Mas-*, extracted from "Tommaso," is followed by the Italian augmentative suffix *-accio*, as in *topaccio*, "great big rat," from *topo*, "rat.") Compare the next name below.

Masolino: Tommaso di Cristofero Fini (1383–*c.*1440), It. painter. The painter's name means "little Tom," presumably referring to his size or stature, possibly by comparison with his pupil, Masaccio *(q.v.)*. (*Mas-*, from "Tommaso," is followed by the diminutive Italian suffix *-olino*, as in *topolino*, "little mouse," from *topo*, "mouse." Topolino is the Italian name for Mickey Mouse.)

Edith **Mason:** Edith Barnes (1898–1973), U.S. opera singer.

Shirley **Mason:** Leona Flugrath (1900–1979), U.S. film actress.

Stuart **Mason:** Christopher Sclater Millard (1872–1927), Br. biographer. The author used this name for his three books on Oscar Wilde (1914, 1915, 1920), but kept his real name for the bibliographical *Printed Work of Claud Lovat Fraser* (1923).

Massachusettensis: Daniel Leonard (1740–1829), U.S. Loyalist writer. The writer used this pseudoclassical pen name for series of contributions to *The Massachusetts Gazette and Post Boy* (1774–1775). These were replied to by Novanglus *(q.v.)*.

Lea **Massari:** Anna Maria Massatani (1933–   ), Fr.-It. film actress.

Ilona **Massey:** Ilona Haymassy (1912–1974), Hung.-born U.S. film actress. Although the actress's screen name clearly resembles her real name, it may well have been additionally suggested by the existing name of film actor Raymond Massey.

Leonide **Massine:** Leonid Fedorovich Miassin (1896–1979), Russ. ballet dancer, choreographer. The dancer not only gallicized his name but at the same time moved slightly away from a Russian surname that in his native language suggests "meat," Russian *myaso*. His son, Lorca Massine (1944–   ), also a ballet dancer, kept the altered name.

Mata Hari: Margarethe Geertruida MacLeod, née Zelle (1876–1917), Du.-born Fr. dancer, spy. The dancer's name for her exotic Eastern temple performance on the French stage perhaps derived from the Malay for "eye of the day," i.e., the sun. Before her arrival in Paris in 1904, Margarethe Zelle had been married briefly to a Dutch colonial officer, Rudolph MacLeod, and with him had stayed, equally briefly, in the Dutch East Indies. She had retained enough of the language to invent the name for her new life in the theatre. Accused of spying for the Germans in the First World War, Mata Hari's days came to an end in 1917 at the age of 41, when she was executed by the French. "Mata Hari" also suggests "Margarethe."

Carmen **Mathé:** Margaretha Matheson (1938–   ), Sc. ballet dancer. The dancer adopted a Spanish-style name rather cleverly from her existing two names, adding "Carmen" as a clincher, the name of the alluring Spanish gypsy girl made famous by Bizet's opera.

Helen **Mathers:** Helen Buckingham Reeves, née Matthews (1853–1921), Eng. novelist.

Anna **Matilda:** [1] Hannay Cowley (1743–1809), Eng. dramatist, poet; [2] Hester Lynch Piozzi, née Salusbury (1741–1821), Eng. writer. The same name was used by both women in their correspondence with the Della Cruscans (see Della Crusca). Hester Piozzi, better known as Mrs. Thrale, after her first husband, had been called "Matilda" by William Gifford in his two satires, *The Baviad* (1794) and *The Maeviad* (1795), both directed against the Dellacruscan school of English poetry.

Julia **Matilda:** Julia Clara Byrne, née Busk (1819–1894), Eng. author.

Matteo: Matteo Marcellus Vittucci (1919–   ), U.S. dancer.

Walter **Matthau:** Walter Mataschanskayasky (1920–   ), U.S. stage, film actor. The actor was the son of a Catholic Eastern Rite Orthodox priest who had fallen afoul of the authorities. Sources vary on his original impressive Slavic surname, but it seems to have been as stated here.

Thomas **Matthew:** John Rogers (1505–1555), Eng. Protestant divine, martyr. The Protestant convert used this name for his English translation of the Bible (1537), assuming a pseudonym for fear of meeting the same fate as his friend William Tyndale, who had earlier translated the New Testament (1525), the Pentateuch (1530) and the Book of Jonah (1531), and who had been burnt at the stake in 1536 as a heretic. But Rogers was accorded exactly the same judgment. . . . His translation is now usually referred to as "Matthew's Bible."

Ian **Matthews:** Ian Matthew MacDonald (1946–   ), Eng. folk rock musician.

Furnley **Maurice:** Frank Wilmot (1881–1942), Austral. poet.

Walter **Maurice:** [Sir] Walter Besant (1836–1901), Eng. novelist.

André **Maurois:** Emile Salomon Wilhelm Herzog (1885–1967), Fr. writer. The writer first used the name for *Les Silences du Colonel Bramble* (1918), in which he described typical British army officers in their mess. The pen name is said to derive from a small front line village called Maurois and the first name of his cousin André who had been killed in the First World War.

Maxim the Greek: Mikhail Trivolis (*c.*1475–1556), Gr. churchman, translator, working in Russia. The scholar was nicknamed for his nationality, but it seems strange that his first name was altered in this way, as both Greek and Russian share a common version of "Michael."

Lois **Maxwell:** Lois Hooker (1927–   ), Can. film actress, working in U.S. One can see why a change of name was desirable in this instance.

Robert **Maxwell:** Jan Ludvik Hoch (1923–   ), Cz.-born Eng. publisher, politician, press baron. The well-known newspaper owner has a fairly complex naming history. He was born near the Czech-Romanian border as the son of a Jewish peasant, Mechel Hoch, who called him Abraham Lyabi. But when the father went to register the boy at the local town hall, the Czech government official insisted on a Czech name for the record. He was thus renamed Jan Ludvik Hoch. Later, in the Second World War, he joined the Czech Pioneer Corps and was posted to Britain, where in 1943 he joined the North Staffs Regiment, taking the name of Private L.I. du Maurier, a name he had chosen from a cigarette packet in order to disguise his true identity if captured by the Germans. A year later, after the D-Day landings, he was working in the intelligence field in Paris, France, using the cover name "Private Jones" (although his actual rank was now higher than this). In due course, his work so impressed the military authorities that he was promoted to second lieutenant and recommended to choose yet another name, as du Maurier and Jones were not regarded as fitting. The Scottish name of Robert Maxwell was suggested, and he adopted it, adding the English form of Jan (Ian) as a first name. For some time after, Robert Maxwell was undecided whether to use "Ian" or "Robert" as his main name [Tom Bower, *Maxwell, the Outsider*, 1988].

Roger **Maxwell:** Roger D. Latham (1900–   ), Eng. stage, film, TV actor.

Elaine **May:** Elaine Berlin (1932–   ), U.S. film actress, director.

Joe **May:** Joseph Otto Mandel (1880–1954), Aust. director of film adventure serials.

Sophie **May:** Rebecca Sophia Clarke (1833–1906), U.S. children's writer.

Rutherford **Mayne:** Samuel J. Waddell (1879–1967), Ir. dramatist.

James **Mayo:** Stephen Coulter (1914–   ), Br. writer of thrillers and spy novels.

Virginia **Mayo:** Virginia May Jones (1920–   ), U.S. film actress. The actress's screen name is almost certainly derived from her real name, although an old Hollywood joke says that she got her name from a cafe counterman's call "Virginia, mayo" when she ordered a ham sandwich with mayonnaise while waiting at a bus station. (Note for British readers: Virginia ham is a special sort of smoked ham got from pigs that have been fed on peanuts.)

Joseph **Mazilier:** Giulio Mazarini (1901–1968), Fr. ballet dancer, choreographer, teacher.

Mike **Mazurki:** Mikhail Mazurwski (1909–   ), U.S. film actor, of Ukrainian descent.

Lillie Thomas (or L.T.) **Meade:** Elizabeth Thomasina Meade Smith (1854–1914), Eng. author of books for girls, mystery, detective fiction writer.

Audrey **Meadows:** Audrey Cotter (1929–   ), U.S. film, TV comedienne, sister of Jayne Meadows.

Jayne **Meadows:** Jayne Cotter (1925–   ), U.S. film actress.

Meat Loaf: Marvin Lee Aday (1948–   ), U.S. rock singer. The singer was so nicknamed by his Dallas school friends on account of his gross size, and he adopted the name soon after, calling his first band alternately Meat Loaf Soul and Popcorn Blizzard. The initials of the name do repeat the true initials of his first and middle names, however.

Kay **Medford:** Kay Regan (1918–1980), U.S. stage actress.

Ralph **Meeker:** Ralph Rathgeber (1920–   ), U.S. stage, film actor.

Mehboob: Ramjankhan Mehboobkhan (1907–1964), Indian film director.

Golda **Meir:** Goldie Myerson, née Mabovitch (1898–1978), Russ.-born Israeli prime minister. After emigrating to the U.S. at the age of eight, Goldie Mabovitch met (in 1917) Morris Myerson, a Russian Jewish immigrant, whom she later married. Back later with her husband in Palestine, Golda changed her name to Meir at the insistence of David Ben Gurion *(q.v.)* when she was appointed (1956) Israeli foreign minister. She chose a name that still suggested "Myerson" (although her marriage had by now broken up), knowing that Meir means "light" in Hebrew.

Melanchthon: Philip Schwarzerd (1497–1560), Ger. humanist, theologian. In the manner of his time, the theologian translated his German name (literally "black earth") into Greek.

Melanie: Melanie Safka (1947–   ), U.S. pop singer, songwriter.

[Dame] Nellie **Melba:** Helen Porter Armstrong, née Mitchell (1861–1931), Austral. opera singer. The singer took her name from Melbourne, the city near which she was born. She first used the name in Brussels in 1887, for her debut as Gilda in *Rigoletto.* She in turn gave her name to those dietetic opposites, Melba toast and peach Melba, the former because she fancied it, the latter because it was as bright and colorful as she was.

Lauritz **Melchior:** Lebrecht Himml (1890–1973), U.S. opera singer, of Dan. parentage.

Jill **Melford:** Jill Melford-Melford (1934–   ), U.S. stage actress.

Courtney **Melmoth:** Samuel Jackson Pratt (1749–1814), Br. poet, prose writer. The writer used the rather flamboyant name for his unsuccessful acting debut in 1773, but later adopted it more generally for his literary pennings. His American wife was more fortunate in her stage career, appearing always as "Mrs. Charlotte Melmoth" after their brief marriage. Her maiden name is unknown.

Sebastian **Melmoth:** Oscar Wilde (1854–1900), Ir. playwright, author, poet. Oscar Wilde adopted this name after his release from Reading Gaol in 1897. He took it from the hero of *Melmoth the Wanderer,* a novel by Charles Maturin, who was a remote ancestor on Wilde's maternal side. The first name Sebastian was suggested by the arrows on his prison uniform, as a reference to classic paintings showing St. Sebastian being shot to death by arrows.

Alan **Melville:** Alan Caverhill (1910–   ), Eng. lyric writer, dramatist.

Jean-Pierre **Melville:** Jean-Pierre Grumbach (1917–1973), Fr. film director.

Jennie **Melville:** Gwendoline Butler (1922–   ), Br. suspense novelist.

Lewis **Melville:** Lewis Samuel Benjamin (1874–1932), Br. author.

Memphis Slim: Peter Chatman (1915–1988), U.S. black blues singer, musician. The singer, who lived in France from the 1960s, was born in Memphis, Tennessee.

Menander: Charles Langbridge Morgan (1894–1958), Br. novelist, essayist. The writer used the name for a series of articles entitled "Menander's Mirror" in the *Times Literary Supplement* during the Second World War. Menander was an Athenian poet of the third century B.C.

Adah Isaacs **Menken:** Dolores Adios Fuertes (?1835–1868), U.S. actress, poet. The actress and poet married (1856) Alexander Isaacs Menken (not to be confused with Henry Louis Mencken, the editor and writer on language) and then, under the impression she was divorced, the boxer John Carmel Heenan (1859). Menken was a Jew, and this may have prompted her to change her first two names to something more specifically Jewish, although she herself was the daughter of a Spanish Jew. She kept her name through subsequent marriages – she is said to have been married four times, one further husband being Orpheus C. Kerr *(q.v.)* – and gained popularity for her role on the London stage as Mazeppa (1864) in a dramatization of Byron's poem. Some sources give her original name as Adelaide McCord.

Gerhardus **Mercator:** Gerhard Kremer (1512–1594), Flemish cartographer, mathematician. In the style of his time, the scholar translated his surname, which literally means "tradesman" (compare modern German *Krämer*), to Latin (compare English "merchant").

T. **Merchant:** Thomas John Dibdin (1771–1841), Eng. playwright, operatic composer, songwriter. The writer used this punning name for some of his writing, but usually used the name of Thomas Pitt, his mother's name. He was illegitimate, and only adopted his father's name of Dibdin to annoy him, as he accused him of having neglected himself and his two brothers when they were children. His elder brother, playwright Charles Pitt (1768–1833), kept his mother's name.

Vivien **Merchant:** Ada Thomson (1929–1982), Eng. stage, film actress.

Freddie **Mercury:** Frederick Bulsara (1946–   ), Zanzibar-born Eng. rock singer.

Anne **Meredith:** Lucy Beatrice Malleson (1899–1973), Eng. crime novelist.

Burgess **Meredith:** George Burgess (1908–   ), U.S. film actor.

Owen **Meredith:** Edward Robert Bulwer Lytton (1831–1891), Br. statesman, poet. The writer adopted the first names of two of his ancestors for his first book, *Clytemnestra, the Earl's Return and Other Poems,* published in 1855, while employed in the diplomatic service.

Bess **Meredyth:** Helen McGlashan (1890–1969), U.S. film scriptwriter.

Merlinus Anglicus: William Lilly (1602–1681), Eng. astrologer. Lilly used the name, meaning "English Merlin," for the many astrological almanacs he published.

Ethel **Merman:** Ethel Zimmerman (1909–1984), U.S. stage, film actress. A rather pleasant conversion of a carpenter (Zimmerman) into a creature of the sea, even if not a feminine one.

May **Merrall:** Mary Lloyd (1890–1976), Eng. stage, film actress. The actress almost certainly changed her name in order to avoid being confused with Marie Lloyd *(q.v.).* She first appeared on the stage in 1907 as Queenie Merrall.

Judith **Merril:** Josephine Judith Zissman (1923–   ), Can. SF writer.

Dina **Merrill:** Nedenia Hutton Rumbough (1928–   ), U.S. film, TV actress, socialite.

Helen **Merrill:** Helen Milcetic (1930–   ), U.S. jazz singer.

Robert **Merrill:** Henry Lavan (1921–   ), U.S. film music composer, lyricist.

Henry Seton **Merriman:** Hugh Stowell Scott (1862–1903), Eng. writer of historical fiction. The writer was obliged by his father to become an underwriter at Lloyds of London, a commercial position that was not to his liking. He chose the name, loosely based on his real name, in order not to incur his family's wrath, first using it for his novel *The Phantom Future* (1889).

Felix **Merry:** Evert Augustus Duychinck (1816–1878), U.S. editor.

Billy **Merson:** William Henry Thompson (1881–1947), Eng. music hall artist.

Ambrose **Merton:** William John Thomas (1803–1885), Eng. antiquary. The founder of the academic journal *Notes and Queries* used this name for a collection of tales and ballads that he published in 1846.

William **Mervyn:** William Mervyn Pickwoad (1912–1976), Eng. stage, film, TV actor.

Pietro **Metastasio:** Pietro Antonio Domenico Bonaventura Trapassi (1698–1782), It. dramatist, librettist. At the age of ten, Pietro was made the heir adoptive of a man of letters, Gian Vincenzo Gravina, who rendered his Italian surname, meaning literally "passage," "transfer" (*trapasso*) into Greek. Compare the medical term "metastasis" used for the spreading of cancer cells.

[Sir] Algernon Methuen Marshall **Methuen:** Algernon Methuen Marshall Stedman (1856–1924), Eng. publisher. The founder of the well-known publishing house of Methuen changed his name officially from Stedman to Methuen (his second name) in 1899. He had used it ten years earlier, however, when branching out into the publishing world while still a schoolmaster, a position that he abandoned in favor of publishing fulltime in 1895.

Giacomo **Meyerbeer:** Jakob Liebmann Meyer Beer (1791–1864), Ger. opera composer, working in Italy and France.

Mezz **Mezzrow:** Milton Mesirow (1899–1972), U.S. jazz musician.

George **Michael:** Yorgos Kyriakou Panayiotou (1963–   ), Br. pop singer, of Gk.-Cypriot/Eng. parentage. "George" is recognizably (and accurately) Yorgos, but "Michael" is a much more casual adaptation of "Kyriakou", which could have been more precisely rendered as "Lord" or even "Lordson." (Greeks have three names, of which the first is their personal name, the second their patronymic, or "son of my father" name, and the third their family name.) The former member of Wham! changed his name when he changed his image at the age of 18, in 1982.

Kathleen **Michael:** Kathleen Smith (1917–   ), Eng. stage actress.

Ralph **Michael:** Ralph Champion Shotter (1907–   ), Eng. film actor.

Karin **Michaëlis:** Katarina Bek (1872–1950), Dan. novelist.

Michelangelo: Michelagniolo di Lodovico Buonarroti Simoni (1475–1564), It. sculptor, painter, architect, poet. It is uncertain whether the great artist's first name was originally Michelangelo or Michelagniolo. The former is more likely, suggesting "Michael the Archangel." The latter name means the same (Italian *angelo* and *agnolo* both mean "angel"), but also suggests "lamb" (*agnello*).

Robert **Middleton:** Samuel G. Messer (1911–1977), U.S. film actor.

Hans **Mikkelsen:** Ludvig von Holberg (1684–1754), Norw.-born Dan. dramatist ("Father of Danish Drama").

Peter **Miles:** Gerald Perreau (1938–   ), U.S. film actor.

Vera **Miles:** Vera Ralston (1929–   ), U.S. film actress.

Lewis **Milestone:** Lev Milshtein (1895–1980), Russ.-born U.S. film director.

Ray **Milland:** Reginald Truscott-Jones (1908–1986), Welsh-born Br. film actor, working in U.S. The actor's first change of name was to Mullane, the surname of his stepfather after his mother's second marriage. Later, a studio publicity man suggested a further change, and recommended the name "Percival Lacy."(Could he really have been serious? Even Polesden Lacy, the name of a country house in Surrey, would have been more effective.) Ray (or Reg), however, was nostalgically thinking back to the rural beauty of his Welsh childhood, and proposed "Mill-land." The publicity man, more reasonable this time, advised a name with three "l"'s might present difficulties, whereupon the actor modified it to the form in which it became popularly known [Ray Milland, *Wide-eyed in Babylon*, 1975].

Mary **Millar:** Mary Wetton (1936–   ), Eng. stage actress, singer. The actress adopted (and adapted) her stage name from her mother's maiden name, which was Mellow.

Ann **Miller:** Lucille Ann Collier (1923–   ), U.S. tap dancer, film actress. The actress's screen name was that of her first husband, Reese Miller.

Joaquin **Miller:** Cincinnatus Hiner Miller (1841–1913), U.S. poet. The poet had the ambition of being "the American Byron." The first name he adopted was originally a nickname, as his earliest writing defended the Mexican bandit Joaquin Murietta. He later preferred to spell his middle name as "Heine"–perhaps alluding to the famous German poet.

Marilyn **Miller:** Mary Ellen Reynolds (1898–1936), U.S. film actress.

Martin **Miller:** Rudolph Muller (1899–1969), Cz. film actor, working in U.K.

Marvin **Miller:** Marvin Mueller (1913–1985), U.S. film actor.

Max **Miller:** Thomas Henry Sargent (1895–1963), Eng. music hall comedian (the "Cheeky Chappie").

Wade **Miller:** Robert Wade (1920–   ), U.S. mystery writer + Bill Miller (1920–1961), U.S. mystery writer.

Carl **Milles:** Wilhelm Carl Emil Andersson (1875–1955), Swe. sculptor.

Millie: Millicent Small (1947–   ), Jamaican pop singer.

Bill **Million:** William Clayton (–   ), U.S. rock musician.

Alan **Mills:** Albert Miller (1914–1977), Can. folk singer.

[Sir] John **Mills:** Lewis Ernest Watts (1908–   ), Br. film actor. The distinguished film actor changed his name when still at school because he considered it "too sissy" [*Sunday Times Magazine*, August 31, 1986]. "Mills" is calligraphically similar to "Watts."

George **Milner:** George Edward Charles Hardinge, Baron Hardinge of Penshurst (1921–   ), Eng. crime novelist.

Sandra **Milo:** Alessandra Marini (1935–   ), It. film actress.

[Cardinal] József **Mindszenty:** József Pehm (1892–1975), Hung. church dignitary. The archbishop adopted the Magyar name from his native village of Szehimindszenty via a protest against Hungary's pro-Hitler stand in the 1930s.

Mary Miles **Minter:** Juliet Reilly (1902–1984), U.S. film actress. The actress began her screen career as a child star, billed as "Little Juliet Shelby." When she was 13, she changed her name to Mary Miles Minter (presumably a random alliteration) and continued under the name as an adult actress until 1923, when she quit the cinema for good after a scandal involving the murder of director William Desmond Taylor (and much talk about silk underwear embroidered "MMM").

Miou-Miou: Sylvette Arri (or Héry) (1950–   ), Fr. film actress. The actress's name probably arose from a child's nickname of endearment, perhaps something on the lines of *mie, minou,* or *mioche,* "darling."

Jean **Mirabaud:** Paul Thiry, Baron d'Holbach (1723–1789), Fr. materialist, atheist philosopher. Holbach frequently used the names of important deceased persons as pseudonyms for his books. This one, which he used for his most important book, *Système de la nature* (1770), he took from the writer and member of the French Academy, Jean Baptiste de Mirabaud, who had died ten years previously. (He must not be confused with the much more eminent French revolutionary, the Comte de Mirabeau, who was his contemporary.)

Carmen **Miranda:** Maria do Carmo Miranda da Cunha (1909–1955), Port.-born U.S. popular singer, film actress. Objectively, the actress's name comes from her middle names; subjectively it evokes the musical gypsy singer heroine of Bizet's *Carmen* and the romantic heroine of Shakespeare's *The Tempest.*

Isa **Miranda:** Ines Isabella Sampietro (1909–1982), It. stage, film actress. No doubt the actress took "Miranda" from the same source as Carmen Miranda *(q.v.)*—unless she was inspired by the latter lady herself.

Miroslava: Miroslava Stern (1926–1955), Cz. film actress, working in Mexico.

Helen **Mirren:** Ilyena Lydia Mironoff (1945–   ), Br. film actress, of Russ. origin.

Mistinguett: Jeanne-Marie Bourgeois (1873–1956), Fr. music hall singer, actress. The singer, popularly known simply as "Miss," was originally named "Miss Helyett" by a revue writer of the day, Saint-Marcel, who used to travel with her regularly on the same train to Enghien, outside Paris, where she lived. *Miss Helyett* was a light opera in vogue at the time. He then suggested the variation "Miss Tinguette," rhyming this with the character in a popular song named Vertinguette. The singer adopted the name in the form "Mistinguette," later dropping the final "e" [France Vernillat and Jacques Charpentreau, *Dictionnaire de la chanson française,* 1968]. The general English-style name is said to have alluded to her prominent front teeth, a characteristic (duly noted by the French) of the British aristocracy. But not all aristocrats have the long legs for which Mistinguette was widely famous.

Gabriela **Mistral:** Lucila Godoy de Alcayaga (1889–1957), Chilean poet. The poet derived her *nom de plume* from two fellow poets, the Italian Gabriele d'Annunzio (1863–1938) and the Provençal Frédérick Mistral (1830–1914). She began to use the name soon after Mistral's death. Thirty years later she was awarded the Nobel prize for literature, as he had been.

Cameron **Mitchell:** Cameron Mizell (1918–), U.S. film actor.

Eddy **Mitchell:** Claude Moine (1942–), Fr. rock singer. The singer adopted the American-style name in 1960 in order to give his persona a more "international" image.

Guy **Mitchell:** Al Cernick (1927–), U.S. pop singer, film actor, of Yugoslav parentage. The singer's real name can be seen reflected, somewhat distortedly, in his professional name.

Joni **Mitchell:** Roberta Joan Anderson (1943–), Can. pop musician. Many source books given the singer's real name thus. But "Joni Mitchell" is just as real, since the first name is a pet form of "Joan" and she married folksinger Chuck Mitchell in 1965 (although soon separating from him).

Yvonne **Mitchell:** Yvonne Joseph (1925–1979), Eng. stage, film actress, writer. The actress adopted her mother's maiden name as her stage name.

Jean **Mitry:** Jean-René-Pierre Goetgheluck Le Rouge Tillard des Acres des Préfontaines (1907–), Fr. film director. With what professional pangs, one wonders, did the filmman reduce his grand array to this?

Mit (or **Mot**) **Yenda:** Timothy (or Thomas) Adney (*fl.*1785), Eng. poet of the Dellacruscan school. The poet simply reversed his name(s). See also Della Crusca.

[President] **Mobutu:** Joseph-Désiré Mobutu (1930–), African statesman, president of Zaire (from 1965). In 1972 the president dropped his Christian name and expanded his surname, which thus officially became Mobutu Sese Seko Kuku Ngdenda Wa Za Banga. According to the *Sunday Times Magazine* (March 7, 1972), this means "invincible warrior cockerel who leaves no chick intact."

Jean-Pierre **Mocky:** Jean Mokiejewski (1929–), Fr. film director.

Helen **Modjeska:** Helena Modrzejewska, née Opid (1840–1909), Pol. actress, working in U.S.

Leonide **Moguy:** Leonid Moguilevsky (1899–1976), Russ. newsreel producer, film director, working in France, U.S.

Molière: Jean-Baptiste Poquelin (1622–1673), Fr. dramatist. This classic pseudonym is also a classic mystery. How did the author of *Tartuffe* and *Le Malade imaginaire* acquire his new name? We do know that he must have first used it in 1643 or 1644, for it is found in a document dated June 28, 1644. It at least has a much more theatrical ring than Poquelin, which to a Frenchman suggests either *poquet*, "seedhole," or *poquer*, a verb meaning "to throw one's ball in the game of *boules* in such a way that it stops still where it lands." As for the name Molière, it did in fact also belong to a second-rank writer who died in the same year that Jean-Baptiste was born (1622). But the commonly held theory is that he derived it not from his lesser codramatist, but from a place of this name—or something like this name—that was visited by the touring company to which young Poquelin belonged. (There are several villages named Molières, for example, and at least one called Molères.).

Ferenc **Molnár:** Ferenc Neumann (1878–1952), Hung. dramatist, working in U.S.

Vyacheslav **Molotov:** Vyacheslav Mikhailovich Skryabin (1890–1986), Russ. diplomat. The politician assumed his party name in 1906, when he became a Bolshevik. It means "hammer," in the meaningful, symbolic manner of the Bolsheviks. Compare the name of Stalin.

Pierre **Mondy:** Pierre Cuq (1925–), Fr. film actor.

Lireve **Monett:** Everil Worrell (1893–1969), U.S. (female) writer of horror stories.

Eddie **Money:** Edward Mahoney (1949–), U.S. rock singer.

Matt **Monro:** Terence Edward Parsons (1930–1985), Eng. popular singer. The singer took "Matt" from a journalist who came to interview him, and "Monro" from the first name of the father of Winifred Atwell, the popular pianist who encouraged him.

Marilyn **Monroe:** Norma Jeane Dougherty, née Mortensen, later Baker (1926–1962), U.S. film actress. Dougherty was the name of Monroe's first husband, whom she married at the age of 16; Baker was a name (not that of a husband) that she used later as her "real" name. When Darryl F. Zanuck signed up the actress in 1946, Ben Lyon wanted to change her name to "Carole Lind," but this was "a rather obvious composite of an opera singer and a dead actress," and didn't sound right. Lyon and his actress wife, Bebe Daniel *(q.v.),* decided they could do better. They invited Norma Jeane to tea. Lyon recalled: "I finally said to her, 'I know who you are. You're Marilyn!' I told her that once there was a lovely actress named Marilyn Miller and that she reminded me of her. 'But what about the last name?' Marilyn said, 'My grandmother's name was Monroe and I'd like to keep that.' I said 'Great! That's got a nice flow, and two Ms should be lucky.' That's how she got her name" [Anthony Summers, *Goddess: The Secret Lives of Marilyn Monroe,* 1985].

Nicholas **Monsarrat:** Nicholas John Turney Montserrat (1910–1979), Eng. novelist. The novelist's name had been incorrectly registered at his birth, with a spelling that was preferred by his mother, who claimed that the family went back to a French nobleman, the Marquis de Montserrat. In his autobiography, Monsarrat recalls that the discrepancy between spellings was to embarrass him both at school and later on joining the Royal Navy [Nicholas Monsarrat, *Life Is a Four-Letter Word,* 1966].

Henry James **Montague:** Henry James Mann (1844–1878), U.S. actor.

Bull **Montana:** Luigi Montagna (1887–1950), It.-U.S. film actor.

Patsy **Montana:** Rubye Blevins (1914–), U.S. country singer, yodeller.

Yves **Montand:** Ivo Livi (1921–), It.-born Fr. film actor, singer. When the singer began his career in Marseille, appearing at the Alcazar, his manager told him that "Ivo Livi" was not right for a professional name: "it's too foreign and it doesn't have a proper ring to it." Montand tells how he arrived at his new name: "When I was a kid, my mother didn't like me to hang around in the street in front of our house. She spoke bad French and would shout, 'Yvo monta, Yvo monta.' [Yvo, come upstairs.] That came back to me, so I frenchified my christian name, Yves, and monta became Montand" [Simone Berteaut, *Piaf,* translated by Ghislaine Boulanger, 1970].

Mlle **Montansier:** Marguerite Brunet (1730–1820), Fr. actress, theatre manager. The actress adopted the name of the aunt who raised her as her stage name.

Montdory: Guillaume des Gilberts (1594–1651), Fr. actor.

Lola **Montez:** Marie Dolores Eliza Rosanna Gilbert (1818–1861), Ir. actress, dancer, courtesan, working in France and U.S. Soon after marrying Ensign Thomas James, of the Indian army, Marie Gilbert called herself "Rose Anne Gilbert," and indeed signed the marriage register in this name when the two eloped to Ireland. Later, as a "Spanish" dancer, she adopted the typical Spanish name of Lola Montez, "Lola" being a pet form of her second name.

Maria **Montez:** María Africa Vidal de Santo Silas (1918–1951), U.S. film actress, born in Dominican Republic ("The Caribbean Cyclone").

Montfleury: Zacharie Jacob (c.1600–1667), Fr. actor.

George **Montgomery:** George Montgomery Letz (1916–   ), U.S. film actor.

Robert **Montgomery:** Henry Montgomery, Jr. (1904–1981), U.S. film actor, politician.

Ron **Moody:** Ronald Moodnick (1924–   ), Eng. stage, TV comedian.

Moondog: Louis Thomas Hardin (1916–   ), U.S. blind "popular-classical" musician. The composer explains: "I began using Moondog as a pen name in 1947, in honor of a dog I had in Hurley, who used to howl at the moon more than any dog I knew of" [jacket notes on record "Moondog," Poseidon Productions/CBS Records, 1969].

Harry **Mooney:** Harry Goodchild (1889–1972), Eng. music hall comedian.

Archie **Moore:** Archibald Lee Wright (1913–   ), U.S. light heavyweight boxer, film actor.

Colleen **Moore:** Kathleen Morrison (1900–1988), U.S. film actress.

Garry **Moore:** Thomas Morfit (1915–   ), U.S. TV comedian, linkman. The TV comic tired of people mispronouncing his surname. A contest was therefore held (1940) to select a new name for him. A Pittsburgh woman suggested "Garry Moore" and won the prize of $50 and a trip to Chicago.

Kieron **Moore:** Kieron O'Hanrahan (1925–   ), Ir. film actor.

Maggie **Moore:** Margaret Sullivan (1851–1926), U.S.-born stage actress, working in Australia.

Terry **Moore:** Helen Koford (1929–   ), U.S. film actress.

Wentworth **Moore:** William Hurrell Mallock (1849–1923), Eng. author, poet.

Lois **Moran:** Lois Darlington Dowling (1909–   ), U.S. film actress.

Alberto **Moravia:** Alberto Pincherle (1907–   ), It. novelist, short story writer.

Jean **Moréas:** Ioannes Papadiamantópoulos (1856–1910), Gk.-born Fr. poet.

Eric **Morecambe:** John Eric Bartholomew (1926–1984), Eng. TV comedian, teaming with Ernie Wise (q.v.). The much-loved comedian described how he came by his name in his and Ernie Wise's joint autobiography: "An early problem was my stage name. Nobody liked Bartholomew and Wise. Bryan Michie [his manager] wanted to call us Bartlett and Wise or Barlow and Wise. The matter was finally settled in Nottingham. My mother was talking to Adelaide Hall, the colored American singer on the bill, when her husband, Bert Hicks, came up. My mother said, 'We're trying to think of a name for Eric.' Bert [. . .] said, 'There's this friend of mine, a colored boy who calls himself Rochester because he comes from Rochester, Minnesota. Where do you come from?' 'Morecambe.' 'That's a good name. Call him Morecambe.' My mother liked it and I liked it, and from there on I was Morecambe on the bill" [Dennis Holman, *Eric & Ernie: The Autobiography of Morecambe and Wise*, 1973].

André **Morell:** André Mesritz (1909–1978), Eng. stage, film actor.

Antonio **Moreno:** Antonio Monteagudo (1886–1967), Sp.-born U.S. film actor.

Rita **Moreno:** Rosita Dolores Alverio (1931–), Puerto Rican stage, film actress, dancer. Spanish *moreno* means "brown," "dark-haired," as many West Indian people are. Rita Moreno has black hair and brown eyes.

Dennis **Morgan:** Stanley Morner (1910–), U.S. film actor.

Frank **Morgan:** Francis Phillip Wupperman (1890–1949), U.S. film actor.

Harry **Morgan:** Henry Bratsburg (1915–), U.S. film actor.

Helen **Morgan:** Helen Riggins (1900–1941), Can. film actress, singer.

Michèle **Morgan:** Simone Roussel (1920–), Fr. film actress.

Ralph **Morgan:** Ralph Wupperman (1882–1956), U.S. film actor, brother of Frank Morgan *(q.v.)*.

Iolo **Morgannwg:** Edward Williams (1746–1826), Welsh poet, antiquary. The poet was born (and died) in Glamorganshire, the Welsh for which is Morgannwg, serving as his bardic name.

Patricia **Morison:** Eileen Morison (1915–), U.S. film actress.

Gaby **Morlay:** Blanche Fumoleau (1897–1964), Fr. film actress.

Karen **Morley:** Mildred Linton (1905–), U.S. film actress.

Mrs. **Morley:** Anne (1665–1714), queen of England. This is the name that Queen Anne used for her correspondence with the Duchess of Marlborough, who called herself Mrs. Freeman *(q.v.)*.

Clara **Morris:** Clara Morrison (1846–1925), U.S. stage actress.

Jan **Morris:** James Humphrey Morris (1926–), Br. journalist, travel writer. The distinguished author underwent a sex-change operation in 1972, having long felt the "victim of a genetic mix-up," and consequently arranged a name change. The experience of the operation and its effects are described in *Conundrum* (1974), where the writer comments: "My new name, though just right for me, I thought, was sometimes itself confusing. 'I thought Jan Morris was a man,' said a jolly Australian at a *Spectator* lunch one day. 'What happened, d'you change your sex or something?' Just that, I replied."

Boris **Morros:** Boris Mikhailovitch (1891–1963), Russ.-born U.S. film producer.

Buddy **Morrow:** Muni "Moe" Zudekoff (1919–), U.S. trombonist.

Jelly Roll **Morton:** Ferdinand Joseph La Menthe Morton (1885–1941), U.S. jazz composer, pianist. The musician's original surname was La Menthe, to which he added Morton, the name of the porter who married his mother after her husband left her. "Jelly Roll" is a nickname (not exclusive to Morton) that implies sexual prowess. In its everyday sense, a jelly roll is a cylindrical cake containing jelly or jam. As with many sweetmeats (such as "crumpet" and "cupcake") the term acquired a more or less specific sexual connotation.

Maurice **Moscovitch:** Morris Maascoff (1871–1940), Russ.-born U.S. film actor, father of Noël Madison *(q.v.).*

Mickie **Most:** Michael Hayes (1938–   ), Eng. record company director, promoter. The record producer first used the name in 1958 for a double act, the Most Brothers, with his friend Alex Murray. The name does, of course, also suggest "Mickey Mouse," and doubtless arose via this when used as a nickname.

Zero **Mostel:** Samuel Joel Mostel (1915–1977), U.S. stage, film actor. The actor adopted his school nickname, given him for his repeated zero marks.

Mounet-Sully: Jean Sully Mounet (1841–1916), Fr. actor.

[Lord] Louis **Mountbatten:** [Prince] Louis Francis Albert Victor Nicholas of Battenberg (1900–1979), Eng. soldier, statesman. Queen Victoria's grandson adopted the English version (part-translation) of "Battenberg" in 1917, when his father, Louis Alexander Mountbatten, relinquished the title at the request of George V. Other members of his branch of German counts living in England did likewise.

Movita: Movita Castenada (1915–   ), Mexican film actress.

George **Mozart:** David Gillins (1864–1947), Eng. music hall comedian, musician.

Leonard **Mudie:** Leonard Mudie Cheetham (1884–1965), Br. film actor, working in U.S.

Elijah **Muhammad:** Elijah (or Robert) Poole (1897–1975), U.S. Black Muslim leader. The meeting of Elijah (or Robert) Poole with Walli Farrad *(q.v.)* started him on a career which took him to the top of the Black Muslim movement. It was he who converted, and named, both Malcolm X and Muhammad Ali *(qq.v.).* His own change of name to that of the founder of Islam is self-evident.

Jean **Muir:** Jean Muir Fullerton (1911–   ), U.S. film actress.

Maria **Muldaur:** Maria Grazia Rosa Domenica d'Amato (1943–   ), U.S. pop singer. The singer's professional name is actually her married name, after Geoff Muldaur, whom she married in the mid–1960s and divorced in 1972. The two worked together, although Maria's solo career has been much more successful.

Multatuli: Eduard Douwes Dekker (1820–1887), Du. novelist. The writer's pen name derives from Latin *multa tuli,* "I have borne many things," referring to his intolerant and impatient nature when expressing his views on many aspects of society that concerned him from the role of women to the morality of roulette. His main work was *Ideeën* ("Ideas") (1862–1877).

Claude **Muncaster:** Grahame Hall (1903–1974), Eng. landscape, marine painter. The painter changed his name to avoid being confused with his father, Oliver Hall, who was also an artist.

Baron **Münchhausen:** Rudolfe Erich Raspe (1737–1794), Ger. scientist, antiquary, writer. The author of the well-known *Marvellous Travels and Campaigns in Russia* (1785), based his fantastic stories on the tales of a real Baron Münchhausen, who had written highly colored accounts of his adventures in the Russian war against the Turks and whose given name was Karl Friedrich Hieronymus von Münchhausen (1720–1797).

Talbot **Mundy:** William Lancaster Gribbon (1879–1940), Eng.-born U.S. writer of adventure novels, historical fantasies.

Paul **Muni:** Frederich Meyer Weisenfreund (1895–1967), U.S. stage, film actor, of Jewish Austr.-Hung. parentage. "Muni" seems to have been the actor's pet name, possibly based on his middle name.

Ona **Munson:** Ona Wolcott (1906–1955), U.S. film actress.

Murad Efendi: Franz von Werner (1836–1881), Austr. poet. The poet was long in the Turkish diplomatic service, and adopted a pen name that reflected this: "Murad" was the name of several Turkish sultans, and "Efendi" (or "Effendi") was a title of respect. He may have deliberately based the name in particular on that of Murad Bey, the Egyptian Mameluke chief who fought with the French against the Turks and who died in 1801.

Friedrich Wilhelm (or F.W.) **Murnau:** Friedrich Wilhelm Plumpe (1889–1931), Ger. film director, working in U.S. The director took his name from the West German town of Murnau, where he lived for some time (but not where he was born, which was Bielefeld).

Dennis Jasper **Murphy:** [Rev.] Charles Robert Maturin (1782–1824), Ir. playwright, novelist. The writer adopted the pseudonym when working as an impoverished curate in Dublin, first using the name for three romances published between 1807 and 1812.

Arthur **Murray:** Arthur Murray Teichman (1895–   ), U.S. TV dancing instructor (of the slogan "Arthur Murray taught me in a hurry").

Braham **Murray:** Braham Goldstein (1943–   ), Eng. stage director.

Brian **Murray:** Brian Bell (1937–   ), S.A. stage actor, working in U.K. The actor adopted his mother's maiden name as his stage name.

Hon. Mrs. **Murray:** Sarah Aust (1741–1811), Eng. topographical writer. The writer's pen name was effectively her real name, for her first husband was the Hon. William Murray. But after his death, in 1786, she married George Aust, and most of her writing was done subsequently. The full title under which she wrote was "The Hon. Mrs. Murray, of Kensington," a name almost as lengthy as that of her best-known work, *A Companion and Useful Guide to the Beauties of Scotland, to the Lakes of Westmoreland, Cumberland, and Lancashire, and to the Curiosities in the District of Craven, in the West Riding of Yorkshire; to which is added a more particular description of Scotland, especially that part of it called the Highlands* (1799).

Ken **Murray:** Don Court (1903–   ), U.S. film comedian, radio, TV entertainer.

Mae **Murray:** Marie Adrienne Koenig (1885–1965), U.S. film actress.

Sinclair **Murray:** Edward Alan Sullivan (1868–1947), Can. novelist.

Musidora: Jeanne Roques (1889–1957), Fr. music hall singer, dancer, film actress. The actress, famous for her "vamp in black" image, took her professional name, at the start of her stage career (1910), from the heroine of Théophile Gautier's novel *Fortunio* (1836), an "Arabian Nights"-like tale set in Paris. The name is found in earlier literature, such as the Musidora who loves Damon in James Thomson's poem *The Seasons* ("Summer," 1727), and it probably means "gift of the Muses," suitably enough for the talented actress.

Ornella **Muti:** Francesca Romane Rivelli (1956–   ), It. film actress.

Eadweard **Muybridge:** Edward James Muggeridge (1830–1904), Eng.-born U.S. photographer, moving picture pioneer. The noted inventor, who photographed people and animals in motion, was born in Kingston-on-Thames, Surrey, and grew up with a keen interest in local history, as many Saxon kings were said to have been crowned in his birthtown (as its name implies). His interest came to a head in 1850, when a special commemorative "coronation" stone was set up in the Market Place. On the plinth were carved the names of the kings who, it was believed, had been crowned in Kingston, among them Eadweard the Elder (crowned 900) and Eadweard the Martyr (975), their names spelled the Saxon way. "This spelling seemed a lot more romantic than plain Edward so the young man decided to adopt the Saxon version and for good measure changed his East-Anglian surname of Muggeridge [. . .] to Muybridge. The only reason for this change of name seems to have been sheer romanticism" [Kevin MacDonnell, *Eadweard Muybridge: The Man Who Invented the Moving Picture*, 1972]. (In point of fact the name of Kingston-upon-Thames does not mean "king's stone" but simply "royal estate," and there is no evidence that kings were crowned there. But this mundanity does not invalidate the origin of Muybridge's name. Come to that, his mutated surname is equally suspect, for Muggeridge is a south of England name, meaning "[person] from [a place called] Mogridge," such as the one in Devon, a county full of Mogridges and Muggeridges.)

Harriet **Myrtle:** Lydia Falconer Miller, née Fraser (1811–1876), Sc. children's writer. The writer seems to have derived her pen name rather fancifully from that of her husband, Hugh Miller, although it was also used by Mary Gillies for *More Fun for Our Little Friends* (1864).

Marmaduke **Myrtle:** [Sir] Richard Steele (1672–1729), Br. essayist, dramatist. The well-known writer used this name for his editorship of the magazine *The Lover* (1714), a paper similar to the better-known *Spectator*.

Minnie **Myrtle:** Anna Cummings Johnson (1818–1892), U.S. writer.

Nadar: Félix Tournachon (1820–1910), Fr. photographer, illustrator, writer. The following account has appeared of the writer's pen name: "He had also found his name: from Tournachon to Tournadard, an obscure epistemological gallic joke, referring either to his satirical *sting*, or else to the tongue of *flame* (also *dard*) above his brow; and thence to the more economical, and generally more marketable, Nadar. This signature now began to appear below little matchstick drawings, and at the age of 27, Nadar published a first caricature on the inside page of *Charivari . . .*" [*The Times*, October 12, 1974].

Anne **Nagel:** Ann Dolan (1912–1966), U.S. film actress.

Laurence **Naismith:** Lawrence Johnson (1908–   ), Eng. stage, film actor.

Nita **Naldi:** Anita Donna Dooley (1899–1961), U.S. film actress.

Lewis Bernstein **Namier:** Ludwik Bernstein (1888–1960), Pol.-born Eng. historian. The historian's father was Joseph Bernstein, originally Niemirowski, and both his parents were polonized Jews who no longer adhered to the Jewish religion. Ludwik came to Britain as a young man, entering Oxford University in 1908. He took British nationality in 1913, and changed his name to Lewis Namier, a version of his father's original name, by deed poll.

Alan **Napier:** Alan Napier-Clavering (1903–   ), Br. film actor, working in U.S.

Diana **Napier:** Molly Ellis (1908–1982), Br. film actress.

Mark **Napier:** John Laffin (1922–   ), Austral. novelist, journalist.

Owen **Nares:** Owen Nares Ramsay (1888–1943), Br. film actor.

Datt **Nargis:** Fatima Rashid (1929–1981), Indian film actress ("Baby Rani" as child actress).

Petroleum Vesuvius **Nasby:** David Ross Locke (1833–1888), U.S. humorous journalist. The writer first used the fiery (and ridiculous) pseudonym when he became editor of the Findlay, Ohio, *Jeffersonian* in 1861. The origin of the surname is uncertain.

Daniel **Nash:** William Reginald Loader (1916–   ), Br. novelist.

Mary **Nash:** Mary Ryan (1885–1976), U.S. stage, film actress.

N. Richard **Nash:** Nathaniel Richard Nusbaum (1913–   ), U.S. dramatist.

Alcofribas **Nasier:** François Rabelais (1495–1553), Fr. satirist. The famous writer used this anagrammatic version of his real name for one of his best-known works, under the deliberately impressive title of *Pantagruel. Les horribles et espoventables faictz et prouesses du très renommé Pantagruel, roy des Dipsodes, filz du grant géant Gargantua, composez nouvellement par Maistre Alcofrybas Nasier* (1532). He also used the name, with an equally grand title, for *Gargantua* (1534), the story of Pantagruel's father, now usually read first. After that, he used his real name for the third and fourth books (respectively 1546 and 1548), continuing the story, as well as for the posthumous fifth book (1562), which may not actually be by Rabelais.

Marie-José **Nat:** Marie-José Benhalassa (1940–   ), Fr. film actress.

Nathalie **Nattier:** Nathalie Belaieff (–   ), Fr. film actress, of Russ. parentage. The actress disposed of her Russian surname by substituting a name based on her real first name, giving it a typical French name-ending. (Nattier is also a surname in its own right.)

John-Antoine **Nau:** Antoine Torquet (1860–1918), U.S.-born Fr. poet and novelist. The writer spent some years "before the mast," and took a surname that means "boat" in origin. (It is a form of French *nef,* related to the Greek root that gave English "nautical.") Compare the next name below.

Nauticus: [1] [Sir] William Laird Clowes (1856–1905), Eng. naval writer, historian; [2] [Sir] Owen Seaman (1861–1936), Eng. editor, humorist. The name is perfectly appropriate for both men, academically for the first, and humorously (of course) for the second.

André **Navarre:** Alexander Wright (? –1940), Austral. music hall impressionist.

Eliot **Naylor:** Pamela Frankau (1908–1967), Br. novelist, short story writer, working in U.S. (from 1942).

Amedeo **Nazzari:** Salvatore Amedeo Buffa (1907–1979), It. film actor.

[Dame] Anna **Neagle:** [Dame] Marjorie Wilcox, née Robertson (1904–1986), Eng. stage, film actress. The actress tells how her change of name came about in her autobiography. When she was beginning to become established in the theatre, after appearing as a chorus girl in Charles Cochran's shows, her manager commented one day: "'I think your name "Marjorie Robertson" has been too much publicized as a "Cochran Young Lady." Now you are turning to serious acting, you must change it.' I stared at him. In my childhood, when I had daydreamed of a stage career, I'd invented the most incredible professional names; but now I'd spent five years putting my real name on to playbills and programs and didn't much like the idea of wasting all that publicity. [. . .] 'It's rather a long name, too,' Mr. Williams went tentatively. His eyes twinkled. 'Think how many electric light-bulbs it would need outside a theatre!' [. . .] I began to see his point. [. . .] If I'd remained 'Marjorie Robertson, Chorus Girl' much longer I would have been type-cast for life. [. . .] 'My mother's name was Neagle . . . ?' 'Nagle?' 'No—Neagle,' I protested. 'Don't worry—they'll call it Nagle,' he said. 'What about Anna Neagle?' I suggested. 'Oh, fine. That's just fine. Anna Neagle? That's it.' And so Marjorie Robertson, successful chorus girl, was quietly, and a little sadly, disposed of in a teashop on the corner of Wardour and Old Compton Streets, on August 21st, 1930. And Anna Neagle, embryo actress and star, was born" [Anna Neagle, *There's Always Tomorrow: An Autobiography*, 1974].

Hilary **Neal:** Olive Marion Norton (1913–   ), Br. children's novelist.

Neera: Anna Radius Zuccari (1846–1919), It. novelist, poet. The writer's pen name seems to represent her first two names, or elements of them.

Hildegarde **Neff:** Hildegarde Knef (1925–   ), Ger. film actress.

Pola **Negri:** Barbara Apollonia Chalupiec (?1894–1987), Pol.-born U.S. film actress. "Pola" from her middle name, and "Negri" allegedly from her black hair.

Thomas **Neill:** Thomas Neill Cream (1850–1892), Sc. physician, murderer. The murderer poisoned his (exclusively female) victims with strychnine, and used the name Thomas Neill, as a doctor, when obtaining the drug from the chemist's shop.

Donald **Neilson:** Donald Nappey (1936–   ), Eng. murderer. The murderer adopted his name from an ice cream van, mainly as he had never liked his original name but also to avoid any future embarrassment for his daughter. (In England, babies' diapers are called nappies.)

Lilian Adelaide **Neilson:** Elizabeth Ann Brown (1846–1880), Br. actress. The actress was the daughter of a woman who at first had the surname Brown but who was later known as Mrs. Bland. Her father's name is not known. On working as a nurse as a young woman, she learned of the somewhat dubious circumstances of her birth, and decided to make her way from the north of England, where she was employed, to London. For the purposes of this she assumed the name Lizzie Ann Bland. She began her stage career (although not in London) in 1865, and soon after this felt confident enough to bloom forth from Lizzie Ann Bland to "Lilian Adelaide Lessont," subsequently changing this last name to "Neilson." She kept the name for her stage appearances, not using her married name (Lee).

Perlita **Neilson:** Margaret Sowden (1933–   ), Eng. stage actress.

Barry **Nelson:** Robert Neilson (1920–   ), U.S. stage, film actor.

Gene **Nelson:** Leander Berg (1920–   ), U.S. stage, film actor, dancer.

Nemo: Phiz *(q.v.)*.

Nadia **Nerina:** Nadine Judd (1927–   ), S.A. ballet dancer, of Russ. parentage. The dancer took her second name from the South African scarlet flower called the Nerine (pronounced "ne-rye-nee"), which grew around Cape Town, where she was born. Her first name, Nadia, is a variant of her real name, with both of these pet forms of her Russian mother's first name, Nadezhda.

Nero: Lucius Domitius Ahenobarbus (37–68), Roman emperor. When the future emperor was only 13, his mother married her uncle, Tiberius Claudius

Drusus Nero Germanicus, otherwise the Emperor Claudius, who adopted the boy and renamed him as Nero Claudius Caesar Drusus Germanicus. Nero was thus a Roman cognomen (surname), not meaning "black," as one might expect, but "strong," "warlike," (i.e. a man of *nerve*).

Franco **Nero:** Francesco Spartanero (1941–   ), It. film actor.

Peter **Nero:** Peter Bernard Nierow (1934–   ), U.S. popular pianist.

Pablo **Neruda:** Neftalí Ricardo Reyes (1904–1973), Chilean poet. The poet adopted a pen name in 1920 so as not to embarrass his father, a railway worker. He took the name from the nineteenth-century Czech writer Jan Neruda, whose story *By the Three Lilies* he had greatly admired. Neruda adopted the name legally in 1946.

Gerard de **Nerval:** Gerard Labrunie (1808–1855), Fr. romantic poet. The writer's second name appears to be a kind of inversion of his real name.

Jimmy **Nervo:** James Henry Holloway (1897–1975), Eng. stage comedian, teaming with Teddy Knox *(q.v.)*. The actor began his public career in the circus, as an artiste whose specialty was balancing and buffoonery – and thus falling and fractures. For such a way of life one needed "nerve." Hence his professional name.

Emma **Nevada:** Emma Wixom (1859–1940), U.S. opera singer. The operatic soprano was born in Austin, Nevada.

Aristarchus **Newlight:** Richard Whately (1786–1863), Eng. logician, theologian. The English theologian, who became Archbishop of Dublin, used this meaningful name to attack German neologism, that is, the German tendency to rationalistic views in religious matters. The name is of course ironic, and intended to ridicule. Aristarchus was a famous Greek critic of the second century B.C.

Ernest **Newman:** William Roberts (1868–1959), Eng. music critic. The critic, famous as an authority on Wagner, first used the pseudonym for his book *Gluck and the Opera* (1895). It was intended to be meaningful, and indicate his innovative approach, but it also seems to have been more generally representative of his attitude to life, as he adopted the name both in his private life and in his writings, although he never legally changed his name. It should be noted that *both* names are significant.

Julie **Newmar:** Julia Newmeyer (1930–   ), Swe. film actress, working in U.S.

Fred **Niblo:** Federico Nobile (1874–1948). U.S. film director, of It. parentage. A rather unconventional shortening of a standard name.

Nicholas II: Gérard (? –1061), Fr. pope.

Nicholas III: Giovanni Gaetano Orsini (*c.*1225–1280), It. pope.

Nicholas IV: Girolamo Masci (1227–1292), It. pope.

Nicholas V: Tommaso Parentucelli (1397–1455), It. pope.

Barbara **Nichols:** Barbara Nickerauer (1929–1976), U.S. film actress.

Mike **Nichols:** Michael Igor Peschkowsky (1931–   ), Ger.-born U.S. cabaret entertainer, film director.

Nico: Christa Paffgen (?1944–1988), Ger. model, pop singer, film actress. The singer took her name from one of her boyfriends, the film producer Nico Papadakis. She came to prominence through her association with Andy Warhol *(q.v.)*.

Nicolino: Nicolò Grimaldi (1673–1732), It. male contralto singer. The singer's adapted name implies "little Nicolò."

Maire **Nic Shiubhlaigh:** Maire Price, née Marie Walker (? –1958), Ir. stage actress. "Nic" in Irish names means "daughter," corresponding to the common "Mac" ("son"). The main name adopted by the actress looks like a genuine Irish name, or an attempt to recreate a family surname. Presumably this comes from her father.

Flora **Nielsen:** Sybil Crawley (1900–1976), Can. opera singer, teacher.

Edouard de **Nieuport:** Edouard de Niéport (1875–1911), Fr. pilot, aircraft designer.

Shmuel **Niger:** Shmuel Charmi (1884–), Russ.-born Jewish literary critic, essayist, working in U.S.

Nikodim: Boris Georgievich Rotov (1929–1978), Russ. Orthodox churchman. The metropolitan of Leningrad may have deliberately chosen a meaningful religious name, as Nikodim (Nicodemus) means "victorious people." But equally he may simply have taken the name of the biblical character. Nikodim is a fairly common Russian first name in its own right. Compare the next name below.

Nikon: Nikita Minov (1605–1681), Russ. Orthodox churchman. The patriarch of Moscow and All Russia seems to have based his religious name on his own personal name. At the same time, it would have been regarded as meaningful, from the Greek word for "victory" or "conquer." Compare the name above, also Greek in origin.

Harry **Nilsson:** Harry Edward Nelson III (1941–), U.S. pop musician.

Nimrod: Charles James Apperley (1777–1843), Eng. sporting writer. The writer semi-punningly adopted the name of the biblical Nimrod, "the mighty hunter" (Genesis 19:9). Did he also intend a name with another sporting connotation, "nim rod"? ("Nim" is an old English word meaning "take," still current in slang use to mean "steal." This interpretation certainly suits the Englishman's third major sport of angling, the three themselves being traditionally "huntin', shootin', and fishin'.")

Nina: Ethel Florence Nelson (1923–), Can. travel writer. Presumably "Nina" reflects the writer's surname. It certainly has more potential panache than "Ethel."

Sir Nicholas **Nipclose,** Bart: David Garrick (1717–1779), Eng. actor, dramatist. The famous actor used this frivolous name for some of his farces and stage adaptations.

Red **Nirt:** Tommy Trinder (1909–1989), Eng. stage, radio comedian. The actor used this comic reversal of his name early in his career, after which he appeared under his own name. On one occasion, when opening a cabaret at the Embassy Club, London, he introduced himself to the actor Orson Welles with the words, "Trinder's the name!" "Well, why don't you change it?" replied Welles. ("Is that a proposal of marriage?" quipped Trinder.)

Greta **Nissen:** Grethe Rutz-Nissen (1906–), Norw. film actress, working in U.S.

David **Niven:** James David Nevins (1909–1983), Sc.-born Br. film actor.

Kwame **Nkrumah:** Francis Nwia Kofi (1909–1972), Ghanaian political leader.

Nobody: William Stevens (1732–1807), Eng. biographer. This, the ultimate in anonymous names, was originally used by the writer in its Hebrew equivalent form of "Ain," as the author of one of his many religious publications, in this case a tract entitled *Review of the Review of a New Preface to the Second Edition of Mr. Jones's Life of Bishop Horne* (1800). The name in turn suggested his pseudonym for collection of his pamphlets published in 1805, *Oudenos erga, Nobody's Works* (the first two words of this in Greek). At about the same time, a club was founded in Stevens's honor entitled the "Society of Nobody's Friends." The name itself is of classical vintage, and occurs in Homer's *Odyssey*, where Odysseus, asked his name by the Cyclops, replies, "My name is Nobody. That is what I am called by my mother and father and by all my friends." (The Cyclops quips, "Of all his company, I will eat Nobody last, and the rest before him.") There are endless possibilities for using the name to disguise or mask a person as Nobody, when that person is, after all, somebody.

Marie **Noël:** Marie Rouget (1883–1967), Fr. writer of religious verse.

Noël-Noël: Lucien Noël (1897–   ), Fr. film comedian.

Victor **Noir:** Yvan Salmon (1848–1870), Fr. journalist.

Mary **Nolan:** Mary Imogen Robertson (1905–1948), U.S. film actress.

Emile **Nolde:** Emil Hansen (1867–1956), Ger. Expressionist painter. The painter adopted the name of his birthplace, the village of Nolde, in what is now North Schleswig (Nord Slesvig), southern Denmark.

Nomad: Norman Ellison (1893–1976), Eng. naturalist, writer, broadcaster. While being purely descriptive of the naturalist's roaming activity, the name at the same time reflects the writer's first name.

Ed **Noon:** Michael Angelo Avallone, Jr. (1924–   ), U.S. thriller, horror story writer.

Jeremiah **Noon:** John Calvin (1828–1871), Br. boxer. The boxer based his name on that of Anthony Noon, who had been killed in a fight against Owen Swift in 1834.

T.R. **Noon:** Olive Marion Norton (1913–   ), Br. children's novelist. An anagram of the writer's surname gives the required genderless pen name that many children's writers favor.

Tommy **Noonan:** Thomas Patrick Noon (1922–1968), U.S. film comedian, writer.

Max Simon **Nordau:** Max Simon Südfeld (1849–1923), Hung.-Ger. physician, author. The name shows a swing of polarity, with the writer's original surname meaning literally "southern field," and his pen name meaning "northern meadow." Südfeld made two radical changes in his life: he emigrated from Budapest to Paris and switched from medicine to literature.

Charles **Norden:** Lawrence George Durrell (1912–   ), Br. novelist, poet. The well-known author adopted this pen name for his early novel *Panic Spring* (1937). This was actually his second novel, but as his first, *Pied Piper of Lovers* (1935), had been a failure, his publishers, Faber & Faber, suggested he adopt a pseudonym as a precautionary measure. Later, the huge success of *The Alexandria Quartet* (1957–1960) ensured that pseudonyms were a recourse of the past.

Christine **Norden:** Mary (Molly) Lydia Thornton (1924–1988), Br. film actress.

Lillian **Nordica:** Lillian Norton (1859–1914), U.S. opera singer. "Nordica" is certainly a more "operatic" name than the singer's real surname, on which it is based.

Norman **Norell:** Norman Levinson (1900–1972), U.S. fashion designer. The designer seems to have derived his new surname from the first syllables of his real two names.

Eidé **Norena:** Kaja Hansen (1884–1968), Norw. opera singer.

Norma Jean: Norma Jean Beasler (1938–   ), U.S. country singer.

Mabel **Norman:** Mabel Fortescue (1894–1930), U.S. film comedienne.

Normyx: George Norman Douglas (1868–1952), Sc. novelist + Elizabeth (Elsa) Theobaldina Douglas, née FitzGibbon, his wife. The two writers used this joint name for *Unprofessional Tales* (1901). Until about 1908, Douglas used the name "G. Norman Douglass" (following the spelling of his father's name) for all his writings, changing this to "Norman Douglas" thereafter. Elsa Douglas was also his cousin: Douglas married her in 1898 but divorced her six years later.

Chuck **Norris:** Carlos Ray (1939–   ), U.S. film actor.

Nedra **Norris:** Nedra Gullette (1914–   ), U.S. film actress.

Captain George **North:** Robert Louis Balfour Stevenson (1850–1894), Sc. essayist, novelist, poet. This was the name adopted by the famous writer for *Treasure Island* when the novel appeared serially in the magazine *Young Folks* (1881–1882). Stevenson used his real name a year later when the story was published in book form. As a Scot, Stevenson came from "North of the Border," and this may have suggested his pseudonym. On the other hand, he could have modeled it on the name of Christopher North *(q.v.)*.

Christopher **North:** John Wilson (1785–1854), Sc. literary critic. The writer used this name for his contribution to many of the dialogues that appeared in the *Noctes Ambrosianae*, published in *Blackwood's Magazine* from 1822 to 1835. "North" relates to the northern country of Scotland, which was the chief subject of the dialogues. (These take place in an inn called "Ambrose's Tavern," based on a real tavern in Edinburgh. Hence their title.)

Sheree **North:** Dawn Bethel (1933–   ), U.S. film actress.

André **Norton:** Alice Mary Norton (*c.*1910–   ), U.S. writer of SF and fantasy fiction for children.

Fleming **Norton:** Frederic Mills (1836–1895), Br. actor, entertainer.

Jack **Norton:** Mortimer Naughton (1889–1958), U.S. film actor.

Red **Norvo:** Kenneth Norville (1908–   ), U.S. jazz musician.

Max **Nosseck:** Alexander Norris (1902–1972), Pol. film director, actor, working in U.S.

Nostradamus: Michel de Nostre-Dame (1503–1566), Fr. astrologer, doctor.

Kim **Novak:** Marilyn Pauline Novak (1933–   ), U.S. film actress. The actress adopted a new first name that she felt went well with her surname. Among other names proposed for her, but mercifully rejected, were "Kavon Novak" (one name reversing the other), "Iris Green" (!), and "Windy City" (Chicago, where Novak was born).

Novalis: Friedrich Leopold von Hardenberg (1772–1801), Ger. romantic poet, novelist. The writer took his pseudonym from the traditional name of certain acres on his father's estate, implying virgin land (ultimately from Latin *novus*, "new"). The Hardenberg family had been known as "de Novali" as far back as the thirteenth century.

Novanglus: John Adams (1735–1828), U.S. statesman, second president of U.S. The name, obviously meaning "New England," was used by Adams for letters of his published in 1775 in the *Boston Gazette* rebutting letters by the Loyalist writer Daniel Leonard, otherwise Massachusettensis *(q.v.).*

Ramon **Novarro:** Jose Ramon Gil Samaniegos (1899–1968), Mexican film actor, working in U.S. The actor's name was given him by director Rex Ingram, who needing a replacement for Rudolph Valentino *(q.v.)*, who had left the company, cast Samaniegos as Rupert of Hentzau in his version of *The Prisoner of Zenda* (1922). The name suggests a new persona and new role in life, while possibly also hinting at Spanish *varón*, "man" (in the "macho" sense).

Ivor **Novello:** David Ivor Davies (1893–1951), Welsh stage actor-manager, dramatist, composer. How did the Welsh actor come to adopt his Italian name? Directly, he inherited it from his mother, Clara Novello Davies, née Davies, whose own Christian name had been given her by her father in admiration of the great singer Clara Anastasia Novello—to whom, incidentally, she was not related, as is sometimes stated, and who was also not her godmother. Clara Novello, otherwise Countess Gigliucci, sang the soprano part in Beethoven's *Missa Solemnis* when she was only 14 (1832), and was praised by Mendelssohn and Schumann. She was the daughter of Vincent Novello, an English organist and composer of sacred music, who himself in turn was the son of an Italian father and English mother. David Davies's pseudonym thus arrived by a somewhat devious route.

Owen **Nox:** Charles Barney Cory (1857–1921), U.S. ornithologist.

Nuitter: Charles-Louis-Etienne Truinet (1828–1899), Fr. playwright, librettist. A straightforward anagrammatic name.

Gary **Numan:** Gary Anthony James Webb (1958–   ), Eng. pop singer. A symbolic name, with a new-style (or nu-style) spelling.

Bill **Nye:** Edgar Wilson Nye (1850–1896), U.S. humorist, editor. The writer used his semi-pseudonymous name for the successful series of books beginning with *Bill Nye and Boomerang* (1881), the latter being the *Laramie Boomerang*, the local newspaper that he edited in Wyoming.

Jack **Oakie:** Lewis Delaney Offield (1898–1978), U.S. film comedian. The actor was born in Sedalia, Missouri, but later his family moved to Muskogee, Oklahoma, where his schoolfriends nicknamed him "Oakie." He added "Jack" to this to fix himself up with a suitable screen name.

Vivian **Oakland:** Vivian Anderson (1895–1958), U.S. film actress.

Annie **Oakley:** Phoebe Anne Oakley Moses (1860–1926), U.S. sharpshooter. The crack markswoman tried out the name "Annie Mozee" when still a girl, but later settled on this more conventional use of her two middle names.

Wheeler **Oakman:** Vivian Eichelberger (1890–1949), U.S. film actor. The actor indirectly translated part of his original name, as German *Eichel* means "acorn." Maybe he had the proverb in mind, "Every oak has been an acorn"?

Merle **Oberon:** Estelle Merle O'Brien Thompson (1911–1979), Eng. film actress.

The actress (born in Tasmania) came to the U.K. in 1928 as a dancer named Queenie O'Brien. In 1939 she married Alexander Korda *(q.v.)*, and he changed her middle names from Merle O'Brien to Merle Oberon. He had intended to change them to "Merle Auberon," but it turned out that there was a Bond Street hairdresser of this name and because of his protests "Auberon" was modified to "Oberon." Oberon is coincidentally a Shakespearean name, but unfortunately the wrong gender, as he is king of the fairies in *A Midsummer Night's Dream.*

Hugh **O'Brian:** Hugh Krampke (1925–   ), U.S. film, TV actor.

Dave **O'Brien:** David Barclay (1912–1969), U.S. film actor.

David **O'Brien:** David Herd (1930–   ), Eng. stage actor.

Flann **O'Brien:** Brian O'Nolan (1912–1966), Ir. novelist. This is the name used by the writer, better known as the columnist Myles na gCopaleen *(q.v.)*, for his first novel, *At Swim-Two-Birds* (1939), and for subsequent fiction. Flann is an old Irish Christian name.

Robert C. **O'Brien:** Robert Leslie Conly (1918–1973), U.S. writer.

Dermot **O'Byrne:** [Sir] Arnold Edward Trevor Bax (1883–1953), Br. composer, writer. The composer had early been attracted to Celtic culture and history, and he used this Irish-style name for three books of stories and sketches about Irish life, published in his early 30s.

Richard **O'Callaghan:** Richard Hayes (1945–   ), Br. TV actor. The actor is the son of the film and TV actress Patricia Hayes (1910–   ), and selected a name to express his individuality and to distinguish his own career and approach from his mother's. He has commented, "I've always had to do things my way, which is why I wanted a different name from hers. I didn't want people giving me jobs because I was her son" [*Sunday Times Magazine,* June 28, 1987].

Sean **O'Casey:** John Casey (1880–1964), Ir. dramatist. The dramatist first wrote, in 1918, under an Irish version of his name, Sean O'Cathasaigh. Later, when his plays were first produced at the Abbey Theatre, Dublin, in the early 1920s, he part-reverted to an anglicized form of this.

Jehu **O'Cataract:** John Neal (1793–1876), U.S. romantic novelist, poet. This pen name, a typical American literary whimsy of the nineteenth century, originally arose as a nickname, given the writer for his impetuosity. He first adopted it for two narrative poems published in 1818, *Battle of Niagara* and *Goldau, or the Maniac Harper.* His feverish, flamboyant writing and editing continued unabated until he was in his 80s.

Maria del **Occidente:** Maria Gowen Brooks (*c.*1794–1845), U.S. poet. The poet was dubbed "Maria of the West" by Southey, who held her writing in high esteem. She herself adopted this name in an italianized form. (She many have been "of the West" to Southey, but she actually came from an eastern state, Massachusetts.)

Billy **Ocean:** Leslie Sebastian Charles (1950–   ), Trinidad pop singer.

Frank **O'Connor:** Michael O'Donovan (1903–1966), Ir. short story writer. The writer adopted his mother's maiden name as his pen name.

Dawn **O'Day:** Dawn Paris (1918–   ), U.S. film actress. A transparent and somewhat twee punning name for the actress early in her career, as a child star. She later settled to the screen as "Anne Shirley."

Odetta: Odetta Holmes Felious Gorden (1930–　), U.S. folk singer.

Odette: Odette Brailly (1912–　), Fr. spy.

Mary **Odette:** Odette Goimbault (1901–　), Fr.-born Eng. film actress.

Cathy **O'Donnell:** Ann Steely (1923–1970), U.S. film actress.

Cornelius **O'Dowd:** Charles James Lever (1806–1872), Eng.-born Ir. novelist. This pseudonym (one of several) was used by the writer for his series of essays entitled *Cornelius O'Dowd upon Men, Women and Other Things in General,* published in *Blackwood's Magazine* in 1864.

Odysseus: [Sir] Charles Norton Edgcumbe Eliot (1862–1931), Br. diplomat, scholar. The diplomat, whose duties took him on travels and voyages to many parts of the world, used his significant pseudonym for *Turkey in Europe* (1901), an account of Macedonia and its different races under the old regime.

Talbot **O'Farrell:** William Parrot (1878–1952), Eng. music hall comedian.

Jacques **Offenbach:** Jakob Eberst (1819–1880), Ger.-born Fr. composer. The composer's father, Isaac Juda Eberst, a cantor at the Cologne Synagogue, had been born in Offenbach, and was known as "Der Offenbacher." When Jakob was 14, his family moved to France, and he himself adopted his father's nickname, modifying his own first name to its French equivalent.

Gavin **Ogilvy:** [Sir] James Matthew Barrie (1860–1937), Sc. novelist, dramatist. The well-known author of *Peter Pan* adopted this name, from his mother's maiden name, for *When a Man's Single, A Tale of Literary Life,* published serially in the *British Weekly* over the two years 1887–8.

George **O'Hanlon:** George Rice (1917–　), U.S. film actor.

Kevin **O'Hara:** Marten Cumberland (1892–1972), Br. thriller writer.

Mary **O'Hara:** Mary O'Hara Alsop (1885–1980), U.S. novelist.

Maureen **O'Hara:** Maureen Fitzsimmons (1920–　), Ir. film actress, working in U.S.

Dennis **O'Keefe:** Edward Vanes Flanagan (1908–1968), U.S. film, TV actor, of Ir. parentage.

Okito: Theodore Bamberg (1875–1963), U.S. magician, of Du. descent.

Pierre **Olaf:** Pierre-Olaf Trivier (1928–　), Fr. stage actor.

Warner **Oland:** Werner Ölund (1880–1938), Swe. film actor, working in U.S.

Sidney **Olcott:** John Sidney Alcott (1873–1949), Ir.-Can. film director, working in U.S. The slight spelling change was probably made to ensure the name's correct pronunciation.

Old Block: Alonzo Delano (?1802–1874), U.S. playwright, humorist. The humorist used this name, doubtless predictably, for *Penknife Sketches, or Chips of the Old Block* (1853).

An **Old Boy:** Thomas Hughes (1822–1896), Eng. author. This was the name under which the writer first published his famous novel of school life, *Tom Brown's Schooldays* (1857), which was semi-autobiographical, evoking the Rugby School he had himself attended.

Humphrey **Oldcastle:** [1] Henry St. John (1672–1751), Eng. magazine contributor; [2] Nicholas Amhurst (1697–1742), Eng. poet, politician. Henry St. John, Viscount Bolingbroke, contributed to *The Craftsman* under this pen name, as did the magazine's originator, Nicholas Amhurst (although he actually founded it as Caleb D'Anvers *[q.v.]*). There is still some doubt about the precise authorship of the articles attributed to Amhurst.

John **Oldcastle:** Wilfrid Meynell (1852–1948), Br. writer, poet. The writer used this pseudonym for *Journals and Journalism* (1880). The name is a punning reference to his birthplace, Newcastle-upon-Tyne.

Old Humphrey: George Mogridge (1787–1854), Eng. writer of moral and religious works for children and adults. Mogridge used more than one pseudonym, with the best known being Peter Parley *(q.v.)*. As "Old Humphrey" he wrote over 40 tracts or tales. He probably took this particular name from some literary character, although it is uncertain who it was. It may even have originated from an existing pseudonym, like the one below.

Jonathan **Oldstyle:** Washington Irving (1783–1859), U.S. essayist, short story writer, historian. This was an early pseudonym by the famous writer, who would later become (singly) Geoffrey Crayon and (jointly) Launcelot Langstaff *(qq.v.)*. He used it for the *Letters of Jonathan Oldstyle, Gent.*, a series of satires on New York society which he wrote for the New York *Morning Chronicle* over the two years 1802 and 1803.

Patrick Albert **O'Leary:** [Dr.] Albert-Marie Edmond Guérisse (1911–1989), Belg. army officer, serving with British Navy. The army officer adopted this name from a peacetime Canadian friend in 1940, when he became first officer of the "Q" ship HMS *Fidelity*, with the rank of lieutenant-commander in the British Royal Navy.

Ole Luk-Oie: [Sir] Ernest Dunlop Swinton (1868–1951), Br. soldier, writer. This unusual pseudonym—a Danish term meaning roughly "Olaf Shut-Eye"—was assumed by the British army officer and military history professor for his book of short stories *The Green Curve* (1909) and other writings. Swinton was the originator of the name "tank" for the original self-propelled armored gun-carrying tracked vehicles when these were disguised for security reasons as railway wagons carrying fuel (tankwagons) in the First World War. A lesser known pen name used by Swinton was Backsight-Forethought *(q.v.)*.

Oliver: William Oliver Swofford (1945–   ), U.S. folk-rock singer.

Edith **Oliver:** Edith Goldsmith (1913–   ), U.S. dramatic critic. Now, who was it wrote *She Stoops to Conquer?*

Edna May **Oliver:** Edna May Cox-Oliver, née Nutter (1883–1942), U.S. film actress.

George **Oliver:** George Oliver Onions (1873–1961), Eng. novelist. This was not the adoption of a pseudonym but a legal name change, made in 1918.

Jane **Oliver:** Helen Rees (1903–1970), Sc. novelist.

Stephen **Oliver:** Stephen John Walzig (*c.*1950–   ), U.S. juvenile TV actor.

Vic **Oliver:** Viktor Oliver von Samek (1898–1964), Austr.-born Br. comedian, musician.

Olivia: Dorothy Bussy, née Strachey (–1960), Br. writer, translator, working in France. The writer used this name for her novel *Olivia* ("by Olivia") (1949), a fictional autobiography of a girl in a French school, preceded by an outline of her earlier years. The account covers a year, involves a passionate affair, and ends in the narrator's suicide. The name Olivia has long been regarded as a romantic one, and even suggests "I love you" if spoken rapidly.

John **O'London:** Wilfred Whitten (? –1942), Br. editor, author, founder of *John O'London's Weekly.* Whitten founded the popular literary weekly in 1919, but it ceased publication in 1936.

Omar Khayyám: Ghiyāthuddīn Abulfath 'Omar bin Ibrāhīm al-Khayyāmi (?1048–1122), Persian poet, astronomer. The famous author of the *Rubáiyát* (which name means "Quatrains" in Arabic) has a name that literally means "Omar Tentmaker," the latter indicating his father's occupation. (The second half of his name, as given here, spells him out more fully as "Omar son of Ibrahim the Tentmaker." Omar was the name of an early caliph of the seventh century.)

Anny **Ondra:** Anny Sophie Ondráková (1903–1987), Ger.-Cz. film actress, working in U.K.

Philothée **O'Neddy:** Théophile Dondey (1811–1875), Fr. poet, short story writer, dramatic critic. To the author's literary accomplishments we might have added "anagrammatist." He was fortunate in having a classical-style first name that could be inverted like this, from "loved of God" (in the original Greek) to "loving God."

Sally **O'Neil:** Virginia Louise Noonan (1913–1968), U.S. film actress.

Egan **O'Neill:** Elizabeth Linington (1921–   ), U.S. mystery writer. There is no great mystery about the writer's pen name, formed from letters of her real name.

Maire **O'Neill:** Molly Allgood (1885–1952), Ir. film actress.

Colette **O'Niel:** [Lady] Constance Malleson, née Annesley (1886–1975), Ir. stage actress, writer. The actress's stage name appears to reflect her married name. Her husband was the English actor Miles Malleson (1888–1969), whom she divorced in 1923. On the other hand, "O'Niel" *may* represent her maiden name.

Marcel **Ophüls:** Marcel Oppenheimer (1927–   ), Ger. film director, son of Max Ophüls *(q.v.).*

Max **Ophüls:** Max Oppenheimer (1902–1957), Ger.-born Fr. film director.

Oliver **Optic:** William Taylor Adams (1822–1897), U.S. novelist, children's writer. The author, who wrote around 1000 short stories and over 100 novels, adopted a name that seems to have been randomly enjoyable. He used it particularly for *Oliver Optic's Magazine for Boys and Girls* (1867–1875).

Katherine **O'Regan:** Kathleen Melville (1904–   ), Ir. film actress.

Miles **O'Reilly:** Charles Graham Halpine (1829–1868), Ir. humorist, soldier, working in U.S. The writer used the name specifically for his humorous description of Civil War events, *The Life and Adventures . . . of Private Miles O'Reilly* (1864).

Max **O'Rell:** Leon Paul Blouet (1848–1903), Fr.-born Eng. humorous writer.

Orinda: Katherine Philips, née Fowler (1631–1664), Eng. poet, letter-writer. The poet adopted the name Orinda as her pseudonym, and this was used for her literary sobriquet, as the "Matchless Orinda." She moved in a society where it was the fashion to adopt a colorful and preferably classical-style name: her husband, James Philips, was "Antenor," and among other friends were "Silvander" (Sir Edward Dering) and "Palaemon" (Jeremy Taylor, the Irish bishop and theological writer). The name Orinda occurs in the writings of Philips' contemporary, the poet

Abraham Cowley, and he may have invented it on classical lines. (Possibly it is meant to suggest Latin *oranda*, "one fit to be entreated," just as the name Amanda means "one fit to be loved.")

Tony **Orlando:** Michael Cassivitis (1944–   ), U.S. pop singer.

Orwell: Walter Chalmers Smith (1824–1908), Sc. poet, preacher. The poet, who was a minister of the Free Church of Scotland, took his name from the parish of Orwell, Kinross-shire, to which he was appointed in 1853.

George **Orwell:** Eric Arthur Blair (1903–1950), Eng. novelist, satirist. The famous author of *Animal Farm, 1984,* and a number of other still popular novels, first used his pen name for *Down and Out in Paris and London* (1933). He felt that Eric was too "Norse" and Blair too Scottish – a more suitable English name was one composed of the name of the patron saint of England and that of the river in Suffolk on whose banks he had lived. He also said that he wished to avoid embarrassing his parents – although friends felt that perhaps he was really seeking to escape from his genteel middleclass background. Somewhat mixed motives, therefore, seem to have led to his decision on a new name. (Another authority claims that the specific choice of George Orwell was made by Victor Gollancz, his publisher.) Blair had also considered other names, among them P.S. Burton, Kenneth Miles, and H. Lewis Allways [Bernard Crick, *George Orwell: A Life,* 1980]. The writer Richard Mayne, reviewing a later book on Orwell, and noting that he had a sense of humor, commented, "I've sometimes wondered whether he concealed a pun in his pen name: jaw-jaw well" [*Times Literary Supplement,* November 26, 1982].

Ozzy **Osbourne:** John Michael Osbourne (1948–   ), Br. rock musician. The name almost certainly arose as a nickname.

Henry **Oscar:** Henry Wale (1891–1969), Br. stage actor, director.

Gilbert **O'Sullivan:** Raymond Edward O'Sullivan (1946–   ), Ir. pop musician. The musician originally intended to call himself simply "Gilbert," but his manager Gordon Mills, who also produced the name of Engelbert Humperdinck *(q.v.),* suggested he keep his surname, doubtless wanting to retain the association with Gilbert and Sullivan, the comic operetta writers.

Richard **Oswald:** Richard Ornstein (1881–1963), Ger. film director.

James **Otis:** James Otis Kaler (1848–1912), U.S. writer of stories for boys.

Johnny **Otis:** John Veliotes (1921–   ), U.S. rhythm and blues musician, of Gk. parentage.

Rudolf **Otreb:** Robert Fludd (1574–1634), Eng. Rosicrucian, philosopher, physician. A straightforward anagrammatic name, with a convincing first name, but a suspect surname.

Ouida: Marie Louise de la Ramée (1839–1908), Eng. novelist, of Anglo-Fr. parentage. The writer adopted her own childhood pronunciation of her name "Louise." By a curious coincidence, the pseudonym happens to combine the words for "yes" in French and Russian. (By another coincidence, one of the author's best-known works was the romantic novel *Under Two Flags.*)

Gérard **Oury:** Max-Gérard Tenenbaum (1919–   ), Fr. film actor, director.

Bill **Owen:** Bill Rowbotham (1916–   ), Eng. stage, film, TV comedian. Unusually, the actor adopted a new stage/screen name only late in his career.

Seena **Owen:** Signe Auen (1894–1966), U.S. film actress, of Dan. descent. A sensible simplification of a name that many would wonder how to pronounce.

Jesse **Owens:** John Cleveland Owens (1913–1980), U.S. black athlete. The athlete's first name was created from his first two initials.

Rochelle **Owens:** Rochelle Bass (1936–), U.S. dramatist.

Elsie **Oxenham:** Elsie Jeanette Dunkerley (? –1960), Br. writer of stories for girls, daughter of John Oxenham *(q.v.)*.

John **Oxenham:** William Arthur Dunkerley (1852–1941), Eng. poet, novelist.

Augustus **Pablo:** Horace Swaby (c.1953–), Jamaican reggae musician.

Pacificus: Alexander Hamilton (1757–1804), U.S. statesman, lawyer ("King of the Feds").

Philo **Pacificus:** Noah Worcester (1758–1837), U.S. clergyman, editor, pacifist. The mock-classical name means "peace-lover," and was used by Worcester for *A Solemn Review of the Custom of War* (1814) and other pacifist works.

Anita **Page:** Anita Pomares (1910–), U.S. film actress.

Annette **Page:** Annette Hynd, née Lees (1932–), Eng. ballet dancer. The dancer adopted her mother's maiden name as her stage name. Her husband is Ronald Hynd *(q.v.)*.

Emma **Page:** Honoria Tirbutt (c.1930–), Br. detective writer.

Gale **Page:** Sally Rutter (1911–1983), U.S. film actress.

Geneviève **Page:** Geneviève Bonjean (1931–), Fr. stage, film actress.

H.A. **Page:** Alexander Hay Japp (1837–1905), Sc. author, publisher. Crossword solvers will quickly spot the reversal of initials and surname (in a fashion) here.

Marco **Page:** Harry Kurnitz (1909–1968), U.S. playwright, novelist, filmwriter.

Patti **Page:** Clara Ann Fowler (1927–), U.S. pop singer. It is possible that the singer took her first name from the surname of Adelina Patti, the (Spanish-born) Italian operatic soprano who died in 1919. She was given her new surname by the Page Company, a dairy in Tulsa, Oklahoma, when she appeared in their radio commercials.

Debra **Paget:** Debralee Griffin (1933–), U.S. film actress.

Elaine **Paige:** Eilene Bickerstaff (1950–), Eng. singer, actress.

Janis **Paige:** Donna Mae Tjaden (1922–), U.S. film actress, singer. The actress took her new first name from the musical comedy star Elsie Janis *(q.v.)*, and her surname from a grandparent.

Robert **Paige:** John Arthur Page (1910–1987), U.S. film actor.

Jack **Palance:** Walter (earlier Vladimir) Jack Palanchik (1920–), U.S. film actor, of Russ. parentage.

Palinurus: Cyril Vernon Connolly (1903–1974), Br. literary critic, novelist. The writer used the name for *The Unquiet Grave* (1944), which he described as "a word-cycle in three or four rhythms: art, love, nature and religion." In classical mythology, Palinurus was the pilot of Aeneas's ship, in Virgil's *Aeneid*, famous for his fall from the ship to the sea. Connolly thought that Palinurus fell through the typically modern will to failure.

Andrea **Palladio:** Andrea di Pietro della Gondola (1508–1580), It. architect.

The artist was named by his patron and tutor, the humanist poet and scholar Count Gian Giorgio Trissino. It was an allusion to the mythological figure Pallas Athene and to a character in Trissino's own poem, "Italia liberata dai goti" ("Italy liberated from the Goths"). The name also aimed to indicate the hopes that Trissino had for his protégé.

Betsy **Palmer:** Patricia Brumek (1929–   ), U.S. film actress, TV panelist.

Gregg **Palmer:** Palmer Lee (1927–   ), U.S. film actor.

Lillie **Palmer:** Lillie Marie Peiser (1911–1986), Ger. film actress.

Luciana **Paluzzi:** Luciana Paoluzzi (1937–   ), It. film actress.

Pansy: Isabella Macdonald Alden (1841–1930), U.S. children's magazine editor. The writer, noted for her sentimental religious fiction, used the name that had been given her as a pet name in childhood. When she became an adult, she did not therefore entirely put away childish things.

Irene **Papas:** Irene Lelekou (1926–   ), Gk. film actress. The actress's screen name is that of her first husband, Alkis Papas.

Joseph **Papp:** Joseph Papirofsky (1921–   ), U.S. stage producer, director.

Paracelsus: Philippus Aureolus Theophrastus Bombast von Hohenheim (1493–1541), Swiss-Ger. physician, alchemist. The medical genius (and charlatan) regarded himself as superior to Celsus, the renowned first-century Roman physician. He was therefore "beyond Celsus," or "para-Celsus." But at the same time there may be a reference to his original surname (a placename), as both Latin *celsus* and German *hohen* mean "high," "lofty."

Harry **Parke:** Parkyakarkus (*q.v.*).

Cecil **Parker:** Cecil Schwabe (1897–1971), Br. film actor.

Dorothy **Parker:** Dorothy Rothschild (1893–1967), U.S. novelist, poet.

Jean **Parker:** Lois Mae Greene, originally Luise-Stephanie Zelinska (1912–   ), U.S. film actress.

Lew **Parker:** Austin Lewis Jacobs (1906–   ), U.S. stage actor.

Willard **Parker:** Worster van Epps (1912–   ), U.S. film actor.

Norman **Parkinson:** Ronald Smith (1913–   ), Eng. society photographer ("Parks"). The famous fashion photographer changed his name in 1934 when he progressed from being a mere photographer's assistant to become a flamboyant society portraitist. He took his new surname from his father, William James Parkinson Smith.

Parkyakarkus: Harry Einstein (1904–1958), U.S. radio comedian. At first, Harry Einstein worked as "Harry Parke." Later, he expanded and embroidered the latter surname to "Parkyakarkus." He reckoned this would be a name easily remembered and pronounced by Americans, who would recognize it as an invitation to take a seat—"park your carcass!"

Peter **Parley:** [1] Samuel Griswold Goodrich (1793–1860), U.S. bookseller, writer of moral tales for children; [2] George Mogridge (*see* **Old Humphrey**); [3] John Bennett (1865–1956), U.S. writer of books for boys; [4] William Martin (1801–1867), Eng. children's writer; [5] William Tegg (1816–1895], Eng. children's writer. A popular name for tellers of children's tales, as the name itself suggests. Samuel Goodrich was the first to use it, however, beginning with *The Tales* *of Peter Parley About America* (1827). It was then adopted by other writers on both sides of the Atlantic, which did not please its originator. But is not imitation the sincerest form of flattery?

Dita **Parlo:** Gerthe Kornstadt (1906–1972), Ger. film actress. Taken literally, the actress's name translates from Italian as "Fingers, I speak" (or "Toes, I speak"). Possibly this was the intended interpretation, referring to the eloquence of gestures made with the fingers?

Martine **Parmain:** Martine Hemmerdinger (1942–   ), Fr. ballet dancer. Although French *par main* happens to mean "by hand," appropriately enough for a ballet dancer, whose hands are as important as her feet, Martine Hemmerdinger was born in the village of Parmain, north of Paris, and took her name from there.

Gram **Parsons:** Cecil Ingram Connor (1946–1973), U.S. country rock musician. The musician's father died when Cecil Connor was only 13. His mother then married again, to Robert Parsons, who shortened his stepson's middle name to "Gram" and provided him with a new surname at the same time.

Louella **Parsons:** Louella Rose Oettinger (1884–1972), U.S. film columnist, actress.

Mrs. **Partington:** Benjamin Penhallow Shillaber (1814–1890), U.S. humorist. The humorist created this lady as a kind of Mrs. Malaprop for his *Life and Sayings of Mrs. Partington* (1854) and other books in which Mrs. Partington chats pleasantly yet ignorantly on a whole range of topics. There had been a real Mrs. Partington, it seems, who during a storm at Sidmouth, England (in 1824) had tried to brush back the sea with her mop. References to her abortive effort became legendary and metaphorical, so that the House of Lords had been compared to her in a speech (1831) attacking the body's opposition to the progress of reform. Shillaber admitted that he borrowed his own character from the English archetype. He originally used her in 1847 for a newspaper on which he was employed.

Paschal II: Ranierus (? –1118), It. pope.

Jules **Pascin:** Julius Pincas (1885–1930), Fr. painter. The painter adopted a more obviously French first name, then anagrammatized his surname likewise.

La **Pasionaria:** Dolores Ibárruri (1895–   ), Sp. Communist leader, writer. The politician first used the name, literally "Passion Flower," when writing articles for the socialist press in 1917. The name is not, of course, meant to suggest romantic passion, but a "fieriness" about social conditions and injustices. She herself was a miner's daughter.

Anthony **Pasquin:** John Williams (1761–1818), Eng. critic, satirist, working in U.S. The writer took the name from the statue called Pasquin in Rome. This was unearthed in 1501 as an incomplete Roman bust, and a habit became established of attaching satirical Latin verses to it on St. Mark's Day. From this practice came the term "pasquinade" to apply to any brief but anonymous satirical comment. (It is not certain how the statue acquired its name: one theory is that it was named after a local shopkeeper whose premises were near the site where it was discovered.)

Joe **Pass:** Joseph Anthony Passalaqua (1929–   ), U.S. guitarist.

George **Pastor:** Emily Morse Symonds (*c.*1870–1936), Br. "feminist" novelist, dramatist.

Tony **Pastor:** Antonio Pestritto (1907–1969), U.S. popular musician.

Wally **Patch:** Walter Vinnicombe (1888–1971), Eng. stage, film comedian.

Gail **Patrick:** Margaret Fitzpatrick (1911–1980), U.S. film actress, TV producer.

John **Patrick:** John Patrick Goggan (1905–   ), U.S. playwright, screenwriter.

Nigel **Patrick:** Nigel Dennis Wemyss (1913–1981), Eng. stage actor, director.

Ted **Pauker:** George Robert Acworth Conquest (1917–   ), Eng. poet, editor, writer on Russia. This is the standard pen name of the British editor and writer Robert Conquest. Its exact origin is not clear, although *Pauker* is German for "kettle-drummer," as well as having a slang meaning "school-teacher," "crammer." Conquest is also a poet, and as Ted Pauker had some of his verse included in *The New Oxford Book of Light Verse* (1978), edited by Kingsley Amis. Shortly before his collection of poems there appears in the book a selection of limericks by one Victor Gray. Gray is given the same birth year as Pauker (1917). A columnist on the *Sunday Times,* in an informal review of the book (June 4, 1978), pointed out that Conquest's full name is George Robert Acworth Conquest, and that if you take the initials of his first three names and precede the name of the unknown rhymster by them you get G.R.A. Victory, otherwise an anagram of Victor Gray, with a victory of course being a conquest! This sleuthwork can hardly have pleased the venerable Oxford University Press.

Paul: Ray Hildebrand (1940–   ), U.S. pop singer, teaming with Paula *(q.v.).*

[Saint] **Paul:** Saul (? –*c.*69), Christian theologian, missionary. When the Christian disciple and missionary was still a Jew he was known by the name of Saul. After his dramatic conversion he took the Roman name Paul, which he used for preference as a proud Roman citizen. (The actual changeover is alluded to in Acts 13, 9 – "Saul, also called Paul.") This was thus one of the earliest well known name changes in history. Why did the Jew Saul choose the name Paul specifically? In Hebrew "Saul" means "asked for"; in Latin "Paul" (Paulus) means "little," and as such was a standard Roman name. The meaning of the new name may perhaps have been significant in some way, but maybe the theologian chose the name simply because it was close in sound to his previous name. It certainly marked a transition: both from Jew to Christian, and to Paul's new role as leader when Barnabas, formerly the leader, handed it over to him.

Paul II: Pietro Barbo (1417–1471), It. pope. A Peter who became a Paul, as did Paul IV (below).

Paul III: Alessandro Farnese (1468–1549), It. pope.

Paul IV: Gian Pietro Carafa (1476–1559), It. pope.

Paul V: Camillo Borghese (1552–1621), It. pope.

Paul VI: Giovanni Battista Montini (1897–1978), It. pope.

Jean **Paul:** Jean Paul Friedrich Richter (1763–1825), Ger. humorist, prose writer.

John **Paul:** Charles Henry Webb (1834–1905), U.S. journalist, editor.

Les **Paul:** Lester Polfuss (1915–   ), U.S. guitarist.

Paula: Jill Jackson (1942–   ), U.S. pop singer, teaming with Paul *(q.v.).* Paul and Paula originally teamed up to sing for a radio station's charity drive in Texas in the early 1960s, becoming a popular attraction with their matching sweaters embroidered with the letter "P." Of course, "Jack and Jill" would have done just as well (considering the lady's name), but no doubt the singers would have regarded this as too juvenile, even too British.

Madame **Paulette:** Pauline de la Bruyère (1900–1984), Fr. hat designer.

Marisa **Pavan:** Marisa Pierangeli (1932–), It. film actress, sister of Pier Angeli *(q.v.)*.

Pax: Mary Cholmondeley (1859–1925), Br. novelist.

Katina **Paxinou:** Katina Constantopoulos (1900–1973), Gk. film actress.

Philip **Paxton:** Samuel Adams Hammett (1816–1865), U.S. humorist, writer of adventure stories.

Johnny **Paycheck:** Donald Lytle (1941–), U.S. country singer.

Minnie **Pearl:** Sarah Ophelia Colley Cannon (1912–), U.S. country singer.

Drew **Pearson:** Andrew Russell (1897–1969), U.S. political columnist.

John **Peel:** John Robert Parker Ravenscroft (1939–), Eng. radio DJ. There may be an implicit pun here. One thinks of the well-known literary John Peel, the huntsman in the Victorian song by John Woodcock Graves ("D'ye ken John Peel with his coat so gray? D'ye ken John Peel at the break of the day?"), and one has it in mind that a DJ is a disc *jockey* (often "at the break of the day," too). As the song continues: "D'ye ken John Peel when he's far far away with his hounds and his horn in the morning?" True, a jockey rides his horse in races rather than in hunts, but there is enough common ground to link the two and and to associate the horseman with the DJ.

Jan **Peerce:** Jacob Pincus Perlemuth (1904–1984), U.S. opera singer.

Baby **Peggy:** Peggy Montgomery (1917–), U.S. child film actress.

Pelé: Edson Arantes do Nascimento (1940–), Brazilian soccer player. The player claimed that he never knew the origin of his "game name," and that it has no meaning in any language known to him. He was apparently nicknamed thus from the age of seven. As he points out, it's easy to say – in many languages [Pelé and Robert L. Fish, *My Life and the Beautiful Game*, 1977]. (But Portuguese *pele* does have a meaning as the word for "skin," "animal hide." Could there be a connection, via the boy or the ball he booted around as a kid?).

A. **Pen,** Esq.: John Leech (1817–1864), Eng. caricaturist.

Pendragon: Henry Sampson (1841–1891), newspaper proprietor, editor, sporting writer. Pendragon was the title given to an ancient British or Welsh chief, and meant literally "head dragon," the "dragon" being the war standard. Possibly Sampson used the name with an implied pun on "dragon with a pen."

Joe **Penner:** Joe Pinter (1904–1941), Hung.-U.S. radio comedian, film actor.

Pennsylvania Farmer: John Dickinson (1732–1800), U.S. lawyer, political writer. The Philadelphia lawyer led the conservative group in the Pennsylvania legislature during the debates on proprietary government, and used the name for his *Letters from a Farmer in Pennsylvania* (1768), published in the *Pennsylvania Chronicle*. The letters criticized England's continuing assertion of its rights of taxation, saying that this was contrary to that country's own constitutional principles.

Hugh **Pentecost:** Judson Pentecost Philips (1903–), U.S. mystery writer.

Pip **Pepperpod:** Charles Warren Stoddard (1843–1909), U.S. traveller, author.

Philemon **Perch:** Richard Malcolm Johnson (1822–1909), U.S. humorous writer, educator.

Percival: Julian Ralph (1853–1903), U.S. journalist.

Edward **Percy:** Edward Percy Smith (1891–1968), Br. playwright, novelist.

Florence **Percy:** Elizabeth Allan, formerly Taylor, then Akers, née Chase (1832–1911), U.S. poet, literary editor. The author used the pseudonym for the one poem for which she is now remembered, "Rock me to sleep," first printed in the *Saturday Evening Post* in 1860. Because of the pseudonym, the authorship was disputed, but Mrs. Akers (as she then was) successfully defended her claim.

Giovanni Battista **Pergolesi:** Giovanni Battista Draghi (1710–1736), It. composer. The composer was born in the family home at Jesi. When the family moved from Jesi to Pergola, however, they became known as the "Pergolesi," meaning "of Pergola."

François **Perier:** François-Gabriel-Marie Pilu (or Pillu) (1919–   ), Fr. stage, film actor.

Eli **Perkins:** Melville de Lancey Landon (1839–1910), U.S. journalist, humorous lecturer.

Perley: Benjamin Perley Poore (1820–1897), U.S. journalist, author, biographer.

Barry **Perowne:** Philip Atkey (1908–1985), Eng. crime, adventure, mystery story writer. The author adopted his uncle's name as his pen name.

Gigi **Perreau:** Ghislaine Elizabeth Marie Therese Perreau-Saussine (1941–   ), U.S. film actress, of Fr. parentage.

Jacques **Perrin:** Jacques Simonet (1941–   ), Fr. film director, producer.

Edgar A. **Perry:** Edgar Allen Poe (1809–1849), U.S. poet, storywriter. This was the name under which the writer enlisted in the U.S. Army in 1827.

Saint-John **Perse:** Marie-René-Auguste-Alexis Léger (1887–1975), Fr. poet.

Il **Perugino:** Pietro di Cristoforo Vannucci (1446–1524), It. painter. The painter took his name from the Umbrian city of Perugia, near which he was born.

Il **Pesellino:** Francesco di Stefano (1422–1457), It. painter. The painter was raised by his grandfather, Giuliano il Pesello, who was also a painter, and worked as his assistant until the old man's death in 1446. His name comes from him, with the *-ino* suffix implying "little."

[Saint] **Peter:** Simon (or Simeon) (? –c.65), Christian leader, pope. St. Peter was the first of the disciples to be called by Jesus, and his "primacy" was affirmed at Caesarea Philippi when, as Simon, son of Jonah, he acknowledged Jesus as "The Christ, the Son of the living God." It was then that he was given his new name, with Jesus saying to him, "Thou art Peter, and upon this rock I will build my church" (Matthew 16:18). The name is a play on words, as in Greek *petros*, in Latin *petrus*, and in Aramaic (Christ's vernacular tongue) *képha* (rendered "Cephas") all mean "rock." The popularity of the name as a Christian name stems entirely from this origin.

Bernadette **Peters:** Bernadette Lazzara (1948–   ), U.S. stage actress, singer.

Elizabeth **Peters:** Barbara Mertz (1927–   ), U.S. mystery writer.

Ellis **Peters:** Edith Pargeter (1913–   ), Br. detective novelist.

Susan **Peters:** Suzanne Carnahan (1921–1952), U.S. film actress.

Olga **Petrova:** Muriel Harding (1886–1977), Eng. film actress, working in U.S.

Ludmila **Petrowa:** Ludmila Petrovna Nacheyeva (1942–), Russ. ballet dancer, teacher, working in Austria. The dancer dropped her surname for professional purposes, then modified her middle name (patronymic) to resemble a surname, with a westernized spelling ("w" for "v").

K.M. **Peyton:** Kathleen Wendy Peyton (1929–), Br. children's writer. There is more to this name than at first glance meets the eye. When the writer was only 15, she completed her first novel, *Sabre, the Horse from the Sea,* which was published four years later under her true maiden name of Kathleen Herald. By then she was studying at Manchester Art School, where she eloped with a fellow student, Michael Peyton. They began producing "potboiler" adventure stories together for a Boy Scout magazine, and these were published under the name of "K. and M. Peyton." Three of the stories were subsequently published in book form, and their publisher, Collins, did not want two authors' names on the title page, so they were stated to be by "K.M. Peyton."

Alazonomastix **Philalethes:** [Dr.] Henry More (1614–1687), Eng. philosopher. More used this mock-Greek name, meaning "impostor Philalethes," for an attack on the alchemical work *Anthroposophia Theomagica* by Eugenius Philalethes (see next entry below).

Eugenius **Philalethes:** Thomas Vaughan (1622–1666), Eng. alchemist. The mock-Greek name literally means "noble-born lover of forgetfulness," and was used by Vaughan for the majority of his works.

Phileleutharus Norfolciensis: [Dr.] Samuel Parr (1747–1825), Eng. pedagogue, classical scholar. Most of Dr. Parr's works were virtually unreadable even in his own day, let alone in ours. But this is just one of the typical, pompous, classical pseudonyms that he used, in this instance for a *Discourse on the Late Fast* (1781), in which the theme (or one of them) is the American Revolution. The name itself is part–Greek, part–Latin, and means "Norfolk freedom-lover." At the time of writing, Parr was a curate in Norwich. For a later work, published in 1809, he was "Philopatris Varvicensis," otherwise "Warwick country-lover."

Philenia: Sarah Wentworth Morton, née Apthorp (1759–1846), U.S. novelist, poet. Mrs. Morton used the full pen name "Philenia, a Lady of Boston" for *Ouâbi; or, The Virtues of Nature* (1790), an Indian tale in four cantos in celebration of the "noble savage," as well as other, similar works. The name Philenia is clearly based on the Greek root element *phil-*, meaning "fond of," "loving," with apparently an arbitrary ending.

François-André **Philidor:** François-André Danican (1727–1795), Fr. musical composer, chessplayer. Both François-André Danican and his father André Danican assumed their surname from the nickname, Philidor, given to an ancestor (Michael Danican, died about 1659) by Louis XIII as a compliment to his musical skill. The name itself means "gift of love" (compare Theodore, "gift of God").

Conrad **Philips:** Conrad Philip Havord (1930–), Eng. film, TV actor.

Esther **Phillips:** Esther May Jones (1935–1984), U.S. pop singer. The singer began her career in 1949 when, as "Little Esther," she won a talent contest in Los

Angeles. She later adopted her new, but hardly original surname from a gas-station hoarding.

Rog **Phillips:** Roger Phillips Graham (1909–1965), U.S. SF writer.

Philomela: Elizabeth Rowe, née Singer (1674–1737), Eng. writer, poet. Mrs. Rowe used this name for a collection of verse published in 1696, *Poems on Several Occasions, by Philomela.* The name is not exactly an original one, deriving from the Philomela of classical mythology, who was the daughter of Pandion, king of Athens. But at least it is appropriate enough for a poet, both because (in the story) Philomela was changed into a nightingale, which sings sweetly, and because it literally means "sweet song." And do not overlook the lady's maiden name!

Phiz: Hablot Knight Browne (1815–1882), illustrator of works by Dickens, Surtees. The artist originally used the name "Nemo" (Latin for "nobody") to illustrate some plates for Dickens's *Pickwick Papers.* Later, he chose a name designed to match Dickens's own pen name of Boz *(q.v.).* At the same time, "phiz" is (or was) a slang word meaning "face" ("physiognomy"), so is suitable in its own right for one who draws portraits and concentrates on facial expressions.

John **Phoenix:** George Horatio Derby (1823–1861), U.S. humorous writer, satirist.

Pat **Phoenix:** Patricia Pilkington (1923–1986), Ir.-born Br. TV actress. The actress who became familiar to millions as the blowzy Elsie Tanner in British television's longest-running soap opera, *Coronation Street,* originally acted under her own name, Pat Pilkington. (She was actually the illegitimate daughter of a man named Mansfield, who claimed to have been married to her mother for 16 years while remaining the husband of his first wife, whom he had never divorced. Later, Pat's mother married Richard Pilkington.) In 1955, the actress temporarily changed her name from Pilkington to Dean so as not to embarrass family and friends when she appeared in the lead role in the sex-crime play *A Girl Called Sadie* that year, at the same time dyeing her hair blonde to complete the physical disguise. She later fell on hard times, and even attempted suicide. But she felt that a change of name might change her fortune, and as she later recounted, "Pat Pilkington did, after all, officially die in London. I changed my name to Phoenix. I took the new name from the book I was reading, Marguerite Steen's *Phoenix Rising"* [*TV Times,* November 1–7, 1986]. And this did seem to help, for Pat began to get small parts in films and stage shows from then on, rising slowly but surely phoenix-like from her days of depression and hunger in her basement flat in London. And from 1960, when she first took the role of Elsie Tanner, Pat Phoenix and her name were assured a lasting place in the British TV popularity polls.

Phranc: Susan Gottlieb (*c.* 1960–   ), U.S. folksinger. The singer changed her name symbolically (in sense and spelling) when she came out as a lesbian at the age of 17, at the same time leaving home, dropping out of high school and cutting off her waist-length hair. For a time she was involved in punk rock, but later progressed to a gentler and more meaningful role as a folksinger, although retaining the name Phranc.

Duncan **Phyfe:** Duncan Fife (1768–1854), Sc. furniture designer, working in U.S.

Edith **Piaf:** Edith Giovanna Gassion (1915–1963), Fr. singer, entertainer. The popular singer was given her stage name in 1935 by her friend, the Paris nightclub owner Louis Leplée. After an audition one day, he asked her her name. When she told him (all three real names) he protested that a name like that was not a show-business name: "'The name is very important. What's your real name again?' 'Edith Gassion, but when I sing I call myself Huguette Elias.' He swept these names aside with a wave of his hand. [. . .] 'Well, *mon petit*, I've got a name for you — *la môme Piaf* [The Little Sparrow].' We weren't wild about *la môme Piaf*, it didn't sound very artistic. That evening, Edith asked [her half-sister], 'Do you like *la môme Piaf?*' 'Not much.' Then she started to think. 'You know, Momone, *la môme Piaf* doesn't sound all that bad. I think Piaf has style. It's cute, it's musical, it's gay, it's like spring, it's like us. That Leplée isn't so dumb after all.'" [Simone Berteaut, *Piaf*, translated by Ghislaine Boulanger, 1970]. Thus the small-statured, birdlike singer, with her peaked face and half-starved look, became the "little sparrow of Paris." (The author of the biography quoted here is the half-sister mentioned.)

Piano Red: William Lee Perryman (1911–1985), U.S. blues singer. See also Dr. Feelgood.

Slim **Pickens:** Louis Bert Lindley, Jr. (1919–1983), U.S. film actor. There must surely be a pun here on "slim pickings."

Jack **Pickford:** Jack Smith (1896–1933), Can. film actor, brother of Mary Pickford *(q.v.).*

Mary **Pickford:** Gladys Mary Smith (1893–1979), Can.-born U.S. film actress. Gladys Smith's name was changed by Broadway producer David Belasco, with the actress adopting a family name that was more distinctive than plain "Smith."

Peregrine **Pickle:** George Putnam Upton (1834–1919), U.S. journalist, music critic. The writer adopted the name of the eponymous hero of Smollett's *Adventures of Peregrine Pickle.*

Pictor Ignotus: William Blake (1757–1827), Eng. artist, poet, mystic. The name is Latin for "Painter Unknown," used on paintings that cannot be confidently attributed to a particular artist. Blake used it occasionally, just as the Anglo-American etcher Joseph Pennell (1857–1926) later used the initials "A.U." ("Artist Unknown").

Piero di Cosimo: Piero di Lorenzo (1462–1521), It. painter. The artist took his name from his master, Cosimo Rosselli, whom he assisted in work on certain frescos in the Sistine Chapel (1481).

[Abbé] **Pierre:** Henri Antoine Grouès (1912–   ), Fr. priest, Resistance fighter.

Pigpen: Ronald McKernan (1946–1973), U.S. rock musician. The name arose as a nickname, alluding to the singer's gross and untidy habits.

Martin **Pike:** David Herbert Parry (1868–1950), Eng. writer of boys' stories, military articles.

Robert L. **Pike:** Robert L. Fish (1912–1981), U.S. mystery writer.

Nova **Pilbeam:** Margery Pilbeam (1919–   ), Br. film actress. The actress had the same first name as her mother, so changed it to Nova, for her mother's family associations with Nova Scotia. It is also, of course, a "new" name in the best sense.

David **Pilgrim:** John Leslie Palmer (1895–1944), Br. thriller writer + Hilary Aidan St. George Saunders (1895–1951), Br. thriller writer. It should not go unnoted that a "palmer" is an old word for a pilgrim (who has been to the Holy Land and returns bearing a palm branch). The two men also wrote jointly as Francis Beeding *(q.v.).*

Paul **Pindar:** John Yonge Akerman (1806–1873), Eng. antiquary, numismatist. The scholar presumably adopted a pen name based on that of Peter Pindar *(q.v.).*

Peter **Pindar:** [1] John Wolcot (1738–1819), Eng. satirical verse writer; [2] C.F. Lawler (1728–1819), Eng. writer. The name was adopted by more than one writer, but notably by John Wolcot. Pindar was a Greek lyric poet of the fourth century B.C., and in his first book, *Lyric Odes to the Royal Academicians for 1782,* Wolcot described himself as "a distant relation to the poet of Thebes." Most of the other Peter Pindars were imitators of Wolcot, some very palely so.

Theodore **Pine:** Emil Pataja (1915–   ), U.S. SF writer.

[Sir] Arthur Wing **Pinero:** Arthur Wing Pinheiro (1855–1934), Br. dramatist, stage actor, of Jewish-Port. descent.

Harold **Pinter:** Harold da Pinta (1930–   ), Br. dramatist, stage actor.

Pinturicchio: Bernardino di Betti di Biago (1454–1513), It. painter. The artist's name arose as a nickname, meaning "little painter," referring to his small stature.

Jeems **Pipes of Pipesville:** Stephen G. Massett (1820–1898), U.S. author.

Marie-France **Pisier:** Claudia Chauchat (1944–   ), Fr. film actress.

Ingrid **Pitt:** Ingoushka Petrova (1944–   ), Pol. film actress, of Russ. parentage, working in U.K.

Augustus Henry **Pitt-Rivers:** Augustus Henry Lane Fox (1827–1900), Eng. soldier, archaeologist. The soldier and scholar was known by his father's name of Fox until 1880, when he eventually inherited the estates of his great-uncle, George Pitt, 2nd Baron Rivers, and assumed his name.

Pius II: Enea Silvio Piccolomini (or Aeneas Silvius) (1405–1464), It. pope.

Pius III: Francesco Todeschini Piccolomini (1439–1503), It. pope, nephew of Pius II *(q.v.).*

Pius IV: Giovanni Angelo de' Medici (1499–1565), It. pope.

[Saint] **Pius V:** Antonio Michele Ghislieri (1504–1572), It. pope.

Pius VI: Giovanni Angelo Braschi (1717–1799), It. pope.

Pius VII: Gregorio Luigi Barnaba Chiaramonti (1742–1823), It. pope.

Pius VIII: Francesco Saverio Castiglioni (1761–1830), It. pope.

Pius IX: Giovanni Maria Mastai-Ferretti (1792–1878), It. pope.

Pius X: Giuseppe Melchiorre Sarto (1835–1914), It. pope.

Pius XI: Ambrogio Damiano Achille Ratti (1857–1939), It. pope.

Pius XII: Eugenio Pacelli (1876–1958), It. pope.

Benjamin **Place:** Edward Thring (1821–1887), Eng. schoolmaster, educationist. The school teacher, famous as the headmaster of Uppingham School, used this pen name for one of his early works, *Thoughts on Life Science* (1869). The pseudonym is probably intended to represent a local street name.

Jacques **Plowert:** Paul Adam (1862–1920), Fr. novelist. The pen name was only an occasional one, and was used by the writer in particular for his *Petit Glossaire pour servir à l'intelligence des auteurs décadents et symbolistes* (1888).

Pocahontas: Matoaka (?1595–1617), American-Indian wife of Eng. colonizer John Rolfe. Motoaka, an Indian chief's daughter, was nicknamed Pocahontas, "sportive," and assumed this name on her marriage (in 1614) to John Rolfe. Little might have been heard of her had she not gone with him to England in 1616, where she died the following year. She had been converted to Christianity in 1812 and given the Christian name Rebecca. Hence the entry in the parish register of St. George's Church, Gravesend, the town where she died, which reads: "1616 [sic], May 2j, Rebecca Wrothe, wyff of Thomas Wroth, gent., a Virginia lady borne, here was buried in ye chauncell" [*Dictionary of National Biography*].

William **Poel:** William Pole (1852–1934), Br. stage actor, producer. The actor changed his surname from Pole to "Poel" out of respect for his father's disapproval of his chosen profession.

Lou **Polan:** Lou Polansky (1904–   ), U.S. stage director.

Boris **Polevoy:** Boris Nikolayevich Kampov (1908–1981), Russ. novelist, journalist. Many English-speaking moviegoers have seen the Russian classic film *Story of a Real Man*, based on the novel of the same name (1946) by Polevoy. The author's original name, Kampov, was changed by the editor of the newspaper *Tverskaya Pravda*, in which he had had an article published (under the pseudonym "B. Ovod") as a 14-year-old schoolboy. The editor regarded the name Kampov as too "Latin," so he russianized it to Polevoy, i.e. translated it from the Latin word for "field" (*campus*) to the corresponding Russian (*pole*) in adjectival form.

Poliarchus: [Sir] Charles Cotterell (1615–?1687), Eng. politician, courtier. The courtier used this name, meaning "ruler of many," for his correspondence with Orinda *(q.v.)*.

Polidor: Ferdinando Guillaume (1887–1977), Fr. film comedian, stage clown. The performer's stage and screen name means "many-gifted," "multitalented."

Antonio **Pollaiuolo:** Antonio Benci (1433–1498), It. painter, sculptor, engraver. The painter obtained his new name, as so often the case, as a nickname. It means "little chicken" (the diminutive of Italian *pollo*), and was given to him affectionately as a younger brother.

Michael J. **Pollard:** Michael J. Pollack (1939–   ), U.S. film actor.

Snub **Pollard:** Harold Fraser (1886–1962), Austral. film comedian, working in U.S.

Pont: Graham Laidler (1908–1940), Br. cartoonist. The cartoonist originally intended to take up a career as an architect, and to this end adopted the name "Pontifex Maximus," literally "great bridge-builder," the title of the Roman pontiff or president, which was already a family nickname for him after he had paid an early visit to Italy. This later became shortened to "Pont," a name familiar to readers of *Punch* where his cartoons appeared. He did not thus adopt his name from London's Pont Street, as has been sometimes suggested [R.G.G. Price, *A History of Punch*, 1957].

Pontormo: Jacopo Carrucci (1494–1557), It. painter. The artist took his name from his birthplace, the village of Pontormo, near Empoli, west of Florence.

Poor Richard: Benjamin Franklin (1709–1790), U.S. statesman, philosopher, writer. Franklin was the author and publisher of *Poor Richard's Almanack* (1733–1758), the most famous of the American almanacs, although he signed the prefaces as "Richard Saunders." The name was almost certainly based on that of the English *Poor Robin's Almanack* (see next entry below), especially as Richard Saunders was the name of the English editor of *Apollo Anglicanus.*

Poor Robin: (?) William Winstanley (?1628–1698), Eng. compiler. The precise author of the various works by "Poor Robin," especially the almanacs published in England from about 1663, is still uncertain. William Winstanley seems the most likely candidate, although others support his brother, Robert Winstanley, possibly simply through the similarity between the names Robert and Robin. Others again suggest that the actual author was the poet Robert Herrick. Either way, the title certainly inspired the name of its American equivalent, *Poor Richard's Almanack* (see entry above).

Iggy Pop: James Jewel Osterburg, Jr. (1947–   ), U.S. rock musician. James Osterburg adopted the name "Iggy" from an early group, The Iguanas. In 1965 he left the Iguanas and joined another group, The Prime Movers. That same year he adopted the name "Iggy Pop," taking the second word from a local junkie, Jim Popp.

Popski: Vladimir Peniakoff (1897–1951), Belg. military commander, of Russ. parentage. The name was a cover name used for military intelligence work in the Second World War. Peniakoff published an account of this work in a book entitled *Popski's Private Army* and this popularized his name.

Peter Porcupine: William Cobbett (1763–1835), Eng. journalist, politician. The author used this name for *The Life and Adventures of Peter Porcupine* (1796), written and published in Philadelphia, as a provocatively pro–English work. A porcupine, after all, has prickly spines.

Porphyry: Malchas (*c.*234–*c.*305), Gk. scholar. The scholar's original Syrian name of Malchas meant "king." This was hellenized at Athens by Cassius Longinus, his teacher of logic, to "Porphyry," meaning "purple," and alluding to the color (imperial purple) associated with kings.

Porte-Crayon: David Hunter Strother (1816–1888), U.S. artist, illustrator. The artist's pen name (literally) is French for "pencil-holder."

Sandy Posey: Martha Sharp (1945–   ), U.S. country-pop singer, songwriter.

Adrienne Posta: Adrienne Poster (1948–   ), Eng. juvenile film actress.

Gillie Potter: Hugh William Peel (1888–1975), Br. humorist, stage, radio comedian. It is doubtless simply a coincidence that the humorist's stage name was identical to that of Stephen Potter (1900–1969), the author of *The Theory and Practice of Gamesmanship* (1947), but it is curious that Gillie Potter's humorous treatment of social material was in many ways similar to that of his namesake.

Jane Powell: Suzanne Burce (1929–   ), U.S. film actress, singer, dancer.

Stefanie Powers: Stefania Zofia Federkiewicz (1942–   ), U.S. film, TV actress.

Stephen Powys: Virginia Bolton, née de Lanty (1907–   ), U.S. playwright, short story writer.

Launce **Poyntz:** Frederick Whittaker (1838–1889), U.S. writer of adventure stories. Was a pun implied here, on "lance" and "points"?

Michael **Praetorius:** Michael Schultheiss (or Schulz) (1571–1621), Ger. composer, writer of music. The composer latinized his German name as nearly as possible. German *Schultheiss* was formerly the title of a village mayor; Latin *praetorius* was the adjectival form of *praetor,* the term for a Roman magistrate (ranking below a consul, just as a village mayor ranked below a town mayor).

Paul **Prendergast:** Douglas William Jerrold (1803–1857), Eng. novelist, journalist, dramatist. The writer used the name for his series of sketches entitled *Heads of the People* (1840–1). The name itself was probably a random alliterative one.

Paul **Prentiss:** Paula Ragusa (1939–), U.S. film actress.

Micheline **Presle:** Micheline Chassagne (1922–), Fr. film actress.

George F. **Preston:** [Baron] John Byrne Leicester Warren (1835–1895), Eng. poet. The writer used this name for some volumes of verse published between 1859 and 1862. The first part of the pseudonym is almost certainly a tribute to his close friend and fellow classmate at Oxford, George Fortescue, who was killed in an accident in 1859. Warren also used the pen name "William Lancaster," and the surnames of both pseudonyms without any doubt derive from the two northern English cities of Preston and Lancaster, both in Lancashire, and not far from his native Cheshire.

Robert **Preston:** Robert Preston Meservey (1917–1987), U.S. stage, film actor.

Préville: Pierre-Louis Dibus (1721–1799), Fr. comic actor.

Marie **Prevost:** Marie Bickford Dunn (1893–1937), Can.-born U.S. film actress.

Dennis **Price:** Dennistoun Franklyn John Rose-Price (1915–1973), Eng. stage, film actor.

Dorothy **Primrose:** Dorothy Buckley (1916–), Sc. stage actress.

Prince: Prince Rogers Nelson (1958–), U.S. soul singer, composer.

Aileen **Pringle:** Aileen Bisbee (1895–), U.S. film actress.

Yvonne **Printemps:** Yvonne Wigniolle (1894–1977), Fr. singer, film, stage comedienne.

James **Prior:** James Prior Kirk (1851–1922), Eng. novelist.

P.J. (Jim) **Proby:** James Marcus Smith (1938–), U.S. rock singer. The singer began his performing career as "Jett Powers," an arbitrary "dynamic" name, and the reversed initials of this give the "P.J." of his stage name. "Proby" appears to have originated as a nickname (?probationer) although it could have tied in with the name of his great friend Elvis Presley, who dated his sister.

Professor Longhair: Henry Roeland "Roy" Byrd (1918–1980), U.S. rock musician.

Lozania **Prole:** Ursula Bloom (1893–1984), Eng. novelist. The unusual name looks like an eccentric variation on the writer's real name, but there may have well been some other origin — unless, of course, it was arbitrary and meaningless. Ursula Bloom also wrote under more conventional pen names, such as "Sheila Burnes," "Mary Essex," and "Rachel Harvey."

Father **Prout:** Francis Sylvester Mahoney (1804–1866), Ir. humorist. The author adopted this name for his *Prout Papers* (1834–6), which purported to be the autobiography of a rural Irish priest. Mahoney had himself abandoned the priesthood for literary pursuits after being expelled from the Jesuit order in 1830.

Marcel **Provence:** Marcel Jouhandeau (1888–1979), Fr. novelist, short story writer, dramatist. The writer took his pen name from Provence, where he was born, disguising his native town of Guéret in his works as "Chaminadour."

Joseph **Prunier:** Guy de Maupassant (1850–1893), Fr. short story writer. Maupassant used this name for his first story, *La Main d'écorché* (1875).

Maureen **Pryor:** Maureen Pook (1924–1977), Ir. stage, film, TV actress.

George **Psalmanazar:** ? (c.1679–1763), Fr. (or Swiss) literary impostor, working in England. The impostor apparently took his name from the biblical character Shalmaneser, with an initial "P" added. For the ins and outs of his disguise and deviousness, see p. 65.

Pseudoplutarch: John Milton (1608–1674), Eng. poet. Milton used this name for addressing Charles II in his *Pro Populo Anglicano Defensio* (1651), written in Latin, in which he replied to the *Defensio Regia* (1649) by the French scholar Salmasius (Claude de Saumaise). The overall work, however, was written under his own name.

Publius: Alexander Hamilton (1757–1804), U.S. statesman + James Madison (1751–1804), U.S. statesman, fourth president + John Jay (1745–1829), U.S. lawyer, statesman. The joint name was adopted by the three influential men for their essays in *The Federalist* in support of the Constitution. They were published in collected form in 1788. The name "Publius" referred to the intention of the writers to address the New York voters publicly, and to persuade them to accept the Constitution. The writers had earlier used the name A Citizen of New York *(q.v.)*.

Punjabee: William Delafield Arnold (1828–1859), Eng. novelist. The Anglo-Indian official was in India as an army officer from 1848, and subsequently became an assistant commissioner in the Punjab. He used his pseudonym, referring to this, for his best-known work, *Oakfield, or Fellowship in the East* (1853). William Delafield Arnold was the son of Thomas Arnold, the educationist and headmaster of Rugby School, and the brother of Matthew Arnold, the poet.

Reginal **Purdell:** Reginald Grasdorf (1896–1953), Br. stage, music hall, film actor.

Bobby **Purify:** Robert Lee Dickey (1939–   ), U.S. black soul singer, teaming with cousin James Purify. The two teamed up as a professional duo in 1965, with Bobby assuming his cousin's name.

Eleanor **Putnam:** Harriet L. Bates, née Vose (1856–1886), U.S. writer.

Isra **Putnam:** Greye La Spina, née Fanny Greye Bragg (1880–1969), U.S. horror story writer. The writer seems to have based her pen name on that of Israel Putnam (1718–1790), the U.S. Revolutionary commander.

Q: [1] Arthur Thomas Quiller-Couch (1863–1944), Br. novelist, short story writer; [2] Douglas William Jerrold (1803–1857), Eng. playwright, humorist. "Q" as a pseudonym usually means little more than "query," otherwise "guess who wrote this." In the case of Quiller-Couch, of course, it was his genuine initial. He first used the name for parodies written when he was a student at Oxford. Douglas

William Jerrold also wrote under the better-known pen name of Paul Prendergast *(q.v.)*, keeping "Q" for social political contributions to *Punch,* the famous humorous journal with which he was associated from its foundation in 1841. See also the next name below.

Q.Q.: Jane Taylor (1783–1824), Eng. children's writer. Jane Taylor used this name, probably meaning simply "query (first name), query (surname)," for her contributions to *The Youth's Magazine,* an evangelical periodical published monthly from 1805 to 1865. Together with her sister Ann, with whom she collaborated in the writing of children's verse, Jane Taylor was the daughter of Isaac Taylor, who wrote a number of instructional works for children. (He should not be confused with the better-known Canon Isaac Taylor, the archaeologist and philologist, author of *Words and Places* and *Names and Their Histories,* who was Jane and Ann Taylor's nephew.)

M. Quad: Charles Bertrand Lewis (1842–1924), U.S. printer, journalist, humorist. The printer's pseudonym reveals his profession, for an "M quad" is a block of type metal the width of a capital letter "M," used in printing for spacing.

John **Qualen:** John Oleson (1899–1987), Can. film actor, of Norw. parentage, working in U.S.

Ellery **Queen:** Frederic Dannay (1905–1982), U.S. crime novelist + Manfred Bennington Lee (1905–1971), U.S. crime novelist. The two crime novelists, whose actual real names were Daniel Nathan and Manford Lepofsky, respectively, were also Brooklyn cousins. (Dannay's commonly quoted name is thus made up of the first two syllables of "Daniel" and "Nathan," while "Manfred" evolved from "Manford" and "Lee" represents the first syllable of "Lepofsky.") They based the name "Ellery Queen" on a mutual boyhood friend called Ellery. To this they added "Queen" as they reasoned this would make the name memorable, especially as it occurs throughout their books as the name of the main detective anyway. They had earlier considered other names, such as "James Griffen" and "Wilbur See," but eventually rejected these.

Peter **Query,** Esq.: Martin Farquhar Tupper (1810–1899), Eng. versifier. The author of the popular *Proverbial Philosophy* (1838–1876, 4 series), which became a bestseller on both sides of the Atlantic for more than a generation, used the pen name quoted here for *Rides and Reveries of Mr. Aesop Smith* (1858), now forgotten, like all his other works. The pseudonym is a transparent attempt to disguise a real name.

Quevedo Redivivus: George Gordon Byron (1788–1824), Eng. poet. Byron used this name for *The Vision of Judgement* (1822), a parody of Southey's poem of the same name published the previous year. The pseudonym means "Quevedo renewed," referring to the seventeenth-century Spanish poet and satirist Francisco Gómez de Quevedo y Villegas, who was imprisoned for his political attacks.

La **Quica:** Francisca González (1907–1967), Span. ballet dancer, teacher. The well-known flamenco dancer assumed a name that doubtless arose as a nickname, for "quica" (from the Portuguese) is an alternative name for the four-eyed opossum, familiar from its big head and small body. The dancer made her debut as a child in a café chantant and may have fancifully been compared to this animal.

Dan **Quin:** Alfred Henry Lewis (c.1858–1914), U.S. journalist, novelist. The writer used this name for his volumes of "Wolfville" stories, presenting a series of whimsical reminiscences of cowboy and mining life in the Southwest by an "Old Cattleman." The first to appear was *Wolfville* itself (1897).

Peter **Quince:** [1] Isaac Story (1774–1803), U.S. satirist, poet; [2] John William McWean Thompson (1920–   ), Eng. editor. Isaac Story adopted his name from the character in Shakespeare's *A Midsummer Night's Dream*, in which Peter Quince, the carpenter, is stage manager of the "Pyramus and Thisbe" interlude. It seems likely that Thompson used the same source, rather than his American namesake. He was appointed editor of the London *Sunday Telegraph* in 1976, and used the name for his book *Country Life* published the previous year.

Simon **Quinn:** Martin Cruz Smith (1942–   ), U.S. mystery writer.

Quiz: [1] [Sir] Max Beerbohm (1872–1956), Br. essayist, caricaturist; [2] Charles Dickens (1812–1870), Eng. novelist, short story writer. The pseudonym is a patent disguise or simply a token anonymity. Dickens used the name for *Sketches of Young Couples* (1840). In this case, however, it happens to blend in well with his other name, Boz *(q.v.)*, and with that of his illustrator, Phiz *(q.v.)*.

John **Quod:** John Treat Irving (1812–1906), U.S. writer on frontier life. The writer, nephew of Washington Irving, used this pseudonym for *The Quod Correspondence* (1842), also titled *The Attorney*, a novel about legal affairs. For the name itself, he may have had the generic name "John Q. Public" or "John Q. Citizen" in mind, as a term for a member of the public or the community. (This name is said to have been based on the name of John Quincy Adams [1767–1848], sixth President of the U.S.)

Richard **Quongti:** Thomas Babington Macaulay (1800–1859), Eng. writer, statesman.

William **Rabbit:** Katay Don Sasorith (1904–1959), Laotian nationalist, writer of resistance pamphlets. The writer adopted the English name from his own name, as "Katay" is the Laotian word for "rabbit." He used it for *Contribution à l'histoire du mouvement d'indépendance national Lao* (1948).

Eddie **Rabbitt:** Edward Thomas (1944–   ), U.S. rock singer, songwriter.

Istvan **Rabovsky:** Istvan Rab (1930–   ), Hung.-U.S. ballet dancer, teacher.

Mlle **Rachel:** Elisabeth (or Elisa) Félix (1820–1858), Fr. tragedienne. The actress's sisters were also on the stage, assuming distinctive names: Sophie (1819–1877) as "Sarah," Adelaide (1828–1872) as "Lia," Rachel (1829–1854) as "Rebecca," and Mélanie Emilie (1836–1909) as "Dinah." Her brother Raphaël (1825–1872) acted under his real name.

Rachilde: Marguerite Vallette, née Eymery (1860–1953), Fr. literary critic.

John **Rackham:** John Thomas Phillifent (1916–1976), Br. SF writer.

Sheila **Radley:** Sheila M. Robinson (1928–   ), Eng. detective novelist.

Charlotte **Rae:** Charlotte Lubotsky (1926–   ), U.S. stage, TV actress, singer.

Anna **Raeburn:** Sally Taylor (1944–   ), Eng. "agony aunt." The lady's assumed name is part real, part false. She was born as Sally Taylor, but later changed Sally to "Anna" in order to avoid confusion with a flatmate. She then married Michael Raeburn, so that she had a new surname. (She subsequently married Nick Lilley, but was by then well established as "Anna Raeburn," and kept this name.)

Chips **Rafferty:** John William Goffage (1909–1971), Austral. film actor. The actor originally considered the name "Slab O'Flaherty," but later rejected this in favor of the name by which he became popularly established as a "rugged" character actor. Possibly his screen surname was intended to suggest "raffish"?

George **Raft:** George Ranft (1895–1980), U.S. film actor.

C.E. **Raimond:** Elizabeth Robins (1865–1952), U.S. stage actress, novelist. The actress used her real name on the stage, keeping "C.E. Raimond" for her novels. She adopted (and adapted) this name from her brother, Raymond.

Raimu: Jules-Auguste-César Muraire (1883–1946), Fr. stage, film actor. The actor's professional name was formed from his surname.

Ferdinand **Raimund:** Jakob Raimann (1790–1836), Austr. playwright, actor.

Allen **Raine:** Anne Adalisa Puddicombe, née Evans (1836–1908), Welsh novelist. The writer's pseudonym is said to have been suggested to her in a dream. If this is so, possibly there was a subconscious connection between "rain" and "puddle"? Anne Puddicombe used it for her love story *A Welsh Singer* (1897), originally titled *Myfanwy* and rejected by six publishers.

Ella **Raines:** Ella Raubes (1921–   ), U.S. film actress.

Ma **Rainey:** Gertrude Malissa Pridgett (1886–1939), U.S. black blues singer. "Rainey" was actually the singer's married name, that of William "Pa" Rainey, who became her husband when she was 18 and he was an established dancer, singer and comedian. The couple toured as "Rainey & Rainey." "Ma" was a compliment to her authority as "Mother of the Blues," while also hinting at her mature style: she did not make her first recording until she was 37.

W.B. **Rainey:** Wyatt Rainey Blassingame (1909–   ), U.S. writer of children's books, reference works. A slight rearrangement of initials enables the writer to use his middle name as a new surname.

Ralph **Rainger:** Ralph Reichenthal (1901–1942), U.S. songwriter. The writer seems to have resisted the temptation to call himself something like "Ralph Rich" (which would have tempted many), instead choosing a more original adaptation of his original name.

Marvin **Rainwater:** Marvin Percy (1925–   ), U.S. country singer, of Cherokee descent. The singer adopted his mother's maiden name as his professional name.

Rosa **Raisi:** Rose Burchstein (1893–1963), Pol. opera singer, working in Italy, U.S.

Jesse **Ralph:** Jessie Ralph Chambers (1864–1944), U.S. film actress.

Vera **Ralston:** Vera Hruba (1919–   ), Cz. ice skater, film actress, working in U.S.

Walter **Ramal:** Walter de la Mare (1873–1956), Eng. poet, anthologist, short story writer. The writer used the name, a part-inversion of his surname, for *Songs of Childhood* (1902), an early volume of poems for children.

Marie **Rambert:** Myriam Ramberg (1888–1982), Pol.-Br. ballet dancer, teacher, director. The dancer's birth certificate showed her first name to be Cyvia. Myriam, therefore, was originally a nickname, given her by her French poet friend, Edmée Delebecque. Myriam's father's family name was Rambam, and her father and his brothers had this name changed to make them seem only children (and thus escape military service), so one son retained the name Rambam, one (her father) took the name Ramberg, one took Rambert, as Myriam herself did, and the fourth, to represent their Polish nationality, assumed the name Warszawski ("from Warsaw") [Marie Rambert, *Quicksilver: An Autobiography*, 1972].

"Ram" **Ramirez:** Roeger Ameres (*c.*1915–   ), West Indian jazz pianist. The musician hispanicized his native name, with his nickname in turn derived from this.

Dee Dee **Ramone:** Douglas Colvin (1952–   ), U.S. punk rock musician, teaming with Joey, Johnny, and Tommy Ramone *(qq.v.* below) to form the Ramones.

Joey **Ramone:** Jeffrey Hyman (1952–   ), U.S. punk rock musician (*see* **Dee Dee Ramone**).

Johnny **Ramone:** John Cummings (1952–   ), U.S. punk rock musician (see Dee Dee Ramone). The group took their collective name vial Paul McCartney of the Beatles, who had briefly performed as "Phil Ramone" when the Beatles were still the Silver Beatles. An early fourth member was Tommy Ramone (Tom Erdelyi), born 1952 like the others.

Sally **Rand:** Helen Gould Beck (1904–1979), U.S. vaudeville dancer.

Tony **Randall:** Leonard Rosenberg (1920–   ), U. S. film actor.

Frank **Randle:** Arthur McEvoy (1901–1957), Eng. music hall, film comedian.

Raoul: High Duff McLauchlan (1920–   ), Sc. music hall dancer, teaming with Babette *(q.v.)*.

Raphael: Raffaello Santi (1483–1520), It. painter.

Renato **Rascel:** Renato Ranucci (1912–   ), It. film actor.

Rasputin: Grigoriy Yefimovich Novykh (?1864–1916), Russ. monk, court favorite, religious fanatic. The infamous monk was born in Siberia as the son of a peasant named Yefim Novykh. He came to lead a dissolute life, and was given the nickname "Rasputin," based on Russian *rasputny,* "dissolute," adopting this subsequently as a surname. An earlier uncomplimentary nickname had been "Varnak," a Siberian word meaning "vagabond." Rasputin was the son of a horse-stealer and became one himself, so establishing his dubious reputation when still quite young [Prince Yousoupoff, *Rasputin,* 1974].

Alexis **Rassine:** Alexis Rays (1919–   ), Lithuanian-Br. ballet dancer. It seems likely that the dancer based his name on that of Leonide Massine *(q.v.),* retaining the initial letter of his surname for distinction.

Thalmus **Rasulala:** Jack Crowder (1939–   ), U.S. black film actor.

Rattlesnake Annie: Annie McGowan (1941–   ), U.S. country singer.

Mlle **Raucourt:** Françoise-Marie-Antoinette-Josèphe Saucerotte (1756–1815), Fr. actress. The actress seems to have based her stage name loosely on her surname.

Genga **Ravan:** Goldie Zelkowitz (1942–   ), Pol.-born U.S. rock musician.

Mike **Raven:** Churton Fairman (1924–   ), Eng. radio DJ.

Aldo **Ray:** Aldo Da Re (1926–   ), U.S. film actor.

Cyril **Ray:** Cyril Rotenberg (1908–   ), Eng. writer on wine. The noted oenophile was given his simpler name by his father.

Jean **Ray:** Jean-Raymond De Kremer (1887–1964), Belg. novelist, short story writer.

Man **Ray:** Emmanuel Rudnitsky (1890–1976), U.S. surrealist painter, photographer, of Jewish-Russ. descent. The painter changed his name when at art school in Manhattan so as to avoid the taunts of his fellow students. His real name long remained unknown, and was publicly revealed only after his death.

Nicholas **Ray:** Raymond Nicholas Kienzle (1911–1979), U.S. film director.

Rene **Ray:** Irene Creese (1912–   ), Eng. stage, film actress.

Ted **Ray:** Charles Olden (*c*.1909–1977), Eng. comedian, violinist. Both the original name and true birthday of the comedian are on the uncertain side. His surname at birth seems to have been Alden, changed by his parents when he was still a boy to Olden. As for his date of birth, it varies between about 1906 and 1910. We do at least know that Charles Olden appeared early in his career as "Nedlo" (his surname reversed) and also as a comic violinist named "Hugh Neek" ("unique!"). Not long after, he selected his permanent stage name – adopting it from a noted golfer of the day, Ted Ray, who was the British winner of the U.S. Open Golf Championship of 1920. And what could be better than a brief, bright name like this for a snappy comic?

Carol **Raye:** Kathleen Corkrey (1923–   ), Austral. film actress, working in U.K.

Martha **Raye:** Margaret Theresa Yvonne Reed (1908–   ), U.S. radio, TV comedienne, singer.

Raymond: Raymondo Pietro Carlo Bessone (1911–   ), Eng. hair stylist, of It. parentage ("Mr. Teasy-Weasy").

Gene **Raymond:** Raymond Guion (1908–   ), U.S. film, TV actor.

Jack **Raymond:** John Caines (1892–1953), Br. film producer.

John T. **Raymond:** John O'Brien (1836–1887), U.S. comedian.

Paula **Raymond:** Paula Ramona Wright (1923–   ), U.S. film actress.

Miss **Read:** Dora Jessie Saint, née Shafe (1913–   ), Eng. author. The author, a former school teacher, became popular for her gentle accounts of life centering on a village school, beginning with *Village School* itself (1955). She has described how she chose her pen name: "That book, *Village School*, was being written in the first person and I remember trying to think of an ordinary kind of name by which this central character would be known. My mother's maiden name was Read. There seemed no reason to seek further. When the time came for it to be published, [. . .] one of the directors of the firm [. . .] which was to publish the book [. . .] suggested that it would be a good idea to let it appear under the pseudonym of 'Miss Read,' thus creating a modest secret" [Dora Saint, "The Birth of Miss Read," *The Countryman*, Winter 1978].

Martin **Redfield:** Alice Brown (1857–1948), U.S. novelist, short story writer, playwright.

Red River Dave: Dave McEnery (1914–   ), U.S. cowboy singer.

Alan **Reed:** Edward Bergman (1908–1977), U.S. film actor.

Donna **Reed:** Donna Belle Mullenger (1921–1986), U.S. film, TV actress, hostess. The actress used the name "Donna Adams" when she began her screen career, later changing the second name to "Reed."

Jerry **Reed:** Jerry Hubbard (1937–), U.S. country guitarist.

Lou **Reed:** Louis Firbank (1942–), U.S. rock musician.

Robert **Reed:** John Robert Rietz (1932–), U.S. TV actor.

Della **Reese:** Dellareese Taliaferro, née Early (1931–), U.S. black pop singer.

Ada **Reeve:** Adelaide Mary Isaacs (1874–1966), Eng. music hall comedienne.

George **Reeves:** George Besselo (1914–1959), U.S. film actor.

Seely **Regester:** Metta Victoria Fuller Victor (1831–1886), U.S. romantic, humorous writer.

Régine: Rachel Zylberberg (1929–), Fr. nightclub owner.

Regiomontanus: Johann Müller (1436–1476), Ger. astronomer, mathematician. The Latin name is the Latin version of his birthplace, Königsberg, now Kaliningrad, in the Soviet Union.

Ada **Rehan:** Ada Crehan (1860–1916), U.S. stage actress.

Max **Reinhardt:** Max Goldmann (1873–1943), Austr. stage actor, manager, director, working in U.S. The actor changed his Orthodox Jewish name for a stage name that would not specifically be regarded as Jewish.

Hans **Reinmar:** Hans Wochinz (1895–1961), Austr. opera singer, working in Germany.

Réjane: Gabrielle-Charlotte Réju (1857–1920), Fr. stage actress, theatre manager.

Uncle **Remus:** Joel Chandler Harris (1848–1908), U.S. writer. The white writer created the character of "Uncle Remus," a wise and friendly old Negro, who told stories about Brer Rabbit, Brer Fox and other animals to the small son of a plantation owner. The formula was new, and was immensely popular. Harris's first Uncle Remus story appeared in the *Atlanta Constitution* in 1879. In 1907 he founded his own *Uncle Remus's Magazine*.

Colonel **Rémy:** Gilbert Renault (1904–1984), Fr. Resistance hero, writer, politician.

Duncan **Renaldo:** Renault Renaldo Duncan (1904–1980), U.S. film actor, painter.

Mary **Renault:** Mary Challans (1905–1983), Br. novelist, working in S.A. Mary Challans began writing when a nurse before the Second World War, and was obliged to keep her activity secret from Matron, her "presiding deity" in the hospital, who might not have approved. She took the name from a character in the *Chroniques* of Froissart, the fourteenth-century French historian and poet. "I never thought of the car!" she said.

Liz **Renay:** Pearl Elizabeth Dobbins (1934–), U.S. film actress.

Elisabeth **Rethberg:** Elisabeth Sättler (1894–1976), Ger. opera singer, working in U.S.

[Baron von] Paul Julius **Reuter:** Israel Beer Josaphat (1816–1899), Ger. founder of Reuters news agency. Originally a Jew, Josaphat became a Christian in 1844 and adopted the name of Reuter, substituting Christian names for Jewish.

Reginald **Reverie:** Grenville Mellen (1799–1841), U.S. author, poet.

Dorothy **Revier:** Doris Velagra (1904–), U.S. film actress.

Alvino **Rey:** Alvin McBurney (1911–), U.S. guitarist, bandleader.

Fernando **Rey:** Fernando Casado Arambillet Veiga (1917–), Sp. film actor.

Monte **Rey:** James Montgomery Fyfe (1900–1982), Sc. radio singer. The singer's name certainly reflects his second name, but also happens to suggest (intentionally?) the California city of Monterey.

Judith **Reyn:** Judith Fisher (1944–), Rhodesian-born Eng. ballet dancer.

Debbie **Reynolds:** Mary Frances Reynolds (1932–), U.S. film actress. The actress's new first name was given her by Jack Warner, of Warner Brothers, when she was starting her stage career in 1948. She is said to dislike it to this day. By popularizing it, however, she gave a boost to similarly abbreviated names, not simply Deborah as Debbie, but Amanda as Mandy, Catherine as Katie, Victoria as Vicky, Linda as Lindy, Jacqueline as Jackie, and so on. Such pet forms seemed "free and easy" and liberated after the Second World War.

Marjorie **Reynolds:** Marjorie Goodspeed (1921–), U.S. film actress. Reynolds is actually the actress's married name.

Peter **Reynolds:** Peter Horrocks (1926–1975), Br. film actor.

Rhäticus: Georg Joachim von Lauchen (1514–1576), Ger. astronomer, mathematician. The astronomer adopted a name derived from his birthplace, the Austrian district of Rhaetia.

John **Rhode:** [1] Honoré de Balzac *(q.v.);* [2] Cecil Charles Street (1884–1964), Br. writer of mystery novels; [3] Miles Burton (1884–1965), Br. detective story writer. For Balzac, the pseudonym was one of many, with this particular one possibly inspired by "Lord R'Hoone," formed as an anagram of his first name. For Cecil Street, the pun of the name is fairly transparent. Miles Burton no doubt took his name from his colleague in crime.

Madlyn **Rhue:** Madeleine Roche (1934–), U.S. film actress. A rather esoteric revamping of the actress's real name.

Jean **Rhys:** Jean Hamer, née Rees Williams (1894–1979), Eng. writer.

Ruggiero **Ricci:** Woodrow Wilson (later, Roger) Rich (1918–), U.S. concert violinist, of It. descent. The musician's father italianized "Roger Rich" to "Ruggiero Ricci," hoping that such a professional-looking name would bring "riches."

Craig **Rice:** Georgiana Ann Randolph (1908–1957), U.S. mystery novelist, filmscript writer. The writer took her surname, Rice, from that of the aunt who raised her, and her new first name, Craig, from another family branch.

Dan **Rice:** Daniel McLaren (1823–1900), U.S. circus clown.

Elmer **Rice:** Elmer Leopold Reizenstein (1892–1967), U.S. playwright, novelist. The writer simplified his name like this in 1914, after becoming tired of constantly having to spell out his real name over the telephone. There is certainly wide scope for confusion between several similar Jewish names, such as Einstein, Eisenstein, Reichstein, Rosenstein and this one.

Irene **Rich:** Irene Luther (1891–1988), U.S. film actress. No doubt "Luther" is not exactly a name for the cinema, although of course there was a movie of the name. But this was long after Ms. Rich's career was over (1973).

Cliff **Richard:** Harold Rodger Webb (1940–), Eng. pop musician, film actor.

Harold Webb is probably not such an exciting name for a pop star and film actor. How did the change come about? Harold, at the start of his career, felt he needed a new name and had always liked Richard but found the choice of a surname difficult. (He toyed with "Richard Webb," but rejected it.) The manager of his group, The Drifters, agreed that a change of name was desirable, and one member of the group proposed "Russ Clifford." Harry Webb thought about it, felt it was too "soft-spoken," and hazarded "Cliff Russard." Almost there. But meanwhile an earlier manager, Johnny Foster, had come up with "Cliff Richard" – "Not Richards, but without the 's.' It's just the name we're looking for. Everybody will call him Cliff Richards and then we can correct them – that way they'll never forget his name." So Cliff Richard he became – the name first being used at the public appearance of Cliff Richard and The Drifters at a ballroom in Derby (in 1958) [David Winter, *New Singer, New Song: The Cliff Richard Story*, 1967].

Francis **Richard:** Frank R. Stockton (1834–1902), U.S. novelist, short story writer.

Pierre **Richard:** Maurice Charles Leopold Defays (1934–   ), Fr. film actor, director. One wonders why the actor chose two completely different names for his screen name. Perhaps "Maurice Charles" was already in use.

Frank **Richards:** Charles Harold St. John Hamilton (1875–1961), Eng. author of school stories. This was the best-known pseudonym of the creator of Billy Bunter and a host of other immortal characters who peopled the writer's fictional Greyfriars School. The choice of the name may appear arbitrary, but in fact the author took much trouble over its selection, as he has recorded: "The chief thing was to select a name totally different from those under which he had hitherto written: so that when he used the name, he would feel like a different person, and in consequence write from a somewhat different angle. I have been told – by men who do not write – that this is all fanciful. [. . .] This only means that they don't understand" [*The Autobiography of Frank Richards*, 1952]. He introduced the name for the first Greyfriars story, published in the school story magazine *The Magnet* in 1908. Hamilton derived the name itself from Frank Osbaldistone, a character in Scott's *Rob Roy*, and his own brother Richard. He identified so closely with it that his entry in *Who's Who* appeared under the name, and (as we have seen), he even used it for his autobiography. Among other pseudonyms used by Hamilton were "Owen Conquest," "Martin Clifford," "Ralph Redway," and "Hilda Richards," this last for some stories featuring Bessie Bunter, the sister of Billy Bunter. However, Hamilton's characterization of Bessie was too crude for his girl readers, and he was replaced by other writers, who continued the stories about the schoolgirl under Hamilton's original name of "Hilda Richards." No doubt readers never noticed. Or did they? (Unusually he wrote his autobiography in the third person.)

Jeff **Richards:** Richard Mansfield Taylor (1922–   ), U.S. film actor.

Richelieu: William Erigena Robinson (1814–1892), U.S. journalist, politician.

Harry **Richman:** Harold Reichman (1895–1972), U.S. entertainer, film actor.

Fiona **Richmond:** Julia Harrison (1947–   ), Eng. stage, film actress.

Kane **Richmond:** Frederick W. Bowditch (1906–1973), U.S. film actor.

John **Ridgeley:** John Huntingdon Rea (1909–1968), U.S. film actor.

Laura **Riding:** Laura Jackson, née Reichenthal (1901–   ), U.S. writer, poet. The author has also published as "Laura (Riding) Jackson." She was married to Schuyler B. Jackson for 27 years from 1941.

Robert **Rietty:** Robert Rietti (1923–   ), Eng. stage actor, playwright, director.

John **Ringling:** John Rüngeling (1866–1936), U.S. circus impresario, of Ger. parentage. "Ringling" is a somehow appropriate name for the circus!

Johnny **Ringo:** Clay Allison (1914–   ), Eng. writer of westerns. The name has the right associations for the world of westerns, with the various senses of "ring" involving animals, especially horses and cattle.

Ringuet: Philippe Panneton (1895–1960), Fr.-Can. novelist.

A. **Riposte:** Elinor Mordaunt, née Evelyn May Clowes (1877–1942), Eng. novelist, travel writer. The author used this name for the U.S. edition, entitled *Gin and Bitters*, of her novel *Full Circle* (1931). The book was intended as a counterblast ("riposte") to Somerset Maugham's *Cakes and Ale*. She hardly carried the guns, however, for this daunting assault.

Elizabeth **Risdon:** Elizabeth Evans (1887–1958), Br. stage, film actress.

Rita: Eliza Margaret Humphreys, née Gollan (? –1938), Sc. romantic novelist. The novelist may now be unread, but her pen name does properly reflect her second name of Margaret, and may well have been her pet name among her family and friends.

Al **Ritz:** Al Joachim (1901–1965), U.S. film comedian, of Austr. parentage, teaming with Harry and Jimmy Ritz (see below) as The Ritz Brothers.

Harry **Ritz:** Harry Joachim (1908–1986), U.S. film comedian (see Al Ritz).

Jimmy **Ritz:** Jimmy Joachim (1904–1985), U.S. film comedian (see Al Ritz). The brothers used the glitzy name of Ritz, the famous hotelkeeper, for their original vaudeville act, first as precision dancers, then as zany comedians.

Chita **Rivera:** Dolores Conchita Figueroa del Rivera (1933–   ), U.S. stage, film actress.

Joan **Rivers:** Joan Rosenberg, née Brookner (1933–   ), U.S. TV comedienne, chat show host, sister of novelist Anita Brookner (1928–   ). As early as 1965 Joan Rivers-to-be decided that neither of the two sisters' careers would be helped by one being associated with the other. She therefore adopted a different name, explaining it in her inimitable way: "Brook–River–geddit?" [*Sunday Times*, November 8, 1987]. The two were raised in Berkshire, England, but parted company when Joan went to the U.S. to achieve her ambition of becoming a stand-up comedienne and chat show host. Anita, the quieter of the two, stayed home to become a leading novelist and, in 1984, winner of the coveted Booker Prize for Fiction with her *Hotel du Lac*.

Johnny **Rivers:** John Ramistella (1942–   ), U.S. pop musician, record company executive.

Larry **Rivers:** Yitzroch Loiza Grossberg (1923–   ), U.S. painter.

Harold **Robbins:** Francis Kane (1916–   ), U.S. novelist.

Jerome **Robbins:** Jerome Rabinowitz (1918–   ), U.S. stage director, choreographer.

Marty **Robbins:** Martin Robertson (1925–1982), U.S. country singer.

Ben **Roberts:** Benjamin Eisenberg (1916–1984), U.S. screenwriter.

Ewan **Roberts:** Ewan Hutchison (1914–   ), Sc. stage actor.

James Hall **Roberts:** Robert L. Duncan (1927–   ), U.S. thriller writer.

Lionel **Roberts:** Robert Lionel Fanthorpe (1935–   ), Eng. SF writer.

Lynne **Roberts:** Mary Hart (1919–   ), U.S. film actress.

E. Arnot **Robertson:** [Lady] Eileen Arbuthnot Turner, née Robertson (1903–1961), Eng. novelist.

[Sir] George **Robey:** George Edward Wade (1869–1954), Eng. stage, film comedian ("The Prime Minister of Mirth"). When George Wade began appearing in amateur theatrical performances at an early age, his family disapproved. He therefore decided to adopt another name, and took "Robey" (originally "Roby") from a builder's business in Birmingham, where he was employed as a clerk in a tram (streetcar) company. He liked the name for its simple, robust appearance and its ease of pronunciation, and later adopted it legally by deed poll [*Dictionary of National Biography*].

Henri **Robin:** Henri-Joseph Dunkell (*c*.1805–1875), Du.-born Fr. conjuror ("The French Wizard").

Mr. and Master **Robinson:** Henry Hawley Crippen (1868–1910), Br. murderer + Ethel Le Neve (1893–1967), his mistress. Following the murder of his wife in London in 1910, Dr. Crippen and his mistress fled to the U.S., of which he was a citizen. They boarded a boat to Quebec with Ethel Le Neve posing as "Master Robinson" and Crippen as "his" father. The master of the ship, however, saw through her disguise and sent a message to the ship's owners in Liverpool. On the ship's arrival in Quebec, the couple were arrested by the police. Crippen was subsequently executed. Various other aliases were used throughout the affair. Crippen's wife, the daughter of a German mother and a Polish father, was christened Kunigunde Mackamotzki. When she was in her late teens in Brooklyn, she began calling herself "Cora Turner." Soon after marrying Crippen, she used the name "Cora Motzki," hoping this would help with a proposed operatic career. For a time she also appeared on the stage as "Belle Elmore." Ethel Le Neve, meanwhile, called herself "Miss Allen" when she again sailed for North America after the trial, and "Miss Nelson" when she returned to England in the First World War. Under this latter name she married one Stanley Smith.

Edward G. **Robinson:** Emanuel Goldenberg (1893–1973), U.S. film actor. The name change is described in interesting detail in the actor's autobiography. Given the need for a change, since Emanuel Goldenberg was "not a name for an actor [. . .] too long, too foreign and [. . .] too Jewish, [. . .] the obvious ploy was translation, but Emanuel Goldenhill didn't work and Goldenmount was too pretentious. [. . .] I continued to debate lists of names in the phone book, catalogs, and encyclopedias I picked up in the Astor Place Library [. . .] and none would satisfy me. Then one night I went to see a play, a highly urbane English drawing room comedy, and from my perch in the rear of the second balcony I heard a butler on stage announce to a lady (could it have been Mrs. Fiske?), 'Madam, a gentleman to see you—a Mr. Robinson.'"

"Mr. Robinson. I liked the ring and strength of it. And, furthermore, it was a common change. I knew many Rosenbergs, Rabinowitzes, and Roths who'd switched to Robinson. Yes, that was it. From this time forward I would be Robinson—Emanuel Robinson. That decision was greeted at the Academy with something less than enthusiasm. Emanuel and Robinson were an odd coupling. What other names began with *E*? Edgar? Egbert? Ellery? Ethan? Edward? Why not Edward, then King of England? [. . .] Edward Robinson. But I could not desert the Goldenberg entirely. That became the *G*, my private treaty with my past. But that wasn't enough. Some managers didn't like the *G*, and quite arbitrarily one of them translated it to Gould. And so, if you ever look at the early programs, you will see me billed as Edward Gould Robinson. . ." [Edward G. Robinson with Leonard Spigelgass, *All My Yesterdays: An Autobiography*, 1974].

Madeleine **Robinson:** Madeleine Svoboda (1916–   ), Fr. stage, film actress.

Ralph **Robinson:** George III (1738–1820), king of England ("Farmer George"). George III used this name, that of his shepherd at Windsor, for his contributions to the *Annals of Agriculture*, the monthly journal published from 1784 to 1809 by the agriculturist Arthur Young. The king was a keen, progressive farmer—hence his nickname.

"Sugar" Ray **Robinson:** Walker Smith (1921–1989), U.S. black world champion boxer. The boxer turned pro in 1940 and acquired his new name that year. Watching a small promotion from ringside one day, he was suddenly asked to substitute for a fighter named Ray Robinson, who had failed to turn up for one of the bouts. Smith won in style, and assumed that boxer's name himself. Later, an observer remarked to Robinson's trainer that he seemed to have a "sweet" fighter. The trainer, George Gainsford, replied, "Yes, he's as sweet as sugar."

Rob Roy: [1] Robert MacGregor (1671–1734), Sc. Highland outlaw; [2] John MacGregor (1825–1892), Eng. traveller, writer, canoe designer. The usual explanation behind the name is that the outlaw signed himself as "Rob Roy," meaning "red Rob" and referring to his dark red hair. However, the motto of the MacGregors was "My tribe is royal," and "Roy" could have derived from this. This origin seems to be supported by the use of the same name by the second MacGregor noted here, although he originally applied the name "Rob Roy" to the canoe he designed and built in 1865. This was built of oak but covered fore and aft in cedar, which is a red wood.

Frederick **Robson:** Thomas Robson Brownhill (1821–1864), Eng. music hall actor.

May **Robson:** Mary Jeanette Robison (1858–1942), Austral.-born U.S. stage, film actress.

Stuart **Robson:** Henry Robson Stuart (1836–1903), U.S. comedian.

Patricia **Roc:** Felicia Riese (1918–   ), Eng. film actress. The actress's adopted name is simply an adaptation of her real name.

Blas **Roca:** Francesco Calederío (1908–1987), Cuban government official. When the political activist joined the Communist Party in 1929, he took the name "Roca," Spanish for "rock." Compare the names of other noted Communists, such as Kamenev (stone) and Stalin (steel).

Mark **Rochester:** William Charles Mark Kent (1823–1902), Eng. author, journalist. Charles Kent (as he was usually known) became editor of the evening newspaper *The Sun* in 1845, and used his pen name for political sketches that he published separately, such as *The Derby Ministry* (1858), later reissued as *Conservative Statesmen*. No doubt the name was inspired by the town of Rochester, in Kent. He himself was born in London.

Rockin' Dopsie: Alton Jay Rubin (1932–   ), U.S. jazz musician.

Jimmy **Rodgers:** James Snow (1933–   ), U.S. folksinger. The singer took his name from the country singer Jimmie Rodgers (1897–1933), the "Singing Brakeman," who died in the year that the folksinger was born. The name was intended commemoratively.

Red **Rodney:** Robert Roland Chudnick (1927–   ), U.S. trumpeter.

William **Roerick:** William Roehrich (1912–   ), U.S. playwright, stage actor.

Ginger **Rogers:** Virginia Katherine McMath (1911–   ), U.S. stage, film actress, dancer. "Ginger" was the actress's childhood pet name (from "Virginia"). "Rogers" came from her mother's second marriage to John Rogers in 1920.

Jean **Rogers:** Eleanor Lovegren (1916–   ), U.S. film actress.

Roy **Rogers:** Leonard Slye (1912–   ), U.S. film actor. When singing early in his career with the Pioneer trio, Slye called himself "Dick Weston." He later adopted the name Roy Rogers, which may have been prompted by the name of either Ginger Rogers *(q.v.)* or, more likely, Will Rogers (1879–1935), the movie actor who had formerly been a cowboy.

Shorty **Rogers:** Milton Michael Rajonsky (1924–   ), U.S. jazz musician.

Eric **Rohmer:** Jean Maurice Scherer (1920–   ), Fr. film director.

Sax **Rohmer:** Arthur Sarsfield Ward (1886–1959), Eng. writer of "oriental" mystery stories. The writer was orginally Arthur Henry Ward, but substituted "Sarsfield" for "Henry" when he was 15. His pen name, Sax Rohmer, has a somewhat convoluted origin. "Sax" came from what he believed was the Anglo-Saxon word for "blade" (which may indirectly lie behind the name of the Saxons themselves, as the word for their weapon, although made of stone, not steel). "Rohmer" he interpreted as meaning "roamer," "wanderer." In other words, he was a "roaming blade," otherwise a freelance! He is best remembered not for this, however, but for Fu Manchu, the central character of his "oriental" stories.

Gilbert **Roland:** Luis Antonio Damaso Alonso (1905–   ), Mexican-born U.S. film, TV actor.

C.H. **Rolph:** Cecil Rolph Hewitt (1901–   ), Eng. writer, editor.

Yvonne **Romain:** Yvonne Warren (1938–   ), Br.-born (Fr.-raised) film actress.

Jules **Romains:** Louis-Henri-Jean Farigoule (1885–1972), Fr. playwright, novelist, poet.

Viviane **Romance:** Pauline Ronacher Ortmanns (1909–   ), Fr. film actress. The actress's new surname neatly combines her real second name and surname. Needless to say, she starred in romantic roles, such as the alluring but faithless wife in *La Belle Equipe*, screened in the U.S. as *They Were Five* (1936).

Michael (or Mike) **Romanoff:** Harry Gerguson (1892–1971), Lithuanian-born U.S. restaurateur, film actor. Harry Gerguson posed (to 1958) as His Imperial

Highness Prince Michael Alexandrovitch Dmitry Obolensky Romanoff. Any émigré Russian will tell you what weight such names carried in the ancien régime. (Earlier, he had used the try-out noble names of William Wellington, Arthur Wellesley, and Count Gladstone.) When once at a party in his role of royal Russian, someone spoke Russian to him. He turned away and said to a friend, "How vulgar, we only spoke French at court." We shall not often see his like again. . . .

Romany: George Bramwell Evans (1884–1943), Eng. writer, broadcaster on the countryside. "Romany" suggests gypsies, of course, as well as someone who roams romantically over the country. (For the record, it should be pointed out that gypsies do not regard themselves as Romany people because they lead a roaming or even romantic way of life, but because their name represents the Romany word *rom*, "man.")

Romark: Ronald Markham (1927–1982), Eng. TV hypnotist. The entertainer formed his professional name rather unusually from the first half of his first name and the first half of his surname, in the manner of a trade name. Nor indeed does the name hint at his specialty, which another performer might have chosen to indicate.

Stewart **Rome:** Septimus William Ryott (1887–1965), Br. film actor. The actor's screen name is virtually extracted from his real name (which, however, contains only one *R*, not two).

Edana **Romney:** Edana Rubenstein (1919–), S.A. film actress.

[Sir] Landon **Ronald:** Landon Russell (1873–1938), Eng. conductor, composer.

Edward **Ronns:** Edward Sidney Aarons (1916–1975), U.S. writer of detective fiction.

Mickey **Rooney:** Joe Jule, Jr. (1920–), U.S. film actor. The actor's original screen name was "Mickey McGuire." Later he adopted the name by which he became famous. Why "Mickey Rooney"? No one seems quite sure, although a reference to the popular song *Little Annie Rooney* may have been intended, especially in view of the actor's small stature. One theory claims that his mother called him "Mickey Looney," and that he adopted this with the necessary small adjustment.

Carl **Rosa:** Karl Rose (1842–1889), Ger. conductor, impresario, founder of Carl Rosa Opera Company.

Rosario: Florencia Pérez Podilla (1918–), Sp. ballet dancer, teaming with cousin Antonio *(q.v.)*.

Françoise **Rosay:** Françoise Bandy de Nalèche (1891–1974), Fr. stage, film actress.

Billy **Rose:** William Samuel Rosenberg (1899–1966), U.S. theatre manager, composer.

Calypso **Rose:** McCartha Lewis (1940–), Tobago calypso singer.

Philip **Rose:** Philip Rosenberg (1921–), U.S. stage producer.

[Saint] **Rose of Lima:** Isabel de Flores y del Oliva (1586–1617), Peruvian virgin recluse, of Sp. parentage.

Rosimond: Claude La Roze (c.1640–1686), Fr. actor.

Carl **Rosini:** John Rosen (1882–), Pol.-born magician, working in U.S.

Emperor **Rosko:** Michael Pasternak (1942–   ), Eng. radio DJ.

Natalia **Roslavleva:** Natalia Petrovna René (1907–1977), Russ.-born Br. writer on ballet. The writer used the name for her contributions to the journal *Ballet Today* in the 1940s, taking her name from the Russian dancer Lyubov Roslavleva (1874–1904) by way of a tribute.

Milton **Rosmer:** Arthur Milton Lunt (1881–1971), Br. stage, film actor, director. The actor took his stage name from that of Johannes Rosmer, the central character in Ibsen's play *Rosmersholm.* For a similar borrowing, compare the name of Rebecca West.

J.H. **Rosny:** Joseph-Henri Boex (1856–1940), Fr. novelist + Séraphin-Justin François Boex (1859–1948), Fr. novelist, his brother. The initials are those of the elder brother ("Rosny aîné"), while the surname appears to have been taken from that of "Baron de Rosny," the name by which the Duc de Sully (1559–1641), the famous minister of Henri IV, was known during the early part of his career.

Adrian **Ross:** Arthur Reed Ropes (1859–1933), Eng. writer of lyrics, librettos for musicals. The lyricist and librettist used the name "Arthur Reed" for the libretto of a vaudeville entertainment, *A Double Event,* written jointly (a "double event") with Arthur Law and staged in 1884. He later adopted the name "Adrian Ross," first using it for the libretto of *Joan of Arc,* produced in 1891. Certainly "Adrian Ross" has something of a musical ring which "Arthur Ropes" does not entirely possess.

Annie **Ross:** Annabella Macauley Lynch, née Short (1930–   ), Eng. jazz singer. Possibly "Ross" evolved out of the singer's maiden name, of which it is a sort of reversal.

Barnaby **Ross:** Ellery Queen *(q.v.).* The Ellery Queen partnership used this name for various crime novels featuring a detective named Drury Lane. Rather surprisingly, the two men did not use this name as their own pseudonym. But no doubt it would have simply looked too corny, or theatrical.

Diana **Ross:** Diane Earl (1944–   ), U.S. black rock singer.

John Hume **Ross:** Thomas Edward Lawrence (1888–1935), Eng. soldier, archaeologist, writer ("Lawrence of Arabia"). This was the name chosen by Lawrence to escape publicity when he enlisted in the Royal Air Force in 1922. A year later he joined the Tank Corps as "T.E. Shaw," adopting the name by deed poll in 1927. The latter name was intended as a mark of respect to Bernard Shaw.

Leonard Q. **Ross:** Leo Calvin Rosten (1908–   ), Pol.-born U.S. humorous writer.

Martin **Ross:** Violet Florence Martin (1862–1915), Ir. author. The writer used her surname as her first name, taking "Ross" from her birthplace, Ross House, County Galway. In collaboration with her cousin, Edith Somerville (1858–1949), she wrote many books and stories about Irish life under the joint name of "Somerville and Ross."

Mike **Ross:** Colin John Novelle (1948–   ), Br. radio DJ.

Shirley **Ross:** Bernice Gaunt (1909–1975), U.S. pianist, singer, film actress.

Robert **Rossen:** Robert Rosen (1908–1966), U.S. film director, screenwriter.

Eleanora **Rossi-Drago:** Palmina Omiccioli (1925–   ), It. film actress.

Lillian **Roth:** Lillian Rutstein (1910–1980), U.S. film actress.

Mark **Rothko:** Marcus Rothkovich (1903–1970), Russ.-born U.S. painter.

Ola **Rotimi:** Emmanuel Gladstone Olawole (1938–   ), Nigerian playwright.

Johnny **Rotten:** John Joseph Lydon (1956–   ), Eng. punk rock musician. The former member of the notorious Sex Pistols group chose a name that was "meaningful" in the same way as those of his fellow punk rockers. The overall attitude was expressed in a contemporary news item: "They call themselves names designed to alienate society: Rat Scabies, Dee Generate, Johnny Rotten, Sid Vicious" [*Sunday Mirror*, June 12, 1977]. (See the last of these names separately.) After the breakup of the group in 1978, soon followed by the death of Vicious, John Lydon reverted to his real name and formed his own group, Public Image Limited (P.I.L.).

Effie Adelaide **Rowlands:** Effie Marie Albanesi, née Henderson (1859–1936), Br. romantic novelist ("Madame Albanesi").

Samuel **Roxy:** Samuel Lionel Rothafel (1882–1936), U.S. film distributor. The name became famous to the public at large through the Roxy cinema chain, typified by New York's Roxy Theatre, which opened in 1927. It was this particular name that lay behind the British rock group Roxy Music, formed in 1970, where of course the name itself suggests "rock."

Marie **Roze:** Hippolyte Ponsin (1846–1926), Fr. opera singer.

Alma **Rubens:** Alma Smith (1897–1931), U.S. film actress.

Harry **Ruby:** Harry Rubenstein (1895–1974), U.S. songwriter.

Steele **Ruby:** Arthur Hoey Davis (1868–1935), Austral. novelist, playwright, short story writer.

Patrick **Ruell:** Reginald Hill (1936–   ), Br. crime novelist.

Titta **Ruffo:** Ruffo Titta (1878–1953), It. opera singer. Unusually, the opera singer's name was taken from a family pet dog. Oresta Titta frequently took his dog, Ruffo, out hunting. One day, on such an expedition, the dog was accidentally shot and killed. Grief-stricken, his master vowed to preserve the dog's name, and later, when his son was born, named Ruffo commemoratively. In due course the boy grew up and started an operatic career. He had come to dislike his dog-derived name, but not wishing to offend his father, chose a new professional name by simply turning his original name around. Thus Ruffo Titta became Titta Ruffo, family honor was satisfied, and the canine commemoration was preserved.

Sig **Ruman:** Siegfried Alban Rumann (1884–1967), Ger. film actor.

Jia **Ruskaya:** Eugenia Borisenko (1902–1970), Russ.-It. ballet dancer. The dancer adopted a name that indicated her Russian parentage, with "Jia" an Italian pet form of her first name.

Anna **Russell:** Anna Claudia Russell-Brown (1911–   ), Br. stage entertainer.

Billy **Russell:** Adam George Brown (1893–1971), Eng. music hall comedian.

Fred **Russell:** Thomas Frederick Parnell (1862–1957), Eng. ventriloquist, variety artist. The performer changed his name to avoid any unpleasant associations with the name of the Irish politician Charles Parnell, who had been involved in a scandal with Kitty O'Shea, the wife of a prominent party member.

Leon **Russell:** Hank Wilson (1941–   ), U.S. rock musician.

Lillian **Russell:** Helen Louise Leonard (1861–1922), U.S. stage actress, singer.

Sarah **Russell:** Marghanita Laski (1915–1988), Br. novelist. The writer used the name for her second novel, *To Bed with Grand Music* (1946).

Mark **Rutherford:** William Hale White (1831–1913), Eng. novelist.

Irene **Ryan:** Irene Riordan (1903–1973), U.S. film comedienne.

Sheila **Ryan:** Katherine McLaughlin (1921–1975), U.S. film actress.

Bobby **Rydell:** Robert Ridarelli (1942–   ), U.S. pop musician.

Alfred **Ryder:** Alfred Jacob Corn (1919–   ), U.S. stage actor, director.

Mitch **Ryder:** William Levise, Jr. (1945–   ), U.S. (white) soul singer.

Poul **Rytter:** Parmo Carl Ploug (1813–1894), Dan. poet, politician.

Umberto **Saba:** Umberto Poli (1883–1957), It. poet.

Sabrina: Norma Sykes (1928–   ), Eng. film, TV actress. The actress may have taken her name arbitrarily, rather than from the Samuel A. Taylor play (or subsequent film) *Sabrina Fair* (1954).

Sabu: Sabu Dastagir (1924–1963), Indian juvenile film actor, working in U.K., U.S.

Sade: Helen Folasade Adu (1959–   ), Nigerian-born pop singer, working in U.K.

Michael **Sadleir:** Michael Thomas Harvey Sadler (1888–1957), Br. novelist, biographer. The writer adopted an earlier spelling of the family name to distinguish himself from his father, Sir Michael Sadler (1861–1943), a noted educationist and art patron, and "my best and wisest friend," as his son called him in his biography.

Françoise **Sagan:** Françoise Quoirez (1935–   ), Fr. novelist. The famous author of *Bonjour Tristesse,* published when she was 19, took her pen name from the Princesse de Sagan, a character in Proust's *A la Recherche du Temps Perdu.*

Leontine **Sagan:** Leontine Schlesinger (1899–1974), Austr. film director.

Sagittarius: [1] Olga Miller, née Katzin (1896–1987), Br. author, satirist, of Russ.-Jewish parentage; [2] Heinrich Schütz (1585–1672), Ger. church music composer. The pseudonym was chosen for quite different reasons by the two quite different people. Olga Miller used the name for her satirical verses in the weekly *New Statesman* (from 1934). These were "barbed," like the arrows shot by the mythological Sagittarius, the Archer. Heinrich Schütz, on the other hand, was simply translating his German name into Latin, in the manner of his time. (Modern German *Schütze* not only means "archer" but is the standard word for "Sagittarius," the sign of the zodiac.) Olga Miller (known to her friends as "Saj") used other names for her satirical socio-political contributions to other publications. For *Time and Tide* she wrote as "Fiddlestick," for the *Manchester Guardian* she was "Mercutio," and in the *Daily Herald* she appeared as "Scorpio."

Michael **St. Clair:** Michael Sinclair MacAuslan Shea (1938–   ), Sc. spy fiction writer. The writer used this name to distinguish his literary activities from his official duties. He was press secretary to Queen Elizabeth from 1978 to 1987.

Renée **St. Cyr:** Marie-Louis Vittore (1907–   ), Fr. film actress.

Michel **Saint-Denis:** Jacques Duchesne (1897–1971), Fr. theatre director, playwright, actor.

Ruth **St. Denis:** Ruth Dennis (1879–1968), U.S. ballet dancer, choreographer.

Raymond **St. Jacques:** James Johnson (1930–   ), U.S. black film actor.

Susan **Saint James:** Susan Miller (1946–   ), U.S. film, TV actress.

Betta **St. John:** Betty Streidler (1930–   ), U.S. film actress.

Christopher Marie **St. John:** Christabel Marshall (? –1960), Br. novelist, playwright, biographer.

Jill **St. John:** Jill Oppenheim (1940–   ), U.S. film actress.

S.Z. Sakall: Eugen Gerő Szakall (1884–1955), Hung. film actor, working in U.S. ("Cuddles"). The actor's screen initials are the first two letters of his real surname.

Alexander **Sakharoff:** Alexander Zuckermann (1886–1963), Russ. ballet dancer, teacher, working in Italy. The dancer translated his name from German to Russian, basically *Zucker* ("sugar") to *sakhar*. People named Sugarman will often be found, in the English-speaking world, to have had a similar Jewish name origin, such as the Welsh-born TV actress Sara Sugarman (1962–   ).

Saki: Hector Hugh Munro (1870–1916), Eng. short story writer. The writer first used the name for his short story collection entitled *Reginald* (1904). According to his sister, the pseudonym comes from a line in Fitzgerald's version of *The Rubáiyát* of Omar Khayyám: "And when like her, O Saki, you shall pass." But another theory claims that the name is a contraction of "Sakya Muni," one of the names of the Buddha [J.W. Lambert, Introduction to *The Bodley Head Saki*, 1963].

Saladin: William Stewart Ross (1844–1906), Sc. author of poems, works on agnosticism. Ross used this name for his contributions to the *Agnostic Journal and Secular Review*, of which he was the editor. The name is a symbolic one, that of the twelfth-century sultan of Egypt who invaded Palestine and defeated the Christians.

Soupy **Sales:** Milton Hines (1926–   ), U.S. TV entertainer, film actor. "Soupy" arose as a childhood nickname, as his surname, Hines, sounded like "Heinz." He changed his surname to "Sales" to match this, and adopted his new name as his screen name in 1952.

Felix **Salten:** Siegmund Salzmann (1869–1947), Hung. novelist, journalist, critic, working in Switzerland.

Galina **Samsova:** Galina Ursuliak (later, Prokovsky), née Samtsova (1937–   ), Russ.-born ballet dancer, working in Canada.

George **Sand:** Amandine-Aurore-Lucile Dudevant, née Dupin (1804–1876), Fr. writer. One of the most famous of literary pseudonyms. The French novelist derived it from her liaison with the writer Jules Sandeau. ("George," it seems, comes from the fact that Sandeau first advised her to write independently, without his assistance, on St. George's Day.) Mme Dudevant first used the name in 1831 for writing done jointly with Sandeau: some articles for *Le Figaro* and their first joint novel *Rose et Blanche*. She herself first used the name independently the following year, for her novel *Indiana*. Earlier she had used the name "Blaise Bonnain," taken from a carpenter she had known as a girl. Note that "George" is so spelled – not in the French manner with an "s". The abbreviated form "Sand" was devised by Jules, and used both by him (as Jules Sand) and Maurice Sand, the son of George Sand and her husband the baron Dudevant.

Paul **Sand:** Paul Sanchez (1944–   ), U.S. film actor.

Dominique **Sanda:** Dominique Varaigne (1948–   ), U.S. film actress.

Cora **Sandel:** Sara Fabricius (1880–1974), Norw. novelist, short story writer.

Baby **Sandy:** Sandra Henville (1938–   ), U.S. child film actress.

Jacopo **Sansovino:** Jacopo Tatti (1486–1570), It. sculptor, architect. The sculptor studied in the workshop of Andrea Sansovino from the age of 16 and adopted the name of his master out of admiration for him and his work.

Santana: Carlos Santana (1947–   ), U.S. rock musician.

George **Santayana:** Jorge Ruiz de Santayana y Borrais (1863–1952), Sp.-born U.S. writer, philosopher.

Sapper: Herman Cyril McNeile (1888–1937), Eng. novelist. The creator of Bulldog Drummond, the ex-army officer who foils the activities of the international crook, Carl Peterson, adopted his pseudonym when an officer in the Royal Engineers, a "sapper" being a term for a military engineer. The name was devised for him by Lord Northcliffe, as no regular serving officer was allowed to publish under his real name. McNeile attempted to use his real name after the First World War, but the public would have none of it, and demanded their familiar "Sapper."

Susan **Sarandon:** Susan Tomalin (1946–   ), U.S. film actress. The actress's screen name is that of her (now divorced) husband, Chris Sarandon.

Gene **Sarazen:** Eugene Saraceni (1902–   ), U.S. golfer, of It. parentage.

Joseph **Sargent:** Giuseppe Sargente (1925–   ), U.S. film director.

Leslie **Sarony:** Leslie Sarony-Frye (1897–   ), Eng. music hall singer.

Andrea del **Sarto:** *see* **Andrea del Sarto**

Lu **Säuberlich:** Liselotte Säuberlich-Lauke (1911–1976), Ger. stage, film actress.

Richard **Saunders:** Poor Richard *(q.v.)*.

George **Sava:** George Alexis Milkomanovich Milkomane (1903–   ), Russ.-born Br. author, consulting surgeon.

Ann **Savage:** Bernie Lyon (1921–   ), U.S. film actress.

Laura **Savage:** Frederic George Stephens (1828–1907), Eng. art critic. The writer used this name early for some contributions on Italian painting to the Pre-Raphaelite journal *The Germ* (1850). He also used the name "John Seward" for his papers that this organ published.

Dany **Saval:** Danielle Nadine Suzanne Salle (1940–   ), Fr. film actress.

Lee **Savold:** Lee Hulver (?1814–1972), U.S. heavyweight boxer.

Joseph **Sawyer:** Joseph Sauer (1901–1982), U.S. film comedian.

John **Saxon:** Carmen Orrico (1935–   ), U.S. film actor.

Peter **Saxon:** Wilfred McNeilly (1921–   ), Sc. detective, occult fiction writer.

Leo **Sayer:** Gerard Hugh Sayer (1948–   ), Eng. rock singer. The singer was given his nickname by the wife of Adam Faith *(q.v.)*, who when she first met him commented on his "mane" of hair, "Hey, he's like a little lion." Sayer liked the name, and adopted it [*Reveille*, January 12, 1979].

Scaeva: John Stubbes (1541–1600), Eng. Puritan zealot. The writer published a pamphlet entitled *The Discovery of a Gaping Gulf* (1579) condemning Queen Elizabeth's proposed marriage with Henry, Duke of Anjou. For this traitorous act, his right hand was ordered to be cut off. *Scaeva* is Latin for "lefthanded."

Gia **Scala:** Giovanna Sgoglio (1934–1972), Br. film actress, of Ir.-It. parentage, working in U.S. The actress's screen name suggests both her own surname and the name of La Scala, Italy's chief opera house, in Milan.

Prunella **Scales:** Prunella West, née Illingworth (1932–   ), Eng. stage, TV actress. The actress adopted her mother's maiden name when she became a professional. Her mother had been on the stage before her marriage, and "I felt my father's name of Illingworth was rather long with Prunella" (personal letter from Prunella Scales, October 6, 1988).

Leon **Schiller:** Leon de Schildenfeld (1887–1954), Pol. theatre director, designer.

Dr. **Schmidt:** Johann Christoph Friedrich von Schiller (1759–1805), Ger. poet, playwright. The famous dramatist was originally a military surgeon in a Württemberg regiment. In 1781 he went absent without leave to attend a performance of his first play, *Die Räuber*. He was arrested by order of the regimental commander-in-chief, the Duke of Württemberg, and condemned to publish nothing but medical treatises. However, the following year he escaped from the Duke under the assumed name of "Dr. Schmidt" and spent several years, his so-called *Wanderjahre*, outside the country. Presumably the choice of name was an arbitrary one, like English "Dr. Smith."

Romy **Schneider:** Rosemarie Magdalena Albach-Retty (1938–1982), Austr. film actress. Although the actress's father was Wolf Albach-Retty, her mother was the movie star Magda Schneider. Rosemarie (pet name, Romy) adopted her mother's name as her screen name when she made her film debut in 1953. Her career took off immediately, and by 1955 Magda Schneider was playing supporting roles to those of her daughter. (Magda Schneider should not be confused with her near-namesake, Maria Schneider, who was a contemporary of Romy but who was French-born.)

A **Scholar:** Samuel Wesley (1662–1735), Eng. clergyman, poet. The father of John Wesley, the founder of Methodism, used this name for a collection of poems published in 1685. The exact title of the work was: *Maggots: or, Poems on Several Subjects, never before handled. By a Schollar*. At the time he was a student at Exeter College, Oxford.

Lotte **Schöne:** Charlotte Bodenstein (1891–1977), Aust.-born Fr. opera singer.

Gordon **Scott:** Gordon M. Werschkul (1927–   ), U.S. film actor.

Jack **Scott:** [1] Jack Scafone (1938–   ), Can. rock singer; [2] Jonathan Escott (1922–   ), Br. crime novelist.

Lizabeth **Scott:** Emma Matzo (1922–   ), U.S. film actress.

Randolph **Scott:** Randolph Crane (1903–1987), U.S. film actor.

Raymond **Scott:** Harry Warnow (1910–   ), U.S. popular music composer, arranger.

Ronnie **Scott:** Ronald Schatt (1927–   ), Eng. jazz club owner.

Sheila **Scott:** Sheila Christine Hopkins (1927–1988), Eng. aviator, lecturer, actress, writer.

Tony **Scott:** Anthony Sciacca (1921–   ), U.S. clarinettist.

Sir Walter **Scott:** James Kirke Paulding (1779–1860), U.S. author. Several writers and plagiarists adopted the name of the great Scottish author for their own works. James Kirke Paulding, a close friend of Washington Irving, used the name for *The Lay of the Scotch Fiddle, a Tale of Havre de Grace* (1813), which was thus itself a "Scotch fiddle." A joint pseudonym shared by Paulding was Launcelot Langstaff *(q.v.)*.

Scotty: Scott Wiseman (1909–1981), U.S. country singer, teaming with Lulu Belle *(q.v.)*.

The **Scout:** Clive Graham (1913–1974), Eng. racing correspondent. The correspondent assumed the byname used by his predecessor on the *Daily Express*, Cyril Luckman. Graham began his journalistic career as "Bendex" in 1931, this name presumably referring to the curve in a racecourse (where one can spot the leaders as they enter the straight).

Martinus **Scriblerus** [1] Alexander Pope (1688–1744), Eng. poet; [2] George Crabbe (1754–1832), Eng. poet. The "Scriblerus Club" was the name of a group of famous writers, including Pope, Swift, and Arbuthnot, formed in about 1713. They undertook the production of the *Memoirs of Martinus Scriblerus*, printed in the second edition of the works of Pope in 1741. The object of the club was to ridicule "all false tastes in learning." The same name was adopted by Fielding for one of his earlier works (see next entry below).

H. **Scriblerus Secundus:** Henry Fielding (1707–1754), Eng. novelist, playwright. Fielding adopted this name for *The Tragedy of Tragedies, or Tom Thumb the Great* (1731), taking it (as a "second scribbler") from the name "Martinus Scriblerus" used jointly by members of the "Scriblerus Club" (see entry above).

George Julius Poulett **Scrope:** George Julius Poulett Thomson (1797–1876), Eng. geologist, politician. The geologist and political economist married Emma Phipps Scrope, heiress of William Scrope, in 1821, and thereupon assumed her name and the Scrope family's arms. William Scrope was the last of the old earls of Wiltshire, and had inherited not only his own father's family estates but those of another branch of the family in Lincolnshire. These all now passed to Emma, and so to the former George Thomson. (He subsequently sold the Wiltshire estates after his wife's premature death, and then remarried. But as there were no children of either marriage, the Scrope inheritance lapsed.)

Barbara **Seagull:** Barbara Hershey *(q.v.)*.

Charles **Sealsfield:** Karl Postl (1793–1864), Swiss monk, author, working in U.S.

Edward **Search:** Abraham Tucker (1705–1774), Eng. philosopher. The writer first used this intentionally meaningful name for his short philosophical work, *Freewill, Foreknowledge, and Fate* (1763). But he also used it for the work by which he is best known, *The Light of Nature Pursued* (1768–1778). Similar names were used by other thinkers and writers, such as Archbishop Whately, who published *Religion and her Name* (1847) as "John Search." Tucker used the name "Cuthbert Comment" for a good-humored little pamphlet, *Man in Quest of Himself* (1763), written in reply to some critics.

January **Searle:** George Searle Phillips (1815–1889), Eng. miscellaneous writer, working in U.S. If "January" does not derive from "George" it presumably alludes to a significant month in the writer's life. It so happened that he died in January.

George **Seaton:** George Stenius (1911–1979), U.S. film writer, director.

Anna **Seghers:** Netti Radványi, née Reiling (1900–1983), Ger. novelist, working in U.S. The writer took her name from the Flemish painter Hercules Seghers (1589–*c.*1638), a pupil of Rembrandt, whom she had always admired. She also used the name in an early story.

Lea **Seidl:** Caroline Mayrseidl (1895–1987), Austr. stage, film actress, singer, working in U.K.

Steve **Sekely:** Istvan Szekely (1899–1979), Hung. film director, working in U.S.

P.T. **Selbit:** Percy Tibbles (1879–1938), Eng. magician. Just a little juggling with the performer's surname, and his new name complete with initials appears. (But isn't his real name better all round?)

Connie **Sellecca:** Concetta Sellecchia (1955–), U.S. TV actress.

Arthur **Sellings:** Robert Arthur Ley (1921–1968), Br. SF writer.

Selmar: [Baron] Karl Gustav von Brinckman (1764–1847), Swe. diplomat, poet.

Morton **Selten:** Morton Richard Stubbs (1860–1940), Eng. stage, film actor.

Tonio **Selwart:** Antonio Franz Thaeus Selmair-Selwart (1896–), Ger. actor.

Lewis J. **Selznick:** Lewis Zeleznik (1870–1933), Russ.-born U.S. film distributor, impresario. Was this man hoping to cash in on the famous Selznick name? Not at all, he was the father of the well-known producer, David O. Selznick (1902–1965).

Mack **Sennett:** Michael Sinnot (1880–1960), U.S. comedy film producer (the "King of Comedy").

Captain **Sensible:** Raymond Burns (1957–), Eng. pop singer. The singer adopted his name in about 1977. Its origins are somewhat vague, but it appears to have had something to do with his habit of wearing a peaked cap, playing the fool on an airplane trip to France with his punk group, The Damned, and announcing himself as "your captain speaking." He later admitted that he would have preferred a more macho name, "something like Duane Zenith or Bert Powerhouse, but I'm lumbered with Captain Sensible" [*Observer Magazine*, February 3, 1985].

Massimo **Serato:** Giuseppe Segato (1917–), It. film actor.

Sergius: [1] Bartholomew Kirillovich (1314–1392), Russ. saint, monk ("Sergius of Radonezh"); [2] Ivan Nikolayevich Stragorodsky (1867–1944), Russ. churchman, patriarch of Moscow and All Russia. St. Sergius of Radonezh was one of Russia's most important spiritual leaders, and was subsequently regarded as the saint protector of Russia. Ivan Stragorodsky almost certainly took his religious name in his honor. This means that the fourteenth-century monk must have taken his own name from an earlier Sergius. He was possibly the third-century Christian martyr St Sergius, who with St Bacchus was put to death by the Romans in about 303. Sergius of Radonezh adopted his religious name in 1337, when consecrated a monk. Stragorodsky similarly took his name in 1890. See also the next name below.

Sergius IV: Pietro Buccaporci (? –1012), It. pope. The pope's original surname was actually a nickname, meaning "pig's snout," and referring to his appearance. He was no doubt all too glad to take a papal name that had been used by three popes before him.

Ernest Evan Thompson **Seton:** Ernest Evan Seton Thompson (1860–1946), Eng. author, artist, naturalist, working in Canada. The writer inverted his two last names when he began his Canadian career as naturalist to the Government of Manitoba. He founded the Woodcraft Movement (later amalgamated with the Boy Scouts), and eventually became Chief Scout of America.

Dr. Seuss: Theodor Seuss Giesel (1904–   ), U.S. writer, illustrator of children's books. The well-known picture book author called himself "Dr." by way of a self-conferred title. In 1955, however, his old college, Dartmouth, awarded him a genuine doctorate.

David **Severn:** David Storr Unwin (1918–   ), Eng. novelist, children's writer.

David **Seville:** Ross Bagdassarian (1919–1972), U.S. music, record company executive.

Anne **Seymour:** Phyllis Digby Morton, née Panting (? –1984), Eng. journalist, broadcaster.

Gordon **Seymour:** [Sir] Charles Waldstein (later, Watson) (1856–1927), U.S.-born Br. archaeologist.

Jane **Seymour:** Joyce Penelope Wilhelmina Frankenberg (1951–   ), Eng. film actress, working in U.S. If the actress's screen name is not derived from the name of Henry VIII's third wife, possibly it is a compliment to Jane Seymour Fonda, her fellow actress?

Lynn **Seymour:** Lynn Berta Springbett (1939–   ), Can. ballet dancer. Despite the possible aptness of her real surname (although it does suggest "bedsprings"), the dancer was advised to find a new name by choreographer Kenneth Macmillan. It was he who proposed "Seymour." The name seems to appeal as a pseudonym (see the three entries above). If the charisma does not stem from the name of Jane Seymour, the third wife of Henry VIII, possibly the lure lies in a name that subconsciously conjures up "see more," which could be regarded as propitious or fulfilling in some way.

William **Seymour:** William Gorman Cunningham (1855–1933), U.S. stage actor. For comments on the apparent charm of "Seymour," see the name above.

John **Shadow:** John Byrom (1692–1763), Eng. poet. The poet (on no account to be confused with Byron!) used this appropriate name for two papers on dreams that he contributed to the *Spectator* (Nos. 586, 593) in 1714.

Mighty **Shadow:** Winston Bailey (*c.*1939–   ), U.S. black calypso singer.

Dell **Shannon:** Elizabeth Linington (1921–   ), U.S. mystery writer.

Del **Shannon:** Charles Westover (1939–   ), U.S. pop singer, songwriter. The near identity of this name and the one above seems a remarkable coincidence. The pop singer is said to have derived his name partly from a friend, Mark Shannon, and partly from his boss's car, a Cadillac Coupe de Ville. But had he also come across the mystery writer and her pen name? And where did *she* get it? Elizabeth Linington had used other pseudonyms, including "Anne Blaisdell," "Lesley Egan," and "Egan O'Neill." These, together with "Dell Shannon," sound somewhat Irish, but otherwise fairly unremarkable. It would be good to have the coincidence satisfactorily accounted for.

Omar **Sharif:** Michel Shalhoub (1932–   ), Egyptian film actor, of Syrian-Lebanese descent. The romantic movie star explains in his autobiography how he arrived at his screen name: "I'd changed my name to do 'The Blazing Sun.' At birth,

I was Michael Shalhoub. My first name, Michael, annoyed me. Anybody could be a Michael. I'd tried to come up with something that sounded Middle Eastern and that could still be spelled in every language. Omar! Two syllables that had a good ring to them and reminded Americans of General Omar Bradley. Next I thought of combining Omar with the Arabic Sherif, but I realized that this would evoke the word 'sheriff,' which was bit too cowboyish. So I opted for a variant—I became Omar Sharif. . ." [Omar Sharif with Marie-Thérèse Guinchard, *The Eternal Male*, 1977]. (A footnote by the translator of the book from the French, Martin Sokolinsky, points out that the Arabic word *sherif* is a form of title applied to one of noble ancestry in a Middle Eastern country.)

Jack **Sharkey:** Joseph Paul Zukauskas (1902–   ), U.S. heavyweight boxer. The boxer took his name from a former leading heavyweight, Sailor Tom Sharkey.

Dee Dee **Sharp:** Diana LaRue (1945–   ), U.S. pop singer.

Luke **Sharp:** Robert Barr (1850–1912), Sc. novelist, working in Canada, U.K. A name of the same punning order as Justin Case *(q.v.)* and his near-cousin, Upton Close *(q.v.)*. Compare also Sandie Shaw (below).

Artie **Shaw:** Arthur Arshawsky (1910–   ), U.S. jazz musician.

Brian **Shaw:** Brian Earnshaw (1928–   ), Eng. ballet dancer.

Roger **Shaw:** Roger Ollerearnshaw (1931–   ), Eng. TV announcer.

Run Run **Shaw:** Shao Yi-fu (1906–   ), Chin. film producer, working in Hong Kong.

Sandie **Shaw:** Sandra Goodrich (1947–   ), Eng. pop singer. A pleasantly punning seaside name, with "Sandie," of course, from her first name.

Susan **Shaw:** Patsy Sloots (1929–1978), Eng. film actress.

T.E. **Shaw:** *see* John Hume **Ross.**

Victoria **Shaw:** Jeanette Elphick (1935–   ), Austral. film actress, working in U.S. In view of the actress's nationality, this sounds like a state-inspired name.

Wini **Shaw:** Winfred Lei Momi (1899–1982), U.S. film actress, singer, of Hawaiian descent.

Dick **Shawn:** Richard Schulefand (1928–1987), U.S. film comedian.

Robert **Shayne:** Robert Shaen Dawe (*c.*1910–   ), U.S. film actor.

Tamara **Shayne:** Tamara Nikoulin (1897–1983), Russ.-U.S. film actress.

N. **Shchedrin:** Mikhail Yevgrafovich Saltykov (-Shchedrin) (1826–1889), Russ. writer. If English-speaking readers are at all familiar with any work of the Russian author born Mikhail Yevgrafovich Saltykov, who is also often called Saltykov-Shchedrin, it will probably be with his famous novel describing the decay of the provincial gentry, *The Golovlëv Family* (1872–6), translated by Natalie Duddington, among others. Saltykov's son has explained how his father came by his pseudonym, which is based on the Russian word *shchedry,* "generous": "It was like this. When he was in government service, he was advised that it was not done to sign one's work with one's real name. So he had to find a pen name, but could not hit on anything suitable. My mother suggested that he should choose a pseudonym based on the word 'shchedry,' as in his writings he was extraordinarily generous with any kind of sarcasm. My father liked his wife's idea, and from then on he called himself Shchedrin." It is possible, however, that the name could have come from a servant in the employ of Saltykov's family, or from a local merchant T. Shchedrin, or some acquaintance of Saltykov, or it could even derive from the word *shchedrina*, "pockmarks," with reference to the "pockmarks" on the face of Russia at the time (1870s) [Dmitriev, pp. 58–9].

Al **Shean:** Alfred Schoenberg (1868–1949), Ger.-born U.S. stage, film comedian.

Moira **Shearer:** Moira Shearer King (1926–   ), Sc. ballet dancer, stage, film actress.

Norma **Shearer:** Edith Norma Fisher (1900–1983), Can. film actress.

Martin **Sheen:** Ramon Estevez (1940–   ), U.S. stage actor. The actor adopted the maiden name of his wife, née Janet Sheen.

Barbara **Shelley:** Barbara Kowin (1933–   ), Br. film actress.

Paul **Shelley:** Paul Matthews (1942–   ), Eng. stage, TV actor.

John **Shelton:** John Price (1917–1972), U.S. film actor.

Sam **Shepard:** Samuel Shepard Rogers (1943–   ), U.S. playwright, film actor.

Michael **Shepley:** Michael Shepley-Smith (1907–1961), Br. stage, film actor.

T.G. **Sheppard:** William Browder (1942–   ), U.S. country singer. The origin of the singer's name is told by Murray Kash in his *Book of Country* (see Bibliography): "T.G. was loathe to use his real name, Bill Browder, feeling that it might conflict with his promotion work. Inspiration struck when looking out of his office window across the street, he saw some dogs of the German Shepherd breed. An office colleague jokingly suggested he call himself 'The German Shepherd.' T.G. was amused at the thought, but on later reflection, decided he liked the idea."

John **Shepperd:** Shepperd Strudwick (1907–1983), U.S. film actor.

Ann **Sheridan:** Clara Lou Sheridan (1915–1967), U.S. film actress (the "Oomph Girl"). The actress's new first name is nicely echoed in her original surname.

Dinah **Sheridan:** Dinah Mec (1920–   ), Br. film actress, of Ger.-Russ. parentage.

Paul **Sheriff:** Paul Schouvalov (or Schouvaloff) (1903–1962), Russ.-born film art director, working in U.K.

Vincent **Sherman:** Abram Orovitz (1906–   ), U.S. film director.

Lydia **Sherwood:** Lily Shavelson (1906–1989), Br. stage, film actress.

Madeleine **Sherwood:** Madeleine Thornton (1926–   ), Can. film actress.

George **Shiels:** George Morsheil (1881–1949), Ir. playwright.

Mother **Shipton:** Ursula Shipton, née Southill (or Southiel) (?*fl.*1486), Eng. prophetess. The lady is probably quite fictional, but her popular biographical data are as here.

Shirley: [Sir] John Skelton (1831–1897), Sc. lawyer, author, literary critic. The writer adopted his pen name from the main character of *Shirley* (1849), the novel by Charlotte Brontë, whose earlier *Jane Eyre* (1847) he had favorably reviewed. (Miss Brontë had written to thank him.) He used the name for his essays and reviews in *The Guardian,* a short-lived Edinburgh periodical, as well as for contributions to the longer-lived *Fraser's Magazine.* He took a pseudonym so as not to jeopardize his professional prospects as an up-and-coming lawyer.

Anne **Shirley:** Dawn Evelyeen Paris (1918–   ), U.S. film actress.

Michelle **Shocked:** [real name unknown] (*c.*1962–   ), U.S. pop singer.

Troy **Shondell:** Gary Shelton (1940–   ), U.S. pop singer, producer.

Dinah **Shore:** Frances Rose Shore (1917–   ), U.S. singer, radio, TV actress. Did the popular singer ever consider that her name might suggest "dinosaur"? The change of name was initially prompted when "everybody down in Nashville" suggested she should use the pet form of her first name, Fanny, quipping and quoting: "Fanny sat on a tack. Fanny Rose. Fanny Rose sat on a tack. Did Fanny rise?" "I had to do something," sighed Frances Rose Shore, so changed her first two names to "Dinah," from the song of that name. (Even so, as a child star, she *had* performed as "Fanny Rose" for some time.)

Bob **Short:** [1] Augustus Baldwin Longstreet (1790–1870), U.S. lawyer, educationist, author; [2] Alexander Pope (1688–1744), Eng. poet. Pope used the name for some contributions to the short-lived periodical *The Guardian* (1713), and it is possible that Longstreet borrowed the pseudonym from him, enjoying the pun on his own surname.

Abel **Shufflebottom:** Robert Southey (1774–1843), Eng. poet. A frivolous nonce pseudonym used by the well-known "Lake Poet."

Nevil **Shute:** Nevil Shute Norway (1899–1960), Br. novelist.

Timothy **Shy:** Dominic Bevan Wyndham Lewis (1894–1969), Br. journalist, novelist, biographer. The writer used this pseudonym for his contributions to the *News Chronicle* from 1934. His better-known pen name was Beachcomber (*q.v.*).

Edward William **Sidney:** Nathaniel Beverley Tucker (1784–1851), U.S. novelist.

George **Sidney:** Sammy Greenfield (1878–1945), U.S. film comedian.

Margaret **Sidney:** Harriet Mulford Lothrop, née Stone (1844–1924), U.S. children's writer.

Sylvia **Sidney:** Sophia Kosow (1910–   ), U.S. stage, film actress. The actress adopted her stepfather's name, Sidney, as her professional name.

Siful Sifadda: Henrik Arnold Wergeland (1808–1845), Norw. poet.

Sigma: [Sir] Douglas Straight (1844–1914), Eng. author. The author's pen name represents the Greek letter corresponding to his initial "S."

Simone **Signoret:** Simone-Henriette-Charlotte Kaminker (1921–1985), Ger.-born Fr. film actress. The actress adopted her mother's maiden name as her screen name in 1945, after the Liberation.

The **Silent Traveller:** Chiang Yee (1903–   ), Chin.-born Eng. writer of popular travel books. The writer, famous for his travel books in the series *The Silent Traveller in* . . . (London, Oxford, New York, Edinburgh, etc.) derived his English pen name from his Chinese pseudonym, Yahsin-che, which meant "dumb walking man."

Beverly **Sills:** Belle Greenough, née Silverman (1929–   ), U.S. opera singer. The syllables of the singer's professional name can be found in "Belle Silverman" (near enough).

Ignazio **Silone:** Secondo Tranquilli (1900–1978), It. anti-fascist writer, novelist. The writer adopted a pseudonym to protect his family from Fascist persecution.

James **Silvain:** James Sullivan (? –1856), Eng. ballet dancer, working in France, U.S.

Silver Pen: Eliza Meteyard (1816–1879), Eng. novelist, miscellaneous writer. The writer was given the name by Douglas Jerrold (see Paul Prendergast, Q) when she contributed an article to the first number of *Douglas Jerrold's Weekly Newspaper* (1846).

Phil **Silvers:** Philip Silver (1912–1985), Russ.-born U.S. film, TV comedian.

Silvia: Zanetta-Rosa-Giovanni Benozzi (*c.*1701–1758), It. actress.

Georges **Sim:** Georges-Joseph-Christian Simenon (1903–1989), Belg. writer of detective fiction.

John **Simm:** John Simmon (1920–   ), U.S. theatre critic.

Gene **Simmons:** Gene Klein (1949–   ), U.S. rock musician.

Ginny **Simms:** Virginia Sims (1916–   ), U.S. singer, film actress.

Hilda **Simms:** Hilda Moses (1920–   ), U.S. stage actress.

Madame **Simone:** Pauline Benda Porche (1877–1985), Fr. stage actress, author. The famous Frenchwoman, whose stage and writing career lasted almost a century, married the actor Charles le Bargy in 1897, and it was he who persuaded her to adopt a stage name derived from that of the Musset heroine.

Nina **Simone:** Eunice Kathleen Waymon (1933–   ), U.S. black jazz musician.

Simplicissimus: Georgy Valentinovich Plekhanov (1857–1918), Russ. socialist. A name adopted for a while by the Russian socialist Plekhanov, who also wrote as Volgin (see Lenin). It derives from the title of a 1669 book by the seventeenth-century German author Hans Jakob Christoffel von Grimmelshausen, in full: *Der Abenteuerliche Simplicissimus Teutsch, das ist: Beschreibung des Lebens eines Seltzamen Vagantens Genannt Melchior Sternfels von Fuchshaim* ("The Adventurous German Simpleton, that is: Description of the life of a Strange Wanderer Named Melchior Sternfels von Fuchshaim"). Canny readers will have noticed that the name of the hero is an anagram of that of the author; moreover, the book was supposedly published by one Hermann Scheifhaim von Sulsfort, a similarly anagrammatic name. And as if this wasn't enough, the author purported to be a certain Samuel Greifensohn von Hirschfeld! The book itself is a picaresque novel about the adventures of a simple youth in various guises (soldier, robber, slave, and the like) and gives a vivid picture of the havoc wrought in Germany by the Thirty Years' War (1618–1648).

Arthur **Sinclair:** Francis Quinto McDonnell (1883–1951), Ir. stage actor.

Clive **Sinclair:** Joshua Smolinsky (1950–   ), Br. writer, of Pol.-Jewish parentage. The writer tells how he came by his present English name: "My mother's father came from Stashev in South-West Poland. How the family got there no one knows. His name in Hebrew was Joshua, though he was known as Shia, its Yiddish diminutive. When he settled in England it was Anglicized and he became Charles. I am named after him, the initial letter sufficing. [. . .] My father's mother was named Shaindel. In England Shane became plain Jane. My middle name, John, comes from her. Smolinsky was her married name, which my father changed to Sinclair when he joined the army in 1939. Thus my disguise, my *nom de vivre*, Clive Sinclair. Joshua Smolinsky (whom I might have been) lives, but only in my stories, as a down-at-heel private eye on the seamy side of Los Angeles. Joshua ben David, by which I am known to God, has not been heard since [. . .] my bar mitzvah [. . .].

The last name ought to be the essential me, but isn't. I am stuck as Clive Sinclair, because my mother tongue is English" [*Times Literary Supplement*, May 3, 1985]. (Strictly speaking, as the writer explains, he never really was Joshua Smolinsky. But he might have been, and his account of the transformation of a series of Jewish names into a pure English one is important for its detail.)

Ronald **Sinclair:** Reginald Teague-Jones (1889–1988), Eng. intelligence officer, working in India, Russia.

Anne **Singleton:** Ruth Benedict, née Fulton (1887–1948), U.S. anthropologist, poet.

Penny **Singleton:** Mariana Dorothy McNulty (1908–   ), U.S. film actress.

John **Sinjohn:** John Galsworthy (1867–1933), Eng. novelist, playwright. The name was an early one used by Galsworthy for his collection of stories, *From the Four Winds*, published in 1897. The name itself refers to his identically named father, John Galsworthy, with "Sin-" apparently intended to mean "son."

Siouxsie **Sioux:** Susan Janet Dallion (1957–   ), Eng. rock singer.

Sirin: Vladimir Vladimirovich Nabokov (1899–1977), Russ.-born U.S. novelist. This was an early pseudonym used by the famous author of *Lolita* when he was still writing in Russian, although already an immigrant resident in the U.S. (from 1919). In Old Russian literature, "Sirin" was the name of a mythical bird with a woman's head and torso, similar to a harpy (but not malignant in the same way). Nabokov used the name so that he would not be confused with his father, Vladimir Dmitrievich Nabokov, a criminologist and political figure who was one of the founders of the "Kadets," the Constitutional Democratic Party led by Milyukov.

Douglas **Sirk:** Hans Detlef Sierk (1900–   ), Ger. film director, of Dan. parentage, working in U.S.

Sixtus IV: Francesco della Rovere (1414–1484), It. pope. This is the pope who built the famous Sistine Chapel, the papal chapel in the Vatican, named after him.

Sixtus V: Felice Peretti (1521–1590), It. pope.

Skanderbeg: George Kastrioti (1405–1468), Albanian national hero. The national leader acquired this name when, as Iskander (for Alexander the Great), he was converted to Islam with the rank of bey. Hence "Skander*beg*." He subsequently rejected his Islam faith and embraced Christianity.

Arthur **Sketchley:** George Rose (1817–1882), Eng. humorous writer, entertainer. The name presumably puns on "sketch."

Skitt: Harden E. Taliaferro (1818–1875), U.S. editor, sketch writer. The link is that between "skit" and "sketch," of course. (Oddly, the two words are themselves quite unrelated in origin.)

Mia **Slavenska:** Mia Corak (1914–   ), Yugoslav-born ballet dancer, working in U.S. The dancer took her stage name from her birthplace, Slavonski-Brod, west of Belgrade. The name happens to indicate her Slavic origins, which is a bonus.

Jonathan **Slick:** Ann Sophia Stephens (1810–1886), U.S. historical novelist. The writer used this name for her quite different *High Life in New York* (1842), based on typical Down East humor.

Sam **Slick:** Thomas Chandler Haliburton (1796–1865), Can. jurist, humorist.

Bumble Bee **Slim:** Amos Easton (*c.*1908–   ), U.S. black blues singer.

Lightnin' **Slim:** Otis Hicks (1915–1974), U.S. blues singer.

Montana **Slim:** Wilf Carter (1904–   ), Can. country singer. "Slim" in names like these implies not so much "slender" as "crafty."

Jonathan Freke **Slingsby:** John Francis Waller (1810–1894), Ir. journalist, poet. The writer used this name, fancifully based on his real name, for his contributions to the *Dublin University Magazine,* of which he was a staff member. He called his articles the *Slingsby Papers,* and they were pieces somewhat in the style of the *Noctes Ambrosianae* (see Christopher North), or an Irish version of them. It is possible that Waller chose the name "Slingsby" after his American fellow-writer, Slingsby Lawrence *(q.v.),* although the name generally seems to have had a contemporary appeal. (Compare also the next entry below.)

Philip **Slingsby:** Nathaniel Parker (1806–1867), U.S. journalist, poet.

Ally **Sloper:** Charles H. Ross (?1842–1897), Eng. humorous writer. The writer was the original creator of this name, which soon became well-known as that of a popular comic cartoon character who was "noted for his dishonest or bungling practices" (*Oxford English Dictionary*). The character's full name was "Alexander Sloper F.O.M.," the latter standing for "Friend of Man." He and his partner in various adventures, Isaac Moses (otherwise known as "Ikey Mo") were seedy conmen who planned to become rich but who never did. The character of the name seems to have been born in a fullpage strip entitled "Some of the Mysteries of Loan and Discount," published in the comic paper *Judy* in 1867. It was not long before Ross's name and that of Ally Sloper became synonymous, especially through the titles of such comics as (the best-known) *Ally Sloper's Half Holiday,* published from 1844 to 1914. Ross's son, Charles Ross, Jr., wrote for this particular comic under the name of "Tootsie Sloper." "Sloper" itself implies someone who "slopes," that is, cheats or tricks, in the slang of the day.

Smectymnuus: Stephen Marshall (?1594–1655), Eng. Presbyterian leader, preacher + Edmund Calamy (1600–1666), Eng. Puritan clergyman + Thomas Young (1587–1655), Sc. clergyman + William Spurstowe (?1605–1666), Eng. clergyman. A rather unattractive joint pseudonym for the five Presbyterian ministers who in a pamphlet of 1641 attacked Bishop Joseph Hall's claim of divine right for the episcopacy. The name is formed from the men's initials, with William Spurstowe's "W" providing the double "u" of the name.

Wentworth **Smee:** George Brown Burgin (1856–1944), Eng. novelist, journalist, critic. The journalist used the name for his contributions to the *Sunday Sun.*

Smilby: Francis Smith (1927–   ), Eng. cartoonist.

Betty **Smith:** Elizabeth Keogh (1896–1972), U.S. novelist.

Cal **Smith:** Calvin Grant Shofner (1932–   ), U.S. country singer.

Cordwainer **Smith:** Paul Myron Anthony Linebarger (1913–1966), U.S. SF writer.

Gamaliel **Smith:** Jeremy Bentham (1748–1832), Eng. jurist, philosopher. The writer used this name for *Not Paul but Jesus* (1823), a didactic work setting out to prove that St. Paul had distorted true Christianity as taught and practiced by Christ. Gamaliel, in the Bible, is the name of the man who had taught Paul (Acts 22:3).

John **Smith:** Robert Van Orden (1931–), U.S. film, TV actor.

Johnston **Smith:** Stephen Crane (1871–1900), U.S. fiction writer. Crane used this name for his first novel, *Maggie: A Girl of the Streets,* published privately in 1893 (but not regularly published until three years later).

S.S. **Smith:** Thames Ross Williamson (1894–), U.S. fiction writer. The author used a number of pseudonyms, especially for children's stories. This particular name was the one he used for mystery stories, basing it on the name of Simmons and Smith College, where he had taught for a time after graduating from the University of Iowa (1917) and studying at Harvard.

Stevie **Smith:** Florence Margaret Smith (1902–1971), Eng. poet.

Harry **Smolka:** Harry Peter Smollett (1912–), Austr.-born Eng. author, journalist.

Phoebe **Snow:** Phoebe Laub (1952–), U.S. pop singer.

[Sir] Henry F.R. **Soame:** [Sir] Henry Edward Bunbury (1778–1860), Eng. historical writer. There seems to be a case of mistaken identity here. This name is usually given as the pseudonym of the soldier, historian, and Member of Parliament Sir Henry Edward Bunbury. The *Dictionary of National Biography* points out, however, that it is the *real* name of Sir Henry Bunbury's cousin, Henry Francis Robert Soame, born ten years earlier (1768). To the twentieth century neither gentleman may seem particularly significant, but the instance is an example of the shaky historical foundation some pseudonyms can have.

Sodoma: Giovanni Antonio Bazzi (1477–1549), It. painter. The painter was nicknamed "Il Sodoma" ("the sodomite") for his homosexual reputation. The name may have been given frivolously, of course, but (somewhat surprisingly) he adopted it, and this is now the name by which the fine artist is always known.

Lydia **Sokolova:** Hilda Munnings (1896–1974), Eng. ballet dancer. The dancer was given her name by Diaghilev himself. He told her, "I have signed your photograph [. . .] with the name Lydia Sokolova, and I hope you will live up to the name of Sokolova, as it is that of a great dancer in Russia" [Richard Buckle, *Dancing for Diaghilev: The Memoirs of Lydia Sokolova,* 1960]. Diaghilev was referring to Yevgenia Pavlovna Sokolova (1850–1925), who was one of the most famous Russian ballerinas of the 1870s and 1880s, and subsequently a noted teacher. (Hilda Munnings studied under Pavlova, who had herself been one of Sokolova's pupils.)

Solomon: Solomon Cutner (1902–1988), Br. concert pianist.

Jane **Somers:** Doris Lessing (1919–), Br. novelist. The famous writer used this name in 1984 for *The Diaries of Jane Somers,* with the aim of "escaping from her reputation."

Suzanne **Somers:** Suzanne Mahoney (1946–), U.S. TV actress.

Franca **Somigli:** Marin Bruce Clark (1901–1974), U.S.-It. opera singer.

Elke **Sommer:** Elke Schletz (1940–), Ger. film actress, working in U.S.

Sonny: Salvatore Bono (1935–), U.S. pop singer, formerly teaming with wife Cher *(q.v.).*

Jack **Soo:** Goro Suzuki (1916–1979), Jap. film actor, working in U.S.

Kaikhosru Shapurji **Sorabji:** Leon Dudley (1892–1988), Eng. pianist. and keyboard composer, of Sp.-Sicilian mother and Parsi father.

Jean **Sorel:** Jean de Rochbrune (1934–   ), Fr. film actor. The actor may have adopted his screen name from that of Julien Sorel, the hero of *Le Rouge et le Noir*, the famous novel by Stendhal *(q.v.).*

Agnes **Sorma:** Martha Karoline Zaremba (1865–1927), Ger. stage actress.

Ann **Sothern:** Harriette Lake (1909–   ), U.S. film actress.

Alain **Souchon:** Alain Kienast (*c.*1950–   ), Fr. pop singer.

David **Soul:** David Solberg (1943–   ), U.S. pop singer, TV actor.

Jimmy **Soul:** James McCleese (1942–   ), U.S. pop singer.

Suzi **Soul:** Suzi Quatro (1950–   ), U.S. pop singer, of It. descent, working in U.K. The singer used this as an early name, when she was a TV go-go dancer at the age of 14, and retained it for a while with her group Suzi Soul and the Pleasure Seekers.

Joe **South:** Joe Souter (1942–   ), U.S. popular musician.

Theophilus **South:** Edward Chitty (1804–1863), Eng. legal reporter. The barrister and legal writer used this name for a publication quite distinct from his professional work, the *Fly Fisher's Text Book* (1841).

Jeri **Southern:** Genevieve Hering (1926–   ) U.S. popular singer.

Southside Johnny: John Lyon (1948–   ), U.S. rock musician. The musician doubtless took his name from jazz jargon, where "Southside" implies playing in small bands in unpromising or unattractive locations (like Chicago's South Side, with its swarming immigrant population). Lyon himself came from New Jersey.

Stephen **Southwold:** Stephen H. Critten (1887–1964), Eng. novelist, short story writer. The writer, who also used the name Neil Bell *(q.v.)*, kept "Stephen Southwold" for his children's fiction. The name refers to his birthplace, Southwold, Suffolk.

Boris **Souvarine:** Boris Lifchitz (1895–1984), Russ.-born Fr. Communist. The political activist, who was prominent in the foundation of the French Communist party, adopted the name, Souvarine, of the intellectual revolutionary depicted in Emile Zola's novel *Germinal.* He also used the name in the form "Boris Souvart."

E. **Souza:** Evelyn Scott (1893–1963), U.S. novelist, poet, short story writer. The writer used this name for her adventure story *Blue Rum* (1930). This was set in Portugal, so merited a Portuguese-style pen name.

Gérard **Souzay:** Gérard Marcel Tisserand (1921–   ), Fr. opera singer.

Bob B. **Soxx:** Robert Sheen (1943–   ), U.S. rock musician. It is not hard to detect the origin of this punning name.

Mark **Spade:** Nigel Marlin Balchin (1908–1970), Br. novelist. The novelist used this name for his humorous contributions to *Punch,* collected in *How to Run a Bassoon Factory, or Business Explained* (1934) and *Pleasures of Business* (1935). The name itself suggests a reference to card-playing.

George **Spalatin:** Georg Burkhardt (1484–1545), Ger. humanist writer. The writer took his pen name from his birthplace, Spalt, Bavaria (now West Germany).

Tony **Spargo:** Anthony Sbarbaro (1897–1969), U.S. jazz musician.

Ned **Sparks:** Edward Sparkman (1883–1957), Can. film actor.

Mighty **Sparrow:** Slinger Francisco (1935–   ), Grenada calypso singer. The singer was so named for jumping about the stage like a sparrow.

Spartakus: Karl Liebknecht (1871–1919), Ger. lawyer, Communist leader. The activist took his name from the Spartacus League, founded by him as the nucleus of the German Communist Party, and itself named for the Roman slave leader, Spartacus.

Speckled Red: Rufus G. Perryman (1892–1973), U.S. black jazz pianist. A pleasant pun on the musician's first name, while borrowing the name of the breed of hens.

Bud **Spencer:** Carlo Pedersoli (1929–   ), It. film actor. Possibly "Bud" evolved from the first syllable of the actor's surname. He would have needed an English-sounding name for the "spaghetti westerns" he played in.

Speranza: [Lady] Jane Francisca Speranza Wilde, née Elgee (1826–1896), Ir. writer, literary hostess, mother of Oscar Wilde.

Spondee: Royall Tyler (1757–1826), U.S. playwright, essayist, satirist, teaming with Colon *(q.v.)*. A spondee is a metrical foot of two long syllables, and as such is an apt name for a (satirical) verse writer.

Dusty **Springfield:** Mary O'Brien (1939–   ), Eng. pop singer, musician, working latterly in U.S. "Springfield" comes from the name of an early folk trio, the Springfields, consisting of "Dusty" (her nickname) herself, her brother Dion, and Tim Field, whose name gave that of the trio.

Mercurius **Spur:** Cuthbert Shaw (1739–1771), Eng. poet. The poet used this name, which is possibly loosely based on his real name, for *The Race* (1766), in which the poets of the day were made to compete for pride of place by running a race. "Mercurius" also suggests Mercury, the fleet-footed messenger of the gods in classical mythology, and "Spur" is a sporting word associated with racing.

Spy: [Sir] Leslie Ward (1851–1922), Eng. illustrator, caricaturist. The artist made many famous contributions to the topical illustrated magazine *Vanity Fair*, founded in 1868 as a periodical designed to "display the vanities of the week." Ward was asked to choose a pen name by the magazine's editor, Thomas Gibson Bowles, and did so by opening a copy of Dr. Johnson's *Dictionary* at random and selecting the first word his eye fell on. This was "spy" – an appropriate name for a man whose professional job was to "spy" on society and produce his observations in pictorial form. Other artists contributing to *Vanity Fair* were Ape, Sir Max Beerbohm (as Ruth, Sulto, and Max) and Walter Sickert (as Sic). (Editor Bowles wrote as Jehu Junior, a name retained by his successors until the magazine closed in 1929.) [1. Leslie Ward, *Forty Years of "Spy,"* 1915; 2. John Arlott, "Ape, Spy, and Jehu Junior," in *Late Extra: A Miscellany by "Evening News" Writers, Artists, and Photographers,* 1952].

Squibob: George Horatio Derby (1823–1861), U.S. humorous writer, satirist. The writer, professionally an army officer, was a noted perpetrator of practical jokes as well as a penner of satirical verse. He thus enjoyed "squibs," or verbal attacks. He also wrote as John Phoenix *(q.v.)*.

Ronald **Squire:** Ronald Squirl (1886–1958), Eng. stage, film actor.

Robert **Stack:** Robert Modini (1919–   ), U.S. film, TV actor.

Hanley **Stafford:** Alfred John Austin (1899–1968), U.S. radio actor.

Stainless Stephen: Arthur Clifford Baynes (1892–1971), Eng. music hall comedian. The performer was born in Sheffield, a city long famous for its manufacture of stainless steel.

Black **Stalin:** Leroy Calliste (1941–   ), Trinidad calypso singer.

Joseph **Stalin:** Iosif Vissarionovich Dzhugashvili (1879–1953), Russ. Communist leader. The Soviet Communist leader did not adopt his pseudonym—basically meaning "steel"–all at once. It took some evolving. He was contributing to Bolshevik magazines such as *Zvezda* ("The Star") under the name K.S. and K. Salin, for example, two or three years before he first used his familiar pseudonym of Stalin (in 1913). Opinions seem divided as to the symbolic intention of the meaning of the name. Undoubtedly Russian *stal'* means "steel," and certainly, after repeated arrest, banishment and imprisonment in czarist days, Dzhugashvili's spirit was unbroken, but it is unlikely that the name was given him by Lenin *(q.v.)*, as legend has it, because of his seeming "steel-like" nature. Another early favorite pseudonym of the Bolshevik activist was Koba—said to be Turkish for "fearless"—and at one time he used the name Kato, perhaps with reference to the forthrightness of Cato the Elder. And these were not all. Among other names favored by the revolutionary were David Bars, Gayoz Nizheradze, I. Besoshvili, Zakhar Gregoryan Melikyants, Ogoness Vartanovich Totomyants, K. Solin (perhaps suggesting Russian *sol'*, "salt"), and K. Stefin. Some of these names are reminiscent of his own real Georgian name [Robert Payne, *Stalin*, 1966].

John **Standing:** [Sir] John Ronald Leon (1934–   ), Eng. stage, film actor, son of Kay Hammond *(q.v.)*. The actor adopted his mother's maiden name as his stage name.

Burt L. **Standish:** William Gilbert Patten (1866–1945), U.S. author of "dime novels."

Konstantin **Stanislavsky:** Konstantin Sergeevich Alekseyev (1865–1938), Russ. stage actor, producer, teacher. The famous actor, originator of the "Stanislavsky method" of acting, seems to have derived his professional name from his real name (the "Stan-" from "Konstantin," for example). He first used it in 1885.

[Sir] Henry Morton **Stanley:** John Rowlands (1841–1904), Welsh-born Br. explorer of Africa. The well-known explorer was the illegitimate son of John Rowlands and Elizabeth Parry. When he was in the U.S. at the age of 18 he was adopted by a New Orleans merchant, Henry Morton Stanley, who gave him his own name.

Kim **Stanley:** Patricia Reid (1921–   ), U.S. stage, film actress.

Barbara **Stanwyck:** Ruby Stevens (1907–   ), U.S. film, TV actress. The actress was given her new name by producer, director, and playwright Willard Mack, when he cast her for *The Noose* on Broadway. "Ruby Stevens is no name for an actress," he told her. He got the name from an old English theatre program, which listed Jane Stanwyck in *Barbara Frietchi* [Jane Ellen Wayne, *Stanwyck*, 1986].

Jean **Stapleton:** Jeanne Murray (1923–   ), U.S. film, TV actress.

Alvin **Stardust:** Bernard William Jewry (1942–   ), Eng. pop singer. The singer began his career as "Shane Fenton." Later, he took his present name from his favorite performers, *Elv*is Presley and Gene *Vinc*ent *(q.v.)*, adding "Stardust" as he thought it more "1974."

Richard **Stark:** Donald E. Westlake (1933–   ), U.S. suspense writer.

Edwin **Starr:** Charles Hatcher (1942–   ), U.S. pop singer.

Freddie **Starr:** Frederick Leslie Fowle (1943–   ), Eng. TV, film entertainer.

Kay **Starr:** Katherine Starks (1922–   ), U.S. popular radio singer.

Ringo **Starr:** Richard Starkey (1940–   ), Eng. pop musician. The former Beatles drummer, who subsequently branched out into a solo career, changed his name in 1961, when appearing with Rory Storm *(q.v.)*. His new second name derives from his original surname (with a "starlike" potential implied), while "Ringo" was his nickname, referring to his fondness for wearing rings.

Vargo **Statten:** John Russell Fearn (1908–1960), Eng. SF writer.

Byron **Steel:** Francis Steegmuller (1906–   ), U.S. novelist, literary critic. The writer used this name for his lesser critical studies.

Bob **Steele:** Robert Bradbury (1907–1966), U.S. film actor.

Tommy **Steele:** Thomas Hicks (1936–   ), Eng. pop singer, stage, film actor. Tommy Hicks was signed up in the mid–1950s by two young promoters, Larry Parnes and John Kennedy, who gave him a more charismatic name in the process. "Hicks," after all, suggests, well, a hick, while "Steele" projects a much more incisive and sharper image.

Saul **Steinberg:** Saul Jacobson (1914–   ), Rom. cartoonist, illustrator, working in U.S. A rather unusual instance of one Jewish name being substituted for another.

Henry Engelhard **Steinway:** Heinrich Engelhardt Steinweg (1797–1871), Ger. piano maker, working in U.S. A simple anglicization took place here, although the "Stein" did not produce a "Stone," as it might have done.

Stella: [1] Esther Johnson (1681–1728), Eng. letter writer, correspondent of Jonathan Swift; [2] Estella Anna Lewes (1824–1880), U.S. author. Swift adopted this name for addressing Esther Johnson through his *Journal to Stella* (1710–13), a series of intimate letters to her and her companion, Rebecca Dingley, chiefly written in baby language. The name hints at "Esther," while also meaning "star." In the case of Estella Lewes, the pseudonym was even closer to her true first name. Because of its meaning, the name has been used by other writers. In the poetry of Sir Philip Sidney (1554–1586), for example, "Stella," in the sonnet sequence *Astrophel and Stella*, was Penelope Rich, the sister of the Earl of Essex. ("Astrophel" was Sidney himself. This name, significantly, means "lover of a star.")

Anna **Sten:** Annel (Anjuschka) Stenskaya Sudakevich (1908–   ), Russ.-born U.S. film actress of Swe.-Ukrainian parentage.

Stendhal: Marie-Henri Beyle (1783–1842), Fr. novelist. Of all the many and varied pseudonyms adopted by the famous French novelist, "Stendhal" is the one by which he is best known. It comes from the name of a small Prussian town, the birthplace of J.J. Winckelmann, a German art critic admired by Beyle, and was first used for his travel account *Rome, Naples et Florence* (1817–1826). Altogether he used up to 200 pseudonyms, many of them Italian. From among them, and to give an idea of their diversity, we may note: Dominique, Salviati (names intended to charm), Cotonnet, Chamier, Baron de Cutendre, William Crocodile (for sheer amusement), Lizio and Viscontini. His first book, *Vies de Haydn, de Mozart et de Métastase* (1814) he wrote as L.-A.-C. Bombet. For his autobiography, published posthumously (1890), he chose the name Henri Brulard, with reference to his passionate nature (French *brûler* meaning "to burn").

Steno: Stefano Vanzina (1917–1988), It. screenwriter, film director. Although obviously deriving from his first name, the writer's pseudonym also suggests "writing" itself, through the *steno-* element in such words as "stenographer" (Italian *stenografo*).

Stephen IX: Frederick of Lorraine (*c*.1000–1058), Fr. pope.

Henry **Stephenson:** Henry Stephenson Garroway (1871–1956), Br. stage, screen actor, working in U.S.

Ford **Sterling:** George Ford Stitch (1883–1939), U.S. film comedian.

Jan **Sterling:** Jane Sterling Adriance (1923–   ), U.S. film actress.

Robert **Sterling:** William John Hart (1917–   ), U.S. film actor.

Daniel **Stern:** Marie Catherine Sophie de Flavigny, Comtesse d'Agoult (1805–1876), Fr. writer. The writer was the mistress of Liszt, and in 1854 published her novel *Nélida*, picturing her relations with him. The pseudonym she selected for the book was based on an anagram of this title.

Paul Frederick **Stern:** Paul Frederick Ernst (1902–   ), U.S. SF writer. It is always convenient to have a surname that can so readily be anagrammatized like this!

Stet: Thomas Earle Welby (1881–1933), Br. journalist, essayist, literary critic. No doubt the writer had more than one occasion to write "stet" when reading the proofs of his articles, this being the term (Latin for "let it stand") to mark a deleted passage that should remain undeleted after all.

Cat **Stevens:** Steven Giorgiou (1947–   ), Eng. pop musician, of Gk.-Swe. parentage. In 1978 the musician turned to Islam, ceased recording, and changed his name yet again to "Yusef Islam."

Connie **Stevens:** Concetta Ann Ingolia (1938–   ), U.S. film actress.

Craig **Stevens:** Gail Shekles (1918–   ), U.S. film actor.

Inger **Stevens:** Inger Stensland (1934–1970), Swe.-born U.S. film, TV actress.

K.T. **Stevens:** Gloria Wood (1919–   ), U.S. film actress.

Onslow **Stevens:** Onslow Ford Stevenson (1902–1977), U.S. stage, film actor.

Shakin' **Stevens:** Michael Barratt (1948–   ), Welsh-born Br. pop singer ("Shaky").

Stella **Stevens:** Estelle Eggleston (1936–   ), U.S. film actress.

Douglas **Stewart:** Edward Askew Sothern (1826–1881), Eng. actor. The actor used this stage name when first appearing in the provinces.

Ed **Stewart:** Edward Stewart Mainwaring (1941–   ), Eng. radio DJ, TV actor ("Stewpot").

Elaine **Stewart:** Elsy Steinberg (1929–   ), U.S. film actress.

James **Stewart:** James Maitland (1908–   ), U.S. film actor.

Michael **Stewart:** Michael Rubin (1924–1987), U.S. popular composer, lyricist.

Sting: Gordon Matthew Sumner (1951–   ), Eng. rock singer. The singer acquired his name by way of a school nickname, referring not only to his "buzzing" energy but more specifically to a black and yellow hooped tee-shirt that he habitually wore.

Wilhelmina **Stitch:** Ruth Collie (1889–1936), Br. author of sentimental verse.

Leopold **Stokes:** Leopold Antoni Stanislaw Boleslawowicz Stokowski (1882–1977), Br. orchestra conductor, of Pol.-Ir. parentage, working in U.S. Was the conductor at one stage known by this English version of his name? His father was Polish, and his mother Irish, and in his obituary notice in *The Times* (1977) mention was made of the fact that it was his father who had so anglicized his name to 1905, from which year the conductor worked mainly in the United States under his more familiar Polish name. However, a few days later (September 24, 1977), *The Times* printed a correction, which ran as follows: "We have been asked to point out that Leopold Stokowski was registered at birth under that name and not under that of Stokes: and that, similarly, he studied at the Royal College of Music under the name of Stokowski." Leopold Stokes would thus appear to have been very short-lived—if he ever lived at all.

[Sir] Oswald **Stoll:** Oswald Gray (1866–1942), Eng. theatre manager. The impresario's mother was widowed when the boy was only three years old, but in 1879 she remarried and gave her son the name of her new husband, John George Stoll.

Cliffie **Stone:** Clifford Gilpin Snyder (1917–   ), U.S. country musician.

George E. **Stone:** George Stein (1903–1967), Pol. film actor, working in U.S.

Hampton **Stone:** Aaron Marc Stein (1906–   ), U.S. mystery writer.

Jesse **Stone:** Charles Calhoun (*c.*1930–   ), U.S. pop music arranger.

Sly **Stone:** Sylvester Stewart (1944–   ), U.S. black rock musician.

Stonehenge: John Henry Walsh (1810–1888), Eng. sporting writer, editor. The famous ancient monument of Stonehenge, on Salisbury Plain, Wiltshire, was a popular venue for hunting and riding in Victorian times. The surrounding area is now largely owned by the army, although local hunts still have the right to hold their meets there on specified occasions.

Tom **Stoppard:** Tom Straussler (1937–   ), Cz.-born Br. dramatist, theatre critic. When the future playwright was still only nine years old, his mother remarried, and he took his new name from his stepfather, Major Kenneth Stoppard. See also William Boot.

Gale **Storm:** Josephine Cottle (1922–   ), U.S. film, TV actress.

Lesley **Storm:** Margaret Clark, née Cowie (1904–1975), Sc. playwright.

Rory **Storm:** Alan Caldwell (1941–   ), Br. pop singer. The singer tried out the name "Jet Storme" early on in his career, then settled for "Rory Storm."

Herbert **Strang:** George Herbert Ely (1866–1958), Eng. children's writer + Charles James L'Estrange (1867–1944), Eng. children's writer. The two men were staff members of the Oxford University Press, writing adventure stories and historical novels for children in the first three decades of the twentieth century. Their joint name is extracted from their real names, as can be seen. They also wrote for girls under the not very original name of "Mrs. Herbert Strang."

Steve **Strange:** Stephen John Harrington (1959–   ), Welsh rock singer. The singer acquired his name thanks to a postman (mail carrier): "I was living in West Hampstead [London] and my hair was white and cut spiky on top. The other girl [sic] I was living with, Suzy, also had white hair and so the postman used to call us Mr. and Mrs. Strange. The name just stuck" [*Observer Colour Supplement*, August 22, 1982].

Joyce **Stranger:** Joyce Muriel Wilson (*c.*1930–   ), Eng. writer of animal stories for children.

Dorothy **Stratten:** Dorothy Ruth Hoogstratten (1960–1980), U.S. film actress, model.

L.B. **Stratten:** Louise B. Hoogstratten (1969–   ), U.S. film actress.

Eugene **Stratton:** Eugene Augustus Ruhlman (1861–1918), U.S. "blackface" music hall singer.

Gene **Stratton-Porter:** Geneva Grace Porter, née Stratton (1863–1924), U.S. writer of books for girls.

Paul Patrick **Streeten:** Paul Patrick Hornig (1917–   ), Austr.-born Br. economist. The writer changed his Germanic name to an English one in 1943, under the Army Council Instruction that year which regulated some name changes. At the time he was serving in the Commandos, but returned to England on being wounded in Sicily.

Hesba **Stretton:** Sarah Smith (1832–1911), Br. writer of evangelical stories for children. How did the rather pleasantly named Sarah Smith devise such an unusual pen name? She took her first name from the initial letters (HESBA) of the names of her brothers and sisters, in order of age (the "E" was Elizabeth, her lifelong companion; the "A" was her younger sister Ann), while her new surname came from the Shropshire village of All Stretton, near the town of Church Stretton, where Ann Smith had been left property by her uncle. Sarah Smith adopted the name in 1858, before her writing career began, choosing the new name because she felt that her real name lacked distinction.

Stringbean: David Akeman (1915–1973), U.S. country singer. The singer's name arose as a nickname, referring to his tall, skinny appearance. According to one story, this originated from a radio announcer, who came to introduce him but forgot his real name.

Patience **Strong:** Winifred May (1905–   ), Eng. "inspirational" poet. The writer took her name from the title of *Patience Strong*, a homely moral (fictional) autobiography by the American author Mrs. A.D.T Whitney (Adeline Dutton Train Whitney [1824–1906]), published in the 1890s. Winifred May was very impressed by the book and its spiritual content. "No words can describe what it did for me. [. . .] The main character, the fictitious Patience Strong, moves through the book with a simplicity that only partially hides a philosophy that is as practical as it is profound. I had found more than a pseudonym. I had turned a corner and found, by chance, my true vocation. [. . .] The charm and the power of that book, *Patience Strong*, is something I cannot define. [. . .] I place it reverently on a pedestal alongside Mrs. Gaskell's *Cranford*, Jane Austen's *Emma* and *Our Village* by Nancy Russell Mitford" [Patience Strong, *With a Poem in My Pocket*, 1981]. The import of the fictional name itself is, of course, transparent enough, and is meaningful for the book's central character, the 38-year-old spinster who shares the old New England home with her mother, and who is thus at a significant stage in her spiritual (and, implicitly, physical) life.

Sheppard **Strudwick:** John Shepperd (1907–   ), U.S. film actor.

Joe **Strummer:** John Mellor (1953–   ), Eng. punk rock musician.

Jan **Struther:** Joyce Maxtone Graham, née Anstruther (1901–1953), Eng. poet, short story writer, novelist.

Gloria **Stuart:** Gloria Stuart Finch (1909–1983), U.S. film actress.

Ian **Stuart:** Alistair Maclean (1922–1987), Sc. novelist. The writer used this name for his SF writing, such as *The Dark Crusader* (1961) and *The Satan Bug* (1962).

John **Stuart:** John Croall (1898–1979), Sc. film, stage actor.

Leslie **Stuart:** Thomas Barrett (1864–1928), Eng. popular songwriter.

Theodore **Sturgeon:** Edward Hamilton Waldo (1918–   ), U.S. SF writer.

Preston **Sturges:** Edmond Preston Biden (1898–1959), U.S. film writer, director. The writer took his new name from his mother's second husband (his stepfather), Solomon Sturges, at the same time dropping his first name.

Jules **Styne:** Jules Stein (1905–1981), Eng. stage producer, composer of musicals. A fairly original variation on the familiar "Stein-to-Stone" transition.

Poly **Styrene:** Marion Elliott (1956–   ), Eng. punk rock musician. The singer, who formed the band X-Ray Spex in 1977, adopted the name because she felt it was suitable for the "plastic" culture and values of the 1970s.

Eugène **Sue:** Marie-Joseph Sue (1804–1857), Fr. novelist. The writer took his new first name from one of his patrons, Prince Eugène de Beauharnais.

Margaret **Sullavan:** Margaret Brooke (1911–1960), U.S. film actress.

Barry **Sullivan:** Patrick Barry (1912–   ), U.S. film actor.

Maxine **Sullivan:** Marietta Williams (1911–1987), U.S. jazz singer.

Yma **Sumac:** Zoila Imperatriz Charrari Sumac del Castillo (1928–   ), Peruvian-born U.S. singer. Despite reports to the contrary, she is *not* a housewife named Amy Camus!

Donna **Summer:** LaDonna Adrian Sommer, née Gaines (1948–   ), U.S. pop singer. The singer married a German, Helmut Sommer, when she was 19, and (conventionally) took his surname, while (slightly unconventionally) altering its spelling to make it look more English. She later divorced him, but kept the anglicized name.

Charles **Summerfield:** Alfred W. Arrington (1810–1967), U.S. lawyer, writer.

Felix **Summerly:** [Sir] Henry Cole (1808–1882), Eng. art patron, educator. The artist first used the name in 1841 for *Felix Summerly's Home Treasury*, a series of children's stories illustrated with woodcuts based on well-known paintings. The name seems to be a fairly arbitrary one suggesting pleasure: Latin *felix* means "fruitful," "lucky," and "Summerly" conjures up summer.

Joe **Sun:** James Paulson (1943–   ), U.S. country singer. The singer's new surname is an imaginative development of the latter half of his original surname.

Colonel **Surry:** John Esten Cooke (1830–1886), U.S. novelist, essayist. The writer used the name for a series of romances, in which the Civil War was seen through the eyes of "Colonel Surry," a fictitious aide of Stonewall Jackson.

Suzy: Aileen Mehle (1952–   ), U.S. "queen of aristocratic tittle-tattle."

Italo **Svevo:** Ettore Schmitz (1861–1928), It. novelist, short story writer. The writer's pseudonym means "Italian Swabian," and was chosen by him to express his feeling of being a hybrid: he was Italian-speaking, Austrian in citizenship, and German in ancestry and education. The name does to an extent reflect or resemble his real name.

Swamp Dogg: Jerry Williams, Jr. (1942–), U.S. pop musician. In real life there ain't no such animal as a "swamp dog," although "swamp dogwood" is the name of various types of trees. Similar names or nicknames have been used by or of others, such as the American soldier Francis Marion, who in the War of Independence was known as "The Swamp Fox."

Gloria **Swanson:** Gloria May Josephine Svensson (1899–1983), U.S. film actress.

Emanuel **Swedenborg:** Emanuel Svedberg (1688–1772), Swe. scientist, philosopher, religious writer.

Tom **Swift:** Thomas Kneafcy (1928–), Br. opera singer.

Nora **Swinburne:** Nora (or Elinore) Swinburne Johnson (1902–), Eng. stage actress.

Basil **Sydney:** Basil Sydney Nugent (1894–1968), Br. film actor.

Urbanus **Sylvan:** Henry Charles Beeching (1859–1919), Eng. poet, essayist. The name was almost certainly adopted from that of Sylvanus Urban *(q.v.)*, and similarly conjured up the town and the country (or forest).

Sylvander: Robert Burns (1756–1796), Sc. poet. This was the name used by Burns when corresponding with Clarinda *(q.v.)*. It was probably intended to mean "forest man," via classical roots, and resembles the familiar Sylvanus of mythology as the name of different sylvan beings or deities.

Sylvia:[1] Sylvia Kirby Allen (1957–), U.S. country singer; [2] Sylvia Vanderpool (1936–), U.S. pop singer.

David **Sylvian:** David Batt (1958–), Eng. rock musician.

Sylvie: Louise Sylvain (1883–1970), Fr. film actress.

T: Joseph Peter Thorp (1873–1962), Br. writer, biographer.

Mr. T: Lawrence Tureaud (or Tero) (1952–), U.S. black TV actor.

Tabarin: Antoine Girard (? –1626), Fr. actor. Sources differ concerning the true identity of the actor. Some say that "Tabarin" was his real name, and that his full name and dates were thus Jean Salomon Tabarin (1584–1633). Either way, his name gave the standard French expression *faire le tabarin*, "play the fool."

Tad: Thomas Aloysius Dorgan (1877–1929), U.S. cartoonist, sports commentator. The cartoonist's initials conveniently gave his acronymic pseudonym. The name has the added advantage of being not only a short personal name (for "Thaddeus") in its own right, but also a colloquial term for "boy."

Taffrail: [Captain] Henry Taprell Dorling (1883–1968), Br. naval writer, broadcaster. The captain's name is obviously based on his middle name, but at the same time is an actual naval term for the upper part of a ship's stern timbers.

Taffy: Nadezhda Aleksandrovna Buchinskaya, née Likhvitskaya (1872–1952), Russ. short story writer, poet, working in France. The writer took her pen name from Taffy, the little prehistoric girl in Rudyard Kipling's story "How the Alphabet Was Made" in the *Just So Stories* (1902). Taffy was herself based at least in part on Kipling's own eldest daughter Josephine.

John **Taine:** Eric Temple Bell (1883–1960), Sc.-born U.S. SF writer.

Howard **Talbot:** Richard Munkittrick (1865–1928), U.S. composer of musicals, working in U.K.

Lyle **Talbot:** Lysle Henderson (1904–1987), U.S. film actor.

Nina **Talbot:** Anita Sokol (1930–   ), U.S. TV comedienne.

Hal **Taliaferro:** Floyd Taliaferro Alperson (1895–1980), U.S. film actor.

Talis Qualis: Carl Vilhelm August Strandberg (1818–1877), Swe. poet, journalist. The pseudonym represents the Latin phrase meaning "of such a kind as."

Richard **Talmadge:** Ricardo Metzetti (1896–1981), U.S. film actor, stunt man.

Talvj: Therese Albertine Louise Robinson, née von Jakob (1797–1870), Ger. author, writing in English. The writer's pseudonym represents the initials of her full maiden name, and was pronounced by her as "Talvey." Her husband was Professor Edward Robinson, the U.S. biblical scholar.

Helen **Tamiris:** Helen Becker (1905–1966), U.S. ballet dancer, choreographer, director.

Tampa Red: Hudson Whittaker (*c.*1900–1981), U.S. black blues singer.

Tania: [1] Haydee Tamara Bunke (1937–1967), Argentine-born agent, of Ger. parentage, working in South America with Che Guevara *(q.v.)*; [2] Patricia Campbell Hearst (1954–   ), U.S. liberationist. Haydee Bunke was a Soviet agent working, and cohabitating, with Che Guevara. When in Havana she used the cover name Laura Gutierrez Bauer. Earlier (1964) when leaving Cuba for Europe she was to become either Vittoria Pancini, and the daughter of German parents living on the Italian-German border, or Marta Iriarte, an Argentinian. Her Cuban cover name above was the outcome: an Italian-Argentinian-German compromise. She was killed, aged 29, in Bolivia when Bolivian forces ran Che Guevara to earth. Tania (or Tanya) had for some time become a popular Soviet or revolutionary cover name, used before her by the young Russian partisan Zoya Kosmodemyanskaya (1923–1941), and after her by the Symbionese Liberation Army agent (who adopted the name in Haydee's honor) Patricia Hearst [1. *Sunday Telegraph*, July 21, 1968; 2. Marta Royas and Mirta Rodriguez Calderon, *Tania*, 1973; 3. David Boulton, *The Making of Tania: The Patty Hearst Story*, 1975].

[Princess] Elizaveta **Tarakanova:** ? (*c.*1745–1775), Russ. royal pretender. For the story behind the dissimulation, see p. 66.

Harry **Tate:** Ronald Macdonald Hutchison (1873–1940), Eng. music hall comedian. The actor took his name from his former employers, the sugar refiners Henry Tate & Sons (now familiar from the name Tate & Lyle).

Jacques **Tati:** Jacques Tatischeff (1908–1982), Fr. comic film actor. The actor was the grandson of Count Dmitri Tatischeff, an attaché at the Russian embassy in Paris who had married a Frenchwoman. His screen name was a shortening of his real name, but at the same time sounds engagingly affectionate to the French ear.

Léo **Taxil:** Gabriel Antoine Jogand-Pagès (1854–1907), Fr. journalist, anticlerical writer.

Estelle **Taylor:** Estelle Boylan (1899–1958), U.S. stage, film actress.

Kent **Taylor:** Louis Weiss (1907–1987), U.S. film actor.

Koko **Taylor:** Cora Walton (1935–   ), U.S. blues singer.

Laurette **Taylor:** Laurette Cooney (1884–1946), U.S. stage, film actress. The actress doubtless felt that her true surname suggested "coon" or "raccoon."

Little Johnny **Taylor:** Johnny Young (1940–   ), U.S. soul, blues singer. The singer took his name from the established soul singer, Ted Taylor.

Robert **Taylor:** Spangler Arlington Brugh (1911–1969), U.S. film actor. The actor was given his screen name in 1934 by MGM head Louis B. Mayer.

Theodore **Taylor:** John Camden Hotten (1832–1873), Eng. writer, publisher. The writer, whose original name was John William Hotten, and who introduced many American authors to the British public, assumed this name for a rather slight biography of Thackeray, published in 1864.

Ludmilla **Tcherina:** Monique Avenirovna Tchemerzina (1924–   ), Fr. ballet dancer.

Conway **Tearle:** Frederick Levy (1878–1938), U.S. film actor.

[Dame] Marie **Tempest:** Mary Susan Etherington (1864–1942), Eng. stage actress. The fine actress took her stage name from her godmother, Lady Susan Vane-Tempest.

Paul **Temple:** Francis Durbridge (1912–   ), Eng. thriller writer + James Douglas Rutherford McConnell (1915–   ), Eng. thriller writer. The two writers used this name for mystery novels which did *not* feature Paul Temple, the famous detective created by Durbridge.

William **Tenn:** Philip Klass (1920–   ), U.S. SF writer. This looks like a pun on "William Penn," but verification is needed.

Kylie **Tennant:** Kylie Tennant Rodd (1912–1988), Austral. novelist, playwright.

Madison **Tensas,** M.D.: [Dr.] Henry Clay Lewis (1825–1850), U.S. humorist.

Teresa: Teresa Viera-Romero (1929–   ), U.S.-Sp. ballet dancer.

[Mother] **Teresa** (of Calcutta): Agnes Gonxha Bojaxhiu (1910–   ), Albanian-born missionary, working chiefly in India. The world-famous missionary went to Ireland in 1928 to join the Institute of the Blessed Virgin Mary. There she took the name Teresa, for St. Teresa of Avila, the sixteenth-century mystic who was one of the greatest religious women of the Roman Catholic Church.

Max **Terpis:** Max Pfister (1889–1958), Swiss ballet dancer, choreographer, teacher. The dancer's professional surname is a near anagram of his real name.

Tammi **Terrell:** Tammy Montgomery (1946–1970), U.S. pop singer. The singer's alliterative name was actually derived from her first husband, the boxer Ernie Terrell. It is therefore a real name, on the same lines as that of Cyd Charisse *(q.v.).* Both ladies had short-lived first marriages, but both retained their married names professionally.

Ellaline **Terriss:** Ellen Hicks, née Lewin (1871–1971), Eng. stage, film actress, daughter of William Terriss *(q.v.).*

William **Terriss:** William Charles James Lewin (1847–1897), Eng. actor. The actor's best work was done at the Adelphi Theatre, London, and consequently he was nicknamed "No. 1, Adelphi Terrace," after a street in this region. He subsequently altered "Terrace" to a spelling that more closely resembled that of a surname. The name also happens to suggest "Terry," a famous theatrical surname. (Ellen Terry, the noted actress, was actually born in the same year as Lewin, so they were exact contemporaries.)

Alice **Terry**: Alice Fances Taafe (1899–1987), U.S. film actress.

C.V. **Terry**: Frank Gill Slaughter (1908–), U.S. novelist.

Don **Terry**: Donald Locher (1902–), U.S. film actor.

Megan **Terry**: Marguerite Duffy (1932–), U.S. dramatist.

Sonny **Terry**: Saunders Terrell (1911–1986), U.S. black jazz, blues musician.

Terry-Thomas: Thomas Terry Hoar-Stevens (1911–), Eng. comic stage, film actor. The actor began his career as "Mot Snevets" (read it backwards), then he tried "Thomas Terry." People started to link him, wrongly, with the theatrical Terrys (such as the Ellen Terry mentioned above, under William Terriss), so he reversed these names and subsequently hyphenated them in about 1947. "The hyphen's the gap between my teeth," the distinctively gap-toothed comedian explained.

Phillida **Terson**: Phyllis Neilson-Terry (1892–1977), Eng. stage actress. The actress's surname is of course a blend of syllables from her real double-barrelled name.

Abram **Tertz**: Andrey Donatovich Sinyavsky (1925–), Russ. novelist, short story writer, critic.

Laurent **Terzieff**: Laurent Tchemerzine (1935–), Fr. film actor.

Joe **Tex**: Joseph Arrington, Jr. (later, as Muslim, Joseph Hazziez) (1933–1982), U.S. soul singer, composer. Needless to say, the singer was born in Texas.

Josephine **Tey**: Elizabeth Mackintosh (1897–1952), Sc. playwright, novelist, short story writer. The writer adopted the name of her great-great-grandmother for her pen name.

[Dame] Maggie **Teyte**: [Dame] Margaret Cottingham, née Tate (1888–1976), Eng. singer. When the soprano went to Paris at the age of 20 she changed the spelling of her surname to ensure the correct pronunciation of "Tate" by the French. This led to doubts about her name's pronunciation in English-speaking countries, a situation that was commented on in the following piece of doggerel (of American origin):

> Tell us ere it be too late,
> Art thou known as Maggie Teyte?
> Or, per contra, art thou hight
> As we figure, Maggie Teyte?

Zare **Thalberg**: Ethel Western (1858–1915), Eng. opera singer, stage actress.

Octave **Thanet**: Alice French (1850–1934), U.S. novelist. "Octave" was the name of a schoolfriend. "Thanet" was a name that the writer spotted chalked on the side of a freight car when her train stopped one day at a way station. Many of her readers assumed she was a man, and wrote her as "My dear Mr. Thanet" accordingly.

Mlle **Théodore**: Marie-Madeleine Crépé (1760–1796), Fr. ballet dancer.

Theodosia: Anne Steel (1716–1778), Eng. writer of religious verse, hymns. The name, which means "gift of God," was doubtless significant for the writer, who adopted it for *Poems on Subjects Chiefly Devotional* (1760).

Sylvanus **Theophrastus:** John Thelwall (1764–1834), Eng. reformer, politician, lecturer on elocution. The writer's pen name is a classical concoction, but may have had specific reference to Johannes Sylvanus, the sixteenth-century German reformer and theologian, and the Greek philosopher Theophrastus.

[Saint] **Theresa of Lisieux:** Marie-Françoise-Thérèse Martin (1873–1897), Fr. virgin, Carmelite nun (the "Little Flower of Jesus").

Danny **Thomas:** Amos Jacobs (1914–   ) U.S. night club comedian, TV actor. For his stage name, the actor adopted the first names of his two brothers.

Olive **Thomas:** Olive Elaine Duffy (1898–1920), U.S. "Ziegfeld girl," film actress.

Carlos **Thompson:** Juan Carlos Mundanschaffter (1916–   ), Argentine stage, film actor.

Jack **Thompson:** John Payne (1940–   ), Austral. film actor.

Sue **Thompson:** Eva Sue McKee (1926–   ), U.S. pop singer.

James **Thomson, B.V.:** James Thomson (1834–1882), Sc. poet. The poet added the initials to his name in order to be distinguished from his namesake, James Thomson (1700–1748), also a Scottish poet. The letters stand for "Bysshe Vanolis," with the first of these names the middle name of Percy Bysshe Shelley, and the second an anagram of the name of Novalis *(q.v.)*. Thomson greatly admired both writers.

Ismay **Thorn:** Edith Caroline Pollock *(fl.*1890), Br. children's writer.

Frank **Thornton:** Francis Bull (1921–   ), Eng. stage, TV actor. The actor adopted his mother's maiden name as his stage name.

Linda **Thorson:** Linda Robinson (1947–   ), Can. stage, TV actress. The actress married Barry Bergthorson, and adopted the latter half of his surname for her stage and screen name.

General Tom **Thumb:** Charles Sherwood Stratton (1838–1883), U.S. midget showman. For his professional name, Charles Stratton adopted the name of the traditional folktale character, who dates back to at least the sixteenth century. His assumed title of "General" was designed to add to his stature, so to speak.

Johnny **Thunder:** John Gonzales (1945–   ), U.S. rock musician.

Chief **Thundercloud:** Victor Daniels (1900–1955), American-Indian film actor.

Henry T. **Thurston:** Francis Turner Palgrave (1824–1897), Eng. poet, anthologist, critic. The compiler of *Palgrave's Golden Treasury* (1861) adopted this name for *The Passionate Pilgrim; or, Eros and Anteros* (1958). Palgrave was the son of the historian Sir Francis Palgrave (1788–1861), who was himself of Jewish origin, with the original surname Cohen. In 1823 he adopted the Christian faith, and in that same year married, changing his name to Palgrave, after the maiden name of his mother-in-law.

Tiffany: Tiffany Renee Darwish (1971–   ), U.S. pop singer.

Pamela **Tiffin:** Pamela Wonso (1942–   ), U.S. film actress, former child model.

Dick **Tiger:** Dick Itehu (1929–1971), Nigerian boxer.

Vesta **Tilley:** Matilda Alice Powles (1864–1952), Br. music hall artiste, male impersonator. The actress began her performing career at the age of six, when she was billed as "Little Tilley" (as a pet form of her first name). This was a provincial debut, made at the Star Music Hall, Gloucester, where her father, William Powles (known as "Harry Ball"), was the manager. When she was 14, she made her first London appearance, now being billed as "The Great Little Tilley." It was soon after this that she adopted the name "Vesta," using "Tilley" as a surname. That way she intrigued even more those members of her audiences who were puzzled as to whether she was a boy or a girl. The selection of "Vesta" may simply have been arbitrary, although it is odd that both "Vesta" and "Tilley" became trade names for a make of stove.

Alice **Tilton:** Phoebe Atwood Taylor (1909–1976), U.S. detective story writer.

Dick **Tinto:** Frank Booth Goodrich (1826–1894), U.S. writer, son of Peter Parley [1] *(q.v.)*. The writer adopted the name of the artist who is the supposed narrator of the story told in Scott's *The Bride of Lammermoor* (1819).

Tintoretto: Jacopo Robusti (1518–1594), It. painter. The painter's name arose as nickname meaning "little dyer," referring to his father, who by profession was a silk dyer (Italian *tintore*).

Tiny Tim: Herbert Khaury (1930–   ), U.S. popular singer, musician. The somewhat bizarre singer adopted his name virtually randomly, but possibly with a nod in the direction of Tiny Tim, the crippled son of Bob Cratchit in Dickens's *A Christmas Carol.* Khaury has taken to alliterative names: others he has tried out have been "Darry Dover" and "Larry Love." In 1969 he married (live, on TV) 17-year-old Victoria May Budinger ("Miss Vicky," as he called her), and their daughter was named Tulip, after Tiny Tim's one (falsetto) hit "Tiptoe Through the Tulips" (1968). Three years later he filed for divorce (finalized 1977).

Timothy **Titcomb:** Josiah Gilbert Holland (1819–1881), U.S. novelist, poet, editor. The writer used this name for *Letters to Young People* (1858).

Titian: Tiziano Vecellio (1488–1576), It. painter. Unlike some of his contemporaries, Titian did not assume (and was apparently not given) a name or nickname that differed from his basic first name.

Michael Angelo **Titmarsh:** William Makepeace Thackeray (1811–1863), Eng. novelist. The famous writer used this name for various tales published from the 1840s. The name is said to have been based on a nickname, "Michael Angelo," given him by a friend who admired the writer's handsome head and shoulders. To this, Thackeray added "Titmarsh" as an absurd contrast.

[Marshal] **Tito:** Josip Broz (1892–1980), Yugoslav soldier, statesman. There are various accounts claiming to explain the famous leader's name. One maintains that it derives from Serbo-Croat *ti to*, literally "you this," meaning "you do this." Tito was always saying "You do this," "You do that," it seems. But Tito himself is said to have adopted the name after reading a book by two Serbo-Croatian writers who had "Tito" as their first name. (As such, it was, and is, a standard Serbo-Croat forename, simply meaning "Titus.") Josip Broz apparently wanted to adopt the name "Rudi," but someone else had already claimed it. The second of these two rival explanations for the name seems the more likely. In the world of partisan warfare in which Tito was involved, he had several underground names, although in Comintern communications he was always "Comrade Walter." The hazardous conditions of guerrilla combat sometimes necessitated a change of cover name as frequently as three times a *day* [Jules Archer, *Red Rebel: Tito of Yugoslavia,* 1968].

Harriet **Toby:** Harriet Katzman (1929–1952), U.S. ballet dancer.

Toby, M.P.: [Sir] Henry William Lucy (1845–1924), Eng. journalist, humorist, satirist. The writer used this name for his contributions to *Punch*. Toby, of course, is the name of Punch's dog in the traditional "Punch and Judy" puppet show. The initials were intended to stand for "Member of Parliament," although Lucy was not an M.P. but a J.P., Justice of the Peace.

Ann **Todd:** Ann Todd Mayfield (1932–   ), U.S. film actress.

Mike **Todd:** Avrom Hirsch Goldenbogen (1907–1958), U.S. film producer. When Avrom Goldenbogen's father died, in 1931, he assumed the first name of his own son, Michael, at the same time changing his surname to "Todd." This represented his own nickname, "Toat."

Tom and Jerry: Art Garfunkel (1937–   ), U.S. pop singer + Paul Simon (1940–   ), U.S. pop singer. The pop singers and composers called themselves thus for the four years 1956–1959, having started in show business as, respectively, Tom Graph and Jerry Landis. In 1959 they vanished from the music scene until 1964, when they re-emerged under their own names (Simon and Garfunkel), subsequently splitting in 1970. The popular pair name Tom and Jerry goes back a good deal further than the well-known cartoon cat and mouse: in 1821 Pierce Egan, an English sports writer, published *Life in London; or, The Day and Night Scenes of Jerry Hawthorn, Esq., and his Elegant Friend Corinthian Tom,* and the names came to typify a couple of roistering young men-about-town.

Jacob **Tonson:** Enoch Arnold Bennett (1867–1931), Br. novelist. Arnold Bennett's early pseudonym was borrowed from that of an eighteenth-century bookseller.

Horne **Tooke:** John Horne (1736–1812), Eng. politician, philologist. John Horne added the name of William Tooke, a friend and political supporter, to his own in 1782, so that from then on he was John Horne Tooke (familiarly, Horne Tooke). William Tooke had a sizeable estate in Surrey, and John Horne had added his name with the intention of indicating that he would be his friend's heir. When Tooke died in 1802, however, Horne Tooke discovered that instead of making him his heir, William Tooke had merely left him £500, apart from cancelling certain outstanding debts.

Topol: Chaim Topol (1935–   ), Israeli film actor.

Peter **Tork:** Peter Torkelson (1942–   ), U.S. pop musician.

Torquemada: Edward Powys Mathers (1892–1939), Br. crossword compiler. The compiler adopted the name of the infamous Spanish Grand Inquisitor, since he aimed to torture his victims, as his historic namesake had done in the fifteenth century.

Raquel **Torres:** Paula Marie Osterman (1908–1987), U.S. film actress.

Malcolm **Torrie:** Gladys Maude Winifred Mitchell (1901–1983), Eng. writer of detective novels, children's fiction.

Peter **Tosh:** Winston Hubert McIntosh (1944–1987), Jamaican reggae singer.

Toto: [1] Antonio de Curtis-Gagliardi Ducas Comneno di Bizanzio (1898–1967),

It. stage, film comedian, circus clown; [2] Armando Novello (? –1938), Swiss circus clown . Circus clown [1] here, whose name was properly Totò, had added the names of two leading Byzantine families, Ducas and Comneno ("of Byzantium"), to his real name, before abandoning this long-winded nomenclature for the little four-letter name that was a pet form of his first name. Circus clown [2] borrowed his own name from him.

Dave **Tough:** David Jarvis (1908–1948), U.S. jazz drummer.

Jennie **Tourel:** Jennie Davidson (1900–1973), Fr.-Can. opera singer, of Russ. parentage.

Maurice **Tourneur:** Maurice Thomas (1876–1961), Fr. film director. Presumably the director based his new name on French *tourner un film*, "to shoot a film."

Peter **Towry:** David Towry Piper (1918–   ), Eng. writer on art, novelist.

Toyah: Toyah Ann Willcox (1958–   ), Br. rock singer, stage, film actress.

Arthur **Tracy:** Harry Rosenberg (1903–   ), U.S. singer, film actor.

F.G. **Trafford:** Charlotte Eliza Lawson Riddell, née Cowan (1832–1906), Ir. novelist. The writer used this name for her first novel, *The Moors and the Fens* (1858), and retained it until 1864, after which she used her real (married) name, Mrs. J.H. Riddell.

Peter **Traill:** Guy Mainwaring Morton (1896–1968), Eng. novelist, playwright.

B. **Traven:** Berick Traven Torsvan (?1890–1969), U.S. novelist, of Swe. (or Ger.) parentage.

Bill **Travers:** William Lindon-Travers (1921–   ), Br. film actor, brother of Linden Travers *(q.v.).*

Graham **Travers:** Margaret Todd (1859–1918), Sc. novelist.

Henry **Travers:** Travers Heagerty (1874–1965), Br. stage, film actor, working in U.S.

Linden **Travers:** Florence Lindon-Travers (1913–   ), Br. stage, film actress.

Richard **Travis:** William Justice (1913–   ), U.S. film actor.

Arthur **Treacher:** Arthur Treacher Veary (1894–1975), Br. film actor, working in U.S.

Lawrence **Treat:** Lawrence Arthur Goldstone (1903–   ), U.S. mystery writer.

Zélia **Trebelli:** Gloria Caroline Gillebert (or Le Bert) (1834–1892), Fr. opera singer.

Pirmin **Trecu:** Pirnon Aldabaldetrecu (1930–   ), Sp. ballet dancer, teacher.

[Sir] Herbert Beerbohm **Tree:** Herbert Beerbohm (1853–1917), Eng. theatre actor, manager. The actor was the son of Julius Beerbohm, a naturalized English grain merchant of German parentage. By taking the name "Tree" he was combining two pseudonymous devices: he not only translated the second element of his original name (corresponding to modern German *Birnbaum*, "pear-tree"), but also added his new name to his existing one. He first used his new stage name (simply "Beerbohm Tree") in 1876. Sir Herbert was the half-brother of the writer, dramatist and critic, Max Beerbohm, who died in 1954.

Trevanian: Rodney Whitaker (1925–   ), U.S. crime novelist.

Hilda **Trevelyan:** Hilda Tucker (1880–1957), Br. stage actress.

John **Trevena:** Ernest George Henham (1870–1946), Eng. poet, novelist, working in Canada.

Austin **Trevor:** Austin Schilsky (1897–1978), Ir.-born Br. film, stage, radio actor.

Claire **Trevor:** Claire Wemlinger (1909–   ), U.S. film actress.

William **Trevor:** William Trevor Cox (1928–   ), Ir. novelist, short story writer.

Trog: Wally Fawkes (1925–   ), Can. cartoonist, working in U.K. The cartoonist took his brief signature from the jazz group, the Troglodytes, of which he had formerly been a member. As their name suggests, the group played in a cellar.

Frances **Trollope:** Paul Feval (1817–1887), Fr. writer of sentimental novels. The writer used the name of the mother of Anthony Trollope, the well-known English novelist. Frances Trollope was an energetic and enterprising woman who eventually wrote about 40 books, including several novels, although few if any of them are remembered today.

Sven **Trost:** [Count] Carl Johan Gustav Snoilsky (1841–1903), Swe. lyric poet.

Leon **Trotsky:** Lev Davidovich Bronstein (1879–1940), Russ. revolutionary leader. There has been a good deal of controversy as to the precise origin of this famous (or infamous) name, adopted by the Russian revolutionary, who was of Jewish parentage. A popular theory is that he picked it at random — writing it in a blank passport handed him by friends — when emerging from exile in Siberia (1902). It is known, however, that Trotsky had been the name of a jailer in the prison of Odessa, where the young Bronstein had been before this. Trotsky is certainly not an invented Russian name, but one that exists in its own right. Even so, with his knowledge of German, Bronstein may have been consciously or unconsciously thinking of the German word *Trotz*, with it symbolic meaning of "defiance, insolence, intrepidity." Certainly, some of his other pseudonyms seem to have been meaningfully selected. At one stage he was Antid-Oto, a word found (*antidoto*) in an Italian dictionary when he started to weight up different pen names, and seen by him as suitable since he "wanted to inject a Marxist antidote into the legal press." At another time (1936) he was Crux, a name he used for articles in the *Bulletin of the Opposition.* At various times he had also been Ensign, Arbuzov, Mr. Sedov (when leaving incognito for Europe in 1932), Pyotr Petrovich (to local Petersburg revolutionaries), Vikentyev (his "official" name in Petersburg in 1905), and Yanovsky (derived from Yanovka Farm, itself named after the colonel who had sold it to his father) [1. Joel Carmichael, *Trotsky: An Appreciation of His Life,* 1975; 2. *Observer Colour Magazine,* October 21, 1979].

Kilgore **Trout:** Philip Jose Farmer (1918–   ), U.S. SF writer. The writer took his pen name from the fictitious SF writer appearing in stories by Kurt Vonnegut, Jr.

Ben **Trovato:** Samuel Lover (1797–1868), Ir. songwriter, novelist, printer. The writer adopted his pseudonym from the Italian phrase *ben trovato*, literally "well found," in other words, "happy invention" — like Lover's pen name itself!

Doris **Troy:** Doris Payne (1937–   ), U.S. pop singer, songwriter.

Henri **Troyat:** Levon Aslanovich Tarasov (1911–   ), Russ.-born Fr. novelist. Although the writer's new surname to some degree resembles his real name, he is said to have taken it from a telephone directory. But the latter circumstance does not necessarily invalidate the former coincidence.

Basil **Truro:** Vassilie Trunoff (1929–1985), Austral.-born Russ. ballet dancer. During the Australian tour of the Ballet Rambert in 1948, Trunoff was invited to fill a vacancy caused when another dancer returned to England. Marie Rambert *(q.v.)* asked him to appear with an English stage name instead of his Russian one, thus rather unusually reversing the usual ballet practice of the day.

H. **Trusta:** Elizabeth Stuart Phelps (1815–1852), U.S. novelist. The writer used this name, formed anagramatically from her middle name and the "h" of her surname, for two semi-autobiographical novels, *A Peep at Number Five* (1851) and *The Angel Over the Right Shoulder* (1851).

Sojourner **Truth:** Isabella Van Wagener (*c.*1797–1883), U.S. black evangelist, reformer. The fine puritanical name was adopted by the evangelist in 1843 when she left New York to "travel up and down the land" singing and preaching. Isabella Van Wagener had been a slave, and her legal name was taken from the family who bought her, then set her free just before the abolition of slavery in New York state in 1827.

Richard **Tucker:** Reuben Ticker (1913–1975), U.S. opera singer.

Sophie **Tucker:** Sophia Abuza (1884–1966), U.S. vaudeville, film actress, of Jewish-Russ. parentage. The actress's father was originally named Kalish, but when he absconded from Russian military service to go to America, he fell in with an Italian named Charles Abuza, also absent without leave. Abuza fell sick and died, whereupon Sophie's father, fearing detection by the Russian authorities, took the Italian's identity papers and also adopted his name. He thus arrived in the U.S. as "Charles Abuza." When she was still a teenager, Sophia Abuza married Louis Tuck, a dancer in Hartford, Connecticut, where her family then lived. Meanwhile, she had gained local success as a singer, and in 1906 went to New York to be auditioned by Harry Von Tilzer, the leading song writer of the day. While waiting for his verdict, she called in at the Café Monopol, on Eighth Street, and asked the proprietor if she could "sing for her supper," as she was hungry and low on funds. He agreed, and asked her name. Sophie Tucker tells what happened next: "I had my mail sent to Mrs. Louis Tuck, care of General Delivery, as of course that was my name. But 'Mrs. Tuck' didn't sound right for a singer. 'Sophie Tucker,' I told him. Right like that a career was born" [Sophie Tucker, *Some of These Days: An Autobiography*, 1948].

Tommy **Tucker:** Robert Higginbotham (1933–1982), U.S. blues singer, pianist. In the nursery rhyme, "Little Tommy Tucker/Sings for his supper," just as any singer has to do if he is to eat. Presumably the blues singer borrowed the name from this well-known source.

Antony **Tudor:** William Cook (1908–1987), Eng. ballet dancer, choreographer, teacher.

Tenpole **Tudor:** Eddie Tudor-Pole (*c.*1950–   ), Br. pop singer. "Tenpole" looks as though it is a nickname (perhaps originally "Tentpole") formed from the singer's real name.

Sonny **Tufts:** Bowen Charleston Tufts (1911–1970), U.S. film actor.

Boris **Tumarin:** Boris Tumarinson (1910–), Latvian stage actor, director, working in U.S.

Yevgeniya **Tur** (or Eugenie Tur): Yelizaveta Vasilyevna Salias-de-Turnemir (1815–1892), Russ. writer. The Russian author is little known in the Western world, and indeed many Russians will not have heard of her (she wrote a number of popular children's books), but her son has given an illuminating account of how she came by her name. This will be of interest both to pseudonymists and admirers of the Russian classic writers: "They have said that 'Yevgeniya Tur' was 'Turgenev' turned round. By sheer coincidence this is so, and you get an almost complete anagram. But there is no secret in this: the stories about my mother's affair with Turgenev are complete nonsense. My mother was called Yelizaveta, but she was extremely fond of the names 'Yevgeny' and 'Yevgeniya.' She was a passionate admirer of Pushkin and of *Eugene Onegin* in particular. That's where I get my own name of Yevgeny from. [. . .] The way her pen name came about is as follows: 'Yevgeniya' was chosen with little hesitation. Then the search began for a surname. 'Yevgeniya Sal' was an abbreviation of 'Salias,' but *sale* in French is 'dirty.' 'Yevgeniya Lias' doesn't sound well, 'Yevgeniya Nemir' is too long. [. . .] Everyone liked 'Yevgeniya Tur'" [Dmitriyev, p. 53].

Turlupin: Henri Legrand (*c.*1587–1637), Fr. actor. The actor used the name Belleville *(q.v.)* for serious parts in tragedy, keeping "Turlupin" for farces. The name itself is of obscure origin.

Lana **Turner:** Julia Jean Mildred Frances Turner (1920–), U.S. film actress. It is uncertain whether Judy Turner (as she usually called herself) chose her new first name, or whether it was given her by her Warner Brothers agent, Mervyn LeRoy. If the latter, LeRoy is said to have taken the unusual name from a girl he knew when he was at school. Either way, Judy Turner adopted the name in 1950, and was anxious that it should be "pronounced Lana as in lah-de-da, not lady" [Joe Morella and Edward Z. Epstein, *Lana: The Public and Private Lives of Miss Turner,* 1983].

Sammy **Turner:** Samuel Black (1932–), U.S. pop singer.

Tina **Turner:** Annie-Mae (or Anna Mabel) Bullock (1938–), U.S. black rock singer. It is really only the first name of the singer that is different, for her surname is that of her husband, Ike Turner (married 1958, divorced 1976), with whom she initially made her name, recording and touring as the Ike and Tina Turner Revue.

Mark **Twain:** Samuel Langhorne Clemens (1835–1910), U.S. novelist, short story writer. Almost everyone knows that the real name behind this famous pseudonym was Samuel Langhorne Clemens. Most people will know, too, that the great American novelist derived his pen name from the call, "Mark twain!" of pilots on the Mississippi River when they wanted a depth sounding (i.e., "mark two fathoms"). But perhaps it is less well known that there was an elderly writer whom Clemens began by satirizing called Mark Twain – his real name being Isaiah Sellers (born possibly in 1802, died in 1864) – and that conceivably *this* was the origin of his pseudonym. Be that as it may, Clemens first used the name, as far as is known, for a contribution to the Virginia City *Territorial Enterprise* (1863). Mencken points out that in the United States the name Mark Twain has become a registered trade name, which may not be used on the jacket, cover, or title page of a book without permission of the Mark Twain Company, through its agent, the publishers Harper & Row.

Twiggy: Lesley Hornby (1950–), Eng. fashion model, film actress, singer. When the fashion model was still at school, she was nicknamed "Sticks," for her thin and skinny appearance. This name was later refashioned as "Twiggy," and she adopted this professionally in 1964 for her fashion career. Her near-anorexic look was regarded as just right for the mini-skirts of the day.

Conway **Twitty:** Harold Lloyd Jenkins (1933–), U.S. country singer. The singer has explained how he got his name: "So we started thinking about all kinds of names, and to make a long story short, what I finally wound up doing was, I got the map out and there's a place called Twitty, Texas. Then I thought if I could get something different to go with this, it might be something. I finally got the map of Arkansas and started looking through that, and there're towns in Arkansas like Baldknob, Walnut Creek, Smackover, and all kinds of crazy names like that. But right outside of Little Rock there's a town called Conway, and that's how it came about—Conway, Arkansas, and Twitty, Texas. So we all agreed that that was an unusual name, and my first record was [. . .] under the name of Conway Twitty. I didn't agree with the idea first because my main interest was I was worried about the people in my hometown that wouldn't know who Conway Twitty is, and I wanted them all to know I had a new record out. [. . .] But I finally realized what the fellow was talking about and I decided he was right, so we went with Conway Twitty" [Shestack, p. 285].

Bonnie **Tyler:** Gaynor Sullivan (1953–), Welsh pop singer.

Tom **Tyler:** Vincent Markowsky (1903–1954), U.S. film actor.

T. Texas **Tyler:** David Luke Myrick (1916–1971), U.S. country singer. As his name implies, the singer came from Texas.

Sarah **Tytler:** Henrietta Keddie (1827–1914), Sc. novelist.

Paolo **Uccello:** Paolo di Dono (1397–1475), It. painter. The painter was nicknamed "Uccello," Italian for "bird," for his fondness for drawing these creatures.

Ulanhu: Yun-Tse (1906–1988), Mongolian political leader. The former Vice-President of the Chinese People's Republic changed his aristocratic name Yun-Tse to Ulanfu in the 1920s, this being the Wade-Giles spelling (the Pinyin spelling is Ulanhu). The change was intended as a tribute both to Lenin *(q.v.)*, whose family name was Ulyanov *(fu* being the Chinese character which transliterates the Russian suffix *-ov)*, and to his Communist beliefs, as *ulan* is the Mongolian word for "red."

Lenore **Ulric:** Lenore Ulrich (1892–1970), U.S. stage, film actress.

Michael **Underwood:** John Michael Evelyn (1916–), Eng. crime novelist. The writer adopted his mother's maiden name as his pen name.

Urban II: Odo of Lagery (*c.*1035–1099), Fr. pope.

Urban III: Uberto Crivelli (? –1187), It. pope.

Urban IV: Jacques Pantaléon (*c.*1200–1264), Fr. pope.

Urban V: Guillaume de Grimoard (*c.*1310–1370), Fr. pope.

Urban VI: Bartolomeo Prignano (*c.*1318–1389), It. pope.

Urban VII: Giambattista Castagna (1521–1590), It. pope.

Urban VIII: Maffeo Vincenzo Barberini (1568–1644), It. pope.

Sylvanus **Urban:** Edward Cave (1691–1754), Eng. printer, founder of *The Gentleman's Magazine.* The writer and editor's pseudo-classical name was designed to reflect his dual interest in both town and country affairs, in other words, things "sylvan" (relating to woodland) and "urban" (relating to cities). Compare the name of Urbanus Sylvan.

Maurice **Utrillo:** Maurice Valadon (1883–1955), Fr. painter. The painter was born as the son of Suzanne Valadon and an artist named Boissy. When he was eight years old, Maurice was formally adopted by a Spanish art critic named Miguel Utrillo, who gave him his own name. Suzanne Valadon had herself undergone a name change, from Marie-Clémentine Valadon to Suzanne. She adopted her new first name when she changed her career from model to artist in 1883, the year that Maurice was born.

Roger **Vadim:** Roger Vadim Plemiannikow (1928–   ), Fr. film writer, director.

Vera **Vague:** Barbara Jo Allen (?1904–1974), U.S. film, radio comedienne.

Ritchie **Valens:** Richard Valenzuela (1941–1959), U.S. pop guitarist.

Dickie **Valentine:** Richard Brice (1929–1971), Br. pop singer.

Joseph **Valentine:** Giuseppe Valentino (1900–1949), It.-U.S. cinematographer.

Rudolph **Valentino:** Rodolfo Alfonzo Raffaelo Pierre Filibert Guglielmi di Valentino d'Antonguolla (1895–1926), It.-born U.S. film actor (the "Great Lover"). It should be noted that, of all these names, the actor's basic real surname was Guglielmi, with "Valentino" derived from his hereditary name. The association with "Valentine" (in the "sweetheart" sense) is thus fortuitous.

Simone **Valere:** Simone Gondoff (1923–   ), Fr. film actress.

Alwina **Valleria:** Alwina Schoening (1848–1925), U.S. opera singer.

Alida **Valli:** Alida Maria Altenburger (1921–   ), It. film actress, of Austr.-It. parentage.

Frankie **Valli:** Frank Castelluccio (1937–   ), U.S. rock musician.

Virginia **Valli:** Virginia McSweeney (1898–1968), U.S. film actress.

Bobby **Van:** Robert King (1930–1980), U.S. dancer, singer, stage actor.

Jan **Van Avond:** Francis Carey Salter (1876–1958), S.A. poet, novelist.

[Dame] Irene **Vanbrugh:** Irene Barnes (1872–1949), Br. stage actress, sister of Violet Vanbrugh (*q.v.*).

Violet **Vanbrugh:** Violet Augusta Mary Barnes (1867–1942), Br. stage actress. The actress adopted her stage name at the suggestion of Ellen Terry, the reference being to the great seventeenth-century dramatist (and architect), Sir John Vanbrugh. (No doubt the alliteration with "Violet" helped.) Her sister, Irene Barnes, then also adopted this name.

Alfred Glenville **Vance:** Alfred Peck Stevens (1839–1888), Eng. music hall character-singer. Presumably "Vance" developed out of "Stevens."

Charles **Vance:** Charles Goldblatt (1929–   ), West Indian stage actor, director.

Ethel **Vance:** Grace Stone, née Zaring (1896–   ), U.S. novelist.

Vivian **Vance:** Vivian Jones (1913–1979), U.S. TV actress.

Margaret **Vandegrift:** Margaret Thomson Janvier (1844–1913), U.S. children's writer, sister of Ivory Black *(q.v.).* There is a hint of "Vandegrift" in the writer's original surname, although the precise origin may lie elsewhere.

S.S. **Van Dine:** Willard Huntington Wright (1888–1939), U.S. literary critic, detective story writer. The writer adopted an old family name, Van Dine, adding the initials whimsically to mean "steamship," as they commonly do before a ship name.

Mamie **Van Doren:** Joan Lucille Olander (1933–   ), U.S. film actress. Presumably the actress's new surname evolved out of her original name.

Peter **Van Eyck:** Götz von Eick (1913–1969), Ger. film actor.

Vangelis: Evangelos D. Papathanassiou (1943–   ), Gk. pop musician.

James **Van Heusen:** Edward Chester Babcock (1913–   ), U.S. composer of musicals, film music.

Eric **Van Lhin:** Lester del Rey (or Rámon Álvarez del Rey) (1915–   ), U.S. SF writer.

Victor **Varconi:** Mihaly Várkonyi (1896–1976), Hung. film actor, working in U.S.

John Philip **Varley:** Langdon Elwyn Mitchell (1862–1935), U.S. playwright.

Comte Paul **Vasili:** Juliette Adam, née Lamber (1836–1936), Fr. novelist, editor. The noted founder of *La Nouvelle Revue* assumed a name that ran counter to reality: she was not a count, but a commoner; not Russian but French; not male, but female!

Frankie **Vaughan:** Frank Abelsohn (1928–   ), Eng. popular singer, dancer, film actor.

Kate **Vaughan:** Catherine Candelin (*c.*1852–1903), Br. stage actress, sister of Susie Vaughan *(q.v.).* The two sisters made their music hall debut as the Sister Vaughan dancers in 1870. A stage name is obviously a tradition, but "Catherine Candelin" is somehow a name with greater glitter than "Kate Vaughan."

Peter **Vaughan:** Peter Ohm (1923–   ), Eng. film, TV actor.

Susie **Vaughan:** Susan Mary Charlotte Candelin (1853–1950), Br. stage actress, sister of Kate Vaughan *(q.v.).*

Bobby **Vee:** Robert Thomas Velline (1943–   ), U.S. pop singer.

Lupe **Velez:** Maria Guadalupe Velez de Villalobos (1908–1944), Mexican film actress.

Lino **Ventura:** Angelino Borrini (1920–1987), It.-born Fr. film actor. The actor adopted his name as a professional wrestler, who needs fortune (Italian *ventura*) in the ring.

Benay **Venuta:** Venuta Rore Crooke (1911–   ), U.S. stage actress, singer.

Vera: [1] [Lady] Gertrude Elizabeth Campbell, née Blood (? –1911), Br. art critic, author; [2] Charlotte Louisa Hawkins Dempster (1835–1913), Br. author. The interesting thing is, of course, that neither lady actually had Vera as an original name. No doubt it was interpreted symbolically, through Latin *vera*, "true," or through Slavonic *vera*, "faith."

Vera-Ellen: Vera-Ellen Westmeyr Rohe (1920–1981), U.S. popular singer, dancer, film actress.

Vercors: Jean Bruller (1902–   ), Fr. writer, illustrator. The writer used this name for his secretly distributed *Le Silence de la Mer* (1942), when running an underground press in Paris. Vercors is the name of an Alpine plateau which was a Resistance center in the Second World War. (For a similar name, compare Forez.)

Violette **Verdy:** Nelly Guillerm (1933–   ), Fr.-born U.S. ballet dancer.

Diana **Vere:** Diana Fox (1942–   ), Trinidad-born Br. ballet dancer.

V. **Veresaeff:** Vikenty Vikentievich Smidovich (1867–1945), Russ. author. The author originally used the pen name "Vikentyev," formed from his patronymic (middle name). In 1892 he adopted the name by which he was subsequently known, taking it from the name of a character in a story by the Russian writer P.P. Gnedich. He felt the name was "attractive and not pretentious" [Dmitriev, p. 61].

Karen **Verne:** Ingabor Katrine Klinckerfuss (1915–1967), Ger. film actress, working in U.S.

Gerald **Verner:** Donald Stuart (1896–1980), Br. thriller writer.

Henri **Verneuil:** Achod Malakian (1920–   ), Turk. film director, of Armenian parentage, working in France.

Anne **Vernon:** Edith Vignaud (1925–   ), Fr. film actress, working in U.K., U.S.

Konstanze **Vernon:** Konstanze Herzfeld (1939–   ), Ger. ballet dancer.

Paolo **Veronese:** Paolo Cogliari (or Caliari) (1528–1588), It. painter. The painter came to be called after his birthplace, Verona.

Andrea del **Verrocchio:** Andrea di Michele Cione (1435–1488), It. sculptor, painter. The artist is said to have adopted the name of his teacher, a goldsmith named Giuliano Verrocchi, and it was in the goldsmith's trade that he was initially trained.

Odile **Versois:** Militza de Poliakoff-Baidarov (1930–1980), Fr. film actress, of Russ. parentage, sister of Marina Vlady *(q.v.)*.

Dziga **Vertov:** Denis Arkadyevich Kaufman (1896–1954), Russ. film documentary director.

Stanley **Vestal:** Walter Stanley Campbell (1887–1957), U.S. author, educator. The author used this name mostly for his writings about the Southwestern frontier, and possibly "Vestal" is meant to suggest "West."

Madame **Vestris:** Lucia Elisabetta Vestris, née Bartolozzi (1787–1856), Eng. actress, singer. As was the tradition of her day, the actress used her married name for her stage name. Her husband was the French ballet dancer, Armand Vestris (who, however, deserted her when she was only 23).

Victoria **Vetri:** Angela Dorian (1944–   ), Austral. film actress. The actress's new first name would have been significant for an Australian.

Sid **Vicious:** John Simon Ritchie (later, Beverly) (1957–1979), Eng. punk rock musician. The Sex Pistols member is said to have received his typical anti-establishment name after making a violent attack with a chain on a journalist.

Martha **Vickers:** Martha MacVicar (1925–1971), U.S. film actress.

Vicky: Victor Weisz (1913–1966), Ger.-born Br. political cartoonist.

Victor II: Gebhard von Dollnstein-Hirschberg (*c.*1018–1057), Ger. pope.

Victor III: Dauferi (later, Desiderius) (1027–1087), It. pope.

Florence **Vidor:** Florence Arto (1895–1977), U.S. film actress.

Jean **Vigo:** Jean Almereyda (1905–1934), Fr. film director.

Charles **Vildrac:** Charles Messager (1882–1971), Fr. poet, novelist, dramatist. The writer adopted a literary name for his pen name, that of Roger Wildrake, the reckless cavalier in Scott's novel *Woodstock*, with the English name rendered in a French manner.

Pancho **Villa:** Doroteo Arango (1878–1923), Mexican revolutionary, guerrilla leader.

Frank **Villard:** François Drouineau (1917–1980), Fr. film actor.

Henry **Villard:** Ferdinand Heinrich Gustav Hilgard (1835–1900), Ger.-born U.S. journalist.

Caroline **Villiers:** Carol Friday (1949–   ), Eng. stage, TV actress.

François **Villon:** François de Montcorbier (1431– ?), Fr. poet. Some uncertainty remains about the real name of the French poet, and his date of death is also not accurately recorded. He seems to have been born as either François de Montcorbier or François des Loges, these two "surnames" being respectively the name of a village on the borders of Burgundy where his father was born and, probably, the name of his father's farm. The name by which we know him is that of the man who adopted him, Guillaume de Villon, a Paris chaplain. Villon used other pseudonyms, among them Michel Mouton ("Michael Sheep").

Jacques **Villon:** Gaston Duchamp (1875–1963), Fr. artist. The artist adopted the latter half of the name of his half-brother, Raymond Duchamp-Villon, also an artist.

Gene **Vincent:** Eugene Vincent Craddock (1935–1971), U.S. rock musician.

Harl **Vincent:** Harl Vincent Schoelphfin (1893–1968), U.S. SF writer.

Barbara **Vine:** Ruth Rendell (1930–   ), Br. detective fiction writer. The "Queen of Crime" took the name from her grandmother. "I know it sounds odd but I feel different when I use it," she says. "It is more feminine." She first used it in 1985 when she was "looking for a different voice."

Vinkbooms: Thomas Griffiths Wainewright (1794–1852), Eng. art critic, writer, forger. This was one of the pseudonyms used by Wainewright for his contributions to the *London Magazine*, others being "Egomet Bonmot" and "Janus Weathercock." After murdering his half-sister, Helen Abercromby, in the hope of claiming on her life insurance (in which he was unsuccessful), and also after issuing a forged cheque, he was arrested and exiled to Tasmania, where he ended his days as a convict. There was a 16th-century Flemish painter named Vinkenbooms.

Helen **Vinson:** Helen Rulfs (1907–   ), U.S. film actress.

Vitalis: Erk Sjöberg (1794–1825), Swe. poet. The poet adopted a Latin name, meaning "likely to live," implying a life struggle. Alas, he died when only 31, the struggle having been too much.

Monica **Vitti:** Maria Luisa Ceciarelli (1931–   ), It. film actress.

Renée **Vivien:** Pauline Tarn (1877–1909), Fr. poet.

Vivienne: Florence Vivienne Entwistle (1887–1982), Br. portrait photographer.

Marina **Vlady:** Marina de Poliakoff-Baidarov (1938–   ), Fr. film actress, of Russ. parentage, sister of Odile Versois *(q.v.)*. The actress's screen surname suggests a Russian family name such as Vladimirovna (as a patronymic) or Vladimirova (as a surname).

Voltaire: François Marie Arouet (1694–1778), Fr. philosopher, poet, dramatist. Possibly the best known of all pseudonyms—and of all pseudonyms, the most uncertain in origin. The commonly held theory is that the name is an anagram of the surname of the great French philosopher and writer François Marie Arouet, with "l.j." standing for *le jeune* (i.e. "The Young") added. (One must also, with this derivation, allow that the 'u' of Arouet becomes 'v,' and the initial 'j' shifts to 'i.') But the name may have been taken from the village of Volterre. Qui sait? We do at least know that the name was first used on the release of its illustrious bearer from the Bastille in 1718. Appendix I gives a complete list of his 173 pseudonyms.

Samuel Greifensohn **von Hirschfeld:** Hans Jakob Christoffel von Grimmelshausen (?1620–1676), Ger. writer. The writer revelled in anagrammatic pseudonyms, of which this is one example. Others were "Erich Stainfels von Grufensholm," "Israel Fromschmit von Hugenfels," "Filarhus Grossus von Trommenhaim," and even "A.c.eee.ff.g.hh.ii.ll.mm.nn.oo.rr.sss.t.uu," which appeared on the title page of *Das wunderbarliche Vogelsnest* (1672). His best-known pen name, however, was "Simplicissimus" *(q.v.)*.

W.O. von Horn: Philip Friedrich Wilhelm Örtel (1798–1867), Ger. writer of popular stories. The writer's pseudonym stands for "Wilhelm Örtel of Horn," the latter being his native town in Germany.

Sasha **von Scherler:** Alexandra-Xenia Elizabeth Anne Marie Fiesola von Schoeler (1939–   ), U.S. stage actress. The actress did the only decent thing, adopting the pet form of her first name and a phonetic rendering of her surname.

Baron **von Schlicht:** [Count] Wolf Heinrich von Baudissin (1789–1878), Ger. literary critic, translator. No doubt significantly, German *schlicht* means "homely," "unpretentious."

Joseph **von Sternberg:** Josef Stern (1894–1969), Austr. film director, working in U.S. An unusual lengthening of a short name, no doubt for distinctiveness.

Erich **von Stroheim:** Hans Erich Maria Stroheim von Nordenwall (1885–1957), Austr. film actor, director, working in U.S. The actor was probably right in judging that "von Stroheim" would have a more memorable effect than "von Nordenwall."

Baron Arminius **von Thunder-Ten-Tronckh:** Matthew Arnold (1822–1888), Eng. poet, critic. An early, bizarre pen name used by the noted writer and critic.

Harry **von Tilzer:** Harry Gumm (1872–1946), U.S. popular song composer. The composer took his mother's maiden name of Tilzer for his professional name.

Bono **Vox:** Paul Hewson (1960–   ), Ir. rock musician. The name suggests, albeit classically, that the singer is in "good voice"!

Henry **Wade:** [Major Sir] Henry Lancelot Aubrey-Fletcher (1887–1969), Eng. detective fiction writer. The writer adopted his mother's maiden name as his pen name.

Michael **Wager:** Emanuel Weisgal (1925–   ), U.S. stage actor, director.

Bunny **Wailer:** Neville O'Reilly Livingston (1947–   ), Jamaican pop singer, songwriter.

Anton **Walbrook:** Adolf Anton Wohlbrück (1900–1967), Austr. film actor, working in U.K.

Jersey Joe **Walcott:** Arnold Raymond Cream (?1914–   ), U.S. heavyweight boxer.

Robert **Walden:** Robert Wolkowitz (1943–   ), U.S. TV actor.

Hubert **Wales:** William Pigott (1870–1943), Br. novelist, writer on psychical research.

Arthur David **Waley:** Arthur David Schloss (1889–1966), Eng. oriental scholar, translator. The writer's family adopted his mother's maiden name as their legal name in 1914, at the outbreak of the First World War.

Jerry Jeff **Walker:** Paul Crosby (1942–   ), U.S. country singer, songwriter.

John **Walker:** John Joseph Mans (1943–   ), U.S. pop singer.

Junior **Walker:** Autry DeWalt (1942–   ), U.S. pop musician.

Nancy **Walker:** Anna Myrtle Swoyer (1922–   ), U.S. pop singer.

Syd **Walker:** Sidney Kirman (1887–1945), Eng. radio comedian.

Max **Wall:** Maxwell George Lorimer (1908–   ), Sc.-born Br. stage, TV actor, comedian. The actor derived his stage name not simply from his first name, split into two, but as a compound of the first half of this name and the first half of his stepfather's name, Wallace.

Edgar **Wallace:** Richard Horatio Edgar Wallace (1875–1932), Eng. novelist, playwright. The writer was born as the son of Polly Richards, née Mary Jane Blair, and Richard Horatio Edgar, both of whom were in the acting business. (His mother had married a Mr. Richards, and was known as "Polly" instead of her actual first name, Marie, which she had "upgraded" from Mary.) The question is: who gave the novelist the "Wallace" of his name? When Polly Richards registered her son's birth, she could not resist giving him the full name of his father, but in the paternity column of the register wrote "Walter Wallace, comedian," in order to disguise the actual identity of the father. It seems likely that "William Wallace, comedian" never existed, and no actor of this name has been traced in theatrical records. Even if he had lived, it seems unlikely that he would have agreed to give his name to a child that was certainly not his. No doubt Polly Richards was giving the boy the name of "a convenient father who could never be traced, and who had his beginning and his end solely in her own imagination" [Margaret Lane, *Edgar Wallace: The Biography of a Phenomenon*, 1939]. By a pleasant irony, one of Edgar Wallace's detective plays was entitled *The Man Who Changed His Name*. It was not a great success, and was full of improbable coincidences.

Irving **Wallace:** Irving Wallechinsky (1911–   ), U.S. novelist, encyclopaedist. The writer is well known for the various editions of *The Book of Lists* (1977), among other works, with this particular book compiled by a family foursome: Irving Wallace, David Wallechinsky (Irving's son), Amy Wallace (his daughter), and Sylvia Wallace (his wife).

Jean **Wallace:** Jean Wallasek (1923–   ), U.S. film actress.

Nellie **Wallace:** Eleanor Jane Liddy (1870–1948), Br. music hall artist.

Lester **Wallack:** John Johnstone Wallack (1820–1888), U.S. actor, playwright, theatre manager.

Fats **Waller:** Thomas Waller (1904–1943), U.S. jazz pianist, composer. The musician's nickname is a descriptive one, and arose to refer to his plump appearance. He then adopted it as his professional name.

Lewis **Waller:** William Waller Lewis (1860–1915), Br. actor, theatre manager. The actor was fortunate enough to have a surname that could readily be adopted as a first name for his stage name.

Max **Waller:** Maurice Warlomont (1866–1895), Belg. lyric poet.

Stella **Walsh:** Stanislawa Walasiewicz (1911–1980), Pol.-born U.S. athlete.

Bruno **Walter:** Bruno Walter Schlesinger (1876–1962), Ger. opera, symphony conductor, working in U.S.

Joseph **Walton:** Joseph Losey (1909–1984), U.S.-born Br. film director. This was one of the pseudonyms under which Losey worked in London in the 1950s when hoping to attract the attention of the critics. He used it for *The Intimate Stranger* (1956), having earlier directed *The Sleeping Tiger* (1954) as "Victor Hanbury."

Walter **Wanger:** Walter Feuchtwanger (1894–1968), U.S. film producer.

Artemus **Ward:** Charles Farrar Browne (1834–1867), U.S. humorous writer. The writer is said to have adopted his pen name from that of an eccentric showman known by him. The name was first used for a character who gave illiterate "commentaries" on various subjects in his letters. In 1861 Browne took to lecturing as Artemus Ward. By a coincidence, there had earlier (1727–1800) been an American Revolutionary commander named Arte*mas* Ward and Artemas Ward was also the name of the advertising manager who gave King C. Gillette valuable advice about hard-hitting advertising when the now famous inventor of the disposable razor blade visited London in the 1880s. No doubt yet more Artemas – or Artemus – Wards are still alive and well and flourishing in the English-speaking world even today.

Burt **Ward:** Herbert Jervis (1945–   ), U.S. juvenile film actor.

Fannie **Ward:** Fannie Buchanan (1872–1952), U.S. stage actress.

Polly **Ward:** Byno Poluski (1908–   ), Br. film actress.

Andy **Warhol:** Andrew Warhola (?1928–1987), U.S. pop artist.

Richard **Waring:** Richard Stephens (1912–   ), Eng. stage actor. The actor adopted his mother's maiden name as his stage name.

Peter **Warlock:** Philip Arnold Heseltine (1894–1930), Eng. composer, writer. The writer's name, adopted around 1921, was intended to signify a change to a new, aggressive personality, one of "wine, women and song." A warlock, after all, is a wizard, a practicer of black magic. Heseltine had first used the name in 1919, after the failure of his early work and a number of rejects. Reviewing a new book on Warlock in the *Times Literary Supplement* (July 11, 1980), Eric Sams points out that the assumed name may be even more meaningful, since Heseltine is said to derive from "hazel," and thus, by means of an associative switch, via "witch hazel," and a sex-change ("witch" to "warlock"), the composer arrived at his new name. One literary pseudonym Warlock did use was Rab Noolas (1929), for *Merry-Go-Down: A Gallery of Gorgeous Drunkards Through the Ages.* (Upend this name to make it meaningful!)

Charles **Warner:** Charles Lickfold (1846–1909), Br. stage actor.

Harry Morris **Warner:** Harry Morris Eichelbaum (1881–1958), U.S. film exhibitor, producer, of Russ. parentage, brother of Jack L. Warner *(q.v.).*

Jack **Warner:** John Waters (1894–1981), Eng. stage, film, TV actor.

Jack L. **Warner:** Jack L. Eichelbaum (1892–1978), U.S. film producer, brother of Harry Morris Warner *(q.v.).* Jack L. Warner was the youngest and best known of the four Warner Brothers, who founded one of the leading film companies in the world.

Harry **Warren:** Salvatore Guaragno (1893–1981), U.S. film songwriter. You can see the germ of the English name in the original Italian.

Leonard **Warren:** Leonard Warenoff (1911–1960), U.S. opera singer.

Lavinia **Warren:** Mercy Lavinia Warren Bumpus (1841–1919), U.S. midget, wife of General Tom Thumb *(q.v.).*

Dionne **Warwick:** Marie Dionne Warrick (1940–   ), U.S. black rock singer.

John **Warwick:** John McIntosh Beattie (1905–1972), Austral. film actor, working in U.K.

Robert **Warwick:** Robert Taylor Bien (1878–1965), U.S. film actor.

Washboard Sam: Robert Brown (1910–   ), U.S. black washboard player, blues singer.

Dinah **Washington:** Ruth Jones (1924–1963), U.S. black blues singer.

Donna Day **Washington:** Donna Day Washington-Smith (1942–   ), Can. ballet dancer.

William **Wastle:** John Gibson Lockhart (1794–1854), Sc. biographer, magazine contributor. The writer used this name for his contributions to *Blackwood's Magazine,* adopting it from that of Willie Wastle, a character in a poem by Robert Burns. This was the name under which Lockhart featured in the *Noctes Ambrosianae* (see Christopher North).

Muddy **Waters:** McKinley Morganfield (1915–1983), U.S. blues singer, musician. The famous blues musician was given this name as a nickname by his grandmother, who raised him on Stovell plantation, near Clarksdale, Mississippi. The name referred to the boy's habit of fishing and playing in a nearby muddy creek.

Dilys **Watling:** Dilys Rhys-Jones (1946–   ), Eng. stage actress.

Claire **Watson:** Claire McLamore (1927–   ), U.S. opera singer.

Wylie **Watson:** John Wylie Robertson (1889–1966), Br. film actor.

Jonathan **Watts:** John B. Leech (1933–   ), U.S. ballet dancer, teacher.

Edward Bradwardine **Waverley:** John Wilson Croker (1780–1857), Ir.-born Br. politician, essayist. The writer adopted this name in two letters (published 1826) replying to Malachi Malagrowther *(q.v.),* concocting the name itself from those of two characters in Scott's *Waverley:* Edward Waverley and the Baron of Bradwardine.

Franz **Waxman:** Franz Wachsmann (1906–1967), Ger. composer of film music, working in U.S.

David **Wayne:** Wayne David McKeekan (1914–   ), U.S. stage, film actor.

Dennis **Wayne:** Dennis Wayne Wendelken (1945–   ), U.S. ballet dancer.

John **Wayne:** Marion Michael Morrison (1907–1979), U.S. film actor. The famous movie star's name change was prompted by head of production Sheehan for the film *The Big Trail* (1930), Sheehan commenting, "I don't like this name, Duke Morrison, it's no name for a leading man." (Earlier Morrison had adopted the first name Duke. This was in fact the name of his Airedale, and the nickname used by firemen in a nearby fire station when young Morrison and dog went past.) Director Raoul Walsh, who admired Mad Anthony Wayne, a general of the American Revolution, suggested Anthony Wayne. Sheehan said that this "sounded too Italian." "Then Tony Wayne," countered Walsh. Here Sol Wurtzel, head of production at Fox, protested that this "sounds like a girl." So Sheehan decreed, "What's the matter with just plain John? John Wayne." Wurtzel approved, "It's American" [Maurice Zolotow, *John Wayne: Shooting Star*, 1974].

Naunton **Wayne:** Henry Wayne Davies (1901–1970), Welsh stage, film, radio, TV actor.

Charley **Weaver:** Clifford Arquette (1905–1974), U.S. entertainer.

Clifton **Webb:** Webb Parmallee Hollenbeck (1893–1966), U.S. film actor.

Arthur **Weegee:** Arthur H. Fellig (1899–1968), Pol.-born U.S. photographer. The story goes that Arthur Fellig was nicknamed "Ouija" for his apparently psychic ability to sniff out a good story. He then altered this to "Weegee."

Barbara **Weisberger:** Barbara Linshen (*c.*1926–   ), U.S. ballet dancer.

Raquel **Welch:** Raquel Tejada (1940–   ), U.S. film actress, of Bolivian parentage. The well-known actress's surname was that of her first husband, James Welch, her high school sweetheart. The marriage collapsed in 1961, but she retained the name.

Ronald **Welch:** Ronald Felton (1909–1982), Br. writer of historical novels for children. The writer took his pen name from his wartime regiment, The Welch Fusiliers.

Tuesday **Weld:** Susan Ker Weld (1943–   ), U.S. film actress. The actress has explained her first name in different ways at different times, but it seems likeliest that "Tuesday" is a corruption of "Susan," perhaps originally as a "baby name."

Colin **Welland:** Colin Williams (1934–   ), Eng. actor, playwright.

Junior **Wells:** Amos Blackmore (1934–   ), U.S. black blues singer.

Kitty **Wells:** Muriel Deason (1918–   ), U.S. country singer. The singer's name was chosen for her by her husband, Johnny Wright, who when courting her recalled the song popularized by the Carter Family, "I'm A-Goin' to Marry Kitty Wells."

John **Wengraf:** Johann Wenngraft (1897–1974), Austr. film actor, working in U.S.

Bessie **Wentworth:** Elizabeth Andrews (1874–1901), Eng. music hall singer.

Patricia **Wentworth:** Dora Amy Elles (1878–1961), Eng. crime novelist.

Oskar **Werner:** Oskar Josef Bschliessmayer (1922–1984), Austr. stage, film actor.

Lina **Wertmüller:** Arcangela Felice Assunta Wertmüller von Elgg (1928–   ), It. film writer, director, of Swiss descent. The writer's first name would doubtless have come via "Arcangelina," an effective diminutive of her real first name.

Adam **West:** William Anderson (1929–   ), U.S. film actor. The actor's screen name draws many of its letters from his real name – all, in fact, except the "t."

Nigel **West:** Rupert Allason (1951–   ), Br. spy writer, professionally an M.P.

Leslie **West:** Leslie Weinstein (1945–   ), U.S. rock guitarist. "West" can be easily picked out of "Weinstein."

Nathaniel **West:** Nathan Wallenstein Weinstein (1903–1940), U.S. novelist, screen writer. "West" can be easily picked out of both "Wallenstein" *and* "Weinstein," with even the last three letters of "Nathaniel" found in the former name.

[Dame] Rebecca **West:** Cicily Isabel Andrews, née Fairchild (1892–1983), Ir.-born Eng. novelist, critic. The well-known writer took her pen name from her character namesake in Ibsen's *Rosmersholm,* where "*R*ebecca *W*est" stood for "*R*ights of *W*omen," her own cause. Cicily Fairchild had also played this part in a London performance of the play. She first used the name in 1911.

Helen **Westcott:** Myrthas Helen Hickman (1929–   ), U.S. film actress.

Helen **Westley:** Henrietta Remsen Meserole Conroy (1879–1942), U.S. stage, film actress.

Mary **Westmacott:** [Dame] Agatha Christie (1890–1976), Br. detective writer (the "Queen of Crime"). The famous novelist, short story writer and playwright (*The Mousetrap*) used this name for six romantic novels, distinctive from her detective genre.

Elizabeth **Wetherell:** Susan Bogert Warner (1819–1885), U.S. sentimental novelist for children, sister of Amy Lothrop *(q.v.).*

Joan **Wetmore:** Joan Dixon, née Deery (1911–   ), Austral. stage actress. The actress must surely have considered the connotations of this name?

Michael **Whalen:** Joseph Kenneth Shovlin (1902–1974), U.S. film actor.

Anthony **Wharton:** Alister McAllister (1877–1943), Ir. author.

Grace **Wharton:** Katharine Thomson, née Byerley (1797–1862), Br. author. The Byerley family were descended from Colonel Anthony Byerley (died 1667), the father of Robert Byerley (1660–1714) who married Mary Wharton, great-niece of Philip, fourth Lord Wharton. Hence Mrs. Thomson's pen name, also adopted by her son, Philip Wharton (see below).

Philip **Wharton:** John Cockburn Thomson (1834–1860), Br. author, son of Grace Wharton (see above).

Peetie **Wheatstraw:** William Bunch (1894–1941), U.S. black blues singer, musician.

Jimmy **Wheeler:** Ernest Remnant (1910–1973), Eng. music hall comedian.

Albert **Whelan:** Albert Waxman (1875–1961), Austral. music hall entertainer.

William and Robert **Whistlecraft:** John Hookham Frere (1769–1846), Eng. diplomat, author. The writer used this double pen name for his humorous poem *The Monks and the Giants* (1817–18). This itself sprang from two cantos entitled *Prospectus and Specimen of an Intended National Work, by William and Robert Whistlecraft of Stowmarket in Suffolk, Harness and Collar Makers. Intended to comprise the most interesting particulars relating to King Arthur and his Round Table* (1817). The work inspired Byron, no less, who wrote to a friend that year: "Mr. Whistlecraft has no greater admirer than myself. I have written a story in eighty-nine stanzas in imitation of him, called 'Beppo.'"

Antonia **White:** Eirene Botting (1899–1980), Eng. author, translator. The writer adopted her mother's maiden name, as she never considered her original name "sufficiently imposing to suit her personality" (*Times Literary Supplement,* August 26–September 1, 1988).

Babington **White:** Mary Elizabeth Maxwell, née Braddon (1837–1915), Eng. novelist. The writer adopted her mother's maiden name as her pen name.

Chris **White:** Chris Costner Sizemore (1927–   ), U.S. "split personality." In 1978 a strange autobiography was published. It was entitled *Eve,* and the author was Chris Sizemore. In it, the writer describes how she developed into that weird psychiatric phenomenon, a multiple personality. It was the story of how one woman became, in effect, 12 different personalities, all existing within the body of a single human being. Naturally, the personalities assumed different names: with Chris White, a "sad, dowdy woman," Chris Costner, a "flamboyant party-goer," and Jane Doe, a "well-bred, refined Southern lady" as the three main women, whose experiences were told in the book, and the film, that swept the United States — *The Three Faces of Eve* (film 1957). The third of these names was the one she used when marrying Don Sizemore, so that the subject of it all has a real name that incorporates her maiden name (Costner) and her married name (Sizemore): Chris Costner Sizemore.

Jesse **White:** Jesse Weidenfeld (1918–   ), U.S. comic film actor.

Joseph Blanco **White:** José María Blanco y Crespo (1775–1841), Sp.-born Eng. poet, journalist, churchman. The writer fled to England as a Roman Catholic priest in 1810. There he took Anglican orders and anglicized his surname while retaining the Spanish original. He referred to this arrangement in another pseudonym, "Don Leucadio Doblado," where the first word indicates his Spanish origin, the second (via Greek) means "white," and the third (in Spanish) means "doubled."

Matthew **White:** William Prynne (1600–1669), Eng. Puritan pamphleteer.

Pearl **White:** Victoria Evans White (1889–1938), U.S. film actress (the "Queen of the Silent Serials").

Slim **Whitman:** Otis Dewey, Jr. (1924–   ), U.S. country singer, yodeller. The singer was a self-styled protégé of Montana Slim *(q.v.).*

Peter **Whitney:** Peter King Engle (1916–1972), U.S. film actor.

Violet **Whyte:** Henrietta Eliza Vaughan Stannard, née Palmer (1856–1911), Eng. novelist. The writer also had the better-known (and less whimsical) pen name of "John Strange Winter" *(q.v.).*

Mary **Wickes:** Mary Wickenhauser (1916–   ), U.S. film comedienne.

Mary **Wigman:** Marie Wiegmann (1886–1973), Ger. ballet dancer, choreographer, teacher.

Helene **Wildbrunn:** Helene Wehrenpfennig (1882–1972), Austr. opera singer.

Kim **Wilde:** Kim Smith (1960–   ), Eng. pop singer, daughter of Marty *(q.v.).*

Marty **Wilde:** Reginald Smith (1939–   ), Eng. pop singer. The singer tells how he came to adopt his new name: "I was 17 when I became Marty Wilde and I've always said that's when I really came alive. Previously I'd been Reg Smith, but Reg Smith was never me. [. . .] Larry Parnes, my manager at the time, did the name change. It was done on the toss of a coin. He tossed the coin and up came Wilde which I hated, and he tossed another coin and that decided Marty which I didn't mind but wasn't mad about. I think I wanted to be Marty Patterson after the World Heavyweight Champion, Floyd Patterson. [. . .] I still say it's important to have a name that looks fantastic in print. The Boomtown Rats – star name. Siouxsie and the Banshees – star name. Cliff Richard is a star-quality name. [. . .] Reg Smith isn't a star-quality name" [*TV Times Magazine,* November 28–December 4, 1981].

Patricia **Wilde:** Patricia White (1930–   ), Can.-born U.S. ballet dancer. The dancer changed her name (slightly) so as to be distinguished from her sister, Nora White, who was also a ballet dancer.

Gene **Wilder:** Gerald Silberman (1934–   ), U.S. film comedian.

John **Wilder:** Keith Magaurn (1936–   ), U.S. film, TV producer.

Warren **William:** Warren William Krech (1895–1948), U.S. film actor.

Andy **Williams:** Howard Andrew (1930–   ), U.S. pop singer.

Barney **Williams:** Bernard O'Flaherty (1824–1876), U.S. actor, of Ir. parentage.

Bert **Williams:** Egbert Austin (*c.*1876–1922), U.S. black stage comedian, songwriter.

Bill **Williams:** William Katt (1916–   ), U.S. film actor.

Bransby **Williams:** Bransby William Pharez (1870–1961), Br. music hall actor.

Cara **Williams:** Bernice Kamiat (1925–   ), U.S. TV, radio, film comedienne.

Daniel **Williams:** Daniel Grossman (1942–   ), U.S. ballet dancer, teacher.

Deniece **Williams:** Deniece Chandler (1951–   ), U.S. black pop singer.

Guy **Williams:** Guy Catalano (1924–   ), U.S. film, TV actor.

Joe **Williams:** Joseph Goreed (1918–   ), U.S. black blues singer.

Otis **Williams:** Otis Miles (1949–   ), U.S. black Motown singer.

Tennessee **Williams:** Thomas Lanier Williams (1911–1983), U.S. dramatist. The famous dramatist was not born in Tennessee but in Mississippi. His father, however, was directly descended from John Williams, first senator of Tennessee, from the brother Valentine of Tennessee's first governor John Sevier (whose own name was itself changed from Xavier by the Huguenots), and from Thomas Lanier Williams I, first chancellor of the Western Territory, as Tennessee was called before it became a state. So "I've just indulged myself in the Southern weakness for climbing a family tree," explained the author of *A Streetcar Named Desire* [Tennessee Williams, *Memoirs,* 1976].

Sonny Boy **Williamson:** Rice Miller (1897–1965), U.S. blues harmonica player, singer. In order to gain greater popularity, Rice Miller claimed to be *the* Sonny Boy Williamson (1914–1948), whose proper name was John Lee Williamson.

Boxcar **Willie:** *see* **Boxcar Willie.**

Meredith **Willson:** Robert Meredith Reiniger (1902–   ), U.S. songwriter, lyricist.

Willy: Henri Gauthier-Villars (1859–1931), Fr. novelist, music critic, husband of Colette *(q.v.).* The name derives from the latter half of the writer's surname.

Henry **Wilson:** Jeremiah Jones Colbath (1812–1875), U.S. statesman. The Republican senator and U.S. vice president (1869–73) was indentured as a farm laborer at the age of 10. When he was freed at the age of 21 he legally changed his name, and soon after determined to devote his life to the anti-slavery cause.

J. Arbuthnot **Wilson:** Grant Allen (1848–1899), Can.-born Eng. author. The writer began his career as a scientist, and down to 1883 all his writings were on scientific subjects. He then found that he could not earn a living on science alone, and took to fiction. It was thus as "J. Arbuthnot Wilson" that he first published some short stories, issued under the collective title of *Strange Stories* in 1884.

Marie **Wilson:** Katherine Elizabeth White (1916–1972), U.S. film actress.

Romer **Wilson:** Florence Roma Muir O'Brien, née Wilson (1891–1930), Br. novelist.

Whip **Wilson:** Charles Meyer (1915–1964), U.S. film actor.

Robb **Wilton:** Robert Wilton Smith (1881–1957), Eng. music hall comedian.

Barbara **Windsor:** Barbara Anne Deeks (1937–   ), Eng. film, TV actress, singer. The popular actress has explained that she took her name "Windsor" from that of a favorite aunt. It is also, of course, the name of the royal family. "I'm very, *very* pro–Royal," Miss Windsor has said, adding that she changed her name when "it was the time of Princess Elizabeth getting married, or was it the Coronation?" (If the former, it would have been 1947, which is surely on the young side for 10-year-old Barbara Deeks. If the latter, it would have been 1953, which seems more likely.)

Claire **Windsor:** Olga Viola Cronk (1902–1972), U.S. film actress.

Marie **Windsor:** Emily Marie Bertelson (1923–   ), U.S. film actress.

Arthur M. **Winfield:** Edward L. Stratemeyer (1863–1930), U.S. author of stories for boys. *Life* magazine carried a letter from the writer explaining how he came by his pen name: "One evening when writing, with my mother sitting near sewing, I remarked that I wanted an unusual name – that I wasn't going to use my own name on the manuscript. She thought a moment and suggested Winfield. 'For then,' she said, 'you may win in that field.' I thought that good. She then supplied the first name saying, 'You are going to be an author, so why not make it Arthur?'" Stratemeyer added the middle "M." himself, reasoning that as it stood for "thousand," it might help to sell thousands of books" [Atkinson, p. 8].

George **Winslow:** George Wenzlaff (1946–   ), U.S. child film actor.

John Strange **Winter:** Henrietta Eliza Vaughan Stannard, née Palmer (1856–1911), Eng. novelist. The author began her literary career under the name "Violet Whyte" *(q.v.)*, with her first writing appearing in the *Family Herald* in 1874. In 1881 her *Cavalry Life* was published, as a collection of regimental sketches, and two years later her *Regimental Legends*. The publisher refused to issue these books under a feminine name, so she selected "John Strange Winter" for them, this being the name of a character in the earlier work. Her readers assumed that the books were by a cavalry officer. The author then kept this name for the remainder of her writing career.

Shelley **Winters:** Shirley Shrift (1922–   ), U.S. stage, film actress. When the actress was about 15, she was in the office of the Group Theatre in New York to read for an understudy in a play by Irwin Shaw. "The secretary asked me my name. 'Shirley Schrift.' [. . .] 'Shirley Schrift isn't a very good name for an actress,' she told me. 'Let's see if we can figure out another one . . . What's your mother's maiden name?' 'Winter,' I told her. She wrote it down. 'Do you like "Shirley"?' she asked. 'God, no, there's millions of Shirleys all over Brooklyn, all named after Shirley Temple.' 'Well, wouldn't you like a name that sounds like Shirley in case someone calls you?' I thought for a moment. 'Shelley is my favorite poet, but that's a last name, isn't it?' She wrote it on the card in front of 'Winter.' She looked at it. 'Not anymore it isn't. Shelley Winter. That's your name.' She handed me the card, and I looked at it. It felt like me. Half poetic and half cold with fright. 'Okay,' I told her. 'Send it in.' Years later, in their infinite wisdom, Universal Studios added an *S* to 'Winter' and made me plural" [Shelley Winters, *Shelley: Also Known as Shirley*, 1981].

Frances **Winwar:** Francesa Vinciguerra Grebanier (1900–), Sicilian-born U.S. novelist. How's your Italian? Mrs. Grebanier translated her maiden name to provide her pen name, using it for her romantic novels, popular biographies, and books on famous poets. She came to the U.S. when only seven years old.

Estelle **Winwood:** Estelle Goodwin (1882–1984), Eng. stage, film actress, working in U.S. A neat transposition of the two halves of the actress's surname, a slight adjustment, and one new stage name emerges.

Norman **Wisdom:** Norman Wisden (1920–), Eng. stage, film, radio comedian.

Ernie **Wise:** Ernest Wiseman (1925–), Eng. TV comedian, teaming with Eric Morecambe *(q.v.)*.

Herbert **Wise:** Herbert Weisz (1924–), Austr.-born stage actor, TV director, working in U.K.

Vic **Wise:** Donald Victor Bloom (1900–), Eng. music hall comedian.

Googie **Withers:** Georgette Lizette Withers (1917–), Eng. stage, film, TV actress. Miss Withers has stuck by her story that the nickname "Googie" was given her by her Indian nurse during her childhood in Karachi, and that it derives from a Punjabi word meaning "dove," or else a Bengali word meaning "clown." But possibly after all it simply developed from her real first name? (Some sources give this as Georgina, rather than Georgette. But the likely explanation still holds true.)

[Sir] Donald **Wolfit:** Donald Woolfitt (1902–1968), Br. stage, film actor, theatre manager.

Stevie **Wonder:** Steveland Judkins (or Steveland Morris Hardaway) (1950–), U.S. black, blind Motown singer. The singer was born Steveland Judkins, later acquiring the surname Morris after his mother's remarriage. He became a singing star at the early age of 12, when he was called "Little Stevie Wonder." Two years later, he had grown to six feet tall, and although he kept the name, he dropped "Little" [Constantine Elsner, *Stevie Wonder*, 1977].

Anna May **Wong:** Wong Liu-Tsong (1907–1961), U.S. film actress, of Chin. parentage. The actress's original Chinese name meant "Frosted Yellow Willow."

Brenton **Wood:** Alfred Jesse Smith (1941–), U.S. pop singer. The singer adopted his professional name from his native Bretton Woods, New Hampshire.

Del **Wood:** Adelaide Hazelwood (1920–), U.S. jazz pianist, singer.

Natalie **Wood:** Natasha Virapaeff, then Gurdin (1938–1981), U.S. film actress, of Russ. parentage. The actress seems to have evolved her new screen name from "Gurdin."

Wee Georgie **Wood:** George Bramlett (1895–1979), Eng. music hall comedian.

Henry **Woodhouse:** Mario Terenzio Enrico Casalegno (1884–   ), It.-born U.S. aeronautics expert. The engineer was able to translate his Italian name into English just as successfully as Frances Winwar *(q.v.)* would do later.

Donald **Woods:** Ralph L. Zink (1904–   ), U.S. film actor.

Sara **Woods:** Lanna Bowen-Judd (1922–1985), Eng.-born Can. detective novelist.

Harry **Worth:** Harry Illingsworth (1918–1989), Eng. radio, TV comedian.

Nicholas **Worth:** Walter Hines Page (1855–1918), U.S. journalist, diplomat.

John **Wray:** John Malloy (1890–1940), U.S. film actor.

Belinda **Wright:** Brenda Wright (1927–   ), Eng. ballet dancer. A small verbal uplift can work wonders for a name in this way, and "Belinda" has the added beauty of French *belle* and the neatness of Italian *linda*, both highly desirable assets for a ballerina (which word is itself suggested by the name).

John **Wyckham:** John Suckling (1926–   ), Eng. theatre consultant, lighting designer.

Julian **Wylie:** Julian Samuelson (1878–1934), Br. theatre manager.

Bill **Wyman:** William Perks (1936–   ), Eng. rock musician.

Jane **Wyman:** Sarah Jane Fulks (1914–   ), U.S. film actress.

Patrick **Wymark:** Patrick Cheeseman (1926–1970), Eng. TV, film actor. The actor's son, Tristram Wymark (1961–   ), also an actor, has preserved his father's name and explains its origin: "I'm the only one to keep Dad's original name, Cheeseman. I keep it for its nostalgia. On my passport I have a nice little a.k.a. [. . .] The name Wymark was borrowed initially from my mum's grandfather" [*Sunday Times Magazine,* August 14, 1988].

[Sir] Charles **Wyndham:** Charles Culverwell (1837–1919), Eng. stage actor, theatre manager.

Esther **Wyndham:** Mary Links, née Lutgens (1908–   ), Eng. writer.

John **Wyndham:** John Wyndham Parkes Lucas Beynon Harris (1903–1969), Eng. SF, short story writer. The writer used all his many forenames as pen names at one stage or another.

Tammy **Wynette:** Virginia Wynette Byrd, née Pugh (1942–   ), U.S. country singer. The singer was asked by Billy Sherrill, her agent in Nashville, what name she wanted to use professionally. Tammy Wynette explains: "It had never occurred to me to change my name but he said, "I didn't think you'd want to use Byrd since you're getting a divorce, and Pugh doesn't fit you.' I said, 'Well, what does fit me?' He thought for a minute, then said, 'With that blond ponytail you look like a Tammy to me,' I said, 'Well, can I at least keep Wynette?' He said 'sure. How about Tammy Wynette?' I left his office saying the name over and over under my breath. It sounded strange, but it sounded right too. 'Tammy Wynette.' I said it out loud. It didn't sound like me, but it sounded like someone I wanted to be. I sensed it was more than just a new name. I felt I was also about to start a new life" [Tammy Wynette, *Stand by Your Man,* 1979].

Ed **Wynn:** Isiah Edwin Leopold (1886–1966), U.S. stage, film, radio, TV comedian.

May **Wynn:** [1] Donna Lee Hickey (1931–   ), U.S. film actress; [2] Mabel Winifred Knowles (1875–1949), Br. writer of popular fiction. The writer's pen name is closer to her true name than that of the actress, but in each case the assumed name has an obvious propitious connotation.

Dana **Wynter:** Dagmar Spencer-Marcus (1930–   ), Br.-born S.A. film actress, working in U.S.

Diana **Wynyard:** Dorothy Isobel Cox (1906–1964), Br. stage actress.

John **Wyse:** John Wise (1904–   ), Eng. stage actor.

X: Eustace Budgell (1686–1737), Br. essayist. The writer can hardly have been the first to adopt this disguise, and he will certainly not be the last!

Flying Officer **X:** Herbert Ernest Bates (1905–1974), Eng. novelist. The well-known novelist H.E. Bates used this rather obvious pseudonym for short stories about the Royal Air Force (in which he was serving as an officer in the Second World War) collected as *The Greatest People in the World* (1942) and *How Sleep the Brave* (1943).

Malcolm **X:** Malcolm Little (1925–1965), U.S. black politician, campaigner for Negro rights. The noted Black Muslim received the conventional Muslim 'X' from Elijah Muhammad *(q.v.)* in 1952. As he explained, "The Muslim's 'X' symbolized the true African family name that he could never know. For me, my 'X' replaced the white slavemaster name of 'Little' which some blue-eyed devil named Little had imposed upon my paternal forebears. [. . .] Mr. Muhammad taught that we would keep this 'X' until God Himself returned and gave us a Holy Name from His own mouth" [*The Listener*, August 8, 1974]. See also Michael X and Muhammad Ali.

Michael **X:** Michael de Freitas Abdul Malik (1933–1975), Br. black power leader. The Trinidad-born activist was the son of a black mother and a Portuguese father, originally named Michael de Freitas. On his conversion to the Muslim religion, this became Michael Abdul Malik and subsequently Michael X.

Xanrof: Léon Fourneau (–   ), Fr. composer, songwriter. The name is certainly distinctive, and was arrived at by translating French *fourneau* ("furnace") into Latin *fornax* and then reversing it. But was it really worth all the trouble?

Xavier: Joseph Xavier Boniface Saintine (1798–1865), Fr. novelist, poet, dramatist.

Ximenes: Derrick Somerset Macnutt (1902–1971), Eng. crossword compiler. Perhaps one of the most imposing and suitable of all pseudonyms, in view of the significant capital letter. It belonged to Derrick Macnutt, professionally a teacher of classics, but a renowned crossword compiler, notably the "Everyman" (to 1963) and harder "Ximenes" ones in *The Observer* (from 1939). He assumed the name in 1943 – it was that of the fifteenth-century Spanish Cardinal and Grand Inquisitor Ximenes – when he succeeded to the compilership vacated by the doyen cross-wordist Torquemada *(q.v.)*. In the 1930s Macnutt had contributed some crosswords to *The Listener* as Tesremos, his middle name reversed.

X.L.: Julian Field (1849–1925), Br. novelist, writer. An obviously meaningful duo of initials, apparently quite unrelated to the writer's real name.

Jean **Yanne:** Jean Gouyé (or Gouillé) (1933–   ), Fr. film actor, director.

Dornford **Yates:** [Major] Cecil William Mercer (1885–1960), Eng. novelist. The author of a series of books about "Berry" Pleydell and his family, popular between the wars, used the maiden names of his grandmothers to form his pen name. It first appeared for a piece he published in *Punch* in 1910. Mercer's cousin was Saki *(q.v.)*.

Yazz: Yasmin Evans (1960–   ), Jamaican-Eng. pop singer.

Yellow Bird: John Rollin Ridge (1827–1867), U.S. writer. The writer and journalist was the son of a Cherokee Indian and a white woman, and his pen name was the translation of his Cherokee name.

Sydney **Yendys:** Sydney Thompson Dobell (1824–1874), Br. poet, critic. Not everyone has a name that can be easily reversed in this way!

Mr. **Yorick:** Laurence Sterne (1713–1768), Ir. writer. The famous author of *Tristram Shandy* used this name for sermons and other writings, as well as in his *Sentimental Journey*, taking it from the "lively, witty, sensible, and heedless parson" in the former work. The character himself believes he was probably descended from Hamlet's gravedigger of this name.

Andrew **York:** Christopher Robin Nicole (1930–   ), Br. thriller writer.

Susannah **York:** Susannah Yolande Fletcher (1939–   ), Eng. film actress. There seem to be two possible accounts behind the name. Susannah York herself claims that it arose when she was learning about the Wars of the Roses as a child and started calling herself "Susannah York Fletcher," substituting "York" for her middle name (which begins with the same two letters). But the actress's sister says that she got her name simply by opening a telephone directory and sticking a pin in [ITV program, *This Is Your Life*, November 11, 1983]. The first version somehow seems the more authentic and the more likely, if only because people who open telephone directories at random usually do so somewhere in the middle, not near the end of the alphabet!

Stephen **Yorke:** Mary Linskill (1840–1891), Eng. novelist. The writer lived in Yorkshire, and many of her novels were set in that county.

Gig **Young:** Byron Ellsworth Barr (1913–1978), U.S. stage, film, TV actor. The actor took his name from the character that he played in the film *The Gay Sisters* (1942). He had earlier used the name "Bryant Fleming." The reason for changing his name in the first place was that there was another actor using the name "Byron Barr."

Loretta **Young:** Gretchen Michaela Young (1913–   ), U.S. film actress. Possibly "Loretta" developed out of "Gretchen," perhaps by way of a pet name. Or maybe the actress deliberately chose a similar name that was easier to pronounce.

Stephen **Young:** Stephen Levy (*c*.1931–   ), Can. film actor.

Marguerite **Yourcenar:** Marguerite de Crayencour (1903–1987), Fr. historical novelist, of Belg.-Fr. parentage, working (from 1947) in U.S. The writer's pen name is a near anagram of her real surname (omitting one "c").

Ysgafell: Jane Williams (1806–1885), Welsh historian, miscellaneous writer. The writer took her name from her family's seventeenth-century home at Ysgafell, near Newtown, Montgomeryshire (now Powys).

P.B. **Yuill:** Gordon Williams (1939–   ), Br. novelist + Terry Venables (1943–   ), Br. football club manager, jointly crime novelists. An anagram?

Yuriko: Yuriko Kikuchi (1920–), U.S. ballet dancer, teacher, choreographer, of Jap. parentage.

Blanche **Yurka:** Blanche Jurka (1887–1974), U.S. stage, film actress. Presumably the actress modified the spelling of her surname to ensure its proper pronunciation, i.e. not as "Jerker" (which could have undesirable associations).

Y.Y.: Robert Lynd (1879–1949), Ir. essayist. The writer used this name for his contributions to weekly magazines, first in the *Nation*, then in the *New Statesman*. Presumably the pseudonym was an elaboration of the vowel in his surname, unless it was intended to suggest "wise."

Zadkiel: Richard James Morrison (1795–1874), Eng. naval officer, astrologer. The writer used the name for his astrological predictions, published in *Zadkiel's Almanack*. The name itself is that of the angel of the planet Jupiter in Rabbinical angelology.

Zélide: Isabelle de Charrière, née Isabella van Tuyll van Serooskerken (1740–1805), Du.-born Fr. novelist, autobiographer. The writer gave herself the name in an early self-portrait, apparently basing it on her birthplace, Zuylen, near Utrecht. See also Abbé de la Tour.

Zico: Artur Antunes Coimbra (1954–), Brazilian footballer.

Anne **Ziegler:** Irene Eastwood (1910–), Eng. romantic singer, teaming with Webster Booth.

Grigory Yevseyevich **Zinoviev:** Grigory Yevseyevich Radomyslsky (1883–1931), Russ. Bolshevik leader.

Miro **Zolan:** Miroslav Zlochovsky (1926–), Cz.-Br. ballet dancer, choreographer.

Vera **Zorina:** Eva Brigitte Hartwig (1917–), Ger. ballet dancer, stage film actress, working in U.S.

Zouzou: Danielle Ciarlet (1944–), Fr. film actress. The actress adopted a childhood nickname as her screen name. The name itself is a characteristic pet doublet name (as for Fifi D'Orsay), and may have derived from the repeated second syllable of *oiseau*, "bird."

Z.Z.: Louis Zangwill (1869–), Eng. novelist, of Jewish-Russ. parentage. The writer, the younger brother of the better-known Israel Zangwill (1864–1926), adopted a name that simply capitalized (literally) on his initial, at the same time ensuring his exclusive position at the end of any alphabetical listing. By hook or by crook, he'll be last in the book (as autograph book signers like to write, entering their name on the final page).

Appendices

The three Appendices that follow are effectively a bonus to the rest of the book. But they are an interesting bonus, and in many ways an important one.

Appendix I is a complete list of the 173 pseudonyms used at one time or another by Voltaire (which is itself a pseudonym of course). They are taken from the Bibliothèque Nationale *Catalogue Général*, ccxiv (1978), i, pp. 162–166 (*Pseudonymes de Voltaire, noms sur lesquels il a écrit, formules ou qualifications sous lesquelles il s'est déguisé* [Pseudonyms of Voltaire, names under which he has written, phrases or designations under which he has disguised himself]. Many of the names were for satirical writings, hence the predominance of religious and professional names and titles for this most outspoken critic of his age. English translations are provided for some of the more obscure (and translatable) French names and titles adopted.

Appendix II is a similar list of 198 pseudonyms adopted by Daniel Defoe. The listing is doubtless not entirely complete, but it is full enough, and in quantity overvaults Voltaire's total. Many of the names were used for Defoe's pamphlets, and reflect the passion and prolificity of his political writings, as well as his vivid imagination and attention to detail. In many ways Defoe's pseudonyms can be compared to those of Voltaire, and both men were outspoken thinkers and polemicists who were active at approximately the period, viz. the first half of the eighteenth century.

Appendix III is quite different in nature, and is of real names, not pseudonyms. It therefore has its own introduction.

I. Pseudonyms Used by Voltaire
(with translations where appropriate)*

Firmin Abauzit
Abbé***
Abbé B**
Un Académicien de Berlin (An Academician from Berlin)
Un Académicien de Londres, de Boulogne, de Pétersbourg, de Berlin, etc. (An Academician from London, Boulogne, Petersburg, Berlin, etc.)
Un Académicien de Lyon (An Academician from Lyons)
Jacques Aimon
Le Docteur Akakia, médecin du pape (Doctor Akakia, physician to the Pope)
Le Rabbin Akib (Rabbi Akib)
Irénée Aléthès, professor du droit dans le canton suisse d'Uri (Irénée Aléthès, professor of law in the Swiss canton of Uri)
Ivan Aléthof, secrétaire de l'Ambassade russe (Ivan Aléthof, secretary at the Russian embassy)
Alexis, archevêque de Novogorod (Alexis, archbishop of Novogorod)
Amabed
Un Amateur de belles-lettres (A Lover of the Humanities)
Archevêque de Cantorbéry (Archbishop of Canterbury)
Abbé d'Arty
Un Auteur célèbre qui s'est retiré de France (A Famous Author Who Has Left France)
L'Auteur de "L'Homme aux quarante écus" (The Author of "The Man with Forty Crowns")
L'Auteur de la tragédie de "Sémiramis" (The Author of the Tragedy "Semiramis")
L'Auteur de la tragédie des "Guèbres" (The Author of the Tragedy "The Gabars")
L'Auteur du "Compère Mathieu" (The Author of "Comrade Mathieu")

Le Sieur Aveline
George Avenger
Un Avocat de Besançon (An Advocate from Besançon)
Un Avocat de province (A Provincial Advocate)
Un Bachelier ubiquiste (A Ubiquitous Graduate)
Feu l'abbé Bazin (The Late Father Bazin)
Beaudinet, citoyen de Neufchâtel (Beaudinet, citizen of Neufchâtel)
Une Belle Dame (A Beautiful Lady)
Ancien Avocat Belleguier (Former Advocate Belleguier)
Un Bénédictin (A Benedictine)
Un Bénédictin de Franche-Comté (A Benedictine from Franche-Comte)
Abbé Bigex
Abbé Bigore
Lord Bolingbroke
Joseph Bourdillon, professor en droit public (Joseph Bourdillon, professor of civil law)
Un Bourgeois de Genève (A Townsman of Geneva)
Le Pasteur Bourn
Abbé Caille
Caius Memmius Gemellus
Dom Calmet
Jérôme Carré
Cass *** , avocat au Conseil du Roi (Cass *** , advocate to the King's Council)
Cassen, avocat au Conseil du Roi (Cassen, advocate to the King's Council)
M. de Chambon
Chapelain du Cte de Chesterfield (Chaplain to the Count of Chesterfield)
Le Papa Nicolas Charisteski
Un Chrétien. . . (A Christian. . .)
Le Chrétien errant (The erring Christian)
Les Cinquante (The Fifty)
Un Citoyen de Genève (A Citizen of Geneva)

*Where pseudonyms resemble first-plus-last-name or contain a surname, they are entered alphabetically under that last name; otherwise arrangement is alphabetical by first main word.

M. Claire
Clocpitre
Cte de Corbera
Lord Cornsbury
Le Corps des Pasteurs du Gévaudan
(The Pastors of Gévaudan)
Robert Covelle
Cubstorf, pasteur de Helmstad (Cubstorf,
pastor of Helmstad)
Le Curé de Frêne (The Vicar of Frêne)
D., chapelain de S.E. Mgr le Cte de
K... (D., chaplain to His Eminence
Monseigneur the Count of K...)
D*** M***
Cte Da...
Damilaville
George Aronger Dardelle
M. de la Caille
De La Lindelle
M. de La Visclède
M. de L'Écluse
Chev^{r} de M...re
Chev^{r} de Molmire
Chev^{r} de Morton
M. de Morza
Démad
Feu M. de Saint-Didier (The Late M. de
Saint-Didier)
Chev^{r} de Saint-Gile
Abbé de Saint-Pierre
Des Amateurs (Some Devotees)
Desjardins
Desmahis
Gaillard d'Étallonde de Morival
Abbé de Tilladet
Cte de Tournay
Mis de Villette (Marquis de Villette)
Mis de Ximénez (Marquis de Ximenez)
John Dreamer
Anne Dubourg
Dumarsais [Du Marsay], philosophe
Dumoulin
M.le Chev^{r} Durand (Knight Durand)
Un Ecclésiastique (An Ecclesiastic)
R.P. Élie, carme chaussé (The Reverend
Father Elias, calced Carmelite)
Ératou
Évhémère
Fatema
Formey
Le P. Fouquet (Father Fouquet)

Un Frère de la Doctrine chrétienne (A
Brother of the Christian Doctrine)
Le Gardien des Capucins de Raguse
(Guardian of the Capuchins of Ragusa)
Un Gentilhomme (A Gentleman)
Gérofle
Dr Good Natur'd Wellwisher
Dr Goodheart
Charles Gouju
Gabriel Grasset et associés
Un Homme de lettres (A Man of Letters)
Hude, échevin d'Amsterdam (Hude,
deputy mayor of Amsterdam)
M. Huet (Hut)
L'Humble Evêque d'Alétopolis (The
Humble Bishop of Alétopolis)
Hume, prêtre écossais (Hume, a Scottish
priest)
L'Ignorant (The Ignorant One)
Imhof
Le Jésuite des anguilles (The Jesuit of
the eels)
Un Jeune Abbé (A Young Priest)
Major Kaiserling
M.L.***
Joseph Laffichard
Lantin, neveu de M.Lantin et de feu
l'abbé Bazin (Lantin, nephew of M.
Lantin and of the Late Father Bazin)
Le Neveu de l'abbé Bazin (The Nephew
of Father Bazin)
R.P. L'Escarbotier
Mairet
M. Mamaki
Abbé Mauduit
M. de Mauléon
Maxime de Madaure
Un Membre du Conseil de Zurich (A
Member of the Zurich Council)
Un Membre des nouveaux conseils (A
Member of the New Council)
Un Membre d'un corps (A Member of
the Body)
Le Curé Meslier
Prêtre Montmolin
Le Muphti
Naigeon
Needham
Docteur Obern
Cte Physicien de Saint-Flour
Plusieurs Aumôniers (Several Chaplains)

Jean Plokof
R.P. Polycarpe, prieur des Bernardins de Chésery (The Reverend Father Polycarp, prior of the Bernardines of Chésery)
Un Professeur de droit public (A Professor of Civil Law)
Un Proposant (A Divinity Student)
Un Quaker (A Quaker)
Le P. Quesnel
Le Dr Ralph
Genest Ramponeau
Rapterre
Don Apuleius Risorius
Josias Rossette
La Roupilière
Sadi
Saint-Hiacinte
Scarmentado
Le Secrétaire de M. de Voltaire (The Secretary to M. de Voltaire)
Le Secrétaire du Prince Dolgorouki (The Secretary to Prince Dolgorouki)
Mr. Sherloc

Une Société de bacheliers en théologie (A Group of Theology Graduates)Soranus, médecin de Trajan (Soranus, physician to Trajan)
Abbé Tamponet
Sieur Tamponet, docteur en Sorbonne (Mr. Tamponet, doctor at the Sorbonne)
Théro
Thomson
Tompson (Thomson)
Trois Avocats d'un Parlement (Three advocates from one Parliament)
Un Turc (A Turk)
Antoine Vadé
Catherine Vadé
Guillaume Vadé
Verzenot
Le Vieillard du Mont-Caucase (The Old Man of Mount Caucasus)
Un Vieux Capitaine de Cavalerie (an Old Cavalry Captain)
Dr Good Natur'd Wellwisher
Youssouf
Dominico Zapata

II. Pseudonyms Used by Daniel Foe, Better Known as Daniel Defoe

A.A.A.
A.B.
A Citizen Who Lives the Whole Time in London
A.G.
A.M.G.
A.Z.
Abed
Abigail
All-Hide
Aminadab
Ancient
Andronicus
Anglipolski of Lithuania
Anne
Antiaethiops
Anti-Bubble
Anti-Bubbler
Anticationist

Hen. Antifogger, Jr.
Anti–Italik
Anti–Jobber
Anti–King-Killer
Anti–Pope
Antiplot
Anthony Antiplot
Antisycoph
The Author of the "Trueborn Englishman"
Bankrupt
Tom Bankrupt
Barinda
Tom Beadle
Tom A. Bedlam
Obadiah Blue Hat
Betty Blueskin
Nicholas Boggle
William Bond

Anthony Broadheart
Bubble
C.M.
Callipedia
Christopher Carefull
Cataline
Caution
Henry Caution, Jr.
Sir Timothy Caution
Celibacy
Sir Malcontent Chagrin
Chesapeake
Combustion
Conscientia
A Converted Thief
The Corporal
Coventry
Credulous
D--
D.D.F.
D.F., Gent.
Daniel De Foe
Daniel Defoe
Democritus
Diogenes
Jeremiah Dry-Boots
E.S.
Eleanor
Elevator
Mr. Eminent
An English Gentleman
An Englishman at the Court of Hanover
Enigma
The Enquirer
Epidemicus
T. Experience
Eye Witness
Dan D.F-e
Count Kidney Face
Frank Faithfull
A Familiar Spirit
Henry Fancy, Jr.
The Farmer
The Father of Modern Prose Fiction
Penelope Firebrand
Florentina
A Freeholder
Harry Freeman
Furioso
Furious
G.

G.B.
G.M.
G.T.
G.Y.
A Gentleman
Grateful
Gunpowder
Gyaris
H.
H.R.
Thomas Horncastle
Autho' Hubble Bubble
Hubble-Bubble
Humanity
Hushai
Anthony Impartiality
Jack Indifferent
The Inoculator
Insolvent
P. Ivy
John-John
Journal
L.L.L.
A Layman
Leicestershire
Libertas
Liberty
Leonard Love-Wit
Theophilus Lovewit
Lionel Lye-Alone
Livery Man
M.G.
Tom Manywife
Lady Marjory
Miranda Meanwell
Meeting House
A Member
A Member of the Honourable House of
   Commons
Meteor
A Ministering Friend of the People
   Called Quakers
Miser
Misericordia
Modern
Moll
Andrew Moreton, Merchant
Myra
N.B.
N-- Upon Trent
Nelly

The New Convert
New Whig
Andrew Newport
Nicety
Oliver Oldway
One, Two, Three, Four
Orthodox
Patience
Abel Peaceable
Phil-Arguros
Mrs. Philo-Britannia
Philo-Royalist
Philygeia
Jonathan Problematick
Protestant Neutrality
Prudential
Quarantine
Anthony Quiet
Quietness
Quinquampoix
Arine Donna Quixota
R.R.
R.S.
Rebel
L.M. Regibus
Anthony Tom Richard
S.
S.B.
T. Sadler
Same Friend Who Wrote to Thomas
    Bradbury, etc.
Fello De Se

Sempronicus
Sincerity
Jeffrey Sing-Song
Spanish
A Sufferer
The Sunny Gentleman
T.B.
T.E.
T.L.
Talonis
T. Taylor
Tea-Table
Termagant
Thelo-Philo
Thunder-Bolt
Sir Fopling Tittle-Tattle
Tranquillity
Timothy Trifle
Boatswain Trinkolo
True Love
The Trustee
Tom Turbulent
Urgentissimus
Vale
W.L.
Wallnutshire
Solomon Waryman
Weeping Winifred
White Witch
Woman Witch'd
A Young Cornish Gentleman

III. Real Names

*I never tell people my real name. It gives me more privacy [Patrick Malahide
(1945–   ), Eng. TV actor, in TV Times, June 4–10, 1988].*

This book has concentrated on those people who have changed their name or
adopted a pseudonym. Yet there are several well-known personalities and individuals who have not done so, and who in some cases have resolutely stuck by
their real name, however unwieldy, unsuitable or incongruous it may have been for
their professional career.

In some instances the persons concerned have taken pains to put the facts
about their real name on the record—*for* the record. Here are some examples.

•When Sydne Rome, the U.S. film actress, once inquired at an airport whether
she could stop off in Nice, the clerk, after asking her name, looked at her carefully
and said, "Madam, I think you would do better to transfer to Qantas" (*Telegraph
Sunday Magazine,* June 3, 1979).

•The United States film actor Bradford Dillman commented, "Bradford Dillman sounded like a distinguished, phoney, theatrical name, so I kept it" (Clarke, p. 250).

•When a Hollywood executive wanted to change the name of Jack Lemmon to "Lennon," the United States film comedian said, "I told him it had taken me most of my life to get used to the traumatic effects of being called Jack U. Lemmon, and that I was used to it now and I wasn't going to change it" (Clarke, p. 250).

•Louella Parsons, the United States film columnist, said of the movie actress Rita Gam, "I *do* wish she would change her name" (Clarke, p. 249).

•The South African actress Janet Suzman adamantly refused to accede to suggestions that she change her surname when she first went on the stage because it was too "foreign." Instead, she sent a telegram to the theatre director: "Imperative remain Suzman" (*TV Times*, April 9, 1976).

•Bridget Fonda, the actress daughter of Peter Fonda and the granddaughter of the famous Henry Fonda, has been frequently tempted to change her name since her childhood, when her father divorced her mother (and attempted to persuade his wife to drop the Fonda name similarly). Bridget acknowledges that having this particular name has its problems: "I did consider changing my name but it does no good to run away and I am proud to be part of the Fonda family," she says (*The Times*, August 1, 1988).

•As a child, the British theatre and TV actress Frances Cuka told her ballerina aunt that she wanted to go on stage and change her name to "Gloria La Raine." "What's wrong with Cuka?" said her aunt sternly. "I was Cuka; your Aunt Eileen acted under the name Cuka. No one can spell it, no one can pronounce it properly—but no one will ever forget it." Says Frances (who actually pronounces her name "Chewka"), "I was too scared to change my name, and I am pleased now I was frightened into keeping it" (*TV Times*, February 14–20, 1987).

•"Of course it's my real name," retorts United States TV star Cloris Leachman, when interviewers raised doubts about it. "Would anyone in his right mind change it *to* Cloris Leachman?" (Andersen, p. 247).

•When Helena Michell, daughter of famous Australian TV actor Keith Michell, first followed in her father's professional footsteps, and was asked how she aimed to preserve her distinct identity, she replied: "What do people want me to do? Change my name? I think my Dad would be upset if I did, as if I were ashamed of it" (*TV Times*, October 22–28, 1988).

•The playwright Timberlake Wertenbaker, who grew up in the French Basque country, finds that critics react with suspicion to her work, since they see her name as an anagram. Yet it is her real name, with her first name a former family surname (*Sunday Times*, April 6, 1986.

For similar reasons, and simply because we expect the names of movie actors and actresses, among others, to be pseudonyms, we tend to imagine non-existent linguistic contrivances and manipulations when we see a real name. Why, Candice Bergen's name clearly contains "iceberg," and must denote her cool, calm beauty and screen presence, while Clara Bow had bow-shaped lips, as the old publicity photos show.

How fitting that Primo Carnera, the heavyweight boxer and wrestler, had such a "meaty" name, suggesting prime beef, or even carnage, while as a kind of converse, Celeste Holm has a name that conjures up a kind of "heavenly home." Thora Hird, the English TV actress, must surely have a name that is an anagram (yes, it must be "Horrid Hat," how droll!), and maybe Anita Loos has a name of this type, too (maybe she was born Tina Olosa or Ilsa Anoto?). Danielle Darrieux, Mireille Mathieu, and Simone Simon have such alliteratively attractive French names that they cannot be their true names, and we all know that William Tubbs was a portly actor.

And so on. Our doubt is also prompted by the knowledge that names such as "Grey" and "Martin" are frequently assumed names. Beryl Grey was originally Beryl Groom, for example, and Joel Grey was Noel Katz. But Zane Grey always used his real name for the westerns that he wrote. Similarly Dean Martin was originally Dino Crocetti, Ross Martin was Martin Rosenblatt, and Tony Martin was Alvin Morris. Yet Mary Martin and Millicent Martin have always performed under their true names. Such duplication of names can cause confusion, so that we tend to think that Audrey Hepburn and Katherine Hepburn are related, or that there is some family relationship between Gloria Holden, Fay Holden and William Holden. But Audrey Hepburn was originally Edda van Heemstra Hepburn-Ruston, while Fay Holden began life as Fay Hammerton and William Holden was born William Beedle.

So there is the apparent artificiality of the name on the one hand or the seeming family kinship on the other, either of which can raise our suspicions.

The list that follows is thus a selection of 250 *real* names that may be thought to be assumed names by some, for whatever reason. The surnames are always genuine, even if in a few instances they are married names (as for Helen Twelvetrees, whose maiden name was Jurgens but whose first husband was one Clark Twelvetrees). The first names may have originated as a nickname (Spike Milligan is properly Terence Milligan, and Rudy Vallee was born Hubert Vallee), or have developed as a pet name (Telly Savalas has the full first name of Aristotle, and Ring Lardner was originally Ringgold Wilmer Lardner), but there was no complete name change to place the person in the main section of this book, rather than in the listing below.

As well as sorting out the sheep from the goats, however (or, more fittingly, the real sheep from the wolves in sheep's clothing), the listing has a further aim. This is to lay one or two popular misconceptions to rest.

It is commonly supposed, for instance, that the "real" name of Adolf Hitler was actually Adolf Schicklgruber, and during the Second World War much satirical play was made of this fact. But the facts of the matter are that the dictator's father, Alois Hitler (born 1837), was an illegitimate child, and for a time bore his mother's surname, which was Schicklgruber. By 1876, however, he had established his claim to the name Hitler, which naturally was passed on to his son. Hitler himself, too, always used this name, and never referred to himself by the longer name.

Again, it was frequently said of the English entertainer Joyce Grenfell that she was "really" Joyce Phipps. But this was simply her maiden name, and she chose to perform professionally under her married name, that of her husband, Reginald Grenfell. This may have been the exception rather than the rule, but there is no denying the authenticity of the name, and it was not one she adopted specially for the stage or screen. (Similar unmaskings are mentioned in the main section of this book.)

For the more improbable-seeming names in the listing, pedigrees or "family trees" can confirm the genuineness. Tyrone Power, for example, acted under his real name, which was exactly the same as that of his father, Tyrone Edmund Power (1869–1931), who in turn acquired his name from his own father, the Irish actor Tyrone Power (1795–1841). And although George Oliver Onions changed his name legally to George Oliver in 1918, he was still Oliver Onions when he married his fellow novelist Berta Ruck as an art student. (He changed his name for the sake of their two sons, although Onions is still a common surname in his native Yorkshire.)

Sometimes an unlikely looking but genuine name may inadvertently be adopted for a fictional character, or coincide with one. This actually happened in the case of Berta Ruck, whose unusual name appeared as that of a character in Virginia Woolf's novel *Jacob's Room* (1922). This caused a dispute between the two women, although subsequently they were reconciled. The matching of real names with fictional names is essentially a topic outside the scope of the present book, however, although this one incidence of it can be mentioned here.

So all credit is due to Ursula Andress, Acker Bilk, Max Factor, Eydie Gorme, John Twist, Fay Wray, et al., who stuck to their guns and stayed by their original names.

Lola Albright (1925–   ), U.S. film actress.
Bibi Andersson (1935–   ), Swe. film actress.
Ursula Andress (1936–   ), Swiss-born U.S. film actress.
Paul Anka (1941–   ), U.S. pop singer.
Alan Arkin (1934–   ), U.S. film actor.
Gene Autry (1907–   ), U.S. film actor.
Burt Bacharach (1929–   ), U.S. popular songwriter.
Joan Baez (1941–   ), U.S. popular singer, of Mexican-Ir. parentage.
Nigel Balchin (1908–1970), Eng. author.
"Long" John Baldry (1941–   ), Eng. blues singer.
Tallulah Bankhead (1902–1968), U.S. stage, film actress.
Shirley Bassey (1937–   ), Br.-born cabaret singer.
Harry Belafonte (1927–   ), U.S. black popular singer, film actor.
Saul Bellow (1915–   ), Can.-born U.S. writer.
Jean-Paul Belmondo (1933–   ), Fr. film actor.
Candice Bergen (1946–   ), U.S. film actress, of Swe.-U.S. parentage.
Ingmar Bergman (1918–   ) Swe. film director (no relation to next).
Ingrid Bergman (1915–1982), Swe. film actress, of Swe.-Ger. parentage.
Theodore Bikel (1924–   ), Austr. film actor, guitarist, singer.
Acker Bilk (1929–   ), Br. jazz clarinettist.
Joan Blondell (1909–1979), U.S. film comedienne.
Humphrey Bogart (1899–1957), U.S. film actor.

Ward Bond (1903–1960), U.S. film, TV actor.
Timothy Bottoms (1949–   ), U.S. film actor.
Clara Bow (1905–1965), U.S. film actress ("the 'it' girl").
Marlon Brando (1924–   ), U.S. film actor.
Eleanor Bron (1934–   ), Br. TV actress.
Pearl Buck (1892–1973), U.S. novelist.
James Caan (1939–   ), U.S. film actor.
Sid Caesar (1922–   ), U.S. film, TV comedian.
James Cagney (1899–1986), U.S. film actor.
Truman Capote (1924–1984), U.S. novelist.
Hoagy Carmichael (1899–1981), U.S. songwriter, lyricist.
Primo Carnera (1906–1967), It. heavyweight boxer, wrestler.
Leslie Caron (1931–   ), Fr. stage, film actress, dancer, working in U.K., U.S.
Enrico Caruso (1873–1921), It. opera singer.
Johnny Cash (1932–   ), U.S. country singer.
David Cassidy (1950–   ), U.S. pop singer.
Harry Champion (1866–1942), Eng. music hall comedian.
Raymond Chandler (1888–1959), U.S. crime novelist.
Lon Chaney, Sr. (1883–1930), U.S. film actor.
Carol Channing (1921–   ), U.S. cabaret comedienne.
Charlie Chaplin (1889–1977), Eng. film comedian.
Maurice Chevalier (1888–1972), Fr. popular singer, film actor.
Julie Christie (1941–   ), Br. film actress.
Petula Clark (1932–   ), Eng. film actress.
Rosemary Clooney (1928–   ), U.S. cabaret singer.
Joe Cocker (1944–   ), Eng. pop singer.
Joan Collins (1933–   ), Eng. film actress, working in U.S.
Alex Comfort (1920–   ), Br. novelist, short story writer, medical biologist.
Ray Conniff (1916–   ), U.S. popular singer.
Billy Connolly (1942–   ), Sc. TV comedian (the "Big Yin").
Jackie Coogan (1914–1984), U.S. film actor, former child star.
Jackie Cooper (1921–   ), U.S. film actor.
Noël Coward (1899–1973), Eng. stage, film actor, writer, composer.
Wally Cox (1924–1976), U.S. comic film actor.
Wendy Craig (1934–   ), Eng. stage, TV actress.
Frances Cuka (1935–   ), Br. stage, TV actress, working in U.K., U.S.
Sinead Cusack (1949–   ), Ir. film actress.
Peter Cushing (1913–   ), U.S. stage, film, TV actor.
Dan Dailey (1914–1978), U.S. film actor, dancer.
Danielle Darrieux (1917–   ), Fr. film actress.
Olivia de Havilland (1916–   ), Eng.-born U.S. film actress, sister of Joan Fontaine
(q.v.).
Judi Dench (1934–   ), Eng. stage, film actress.
Neil Diamond (1945–   ), U.S. pop singer.
Bradford Dillman (1930–   ), U.S. film actor.
Ken Dodd (1927–   ), Eng. vaudeville, TV comedian.
Val Doonican (1927–   ), Ir. popular singer.
Faye Dunaway (1941–   ), U.S. film actress.
Jimmy Durante (1893–1980), U.S. film comedian.

Clint Eastwood (1930–   ), U.S. film actor.
Nelson Eddy (1901–1967), U.S. film actor, popular singer.
Samantha Eggar (1939–   ), Eng. film actress.
Anita Ekberg (1931–   ), Swe. film actress.
Hope Emerson (1897–1960), U.S. film actress.
Dick Emery (1918–1983), Eng. TV comedian.
Max Factor (1876–1937), Pol. cosmetician, working in U.S.
Marianne Faithfull (1947–   ), Eng. film actress, singer.
Mia Farrow (1945–   ), U.S. film actress.
Marty Feldman (1933–1982), Eng. TV comedian.
Mel Ferrer (1917–   ), U.S. film actor.
Roberta Flack (1937–   ), U.S. pop singer.
Errol Flynn (1909–1959), Tasmanian-born U.S. film actor.
Jane Fonda (1937–   ), U.S. film actress.
Lynn Fontanne (1887–1983), Eng. stage actress, working in U.S.
Aretha Franklin (1942–   ), U.S. soul singer.
Allen Funt (1914–   ), U.S. TV actor.
Will Fyffe (1884–1947), Sc. film comedian, music hall singer.
Clark Gable (1901–1960), U.S. film actor.
Rita Gam (1928–   ), U.S. stage, film actress.
Art Garfunkel (1937–   ), U.S. pop singer, formerly teaming with Paul Simon.
Greer Garson (1908–   ), Eng.-Ir. film actress, working in U.S.
Leo Genn (1905–1978), Eng. film actor.
Dizzy Gillespie (1917–   ), U.S. jazz trumpeter, composer.
Hermione Gingold (1897–1987), Eng. revue, film comedienne.
Rumer Godden (1907–   ), Br. novelist, short story writer.
Eydie Gorme (1932–   ), U.S. stage, TV singer.
Betty Grable (1916–1973), U.S. film actress.
Joyce Grenfell (1910–1979), Eng. film comedienne, solo revue artist.
Zane Grey (1875–1939), U.S. writer of westerns.
Alec Guinness (1914–   ), Eng. stage, film actor.
Edmund Gwenn (1875–1959), Eng. film actor.
Rider Haggard (1856–1925), Eng. writer of romantic adventure fiction.
Susan Hampshire (1938–   ), Eng. film actress.
Jack Hawkins (1910–1973), Eng. film actor.
Goldie Hawn (1945–   ), U.S. film actress.
Will Hay (1888–1949), Eng. film comedian.
Sessue Hayakawa (1889–1973), Japanese film actor, working in U.S.
George "Gabby" Hayes (1885–1969), U.S. comic film actor.
Katharine Hepburn (1907–   ), U.S. film actress.
Thora Hird (1914–   ), Eng. film, TV comedienne.
Adolf Hitler (1889–1945), Ger. Nazi dictator.
Dustin Hoffman (1937–   ), U.S. film actor.
Gloria Holden (1908–   ), Br. film actress, working in U.S.
Celeste Holm (1919–   ), U.S. stage, film actress.
Lena Horne (1917–   ), U.S. black popular singer, film actress.
Trevor Howard (1916–1988), Br. film actor.
Roy Hudd (1936–   ), Eng. TV comedian.
Rod Hull (1935–   ), Eng. TV comedian.

Gayle Hunnicutt (1942–   ), U.S. film actress.
John Hurt (1940–   ), Eng. stage, film, TV actor.
Olivia Hussey (1951–   ), Argentine-born Br. film actress.
Hammond Innes (1913–   ), Eng. writer of adventure, mystery stories.
Mick Jagger (1939–   ), Eng. pop musician.
Peter Jeffrey (1929–   ), Eng. TV actor.
Glynis Johns (1923–   ), Br. film actress.
Ben Johnson (1919–   ), U.S. film actor.
Janis Joplin (1943–1970), U.S. blues singer.
Yootha Joyce (1927–1980), Eng. TV comedienne.
Rosco Karns (1893–1970), U.S. film actor.
Gene Kelly (1912–   ), U.S. film actor, dancer.
Grace Kelly (1928–1982), U.S. film actress, later Princess Grace of Monaco.
Eartha Kitt (1928–   ), U.S. Creole cabaret singer.
Alan Ladd (1913–1964), U.S. film actor.
Dinsdale Landen (1932–   ), Eng. TV actor.
Ring Lardner (1885–1933), U.S. short story writer, journalist.
Cloris Leachman (1925–   ), U.S. TV actress.
Jack Lemmon (1925–   ), U.S. comic film actor.
Jennie Linden (1939–   ), Eng. film actress.
Gina Lollobrigida (1927–   ), It. film actress.
Anita Loos (1893–1981), U.S. humorist, screenwriter.
Joanna Lumley (1946–   ), Eng. TV actress.
Ida Lupino (1914–   ), Eng. film actress, daughter of Stanley Lupino (below).
Stanley Lupino (1893–1942), Eng. stage, film comedian.
Carol Lynley (1942–   ), U.S. film actress.
Ben Lyon (1901–1979), U.S. film actor, husband of Bebe Daniels *(q.v.)* with whom
teamed.
Mercedes McCambridge (1918–   ), U.S. film actress.
Ali MacGraw (1938–   ), U.S. film actress.
Steve McQueen (1930–1980), U.S. film actor.
Melissa Manchester (1951–   ), U.S. pop singer.
Barbara Mandrell (1948–   ), U.S. pop singer.
Mary Martin (1923–   ), U.S. musical comedienne.
Millicent Martin (1934–   ), Eng. stage, TV singer.
Lee Marvin (1924–1987), U.S. film actor.
James Mason (1909–1984), Eng. film actor.
Raymond Massey (1896–1983), Can. stage, film actor, working in U.K.
Mireille Mathieu (1946–   ), Fr. film actress.
Melina Mercouri (1923–   ), Gk. film actress.
Bette Midler (1945–   ), U.S. entertainer.
Spike Milligan (1918–   ), Ir. stage, radio, TV comedian.
Robert Mitchum (1917–   ), U.S. film actor.
Tom Mix (1880–1940), U.S. film actor.
Patrick Mower (1940–   ), Eng. TV actor.
Carry Nation (1846–1911), U.S. temperance reformer.
Paul Newman (1925–   ), U.S. film actor.
Robert Newton (1905–1956), Eng. film actor.
Derek Nimmo (1931–   ), Eng. film, TV actor.

Anaïs Nin (1903–1977), U.S. novelist.
Des O'Connor (1932–   ), Eng. pop. singer.
Jimmy O'Dea (1899–1965), Ir. film comedian.
Oliver Onions (1872–1961), Eng. novelist, married Berta Ruck (below).
Milo O'Shea (1926–   ), Ir. film actor.
Dolly Parton (1946–   ), U.S. country singer.
Gregory Peck (1916–   ), U.S. film actor.
Sam Peckinpah (1926–1984), U.S. film director.
Susan Penhaligon (1950–   ), Eng. TV actress.
Walter Pidgeon (1897–1984), Can. film actor, working in U.S.
Lili Pons (1904–1976), Fr. opera singer.
Oleg Popov (1930–   ), Russ. circus clown.
Cole Porter (1893–1964), U.S. songwriter, composer.
Tyrone Power (1913–1958), U.S. film actor.
Tom Powers (1890–1955), U.S. film actor.
Elvis Presley (1935–1978), U.S. pop singer.
Victoria Principal (1950–   ), U.S. TV actress.
Suzi Quatro (1950–   ), U.S. pop musician, working in U.K. (see Suzi Soul).
Anthony Quayle (1913–   ), Eng. stage, film actor, director.
Diana Quick (1946–   ), Br. film actress.
Anthony Quinn (1915–   ), Mexican-born U.S. film actor.
Gregory Ratoff (1897–1960), Russ.-born film actor, working in U.S., U.K.
Lee Remick (1935–   ), U.S. film actress.
Burt Reynolds (1936–   ), U.S. film actor.
Diana Rigg (1938–   ), Eng. film, TV. actress.
Sydne Rome (1946–   ), U.S. film actress.
Cesar Romero (1907–   ), U.S. film actor.
Berta Ruck (1878–1978), Eng. novelist, married Oliver Onions (above).
Charles Ruggles (1886–1970), U.S. film comedian.
Damon Runyon (1884–1946), U.S. short story writer, journalist.
Gail Russell (1924–1961), U.S. film actress.
Robert Ryan (1909–1973), U.S. film actor.
Telly Savalas (1924–   ), Gk.-U.S. film, TV actor.
Maria Schneider (1952–   ), Ger. film actress.
Jean Seberg (1938–1979), U.S. film actress.
Neil Sedaka (1939–   ), U.S. popular songwriter, performer.
Pete Seeger (1919–   ), U.S. popular musician.
Blossom Seeley (1892–1974), U.S. nightclub entertainer.
William Shatner (1931–   ), Can. film, TV actor.
Dinah Sheridan (1920–   ), Br. film actress.
Brooke Shields (1965–   ), U.S. juvenile film actress.
Victor Silvester (1901–1978), Br. dance band leader.
Alastair Sim (1900–1976), Sc. film actor.
Jean Simmons (1929–   ), Eng. film actress, working in U.S.
Simone Simon (1910–   ), Fr. film actress.
Frank Sinatra (1915–   ), U.S. film actor, singer.
Donald Sinden (1923–   ), Eng. film actor.
Cornelia Otis Skinner (1901–1979), U.S. stage, film actress.
Koo Stark (1956–   ), Eng. film actress, photographer.

Rod Stewart (1945–   ), Br. pop singer.
Janet Street-Porter (1947–   ), Eng. TV hostess.
Elaine Stritch (1922–   ), U.S. stage, film comedienne.
Booth Tarkington (1869–1946), U.S. novelist.
Shirley Temple (1928–   ), U.S. child film actress.
John Thaw (1942–   ), Eng. TV actor.
Gene Tierney (1920–   ), U.S. film actress.
Ann Todd (1909–   ), Br. film actress (not to be confused with Ann Todd *(q.v.)*).
Richard Todd (1919–   ), Br. film actor.
Franchot Tone (1905–1968), U.S. stage, film actor.
Mel Torme (1923–   ), U.S. ballad singer.
Spencer Tracy (1900–1967), U.S. film actor.
William Tubbs (1909–1953), U.S. film actor.
Forrest Tucker (1919–1986), U.S. film actor.
Ben Turpin (1874–1940), U.S. film comedian.
Helen Twelvetrees (1908–1958), U.S. film actress.
John Twist (1895–1976), U.S. screenwriter.
Edward Underdown (1908–   ), Br. stage, film actor.
Rudy Vallee (1901–1986), U.S. film comedian, singer.
Robert Vaughn (1932–   ), U.S. film actor.
Gore Vidal (1925–   ), U.S. writer.
King Vidor (1894–1982), U.S. film director.
Sam Wanamaker (1919–   ), U.S. film director, actor.
Ethel Waters (1900–1977), U.S. black film actress, singer.
Orson Welles (1915–1985), U.S. film actor, producer, director.
Timberlake Wertenbaker (*c.*1945–), Fr.-born Br. (female) playwright.
Mae West (1892–1980), U.S. film actress.
Cornel Wilde (1915–   ), U.S. film actor.
Michael Wilding (1912–1979), Eng. film actor.
Esther Williams (1923–   ), U.S. film actress.
Frank Windsor (1926–   ), Eng. TV actor.
Terry Wogan (1928–   ), Ir. TV host.
Fay Wray (1907–   ), U.S. film actress.
Frank Zappa (1940–   ), U.S. rock musician.

Bibliography

Clearly, any bibliography on the vast subject of pseudonyms and name changes is bound to be selective. The bibliography that follows concentrates on those works that were found to be the most helpful in establishing a pseudonymous person's real name, or in recording permanent name changes, and if anything it covers the popular rather than the esoteric, if only as such names are the most readily documented.

At the same time, the reader of this book should know that many more books than those actually listed here were consulted during its compilation. This particularly applies to books shown as published in a numbered edition ("2nd ed.," "4th ed." and so on), where the earlier editions will also have been consulted and exploited.

In the main, the books are English-language publications. A few, however, are in a foreign language, and in such cases the title is translated into English for ease of reference.

Agee, Patrick. *Where Are They Now?* London, Everest, 1977.

Andersen, Christopher P. *The Book of People.* New York: Perigee, 1981.

Ash, Brian. *Who's Who in Science Fiction.* London: Sphere, rev. ed., 1977.

Ashley, Leonard R.N. "Flicks, Flacks, and Flux: Tides of Taste in the Onomasticon of the Moving Picture Industry," *Names (Journal of the American Name Society)* 23:4 (December 1975).

Ashley, Mike. *Who's Who in Horror and Fantasy Fiction.* London: Elm Tree, 1977.

Atkinson, Frank. *Dictionary of Literary Pseudonyms.* London: Clive Bingley, 4th enl. ed., 1987.

Attwater, Donald. *The Penguin Dictionary of Saints.* Harmondsworth: Penguin, 1965.

Baker, Glenn A. *The Name Game: Their Real Names Revealed.* London: GRR/Pavilion, 1986.

Bateman, Michael. *Funny Way to Earn a Living: A Book of Cartoons and Cartoonists.* London: Leslie Frewin, 1966.

Benét, William Rose. *The Reader's Encyclopedia.* London: A. & C. Black, 3rd ed., 1988.

Browning, D.C., comp. *Everyman's Dictionary of Literary Biography, English and American.* London: Dent, 1969.

Busby, Roy. *The British Music Hall: An Illustrated Who's Who from 1850 to the Present Day.* London: Paul Elek, 1976.

Carpenter, Humphrey, and Mari Pritchard. *The Oxford Companion to Children's Literature.* Oxford: Oxford University Press, 1984.

Case, Brian, and Stan Britt. *The Illustrated Encyclopaedia of Jazz.* London: Salamander, 1978.

Chaneles, S., and A. Wolsky. *The Movie Makers.* London: Octopus, 1974.

Clarke, Donald, ed. *The Penguin Encyclopedia of Popular Music.* London: Viking Penguin, 1989.

Clarke, J.F. *Pseudonyms.* London: Elm Tree, 1977.

Clifford, Mike, consult. *The Illustrated Rock Handbook.* London: Salamander, 1983.

Cooper, John, and B.A. Pike. *Detective Fiction: The Collector's Guide.* Taunton: Barn Owl Books, 1988.

Coston, Henri. *Dictionnaire des Pseudonymes [Dictionary of Pseudonyms].* Paris: Lectures Françaises, 1965 (vol. I), 1969 (vol. II).

Crosland, Margaret. *Ballet Carnival: A Companion to Ballet.* London: Arco, 1977.

Crowther, Jonathan, ed. *The AZED Book of Crosswords.* London: Pan, 1977.

Dawson, Lawrence H. *Nicknames and Pseudonyms: Including Sobriquets of Persons in History, Literature, and the Arts Generally, Titles Given to Monarchs, and the Nicknames of the British Regiments and the States of North America.* London: Routledge, 1908.

Dmitriev, V.G. *Pridumannye Imena (Rasskazy o Psevdonimakh) [Invented Names (Stories About Pseudonyms)].* Moscow: Sovremennik, 1986.

————. *Skryvshie Svoë Imya (iz Istorii Anonimov i Psevdonimov) [The Name Concealers (A History of Anonyms and Pseudonyms)].* Moscow: Nauka, 2nd enl. ed., 1977.

Drabble, Margaret, ed. *The Oxford Companion to English Literature.* Oxford: Oxford University Press, 5th ed., 1985.

Dunkling, Leslie Alan. *The Guinness Book of Names.* Enfield: Guinness Publishing, rev. & updated ed., 1989.

————. *Our Secret Names.* London: Sidgwick & Jackson, 1981.

Elson, Howard, and John Brunton. *Whatever Happened To . . . ? The Great Rock and Pop Nostalgia Book.* London: Proteus, 1981.

Encyclopaedia Britannica, 5th ed., 1976.

Farmer, David Hugh. *The Oxford Dictionary of Saints.* Oxford: Clarendon, 1978.

Fisher, John. *Funny Way to Be a Hero.* St. Albans: Paladin, 1976.

Gammond, Peter, and Peter Clayton. *A Guide to Popular Music.* London: Phoenix, 1960.

Greif, Martin. *The Gay Book of Days.* London: W.H. Allen, 1985.

Halliwell, Leslie. *Halliwell's Filmgoer's Companion.* London: Paladin, 9th ed., 1988.

————, with Philip Purser. *Halliwell's Television Companion.* London: Grafton, 3rd ed., 1986.

Hamst, Olphar. *Handbook of Fictitious Names (Being a Guide to Authors, Chiefly in the Lighter Literature of the XIXth Century, Who Have Written Under Assumed Names; and to Literary Forgers, Imposters, Plagiarists, and Imitators).* London: John Russell Smith, 1868.

Hanks, Patrick, and Flavia Hodges. *A Dictionary of Surnames.* Oxford: Oxford University Press, 1988.

Hardy, Phil, and Dave Laing, eds., with additional material by Stephen Barnard and Don Perretta. *Encyclopaedia of Rock.* London: Macdonald Orbis, 1987.

Hart, James D. *The Oxford Companion to American Literature.* Oxford: Oxford University Press, 5th ed., 1983.

Hartnoll, Phyllis, ed. *The Oxford Companion to the Theatre.* Oxford: Oxford University Press, 4th ed., 1983.

Harvey, Sir Paul, and J.E. Heseltine, comps. and eds. *The Oxford Companion to French Literature.* Oxford: Oxford University Press, 1961.

Herbert, Ian, ed. *Who's Who in the Theatre. Vol 1: Biographies.* Detroit: Gale, 17th ed., 1981.

Hildreth, Peter. *Name Dropper.* London: McWhirter, 1970.

Illustrated Encyclopaedia of World Theatre. London: Thames & Hudson, 1977.

International Authors and Writers Who's Who. Cambridge: International Biographical Centre, 11th ed., 1989.

Jares, Joe. *Whatever Happened to Gorgeous George?* New York: Grosset & Dunlap, 1974.

Jasper, Tony. *The 70's: A Book of Records.* London: Macdonald Futura, 1980.

Jones, Maldwyn A. *Destination America.* London: Weidenfeld & Nicolson, 1976.

Josling, J.F. *Change of Name.* London: Oyez, 11th ed., 1978.

Kaganoff, Benzion C. *A Dictionary of Jewish Names and Their History.* London: Routledge & Kegan Paul, 1978.

Kaplan, Justin. "The Naked Self and Other Problems," in Marc Pachter, ed. *Telling Lives, The Biographer's Art.* Philadelphia: University of Pennsylvania Press, 1981.

Kash, Murray. *Murray Kash's Book of Country.* London: W.H. Allen, 1981.

Keating, H.R.F., ed. *Whodunit? A Guide to Crime, Suspense and Spy Fiction.* London: Windward, 1982.

Klymasz, R.B. *A Classified Dictionary of Slavic Surname Changes in Canada.* Winnipeg: Ukrainian Free Academy of Sciences, 1961. (Onomastica No. 22).

Koegler, Horst. *The Concise Oxford Dictionary of Ballet.* Oxford: Oxford University Press, 2nd rev. ed., 1987.

Lamb, Geoffrey. *Magic Illustrated Dictionary:* London: Kaye & Ward, 1979.

Lloyd, Ann, and Graham Fuller, eds. *The Illustrated Who's Who of the Cinema.* London: Orbis, 1983.

McCormick, Donald. *Who's Who in Spy Fiction.* London: Elm Tree, 1977.

Masanov, I.F. *Slovar' Psevdonimov Russkikh Pisateley, Uchënykh i Obshchestvennykh Deyateley [Dictionary of Pseudonyms of Russian Writers, Scholars and Public Figures].* Moscow: Izdatel'stvo Vsesoyuznoy Knizhnoy Palaty, 1956. 4 vols.

Meades, Jonathan. *This Is Your Life: An Insight into the Unseen Lives of Your Favourite TV Personalities.* London: Salamander, 1979.

Mencken, H.L. *The American Language.* London: Routledge & Kegan Paul, 1963.

Miller, Compton: *Who's Really Who.* London: Sphere, 3rd ed., 1987.

Morgan, Jane, Christopher O'Neill, and Rom Harré. *Nicknames: Their Origins and Social Consequences.* London: Routledge & Kegan Paul, 1979.

Mossman, Jennifer, ed. *New Pseudonyms and Nicknames.* Detroit: Gale, supp. to 1st ed., 1981.
_____, ed. *Pseudonyms and Nicknames Dictionary.* Detroit: Gale, 1st ed., 1980.

Neuberg, Victor E. *The Batsford Companion to Popular Literature.* London: Batsford Academic and Educational, 1982.

New Catholic Encyclopedia. New York: McGraw-Hill, 1967.

Noble, Peter, ed. *Screen International Film and Television Yearbook 1988–89.* London: King, 1988.

Ousby, Ian, ed. *The Cambridge Guide to Literature in English.* Cambridge: Cambridge University Press, 1988.

Panassié, Hugues, and Madeleine Gautier. *Dictionary of Jazz.* London: Cassell, 1956.

Pareles, Jon, and Patricia Romanowski, eds. *The Rolling Stone Encyclopedia of Rock & Roll.* London: Rolling Stone/Michael Joseph, 1983.

Parish, James Robert. *Great Child Stars.* New York: Ace, 1976.

Pascall, Jeremy, and Rob Burt. *The Stars and Superstars of Black Music.* London: Phoebus, 1977.

Pedder, Eddie, ed. *Who's Who on Television.* London: ITV, 4th ed., 1988.

Phoebus Publishing Co., comps. *The Story of Pop.* London: Octopus, 1974.

Quinlan, David. *Quinlan's Illustrated Dictionary of Film Stars.* London: B.T. Batsford, 1986.

Rees, Dafydd, and Luke Crampton, with Barry Lazell. *Book of Rock Stars.* Enfield: Guinness Publishing, 1989.

Reyna, Ferdina. *Concise Encyclopedia of Ballet.* London: Collins, 1974.

Rigdon, Walter, ed. *The Biographical Encyclopedia and Who's Who of the American Theatre.* New York: J.H. Heinemann, 1966.

Roberts, Frank C., comp. *Obituaries from The Times 1961–1970.* Reading: Newspaper Archive Developments, 1975; . . .*1971–75*, 1978; . . .*1951–1960*, 1979.

Robertson, Patrick. *The Guinness Book of Almost Everything You Didn't Need to Know About the Movies.* Enfield: Guinness Publishing, 1986.

Rosenthal, Harold, and John Warrack. *The Concise Oxford Dictionary of Opera*. Oxford: Oxford University Press, 2nd ed., 1979.

Roxon, Lillian. *Rock Encyclopedia*. New York: Grosset & Dunlap, 1971.

Sharp, Harold S., comp. *Handbook of Pseudonyms and Personal Nicknames*. Metuchen, N.J.: Scarecrow, 1972. *First Supplement*, 1975.

Shestack, Melvin. *The Country Music Encyclopaedia*. London: Omnibus, 1977.

Shneyer, A. Ya., and R. Ye. Slavsky. *Tsirk: Malen'kaya Entsiklopediya [The Circus: A Little Encyclopaedia]*. Moscow: Sovetskaya Entsiklopediya, 1979.

Stacey, Chris, and Darcy Sullivan. *Supersoaps*. London: Independent Television Publications, 1988.

Stambler, Irwin. *Encyclopaedia of Pop, Rock and Soul*. London: St. James, 1974.

Stevens, Andy. *World of Stars: Your 200 Favourite Personalities*. London: Fontana, 1980.

Thomson, David. *A Biographical Dictionary of the Cinema*. London: Secker & Warburg, 1975.

Thomson, Ronald W. *Who's Who of Hymn Writers*. London: Epworth, 1967.

Tobler, John, and Alan Jones. *The Rock Lists Album*. London: Plexus, 1982.

Uglow, Jennifer, comp. and ed. *The Macmillan Dictionary of Women's Biography*. London and Basingstoke: Macmillan, 2nd ed., 1989.

Vinson, James, ed. *The International Dictionary of Films and Filmmakers. Vol. III: Actors and Actresses*. London: St. James, 1986.

Ward, A.C. *Longman Companion to Twentieth Century Literature*. London: Longman, 3rd ed., 1981.

Webster's Biographical Dictionary. Springfield, Mass.: Merriam, 1976.

Webster's New Biographical Dictionary. Springfield, Mass.: Merriam-Webster, 1988.

Wheeler, William A. *A Dictionary of the Noted Names of Fiction (Including Also Familiar Pseudonyms, Surnames Bestowed on Eminent Men, and Analogous Popular Appellations Often Referred to in Literature and Conversation)*. London: George Bell, 1892.

Who Was Who. London: A. & C. Black, decennially (1920–1981). 7 vols.

Who Was Who in the Theatre: 1912–1976. Detroit: Gale, 1978. 4 vols.

Who's Who. London: A. & C. Black, annually (from 1897).

Williams, Sir Edgar, ed. *Dictionary of National Biography*. Oxford: Oxford University Press, 1975.

Winchester, Clarence, ed. *The World Film Encyclopaedia*. London: Amalgamated Press, 1933.

Wlaschin, Ken. *The World's Great Movie Stars and Their Films*. London: Peerage, rev. ed., 1984.

Yutkevich, S.I., chief ed. *Kino: Entsiklopedicheskiy Slovar' [The Cinema: An Encyclopedic Dictionary]*. Moscow: Sovetskaya Entsiklopediya, 1986.

Zec, Donald. *Some Enchanted Egos*. London: Allison & Busby, 1972.